Multicultural Education
A Generation of Advocacy

Multicultural Education
A Generation of Advocacy

José A. Cárdenas
Intercultural Development Research Association

SIMON & SCHUSTER
CUSTOM PUBLISHING

Cover photograph by Craig Stafford

Printed in the United States of America

10 9 8 7 6 5 4 3 2 1

ISBN 0-536-58760-4
BA 1480

SIMON & SCHUSTER CUSTOM PUBLISHING
160 Gould Street/Needham Heights, MA 02194
Simon & Schuster Higher Education Publishing Group

COPYRIGHT ACKNOWLEDGMENTS

Grateful acknowledgment is made to the following sources for permission to reprint material copyrighted or controlled by them:

"Seven Cities of Gold," by Dr. José A. Cárdenas, reprinted from *Bulletin*, Vol. XV, No. 3, October 1970 published by Delta Epsilon Sigma. Reprinted by permission of Delta Epsilon Sigma Journal.

The following articles, by Dr. José A. Cárdenas unless otherwise indicated, appeared in the *IDRA Newsletter* and are reprinted by permission of the Intercultural Development Research Association: "Poverty in Texas" (1974); "Legislative Issues in Mexican American Education" (March 1983); "VSP: Key to Minority Education" (June 1987); "Struggle for Bilingual Education Enters Courts" (June 1975); "*U.S. v. Texas* in a Historical Context" (May 1981); "Fifth Circuit Rules in *U.S. v. Texas*" (August 1982); "Legal Basis of Bilingual Education" (May 1976); "Lau Remedies Outlined" (January 1976); "Legal Status of Bilingual Education" (May 1976); "*Keyes v. Denver*" (May 1976); "Bilingual Education: Its Analysis, Needs, and Cost" (February 1977); "*Rios v. Read*" (March 1977); "AIR Evaluation of Bilingual Education" (June 1977); "The Role of Native-Language Instruction in Bilingual Education" (January 1984); "The English Only Legislative Movement" (August 1985); "Education Secretary Bennett and the Big Lie" (October 1985); "Al Shanker, the AFT, and Minority Issues" (November 1985); "U.S. English Strikes Again" (September 1986); "Bilingual Education in Heterogeneous Groups" (September 1985); "Flexibility in Bilingual Programs" (January 1986); "Current Problems in Bilingual Education" (September 1993); "An Open Letter to Our Readers" (1979); "No Pass, No Nothing" (May 1990); "School-Based Management: Are We Ready?" (April 1991) by Gladys J. Gibbs; and "Widening, Not Narrowing, the Gap" (June 1991).

"Education Problems of Migrant Children" (originally published as "Education and the Children of Migrant Farmworkers: An Overview"), by Dr. José A. Cárdenas, reprinted from *Inequality in Education*, No. 21, June 1976, published by the Center for Law and Education at Harvard University. Reprinted with permission.

"Response to Noel Epstein," by Dr. José A. Cárdenas, reprinted from a report by the Institute for Educational Leadership at George Washington University, 1977. Reprinted with permission.

"Children at Risk," by Dr. José A. Cárdenas and Joan McCarty, reprinted from *Educational Leadership*, Vol. 43, No. 1, September 1985, published by Association for Supervision and Curriculum Development.

"The Impact of *Doe v. Plyler* Upon Texas Public Schools," by Dr. José A. Cárdenas and Albert Cortez, reprinted from the *Journal of Law and Education*, published by M. Jefferson Law Books.

"Use of Tests: Educational Administration," reprinted from *Report of the Tenth National Conference of Civil and Human Rights in Education*, published by National Education Association, Washington, D.C., 1972.

"Political Limits to an Education of Value: The Role of the State," by Dr. José A. Cárdenas, reprinted from *Access to Knowledge: An Agenda for Our Nation's Schools*, published by the College Entrance Examination Board, 1990.

Intercultural Development Research Association (IDRA) is an independent nonprofit organization dedicated to equity and excellence in education for all children.

Founded in 1973, IDRA has worked since its inception for the rights of minority and other special populations. IDRA ful-fills its mission through targeted research and evaluation projects, the provision of training and technical assistance, the development of appropriate instructional materials, and the aggressive dissemination of information.

IDRA targets specific pressing concerns through its Center for the Prevention and Recovery of Dropouts, which seeks to turn the school dropout tide through in-school programs such as the national, award-winning Coca-Cola Valued Youth Program, and its Center for Policy and Leadership, which informs decision-makers on school finance and other policy issues.

As IDRA enters a new century, it maintains its commitment to educational equity, the potential within each student, and the right of every child to the brightest possible future as only such equity can provide.

Intercultural Development Research Association
5838 Callaghan Road, Suite 350
San Antonio, Texas 78228-1190

Contents

PREFACE

This publication addresses the purpose of TEE/IDRA, to inform decision-makers and the general public on issues affecting the education of all Americans. It is hoped that this publication will provide much deserved recognition for the role that IDRA has played in its twenty-year effort to improve educational opportunities for students through research and evaluation, materials development, training and technical assistance and dissemination of information.

In general, all of the articles included in this anthology were written predominantly by me. Contributions of others to the writing of an article is acknowledged in the article. This is not necessarily true of the earliest articles in the anthology. Some of the first articles (1969–1972) reflect joint input by myself and Dr. Blandina "Bambi" Cárdenas Ramírez. Most of the early TEE articles (1973–1974) were cooperatively drafted by myself and Ms. Rosa Maria Catacalos. Articles written predominantly by other persons have not been included in this anthology.

IDRA has been commonly referred to as a "think tank." One of its salient characteristics is a work style based on cooperation, rather than on individual effort and competition. In such a relationship, it is inevitable that the creative ideas found in these works were the creative efforts of many persons rather than the author alone. This consistent contribution by an extensive number of creative staff members as well as countless other persons not directly associated with IDRA is duly acknowledged at this time.

Special acknowledgements are due to the members of the board of IDRA for support provided, IDRA Executive Director Dr. María Robledo Montecel for her extensive assistance, Mrs. Evelyn Reed for editing suggestions, and Dr. Frances A. MacÉinrí for recommendations for chapter discussion questions.

I imagine that since the advent of civilization, each writer has had to face the embarrassment of reading his/her earlier writings. This potential embarrassment served as a deterrent to my publishing educational material for many years. It wasn't until a colleague of mine, Dr. Richard Foster, Superintendent of the Berkeley school district in California, urged me to write freely with the understanding that reviewing the article in the future would indicate how much I had grown, that I was able to put thoughts down on paper. In this light, I ask the reader to refrain from focusing on how little we knew in the past, but rather on how much we have learned in the intervening years.

J.A.C.
1993

FOREWORD

Education, says the adage, begins at home. And so it does. Home is where our first words were heard and our first steps celebrated. Once in school, some children continue to be heard, celebrated and educated; many others—mostly poor, minority, and non-English-speaking children — do not.

In 1980, *A Nation at Risk* declared that continued failure to educate students constrained national economic productivity and the ability to remain competitive in a global market. Today, after dozens of blue ribbon reports have echoed the same concerns and after at least four waves of top-down, up-down, inside-out and outside-in education reform efforts, our nation is still at risk—perhaps more so.

Why? One set of explanations fall into the more and better perspective that is so unique to the American experience. We need more and better standards, more and better tests, more and better teachers, more and better teaching methods, more and better structures. A second set of explanations converge around schools as an institution. Schools do not work because they lack the logistical capacity of the military or the management of the private sector or the competitiveness of the free marketplace. Finally, there are the society-has-lost-its-way explanations: television is the problem, crime is the problem, poverty is the problem, absent parents are the problem, the demographics are the problem, immigration is the problem, wrong values are the problem, political correctness is the problem.

The debate rages on. The ideological spectrum shines brightly. We retool, restructure, and reinvent with insufficient results.

Explanations, of whatever ilk, will not successfully move us into the next millennium. More than anything, what is needed is a place to stand, a place to come from as we create workable solutions. In this compilation and examination of twenty-five years of advocacy, Dr. José A. Cárdenas offers such a place. His is a consistent voice. The premise is simple: all children are valuable and schooling must acknowledge, nurture, and build on that value.

This book is an urgent and always insightful call for clarity of purpose. Through the myriad of circumstances in an entire generation, Dr. Cárdenas examines educational issues with one unswerving purpose: advocacy for children. The urgency, the insights, and the purpose will move us into a generation of schools that hear, celebrate, and educate all of our children.

María Robledo Montecel, Ph.D.
October, 1993

INTRODUCTION

This publication is a collection of articles written by the author over a twenty-five year period, from 1968 to 1993. This is a unique period in American education, a time which should have resulted in the formulation of an educational policy for previously disenfranchised segments of the school population—minority, disadvantaged, limited English proficient, immigrant, migrant and female children.

Three stimuli provided the basis for an initial attempt to provide equality of educational opportunity for these children during this period.

The first was the Supreme Court decision in *Brown v. Board of Education* which as subsequently implemented, addressed not only the elimination of segregated schools, but also the elimination of cultural isolation through the integration of minorities in school activities.

Second, the Civil Rights Act of 1964 provided the legal framework for addressing inequities in educational opportunity.

The Civil Rights Act created the Office of Civil Rights in the Department of Health, Education and Welfare, which was subsequently moved to the Department of Education. This office was given a monitoring and regulatory role never before found at the federal level.

Third, in 1965 the Elementary and Secondary Education Act (ESEA) provided the largest federal financial subsidy ever experienced in the history of education. Its various titles provided ample funds for the development and implementation of a new strategy for the education of a previously disenfranchised school population.

Brown and the Civil Rights Act provided the sticks to awaken the American school to the needs of atypical children; ESEA provided the carrots necessary for an educational response.

Though the legal basis and the funds were readily available, the provision of equal educational opportunity was severely constrained by the lack of an educational plan for the integration of atypical school populations. Since its inception, the American public school has focused on meeting the educational needs of a select segment of the population. Educational programs were designed by and for white, Anglo, English-speaking, middle and upper class students which came from the cultural mainstream.

Instructional programs designed for the cultural mainstream provided little compatibility between the educational system and the unique characteristics of different segments of the population. This absence of compatibility, when addressed, was inevitably placed on the shoulders of the target population, requiring the atypical student to become typical in order to have a chance of succeeding in school. Thus minority students were expected to learn and accept the customs, traditions and orientations of the cultural mainstream in order for schooling to become relevant. The economically disadvantaged were supposed to adopt middle class values and somehow make up the deprivations of poverty in order to fit it with middle class students. Limited English proficient students were to acquire English as a dominant language as cognitive development atrophied and basic skill and content acquisition was postponed while this command of the English language was being acquired, and girls were expected to act like girls and adhere to the antiquated female roles of an antiquated era.

The epitome of school tractiveness during what should have been a dynamic era of change was the need for the United States Supreme Court to point out in *Lau v. Nichols* that 1,800 Chinese students who spoke no English taught in a tradition English program by teachers who spoke no Chinese were being denied equality of educational opportunity. The school's argument that it was the responsibility of the parents to teach them English was struck down by the Supreme Court by pointing out that few of the parents spoke English, and the learning of English was one of the primary reasons for sending the children to school.

Lau set the precedent that providing a uniform instructional program for children with differing characteristics constitutes a denial of equal educational opportunity. Instead of responding to this mandate, the schools continued traditional school programs.

The inevitable prescription for the under-performance of atypical students became an increase in the dose of traditional programs. The school focused its energies, its time and its resources in doing the wrong things better, in doing the wrong things longer, in doing the wrong things more often. Students who did not perform well during the regular nine months of instruction were given additional schooling during the summer months, invariably using the same materials, methodologies and teachers that had proved unsuccessful during the regular term. Migrant students were placed in extended day programs based on the rationale that if the extended number of hours of school attendance each day were to be multiplied by the shortened number of days spent in school, the achievement of an equal number of hours would inevitably produce educational achievement equal to their geographic stable peers.

Even the massive educational reform movement of today is dysfunctional for atypical school populations in that reform efforts are characterized by a "trickle down" educational theory. It is assumed that an improvement in the general performance of the school will eventually trickle down to the atypical populations. This approach has failed miserably in the past; it will continue to fail in the future.

This publication serves various purposes. First, it should be of historical interest to present and future scholars seeking insights into the historical period covered in the publication. Introductions to the various articles provide background information, not only about the topic, but about the context in which the topic was originally addressed.

However, the publication serves a more important need. Though almost forty years have elapsed since the Supreme Court ruling in *Brown v. Board of Education*, minorities are still far from enjoying equality of educational opportunity in the schools. Neither the Civil Rights Act nor the Elementary and Secondary Schools Act, nor subsequent federal and state legislation, have brought about a dramatic improvement in the performance of the school. If anything, the overall performance of the school has deteriorated, since its concern for an elitist population has been watered down considerably by the inclusion of a host of students from those segments of the population outside of the cultural mainstream.

George Santayana observed that a people ignorant of its history are doomed to repeat the mistakes of the past. It behooves us to look at the history of the early era of minority education, understand its relationship to current educational conditions and problems, and seek new avenues in our present efforts to extend educational opportunities to all.

Just as past litigation and legislation opened up new vistas in public school education, there is a new stimulus which demands that we analyze past successes and failures in the education of atypical students. This new stimulus is the drastic change in the economic base of the country and the subsequent change in the characteristics of the work force in support of this new economy. The move from an economy based on agricultural, mineral and heavy industry to a new economy based on service, information and technology has placed a new burden on our schools, no lighter than the burden placed on the past generation by equal rights litigation and legislation.

The need for improved and equal educational opportunities based on social justice for atypical populations, takes a new significance when based on an economic need affecting the entire population. The past need for improved education was critical for the minority populations. The present need is critical for the survival of our country in its world leadership role.

The American economy can no longer absorb the failures of the American school. The prohibitive cost of support for non-productive elements of our society is exceeded only by the impact of our failure to produce a modern work force which can maintain America competitive in a shrinking world.

I trust that twenty-five years from now we will not regret our failure to address the education needs of minority and disadvantaged students as we have done these past twenty-five years.

1

Minority Education

SEVEN CITIES OF GOLD

March 21, 1970

PREFACE

More than 130 years ago, Arthur Hugh Clough observed, "The more things change, the more they remain the same. . . . And as things have been, things remain." The following article, *Seven Cities of Gold,* certainly substantiates the correctness of this saying.

First presented on March 21, 1970 to the San Antonio Chapter of Delta Epsilon Sigma, this article addresses seven myths in American education that I deem detrimental to the education of minority and disadvantaged children. The seven concepts presented in the article are unique for three reasons. First, subsequent developments proved that I was right; each of the seven was subsequently identified as a barrier to the education of minority and disadvantaged children. Second, each of the seven concepts developed into a major educational issue, with additional and extensive coverage in the educational media. In this anthology, there are many articles that address at least five of the seven concepts discussed in the original paper. Third, each of the seven concepts remains in educational practice today, continuing to be a barrier to educational opportunities for minority and disadvantaged children.

This article also predicts the emergence of educational change as a priority consideration and calls for drastic changes in the pre-service preparation of teachers.

It is remarkable that although the schools have undergone twenty-two years of change since this article was first presented, none of the seven topics has been more than superficially addressed. The need for minority sensitivity in the preparation of teachers is no less urgent today than it was in 1970.

The article does contain one glaring error. I mentioned in 1970 the need for schools to compensate "for the negative self-concept which disadvantaged children traditionally bring to school." Subsequent study and observation indicate that disadvantaged children do not automatically bring a negative self-concept to school; that negative self-concept is usually created in the school.

This article appeared in the Delta Epsilon Sigma *Bulletin* of October, 1970, and was distributed nationally.

I began my professional career as a classroom teacher full of that enthusiasm which this season is paying off handsomely for television producers who market it in "Room 222" and the like. Nonetheless, when a promotion to a higher position was offered me, I jumped at the opportunity, not because I felt particularly competent that I could do the work, but because I felt that perhaps in the new position I would find the answers to the classroom enigmas that had puzzled me. Thus I went from teacher to vice-principal, to supervisor, to principal, to college professor, to educational researcher, and on to superintendent.

I've known the frustration of Socrates, certain that the oracle erred, but unable to find the answer elsewhere. My frustration has been heightened by the circumstance of my ethnicity, on the one hand, and the reality of my commitment on the other.

Although the answers still elude me, I have reached in my journey certain milestones that have given me clues to the nature of the educational puzzle; and although the ultimate answer will probably not be mine, I feel that I have formed certain sections that when brought together will form the picture I have been seeking.

The sections of the puzzle I have formed indicate to me that we as educators have been misled by educational practice, and that many of the basic premises in education, some of long standing and some relatively recent, are based on fallacies that tend to perpetuate our persistence in a wrong, perhaps circuitous, course.

At a recent meeting in Washington, D.C., a group of people—some educators, some non-educators, and some anti-educators—in less than a quarter of an hour listed forty to fifty such fallacies, which, although readily accepted as fallacies by educational researchers, still dominate educational practice today and may easily account for a large portion of our educational failures.

Today I am going to focus on seven of these fallacies, which in my opinion constitute the greatest deterrent to equality of educational opportunity for the culturally different, and perhaps, in fact, for all children.

1. *Culturally Disadvantaged*

Perhaps the most erroneous fallacy is the concept that children who are atypical, that is, children with different values, traditions, and orientations, are culturally disadvantaged, culturally poor, or culturally deprived. Recently, some educators like Frank Reissman have looked on the positives of culturally different children as a solution to the problem of meeting their educational needs (Reissman, 1966). Unfortunately, educational practice today tends to agree more closely with Robert J. Havighurst (1964) who stated, "There is substantial doubt that the socially disadvantaged children in our big cities have any positive qualities of potential value in urban society. . . ."

In the case of the disadvantaged in the southwestern United States, this fallacy has had devastating results. Because minority group culture has been so greatly devalued by the institutions of society, its great "levelling" institution, the school, has sought to do the disadvantaged student the great favor of ridding him of all that is his disadvantage—his culture.

At the same time, the dominant culture has refused to open its gates to the brown and the black minorities in the Southwest. Having come close to giving up their culture and through prejudice and discrimination not being accepted into a new culture, the black and the brown have been led to a dangerous social disorientation, particularly the young, whose cultural ties with the past have been weakened. It is no surprise, then, that as a response to the questions, "Who am I? What am I?" minority group members have sought to strengthen their egos by extending new roots into their heritage with the resulting minority group "power" movements.

2. *Homogeneous Grouping*

Typical of educational fallacies is the concept of homogeneous grouping. It has long been believed that higher educational gains can be achieved by grouping students through the application of some criterion that results in a group that shares an equal propensity for learning through common educational experience.

Such a concept forms the basis for assignment to "slow" groups, to "fast" groups, to the red-bird group, to classes for the mentally retarded, to special classes for migrant children, special classes for the non-English speaking, and special classes for the racially and ethnically different.

These groupings exist in spite of the fact that educational evaluation has failed to show that such segregation of children on the basis of IQ, or language, past achievement, geographic stability or any other criteria has produced increased learning, and there is an abundance of evidence on the detrimental educational, psychological, and social effects of such groupings.

I dare any of you to spend an extended period of time in a special class for low-ability children and not come out mentally retarded.

Perhaps the human being is so unique that a group as small as two fails to produce two individuals sharing an equal propensity for learning the same way, at the same time.

3. *Non-Motivation*

Related to the fallacy of "cultural disadvantages" or "minus-culture" is the fallacy of non-motivation. Simply stated, this concept tells us that a human being can achieve the status of a vegetable or the proverbial "bump on a log" and while in this happy state may not be motivated to learn or to do. The basic concepts of psychology known to us for years state that this cannot be so. The drive for satisfaction of basic physiological needs used to dominate our every move. With the satisfaction of physiological needs the human being strives for the satisfaction of psychological needs, which, being relatively insatiable, keep us in a constant state of motivation. Therefore, rather than stating that an individual is not motivated, we should state that he fails to see, in the activity we have prescribed, the opportunity for achieving satisfaction. Instead of not being motivated, the non-participant is saying to us, "I don't want to play your game; I don't like the odds."

Yet when responding to the problems of the non-achiever, the under-achiever, the failure, and the school dropout, we invariably clutch at our favorite tranquilizer, the same fallacy of non-motivation, just as we find comfort in the concept of "minus-culture." Determining that non-motivation exists, we then go to the extent of trying out all kinds of little games, only to find that we have failed to produce that which to us should supplant what we have called non-motivation. Perhaps a more realistic explanation for the phenomenon of our failure might be that as a child grows up, especially if he is a child of the poor, but more and more in our middle class society, as a student he is motivated to resist more actively an education that is dysfunctional for him and that assaults his sensibilities.

4. *IQ Testing*

A fourth fallacy that I wish to attack is the fallacy of intelligence testing. Educational practice has gone so far up this wrong creek that it has lost sight of the original direction and we are hopelessly lost seeking the right branch in the wrong stream.

The basic assumption of this kind of testing, namely that children share typical experiences, again is contrary to my experiences and my perceptions of the uniqueness of the individual. Efforts to seek valid measurement through "culture-fair tests" (which are culturally unfair!) and through non-language tests based on non-verbal communication, are gnats we strain on after having swallowed the camel.

The pioneering work of J. Paul Torrance in creativity and J.P. Guilford in intelligence more than a decade ago should have led us to discontinue intelligence testing, especially when it became evident that there was more about intelligence that was unknown than known (Guilford, 1971).

The use of Wechslers, Binets and PPVIs, particularly for children from disadvantaged homes, ethnic minorities, and other obviously atypical children, should be discontinued immediately. *Pygmalion in the Classroom*, the studies of Kesler and Jimenez, and of many others, indicate that (first) erroneous IQs are being obtained and (second) that subsequent educational practice tends to perpetuate these scores.

In his "Overlooked Positives," Reissman (1966) points to sub-fallacies *within* the fallacy of intelligence testing. These include the equation of slowness with dullness and the determination that "disadvantaged" groups are inarticulate and non-verbal. Although there is no evidence to support the fact that there are not many slow gifted children, the school in general does not pay much attention to the slow gifted child, but rather is alert to discover fast gifted children. This matter is complicated by the realization that the assumption that the slow pupil is not bright functions as a self-fulfilling prophecy.

The strongest evidence against IQ testing, however, lies in the effective domain, and it needs very little documentation. To label a child with a "permanent" stratification index (IQ) may well be the equivalent of sentencing him to life imprisonment in a world of negative self-concepts that will affect his goals, his motivation, and his achievements. We see the tragic effects of such labelling every day. Most teachers and administrators can recite instances where experience refutes the results of intelligence tests, yet every educational agency continues to embrace them.

5. *Failures*

Another fallacy in educational practice is the concept of failure. This concept uses the promise of success or promotion as a long-range motivation device, with its corollary, failure or the threat of failure, as a negative incentive.

I have two major objections to this concept. First, the promise of course or grade promotion is too long-range to be of any significant motivational value. Children's temporal horizons are not so vast that pass/fail decisions in May will affect performance during the previous September. Second, especially in the case of disadvantaged children, the implications of failure for an already negative self-concept are devastating.

Our experiences show that the threat of failure has not succeeded in preventing failure. A related fallacy is that failure and the repetition of a grade (or courses) allow the student to add to previous learning and that the cumulative learning of two or three sessions will produce enough knowledge to meet our arbitrarily determined minimum standards for promotion. Yet studies of retention indicate that three-fourths of all children retained do no better upon repetition of a grade, and one-fourth of all children actually do *worse* the second time around!

In order to compensate for the negative self-concept that disadvantaged children traditionally bring to school, instructional programs need to be scaled at such minute intervals that school performance automatically becomes a series of successful experiences. Experiments in programmed learning have amply demonstrated that success can be one of the strongest motivating factors for desirable school performance. Relying on the motivation that develops retroactively from successful educational achievement further promises to be a more effective method of developing intrinsic motivation.

6. *The "Right" Method*

A fallacy of long standing in educational practice has been the dream that there is a "right" way or method of teaching a specific concept. Again, the uniqueness of the individual seems to produce varying learning in varying situations.

I can best illustrate this fallacy by recounting one of my experiences as a teacher and administrator. One day soon after the opening of a school year, a first grade teacher brought a six-year-old to my office in order to demonstrate an unusual phenomenon. It appeared that the young man had been taught to read at home by an older brother now in the second grade. The unusual thing was that the six-year-old was capable of reading fourth- and fifth-grade books, and although some of the words may have been new, he had no difficulty in comprehending what he was reading! Needless to say, in a school where three-fourths of the children were retarded in reading development, such a case was both unusual and bewildering. Many times since then I wondered how this child would have fared if instead of having been taught in some unusual manner by a seven-year-old pedagogue, he would have had the "benefits" of the "right" methodology, with an abundance of audio and visual discrimination exercises, left-to-right eye movement training, and the proper development of word attack skills, either the use of context clues or phonetic analysis, depending on the "right" methodology in vogue at the time. Would he have turned out to be a functional illiterate like most of his classmates? The fact is, I am not sure that participation in such exercises with the rest of his classmates did not eventually do this, in spite of the five-year headstart he brought to school.

Equally erroneous were my curious investigations as to the methodology employed by the seven-year-old, although today I am glad that I never uncovered the system, for if I had I would have been tempted to try it with all the other youngsters in the hope of solving the school's most serious problem. I now feel that the magic was in neither the children nor the methodology. The magic was the merging of the right child, in the right place, at the right time with the right method. I am certain that the method is no more a constant in a learning situation than the child, the place, or the time.

7. *Competition*

Another fallacy prevalent in educational procedures is the concept of competition. Educational methodology and educational curricula contain an abundance of practices based on the mistaken notion that it is necessary that children be kept in a constant state of competition. Unfortunately, these practices do not promote educational dividends. For one, carried to an extreme, the competition leads to one winner for whom the competition may prove motivating and rewarding and a host of losers who find the experience educationally frustrating. Witness the spelling bee which for weeks-on-end provides extensive repetitious reinforcing experiences for the children who need it the least while the children most in need of spelling instruction wait on the sidelines after the first round. At best, the many competitive experiences provided in school programs equip children to perpetuate the dog-eat-dog world in which we want them to live.

The strongest advocacy of competition in the schools usually stems from athletic departments, which are quick to point out the tremendous achievements of their football teams. Yet this is the group I criticize the most. Through their competition, they have created a nation of non-competitors, whose only participation in sports consists of opening a can of beer and sitting in front of the television set in order to identify with those more talented, rather than risk failure by participation in a sports activity.

This has also led to the development of super-athletes, with definite professional orientation, at the expense of lifetime sports. It is interesting to note that the University of Texas now has a $2,000,000 budget for some two-hundred student competitors in Southwest Conference Sports and less than $200,000 for the other 30,000 students who should be participating in individual and intramural activities. The public school budgets for athletic programs have not reached these proportions, but give us time; we are slowly getting there.

The reason for this attack on athletic programs is not my specific concern with them at the moment, but rather that they serve as an analogy to what may be happening in other areas. The same concept that has led to non-participation in sports activities is equally responsible for non-participation in the humanities, the sciences and the arts. Competition in the classroom is responsible for much of the non-participation in the classroom.

Competition has been especially harmful to the ethnically different youngster who brings to school a culture that does not embrace the concept of competition and a family tradition that frowns upon competitive excellence at the expense of others.

Equally damaging is classroom competition in which a youngster refuses to compete because of a handicap being given to him as a result of the inappropriateness of the instructional program for his unique characteristics, or because of the handicap of a previously developed and consistently reinforced negative self-concept.

The tenacity of these fallacies in educational practice is amazing, especially in view of the education profession's ready acceptance of each one as a fallacy. Why do we maintain them?

Alternatives must be sought. The indictment of the educational system as it relates to the atypical is coming in from assorted juries. While we can measure with some accuracy its failure with groups such as the disadvantaged, we have not yet begun to measure on a broad scale the system's failure with the children for whom it *was* designed: typical children in typical schools. Perhaps this system is also tragically failing *them,* even if they are not necessarily failing the system. If I may play the roll of the seer (as most people are prone to do in years ending with zero) and gaze into my crystal ball, the one item that will dominate education in this decade will be the question of change. For unless educators are willing to put their houses in order and replace myths and fallacies in educational practice with new practices based on sound principles and research findings, the educational system we now know will be at an end. The beginning of that end is at hand. An experiment is being conducted in Texarkana, Arkansas, which may turn out to be the most significant influence on the educational systems since the Kalamazoo decision. In Texarkana, the Dorset Press received a contract, complete with specifications, for the implementation of a reading program. Payment for Dorset Press services will be dependent on the gains made by the students participating in the project. This experiment has one saving feature for current educational systems, and that is turn over. Texarkana teachers are being trained to continue the reading project if it proves successful. These teachers must adhere to the innovative practices that prove successful. Regression to the typical program, with its myths and fallacies, will lead to educational institutions acquiring more and more contracted services so that the future role of the public school educator will be one of writing specifications and opening bids.

Perhaps if education in its present form should be continued, the key will lie with teacher education institutions and students in teacher education programs. I beg them to stop sending us new teachers well-versed in obsolete practices. We need, and desperately so, new people unprejudiced by the educational fallacies being practiced today people who can give a better justification for educational practices than "It has always been done this way."

THE CHASM OF CONFLICTING CONCERNS

November, 1970

In November, 1970, after having served as superintendent of the Edgewood Independent School District for about one and one-half years, I was asked to make a presentation to the annual conference of the Texas United Community Services.

It was extremely unusual for a minority person to be asked to address this or any other conference, and through the morning of the presentation there was an aura of curiosity about the content. Conversations with conference participants indicated that they expected the Mexican-American superintendent, probably one of only three Mexican-American superintendents in the entire country, to address the poverty of Mexican-Americans and make a plea for their inclusion in the services provided by social service institutions.

Bambi Cárdenas and I spent considerable time in the preparation of this paper. We intended to address the need for a massive reformation in the nature of social institutions, rather than asking for an expanded service delivery. The paper addressed the history of prejudice and discrimination against Mexican-Americans, the changing social and political context of the country, and a warning, if not a threat, of the consequences of continued neglect of a restless and growing segment of the population.

Considering the early date of this paper, it is amazing in its content. In education, it calls for adapting the school to the characteristics of the minority child, a concept that was unthinkable at the time, but was subsequently made the law of the land in the *Lau v. Nichols* case and subsequent federal policies formulated under the U.S. Supreme Court ruling (*Lau v. Nichols*, 1974).

The article advocates bilingual education, early childhood education, individually-prescribed instruction, and community involvement at a time when such practices were relatively unknown, let alone understood or accepted.

Dropout rates, retentions in grade, and measures of underachievement are cited as performance indicators more than twenty years before they were adopted as such by the National Education Goals Panel (*National Education Goals Report*, 1991).

This marks the first appearance of the concept of educational incompatibilities, a concept that was subsequently to provide the framework for twenty years of IDRA contributions to the education of atypical students. This concept also provided the framework for the San Antonio New Schools Development Foundation's education plan in 1992 (*San Antonio New Schools Development Foundation*, 1992).

Other key concepts that were to become a part of the national education agenda include the impact of invalid testing, low levels of expectation, self-fulfilling prophecies, participation in school decision-making, and institutional accountability—topics that would dominate as educational issues over the next twenty-two years.

As the presentation proceeded that November morning in 1970, a restless audience quieted down and listened intently. After the presentation was finished, there was a long period of silence, finally broken by a short period of decent applause by the majority of the participants, but a long, wild period of applause and cheering by Mexican-Americans in the group. Requests for copies of the presentation were freely handed out, since we had anticipated this and had an extensive supply ready.

A representative from Southwestern Bell later requested permission to disseminate the document, and several thousand copies were distributed by Southwestern Bell throughout its service area.

INTRODUCTION

For the last twenty years I have been involved in the education of Mexican-American children. Much of my energy during that time has been devoted to a reconciliation of what I consider to be an erroneous strategy: that of attempting to adapt the child to the curriculum. I think the failure of that strategy is amply substantiated by an 80 to 90 percent school dropout rate among Mexican-Americans. I have been thoroughly convinced for several years now that the educational problems of Mexican-Americans will not diminish until all educators drop the concept of "adapting the child to the curriculum" and substitute this with a program of adapting the curriculum, and the school, to the child. I call your attention to this because I think a parallel exists in the response of most social institutions to the Mexican-American. Almost daily we still hear of "the Mexican-American problem," in health, in community services, in economics, and in politics; and in my opinion, social agencies are no closer to solving the social problems of Mexican-Americans than I am to solving their educational problems—at least, not until we think in terms of adapting social institutions to the Mexican-American rather than attempting to adapt the Mexican-American to the institutions.

My commitment to education has caused me to continuously criticize its inefficiencies and promote its most promising innovations. I have been an advocate of bilingual education, of early childhood education, of multicultural education, of individually prescribed instruction, and of community involvement. I still support the merits of these educational strategies as necessary to equality of educational opportunity.

In the last few years, however, I have begun to crystalize the conviction that we can expect little beyond minimal success in the education of the Mexican-American so long as the reality of his environment provides full justification for the negative self-concept he begins to nurture at his first encounter with the dominant culture, and extends during his tenure at school. Although I do not have substantive research supporting my prognosis (theoretical basis may be found in the writings of Fromme, Alport, Rogers, et al.), I feel sufficiently justified in my opinion to join the ranks of those who expound the urgency of an accelerated resolution to the inequalities in health, housing, and economics that are to a great extent responsible for the present plight of the Mexican-American, before great strides can be made in solving the problem of educational inequalities in the school. It is to this cry, this quest for equality that many Mexican-Americans choose to call "La Causa," that I would like to speak today.

CLARIFICATION OF THE RESPONSE

The Mexican-American movement is as complex as the field within which it operates. Symbolically, it is young Mexican-American leaders attempting to change a local, state, and national government's response to a problem these governments fail to recognize—and it is much more. Its complexity, and the complexity of the field within which it operates, necessitate clarification.

This is a movement encompassing a broad spectrum of individuals, strategies, motivations, and concerns. It includes the rhetoric of revolution and of reaction. Although its language has been a part of the Southwest for centuries, that language suddenly seems very loud, very foreign, and very threatening to people who never bothered to hear it before. It is a fire fed by the young at a time when the traditional gap between the young and the not-so-young seems to have reached unprecedented proportions. It is strategies which might have been better implemented ten years ago, and it is a call for morality which was clearly heard almost 2,000 years ago.

The problem as it affects the Mexican-American is enormous. In schools, dropout rates are reduced at such a slow pace as to negate the efficiency of the schools as instruments of upward mobility. Retention rates and underachievement aggravate the problem. In the area of civil rights, equal employment opportunity, justice, health, and welfare, the problem is at least of equal magnitude.

The last few years have brought an increased awareness, if not understanding, of the Mexican-American and his perception of and attempts to resolve, the bleakness of his existence. The Valley Farmworkers March and subsequent confrontation with a governor of the State of Texas, the Civil Rights Commission Hearings, various walkouts in area schools, the Del Rio March, and the Crystal City situation, even when adversely reported, have at least testified to the growing willingness of Mexican-Americans, especially the young, to attack their problems collectively as well as individually. The violence erupting in association with Mexican-American civil rights activities in recent weeks has been covered extensively by the news media and certainly added a new dimension to the meaning of commitment for Mexican-Americans.

The emerging purposeful collectivity among Mexican-Americans has been recognized by individuals in politics. It was perhaps during John F. Kennedy's campaign that the political potential of Mexican-Americans as a group became apparent both nationally and locally. Since then, a Mexican-American strategy has been a major feature of most political campaigns in the Southwest. The advent of La Raza Unida Party in south Texas will undoubtedly increase the awareness of ethnicity in the quest for political support.

Several factors have contributed to the emerging political importance of Mexican-Americans. The elimination of the poll tax, massive voter registration drives, and sporadic attempts at voter education have done much to curtail the previous disenfranchisement of minorities. Equally relevant to the political importance of emerging minorities like Mexican-Americans, however, is the increasing divisiveness in the country.

The possibility exists that this increased awareness of the problems of Mexican-Americans may have an adverse effect, in terms of short-range goals, on the Mexican-American's quest for equal opportunity. The problem is turbulent and it is constrained by the tolerance for turbulent phenomena. Just as the wrongness of an eighty percent drop out rate among Mexican-Americans is a reality, so the existence of other, perhaps more threatening, national and international concerns is a reality. Americans live under the threat of Red China and the communist world. Conservationists (and our children) tell us that our most serious problem is the ecosystem. The threat of a nuclear holocaust is brought home to us by at least one novel and several new movies per year. Student unrest and the drug problem widen the gap between the generations, and we are all, of course, worrying about our shrinking American dollar. On the national scene, the Mexican-American competes for priority with these and other concerns. On the local scene, the competition for priority among concerns is almost as keen. There is also the possibility that the introduction into this scene of the problems of the

Mexican-American may well push many apprehensive middle class Americans beyond their thresholds of tolerance.

In addition to the tolerance for turbulence phenomena, the Mexican-American movement must exist within the framework of Newton's Law. For every action of the Mexican-American, there is a reaction of the dominant ethnic group. Opposition to change is usually manifested in a reactionary response that in most cases causes a comparable response from the proponents of change. Defense mechanisms are set up both at the psychological and physical level. We hear accusations from the dominant ethnic group that Mexican-Americans are ungrateful for "what has been done for them." The "some of my best friends are Mexicans" approach is still very much in practice, amazingly so in view of all the bad jokes about this. Other defenses are obvious perhaps only to the Mexican-American. Almost always these are most costly to the persons employing them. The use of "in-house Mexicans" in negotiations with activist groups is perhaps the most symptomatic of the lack of understanding. To expect to appear sincere to activist Mexican-Americans by having as your spokespersons Mexican-Americans who are perceived as sell-outs by those activists is strategically questionable if not foolhardy.

STATUS OF THE PROBLEM

The reality of the historical presence of Mexicans and Mexican-Americans in the Southwest is evidenced by their influence on present Southwestern culture, if not by the history books. The Conquistadores, often portrayed as nothing more than fortune-seeking pursuers of Indian myths, were followed by Spanish settlers, whose descendants are still living in Texas, having been Mexicans only for that short period between Mexican independence from Spain and Texas' secession from Mexico. With Anglo settlement of the Southwest came the loss of the lands and other wealth, leaving deep fissures in the relations between the Anglo- and Spanish-speaking populations.

Although the Treaty of Guadalupe Hidalgo guaranteed the Spanish- speaking population its language, religion, and culture, and the United States theoretically recognized the claim of inhabitants to all the land rights proved by Spanish grant, few of these rights were recognized and respected. The non-compliance of the United States' government with the terms of the treaty poses an interesting, if strictly academic, legal question, since it was under this treaty that Mexico ceded the states of California, Arizona, and New Mexico to this country.

Many factors have contributed to the lack of cultural assimilation on the part of Mexican-Americans. The geographic proximity of the mother country and the fact that geographically the Southwest is a part of Mexico has helped to maintain cultural integrity, as has reinforcement of that culture through immigration. Physiological differences were another barrier to cultural assimilation. Discriminatory practices on the part of institutions that were the avenues to cultural assimilation were probably the greatest barriers.

Inequality of opportunity has pervaded life for Mexican-Americans in the Southwest and persists in education, housing, employment, the administration of justice, and business.

In education, Mexican-American progress is hampered by a system that has not accepted the responsibility for implementing an instructional program compatible with cultural and learning characteristics. The most blatant disregard for the cultural and learning characteristics of Mexican-American children is evidenced by the practice of prohibiting the children's use of their home language. Not only has the child's primary language been ignored as a vehicle for instruction, a questionable pedagogical practice, but the move in many areas has been to eliminate Spanish altogether. The impact in terms of loss to human dignity of this practice alone will probably be felt over the next fifty years.

Similarly, the complete disregard for the culture of the Mexican-American has done much to alienate these people. The educational problems related to this disregard for culture can be summarized in three statements: 1. Few teachers are aware that Mexican-Americans have a culture. 2. The teachers who are aware of a Mexican-American culture rarely do anything about it in terms of curricular content. And 3., the one in a thousand teacher who attempts to do something about it invariably does the wrong thing. Educational literature commonly describes Mexican-Americans as "culturally deprived children," when with only a single look it is readily evident that they are not. As Dr. John Aragon of the University of New Mexico once stated, "These are not culturally deprived children, they are culturally atypical children, being taught by culturally deprived teachers."

Illogical testing practices further hamper educational progress for Mexican-Americans. In California, Mexican-Americans account for more than 40 percent of the so-called "mentally handicapped." Even when escape from the special education classes is possible for Mexican-American children, unfair testing undermines their success in school by contributing to the low level of expectation evident in many teachers, both Anglo and Mexican-American. In the style researched by Jacobson and Rosenthal and reported in *Pygmalion in the Classroom*, teachers of Mexican-American children, influenced by the non-school culture, have traditionally expected Mexican-American children to achieve less (Jacobson and Rosenthal, 1968). The prophecy becomes self-fulfilling.

In housing, Mexican-Americans have been hampered by a traditional unwillingness on the part of lending institutions to make monies available for construction and repair of homes in the barrio. The resultant decay of the barrios adds to the stereotypical image of Mexican-Americans who are uncaring about their surroundings. One alternative to this lack of capital has been the use of mechanics' or builders' liens in upgrading homes in the barrio. These liens constitute a menace to many Mexican-Americans in that they provide for the construction or repair of a home with the lien-holding company maintaining the power to take possession of the home should a specified number of monthly payments not be forthcoming. Ignorance of homestead and other protective laws, as well as insecurities about jobs, keeps many Mexican-Americans from risking the loss of a home, however humble.

Discriminatory practices on the part of the Federal Housing Administration that tend to benefit the middle and upper-middle classes, have also succeeded in keeping the Mexican-American from availing himself of the services of that institution. Those FHA services that have finally reached the Mexican-American have to a great extent been detrimental to the cause of an integrated society.

FHA practices of the last twenty years have tended to create ghettos in the cities with the primary consideration in site selection for public housing being the racial or ethnic concentration of the neighborhoods.

The Report of the National Advisory Commission on Civil Disorders, also known as the U.S. Riot Commission Report, took note of this practice in recommending:

> To date, housing programs serving low-income groups have been concentrated in the ghettos. Non-ghetto areas, particularly suburbs, for the most part have steadfastly opposed low-income, rent supplement, or below-market interest rate housing, and have successfully restricted use of these programs

> outside the ghetto. We believe that federally aided low and moderate income housing programs must be re-orientated so that the major thrust is in non-ghetto areas. Public housing programs should emphasize scattered site construction, rent supplements should, wherever possible, be used in non-ghetto areas, and an intensive effort should be made to recruit below-market interest rate sponsors willing to build outside the ghettos (*National Commission on Civil Disorders*, 1968).

In spite of the Riot Commission's report and after almost a year of strong citizen objection to this further ghettoizing, and in spite of Secretary George Romney's recent admission to the Senate Select Committee on Equal Education Opportunity of past FHA and Department of Housing and Urban Development contributions to racial and ethnic social problems, there is still lacking, in most cities, a comprehensive plan for housing that will eliminate the further polarization of our society and the continued destruction of human lives.

Perhaps the greatest alienation between Mexican-Americans and Southwestern institutions exists in the area of the administration of justice. In February 1970, the Texas Advisory to the U.S. Civil Rights Commission stated in a report:

> Definitive evidence exists that black and Mexican-American citizens of Texas suffer discrimination in the administration of the law. This is particularly so in rural areas of the State. Even clearer, and perhaps even more important in its possible consequences, is the evidence that minority citizens tend to regard those who administer the law—including police officers, the courts, and correctional officials—as agents of discrimination and oppression (*Texas Advisory to the U.S. Civil Rights Commission*, 1970).

The use of Texas Rangers and Department of Public Safety personnel in areas experiencing civil rights, or labor activities, promises to do little to curtail the attitude identified by the Civil Rights Advisory. In Starr County, in Mathis, and in Uvalde, Texas, Mexican-Americans perceive law enforcement personnel as opponents of the struggles for equality they have chosen. The damage may well be irreparable.

Their value before the law is questioned by Mexican-Americans for less obvious reasons. The national paradox that shows a relatively low level of concern for problems of drug abuse, other than mandatory and more severe prison sentences, until it becomes a middle class, white, Anglo-Saxon Protestant problem, is very obviously apparent to Mexican-Americans in the barrio. The practice of excluding Mexican-Americans from juries in many south Texas towns still exists, although most have shifted to the practice of including a token Mexican in juries so long as he is the "right kind" of Mexican. The far-reaching effects of this practice are perhaps more apparent when you consider a civil case wherein an all-Anglo jury, with its opinion of the value of a Mexican-American's day work, is called upon to determine compensation for a Mexican-American disabled through personal injury.

While a small percentage of Mexican-Americans have enjoyed social and economic mobility, most Mexican-Americans suffer the lack of socioeconomic mobility. This fact is emphasized, almost indisputably, by the high drop out rate among Mexican-Americans, the high unemployment, and underemployment, prevalent in the barrio.

Lack of socioeconomic mobility is perhaps the most crippling condition of Mexican-American life. A tradition of discriminatory practices and the ever-widening present-day gap between the lower and middle class standards of living presents a rather hopeless picture to Mexican-Americans. Sociologists and anthropologists have stated often that the Mexican-American is held back by a low level of aspiration. I submit that what exists is a low level of expectation, reinforced by successive failures in the school, negatively stereotyped images in the media, and what often become self-fulfilling prophecies about Mexican-Americans' ambitions and capabilities.

Because institutions seem not to serve them, Mexican-Americans see themselves as an exploited people. This exploitation manifests itself through low wages, unfair labor practices, lack of equal employment opportunity, and discrimination in upward job mobility. Nowhere is the economic exploitation of the Mexican-American more apparent than in the plight of the agricultural migrants. Employers with vested interests, and frequently with the assistance of government officials, have successfully impeded most legislation aimed at improving the lot of the migrants.

These efforts deny the migrant coverage under minimum wage laws, coverage under the National Labor Relations Act, and in the state of Texas, adequate housing, rest stops, transportation safety, and the unfair competition of foreign green card holders. Texas Ranger efforts to maintain law and order in the Rio Grande Valley, very conveniently for the growers, also all but ended unionizing activities.

A second form of exploitation experienced by Mexican-Americans is cultural exploitation. Mexican-Americans shopping in downtown San Antonio see the large amounts of money being expended by Mexican citizens who can feel quite at home because they find Spanish-speaking personnel eager to serve them. On the other hand, U.S. tourists are attracted to San Antonio by the quaint Mexican atmosphere, complete with strolling mariachi bands. It is not surprising then that a stroll down the San Antonio Riverwalk is a bitter experience for a Mexican-American who can see that, for the most part, other Mexican-Americans are able to enjoy the beautiful surroundings, expensive shops and the fiesta atmosphere only in their capacity as waiters, busboys, and bartenders.

So entrenched is the feeling of exploitation among Mexican-Americans, especially those in the urban barrio who experience on a daily basis the ploys of money lenders, salesmen with gimmicks, and bill collectors, that efforts to provide self-help opportunities are often viewed with real skepticism. Recently, a federally funded program offering benefits totaling thousands of dollars to participants was implemented in west San Antonio. After the Project Director had explained all of the program to the participants, a stillness pervaded the room which seemed to indicate that there remained some questions. Finally, one program participant broke the silence. "All right," he said, "Now tell us the catch!" And, unfortunately, many programs do carry their own "Catch-22s."

A third form of exploitation is political exploitation. The history of political exploitation of Mexican-Americans is reaching its climax today, when young Mexican-Americans are seeking to establish a third party in the hope of enjoying increased responsiveness. The failure of either major party to institute a program of voter education among Mexican-Americans is perhaps indicative of what has tended to be their philosophy towards this group. Most politicians continue to believe that with enough rallies with free beer and tamales they can secure the support of the Mexican-American community; Mexican-Americans resent this. The lack of concern for the integrity of the Mexican-American voter may well be the clue to the lack of concern for this need. It is not difficult to understand why young Mexican-Americans would choose to work for the unseating of a Texas State Senator, who, with a 65 percent Mexican-American constituency, attempted to filibuster the minimum wage law introduced in the legislature last year (1969).

In recent years, Mexican-Americans have begun to recognize or perceive a fourth type of exploitation. The pride felt by most Mexican-Americans after the exemplary record of Mexican-Americans in World War II and Korea is fast converting into bitter cynicism as a disproportionate percentage of Viet Nam War casualties are Mexican-Americans. Even more bitter is the recognition that in many instances, those same heroes have been unable to enjoy the fruits of life in this country.

All of the conditions I have described combine to create the atmosphere for protest. The reporters of these conditions are frequently those individuals who, having reached their own tolerance for turbulence threshold, react in a manner that causes the protestors to be viewed as troublemakers, outside agitators, egotistical juveniles, effete snobs, criminals, and communists by those who desire that the condition not be reported.

One overriding motivation pervades the Mexican-American protest. It is an unwillingness to perpetuate second-class citizenship. Mexican-Americans are demanding equality before the institutions which have either ignored their needs or misread their needs in the past; they are demanding upward mobility and that means the opening of doors to those institutions that have heretofore been closed to Mexican-American entry.

Mexican-Americans are demanding freedom. In politics it means an end to delivery of the Mexican-American vote by boss politicians, whether they be brown, black, or white. It means alternatives to leadership so that they are not saddled with only a few leaders who might reach their own tolerance for temptation and begin to ignore the needs of the Mexican-Americans; and it means political education, so that the people can choose their candidate because he is responsive, and not because he has the most advertising or the highest endorsement by all the right Mexican-Americans. Most of all, the Mexican-American demand for freedom means the demand for the right to alternatives: alternatives in life styles, alternatives in aspirations, and alternatives in values.

The complexity of Mexican-American needs, values, and aspirations is multiplied by the complexity of the needs, values, and aspirations of the dominant middle-class society. There is no absence of concern for the future course of society; the gap that exists is between the focal points of concerns, many of which are in conflict. The question I bring before you today is, "What is the nature of this chasm of conflicting concerns and how can this chasm be bridged?"

THE CHASM OF CONFLICTING CONCERNS

The chasm is many-faceted. It includes nationalism versus cultural pluralism, participation in institutions versus the preservation of institutions, civil rights versus property rights, and shared political power versus maintenance of the status quo.

The conflict between the growing nationalism among middle America and the surging culturalism among Mexican-Americans is exemplary of the chasm of conflicting concerns. Recently, Mexican-American youth in San Antonio, Texas celebrated La Semana de la Raza, a week-long observance culminating on September 16th, Mexico's Day of Independence. This observance, as well as the Mexican-American's insistence on retaining his language, is viewed as un-American by many, especially those individuals caught up in the wave of renewed patriotism. What is lacking is the realization that Mexican-American activities of this type are celebrations of the Mexican-American's own culturalism rather than of a return-to-Mexico type of nationalism. The conflict is reinforced by the fact that each group has an equal need for its own mechanism. The Mexican-American, too long aware of a slipping away of his values and identity, asserts himself in a celebration of his culture, especially in its exclusion of the dominant culture, and the middle American also feels the need to assert a nationalism, especially in its exclusion of anything foreign or threatening.

Conflicting concerns are manifested in terms of the Mexican-American's urgent push for participation in the institutions that have been closed to him thus far, while middle America is pushing to preserve these institutions as they presently exist. Mexican-American techniques to open the doors of those institutions must often be perceived as battering rams threatening to break down the walls upon which middle America is attempting to build improvements.

Illustrative of this phenomenon are current Mexican-American efforts to participate in the decision-making process of the schools. In the extreme, we are faced with the reality that while universal matriculation is taken for granted in this county, studies have shown that 20 percent of migrant children in Texas never enroll in schools. In institutions of higher learning too, Mexican-Americans are attempting to gain entry—a move seen by many as an attempt to weaken the institutions through a lowering of standards.

In the area of health, too, we see a chasm between a medical profession that daily moves towards increased specialization and a need for improved health delivery services. The irony of the situation becomes evident when one considers that, in a time when organ transplants have become a reality and aerospace medicine is a maturing specialization, there are still Americans who do not have access to the most basic medical and dental services.

In the area of the administration of justice, we are faced with another chasm: a middle America concerned about the protection of public property, and Mexican-Americans and minority groups in general perceiving the tools of justice as something to which they must gain access in order to protect their civil rights. Mexican-American clashes with the instruments of the administration of justice have put the problem into a new perspective. Violent outbreaks in association with civil rights activities usually reflect on the groups initiating those activities, regardless of the findings of commissions and other investigatory bodies. To this concern, many young Mexican-Americans are responding that violence is perpetrated against the Mexican-American every day of his life in the form of systems that sentence him to a life lacking in the joy of taking all that this country has to offer. The consensus seems to be that sentencing a child to a life without an education cripples him as surely as if a gun had been aimed at his limbs, and represents an act of equal violence.

Middle America's political aspirations are also in direct conflict with the political aspirations of Mexican-Americans. In this field we see the maintenance of the status quo as the primary objective of the dominant group while, logically, the Mexican-American attempts entry into the political arena, a move seen as threatening to the status quo by the dominant group.

The political conflict goes beyond the obvious electoral processes for Mexican-Americans. More and more Mexican-American resentment of patronage is evident. The Mexican-American wants to be a full member of the political process, with self-determination as a goal. Participation that is short on self-determination is seen as little more than tokenism and is clearly the object of contempt.

SOME SOLUTIONS

If in fact there is no absence of concern for the future course of our society and the world, then it becomes obvious that those concerns which are today in such great conflict must be harnessed into a force that will bring about the realization of the American Dream for all concerned. If we are to survive and accomplish our goals as a nation, we must begin by implementing several strategies.

First: It might not be totally irrelevant to look to the advice of a great American who became Mexico's first Indian President. Benito Juarez advised his countrymen that ("El respecto al derecho ageno es la paz") "Respect for the rights of others is peace."

Second: We are going to have to do more than pay lip service to the concept of better communications. It may serve us well to remember that communication need not always be verbal, and, in fact, physical exposure to the realities of the differing life styles in our society may be the only effective avenue to real communication.

Third: We must beware of over-reaction and of blind reaction. I can think of no greater deterrent to a solution to the problems of our society than those individuals who resort to fear and hate-mongering as a response to protest.

Fourth: We must implement the concept of change in relationship to all of our institutions. We are going to have to put into practice our conviction that institutions were established to serve individuals. When these institutions fail to serve the needs of individuals, or groups of individuals, they must be changed, expanded, or replaced with those that will not be found wanting under the scrutiny of accountability.

Fifth: We must learn to appreciate and exploit our cultural pluralism. The melting-pot myth must be recognized for what it is, and we must begin to accommodate peoples who are ethnically, racially, and culturally different and have much to offer this country, and indeed the world.

Today, I have attempted to accomplish three things. First, to familiarize you (perhaps needlessly or repetitiously) with the problems of Mexican-Americans as an ethnic group in our society. Second, I have attempted to explain the rapid polarization occurring in our society in terms of conflicting concerns. And finally, I have attempted to seek a way out of the precarious dilemma gripping our entire country.

I can only hope that members of all ethnic and racial groups gathered here today can develop the necessary insights for the diminishing of and eventual solution to, the problem—lest we *all* fall into the ever-widening chasm.

THE THEORY OF INCOMPATIBILITIES

José A. Cárdenas and Blandina "Bambi" Cárdenas

1973

PREFACE

As I approach my forty-third year as a professional educator, if I were asked what I consider to be my single most notable contribution to education, I would immediately respond, "The Theory of Incompatibilities." This document is both a comprehensive analysis of the educational problems of atypical students *and* a framework for the development of a comprehensive educational system responsive to the needs of Hispanics, African Americans, Native Americans and other minorities (those not proficient in English, migrants, immigrants, the disadvantaged, and female students.)

Since its conception twenty-five years ago by Dr. Blandina "Bambi" Cárdenas Ramírez and me, there has never been any question in my mind that the use of such a plan in the education of atypical school populations, notably underserved in the past and the present, could eliminate overnight most of the problems, issues, frustrations, and failures in our educational system.

There has been little improvement of educational opportunity for atypical students during the past twenty-five years that has not been brought about by a school effort that is compatible with some portion of this education plan, and there have been few successful school programs for atypical students that are not consistent with the contents of its framework.

Many of the elements of this plan were not original to the authors. Our contribution lay in providing a comprehensive rationale that could provide the basis for a much-needed overhaul of the schools, rather than the hit-and-miss, piecemeal approaches of the past.

The "Theory of Incompatibilities" originated from a series of conferences on migrant education held by the Texas Migrant Educational Development Center, a program directed by me at the Southwest Educational Development Laboratory (SEDL) in Austin, Texas. Under the mentorship of two consultants, Egon Guba and Dan Stufflebeam (hired by Dr. Edwin Hindsman, SEDL Executive Director), we conducted conferences with migrant parents, teachers, administrators, school board members, and community leaders concerning the education of migrant children. The conferences resulted in the identification of many problems as perceived by the conference participants and recommendations for addressing those problems.

As we analyzed conference proceedings, we were struck by the repetitiveness of the word *incompatible* in the records. The language used by the school was incompatible with the language spoken by the students; the school calendar was incompatible with the geographic lifestyles of the migrant population; and instructional materials were incompatible with the culture of the migrant family. Grouping these incompatibilities into the three areas of culture, language, and mobility, the authors later conceptualized the areas of poverty (socio-economic class) and societal perceptions (self-concept and school perceptions). Brainstorming over a number of months produced the ten elements of school activity and the principles of inter-relatedness and adaptability that completed the model.

The Theory of Incompatibilities was published a few times, presented at conferences, workshops, and seminars several hundred times, and distributed to thousands of interested parties as a handout and as an independent publication.

The document was changed so many times by a succession of editors, that upon reviewing the latest version recently used in an education class at one of the local universities, Bambi and I were surprised at its condition. The version included here is a copy of a 1973 draft that I located in my files.

Even before its original publication, The Theory of Incompatibilities served as the framework for four years of sensational pioneering work in the education of minority children in the Edgewood Independent School District, from 1969 to 1973. It also served as the framework for the Edgewood Experimental Schools Program, a large reform effort funded by the research division of what was then the United States Office of Education.

At Texans for Educational Excellence (TEE)/Intercultural Development Research Association (IDRA), The Theory of Incompatibilities has served for twenty years as the guide for most of the organization's activity. Innovative programs in multicultural education, bilingual education, staff training, parent involvement and materials development were based on this model. Technical assistance provided to hundreds of school systems through national origin, and race desegregation assistance centers were also based on the model, and it has served as a conceptual framework for *Amanecer, Nuevo Amanecer,* the Coca-Cola Valued Youth Program, and most other successful materials and programs of IDRA (IDRA, 1979; IDRA, 1985).

The Theory of Incompatibilities served as the model for the education plan ordered by the federal court in the San Felipe Del Rio intervention motion in *U.S. v. Texas,* in *Keyes v. Denver,* and in some sixty other court cases and administrative hearings on the denial of equality of educational opportunity (*United States v. Texas,* 1971; *Keyes v. School District No. 1,* 1983).

At various times, the model has been adapted for presentation to health organizations, social work institutions, the Immigration and Naturalization Service, U.S. Customs Service, and a host of other institutions. The warm reception received at such presentations would indicate that in addition to serving as a model for a comprehensive plan for the education of minority students, it could well serve as the framework for the successful delivery of services by *all* social institutions serving a culturally diverse population.

Although the use of this model has resulted in a number of successful efforts, it has certainly not led to any large or drastic changes in educational practice.

Schools are extremely intractable institutions, highly limited in the amount of change they can assimilate at any one time. Following a presentation of the model to an educational institution, it was not unusual for the institution to respond, "It sounds wonderful, but we aren't interested in such a big program; we just want something to improve the performance of the students." Needless to say, educational practitioners have limited capacity for turbulence and persistently seek quick fixes for massive educational programs. The typical teacher is seeking a solution to be found in a hand puppet, a little song, or a one-page worksheet that will bring about a dramatic improvement in educational performance.

School administrators are still looking for some kind of an electronic device that can be plugged into the student to eliminate failure. It is difficult for school leadership to comprehend, let alone implement, substantial change in school activity.

The training of school personnel at all levels is still divorced from the realities of the education of minority and disadvantaged children. Education professors in institutions of higher education, seldom members of minorities and almost never economically disadvantaged, have few relationships with the education of minority and disadvantaged students.

It is hoped that at some future date, professional accountability for the dismal failure in the education of atypical school populations will force educators to look at a model for bringing about a culturally democratic learning environment that will provide an avenue for the improved educational performance of minority and disadvantaged students. Perhaps at this future date the following article will receive the attention we feel it deserves.

INTRODUCTION

An awareness of problems in the education of Hispanic Americans during the 1960s led to the development and implementation of a comprehensive education plan in response to these problems. This comprehensive plan, developed and first published in 1969, by José A. Cárdenas and Blandina Cárdenas, provided a rationale for the development and implementation of educational strategies compatible with the characteristics and needs of Hispanic American children. Entitled "A Theory of Incompatibilities," the model is based on the concept that the poor performance of Hispanic American children can be attributed to incompatibilities between the characteristics of the children and the characteristics of the instructional program. The last nine years have presented no new findings that suggest a need for altering the conceptual framework for this response. On the contrary, during the last nine years, the authors' continuous involvement in minority and Hispanic education has only reinforced the original concept as a theoretically sound and educationally practical solution to the problems of educating minority populations.

Black, Mexican-American, and economically disadvantaged children have not enjoyed the same success in school as that of the typical middle-class American. The Cárdenas-Cárdenas Theory of Incompatibilities is a tested belief that the failure of such children can be attributed to a lack of compatibility between the characteristics of minority children and the characteristics of a typical instructional program (Cárdenas and Cárdenas, 1973).

An instructional program developed for a white, Anglo-Saxon, English-speaking middle class school population cannot be, and is not, adequate for a non-white, non-Anglo-Saxon, non-English-speaking, or non-middle-class population.

To reverse the pattern of failure for non-typical children, it is necessary that the instructional program and the characteristics of the learner be compatible, and in order to develop such an instructional program, these incompatibilities need to be identified and eliminated.

We have identified over forty such incompatibilities and have grouped them into five areas: poverty, culture, language, mobility, and societal perceptions.

AREAS OF INCOMPATIBILITY

POVERTY

Many of this country's minority children are raised in an environment of poverty. Much has been written about the effects of poverty on the development of the individual. In general, it can be concluded that the growth of a child living in such circumstances leads to a non-typical development pattern that differs significantly from the developmental patterns of middle-class children.

Large child-to-adult ratios lead to the development of atypical speech patterns when the amount of interaction between child and adults is constrained. The frequent absence of one of the typical adults in the home and the dissipation of adult energies in meeting the basic essentials of life further compound this problem. The relative absence of communication media (TV, radio, newspapers, magazines, and books) contributes to the development of an atypical developmental pattern. An absence of success models and an academic-oriented tradition develops differing attitudes toward schools and schooling. Poverty also leads to a relative unavailability of intellectually stimulating toys, games, and activities. The deprivational effects of inadequate housing, malnutrition and poor health similarly influence the development of poor children.

Evidence of this type has led educators to an erroneous conclusion: namely, the development of a "deficit" philosophy, which attributes poor school performance of poverty children to a deficiency caused by growing up in a deficient environment. Although there is often an educational development retardation, it is our opinion that this retardation is not a serious educational handicap, and that this retardation can be overcome by the placement of the child in a school environment that stimulates development and rapidly produces an accelerated development in those areas critical to educational success in typical school situations.

The educational handicap of poverty children occurs when they are placed in an educational program that fails to take into account these unique early development patterns and assumes (and requires) the same developmental level normally found in middle-class children.

For example, it has been extensively documented that children growing up in the noisy environment of an overcrowded ghetto home located in a poor residential area develop listening skills in a different manner from children raised in the relative quiet and order of a middle-class home. Poor children tend to learn to block out sounds rather than learn finer and finer sound discriminations, as is the case with middle-class children. Upon entering school, it is possible to place a poor child in an auditory-discrimination program. In a matter of weeks, the auditory developmental retardation may be successfully overcome.

But instead of being placed in such a program, he is usually placed in a typical reading-readiness program that assumes that the child has the auditory-discrimination development of the middle-class child for whom the program was designed. The results of such a placement are disastrous.

Therefore, the failure of the child in this case is not caused by the type of *home* in which he was *raised*, but rather the type of *school program* in which he was *placed*. Auditory-discrimination retardation is *not* an educational problem! Research at the José A. Cárdenas Early Childhood Education Center in the Edgewood Independent School District showed that two weeks of audio-discrimination training completely eliminated this "problem." The incompatibility between the existing level of development and the level of development assumed in the instructional program and needed for success is the educational problem.

CULTURE

A second incompatibility between the characteristics of minority children and instructional programs lies in the area of culture. This incompatibility between minority children and most school systems can be summarized in three generalizations:

1. Most school personnel know nothing about the cultural characteristics of the minority school population;
2. The few school personnel who are aware of these cultural characteristics seldom do anything about them; and
3. On those rare occasions when the school *does* attempt to do something about the culture of minority groups, it almost always does the *wrong things*.

Much has been written about the cultural irrelevance of instructional materials. In general, typical instructional materials developed by and for white, Anglo, middle-class personnel present surroundings, situations, dialogue, and conclusions that are foreign and incongruous to the culturally atypical child. The absence of minority traditions, values, and orientations in instructional materials makes them irrelevant, meaningless, and inferior in educational value for use by minority children.

School responses to this incompatibility have been dysfunctional. The use of black or brown ink to color the physical features of some of the people portrayed in some textbooks has done little to reduce the incompatibility, and in fact, the inclusion of negative stereotypes has frequently aggravated this problem rather than diminished it.

Although incompatibilities in instructional materials have received much attention in recent years, no such attention has been drawn to the incompatibilities in instructional methodologies. Professor Lesser, at Harvard, conducted interesting experiments that give us some insights into the nature of this problem. In studying learning characteristics of children from different ethnic backgrounds, he discovered that children from different ethnic groups display some marked preferences for ethnically compatible learning styles. For example, Jewish children did better than Chinese children in instructional activities based on verbalization. On the other hand, Chinese children outperformed Jewish children in instructional activities presented in the abstract. Regardless of socio-economic background, the amount of learning correlated with the ethnicity and preferred learning style (Lesser, 1965).

In a similar experiment at UCLA, Kagan and Madsen conducted learning activities with Mexican National, Mexican-American, and Anglo children. In a learning activity based on typical middle-class Anglo competition, the Anglo children outperformed the Mexican children (Kagan and Madsen, 1971). But upon presenting the same learning activity, but basing it on *cooperation* rather than *competition*, the Mexican children outperformed the Anglo children.

The conclusions of these and other similar studies indicate that the amount children learn in a classroom is dependent on their race or ethnicity, the related cultural characteristics, their culturally related preferred learning styles, and the style used by the school.

Obviously, if learning styles compatible with Anglo children are used exclusively, the instructional program is biased against, and incompatible with, minority children.

Dr. Manuel Ramirez and Dr. Alfredo Castañeda, at Stanford University, developed an instructional approach based on a "Culturally Democratic Learning Environment" that allows children options in selecting learning activities compatible with their culturally dependent learning styles (Ramirez and Castañeda, 1973).

In distinguishing between these first two areas of incompatibility, the school is warned that it is responsible for differentiating between the "culture of poverty" and "cultural poverty." Responsiveness to the characteristics of poverty is a prerequisite to providing equal access to the full benefits of the educational program to minority group children. It is incumbent on the school district to remove the constraints that poverty places on the educational success of children and to compensate for deprivations that are correlated with poverty.

There is a fine distinction, however, between the effects of poverty and the effects of culture. While it is the school district's responsibility to eradicate the effect of poverty, it is not the school's prerogative to reverse the effects of culture. Mexican-American and Black children are culturally different children who are deprived because they are poor; cultural difference becomes cultural deprivation only after culturally biased institutions succeed in damaging the fabric of culture through consistent attack.

LANGUAGE

Language is an element of culture so significant in its role as an impediment to learning that it must be listed as a separate incompatibility.

It is obvious that an incompatibility exists when a Spanish-speaking child is placed in an English-language instructional program. The incompatibility is not so apparent when the language differences are attributed to dialect (as in some Black children) or socio-economic background. The language used in most textbooks in the early grades is so incompatible with the language of minority and disadvantaged children that it frequently appears to be a foreign language.

We make no value judgement as to the relative worth or adequacy of the various languages and dialects that can be used in our country. The important point, as in the two preceding areas of incompatibility, is that a child cannot be taught successfully in a language system that he does not understand.

Past attempts to eliminate this incompatibility have been detrimental to the minority child. Psychologically, the trauma produced by the sudden immersion into an incomprehensible situation, coupled with the identification of the native language as undesirable, detrimental, and inadequate, still remains with many of us. Pedagogically, the cold-turkey approach to the acquisition of a new language commonly requires that the beginning child master a new language, plus skills in that new language such as reading and arithmetic, *and* a variety of content materials—all at the same time. The common failure of the child to achieve all three marks the beginning of the cumulative "deficit" phenomenon.

The introduction of English as a Second Language (ESL) programs may have improved the situation, but in itself it has failed to solve the problem. The postponement of basic skill development and content acquisition until a new language system has been mastered has led to delays for periods of as long as one year, with a resultant academic retardation. ESL, with its inevitable non-acceptance, and subsequent elimination of, the Spanish language, can only give the child a sense of language valuing that tells him his native tongue is inferior.

The only sensible solution for the elimination of this incompatibility has been the development of bilingual programs in recent years. Typically, bilingual programs consist of three basic elements:

1. The continued cognitive development of the child, with accompanying development of basic skills and content acquisition in his dominant language;
2. The development of English as a second language; and
3. A transition of instructional activity from the native language to English when there is sufficient assurance that the student can handle English language instruction.

A fourth basic element, which is optional, is the further extension of the student's native language. Since the mastery of languages other than English has long been an objective of the school, it would be ridiculous to allow native language proficiency to atrophy, only to reintroduce the language as "foreign" at a later age, when the student may have less physiological and psychological propensity for language acquisition.

MOBILITY

To a large extent, the instructional program for typical children is one designed for a geographically stable population. Such a program is incompatible with a highly mobile child. Although this characteristic was originally identified in the children of migrant agricultural laborers, it was soon apparent that urban minority children are no less mobile. The advent of urban development, with accompanying urban renewal and government-subsidized housing, coupled with financial and social problems, has led to the mobility of minority and disadvantaged children.

The typical instructional program, with built-in continuity and sequences that assume that the child in the classroom today was there yesterday and will be there tomorrow, is incompatible with this mobility. This program discontinuity problem must be faced with either a mobile curriculum or with a highly individualized instructional program.

SOCIETAL PERCEPTIONS

The last area of incompatibility is between the instructional program and the way the minority child is perceived.

After negative interactions with the school, minority children tend to perceive themselves in negative terms. If the child does not have negative perceptions on entering school, the alien environment, with its continuous negative valuing of the child, his home, his language, and his culture, will rapidly develop this negative self-concept in him.

Typical instructional programs are developed for dominant-culture children who have positive, often very positive, concepts of self in school. These instructional materials and methodologies do not have the frequent, strong, and immediate positive feedback mechanism needed in order for a child who perceives himself as a non-learner to change his concept and perceive himself as a successful learner.

On the contrary, the erroneous assumption of the existence of prerequisite skills, the large increments of difficulty, and the inadequacies of the program tend to develop or even strengthen a negative concept. Yet just as nothing succeeds like success, nothing is as educationally motivating to a child as experiencing success in a learning situation.

A similar situation exists in regard to the perceptions the school has of the minority child. In general, the negative feelings schools hold and express about minority children lead to the development of very low levels of expectation for the performance of these children, and all children tend to perform in keeping with what is expected of them. Just as Jacobson and Rosenthal were able to improve children's school performance, and subsequently, even intellectual abilities, by giving teachers false information about the innate potential of children in their classic experiment, *Pygmalion in the Classroom*, so too, can teachers downgrade the performance of minority children by low levels of expectation based on equally false information (Jacobson and Rosenthal, 1968).

SUMMARY

In general, the Cárdenas-Cárdenas Theory of Incompatibilities attributes the poor school performance of minority and disadvantaged children to differences between the characteristics of the children and the characteristics of typical instructional programs developed for typical children.

No deliberate attempt is made to criticize instructional programs when used with the children for whom the programs were developed. On the other hand, no criticism is made of the characteristics of minority children. The situation is analogous to a square peg and a round hole. The incompatibility between the two shapes speaks for itself.

INTERRELATEDNESS AND INTERDEPENDENCE

Two additional principles are necessary for understanding the educational implications of the Theory of Incompatibilities. The first is the principle of interrelatedness and interdependence.

Up to this point, various areas of incompatibility have been presented individually. It is dangerous to assume that each of these areas is an independent variable that can be studied, analyzed, and responded to independent of the other four areas. The five areas are so interrelated that it is impossible (as well as fruitless) to consider one in the absence of the others.

For instance, it has been stated that mobility is an area of incompatibility that accounts for the poor academic performance of minority and disadvantaged children. Yet we can cite many examples of other types of "mobile" children, such as the children of military personnel, chain store executives, and certain civil service workers, who experience a similar degree of mobility and still do not suffer from the effects of program discontinuity. In fact, many of these children, in spite of, or because of, their mobility, tend to out-perform children from geographically stable homes!

Therefore, mobility can be an asset *or* a liability. It is only when mobility is coupled with poverty, culture, language, or societal perceptions that it becomes a liability for the minority child. Perhaps it is the combination of some, or even all, the other areas of incompatibility with mobility that produces the disastrous educational effects characteristic of mobile minority children.

Another example is the incompatibility of language, which is frequently described as the cause of all of the educational problems of Mexican-Americans. Yet educators who have taught along the Mexican border, where there is a large influx of new immigrants, are well acquainted with a phenomenon characteristic of these children. Although immigrant children who have previously attended school in the mother country may enter our schools without any knowledge of the English language, after a brief period of instability as they acquire English language skills, they will consistently outperform native-born minority children. Therefore, the incompatibility of language, even coupled with culture, is not the sole source of the problem. It is language, *and* culture, *and* poverty, *and* mobility, *and* perceptions *in tandem* that account for the poor performance of minority children.

This principle has two major implications for our purposes. First, the development of education programs that respond to one of the incompatibilities and ignores the others is doomed to failure. This principle accounts for the past failure of our school systems to develop successful programs for minority children. In most cases, billions of federal dollars have been poured into programs aimed at responding to some characteristics of the minority child in the absence of the others, and have failed to make a significant change in the performance of the children.

The second implication is that the development of an education plan that responds to the needs of minority children must be a comprehensive plan that takes into account all the areas of incompatibility, rather than a piecemeal effort. A bilingual program, a Black studies program, or a poverty program developed in the absence of a comprehensive attack will *not* bring about improved performance of minority children.

ADAPTABILITY

A second principle that must be considered before the development of an educational plan is the principle of adaptability.

As we said before, an incompatibility exists between the characteristics of the minority child and the characteristics of the instructional program. One of two options exists: either the child must be changed to fit the instructional program, or the instructional program must be changed to fit the child.

Past attempts on the part of school systems to develop functionally responsive instructional programs indicate an eclectic philosophy. When the atypicality was a characteristic falling within the area of the dominant cultural group, the school modified its program to fit the child. Thus, we commonly see elevators for handicapped children, Braille materials for the blind, and elaborate schemes, materials, and equipment to fill the needs of a limitless assortment of atypical children.

But when the atypical characteristic has been attributed to race or ethnicity, the school has placed the burden of adaptability on the child. Thus, schools have acted in a racist manner in the application of this double standard for adaptability. In addition to this inherent racism in the concept of having minority children adapt to a typical program, such an approach can no longer be tolerated for the following reasons:

1. It has failed. There is no way to change a non-white into a white or to change a Mexican-American boy or girl into a child of northern European descent. Mass efforts in welfare legislation have barely made a dent in the incidence and extent of poverty. Past legislation in various states prohibiting the use of any language other than English for instructional activities in schools did little to reduce, let alone eliminate, the speaking of Spanish among Mexican-Americans.

2. The melting-pot myth is rapidly being replaced by concepts of cultural pluralism. Before attempts to change the characteristics of the learner are implemented, we must raise the question: Is it desirable to do so?

3. Changing the individual in order to produce compatibility between the instructional program and the learner is futile unless the changed individual is *also* accepted into the larger society. Social, political, military, and economic discrimination against Blacks and Mexican-Americans in this country will continue to constrain any ethnic disposition to change for the sole purpose of participating in the educational program.

4. The process of change is destructive when it calls on Blacks and Mexican-Americans to reject themselves in order to assume a new identity.

ELEMENTS OF AN EDUCATIONAL PLAN

A comprehensive education plan aimed at eliminating the incompatibilities between the school and minority children cannot be effective if it addresses itself only to the physical assignment of students or the implementation of a smattering of isolated programs. The entire institution must develop a sensitivity to the problem, and all aspects of the school must be affected.

The institution of a course for the educational improvement of minority children is of no value if the teacher is not trained to teach the course. The assignment of children to mixed classes on the basis of racial equality is useless if the child encounters racist manifestations in the school policies, the curriculum, materials, or on the football team.

Therefore, the schools must consider a wide array of change, a comprehensive program coupled with an intense and massive compensatory program for the students if it is to be successful and involve the entire community, the schoolboard, the school staff, and the pupils.

EDUCATIONAL PHILOSOPHIES

Problems in the education of minority children would be eliminated almost overnight if educational institutions would develop and implement positive educational philosophies. It is hoped that these institutions would develop such philosophies of their own accord, but in the absence of any initiative, these philosophies must be imposed by external agencies. Thus, a court order may lay down the rules under which schools are to operate.

Basic policies that must be adopted, regardless of origin, include the following:

1. Minority children can learn, regardless of any characteristic they may exhibit because of economic, cultural, language, social, ethnic, or racial background. There is *nothing* inherent in minority children that is an impediment to learning. Past failures of minority children are the result of inadequate school programs, and *not* the fault of the child and his background.

2. Cultural pluralism is a desirable condition in our society. It is the pluralistic element in our society that made this country great. It is impossible to predict those cultural characteristics that will be conducive to the continued development, or perhaps survival, of our society. The co-existence of differing lifestyles will allow alternatives that provide the natural variations needed for subsequent selection.

3. A facility in more than one language is a desirable educational goal. The United States is probably the only country in the world where a person is considered educated in spite of an inability to speak a foreign language. Although schools pay lip service to this philosophy, neither the teaching of foreign languages, nor the retention and expansion of non-English native languages has been accomplished by our schools. The cost of this shortcoming in terms of international relations, and economic, social, diplomatic, political, and military effects, has been disastrous.
4. The individualization of instruction is an essential element of all instructional programs for all children. The different characteristics of children lead to different needs, interests, efforts, motivations, styles, and programs. The lockstep concept of education, with similar programs for all children has led to the waste of a good portion of our personal resources—minorities, the disadvantaged, the gifted, and the handicapped.
5. Children, *all* children, are a natural resource of our country. As humans, they have an intrinsic worth; as resources, they have a potential value. Each child must be developed to the point where he becomes an integral and positive part of our society, a contributing member, and a participant in the fruits of this bountiful land.
6. The final result of an educational program for minority children is freedom. Freedom is manifested through freedom of choice, and freedom of choice in turn requires feasible alternatives from which to choose. It is incumbent on the schools to develop in children the necessary skills that make feasible alternatives available to them. Vocational choices, lifestyles, and economic levels should be dependent on an individual's free choice, and not by accident of birth, parents' economic conditions, geographic location, race, ethnicity, or any of the monolithic cultural constraints now found in social institutions and which lock out people through the absence of alternatives.

GOVERNANCE—POLICIES, RULES, AND REGULATIONS

The racism inherent in our social institutions commonly manifests itself through racially biased policies, rules, and regulations. These governances are usually biased in favor of the dominant cultural group in that they reflect its values, traditions, and orientations. The school system must analyze its governance as it affects economic conditions, culture, language, mobility, and the perceptual characteristics of children.

SCOPE AND SEQUENCE

The scope and sequence of the instructional program must be flexible to the needs of individual children and the varying elements in the community. A barrio child may benefit greatly from early interventions by the school. The nutritional aspects of a free lunch at the age of three may require that such a program be made available to the child. The educational level of an adult group may be such that considerable benefits may be derived from an adult education program.

CURRICULUM

The changes which the school must make in order to eliminate incompatibilities between child and school are most evident in the curriculum element. In general, the school should identify, acquire, adopt, or develop instructional materials and methodologies that are compatible with the characteristics of minority children.

STAFFING

The implementation of an adequate curriculum requires that schools devote considerable attention to this area.

Four concepts must be included in the education plan.

1. It is the responsibility of the school district to identify, recruit, and employ educational personnel sufficiently cognizant of the characteristics of minority children to insure the adequate development and implementation of a responsive instructional program. Not only must training and experience be taken into consideration, but at least a portion of this staff must be reflective of the characteristics of the minority child. Teachers who are members of minority groups have the highest propensity for understanding and responding to the characteristics of minority children. It is the responsibility of the system to acquire minority staff at least in equal proportions to the numbers of minority children.

2. An adequate curriculum requires staff differentiation patterns. An educational institution may react negatively to the seemingly awesome implications of this education plan. The chances of a successful implementation are considerably diminished in light of the staff expertise that will be required. Staff differentiation is the use of a variety of professional and paraprofessional personnel for instructional purposes. The type of personnel is very much determined by the skills required for a specific instructional activity.

3. The successful implementation of this plan will require a massive effort in the training and retraining of all levels of educational personnel. Beginning with the basic assumption that traditional practices have not been successful and alternative programs must be developed and implemented, it is apparent that an in-service teacher training program must be implemented for the understanding and synthesis of the rationale of this education plan. Further training would be needed for the identification of the characteristics of minority children, the development of alternative activities, and the acquisition of the necessary skills for program implementation.

   The development and implementation of a staff training program will require the identification and acquisition of personnel resources very different from the conventional higher education trainers of teachers, locked in their ivory towers and cranking out dysfunctional teachers completely unprepared to teach the atypical minority child.

4. Staffing also implies the development of a program that affords upward and lateral mobility for minority personnel. The use of minority persons in paraprofessional positions may become detrimental when the child perceives that assistants and aides reflect minority characteristics, but professional personnel and authority figures always reflect an alien cultural group. An adequate staffing program will also provide the necessary training and experience for minority teachers to move into counseling, supervisory, and administrative positions. This upward mobility must extend into the highest-level administrative position of the school system.

CO-CURRICULAR ACTIVITIES

The effective integration of minority children must extend beyond the confines of school integration and an integrated instructional program. The various co-curricular activities must provide an opportunity for minority children to perceive themselves as equal participants in these activities. Various impediments such as cost, policies, and procedures must be reviewed in order to afford minority children a full opportunity for effective participation in all aspects of school activities.

STUDENT PERSONNEL SERVICES

The various services provided to students, such as advisory, counseling, guidance, and health, usually contain the same incompatibilities found in the classroom. The use of invalid and biased tests has been extremely detrimental to minority children. This aspect of the school program must be drastically revised in order to afford equality of educational opportunity.

NON-INSTRUCTIONAL NEEDS

Not all the needs of minority children can be met in the classroom. The effects of hunger, malnutrition, inadequate housing, and poor dental and medical attention have a direct and strong influence on educational outcomes. A failure to provide adequately for the non-instructional needs of children can be a contributing factor to the lack of school success.

COMMUNITY INVOLVEMENT

Schools have generally failed to effectively involve some segment of the community in planning, implementing, and evaluating school programs. Sometimes this failure can be attributed to preconceived notions that the school, and the larger society, have of minorities. An erroneous myth still persists that minority cultures do not have an interest in their children. Anthropological studies support the rejection of this myth. The fact that minority communities have different customs not understood by the schools, the failure of the schools to communicate effectively with parents, and the negative relationship that exists between the two, all fail to provide the necessary bridge for the chasm that exists between the school and the home.

Parents continually complain that they are degraded and insulted in school interactions. Communicating with parents only when a negative situation develops, such as a disciplinary problem, makes parents shy away from any relationship. The failure of schools to provide personnel cognizant of minority lifestyles and fluent in the language of the home creates a barrier to an effective relationship.

EVALUATION

The evaluation designs, materials, and techniques commonly used by the school are frequently most inappropriate for use with minority populations. Not only are the tools inadequate, but conclusions based on cultural and language biases can be extremely erroneous and detrimental to the student. Incompatibilities existing between this element and the characteristics of minority children must be eliminated.

THE DEVELOPMENTAL MATRIX

The five areas of incompatibility (poverty, culture, language, mobility, and societal perceptions) crossed with the ten elements of an education plan produce a developmental matrix of fifty cells. Each of these cells is the intersection of an area of incompatibility with a particular school element. For example, the incompatibility of language relates to educational philosophies, school policies, scope and sequence, curriculum, staffing, co-curricular activities, student services, non-instructional needs, community involvement, and evaluation. Similarly each of the elements of school activity intersects with each area of incompatibility. For example, the curriculum must be compatible with the minority characteristics of poverty, culture, language, mobility and societal perceptions. The same is true for each element in the list.

The following table is the developmental matrix produced by the crossing of incompatibilities with elements. This matrix serves as the basis for an instructional program that will improve the performance of minority children, protect the rights of minority children, and provide equality of educational opportunity (See Table 1).

TABLE 1

THE DEVELOPMENTAL MATRIX AREAS OF INCOMPATIBILITY

ELEMENTS:	POVERTY	CULTURE	LANGUAGE	MOBILITY	SOCIETAL PERCEP-TIONS
PHILOSOPHIES					
POLICIES					
SCOPE & SEQUENCE					
CURRICULUM					
STAFFING					
CO-CURRICULUM					
STUDENT SERVICES					
NON-INSTRUCTIONAL NEEDS					
COMMUNITY INVOLVEMENT					
EVALUATION					

TESTIMONY IN *U.S. v. TEXAS*

1971

PREFACE

This portion of the litigation in the protracted Texas desegregation court case is one of the most unusual ever encountered in the attempt by the Department of Justice to dismantle the system of segregated schools in this country. It is unusual in that the intervention was sought by the defendant school district with a petition to the Federal Court of the Eastern District of Texas to integrate this white majority school district with an adjacent predominantly minority school district. The legal basis for the request was that the majority school district, the Del Rio Independent School District in Val Verde County, Texas, claimed that in its formation it had intentionally excluded for discriminatory reasons a portion of the city's minority population, patrons of the San Felipe Independent School District.

The school district presented a reasonably acceptable argument that since it had acted illegally in its own creation, the resulting entity was illegal!

The history of desegregation and civil rights litigation has produced few cases in which the defendant school district admits to discriminatory treatment of minorities, let alone volunteers such information with a request for remedy at court to correct such discriminatory treatment.

The basis for this request was the existence of Laughlin Air Force Base in the San Felipe district, which sent, through inter-district transfers, most of the military-related children in Laughlin Air Force Base to the Del Rio District. In *U.S. v. Texas*, Judge William Wayne Justice issued a court order, known as Civil Action 5281, which prohibited school district transfers in the state of Texas that exacerbated racial or ethnic segregation (*United States v. Texas*, 1971). Since most of the children at Laughlin were white and Anglo, the traditional transfer of these students resulted in a higher concentration of minority students in San Felipe and a higher concentration of non-minority students in Del Rio.

The transfer students provided the Del Rio School District with a financial windfall. The enrolling school district received extensive financial aid under the Federal Impact Aid Program, with Public Law 874 providing funds for the maintenance and operation of the schools and Public Law 815 providing extensive funds for the building of school facilities.

The failure of the Texas Education Agency (TEA) to approve the transfer of the students, in keeping with Civil Action 5281, resulted in a request for the consolidation of the two districts in order to prevent the military-related students from attending a predominantly Mexican-American school district.

In response to the request by Del Rio, Judge Justice ordered the consolidation of the two school districts into a new entity, the San Felipe Del Rio Independent School District. Officials of the former San Felipe District opposed the consolidation, arguing that minority interests would be lost in the newly formed district.

Attorney John Conroy, of the Department of Justice, and Mrs. Dorothy Stuck, of the Department of Health, Education, and Welfare's Office of Civil Rights, asked me to testify in court on behalf of the Mexican-American students in the newly consolidated school district and for the development of a court-ordered, comprehensive educational plan that would safeguard the rights of Mexican-American students and guarantee them equal educational opportunity.

At the time, I was superintendent of the Edgewood School District in San Antonio, Texas, which, like San Felipe, was predominantly Mexican-American. With a Board of Trustees made up entirely of Mexican-Americans, I had had little difficulty in making massive changes in the district, with the implementation of a large number of innovative programs designed to expand educational opportunities by making the schools compatible with the characteristics of minority students. New initiatives in Edgewood included bilingual education, multicultural education, an unbelievably extensive early childhood program, which included everything from pre-natal care for expectant mothers to pre-school programs for three-, four-, and five-year-old children. Other innovations included an infant stimulation program, a cross-age tutoring program as a successful dropout prevention strategy, extensive parent and community development programs, career development for high school graduates, the use of social workers, and even employment and financial assistance programs for parents. My testimony resulted in Judge Justice's handing down a comprehensive order described by state officials as "the goddamnedest cradle-to-grave order in legal history" (Kemerer, 1991).

In his ruling, Judge Justice wrote:

> The Court was particularly impressed by the testimony of Dr. José Cárdenas who presented a lengthy commentary on the problems commonly faced by Mexican-American students. This testimony demonstrated that Mexican-American students exhibit numerous characteristics which have a causal connection with their general ability to benefit from an educational program designed primarily to meet the needs of so-called Anglo-Americans. These characteristics include "cultural incompatibilities" and English language deficiencies—two traits which immediately and effectively identify those students sharing them as members of a definite group whose performance norm habitually will fall below that of Anglo-American students who do not exhibit these traits. It would appear, therefore, from Dr. Cárdenas' testimony that it is largely these ethnically-linked traits—albeit combined with other factors such as poverty, malnutrition and the effects of past educational deprivation—which account for the identification of Mexican-American students as a group and which have, as a consequence, elicited from many school boards throughout Texas and, indeed, throughout the southwestern United States, the different and often discriminatory treatment shown on the record in this case.

Virtually all of the areas of incompatibility and all of the elements in the Cárdenas-Cárdenas Theory of Incompatibilities were included in the court ordered plan. The action taken by the court had a strong effect on the education of Mexican-Americans and other minorities nationwide. The court concluded that Mexican-Americans were an identifiable ethnic group and were afforded the same desegregation guarantees African American students enjoyed under *Brown v. Board of Education* (*Brown v. Board of Education*, 1954). This finding curtailed a tendency for school officials to respond to court-ordered desegregation mandates by integrating African Americans and Mexican-Americans, while perpetuating the segregation of white Anglo students. Tri-ethnic desegregation was subsequently practiced in Corpus Christi, Dallas, Ft. Worth, Texas, Denver, Colorado, and in most other urban centers.

The court order established a precedent not only for desegregation, but also for addressing the characteristics and needs of a unique ethnic group in the educational program. The principle of adaptability placed the onus for adaptation on the educational system rather than on the students. This principle of school adaptability subsequently became the key issue in *Lau v. Nichols* and was affirmed by the U.S. Supreme Court (*Lau v. Nichols*, 1974).

The comprehensive educational plan based on our Theory of Incompatibilities became a routine part of desegregation court cases, as I presented similar testimony in Denver and Grand Junction, Colorado; Bakersfield and Los Angeles, California; Tucson, Arizona; Dallas, Harlingen, Raymondville, El Paso, and Uvalde, Texas, and many other court cases and administrative hearings. I also participated in the development of comprehensive education plans for San Francisco, California; Chicago, Illinois; Seattle, Washington; Victoria, Texas; Puerto Rico, and Alaska.

In recent years, I have been asked by several historians why I did not develop these comprehensive education plans any further than I did. My response is that I never had the luxury of time to do so. During most of this time I was employed as a full-time superintendent of schools in one of the dozen largest school districts in Texas, and it was extremely difficult to devote an extensive amount of time to the refinement of locally implemented court plans. Although I worked as a consultant in some sixty or seventy court cases, due to the financial constraints of civil rights organizations and the extensive bureaucracy of the federal government, I seldom received any pay for my services. On many occasions I wasn't even reimbursed for my travel expenses, and I frequently had to pay for transportation, lodging, and meals with personal funds. At other times, I depended on the cooperation and generosity of the Edgewood Board, which gave me the necessary time off and sometimes even took care of travel expenses.

It is ironic, but also admirable, that the Edgewood School District, which was one of the poorest out of 1,200 in Texas, did so much for the improvement of educational opportunities for minority students nationwide.

But the implementation of the comprehensive education plan in the new San Felipe Del Rio School District was never realized for various reasons. First, there was an extreme lack of support and effort by the school officials in the district. The old adage proved true, "You can lead a horse to water, but you can't make him drink." Only feeble attempts were made to implement the plan, with extensive foot-dragging and a typical school recalcitrance to change.

Second, funds for the implementation of the new programs never materialized. Testimony presented by Gilbert Chavez in court that an abundance of funding was available from the federal government was interpreted by the court to mean that it would be easy to acquire all the funds as entitlements for the school district. Although extensive funding was available from federal agencies, as indicated by Chavez, most of the funds were allocated through competitive proposals, and the school officials did not break their backs writing sophisticated and competitive proposals for programs they did not want.

Third, extensive opposition to the adaptation of educational programs for minority populations developed in the Texas Education Agency. For two decades, from 1971 through

1991, the state agency consistently opposed all new programs for minority, disadvantaged, and limited-English-proficient students. Almost without exception, and as stated by State Senator Carlos Truan, all improvements in minority education and school finance reform in Texas came about by dragging the Texas Education Agency and its educational leadership through the courts and into the twentieth century.

Fourth, the San Felipe Del Rio School District was successful in having jurisdiction in the court case and in the implementation of the comprehensive educational plan transferred from Judge Justice's court in Tyler, Texas, to John Wood's court in San Antonio. Although most court and administrative judges reacted favorably to my arguments for adapting educational programs to the characteristics of students, my suggestions had not been very favorably received by Judge Woods in the Uvalde court case. When I testified to the need for individualized education plans for students with special needs, Judge John Wood responded, "That is the stupidest thing I have ever heard of" (*Morales v. Shanon*, 1975). Needless to say, he did not spend an extensive amount of time checking on the implementation of the comprehensive plan for San Felipe Del Rio.

One other interesting aspect of this court case is the transfer policy of Laughlin AFB students to the Del Rio schools. It serves as a precursor of the "choice" movement twenty years later and provides some insights on minority skepticism on choice and voucher systems being proposed today.

Given a choice of which schools to attend, the Laughlin personnel inevitably selected the predominantly white Anglo Del Rio schools over the minority San Felipe schools. Choice was a reality only for the middle-class students from the Laughlin portion of San Felipe and certainly not for the poorer students in the rest of the district. The Department of Defense provided free transportation in support of the Laughlin students' choices; no similar transportation was available to the Mexican-American students from San Felipe. And, as can be expected in currently proposed choice programs, Del Rio accepted unconditionally all students transferring from the Laughlin AFT portion of San Felipe. No such consideration was tendered to the minority and disadvantaged students from the rest of the San Felipe School District.

As practiced in Del Rio, Texas, school choice perpetuated and exacerbated the segregation of the two ethnic groups, a potential danger in currently proposed school choice plans today.

JOSÉ CÁRDENAS, a witness called by the Government, having previously been duly cautioned and sworn to testify the truth, the whole truth and nothing but the truth, testified as follows:

DIRECT EXAMINATION

BY MR. CONROY:

Q: Dr. Cárdenas, would you please state your full name, your place of residence and your occupation, please?

A: My name is José Cárdenas. My place of residence is San Antonio and my occupation is school superintendent.

Q: And where are you the school superintendent, Dr. Cárdenas?

A: Edgewood Independent School District in the west side of San Antonio.

Q: How long have you held that position?

A: Two years, sir.

Q: Can you briefly describe without any false modesty on your own part your educational experiences.

A: Yes, sir, I have a Doctorate Degree from the University of Texas at Austin. I have a Master's Degree from Our Lady of the Lake College in San Antonio, and I have a Bachelor's Degree from the University of Texas at Austin, sir.

Q: Can you describe your occupational history.

A: Prior to becoming superintendent of schools of the Edgewood School District I was with the Southwest Educational Development Laboratory, the regional laboratory funded under Title IV of the Elementary-Secondary Education Act in Austin. At that time—I held several positions. One of them was Director of Field Test Centers. Another one was Director of Texas Migrant Educational Development Center, and a third position as Director of all programs dealing with Mexican-American populations within the two-state area that was under the jurisdiction of the laboratory.

Prior to this I was Chairman of the Education Department at St. Mary's University in San Antonio. I was Chairman for three years. I was Associate Professor of education for six years at St. Mary's University. Prior to this I spent—the experience in public education for the grand total is twenty-one years. I have taught elementary school, junior high, high school. I have done elementary school administration, secondary school administration, all level supervision and some other related activities, sir.

Q: Do you have a particular connection in the area of Mexican- American education?

A: Yes, sir, a lot of the work that I have done has been specifically in the area of Mexican-American education, both in my regular employment, as well as advisory and consultant work with other agencies, sir.

Q: Could you briefly give us a description of some of the consultant and advisory work you have done for other agencies?

A: Well, I am consultant to the Department of Health, Education and Welfare, have been a consultant to the Department of Labor. I have done very extensive work with the Bureau of Education Personnel Development and the U.S. Office of Education in the six-state area, as well as the island of Puerto Rico. I have worked with the development and implementation of the Career Opportunities Program, the Urban Rural Program, the Experimental School Program, many bilingual and multi-cultural training—teacher training institutes and other types of similar activities, sir.

Q: Were you at one time or are you presently a consultant to the Secretary of Health, Education and Welfare?

A: Yes, sir, I am a consultant and a member of a team to develop an instructional program for the consolidated school districts.

Q: Have you background in the area of migrant education?

A: Yes, sir. I have taught and have been in administrative positions with migrant students, and then I developed and organized and directed the Texas Migrant Educational Developmental Center, which resulted in two major documents. One of them is the Evaluation of Migr*ant Education in the State of Texas* and then *Alternate Strategies for the Education of Migrant Children*. This was in cooperation with the Texas Education Agency.

Q: Do you have some special knowledge in the area of special education?

A: Yes, sir, I have done quite a bit of consultant work in special education, and I have participated in the development of alternate plans for special education and have done some work in the assessment and measurement of intellectual abilities of multi-cultural and bilingual children.

Q: In your spare time were you a member of a committee which was sent to Del Rio in order to develop an educational plan for the newly consolidated school district?

A: Yes, sir, I am a member of the committee that was in Del Rio.

Q: Would you briefly describe some of the other members of the committee that was in Del Rio for this purpose?

A: Among the members that I met over there was Miss Bambi Cárdenas that is from Del Rio and has been in education and has been working with me for some time, Dr. Tom Arciniega from the University of Texas at El Paso.

THE COURT: Sir, we are not very familiar with Spanish names. Would you be kind enough to spell these for the reporter as you go along?

THE WITNESS: Yes, sir.

THE REPORTER: Bambi Cárdenas, the last name same as yours?

THE WITNESS: Spelled the same as mine.

THE REPORTER: All right, and about Dr. Tom —?

THE WITNESS: Arciniega, A-r-c-i-n-i-e-g-a.

THE COURT: Thank you, and the other members of the committee?

THE WITNESS: Mrs. Dorothy Stuck, from the Department of Health, Education and Welfare.

THE COURT: S-t-u-c-k, I presume, is that what you said?

THE WITNESS: S-t-u-c-k.

THE COURT: All right.

THE WITNESS: Marty Gerry from the Washington office of Health, Education and Welfare. I believe Mr. Gilbert Chavez from the Office of Spanish-Surnamed Americans in Washington.

THE COURT: That is C-h-a-v-e-z, I presume?

THE WITNESS: That is right, I'm sorry. There were Texas Education Agency personnel, including Mr. Conoley, who testified here and spelled his name earlier.

THE COURT: Yes.

THE WITNESS: Juan Ybarra, Y-b-a-r-r-a, who also is with the Department of Health, Education and Welfare, and Mr. Ernie Robles, R-o-b-l-e-s. Several of the members that were there were former residents of Del Rio, and we also met with some people from Del Rio concerning the development of a plan for assuring that the resulting consolidated school district would offer a responsive program to the needs of all the children.

THE COURT: Thank you.

BY MR. CONROY:

Q: Would it be your educational judgment that the personnel who were assigned to assist in the formulation of this plan were educationally qualified to do so?

A: It is my opinion that they were very highly educationally qualified to do so.

MR. CONROY: The plan that was developed, Your Honor, has been marked for identification as Government's Exhibit No. 308. It is in the record at this time.

(THE GOVERNMENT'S EDUCATIONAL PLAN—was previously duly marked as: GOVERNMENT'S EXHIBIT NO. 308)

Q: Dr. Cárdenas, rather than have you refer to the document itself, which we have filed with the Court for the purposes that the Court would wish to use it in the development of an Order in this case, would you like to in your own style give us an overview of the problem that confronts the Mexican-American student in public education in the Southwest?

A: Yes, sir.

Q: Would you like to get off the stand to do it?

A: It helps me sometimes in listing some of the things.

THE COURT: Yes, right over here. I don't know whether that will be large enough for your purposes or not (indicating).

(REPORTER'S NOTE: The witness approaches the blackboard.)

THE WITNESS: I think it will be large enough, sir.

Your Honor, during the time that I have been involved in the education of Mexican-American children and members of other ethnic groups, there are certain characteristics, demographic characteristics, of the performance of children in Texas schools as well as in schools throughout the Southwest and throughout the whole country that stand out. These are things that I identify as problem areas.

One of the things that concerns me tremendously is the amount of underachievement of Mexican-American children in our schools. Looking at the demographic information made available to us on the performance of Del Rio children, for instance, on standardized achievement tests, the general pattern repeats itself. Mainly, the children, and it is documented in the recommendation in the plan—the children are underachieving at early grade levels, and beyond this there seems to be an increase in the amount of underachievement as they continue through school.

This has been described previously as a cumulative deficit, in which their initial performance is substandard, and then it become more substandard as the child progresses through the educational system.

The second thing that stands out is that invariably in the education of Mexican-American children, and I think I can later explain reasons for this, the children are over-aged, and it is not unusual, for instance, in our studies of migrant education throughout the whole State of Texas and Mexican-American education it is not unusual to identify thirteen, fourteen, fifteen and sixteen year-old children in the fifth and sixth grade classes in the State of Texas, these children being Mexican-American.

The third thing that stands out and is of tremendous concern to me is the number of children that drop out of school from the Mexican-American group. Invariably in most school districts you will find that the percentage of Mexican-American children who do not complete school runs anywhere from fifty to eighty and ninety per cent. Dealing with the migrant population, estimates have gone as high as the mid ninety per cents. In fact, in the State of Texas we identified that twenty per cent of all migrant children never even enrolled in school, that they are dropouts before they are even five or six years old.

This type of information, I would imagine, would create a lot of concern for a lot of people, and, of course, the United States Office of Education and the State of Texas has expended a tremendous amount of money trying to respond to this problem and solve some of the problems that exist. However, not all of the efforts have been successful, and I am of the opinion that the reason the efforts have not been successful is because on the whole they have been misdirected.

We find that the Mexican-American children are a unique ethnic group, and they have unique characteristics, like Black children. They have characteristics that make them atypical.

However, the instructional programs that are presented in the State of Texas and many other states of this country are programs that are designed for white Anglo-Saxon, English speaking, middle-class population, and I don't care to knock the instructional program for the white Anglo-Saxon, English-speaking, middle-class children, but this program which this develops has this characteristic, that it responds to the characteristics of the children and, therefore, there is a certain amount of compatibility between the characteristics of the learner and the characteristics of the instructional program.

However, if a child is not a typical child, and when a child is a non-white or when he is non Anglo-Saxon, you develop an incompatibility between the characteristics of the learner and the characteristics of the instructional program, and I think that it is these incompatibilities that exist that lead to, first, the problem performance of children, Mexican-American and black children, and disadvantaged children in our American schools, but in addition to this, I think that unless the incompatibilities are eliminated, that we will not be able to ever achieve better performance on the part of the children.

Now, up to now, many educators have understood that the incompatibilities have existed. However, invariably the effort has always been to bring about changes on the part of the kids in order to make them compatible with the instructional program which is provided in the schools, and this has been rather ridiculous, because there is no way that you can make a white out of a black child. There is no way that you can make an Anglo-Saxon out of a Mexican-American, and efforts to do so and even efforts to acculturate, efforts to eliminate a dominant language have been unsuccessful, and it is fairly obvious that if we are going to enjoy immediate success it is necessary that we abandon these efforts to change the characteristics of the child and do something immediately about changing the characteristics of the instructional programs, so that it will be compatible with the characteristics of the child.

The next obvious question, and the question that comes to my mind, is what are the essential characteristics of the Mexican-American that leads to these incompatibilities with the instructional program, and I have identified five rather general areas, and I would like to present to the Court a very brief summary of these things and the implications that they have for the development of an instructional program of Mexican-American children in Del Rio.

The first characteristic we think of is a product of the population, the fact that ninety-eight per cent of the kindergarten children are Mexican-American in Del Rio would indicate that the need for poverty guidelines or some other type of deprivation which qualifies them for participation in the kindergarten program of the State of Texas. I think that demographic information available from the San Felipe School District on the Mexican-American population in Del Rio will substantiate the fact that we are working with a poverty population.

Now, getting back to the concept of the incompatibilities, the instructional program that is invariably presented to these kinds fails to take into account that this characteristic exists, and this characteristic has serious implications. One of the most serious, for instance, is the fact that in poverty homes you tend to find a very high child-to-adult ratio, whereas, in middle-class homes very frequently the child-to-adult ratio is as low as one-to-one, there being two children and perhaps none. In poverty homes it is not unusual to find four-to-one and even higher ratios. Not only this, but very frequently because of the poverty itself, father and mother have to dissipate a lot of their energies acquiring the basic necessities of life, and it is not unusual to have a mother in some towns spending a full day at the food stamp distribution center or perhaps daddy seeking employment or being employed in a number of jobs. It is also not unusual to have the adult members of the family trying to secure welfare health services for members of the family. As a result, you have children who grew up in relative isolation and have very limited interactions between themselves and adult persons that can provide a stimulating influence on their intellectual or cognitive development.

Not only do we find this type of situation, but very frequently we find that there is an absence of the educational toys, which are intellectually and psychomotor stimulating, but there may be an absence of communications media or a relative absence of communications media, so that when you have some form of deprivation or lack of stimulation for the intellectual and the cognitive development of the children.

Now, a lot of the child psychologists in recent years, Piaget, Bloom, Brunner, and almost all of them, are very much concerned with the effect of this type of deprivation, intellectual deprivation, or lack of intellectual stimulation on the development of the child, and it is generally agreed that the formative years for intellectual development take place between let's say one and a half years of age all the way through nine, with perhaps as much as—well, more than fifty per cent of the intellectual development being complete by the time the child is six years old. I would imagine that fifty per cent of the development may be complete by the time that the child is five years old.

There is another principle that has been identified that has a lot of relevance to the children of San Felipe and Del Rio, and that is that it is assumed, and there is substantial proof for the fact that being raised in a non-stimulating environment stunts the development of intellectual abilities, and the people and the children that are raised in homes where you have the deprivations of poverty tend to suffer in the area of cognitive development, because of the poorness of the environment.

A third principle that I think is very relevant is the fact that after the period of growth has been completed, let's say at the age of nine, or most of it has been completed let's say at the age of six, it is impossible to bring about some type of stimulation that would result in making up the amount of loss that took place during the period of development.

If I may make an analogy, sir, we say that physical development is relatively complete by the time that a person is nineteen years old. The same principles apply. Most of the development is complete by the time the child is nineteen years old. If a person were raised in a physically deprived environment, malnutrition, poor health and so forth, the person may not develop to his genetic potential, and let's say arbitrarily that his genetic potential was be to six feet tall.

Because of the deprivation of his environment, he only grew by the time we was nineteen years old to a height of let's say five feet six inches. This happens very commonly, and there is a lot of documentation of this happening in the physical area.

Now, the third principle which I mentioned is that taking an individual that did not fulfill his potential for growth because of a deprived environment during the growing period and taking this individual at a subsequent age, such as thirty, and giving him an adequate diet and vitamins and medical attention and so forth will probably not result in after the age of thirty this individual making up the six inches and growing to the height of six feet after the age of thirty.

The analogy here is that unless this type of stimulation is presented during the years of cognitive growth, a lot of potential for intellectual development is lost and cannot be replaced later. This is one of the reasons why the plan that we have submitted puts so much emphasis on early childhood education, and not only the kindergarten type that the State supports, but programs for three-, four-, and five-year-old kids that are much younger than the program which the State makes available. I think this is the reason why the Office of Child Development in Washington is making tremendous amounts of money available for providing stimulating experiences in very young children, and in the Edgewood School District we go down to one and a half years of age in an infant stimulation program in cooperation with Texas A & M University, and then you put the children in school, regular school, at the age of three and carry them through the age of four, five, six and all the way through.

We have found some things that are rather startling. For instance, we find from testing the three and four and five-year-old population of the school district prior to the implementation of the Early Childhood Education Program, we took the three and the four and the five-year-old children and administered some rather non-cultural, non-verbal measures of intellectual development. We chose the Leiter because it is really a non-verbal test, and although the resulting I.Q. scores may have no absolute value, I would like to present them because of their relative value. Assuming that the I.Q. of the whole United States would average out at one hundred, and theoretically it does, the children in the Edgewood School District that were three years old averaged a hundred and three I.Q., which is above the average for the country, and this is a very deprived population, economically deprived, and the four-year-olds, however, upon being tested, averaged an I.Q. of approximately ninety, and the five-year-olds that were tested averaged an I.Q. of approximately seventy.

Now, this is in keeping with almost every study that has been made of the intellectual development of children. None of these kids had attended school before. The assumption or conclusion is that unless some type of an intervention is made at an early age, you have your progressive decline, which means that the individual functions at a lower and lower mental level, not that his mental abilities are not developing, but the development of his mental abilities is not in keeping with his chronological development, and since I.Q. is nothing more than the division of the mental age by the chronological age, if mental age is not developing through lack of stimulation, then this progressive decline indicates that the I.Q. will continue to be lower and lower with the person functioning at a lower and lower level of mental ability.

Incidentally, and I would like to present this now, lest I forget, after seven months in the Early Childhood Education Program in the Edgewood School District, the three-year-olds averaged I.Q.'s of a hundred twenty. The four-year-olds averaged I.Q.'s of a hundred eight, and the five-year-olds averaged I.Q.'s of seventy-seven. I think that this has a lot of significance in that if we are to draw the same type of curve that we had before, it would show that the investment of money for education at an early age pays such a tremendously bigger dividend that it may be much more economical, and in my opinion it is much more economical to make the investment at the age of three than to make the investment let's say at the age of five, six or some subsequent age.

I don't think that this showed any new information. I think it just substantiated that what the psychologists have been saying is true and it held true in this school district where the program was implemented.

Prior to my becoming superintendent of the Edgewood School District we implemented this program in McAllen and Fort Worth and subsequent to this it has been implemented in other cities, and in every case that they have worked with the three and four-year-old populations we have found dramatic increases in I.Q. and in levels of mental functioning on the part of the kids as a result of the participation in this program.

The second characteristic—I will try not to go further into this—but the second characteristic that I am very much concerned with is the cultural characteristics of so many of the pupils in Del Rio. It becomes very obvious that you have some sixty-five per cent of the population of Del Rio having values, traditions and orientations which are very much incompatible with the values, traditions and orientations which are presented in the traditional and structural program for a white Anglo-Saxon population, and I feel that a lot of the poor performance on the part of the children can also be attributed to the fact that you have these cultural incompatibilities.

I am not particularly concerned at this point—I will get to it in another area of incompatibility—I will not say that the celebration of the 16th of September or the 5th of May is going to add much to the educational gains of Mexican-American children directly. It may indirectly, but what I am concerned about is that there is an increasing amount of evidence that learning is culturally oriented, and that different types of populations have different types of learning styles, respond differently to different types of motivations, so that a child may learn or not learn, depending on the extent to which the instructional program is comparable with his cultural characteristics.

The work of Fishman (phonetic) and Lesser (phonetic) in the East, Joshua Fishman, the work of Dr. Manuel Ramirez and Dr. Al Castañeda at Riverside, the work of Dr. John Aragon at the Cultural Learning Center in Albuquerque, New Mexico, substantiate that this is so (Fishman, 1966).

As some examples, so it won't all be in the abstract, William Madsen, the anthropologist, found Mexican-American children working in cooperation performed and out-performed Anglo-American children and other ethnic groups that were evaluated, as long as it required cooperativeness in performing in the educational tasks.

On the other hand, when Mexican-American children were given a similar type of educational task that required competitiveness, the Mexican-American children performed very poorly as compared to the Anglo-Saxon control group.

The implications are that there is such a thing as a learning style, in that perhaps if we educators develop an instructional program which capitalized on cooperativeness, rather than competitiveness, for Mexican-American children, that the performance of these children may be enhanced tremendously.

There are other aspects of culture that I think are very important. I think that the methodology which I have been talking about is very important. Another area is the instructional materials used. In many cases the instructional material [sic] are disfunctional. [sic] I can give as an example, a very concrete example of this, where I saw in McAllen, Texas, a Mexican-American child being taught by a teacher, and the materials that were used reflected a middle-class, Anglo-Saxon family, the mother looked like Betty Grable—let's put it that way, and the child was told by the teacher, "Find mother in the picture," and the kid looked at the picture, and he just shook his head and shook his head, and the teacher said, "He doesn't know much English and things like that," and she kept saying, "Come on, find mother in the picture. Mother is in there," and then the teacher said point blank, "Do you see your mother in that picture," and the child said, if you will pardon the expression, "Hell, no," indicating that it wasn't a conceptual problem that he had, but the fact that the White or Anglo or Teutonic characteristics of the mother pictured in the picture did not lead to any association on the part of the child to the mother that he has at home, and I think that this type of irrelevancy and incompatibility in instructional materials has been very detrimental to the learning of children.

Another area that I am very much concerned about is rules and regulations of schools that in many places and in most cases reflect middle-class values and may be disfunctional [sic] for Mexican-American and black children. Just the other day I was observing a group of my own counselors talking about absenteeism among Mexican-American Students, and they were very concerned, and they said that Mexican-American students had a high rate of absenteeism, because very frequently they have to stay out of school in order to baby-sit while mother attends to some personal business, or else they have to run errands for mother, and the counselors and the attendance office were trying to develop strategies and put pressure on the kids, the law if necessary, compulsory attendance laws, in order to have the kids not miss school in order to devote time to family problems and family activities, and I got to thinking about this, and I got very concerned, particularly when William Madsen, the anthropologist and Arthur Ruble and other anthropologists say that one of the outstanding characteristics and one of the most unique characteristics of the Mexican-American that they identified was the sense of responsibility of the individual to the family. The family is a close-knit group, and there is a sense of responsibility of the individual to the family.

They argue as anthropologists that in the Anglo-Saxon family structure there is very little responsibility of the individual to the family as a group, and then I get to thinking what Smith, Stanley and Shores said in their book, *Principles of Curriculum Development*, most of the major social ills of this country can be attributed to the dissolution of the family as a social unit, to the breakup of the family as a social unit, and then I say, "Well, we find here in the Mexican-American population a unique group that still has the family as a strong unit, and we as educators develop regulations and policies which say that we want to break up this unity that the family has."

Now, it is very obvious that the kids when the school system says, "You cannot be absent from school in order to take your mother to the hospital or to the doctor," is [sic] placed in a value conflict, and I can't say which is the choice that the child should make or the school should make, because I don't think that I should make the choice, but I think that the school should enact policies and use methodologies to reduce this value conflict, and at the same time to allow the individual to have a certain amount of cultural freedom and cultural mobility and function within the cultural traditions and orientations and the value system that he has.

In the area of culture we have another area, which I think is of tremendous significance.

THE COURT: Sir, before we go on with that, I am very interested in your presentation. I want to hear it in full, but I think we need a recess.

THE WITNESS: Sure.

THE COURT: The court will be in recess for fifteen minutes.

(REPORTER'S NOTE: The Court then, at 4:45 o'clock, P.M., August 19, 1971, recessed until 5:00 o'clock, P.M., the same date, at which time it reconvened.)

THE COURT: Please be seated. Are you ready to proceed, sir?

THE WITNESS: Your Honor, the last thing that I said before the recess was that there are these cultural incompatibilities that exist, and that the disability in learning can be attributed, and some of them are attributed to the fact that these cultural incompatibilities exist, and this is one of the reasons why our recommendation for the instructional program for the consolidated school district takes in not only the Early Childhood Education recommendations, but also that throughout the educational program that there be cultural compatibility between the instructional program and the characteristics of all students of the San Felipe-Del Rio School District.

The third factor or characteristic that I think has relevance that has been mentioned rather extensively is the language characteristic, and granting that it is a sub-aspect of culture, I prefer to list it separately, because the implications are tremendous. I think it is very obvious that a child that speaks Spanish cannot learn as long as the instructional program is presented in the English [sic] or any other language which he cannot speak.

We have been aware of this as educators for many years. Two things have been done previous to this. One approach had always been putting the child into an English-as-a-second-language program, and the kid enrolled at the age of six in school, and while he learned the English language did not really have any serious experience in the development of skills or the acquisition of content material until such time as he developed English language proficiency.

The other alternative that has been tried is—I call it the cold turkey approach—and that is where you put him in the classroom and you throw a new language system at him, basic skills, such as reading and writing and arithmetic in the language system and content material, such as science, social studies and other areas of curriculum all at the same time, and I think that this is just too much to expect the child to function when he is trying to acquire a new language system, basic skills and content at the same time.

The fact that the instructional program is invariably in English prohibits his acquiring the basic skills and the content material. Now, in both of the plans it leads to inevitable retardation of the child. If he spends one year acquiring English as a second language, it would take him then another year in the first grade to acquire the basic skills and the content material. Therefore, I would prefer to go into some other alternative, such as the one that was tried in the Del Rio and San Felipe School Districts, namely, a bilingual approach to education, and although I agree with everybody that has stated that bilingual education is education in two languages, I think I can come up with a much better operational definition of bilingual education.

In this case it is the education of the kids or the acquisition of cognitive and effective learnings in the vernacular, while another language is being learned as a second language. In the case of the Mexican-American children bilingual education then would be the acquisition of let's say basic skills and content information in his vernacular, being Spanish, while English is being learned as a second language.

Now, while this is being done, you have the parallel development of cognitive development on the part of the kid and learning of content material with the development of English as a second language with a gap or transition made so that the learnings acquired in the Spanish language system can be transferred into the English language system. It doesn't have any great formidable problems. It has long been established in other countries, for instance, that learning to read is an activity that an individual goes through once in his life, and once you learn how to read, all you have to do is apply the information to new language systems that are acquired.

Therefore, if we teach the child to read in Spanish, it is very easy to make the transition and have the child learn to read in English, when he has mastered English as a second language system.

The characteristics, I would say, of a good bilingual education program would be three. One of them is that it would provide a program in which learning continues to take place and cognitive stimulation, intellectual stimulation, takes place without having to interrupt the cognitive development or the intellectual development while the kid sits in a classroom for any extended period of time while acquiring a new language system.

A second characteristic of a bilingual program would be that he would acquire a new language system. In this case it would be English as a second language for the Mexican-American population, and Spanish as a second language for the non-Spanish speaking population.

THE COURT: Well now, isn't something like that done all the time in Europe?

THE WITNESS: Very frequently in Europe you have extensive bilingual programs, and in many cases they do inject three, four, five languages, and there is very little problem, if it is presented at an early enough age.

THE COURT: Proceed.

THE WITNESS: The third thing that would be characteristic of bilingual educational programs in my opinion would be further extension of your original language system. In this case with Spanish or English being the original language system, you would want to see further development, and I see where in Texas, for instance, the acquisition of a foreign language, such as Spanish, is so valued that it is mandatory in the secondary schools and in the colleges.

Unfortunately, they are offering the language training at an age when the individual has a lot less propensity, physiological and pedagogical, for learning a new language than if they were offered let's say at the age of one and a half or at the age of one, two, three, four, five. In other words, what we stated previously would hold, that the earlier the child goes into the bilingual education program, as far as the second language, the better the proficiency in that language would be. The result of early activities in bilingual education indicate [sic] not only that it is feasible, not only that it can be done, but some startling information.

For instance, we find in our own bilingual programs that children that are taught English as a second language and continue learnings in their Spanish language vernacular do better in English than children that are put directly into English language programs. In other words, when the child is allowed to continue his educational activities in a non-English vernacular, he learns English better than if all his energies were directed toward the acquisition of English as a second language, and the results are rather conclusive.

There has been some question about the methodology under which a bilingual educational program can be implemented. There are various alternatives. As has been stated, Tug Anderson and Tootie Boyer did a rather extensive study and came up with a two-volume document that has been described.

However, in general, for a Spanish-speaking population, you would say that you have a—and this is a two-variable matrix, and this one would be language over here (indicating), and this would be time you would start with all of the instructional program being in the language system, which the child brings to school, and all of your activities are conducted like this, and they [sic] you will have a tapering off, in which as English is acquired as a second language, you have crossovers, so that the information, as in the United Consolidated School District in Laredo, can be taught in both languages, and the ultimate end is that you would produce an individual that has a tremendous amount of not only vernacular but technical competency in two languages, which is a resource that this country needs very sorely.

It can be done by a teacher that is bilingual, and you can have instructional periods in which instruction is done in the vernacular, and then the other language is introduced.

Laredo has experimented with the use of co-stimuli being presented, in which a learning is presented in one language, immediately followed by the other language, and have the child identify that both languages are saying the same thing, that is, it is just two different ways of saying the same thing, and, of course, he can make his response in either of the two languages. This does produce an individual that can learn and can function in either of the two language systems.

There are groupings that can be made, and I would like to present one later, that will allow staff differentiations so that you can have in the same classroom persons, instructional staff, that are English-speaking, and instructional staff are Spanish-speaking, and by grouping students, you are able to have two programs going on at the same time in both language.

In Dade County, Florida, Coral Gables School, they have done this very extensively. In fact they have large rooms in which you have teachers presenting the same instructional program in two languages in opposite ends of the room with the kids free to turn their chairs around and participate in either an English-speaking program or a Spanish-speaking program.

There are many other technical ways in which this can be presented. You can have a morning assigned to English language instruction and an afternoon assigned to Spanish language instruction with the understanding that for the person that does not speak a language system, rather than initially introducing basic skills and content, you would introduce a second language acquisition type of instructional program.

I will go ahead to another one of the incompatibilities.

The fourth incompatibility which has become apparent in the Del Rio-San Felipe area is the problem of mobility, or actually it is a characteristic of mobility, the problem being program discontinuity. It has been stated that there is a large number of migrant students in the consolidated school district. The instructional programs which are developed and are invariably introduced are instructional programs that depend upon a sequence and continuity with the assumption being that the child is there continuously.

Now, this doesn't hold true for the migrant population, and in many cases it doesn't hold true for urban populations that are becoming increasingly mobile. Therefore, it is necessary that the instructional program be so structured that you do provide sequence and continuity. One way may be to transport instructional programs with children. However, the mechanics of this become almost prohibitive. The second alternative, and this is the one that we are recommending, is that the program be extremely individualized so that on the basis of diagnosis and prescription you bring the child into an entrance level in the instructional program that is compatible with his past learnings, and in this way give the necessary sequence and continuity to the instructional program.

A fifth characteristic that we have been working with is the perceptual. Again, there are various ways of looking at this. The one I am most concerned with is the concept that the child has of himself, and in most cases Mexican-American and Black children tend to have negative self-concepts. If they don't, invariably, because of the inadequacies of the instructional program, they develop them soon after they are enrolled in school. A child that has a negative self-concept has a barrier to learning. He thinks of himself as inferior when participating in a learning activity, and then you have the self-fulfilling prophecy that he does very poorly in his learning activity, because he sets very low levels of expectations for his own performance.

The instructional programs that are typically used are very much based on middle-classed motivation and middle-classed posture concepts that children bring to school. Now, when the child comes in there and has a negative self-concept, it is necessary that you have teaching methodologies that are immediately positively reinforcing. In other words, the increments of difficulty of the material and the amount of readiness which the child has for participating in the learning activity—the readiness has be to so great and the increment so small that you have a successful experience in a learning situation, and then you would have to provide feed back information so that he realizes immediately that he has performed well, and this becomes self-motivating, and those that learn tend to learn more, and those that did not learn tend to learn less.

And another—area and incidentally, in this area of perceptual—I said I would bring out some of the cultural aspects over here, and I think that it is very important that in the consolidated school district that you have policies and participation particularly in learning activities and in co-curricular activities that assures us that the child is going to have and maintain a positive self-image. In other words, if a child were to go into a new school system and he did not participate in a leadership role, let's say in all of the co-curricular activities, I think that this would develop a negative self-concept, and that educationally it would be detrimental.

Therefore, we include a lot of recommendations in the area of co-curricular activities to assure the perceptions that the child has of himself in a new school system is a positive perception. I am most concerned about the perceptions which the adults have of the child. I have been in the past very critical of institutions of higher education in the State of Texas that fail to provide programs for training teachers to teach disadvantaged and minority group children. For the most part, the teachers are really disfunctional [sic], and over the last twenty-one years I have become very much aware that so many people that go into teaching have a lot of potential as teachers, and in many cases some of them are wanting to do a lot for the disadvantaged and minority group child, but unless they have training and understanding of the problem of the minority kids and the educational implementations of the incompatibilities, they tend to have negative experiences. They fail with the kids, and just looking at the standardized achievement test data, it becomes rather obvious that somebody has failed.

Now, this can be very bad for a teacher psychologically. There is a lot of stress associated with failure, and if the teacher cannot experience success because of the inadequacies of the training that they have received, the instructional materials which are used and the methodologies which are employed, then I think that there is a tendency for the teacher to rationalize the ineffectiveness of the interaction between teacher and student and start coming up with some dysfunctional reasons for the student performing poorly in school, and this is why I have heard many teachers say that Mexican-American children don't want to learn, that Mexican-Americans don't value education. I have even heard teachers tell me that Mexican-Americans are genetically inferior and that, therefore, they cannot learn.

The development of these defense mechanisms on the part of the teachers could be changed if the teacher had more insights into the problems of minority group children and the educational implications of these problems.

Before moving out of this area, Your Honor, I would like to state that in recent months I have become concerned with the fact that all these incompatibilities are interrelated and interdependent, and that it isn't just mobility itself which created an educational barrier for the child, because in Del Rio they have a lot of children from Laughlin Air Force Base that are highly mobile, because they are related to families that are military-connected and move tremendously. My experience with these types of children is that the mobility enhances their educational performance, and the reason for this is that it is not mobility in itself which is crippling but mobility coupled with some of the other incompatibilities, which I have listed here.

Another example of this, it was stated this morning by Dr. Tom Carter, that his child learned a new language in six weeks. I don't think there is anything amazing about this, and I am of the opinion that children can learn a new language system certainly with enough facility to be able to function in the classroom in that language system in six weeks. We see this quite a bit with immigrants, recent immigrants from Mexico, where we have people coming in, students coming in from Mexico from higher socio-economic levels that have tremendous cultural and language incompatibilities, and the reason—well, and we put them in the classrooms and then give them an intensive English language program, and at the end of six weeks these children out-perform native-born Mexican-American children, and the reason for this is not only the language and cultural incompatibilities, which cripples, but it is the language and cultural incompatibilities coupled with poverty problems, coupled with mobility, coupled with the perceptual, which is the crippling or the crippler of children of minority ethnic and racial groups, and this is the reason why we find it very difficult to fragmentize and present options and say that a school system serving minority group children can shop around and pick some elements of an educational plan where you respond to the cultural characteristic and the language characteristic but may fail to respond to the poverty or the perceptual or the mobility characteristics.

In other words, it has to be an educational program which is developed on the basis of—with a table of specifications with guarantees that you are responding to all of the incompatibilities.

If I may make an analogy, because I think this is a very important point, if a patient were taken to the hospital, and he was having a heart attack, and he was having a cerebral hemorrhage, and he was having appendicitis, and the surgeon zeroed in on his appendix and performed a beautiful appendectomy, the patient may still die, because it is necessary that they respond to all of the illnesses that he has, rather than to say, "We are responding to the language incompatibility," while doing nothing in some of the other areas.

The plan that we have presented will, I think, respond to all of these incompatibilities that we have.

I have a chart that illustrates—.

(PAUSE)

THE WITNESS: Your Honor, while the attorney is getting the chart, may I say that I am thoroughly convinced that bandaids for instructional programs as they exist now for minority group children is not going to solve the educational problem of these minority group kids. I think that we have to implement in our schools rather drastic and tremendously innovative approaches to the education of these children.

If I could have this right here (indicating).

Here we have the plan, and it does not include all of the elements which are presented in the—.

THE COURT: If you would, please put that out beyond the lectern.

(REPORTER'S NOTE: The charts are placed for better viewing.)

THE COURT: That's fine.

THE WITNESS: This plan that we have in here responds to some of the incompatibilities that I have mentioned. One of the most essential things that we have here is the fact that we do include an Early Childhood Education Program. This Early Childhood Education Program should be bilingual in order that you can have the cognitive development that is necessary in the vernacular. I think that cognitive development is the main target, a problem-solving type of program with a lot of intellectual stimulation in there. I think that it should have parental involvement responsible to the cultural incompatibilities and language incompatibilities and the fact it is possible through an educational program, thus involving parents and volunteers on a parent-professional personnel basis to increase the number of adults that have contact with the kids, so that you have optimum conditions for a lot of individual attention for the child.

In our Early Childhood Education Program, and maybe this accounts for the I.Q. gains which we had, we limit the enrollment of the children to twenty per classroom. We have a full-time teacher. We have a full-time teacher aide. We have on a daily basis, a parent volunteer, and then we bring in high school kids and other types of personnel in order to provide a tremendous amount of adults and through the process of staff differentiation have these people working with kids in instructional activities.

Parental involvement can do a lot of things. It can establish the communication between the parent and the school. Invariably, the school is seeking that the parent understand and support the role of the school. I think invariably also the parent is seeking that the school understand and support the role of the parent, and I think that both of these can be accomplished through parental involvement programs.

Then it is necessary that we respond to the non-instructional needs of the children, such things as food, clothing and shoes and health services and other types of things, which, if they go unattended, would be detrimental to learning in the classroom.

In eight to twelve we have the bilingual bicultural teaching, and I would like to make a recommendation for team teaching or an organization that would allow for this, the utilization of bilingual aids, the utilization of bilingual community personnel, and then an intensive effort in curriculum development. This can be implemented now, and I think that it will be carried over from the 1971–'72, at least through '72–'73 school year.

In the fifth and sixth grades I think that more preparation would be necessary, so we decided to split this and provide English as a second language training and Spanish as a second language training for the children, and then have curriculum development in order to implement in subsequent years bilingual, bicultural programs and to support programs of staff development and community and parental involvement, thus having the type of responsive instructional program which the children need.

In grades seven and eight immediately you may have implemented Spanish as a second language program and English as a second language program, bilingual bicultural counseling, cultural awareness, group work and curriculum development and members of the team said that social studies was one of the areas which was very much responsive to the cultural incompatibilities, and through the study or the teaching of social studies this could be brought about.

Then we have curriculum development and all these things over here (indicating) carrying over into the '72–'73 school year, in which both the bilingual and bicultural instructional programs could be implemented.

In grades nine through twelve we make recommendations for ethnic studies courses in order to better teach the child about himself, Spanish as a foreign language and then bilingual bicultural counseling and then intensive scholarship financial assistance programs that would allow the kids to stay in school and perhaps go on to higher education, and then have such things as culturally pluralistic literature programs, social studies, home economics, different areas of the curriculum being responsive to the Mexican-American and Anglo-American characteristics of all these children.

I would like to mention that we have included in here Early Childhood Education, bilingual education, bicultural education. I would like to make a recommendation for the continuation of the migrant education program with one additional recommendation, namely, that I think it is detrimental that migrant children be segregated, and I think that there are provisions within the Texas Education Agency Migrant Program so that migrant kids can be placed in regular classrooms, so that you would have heterogeneous grouping of children and not homogeneous groupings of migrant children.

In fact, it is possible through the Texas Education Agency, Title I Migrant Program, for children to be assigned to classes at the beginning of the school year, leaving empty spaces until such time as the migrant children come into the community and then these migrant children will fill in those empty spaces.

THE COURT: How are migrant children able to fit into a classroom after say two months and the class has already been at work?

THE WITNESS: If the instructional program is individualized, and if you have staff differentiation, this would be no problem whatsoever. In fact educators are always saying, "How can any two kids function in the same instructional activity in the same way?" because if you take any two kids and start them off in an instructional program, just like in a foot race, it would be only a matter of seconds before one of them was already ahead of the other, and the migrant children are no exception.

Now, it is possible for the migrant children, if you have individualized instructional programs, the implementation of youth-tutoring-youth type of programs that the kids can receive and can make up what they lost while they were not in the classroom.

Another recommendation that we are making is that special education classes, particularly classes for the educable mentally retarded, be integrated, that the children be integrated into the regular school program. We feel it is extremely detrimental, particularly when there are great doubts about the validity of the intelligence tests that identify an educable mentally retarded child. Therefore, it is greatly desirable that the kids be placed in heterogeneous classes and that we provide resource teachers, both for the children to work with them and to help them develop.

Incidentally, this is another technique that can be used for the migrant children; that a resource teacher can be made available, and this resource teacher can help the kid catch up if he comes in after the beginning of the school program.

We have included the co-curricular activities, and then we have included some recommendations for meeting non-instructional needs of the children. We have recommended two very strong support programs. We feel that community involvement is desirable and that the community must be involved in an advisory capacity. It should be advised in instructional activities, and I am very much astounded and pleased with the fact that we have had a tremendous amount of success using community para-professional personnel and community parents in a summer program that we operated this summer, high school and elementary kids in presenting instructional programs to kids. I think that we tend to overrate the amount of professionalism that is needed in order to conduct some of the instructional activities, and that it is possible to take community people, lay people from the community, provided that they are trained, and provided that the teacher works with them they can present instructional programs to the children.

We feel that there should be some type of a planning, designing, implementing and evaluating system that involves the community. Therefore, we are making a recommendation for the establishment of school community councils that will allow the lay members of the community at the various schools to participate and become a complement to the instructional staff in the development of educational programs. The Urban Rural Program by the Bureau of Education Personnel Development is funding many programs this year. In the area of staff development I have taken the liberty to bring a chart with me. We present a program so that in a very limited time there could be, following the Court order of consolidation of the Del Rio and San Felipe School Districts, the presentation of a tentative plan, and then the decision being made as to the type of staff development program that is implemented. We feel that by September 30, 1971, it is possible to develop and submit for approval a staff development plan for the San Felipe-Del Rio Consolidated School District.

Some of the essential elements again is that there be community representatives involved and that all professional staff also be involved in the development of the staff development plan.

We feel it is feasible by October 30, 1971, at this point over here (indicating) that we could have the appointment of a Director for the Staff Development Plan, and this individual would start immediately developing a systematic management plan for staff development, as well as initiate such programs as Career Development Programs for the community and for teachers, administrative personnel and other types of persons.

We think that by January 30, 1972, we could arrive here, although, personally I would rather reverse these and have the cooperative agreement between the school district and the teacher training institution and then follow this up with the initiation of a system-wide staff training program.

Certainly, I think that by the beginning of the second semester that you could have the implementation of the staff development program that would continue to the end of the school year and through the summer, and then I would select as a target date between June '72 and August '72 a target date for the evaluation of the staff development program.

One last chart that I would like to present, sir, is a type of organization for team teaching that can be implemented that would facilitate the implementation of some of the innovative programs that we are recommending.

THE COURT: This is what I am eager to see.

THE WITNESS: Well, you have thirty-two hundred children, including migrants, I am told, in grades K to four. At least, this is the figure that was made available to us. I think that we can have in a typical classroom anywhere from fifty-five to sixty students different types of resource personnel. Some are available already to the school district and are listed here. We have resource personnel that would be made available through the staff development program. We have sixty-six bilingual teachers in K through six. At the beginning of the school year in the consolidated school district you have about approximately one hundred multi-lingual teachers. I think it is possible to staff fifty-five to sixty students with a bilingual teacher and a monolingual teacher. We could bring two community aides, para-professional personnel in here through the staff development program. Title I and other funds can be utilized for this purpose, as well as ESAP money. You could bring in fifty-four volunteer bilingual personnel taken from a school-community council type structure and bring them into the classroom over here. Then you have in here a bilingual teacher, a monolingual teacher, two bilingual community aides and at least one bilingual volunteer parent aide. This would give you a total of five people working with fifty-five to sixty students, and it gives you a very nice child-to-adult ratio to utilize the capabilities and the language abilities and the cultural experiences of all of the personnel that you have over here (indicating).

All of the resources that are utilized are fifty-four bilingual, fifty-four monolingual and fifty-four classroom, a hundred eight bilingual community aides and fifty-four volunteer bilingual parents.

BY MR. CONROY:

Q: Dr. Cárdenas, this does not require that any given classroom be for fifty-five to sixty students?

A: That's right.

Q: It can be broken up into smaller classrooms?

A: That's right, and this can be broken into instructional areas where you have individual instruction and small group instruction, and you can also have large group instruction, which, incidentally, could release quite a few of these people for further staff development activities. We are doing quite a bit of this in the Edgewood School District.

One last statement that I would like to make, sir, being a school superintendent, I have the same obsession with money as other school superintendents. We have as fiscal resources available to us such things as Public Law 874, the Federal Impact money, which are made available because of the children and people living or employed in Laughlin Air Force Base. Title I money can be used for financing this type of instructional program. The Emergency School Assistance Plan money can be utilized for this purpose. Title VII money can be utilized for this, and it is not inconceivable that contracts can be modified to allow even greater resources.

The Bureau of Education Personnel Development has a lot of money that can be brought to bear for staff development activities. When we met with Mr. Gil Chavez from the Office of Spanish Surnamed Americans, he gave me a document which indicates that at the present time there are six hundred seventy-five million dollars in discretionary funds available in the U.S. Office of Education alone. These are monies that are not earmarked for any one program or do not have to meet requirements, let's say, for a proposal, but can be given at the discretion of the Commissioner of Education, so we realize that there is a need for money. I think that the fiscal resources are available.

We realize that there is a need for personnel resources. I think that there are a lot of personnel resources, as has been illustrated by the San Felipe Del Rio Consolidated School District. There are a lot of resources within that school district. I think that the U.S. Office of Education, Title IV, which provides technical assistance, can provide personnel resources. There is a lot of program personnel with the U.S. Office of Education. There are regional laboratories, regional service centers. The University of Texas systems and other institutions of higher education and certainly the Texas Education Agency. As far as materials, instructional materials, the regional laboratories have instructional materials which can be made available. The Texas Education Agency also has them. There are special projects that provide materials, and the U.S. Office of Education can provide these too.

THE COURT: Does this conclude the direct examination?

BY MR. CONROY:

Q: The program to which you have just had reference, Dr. Cárdenas—.

THE COURT: Would you excuse me just a minute? Government's Exhibits 308, 309, 310 and 311 are received in evidence.

(THE GOVERNMENT'S EDUCATIONAL PLAN—was previously duly marked as: GOVERNMENT'S EXHIBIT NO. 309)

(THE GOVERNMENT'S EDUCATIONAL PLAN—was previously duly marked as: GOVERNMENT'S EXHIBIT NO. 310)

(THE GOVERNMENT'S EDUCATIONAL PLAN—was previously duly marked as: GOVERNMENT'S EXHIBIT NO. 311)

Q: The program to which you have just had reference, is it presently in operation in the Edgewood Independent School District?

A: Yes, sir, this program—most of the features of this program—all of the features of this program are in operation in the Edgewood School District.

Q: Would you describe the Edgewood Independent School District as a wealthy school district?

A: No, sir, it is the fourth poorest out of twelve hundred in the state of Texas. It is a very poor school district.

Q: Yet, you have not had any difficulty implementing this program?

A: No, sir.

MR. CONROY: Your Honor, I would like to state for the record that if the Court would deem it appropriate, the United States would deem it appropriate that we be ordered to assist the district in finding any funding that would be necessary to effect the program.

Q: Now, is this the program that has some serious depth of thought into it, or is it something that was just—?

A: I'm sorry. I did not get the question, sir.

Q: I'm sorry. Is this something that has had years of development before it has been presented, each aspect of it?

A: Different aspects of the program have different lengths of time in development. Some of them are relatively new and are implemented just this year. For instance, in the Urban Rural Program where we implemented the school-community council concept this year. Other aspects of the program, such as the migrant—I have been working on this—and members of the team have been working for many years. Some of the members of the team have been working for as long as ten or fifteen years in the development of these programs.

MR. CONROY: Pass the witness.

THE COURT: I believe we will forego the cross-examination at this time. How many more witnesses do you have?

MR. CONROY: None, Your Honor.

THE COURT: Do the parties anticipate that there will be rebuttal testimony?

MR. OCHOA: Excuse me, Your Honor. What was the Court's ruling on cross-examination?

THE COURT: I said I was contemplating putting off the cross-examination until tomorrow, but I have just learned that this was the Government's last witness. Do I anticipate that you will have rebuttal evidence?

MR. OCHOA: No, sir.

THE COURT: Do you anticipate that you will have any—?

MR. MURRAH: Might I have just a moment, Your Honor?

MR. OCHOA: Our cross-examination will be very, very little.

MR. McCOY: The State of Texas anticipates no rebuttal witnesses, Your Honor.

THE COURT: Thank you, sir. The Court has been in session until about 7:00 o'clock every day this week, as I recall it. I am beginning to believe there are limitations.

MR. DOBBINS: Your Honor, did I understand you to say that you contemplated putting off cross-examination until tomorrow unless there was some objection? Is that what the Court said?

THE COURT: Well, if the cross-examination is going to be relatively short, I guess we can finish it up today. If, however, you contemplate some extensive cross-examination, I want to put it off until tomorrow.

MR. DOBBINS: To be perfectly frank with you, Your Honor, this is going to require a little thought before we decide exactly what type or length of cross-examination we will have.

THE COURT: Well, I can understand. This has been a very complicated set of facts that have been set forth in a very short time.

MR. DOBBINS: That's right, and it is very innovative, as the witness says, and to me it is startling. I would like to think about it a little bit.

THE COURT: I appreciate your position, and if you desire more time to think about it and to be able to frame your cross-examination, I will give it to you.

MR. DOBBINS: Thank you.

THE COURT: Do you feel that you need it?

MR. DOBBINS: I think so, I really do.

THE COURT: Very well, I am going to recess this hearing at this time until 9:00 o'clock tomorrow morning. I have another matter set at that time, a habeas corpus hearing, but I don't believe there will be any difficulty in setting it off until this cross-examination is concluded.

MR. DOBBINS: Your Honor, I want to be fair with the Court. We might retire here in a few minutes and discuss this and maybe reach a conclusion, you know, as to just a few questions. We don't know. We haven't given it any—like I say, it is difficult to work it out.

THE COURT: All right. This is some information that I ask that the parties furnish me by 9:00 o'clock tomorrow morning, if possible. If not, at the earliest time possible. What are the population figures for—?

MR. DOBBINS: Population of—.

THE COURT: Del Rio, all of Del Rio, excluding the former San Felipe District, and then the population of San Felipe alone. Are those figures available?

MR. MURRAH: You mean just the population, not the student population?

THE COURT: The population. I am not speaking about the student population, but just the population. Are those figures available?

MR. MURRAH: I am sure they are, Your Honor. I don't know where they are.

THE COURT: Is San Felipe a part of the corporate limits of the City of Del Rio?

MR. GONSALEZ: Yes, sir, it is one city.

THE COURT: It might be that the information I am asking of you then is not available. If not, why, so inform the Court.

MR. DOBBINS: Your Honor, before we adjourn, we probably should introduce our exhibits.

THE COURT: I will let you do that tomorrow, if you please. I am particularly eager to close these proceedings down at this time. Court will be adjourned.

(REPORTER'S NOTE: The Court then, at 5:45 o'clock, P.M., August 19, 1971, adjourned until 9:00 o'clock, A.M., August 20, 1971, at which time it was reconvened.)

POVERTY IN TEXAS

1974

PREFACE

Since its inception, Intercultural Development Research Association (IDRA) has acted as an advocate for economically disadvantaged children. Although IDRA is interested in the successful educational performance of all children, we realize that middle- and upper-class children usually have an abundance of advocacy in the home and in the larger community. One outstanding distinction between the haves and the have-nots is the access of the haves to social institutions. No such access is found among the poor; for the most part, they find themselves disenfranchised and powerless in the social and political currents of the community.

IDRA attempts to fill this void by acting on behalf of economically disadvantaged children. The contents of the following article attest to the educational dilemma of these children. Other data attest to the cyclic nature of poverty; children born into poverty tend to remain poor and bring a subsequent generation of children into poverty.

IDRA believes that schools should have both the responsibility and the capability of breaking this cycle of poverty, although historically, schools have demonstrated neither. Contrary to popular belief, American schools have not provided an avenue for socio-economic mobility. Although limited numbers of disadvantaged students may have capitalized on the school as a stepping stone for upward mobility, the vast majority have not. Evidence of the school's failure to break the cycle of poverty lies in the well-known statistic that the most reliable indicator of student performance in school is the socio-economic background of the student. With limited exceptions, students from middle- and upper-class homes do well in school; students from lower-class homes experience frustration and failure.

The inability of the school to break the cycle of poverty does not preclude its doing so. It is our expert opinion that the main reason for the school's inability to provide successful educational experiences for poor students is the failure of the school to adjust a middle-class institution to the characteristics and needs of the economically disadvantaged. Philosophies of education, rules and regulations, materials and methodologies, parent involvement, and virtually each and every element of school activity follow a middle-class paradigm that penalizes students without a middle-class tradition, orientation, and experience.

Disadvantaged students are perceived by the school as a conglomeration of deficits, negative characteristics that preclude successful performance in school. Experiential limitations of poverty are commonly interpreted by the school as evidence of a lack of mental competency and are so addressed in instructional programs. Human subjectivity and prejudice is "scientifically" substantiated by standardized measures of mental ability that are similarly based on middle-class values, traditions, orientations, and experiences. The failure of disadvantaged students to profit from middle-class experiences is measured in standardized tests and reported as a mental deficit.

IDRA staff perceive disadvantaged children as children who have unique home and community experiences. They are disadvantaged mostly in light of the middle-class characteristics of social institutions. Within the context of their own class and in the world in which they live, they may have great strengths and advantages. Their disadvantage in a middle-class context is not different than the "disadvantaged" position that middle-class persons experience when they find themselves in the strange and ofttimes terrifying environment of urban ghettos and barrios. Although economically disadvantaged children may not be prepared to deal with schooling in the middle-class context in which it is offered, they frequently have great strengths, although these strengths are seldom perceived by middle-class educators.

A solution to the dilemma of educating disadvantaged children can readily be found in the adaptation of the school to the characteristics of these children. Experiential constraints can be eliminated by experientially enriching activities. Experiential advantages can be used as the basis for expanded learning. The key for successful performance is the elimination of artificial barriers imposed by the school and the creation of viable bridges between poverty and school performance.

This elimination of barriers and the building of bridges between economically disadvantaged children and the schools was addressed in a publication developed by IDRA in 1989 for the Texas Education Agency's Dropout Information Clearinghouse. The publication, *Successful Schooling for Economically Disadvantaged At-Risk Youth,* is one of the best products available for the improvement of educational opportunities for disadvantaged children (IDRA, 1989).

Texas ranks second among the states in the number of poor persons (2 million) and twelfth in the "incidence of poverty" category. These findings are the result of an analysis of economic conditions in Texas conducted by the Texas Office of Economic Opportunity, a Division of the Texas Department of Community Affairs.

Poverty in Texas—1973 analyzes poverty according to nine categories: ethnicity, age, household characteristics, education, employment, labor force characteristics, housing, health, and geographic distribution (Texas Department of Community Affairs, 1974).

The data on education are striking. There is a direct relationship between income levels and educational attainment. As the educational attainment level increases, there is a downward trend in the incidence of poverty. At every level of education, Texas shows higher rates of poverty than the nation as a whole. The incidence of poverty for individuals with an eighth-grade education or less is 32.2 percent in Texas, while it is 23.9 percent nationally. Even among those with some college education, Texas ranks lower than the national average: 7.2 percent as compared to 4.9 percent.

Although minorities in Texas have improved their educational attainment during the past two decades, they are still behind the predominant Anglo population. "Among the poor population as well as the total population, far greater proportions of Anglos than minorities were found in the upper educational groups" (page 48, *Poverty in Texas—1973*). For example, only 24.1 percent of the total Mexican-American population had graduated from high school as compared to 54.8 percent of the total Anglo population. In terms of four years of college or more completed, the percentage of Anglos was 13.3 percent as compared to 4.1 percent for Mexican-Americans. The Black population in Texas fared only slightly better than the Mexican-American population. Among Blacks, the percentage of high school graduates was 29.8 percent; and the percentage of individuals with four years of college or more was 5.2 percent.

A surprising fact noted is the number of individuals "...whose income was only slightly higher than the two million Texans living within the poverty income guidelines." The study reports that there are 750,000 Texans in this category. Copies of the study may be obtained by contacting Ben F. McDonald, executive director of the Texas Department of Community Affairs, 611 South Congress Avenue, Austin, Texas 78711; telephone (512) 478-9601.

IMPLEMENTATION OF INNOVATION IN MULTICULTURAL EDUCATION

1975

PREFACE

The following article was printed in the IDRA *Newsletter* in September, 1975. It was written by me with the assistance of staff members who joined the organization as a result of funding received for the creation of a technical assistance center for national-origin minority students. This new center was created at a time when new state mandates for multicultural education were being enacted into law.

The article makes a strong case for addressing not only the characteristics of an innovative school program, but also the school environment in which the new program would operate. Although it is directed to school districts implementing bilingual and other multicultural programs, it really addresses all forms of innovation. Much of the content is readily applicable to the recent movement toward site-based management and other school reform concepts being implemented today.

The article looks into the causes of the resistance to change so characteristic of educational institutions, and it seeks ways to reduce this resistance.

IDRA staff anticipated so many problems in creating a school setting receptive to innovation that the new technical assistance center was named by its first director, Dr. Blandina "Bambi" Cárdenas, the Center for the Management of Innovation in Multicultural Education (MIME).

The content of this article should be a key part of a staff development program for the introduction of any innovation that can be expected to upset the status quo of a school.

The advent of state supported bilingual education, the implementation of the *Lau v. Nichols* decision, and the expansion of federally funded bilingual education programs all point to increased school district commitments to the implementation of multicultural education strategies (*Lau v. Nichols*, 1973). The Texas State Board of Education has adopted multicultural education goals for the state, and the trend appears healthy and irreversible.

It is important, therefore, to examine the needs of educational institutions as they proceed to implement innovations in bilingual and multicultural education. Since the inception of the federal effort in bilingual education, much research into, and development of, alternative approaches to implementation have occurred. While many would suggest alternative approaches that focus on ascertaining the most appropriate strategies for the implementation of successful bilingual and multicultural education, it is fair to say that for the most part, only those issues focusing on innovation itself are currently under broad examination. Unfortunately, little attention is being given to issues in organizational and human relation needs that affect the successful implementation of all innovations and bilingual and multicultural education in particular.

ORGANIZATIONAL NEEDS

Behavioral scientists tell us that any particular innovation is deeply conditioned by the state of the system in which it takes place. Most teachers and parents involved in bilingual education programs would tend to agree on the relationship between the innovation and the system, although in many cases the argument would be verbalized through negative and blame-setting statements such as: "They don't really want bilingual education," or "All they are interested in is the federal money," and the even more destructive "This is a racist system."

While these statements may reflect differing degrees of truth, they often obscure the need for more comprehensive responses to the organizational needs that must be met if innovation in multicultural education is to have a fair chance to succeed.

Matthew B. Miles, a noted behavioral scientist, has identified ten dimensions of healthy organizations that appear particularly relevant to school districts bringing about change through multicultural education:

1. Goals are reasonably clear to the members of an organization and reasonably well accepted by them. They are achievable and appropriate.

2. There is communication adequacy. The movement of information is relatively distortion-free, "vertically," "horizontally," and outside and into the system.

3. The distribution of influence is relatively equitable, presumably based on competence, interest, or commitment, and the amount of knowledge or data the individual has.

4. Resource use is effective. People may be working very hard indeed, but they must feel that they are not working against themselves, or against the organization.

5 Cohesiveness exists. Members want to stay with the organization, be influenced by it, and exert their own influence in a spirit of collaboration.

6. Morale is healthy. The members of the organization share feelings of well-being, satisfaction, and pleasure.

7. Innovation is ongoing. The organization is growing, developing, and changing rather than remaining routinized, and standard.

8. Autonomy promotes responses to the outside environment that are neither passive nor destructive or rebellious.

9. Adaptation occurs in the organization when necessary because of environmental demands.

10. Finally, the organization has problem-solving adequacy. The organization must have well-developed structures and procedures for sensing the existence of problems, for finding possible solutions, for deciding on those solutions, for implementing them, and for evaluating their effectiveness.

Obviously, just as bilingual and multicultural education cannot be achieved overnight, creating these conditions in school districts requires a long-term commitment of resources, including time and energy. Equally obvious is the fact that innovations in bilingual and multicultural education, no matter how strong and thorough, in and of themselves cannot achieve optimum success in school districts organizationally predisposed to have things "remain as they have always been."

The management of bilingual/multicultural education as an innovation requires the implementation of strategies that create appropriate organizational conditions as the educational innovation is introduced.

HUMAN RELATIONS NEEDS

Key to meeting the organizational needs of a school district undertaking bilingual and multicultural education is an understanding of the human relations needs created by innovation in general and by particular innovations that touch on deep-rooted, culturally-focused attitudes. Conversely, meeting the human relations needs of individuals involved in bilingual and multicultural education requires not only an understanding of those needs, heightened by the content of the innovation (cultural awareness, self-awareness, examination of prejudices, and so on), but perhaps more importantly, those needs that are heightened by the tension between the process of innovation bringing about change and the organizational demands inherent in school districts.

Concealed misgivings about bilingual education are probably widespread among school personnel involved in bilingual and multicultural education, whether they be members of the dominant cultural group or minority group members. These are motivated as much by a concern for the needs of the students as they are by the promise of new demands on the professional.

The first concern is easily understood when viewed in the light of the history of repression of alternative cultural and linguistic expression through educational, economic, political, and social sanctions. It will be overcome only as institutions, including the schools, provide for the full participation of diverse members of the population in the decision-making, implementation, and maintenance of the institution's mission.

Minority group teachers will not be convinced that competence in more than one culture and language is an asset until they perceive themselves as not handicapped by virtue of their own cultural and linguistic difference. Likewise, school personnel of the dominant cultural group must perceive bilingual and bicultural individuals as being of equal value to themselves and to the institution before they can lessen their latent and extant fear of bilingual and multicultural education.

Fears about increased professional demands affect both bilingual and monolingual personnel. Because the funds that facilitate additional staff training, supervision, and evaluation often are funds intended to focus on the educationally disadvantaged (most often minority populations), there is a tendency to scapegoat the disadvantaged populations as school personnel perceive greater demands avalanching upon them. When those demands are made in terms of linguistic or cultural competence, the fears of those who perceive themselves as culturally and linguistically limited are realistically heightened.

Responding to these fears requires more than appeasement. In fact, school personnel are due to experience greater (certainly different) professional demands regardless of the ethnicity or linguistic characteristics of the population. The technology of education is undergoing constant study, revision, and improvement. If these advances are to reach children, the educational practitioner, too, must undergo consistent growth, just as the school does.

The other side of the fear of increased professional demands is the fear of exclusion from professional growth. Minority and non-minority personnel involved in bilingual education customarily undertake extensive staff development. At its best, this training empowers the trainee with feelings of self-assuredness, confidence, and (oftentimes) a missionary zeal that finds its expression in the classroom, the teachers' lounge, and in social settings. The trainee also learns theory, methods, and technology more effectively than he did in preservice learning experiences. The trainee learns the vocabulary and diction of new educational approaches. Often, the trainee knows more about a program than a supervisor, principal, or superintendent does. He or she has acquired this new knowledge in training settings that stress self-expression, openness, and self-evaluation.

ACCURATE DIAGNOSIS

The provision of paraprofessional aides, increased staff training, and increased instructional materials also serves to increase the human relations problem within staffs when resources are not uniformly available. Staff that is not part of the "special project" may feel left out, less important, and deprived of resources. Again, often the innovation itself (i.e., bilingual education) becomes the scapegoat for the legitimate hostility of "excluded" teachers. Thus the "bandaid" innovation often serves to uncover other sore spots within the organization. The inaccurate assessment of this situation may result in a decision to: (a) curtail the resources of the innovative program because of the human relations problem; or (b) provide "human rélations" training to "cure" the ill-feelings of the excluded teachers.

A better way to proceed would be to assess the organization's needs and set about strengthening those dimensions of a healthy organization that would diminish this hostility and create a positive environment.

The organizational and human relations needs of school districts implementing bilingual and multicultural education are obviously much greater in number and complexity than can be examined in this brief article. What is intended is to acknowledge their existence, their critical relationship to the innovation itself, and the need for school districts to assess these accurately in relation to bilingual and bicultural education. Only when an accurate assessment of the need has occurred can the school district or project implement the appropriate problem-solving strategies necessary to the successful management of innovation.

EDUCATION PROBLEMS OF MIGRANT CHILDREN

1976

PREFACE

This article was published in the October, 1976 issue of the IDRA *Newsletter*. It was originally published as "Education and the Children of Migrant Farmworkers: An Overview" in the June, 1976, issue of *Inequality in Education*, a publication of the Center for Law and Education at Harvard University (Cárdenas, 1976).

It is disheartening that no major breakthrough has occurred in the education of children of migrant farmworkers. Although a new generation of children finds itself in the educational predicament described in the article, the performance of these children is as dismal as the performance of the preceding generation.

Barring a major and dramatic change in educational procedures, we can anticipate several subsequent generations of children born into a subcultural lifestyle from which there is no escape.

If one had to identify a group of American children who underperform all others in school, the group with the highest dropout rates, the lowest achievement levels and the most failures, that group would undoubtedly be the children of migrant agricultural workers.

Statistics concerning the education of these children are almost unbelievable. Their performance deviates so drastically from the norm that common evaluation techniques are not even valid for this group. For instance, in an evaluation of migrant education in Texas conducted in 1968, an attempt was made to determine the percentage of migrants who dropped out of school prior to completion of the twelfth grade. Statistics derived were realized to be meaningless when it was discovered that an estimated 20 percent of all migrant children in Texas never even enrolled in school at any age.[1] Attempts to measure performance in school are consistently invalidated because of the migrants' absence during testing periods, the difficulty in attaining test/post-test scores, the inability of the tester to speak the language of the children, and the difficulty of establishing rapport.

The vast majority of migrant farmworkers in the United States are Mexican-American, Black and Puerto Rican; their children suffer the deprivations common to their ethnic or racial minority group, plus additional deprivations caused by their economic plight, their mobility, and the low social status given to them by a more stable society. In effect, migrant students are treated as the third-class baggage of second-class citizens.

This article will discuss the unique set of problems faced by migrant children and the schools from which they are supposed to be receiving an education.

Segregation

Perhaps the most detrimental educational situation migrant children face is their almost complete exclusion from mainstream educational programs. In following agricultural employment patterns, they spend the winter in the agricultural areas of the southern states. Several months before the end of the school year, they begin to withdraw from school in order to accompany their families north in search of work. Some re-enroll in another school for the last weeks of the school year; most do not. Students who do enroll in school this late have a difficult time integrating with the permanent students. If the number of migrants is large, schools invariably enroll them in "new" and separate classes, and in segregated facilities.

Not only is it difficult for the migrant child to adapt to the instructional program, but it is nearly impossible to participate in extracurricular activities and other events of the school community. After having spent the late spring, summer, and early fall seasons as a transient, the migrant child returns to his or her home base in the late fall, several weeks, and perhaps months, after the school year has started. By then, classes have been formed, teachers have been hired, and the returning migrant child fails to become integrated into the mainstream program. During the years of bulging school enrollments, a barracks or obsolete school building was likely to be reopened to provide space for migrants. Most school districts anticipating an influx will place a child on "hold" until the arrival of a sufficient number of migrants to start a new class and hire a new teacher. In many cases, home districts beginning new classes in November do not arrange for a competent staff to be available to instruct the children entering school at that time.

Many school districts, therefore, organized schools for migrants on a shortened school year and on an extended-day basis. The operation of segregated facilities locked the migrant child into a separate world, where he or she was oftentimes unaware of, or totally out of contact with, other groups of children. When migrants were assigned to schools with non-migrant children, the migrant child saw the other children leave at 3:00 p.m. and interpreted the two additional hours he or she spent in school as punishment for being a migrant.

School Finance

In most of the states in which migrant children attend school, the standard provision for allocating state resources to a school district is the use of average daily attendance (ADA) or average daily membership (ADM). Under this concept, a school district receives state funds on the basis of the number of children attending school (ADA) or enrolled (ADM). If a migrant child is in a school district for less than the total number of days in the school year, state funds received are for a fraction of the school year, i.e., if he attends school in a district for 120 days out of a 180 day term, funds in the amount of 120/180 or two-thirds of the annual rate are paid to the district.

On the surface, this arrangement may seem justifiable, but school personnel face the dilemma of employing two-thirds of a teacher, buying two-thirds of a desk, or using two-thirds of a textbook. Physical facilities, equipment, books, materials, and personnel must be obtained for maximum enrollments, yet allocations are based on averages. The problem is further compounded by the fact that, unlike the case with other mobile populations, where arrivals and departures tend to even out, migrant children tend to arrive and depart at the same time, in keeping with the agricultural rhythm of the community, and severely distort enrollment figures.

The financial problems faced by school districts facing an influx of migrant children tend to encourage the development of negative perceptions and attitudes toward these children. Other types of highly mobile children, such as the children of military personnel who bring PL874 and PL815 (Federal Impact Aid) monies, which are discretionary and labeled as local funds, are made to feel much more welcome. The advent of the Migrant Amendment to Title I, ESEA provided additional funds for the education of migrant children, yet the educational impact of this federal funding was negligible. Although Title I, ESEA funds are available to school districts for migrant children, these funds must supplement, not supplant, local and state resources.[2] Thus federal migrant programs are built on inadequate local and state foundations.

Staffing

The arrival of agricultural migrants in a community necessitates the acquisition of additional staff at unusual times in the educational calendar. Administrative personnel in home-based schools are reluctant not to employ the best teachers at the beginning of the school year, in anticipation of the arrival of migrant children later in the year. Therefore, personnel hired "as necessary" during the year to accommodate migrant students often do not meet the highest professional standards.

Very few migrants ever finish school, let alone go on to college and become educators, so it is unusual to find a teacher with personal experiences or even deep insights into the problems and rigors of a nomadic existence. In evaluating migrant educational programs it was not unusual to find that where migrant children were integrated into mainstream classes, a large number of teachers were completely unaware of migrant children in their classes. Although all were aware that the children had entered late or withdrawn early, the teachers had not associated these attendance patterns with migrancy.[3]

Training school personnel to deal with the migrant child has not been very extensive or productive. Workshops for teaching migrant children usually involve only those teachers dealing exclusively with migrants, and much of the training is remedially oriented and dysfunctional.

Instructional Programs

In spite of the fact that school districts have enrolled migrant children for many years, no major revision has been made in instructional materials or methodologies in order to accommodate the migrant child. Migrant children use materials developed for white, English-speaking, middle-class, geographically stable children that are grossly incompatible with the characteristics of migrant children.

Materials and methodologies are not only culturally irrelevant, but are also linguistically irrelevant, economically irrelevant, and perceptually irrelevant.

Ninety-nine percent of the migrants in Texas are Spanish-speaking, yet only in recent years have some school districts employed bilingual programs, and the percentage of migrants participating is insignificant. In other states, similar problems exist for Spanish-speaking and other linguistically different migrant children.[4]

Few school districts use materials reflecting the culture, work, or experience of migrants. In math classes, they add cream puffs, multiply hot dogs, and divide model airplanes without a clear notion of what they are. They read about the shopping mall although they may never have seen one, and the amusement park or circus is as fantastic and remote as the giant's house on top of Jack's beanstalk. The family in school books not only looks different, but it sets up a standard of father, mother and baby that excludes the rest of the migrant's siblings and shameful family appendages such as aunts, cousins, and "comrades." Migrant children who live in substandard housing without running water feel pressured to report the time of day they took a shower in order to qualify for the Cleanliness Gold Star, and in health class they learn the value of "enriched" bread, although they have never eaten anything but tortillas with their meals.

In one work book, a picture of a businessman, a laborer, and a hobo was presented to a group of migrant children. Asked to circle "Daddy" in the picture, most of the children circled the hobo. The teacher not only informed them of their incorrect performance, but gave a long tirade on the evils of hoboes, their non-contributing to the community, their laziness and dirtiness. What a horrible and traumatic experience it must be for a child to have a "Daddy" who looks like that!

School curricula have built-in continuity and sequence, and the materials assume that prerequisite skills have been presented and mastered. For example, a migrant child may run into division before he encounters multiplication. As he grows up in the educational system, instead of moving from the known to the unknown, he systematically moves from the unknown to the less known.

Few of the materials developed for middle-class children provide sufficient immediate positive reinforcement for the migrant child. Deferred rewards are meaningless if the child will be in Michigan when the award is being made back in Texas.

Teachers rarely capitalize on the extensive travel and agricultural experiences of migrant children. The middle-class child who has visited Europe writes essays on the trip, makes substantial contributions to geography units, and may even make a presentation to the class on dolls acquired in Germany, wooden shoes from Holland, or "banderillas" from Spain. Teachers of migrant children do not incorporate migrant travel into the curriculum, and the reading, writing, and arithmetic are far removed from the migrant's experiences.

The worst aspect of school relations with migrant children is the negative perception held by the school and consequently passed on to the children. Regardless of funding, staffing, and assignment, as long as the school views their culture, language, work, and instability negatively, the performance of migrant children in school will be inadequate.

The entire instructional program is often one huge trauma, so that finding employment in a community where school officials look the other way as children work in the fields becomes a welcome relief to the migrant child and his or her family.

Dysfunctional Responses

One very important by-product of the evaluation of migrant education in Texas[5] has been the identification of a large and diverse number of dysfunctional responses to the problems of migrant children. In general, the school either provides a response irrelevant to the nature of the problem, or persists in further punishing the children for being migrants.

Thus, during the short period the migrants are in the system, they are further handicapped by the school! The school day may be extended, but instruction is not individualized to provide continuity and sequence.

Like other Title I children, migrants are the recipients of dysfunctional extensions and repetitions of unsuccessful techniques. The same teachers who have not been able to teach them all day are employed to extend their lack of success for extra hours in the afternoon. Even in special classes for migrant children, the same inappropriate educational techniques persist. For example, movies, filmstrips, audio tapes, and other audio-visual aids purchased with Title I Migrant Program funds are used, despite the fact that they were developed for white, English-speaking, middle-class children.

Perhaps the most dysfunctional responses are in the administrative area. In order to "encourage" migrants to leave later and return earlier, school districts often tend to enact local policies that turn out to be impractical and dysfunctional. For example, almost every home district has some type of regulation regarding late entries and early withdrawals. Children who withdraw from school before some arbitrary cut-off date do not receive credit for that semester regardless of classroom performance. Similarly, children enrolling past an arbitrary date do not receive credit for work performed in the first semester. Such policies, rigorously enforced in secondary schools, preclude the acquisition of Carnegie units, the standardized unit for credit in high school work. It is easy to see how a student unable to acquire the credits necessary for promotion and graduation would be strongly tempted to withdraw from school at an early age and forgo an education. The different policies that prevail in various states and school districts further compound this problem.

Other Social Institutions

The school is not the only institution that fails to respond to the needs of migrants. The areas of government employment, housing, social services, medicine, welfare, and justice also have an abundance of policies and practices developed for, and compatible with, a primarily white, English-speaking, middle-class, and less mobile population. Migrant agricultural workers are commonly excluded from National Labor Relations Board coverage, minimum wage laws, participation in the democratic political process, eligibility for service, and continuity of treatment. It appears that not only the schools, but the entire social system excludes migrants from receiving basic goods and services, and locks them into successive generations of hopelessness.

Recommendations

Children of migrant agricultural workers stand out in their lack of success in education. In terms of dropout rates, underachievement, grade retention, and failure, they do worse than any other minority group. Past efforts to alleviate their plight have been unsuccessful because of the emphasis placed on attempting to extend a system of education incompatible with the characteristics of the migrant. A traditional approach to the education of migrant children has been to afford them the same, or more of the same, instructional programs developed for other children.

The recent *Lau v. Nichols*[6] Supreme Court decision declared that equal treatment does not constitute equality of educational opportunity. The school may not ignore special characteristics of children and have the children assume the responsibility for adapting to an irrelevant school experience.

In the education of migrant children there are three needs which must be met by school districts and the state educational system in order to remedy their continued failure. These are adaptability, comprehensiveness, and resources.

The entire educational structure must be revamped in order to make it compatible with the characteristics of disadvantaged, minority, and migrant children. This revamping must go beyond coloring pictures of brown or black children in textbooks and labeling it the "multicultural series." Change must be made in institutional philosophies, administrative policies, scope and sequence, the curriculum, the extra-curriculum, staffing, student personnel services, non-instructional needs, community involvement, and evaluation.

Educational responses to the characteristics of disadvantaged, minority, and migrant children must be comprehensive. The piecemeal effort now exerted by local, state, and federal agencies does little to remedy the existing situation. The migrant child does poorly in school not because he is culturally and linguistically different. All of these characteristics, which are perceived as negative attributes by society, are expressed by the schools and learned by the child. School systems require the necessary financial and personnel resources for coping with this problem. The imposition of financial penalties in addition to already existing financial constraints further aggravates the problem and will assure its perpetuation. Until a comprehensive change in educational practices is brought about, this unfortunate segment of our society will continue to be denied equality of educational opportunity.

NOTES

1. "Evaluation of Migrant Education in Texas," conducted by the Southwest Educational Development Laboratory, Austin, Texas, 1968.
2. For a complete discussion of the Title I Migrant Program, see Masurofsky, pp. 11 to 23, in this issue.
3. Documented in "Evaluation of Migrant Education in Texas," supra, and subsequently reinforced by the author's personal observations in San Antonio, Texas, 1969–1973.
4. See, for example, Masurofsky, pp. 11 to 23, and note 56, in this issue.
5. "Texas Evaluation," supra.
6. 414 U.S. 563 (1974).

RESPONSE TO NOEL EPSTEIN

1977

PREFACE

In 1977, I was contacted by Samuel Halperin, Director of the Institute for Educational Leadership at George Washington University, with a request that I review a manuscript on bilingual and multicultural education by Noel Epstein, a former educational writer for the *Washington Post*. Epstein had been hired by Halperin to conduct a comprehensive review of bilingual and multicultural education in the United States. Another review of the manuscript was to be conducted by Gary Orfield, a nationally prominent specialist in school desegregation.

I was intimately familiar with Noel Epstein, having met with him on many occasions concerning his prejudicial reporting on bilingual and multicultural education. On many occasions I had extensive arguments with him concerning his obsession with "Affirmative Ethnicity," which to him represented a separatist movement by language minorities. Epstein viewed American schools, educational programs, materials, and methodologies as culturally neutral, based upon "the common English language and the common national history." Multicultural education for him consisted of affirmative ethnicity, an attempt by minorities to inject into education cultural content, the inclusion of the history and culture of minority groups into the curriculum, particularly by federally funded program initiatives.

No amount of argument could convince Epstein that American schools and their programs, materials, and methodologies are far from being culturally neutral. Virtually all school activity has clear and strong cultural nuances, although such nuances strongly reflect a Northern European culture, the history, values, traditions and orientations of the cultural mainstream. American history begins with our pilgrim fathers, and Texas history begins with Moses Austin's first visit to the Lone Star State.

Epstein's cultural naivete gave rise to a long series of xenophobics such as Albert Shanker of the American Federation of Teachers, S.I. Hayakawa, U.S. Senator from California, Linda Chavez of the Office for Civil Rights, and William Bennett, Secretary of Education, who elevated the Affirmative Ethnicity alarm to ridiculous heights.

Halperin's request that I respond to Epstein's manuscript placed me as spokesperson for twenty million Hispanics who overwhelmingly supported bilingual and multicultural education. Since I attended hundreds of meetings, conferences, seminars, workshops, and other activities in which I was the only Hispanic present, I frequently found myself in such a position. Subsequent communications with the country's Hispanic leadership inevitably provided favorable and extensive support for my statements.

The Institute for Educational Leadership publication by Noel Epstein, *Language, Ethnicity, and the Schools*, provided an immense disservice to language minorities and specifically to language-minority children in our schools (Epstein, 1977). I still object to its publication for the following reasons:

1. Noel Epstein was not an impartial researcher on the topic of bilingual and multicultural education. He had a reputation as a strong opponent to these issues, and his prejudicial attitudes are reflected in every page of the publication.

2. Advocates for and against bilingual and multicultural education were not afforded equal treatment. The publication was written solely by Epstein; twelve and one-half pages of rebuttal at the end does not provide a balanced perspective.

3. A copy of my criticisms was given to Epstein prior to publication. Epstein subsequently toned down various racist statements prior to publication. The overt racism in the original draft was replaced with a covert racism much more difficult to detect and address.

4. Epstein's publication perpetuates the myth that American education is culturally neutral. There is little that goes on in the schools that does not reflect the values, traditions, orientations, and history of the dominant mainstream culture.

5. Gary Orfield was hardly qualified to respond to the criticisms about Affirmative Ethnicity. After praising Epstein for his work, he concentrated on his specialty, which is the desegregation of schools. Orfield made no attempt to react to the constricting choice between desegregation and bilingual education by proposing a third alternative, namely bilingual education in a desegregated setting as presented by me in the article, "Bilingual Education, Segregation, and a Third Alternative" found elsewhere in this anthology.

   Furthermore, Orfield has never understood the relationship between desgregation and cultural pluralism in the instructional program. The elimination of cultural isolation through the use of culturally pluralistic materials and methodologies is just as important to the schooling of minorities as the elimination of the physical isolation of segregated campuses.

6. The Institute for Education Leadership distribution of this biased publication promulgated relatively unchallenged misconceptions about bilingual and multicultural education still with us today. Epstein's publication became the "Holy Book" to accompany the "Sacred Cows" on which prejudice and discrimination rely for the denial of equal educational opportunity.

Bilingual education has been defined as education conducted in two languages. This does little to clarify the rationale of current bilingual education efforts in this country. A much better definition of these efforts would be "the use of a child's native language as a medium of instruction while English is being acquired as a second language."

The basic rationale is a response to the problems encountered by school systems in the education of children of limited English-speaking ability. Although the problem has been with us for well over a century, no effective solution has been identified. For many years, common educational practice consisted of placement of children of limited English-speaking ability in a regular English language program, very similar to the immersion concept described by Mr. Epstein. This practice proved remarkably unsuccessful, as shown by the educational characteristics of language-minority children throughout the country.

There are few insights as to the nature of this failure, especially since there was little interest in the education of language minority children or in the reasons why traditional educational practices were so remarkably unsuccessful. Neither the federal government, nor institutions of higher education, nor education professionals were motivated to conduct any extensive study into reasons for the massive failure of our schools in dealing with the education of language minority children. Studies in the mid-1960s *did* substantiate the failure of traditional programs, as evidenced by dropouts, retention in grades, underachievement, assignment to classes for the mentally retarded and disciplinary measures used by schools.

In the 1960s, an alternative approach surfaced that was used extensively in the education of language-minority children. This consisted of a highly structured approach to the teaching of English as a second language. This alternative was deemed unsuccessful in that it did little to eliminate the academic retardation of language-minority children. In general, the acquisition of English as a second language led to a discontinuity in the child's cognitive development, with the acquisition of content material in all subject areas being delayed until the child had a sufficient mastery of the English language to cope with basic skill acquisition and content learning.

Another alternative was developed in the last decade that incorporated the previously given definition of bilingual education. The rationale for this approach was that as English was being learned as a second language, the child could proceed with cognitive development and skill acquisition in his native language. Thus, the rationale of a bilingual education program consisted of an English as a second language (ESL) program, with initial instruction being conducted in the native language until the learner had sufficient mastery of the English language and a transition could be made from the native language to English.

Since the acquisition of languages other than English was a desirable outcome of education—as evidenced by curriculum offerings in secondary schools and institutions of higher education as well as in legislation and in graduation and college entrance requirements—it was suggested that native skills in languages other than English be maintained and developed in order to avoid the loss of language facility and the need for subsequent reintroduction as a foreign language several years later.

The failure of prior efforts in the education of language-minority children may be attributed largely to the negative perceptions of speakers of languages other than English and the accompanying rejection of language-minority children through the valuing expressed by the curriculum of the school.

Early efforts in bilingual education were viewed positively by minority populations in that they would eliminate the academic retardation of children of limited English-speaking ability evidenced in traditional and ESL programs; avoid the traumatic experience of language rejection; and maintain and perhaps develop a language resource already held by the student.

THE CURRENT STATUS OF BILINGUAL EDUCATION

A. Classification of Programs

In spite of the implementation of large numbers of bilingual education programs through federal, state, and local efforts, current programs have made little change in the educational methodology used in teaching children of limited English-speaking ability. Despite analysis and estimates made by various organizations, current bilingual education programs may be described as follows:

1. The vast majority are really ESL programs that contain structured activities for the acquisition of English as a second language and that *may* contain some communication in the language other than English.
2. There is a limited number of transitional bilingual education programs in which an attempt is made to conduct language activities in a language other than English while English is being learned as a second language. I have never encountered a single bilingual education program in which all subject matter and skill-development activities are conducted in a language other than English, thereby meeting even the most limited definition and rationale of a bilingual education program.
3. There is an insignificant number of maintenance programs in which the continued development of native language proficiency is nurtured or expanded.
4. Many bilingual education programs are viewed by the language minorities as token programs responding to legislation, litigation, and consumer demand, or program popularity.

B. Characteristics of Programs

1. There is an extensive variety of untested organizational patterns in current bilingual education programs. These patterns reflect the use of native languages in limited subject areas. Native language use may be found in one or more of the following subjects: reading, arithmetic, culture, social studies, natural science, art, and music. Some students are assigned to full-time classes, others are traded, and still others are "pulled out" for bilingual instruction.
2. The time devoted to the native language in bilingual education programs may range from five minutes a day, three times a week, to a majority of the school day.
3. In general, bilingual education programs have failed to identify, recruit, employ, or train the staff necessary to implement a bilingual education program. In one major city with an extensive enrollment in bilingual education programs, 92 percent of the staff in the programs were monolingual English speakers. In another community, teachers were certified as bilingual, with a minimum proficiency of 750 words in the language other than English.

4. There is no available collection of curriculum materials that affords compatibility between the instructional program and a child speaking a language other than English. Although there is a scattering of bilingual materials in almost every subject and at almost every elementary grade level, there is no complete set which includes every subject matter area and extends over several years.
5. There has been no attempt to develop educational methodologies consistent with the characteristics of languages other than English. For example, phonetic inconsistencies in the English language have led to a rejection of phonetic approaches in the teaching of reading in English. Such rejection has been translated and has become a part of teaching methodologies in reading by English-trained teachers in spite of phonetic consistencies in languages other than English.
6. There is an absence of support materials for an instructional program in a language other than English. Neither resource books nor audio-visual aids are extensively available.
7. Instrumentation for the determination of language characteristics and educational achievement in languages other than English is only now being developed.

STATUS OF RESEARCH IN BILINGUAL EDUCATION

Not only is there a limited amount of educational research on bilingual education, but research findings on the accomplishments of bilingual education are almost nonexistent. The few studies that are available lack adequate depth, scope, time, and methodology to provide a valid measurement of the outcomes of bilingual education. The studies currently available also swallow elephants and strain on gnats in analyzing the effectiveness of this instructional approach.

The much-awaited American Institutes for Research (AIR) study recently released by the U.S. Office of Education is no more effective than prior attempts to evaluate bilingual education programs (American Institutes for Research, 1977). An analysis of the AIR study conducted by the Intercultural Development Research Association (IDRA) identifies major discrepancies in the identification of the target population, the selection of comparable control groups, test instruments used in the study, the amount of time between pre- and post-testing, lack of consistency in programs being studied, adequacy of instructional staff, and the source of funds being used.

Space limits do not allow a thorough examination of all the flaws IDRA found in the study, but the following examples will suffice:

1. Language classifications were done subjectively by teachers in spite of a body of research that points to the unreliability of teacher judgment as an indicator of the language characteristics of students.
2. Half of the teachers classifying students in the various language categories did not speak any language other than English.
3. District Title VII personnel were allowed to nominate groups to be used for comparisons from classrooms outside of their own. Differences be-

tween school districts—in organizations, teaching methodologies, teacher training, teacher qualifications and competence—and varying financial resources were not controlled.

4. About one-third of the *non*-Title VII teachers and aides were involved in a bilingual program. This raises the possibility that the comparison groups had "bilingual treatment," thus invalidating them as a comparison. Instead of concluding that students were not doing well in some aspects of the Title VII bilingual program, an alternative conclusion may have been reached that students do better in state or locally funded bilingual programs.

5. Although in theory the interim between pre- and post-testing could have been seven months, only six of the thirty-seven projects involved more than six months, and eighteen of the projects (almost 50 percent) were pre-post tested within five months or less.

6. Using a definition based on the placement of students and not on the characteristics of the program itself, the study concludes that most bilingual programs are of the maintenance type. "Maintenance" is not defined.

7. Program characteristics varied considerably as to instructional time, content, and instructional methodologies. Impact findings did not control for such differences.

8. IDRA's secondary analysis of the AIR data shows that only 26 percent of the teachers participating in the study reported having a bilingual teaching credential, which is the minimum criterion for adequate training, as determined by many states.

9. Although the study reports that 93.8 percent of the Title VII teachers had participated in bilingual in-service training, the training could have been taken within a five-year span and could have consisted of as little as one day or less. IDRA's analysis of the individualized project descriptions revealed that 6.6 percent of the teachers involved in the Title VII programs received no training whatsoever, and that 7.4 percent received one day or less. It is possible that as many as 46 percent of the teachers received less than three days of in-service training over a five-year span in the implementation of a new and drastically different instructional methodology. There is also no indication of the quality of such in-service training.

10. Analysis of the study indicates that 49.6 percent of the teachers in the Title VII bilingual programs admit to not being proficient in the other language!

If nothing else, the AIR study substantiates one imperative need in bilingual education, namely, the need for leadership in developing, implementing, and monitoring the federal Title VII investment in bilingual education.

The number of requests for the implementation of Title VII programs far exceeds the small number that are being funded. Shouldn't approval of proposals and allocation of funds be governed by the school district's willingness to provide adequate staffing, training for staff, and valid pupil assessment procedures?

It seems inconceivable the Congress would "throw out the baby with the bathwater," that is, diminish support for bilingual education, because of inadequacies in federal supervision. Accountability should be directed toward the guilty, not toward the victim.

ISSUES RAISED BY THE EPSTEIN STUDY

A. Legal Status of Bilingual Education

It is difficult to concur with Mr. Epstein's statement that "there is no federal legal requirement for schools to provide bilingual or bicultural education."

Although the Supreme Court in *Lau v. Nichols* did not provide such a legal requirement, it must be remembered that the plaintiffs made no such request in the case (*Lau v. Nichols*, 1974). The San Francisco Unified School District did have a policy toward bilingual and bicultural education, including operational programs. The issue before the Supreme Court was the exclusion of massive numbers of children from such programs.

Other court cases have resulted in far more explicit interpretations of federal law in regard to bilingual education.

In *U.S. v. Texas* (December 6, 1971, San Felipe Del Rio intervention suit), the Federal Court for the U.S. Eastern District of Texas held that the absence of a bilingual education program was in violation of the 14th Amendment of the U.S. Constitution and Title VI of the Civil Rights Act of 1964 (*United States v. Texas*, 1971). The court prescribed curricula that recognized the value and cultural environment and language of Mexican-American students; language programs that developed and reinforced the student's primary and secondary language from early childhood through the 12th grade; bilingual counseling; intercultural awareness programs and ethnic studies courses; the establishment of multi-ethnic community councils to assist in the formulation and evaluation of the program; and the development of a plan to insure the hiring and retention of competent bilingual and bicultural staff. It also recommended provisions for language and cultural awareness training and the appointment of bilingual and bicultural teachers for special education classes.

In the review of *Portales v. Serna*, the Federal 10th Circuit Court of Appeals stated, "Under Title VI of the Civil Rights Act of 1964 [children of limited English-speaking ability] have a right to bilingual education" (*Serna v. Portales*, 1974). A similar finding was made in the *Overton v. Austin* case, when the Federal Fifth Circuit Court of Appeals in New Orleans observed that bilingual education programs had been implemented by the Austin School District as required by the law (*Overton v. City of Austin*, 1984). Recently, a New York federal court handed down a similar legal interpretation in *Rios v. Reed* (*Rios v. Reed*, 1977).

The federal courts' interpretations of the Civil Rights Act of 1964 is that this law is a specific legal mandate for bilingual education programs. Mr. Epstein's study expresses a strong fixation that bilingual education programs comprise a separatist movement by language minorities. Neither the rationale of bilingual education nor the programs being implemented reflect a separatist movement in this activity. This study depicts bilingual education and bicultural programs as ends in themselves, which are sought by minority populations to establish and maintain a cultural identity different from the American mainstream. This has never been an objective in bilingual and bicultural education. It is not occurring in school programs and is not likely to occur.

The education of children does not take place in a cultural vacuum. Each subject matter area introduced in the schools is saturated with culture both in the content of the materials and in the methodology utilized. The cry for cultural pluralism in education is for materials and methodologies to be representative of the various cultures found in our American society rather than unfairly representing solely the cultural characteristics of Northern Europeans.

American Indians are sick of hearing that America was "discovered in 1492," with the assumption that other populations did not exist before that or that they were not worthy of mention. American Blacks resent their status in the history books as carefree darkies for over 100 years, the cause of the American Civil War, and a problem ever since. Mexican-Americans take little pride in being the villains of the Alamo who murdered John Wayne, disappeared for 100 years, and have recently surfaced as the culturally disadvantaged.

American minorities request that their ethnicity be represented in art, music, sociology, anthropology, science, reading, arithmetic, and all other aspects of the instructional program.

The author questions whether the cultural enrichment of language minorities is related to student achievement. I am of the opinion that the learner's perception of self may be the strongest determinant of success or failure in educational activities.

Mr. Epstein has completely missed the boat by his failure to understand that one main purpose of multicultural education is to promote an understanding that my ethnic culture is a part of this American culture.

The author also expresses strong concern about segregation. If ethnic minorities have been less than enthusiastic over desegregation efforts, the reason is that past desegregation efforts have led to the following:

1. The burden of desegregation has fallen upon the minority populations. As a result of desegregation efforts, minority schools have closed or enrollments have been reduced, with the minority population being transported to white majority schools.

2. The reassignment of minority pupils to other schools inevitably will lead to the minority pupil's becoming a minority in each of the desegregated schools. Community personnel enjoyed wide powers in the decision-making, staffing, and operation of segregated, predominantly minority schools. Such prerogatives vanish when the minority population is dispersed and becomes 15 percent of every school in the system.

3. Pupil assignment plans that have dispersed minority populations have consistently failed to provide adequate transportation for participants in extra-curricular activities and for parental involvement activities, and in responding to emergency situations.

4. Desegregation efforts consistently have jeopardized special programs for minority populations.

School districts threatened with desegregation have been presented a choice between participation in bilingual and multicultural education and/or the desegregation of schools. In the Denver case, the school district displayed an unwillingness to trouble itself with administrative reorganization and maintained that continued segregation was essential to bilingual program implementation.

School authorities also consistently warn minority parents that desegregating pupil assignment plans may result in their children no longer being eligible for participation in Title I programs for disadvantaged students. This constitutes a half-truth; although concentrations used for determining school plan participation may change, the number of participating students should remain the same.

B. Language Immersion Programs

Mr. Epstein's study makes several interesting and promising recommendations for future programs. One such recommendation, however, is dysfunctional. It is the recommendation that language immersion programs be tested as an alternative. In the eyes of the language minorities, such an approach would lead to regression in the education of their children.

The author fails to understand that his concept of language immersion is not an innovative practice, but rather a return to the traditional practices in the schools that accounted for massive failure by the minority population.

Although a few studies document the success of bilingual education, there is an abundance of studies that adequately evaluate the effect of past immersion programs.

In such programs, anywhere from 50 to 100 percent of language minorities dropped out of school before the completion of the twelfth grade, achievement was consistently one year below national norms at the third grade, one and one-half years below national norms at the sixth grade, and two years behind at the seventh grade. In Texas, the result of immersion programs produced such a high level of retentions that 86 percent of all Mexican-American children in that state had repeated at least one grade prior to the completion of the third grade.

Perhaps Hispanic minorities are so overwhelmingly in favor of bilingual education regardless of lack of evidence of its success because the experiences with past programs have been so negative that any alternative seems a step in the right direction. If, as documented by the Texas Education Agency, the dropout rate of Mexican-American children in a South Texas school system is 90 percent, the parents cannot be blamed for strongly recommending an untested alternative.

Another consideration for the rejection of immersion programs as an alternative to the education of children of limited English-speaking ability is that, in my opinion, and it is not contradicted by research findings, such immersion programs, although adequate for adults and for higher grade levels, produce too much of a psychological trauma in young children. Placement in a language immersion program today would constitute for me a fun activity, although I can still remember the horror of this experience when I was six years old.

C. Specific Exceptions

It is almost impossible to critique the many erroneous or opinionated statements found in Mr. Epstein's study. Efforts to group them invariably lead to an excess of classifications, making the critique extremely long, repetitious, and shallow.

However, to illustrate the unfairness of Hispanic treatment in this study, I will meticulously critique three consecutive pages of the study's summary, hoping that the identification of specific discrepancies will develop reader sensitivity to other discrepancies in the study.

1. The Congress has not, as Mr. Epstein states, expanded significantly its commitment to bilingual education. Figures presented in the study indicate 425 projects in fifty states in sixty-eight languages and dialects. Spanish projects account for about 340 projects in fifty states. These 340 projects are not only dispersed nationally, but represent a variety of Hispanic groups, including Mexican-American, Puerto Rican, Cuban, and others. The remaining 85 projects represent sixty-seven language groups, indicating not much more than one project in the nation for each of these language groups.

The number of pupils participating in these projects cannot be more than 1 or 2 percent of the total eligible population. Regardless of the quality of the "piloting" taking place in the various projects (a federal government responsibility in terms of goals, approaches, training, and development), the number and percentages of participants does not remotely denote an "educational service program."

Program activity in bicultural education does not constitute teaching students about their own ethnic groups, but rather the use of information about their own ethnic groups as background for skill development and further content acquisition. Teaching minority children to add, subtract, multiply, or divide "creampuffs" is an unnecessary complication of mathematical processes if the pupil does not know what a creampuff is. This bakery item is so remote from non-affluent Hispanic minorities that there is no such lexical equivalent in the Spanish language. As stated previously, American English language textbooks are full of such inconsistencies that make education unnecessarily difficult for the minority child.

2. The study claims that there is no federal legal requirement for schools to provide bilingual or bicultural education, and that OCR policy therefore is difficult to explain.

This assumption has been refuted in a previous section, but further elaboration is needed to clarify the OCR position. In *Lau v. Nichols,* meeting the needs of children of limited English-speaking ability was not solely dependent on the Civil Rights Act of 1964, but the Supreme Court did act on OCR regulations that had been issued under that act.

In a memorandum to all school districts on May 25, 1970, the director of the Office for Civil Rights, J. Stanley Pottinger, stated, "Where inability to speak and understand the English language excludes national origin-minority group children from effective participation in the educational program offered by a school district, the district must take affirmative steps to rectify the language deficiency in order to open its instructional program to these students."

The memorandum thus reflects a finding by HEW, the federal agency with special competence in the area of education, that, where a school system employs English as the basic language of instruction but provides no special assistance to non-English-speaking students who comprise a significant portion of the system's enrollment, those students are impermissibly excluded from participation in, denied the benefits of, and subjected to discrimination under the system's educational program on account of their national origin.

In *Lau v. Nichols,* the Supreme Court recognized the authority of the May 25 Memorandum and set a legal precedent for subsequent OCR regulations such as the "Lau Remedies" issued to the 334 school districts in question.

3. The national government has spent more than half a billion dollars without demonstrating the effectiveness of bilingual and bicultural

education, not because of the size of the task or the impossibility of proving such effectiveness, but because of the lack of effectiveness and efficiency by the federal government. In general, funds for bilingual education have been dispersed throughout the country without regard to staff adequacy, availability of materials, evaluation designs, and accountability procedures. Even special research studies such as the aforementioned AIR/Office of Education study were unbelievably bad.

Unfortunately, the response to such incompetence is to penalize the victim through a proposed discontinuity of service, rather than to hold the dispenser of funds accountable.

On the other hand, traditional educational programs for minority children expend billions of dollars a year with a most remarkable consistency of failure and are replicated year after year at federal, state and local expense with not only no evidence of success, but rather with substantial and conclusive proof of failure.

4. The question of whether federal funds are aimed at or reaching the target students should not be directed toward either Congressional or OCR policies, but should be directed toward the U.S. Office of Education, and specifically toward the Office of Bilingual Education.

Advocates of bilingual education are cognizant that Title VII funds involve less than 2 percent of the eligible population and are extremely concerned with either a lack of priorities that may deny a bilingual program to the children who need it the most, or gross inefficiencies in selection criteria that produce the same effect. Yet, there is little assurance that pupil selection is all that bad. Although the USOE-sponsored study judged 70 percent of pupils in a sample to be dominant in English, not Spanish, for test-taking purposes, keep in mind that: (1) pupil selection criteria can (and should) be controlled by the granting source; (2) half of the teachers who made the judgments were not proficient in any language other than English and therefore had no way of measuring bilinguality; and (3) it is my contention, reinforced by the evidence of lack of teacher bilinguality in bilingual programs, that most bilingual education activities are still conducted in the English language and, therefore, it is not surprising that 70 percent of the pupils having been taught in English demonstrated an English preference for test-taking purposes.

5. Most of the controversy created by this study stems from statements in the third page of Mr. Epstein's summary. Previous sections of this critique have attempted to show that instructional materials and methodologies are biased toward certain language and ethnic groups.

Although most bilingual education advocates give highest priority to children of limited English-speaking ability, they share an ideal in which American schools will value other languages to the point of teaching them in our schools and maintaining and developing them in the case of language minorities.

In many years of involvement in minority education, I have never heard the term nor encountered the concept of "cultural maintenance programs." I have heard of intercultural, multicultural, and bicultural programs in which the purpose of the programs is either intercultural understanding or the ability to function in more than one cultural milieu.

The federal government does not finance or promote pupil attachments to our ethnicity—these attachments we formed at our mothers' breasts. The federal government finances and promotes understanding, respect and acceptance of other cultures; that is, other heritages, other traditions, values, and orientations, and other lifestyles. As an American, I value freedom, freedom of choice, and feasible alternatives from which to choose. I wish for the school to help me hold these options open for my children so that they continue to be options until they are old enough to choose.

I would, for example, detest an American textbook that stated, "Parents, when they get old, are a pain in the rear, and should be placed in an institution." My ethnic heritage rebels at such a concept, since parents are valued and respected for their wisdom, experience, and affection, and play a continuing role in family activity and decision-making even at an advanced age. Such is the role my mother plays, and I would wish to play in my old age. I would, therefore, resent the school's eliminating such an option or denoting that people who like to have old parents around are weird.

In coping with such a conflict, the school should state that some people find it more convenient to place parents in an institution, others prefer to keep them at home, others allow them to go into the snow and die, or perhaps the school should state nothing at all!

Perhaps I belabor the point. I am not attempting to stereotype a specific ethnic group, and if the previous example seems exaggerated, it is because I have already tried to explain this to the study author twenty times, and he still perceives bicultural education as "affirmative ethnicity," with all kinds of innuendos about separatism, unAmericanism and minority power.

6. Most bilingual education programs, both transitional and maintenance, are highly segregated because they are implemented in school districts that are highly segregated.

J.P. Guilford, in his introduction to statistics textbooks, states that the most common correlation error made by neophyte statisticians is to observe a relationship between two variables and project a causal relationship (Guilford, 1965). This study depicts this error admirably.

Since 1945, Hispanics have been challenging *de jure* segregation in American schools, and a short listing of desegregation cases such as *Delgado, Hernandez, Alvardo, Cisneros,* and *Morales* indicates the willingness of Hispanics to oppose segregation and act as plaintiffs in desegregation cases.

In spite of these efforts, Hispanics are still the recipients of segregation, *de facto* in most cases and *de jure* in some. It is not surprising that bilingual education programs are highly segregated when in fact non-bilingual education programs are similarly highly segregated.

7. It is impossible to follow the study's logic that concludes that, if maintenance programs were to succeed, they would be just as likely to lead to an attrition in the use of native languages as to nourish them. If concentrated efforts by the schools to stamp out the use of languages other than English through negative valuing and even extensive punitive measures have been notoriously unsuccessful, I find it difficult to understand how the acceptance of the language by the school and its maintenance and development would accelerate attrition.

Personally, I have not only retained Spanish language competence in a 96 percent English-speaking society, but my competence, vocabulary, and use have increased over the years. Bilingualism in radio and television also has increased in recent years. Newspaper bilingualism, which had been declining, has now experienced a reversal, and is increasing.

Several new Spanish-language national magazines have come into being in the last few years.

Ironically, the reason for this increase is not caused by school efforts or bilingual programs. Instead, advertisers, business, and industry have realized that if they want to carry their message to the consumer, it is highly desirable to express that message in the language used by the consumer, a truism that the schools have never understood or accepted.

8. The ethnic political wave that has been sweeping the globe has done very little to increase the economic and political power and prestige of language minorities. Simple mathematical calculations will determine that Hispanic Americans are underrepresented in medium- and high-level positions in each and every hierarchy in this country, including federal, state, and local political structures and social and economic institutions.

Hispanic Americans feel that equality of educational opportunity is the key to an increase in upward mobility that will allow them to attain a socio-economic position comparable to that of the white Anglo.

The protection of civil rights and federal intervention to enhance equality of educational opportunity are desirable goals and not the controversial question posed by the study. "The most socially sensitive aspects of the local school curriculum" deserve federal inquiry and intervention if these local prerogatives lead to a denial of equal protection or equal educational opportunity.

Bilingual education programs are not alone in setting segments of the American population against each other; so do desegregation, evaluation, progressive education, busing, ROTC, and football. Allow the Greek Americans in Chicago to settle their differences just as Hispanic Americans settle their differences, and thank the Lord that we enjoy the freedom to differ and to choose from varying options.

SUMMARY STATEMENT

The past eight criticisms denote exceptions taken to each of nine consecutive paragraphs in the first section of the Epstein study. Further analysis would result in a critique several times the size of the study and may serve no useful purpose. It is evident that the study identifies problems in the development and implementation of bilingual education programs, but these problems are for the most part administrative and do not indicate an erosion of American principles. On the contrary, bilingual and bicultural education are not only pedagogically sound concepts, but are a positive step in bringing about equality of opportunity and the realization of the American dream for populations being excluded from the political, social, economic, and educational mainstream.

IMPRESSIONS OF EDUCATION IN THE SOVIET UNION

1977

The National Institute of Education and the State Department afforded me the opportunity to be a part of a nine-person delegation to the Soviet Union and to conduct a study and exchange program in educational research methodology. The nine-person delegation was in the Soviet Union from Saturday, September 17, through Sunday, October 2. Our visit included activities in the three largest cities in the Soviet Union—Moscow, with a population of over eight million; Leningrad, with a population of over three million; and Kiev, the capital of the Ukraine, with a population of over two million.

Activities during this trip may be categorized in four classes, as follows:

1. the presentation of formal papers by members of the Soviet Academy of Pedagogical Sciences, the Ministry of Education, and research institutes, followed by rather lengthy discussions for clarification, the answering of questions, and presentations on comparable activities in educational systems in the United States;
2. visits to educational institutions, including research institutes, universities, teacher training institutions, pioneer palaces, experimental schools, and pre-school programs;
3. almost nightly entertainment, including Soviet opera, ballet, concerts, circuses, museums, and monuments; and
4. dinners and luncheons arranged by our hosts in the Soviet Union, the U.S. Embassy, and members of the American delegation.

The hospitality extended to us by our Russian hosts was warm and generous. Three staff members of the Academy of Pedagogical Sciences, fluent in English, accompanied us from arrival to departure.

A CENTRALIZED EDUCATIONAL SYSTEM

Any understanding of educational activities in the Soviet Union must be preceded by an understanding of the highly centralized nature of the Soviet educational system. The American system of education, with its lack of federal responsibility and authority, and 10,000 independent school districts loosely supervised by fifty separate and independent state agencies, presents a most unusual situation not readily perceived or understood by the Soviet Union or other countries. The Soviet Union's Ministry of Education is centralized, with complete authority over every aspect of the educational system. However, each of the fifteen republics in the Soviet Union has a Ministry of Education, similar to our own state education agencies, but under the control of the Supreme Soviet. The role of the Communist Party is difficult to comprehend, since it is an independent hierarchy, although party education officials and Soviet ministers are one and the same, especially at the very high levels.

The highly centralized nature of Soviet education is particularly noticeable in research and development efforts. Research conducted by the Academy of Pedagogical Sciences, the many research institutes, and problem councils, is relatively easy to synthesize, convert into educational practice, and implement in their schools. This contrasts sharply with the almost unbelievable situation in the U.S. in which there is little, and on occasion, no formal relationship between research activities and educational practice. The Academy of Pedagogical Sciences operates fifteen experimental schools with at least one-third of all teachers in these experimental schools directly involved in research projects and receiving supplementary salaries from the academy. In specific instances, and for particular purposes, the number of experimental schools and participating teachers may be extended.

A second consideration when analyzing Soviet education is the economic condition of the country. The inability to develop their natural resources, the need for qualified technicians, the devastating effects of World War II, and the failures in agricultural development present a dismal environment for the development of educational programs.

It must also be understood that on-site visits for the American delegation were limited to experimental schools, schools with new physical facilities, and exclusively in the urban areas. By necessity, all observations made and conclusions reached may be colored by an extremely biased sampling in the institutions observed. Educational methodology, staff training, technology, and audio-visual equipment observed in the experimental schools may not be available in rural areas until many years from now.

The following are a few of my impressions of Soviet education:

RESEARCH BACKGROUND

The Soviet Union is in the last phase of a five-year plan for extensive, comprehensive, educational change. During the five-year period, the entire educational system of the Soviet Union has been revamped. This effort has resulted in a modernization of the educational system, with a complete restructuring of the curriculum. The elementary school has been shortened from four to three years, and the secondary school has been lengthened from four to seven years. Prior to the massive implementation of the new program, the new curriculum was field-tested in over 2,000 schools throughout the Soviet Union.

The effort was an extensive attempt to change education in keeping with Soviet ideology; the results of fifteen years of research in educational methodology; a new psychological rationale based on the need for the cognitive development of children; changes in social institutions such as the family, industry, and the economy; and a realistic appraisal of the labor needs of the Soviet Union in the last part of the twentieth century and the beginning of the twenty-first.

The most important characteristic of the recent educational change was the comprehensive effort by which it was implemented. The defining of educational philosophy, the use of research findings, changes in scope and sequence, the production of a new syllabus for each course in each grade, the massive retraining of teachers, and extensive pilot testing and evaluation are far superior to the piecemeal efforts so characteristic of the American system.

In spite of the extensive planning and extensive support for the change effort, numerous problems manifested themselves. Not all educational personnel shared the enthusiasm and optimism necessary in support of the effort. It was found that many participants found it difficult to break with tradition, and the new system was viewed with prejudice by both parents and teachers. As stated by one speaker, their failure to extend parental participation in the initial stages was a costly mistake which created extensive problems in its implementation.

The Soviet concept of comprehensive educational planning for innovation and change closely parallels our own experiences in these activities. The failure of the educational system in the U.S. to do extensive planning for the implementation of change and innovation has led to failure, waste, and inefficiency in much of the federal effort of the last fifteen years.

EARLY CHILDHOOD EDUCATION

The Soviet Union has made extensive strides in the implementation of comprehensive pre-school programs. It was estimated at various times that as many as 50 percent of all pre-school age children are enrolled in a pre-school institution. This impressive statistic corresponds to the increase of women in the labor force of the Soviet Union. Women, who constituted less than 10 percent of the total labor force in 1920, now constitute 49.4 percent of the Soviet labor force. The pre-school we visited is one of many serving large, multiple-family units that have grown up in the suburbs. Incidently, the growth of the suburbs has led to a severe pupil decline in the metropolitan central areas. It is ironic to note that Russia is experiencing extensive and unmanageable white-flight in the absence of a Black population.

The pre-school center operates from 7 a.m. to 7 p.m. and serves approximately 1000 children ages one to six, who are placed in groups of twenty-four. Every twenty-four children have a cluster of rooms that include work area, play area, dormitory, and bathroom. A full-time doctor and nurse are available at the center. Participation is voluntary, and children may stay any number of hours up to twelve at no cost to the parent. There is extensive support for non-instructional needs, with food and milk readily available free or at reduced prices. Instructional activities at the pre-school level as well as other levels of education are cognitive-development-oriented. All toys used are educationally oriented. In fact, it was stated that all toys manufactured in the Soviet Union for use in the school or in the home must be approved by the appropriate research institute. Toys and materials used are in good shape and immaculately stored by the child after use. Even at this early age, the individual needs and characteristics of the student are tempered with social responsibility.

SCIENCE AND FOREIGN LANGUAGES

Visits to elementary and secondary schools were particularly impressive in science and foreign language instruction. Scientists appear to be worshipped in the Soviet Union and educational methodologies, facilities, and equipment readily reflect this condition. The instruction in mathematics and sciences is modern, and methodologies are problem-solving and experimentation-oriented. In the experimental schools, there is an abundance of audio-visual aids that are extensively used in the instructional program. In the experimental schools we visited, three out of six classrooms inspected had T.V. sets with video-taping equipment.

Language instruction was extremely sophisticated in the experimental schools. In one school in Leningrad, most, if not all of the children were studying English as a second language. Language development used modern language laboratories with electronic equipment, although the language tapes displayed a British orientation rather than American. Language instruction is augmented by extensive English language literature, current events, and history. Every student interviewed readily discussed Mark Twain, Jack London, Ernest Hemingway, A.J. Cronin, and a host of other American and English authors. Students also belong to international friendship clubs that carry on extensive correspondence with children throughout the world.

PIONEER PALACES

The most unexpected and surprising institutions in the Soviet Union were the Moscow and Leningrad pioneer palaces. These institutions are not a part of the schools, although it appears that they are administered by the Ministry of Education. The best way to describe a pioneer palace, since there is no comparable institution in our country, is as a combination of the YMCA, Scouts, Campfire groups, athletic centers, hobby centers, cultural centers, and a host of other activities scattered in our country among churches, civic organizations, and private institutions.

These pioneer palaces serve children from the time school dismisses through the evening hours. Participation is voluntary, although parents are responsible for transportation to and from the palace. In each of the two institutes visited, the range of activities was unbelievable. In one institution, activities included folk dancing, ballet, art, sculpture, advanced chemistry, international friendship clubs, botany, zoology (including the raising, feeding, and care of every type of animal, from insects to alligators), sewing, cooking, baking, radio (electronics as well as Morse Code), storytelling, random play, model railroading, model airplane making and flying, pilot training (including two computerized Link simulators), literary, and political activities.

The pioneer palaces serve as a place to keep children out of the streets, for amusement, for school enrichment activities, for the development of academic, vocational, and recreational interests, and for the identification and development of unusually talented and gifted children. Each activity is closely supervised by a staff that includes paid professionals, aides, specialists, volunteers, and guest consultants, which may include anyone who is an expert in the field, from a cosmonaut to the vice president of Moscow University. Supervisory personnel keep detailed observational and anecdotal records of all children.

BILINGUAL EDUCATION

My interest in bilingual and multicultural education created a certain amount of apprehension and frustration during our first few days in the Soviet Union. Neither of the two topics was included in any of the research institutes, and my inquiries produced little information. I had almost come to the conclusion that U.S. reports about bilingual and multicultural education in the Soviet Union were extremely erroneous until it finally dawned on me that bilingual and multicultural education has been a characteristic of Soviet education and of the 15 republics since 1920, and is so institutionalized that there is little research, experimentation, or developmental concern.

This realization was completely substantiated by our visits to schools in the Ukraine. Initial native language instruction is universal, whether the initial language is Russian or Ukrainian. The other language is introduced as a second language in the second year, and the schools have a parallel system of instruction offered in all subject matter in both languages. Under no circumstances does a student cover the same material in both languages. A child may opt to study mathematics in Russian or Ukrainian, and may even change languages in subsequent years. I observed similar classes in both languages, and out of 100 teachers in one school, ninety-eight of them were reported to be bilingual.

It was reported that a similar policy exists in each of the fourteen republics where a language other than Russian is spoken.

It is interesting to note that Leningrad schools operate special programs for "people from the far north" who speak a language other than Russian. Leningrad teacher training institutes also prepare teachers for teaching children from the far north. I assume that this reference was to Eskimos and Laplanders scattered throughout Russia and areas above the Arctic Circle. I was informed that both the schools as well as the teacher training institutions are completely bilingual. When a question was raised about instructional activities relating to the use of bilingual instruction for small groups of far north children numbering only three or four, the Russian Ministry of Education asserted that the instruction must be bilingual because of the necessity of preserving the native language and culture. Unfortunately, time did not allow us to pursue this official policy, which describes cultural and language pluralism as a necessity.

INTERDEPENDENCE AND SOCIALIZATION

Another extremely interesting area in Soviet education is the relationship between the development of a child as an individual and the socialization of the child. The new educational system of the Soviet Union proports to socialize the child while at the same time preserving the uniqueness and individuality of the child. The unbelievably good discipline and order in every institution we visited constitutes proof of the success in the socialization of the children. Proof of the individualization is much more difficult to perceive.

Strictly on subjective observations, I assume that the relationship between the individual and socialization is a two-dimensional continuum, as depicted in the following graph.

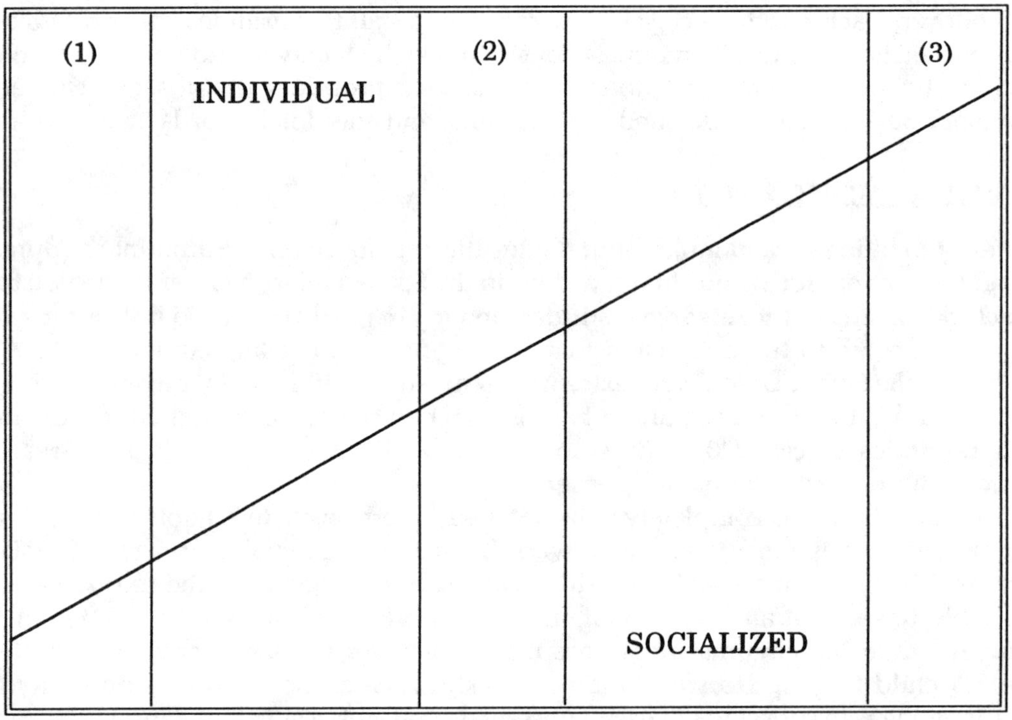

At the extreme left (1) is a situation in which an individual functions as such with little relationship to other members of his society. Such an individual may enjoy large prerogatives concerning his own conduct but may be ignorant of his responsibility to the larger society. At the extreme right (3), we would find a socialized individual who is completely dependent on the society for everything he needs or does, and is completely void of any independent thought, ability, or creativity. Somewhere in the middle (2) is an area in which there exists an ideal balance between independent and social responsibility. If I were to stereotype American children, I would place them close to #1 in the continuum. The stereotyped child in a communist society would be located in area 3 of the continuum. The Soviets purport to be making an effort through their educational institutions to move toward the left in the continuum in developing a better balance between socialization and independence. Perhaps American schools should also start moving toward the middle of the continuum in order to achieve an optimum balance.

TEACHER TRAINING

The most interesting facet of teacher training in the Soviet Union is a regulation that after each five years of teaching, professional personnel must participate in four months of retraining. Teachers are given a paid leave of absence during this four-month period.

Training is done in an institution of higher education, and the program is mostly determined by the teacher and advisory staff. Approximately one-third of the time is spent on subject matter updating and a study of new educational methodology. The remaining two-thirds is dependent on the individual interests of the teacher, and may include special studies, readings, experimentation, research, or other approved activities.

NEGATIVE FINDINGS

The educational situation in the Soviet Union is not all roses. Three massive problems manifest themselves and form the challenge to Soviet education during the next few decades. The problems are as follows:

1. Technology—As stated by one researcher, "The Soviet Union educational system is full of ideas. What we lack is your American technology." I cannot believe that the technology seen in the experimental schools is readily available throughout the Soviet Union. In looking at the products of Soviet technology in hotel rooms, bathrooms, department stores, and on the streets, it is apparent that Soviet technology is many years behind the U.S. Their ability to make technological advances is probably dependent on the products of the most advanced schools, as well as on agricultural, economic, political, and military factors.

2. Rural Areas—It appears that the vast majority of the Soviet Union is made up of impoverished, backward, rural areas. Some educational authorities readily admit that little of the new educational system has been, or can be, implemented in the rural areas. Educators in the Ukraine admitted to the impossibility of implementing the ten-year compulsory education program; and resources, including trained teachers, are too scarce for the immediate reform of rural education.

3. Family—As in most non-industrial, non-urban societies, Russia appears to have a strong sense of family unity. With 50 percent of their pre-school children enrolled in pre-school institutions for as long as twelve hours per day, there is no question but that family relationships will change abruptly in the near future. It is undetermined how Soviet society will cope with this dissolution of the family, which, in our country, social scientists agree has become the largest evil of urbanization.

LEGISLATIVE ISSUES IN MEXICAN-AMERICAN EDUCATION

1983

(with Dr. Albert Cortez)

PREFACE

When Texans for Educational Excellence (TEE), which subsequently became Intercultural Development Research Association (IDRA), was established in 1973, four fields of activity were projected for the organization: research and evaluation, materials development, training and technical assistance, and dissemination of information. Although programmatic activity has varied considerably during the life of the organization, the four areas of activity have remained fairly consistent, so much so that these four areas have formed the basis for organization and management.

The dissemination function commanded most of the attention and resources of the organization for its first two years and has remained an important function of the organization, although the Division of Training and Technical Assistance has dominated IDRA activity for the past seventeen years.

Activities in the dissemination function have always included the more traditional methods of disseminating information, such as the distribution of a monthly newsletter, periodic bulletins, and research reports; but there have been two rather unusual avenues for the dissemination of information at IDRA, in keeping with the mission statement of making information available to decision makers.

One is the provision of testimony in pertinent court cases; the other is the provision of information to legislative bodies such as the Congress of the United States and state legislatures. Far more information has been provided to the Texas Legislature than to any other legislative body.

During the TEE years, it was not unusual for the entire staff of the organization to camp out in Austin for entire legislative sessions. As programmatic activity increased at IDRA, I still played the role of legislative liaison for several years. Eventually Dr. Albert Cortez assumed this responsibility, and recently another staff member, Ms. Consuelo "Conchi" Salas, has been added to this effort.

Although IDRA has always been a non-lobbying organization and has not lobbied for or against any specific legislation, information has been provided consistently to the legislature as a whole, to the various relevant committees of the legislature, and to various groups in the legislature, such as the Mexican-American and African American legislative caucuses.

Since school finance reform was the original mission of TEE, much of the early dissemination of information dealt with this issue, and it has remained a major topic throughout the life of the organization. IDRA has provided legislative bodies with research information, alternative funding plans, analyses, and reviews of proposed legislation, and testimony at the invitation of various committees. On occasion, IDRA staff have presented testimony as individuals, and not as representatives of the organization.

I remember one time when I was scheduled to present testimony on school financing before the House Committee on Education of the Texas Legislature. While waiting for the school finance legislation to come up in committee, other proposed legislation was being considered. A bill submitted by a legislator on behalf of a professional administrators' group came up for consideration. A member of the professional organization testified on behalf of a bill that would have eliminated the state's compulsory school attendance law for students past the fifth grade. The witness explained to the Education Committee members that many students had no interest in school and wanted to drop out but were prohibited from doing so because of the compulsory attendance law. He further testified that there was no sense in keeping the unhappy students around and detracting from the education of other students.

At the end of the testimony for the bill, the chairperson asked the audience if there was anybody wanting to testify on the bill. When no one responded he then asked, "Does anybody wish to testify against the bill?" He repeated the question twice, and when it was evident that there was to be no testimony against the bill, I stood up and walked up to the committee.

"Dr. Cárdenas, do you wish to testify on behalf of IDRA against the bill?" asked the chairperson.

"No sir, I am here to testify on behalf of IDRA on the school finance bill. But while I'm here, I would like to present personal testimony against this bill."

Following my unexpected and unprepared testimony, the chairperson of the Education Committee called for a committee vote on the bill. It was defeated unanimously.

"I have never before been treated so shabbily in a committee hearing on any legislation I have introduced," said the representative who authored the bill.

"You have never before introduced such a shabby piece of legislation," answered the chairperson.

IDRA has provided technical assistance to the Texas Legislature on other topics. We participated in the legislative study that led to the repeal of the Texas law that prohibited the teaching of any subject other than foreign languages in a language other than English. IDRA subsequently submitted a study on the cost of bilingual education that led to the first state categorical financial support for bilingual and English as a second language programs.

The same IDRA staff that provided testimony in the bilingual education intervention suit in *U.S. v. Texas* provided technical assistance to the State Task Force on Bilingual Education and to the Senate Education Committee in the design of Senate Bill 477, which provides the basis for the education of limited-English-proficient students today. The court order on bilingual education in *U.S. v. Texas*, the recommendations of the State Task Force, and Senate Bill 477 contain common strands that reflect IDRA staff assistance to the three efforts.

Following enactment of the Bilingual Education Bill, IDRA was inundated with calls from educators wanting to know what an "LPAC" was. IDRA staff had borrowed the concept from special education's Admission, Review, and Dismissal committees (ARD) and created the Language Proficiency Assessment Committee (LPAC), made up of teachers, parents, administrators, and student service personnel to determine student placement and continuity in a bilingual program. With its capability to respond quickly to problem situations, IDRA immediately wrote and printed a guide for the LPAC that was distributed state wide for several years before the concept appeared in state bilingual program guidelines.

IDRA has also provided input to the development and implementation of testing programs. In general, we recognize the diagnostic need for assessment and the accountability need for evaluation, but we are extremely sensitive to the stigmatizing of students, particularly through the use of cultural and language-biased and invalid instruments.

The following article appeared in the IDRA *Newsletter* in March, 1983, and illustrates IDRA's interest in legislative issues.

Each session of the legislature is inundated with a proliferation of proposed legislation affecting Mexican-Americans in Texas. The 68th session is no exception and a number of bills have been introduced that impact the availability of equal educational opportunities for Mexican-American children. The purpose of this article is to highlight some of the important issues and relate them to legislative activity.

SCHOOL FINANCE

Perhaps the most pressing and demanding educational issues deal with the financing of public schools. This continues to be a crucial topic since the loss of the Rodriguez case in the federal courts in 1973. This topic has been a consistent priority in every legislative session since then.

The Rodriguez case was filed by a group of Mexican-American parents in the Edgewood Independent School District in the late 1960s. Plaintiffs claimed that the system of school finance in Texas discriminated against children in low-wealth school districts. After having won the case in the lower courts, it was lost in the Supreme Court in a heartrending five to four decision. The Supreme Court pointed out that the Texas school finance situation was most unfair, but that relief had to come from the legislature rather than the federal courts. During the arguments in the courts the State of Texas asserted that disparities between high- and low-wealth districts existed, were unfair, and would be addressed, without the need for the federal courts to force a change in the system.

In spite of the priority given school finance in each legislative session following the court decision, the legislature has failed to provide adequate relief for low-wealth school districts or to diminish the disparities between high- and low-wealth districts. At best, the limited legislation enacted has slowed down the rate of growth of disparities. Nonetheless, the disparities are still there, and they are still growing.

This issue is of particular interest to Mexican-Americans because a majority of Mexican-Americans live in low-wealth school districts. There is a high correlation between the wealth of school district and the number and percentages of Mexican-Americans. IDRA's research shows that, in general, the larger the number of Mexican-American children residing in a Texas school district, the lower the wealth of that school district.

The need to reform school financing in Texas in order to improve educational opportunities for Mexican-American children can be met through the following agenda:

1. **Equalization Aid**—The foundation school program in Texas is not adequately funded to provide anything but "bare bones," minimum

educational programs. For this reason, almost every school district in Texas has to raise additional money to enrich the educational program through local school taxes in addition to the local taxes required as part of the foundation school program. The problem is that, in spite of high tax rates, low-wealth school districts cannot produce sufficient revenues for enrichment purposes. Although there exists a common conservative belief that these poor districts suffer because of an unwillingness to tax themselves, this is an erroneous myth. Our research shows that the higher the percentage of Mexican-Americans in a school district, the higher the tax rate for that district. Therefore, in spite of overtaxation, Mexican-American children have fewer funds for their educational programs.

The solution to this dilemma has been district power equalization, an effort by the state to compensate for the lack of taxable wealth in school districts. As provided in past legislation, the state provides equalization aid to low-wealth districts to compensate for their low tax bases. The problem is that the amount of aid being provided is insufficient to meet the needs in a depressed economy with high utility costs and diminishing tax bases. If disparities between districts are to be reduced, it is necessary that the amount of equalization aid be increased. Present aid amounts to about one-half the average amount of enrichment being expended in districts throughout the state. A realistic goal is that the amount of enrichment funds provided should be raised to the average amount of enrichment expended in the State—an amount of approximately $750 per-pupil this year.

2. **School Construction**—The state of Texas is unique in being one of the few states in the country that does not provide state funds for school construction. Other states provide grants, foundation provisions, loans, and other types of assistance to needy school districts.

A recent fact-finding tour of south Texas by the authors indicates that this problem is increasing. The absence of state help, coupled with diminishing tax bases in a depressed economy, the high cost of construction, and high interest rates, are making it increasingly difficult for low-wealth school districts to generate necessary construction funds. State constraints on amounts of bonded indebtedness and district tax rates have made it impossible for school districts to construct even high-priority facilities.

Since most of the opposition heard on the provision of state funds for construction centers on the arguments that the state of Texas has never provided such funds, the highest priority for advocates of construction aid is to *start* such a practice. Two approaches appear feasible, although it is not necessary to select between the two, because both should be implemented.

The first approach is to provide funds for construction, repair, remodeling, and equipment through a formula grant program. The formula can be based on the tax wealth of the school district and adjusted for other variables such as past effort (the amount the district has already raised through bond issues), increasing enrollments, and age of existing facilities. The second approach is through the use of the permanent school fund for the *purchase* of school bonds at a low interest rate.

3. **Continued Emphasis on Local District Contributions in Proportion to Their Ability to Pay**—The foundation school program is an equalized program. After the cost of implementing a minimal school program is computed, the cost is divided between the state and the local school district. The program provides for the amount each district pays, to be determined by the taxable wealth of the school district. Low-wealth school districts pay a small amount of the foundation program; high-wealth school districts pay a larger portion of the program from local funds. The amount that each district pays is called the Local Fund Assignment.

   Unfortunately, and unbelievable as it may seem, in spite of the need to increase equalization, the legislature has been providing state funds that actually *reduce* equalization! This increase in the disparity between high- and low-wealth districts has been brought about by limiting the amount a local district has to contribute as its share of the foundation school program. This approach appears attractive to school districts because all districts pay less from local funds, but when one considers that the local fund assignment is proportionate to wealth, an across-the-board limitation on the local share means a tiny savings for low-wealth districts and a huge savings for high-wealth districts.

   Another factor contributing to inequality has been "save harmless" provisions and "minimum aid" provisions in state legislation. These provisions state that regardless of the amount that constitutes a fair share of the foundation program, a school district will receive no less, or have to pay no more, than they did before the legislation was enacted. These provisions are frustrating and dysfunctional because they say in effect, "This legislation eliminates the problem, except that the situation must not be changed." A recent proposal to the legislature to freeze Local Fund Assignments at past levels is similarly disequalizing.

4. **Categorical Funding**—Special funds have been made available to school districts on the basis of special needs of children over and above the foundation school program. These funds are aimed at providing assistance in the education of children with special needs and characteristics that require special programs at additional costs. Examples of categorical funds include special education for handicapped children, bilingual education for limited-English-proficient children, and compensatory education for the disadvantaged. Such funds are usually not adequate to meet the need. Research indicates that the Texas level of funding is far below the minimum costs required for such programs. If

these programs are to be fully implemented, it is necessary that their funding be increased significantly.

Bilingual advocacy groups are recommending that the amount of funding be increased by $150 to $200 per pupil eligible for bilingual education programs.

Recent research findings reveal that minority students continue to lag behind in academic performance and that a significant percentage are failing to demonstrate mastery in basic skills. If the need to upgrade existing efforts is to be met, funding for compensatory education programs would have to be increased to $100 per pupil.

In addition, recommendations have been made for a new category of funding, known as impact funds, for school districts on the basis of the number of undocumented alien children enrolled as a result of the recent Supreme Court decision. Impacted school districts are requesting $400 per pupil.

5. **Available School Fund Redistribution**—Income derived from the permanent school fund is placed in a separate fund called the available school fund and distributed on a per capita (unequalized) basis to all school districts in Texas. This means that the wealthiest school districts in the state receive the same amount per pupil as the poorest school districts in the state. Very high-tax-wealth school districts that receive little or no state aid for the foundation school program receive their share of the available school fund. Although the distribution of income from the permanent school fund is constitutionally mandated and cannot be changed by legislation, a portion of the available school fund comes from taxes on tobacco, motor vehicle sales, and liquor and beer, which *is* legislated and *can* be distributed on an equalized basis through new legislation. Advocates of school finance reform are calling for the elimination of tax income from the available school fund and the distribution of this income in support of equalization programs.

   In general, school finance reform advocates are recommending steps to guarantee that quality educational programs be made available to all children on the basis of the wealth of the state as a whole rather than on the peculiar economic characteristics of the school district in which a specific child resides.

BILINGUAL EDUCATION

In 1981, during the 67th session of the Texas legislature, a bill was enacted that sets standards for bilingual education in the state of Texas. This bill, S.B. 477, outlines minimal services to be provided and procedures to be followed in the identification, assignment, and instruction of children of limited-English proficiency.

These requirements closely parallel orders of the federal court in *U.S. v. Texas* and recommendations by the State Task Force on Bilingual Education.

Although there are some problems and weaknesses in the existing law, there is no widespread movement for making changes in the law at this time. It is believed that S.B. 477 is sufficient for the present because many of its provisions are just being implemented at this time. Meeting the letter of this legislation may take several more years, at which time necessary legislative revisions can be made.

On the other hand, there is a definite resolve that the 68th Legislature not regress by eliminating any of the provisions of S.B. 477. This bill is the bottom line of what is acceptable to Mexican-Americans in the form of a state program in bilingual education although, as stated previously, there is a need for increasing the level of funding in order to carry out the provisions of the 1981 legislation.

COMPETENCY TESTING

In 1979, the Texas Legislature enacted a bill for the establishment of a competency testing program for children in grades three, five, and nine. This program, called the Texas Assessment of Basic Skills (TABS), is designed to provide general and comprehensive information on student mastery of basic skills in the respective grades. The Texas Education Agency suggests that these tests are quite invalid for determining grade placement and graduation because their primary purposes are the assessment of instructional curriculum and practice, and the diagnosis of pupil and program needs.

Since the TABS program was introduced in the legislature, there has been a movement for using the test as a requirement for promotion and graduation. In fact, some school districts have initiated such requirements in the past few years. Not only is the practice educationally unsound, but it is also probably illegal. Court suits in various other states have held that a standardized test may not be used for promotion or graduation unless every aspect of the test has been taught in the school curriculum. Because this has not happened in Texas, and the state education agency admits that promotion and graduation are not the purpose of the test, the use of the test for that purpose is probably illegal. The use of TABS scores for promotion and graduation is also undesirable in that mastering the content of the test can easily become the major preoccupation of the school. This is undesirable because there are many types of learning, including all the higher forms, that are *not* measured by the TABS test.

HIGHER EDUCATION

The dominant issue in higher education during the 68th session of the Texas Legislature has been the dispersal of the Permanent University Fund (PUF). Originally this fund was set up for the University of Texas and it has grown into an almost inconceivably large amount. Proceeds from this fund were used exclusively for the University of Texas. Later, Texas A&M was added as a recipient of PUF funding.

Reaction to the current system can be divided into three camps. The first camp is a group that maintains that the University of Texas and Texas A&M are designated as universities of the "first class" and must compete with other first-class universities worldwide. In order to do so, they require the proceeds of the PUF for facilities, equipment, research, special programs, and the recruitment of world-recognized expert faculty. The dispersal of these funds to all universities in the state would assure that not one of them would be distinguished as a first-class university. Because students enroll from throughout the state, all parts of the state benefit from preserving this selectivity in the use of PUF funds. Needs of other universities should be met by special appropriations for those universities.

The second camp maintains that the PUF belongs to the entire state of Texas and that proceeds from this fund should be distributed to all 106 public institutions of higher education in the state. They maintain that although the needs of other universities should be met by special appropriations, they never *have* been met. All other universities compete with the needs of highways, teacher salaries, social programs, etc. This group believes that it is unfair for such huge sums of money to be readily available to two institutions while other institutions are hard pressed to make ends meet.

A third camp makes a compromise. Although they agree with the need for a first-class university system, they also feel that its distribution to two institutions is too limited. Their recommendation is that the permanent school fund proceeds be distributed to all institutions in the University of Texas system and in the Texas A&M system and that legislated funds be provided for all other institutions.

Events in Austin during the last few weeks indicate that the third camp will prevail and that participation in the distribution of the PUF funds will be extended to the two systems, with some $75 million in funding for all other institutions.

CONCLUSION

Although previous legislative sessions have given lip-service to the various issues outlined, adequate levels of funding or the introduction and passage of innovative, progressive approaches have been lacking. Faced with a growing proportion of minority students in the schools and growing community dissatisfaction with the inequitable status quo, the 68th legislature will need to deal with these issues. The subjects have been outlined for the legislative class of 1983; their report cards will be issued at the close of this session. Should the report cards indicate bad grades, there is no question but that advocates of reform will resort to the courts in an effort to obtain relief.

CHILDREN AT RISK

1985

PREFACE

This article was jointly written by José A. Cárdenas and Joan McCarty First of the Boston-based National Coalition of Advocates for Students. It was published in the September, 1985 issue of *Educational Leadership,* the journal of the Association for Supervision and Curriculum Development.

The doors to public schools are more open than they were twenty years ago to low-income persons, blacks, Hispanics, and the learning-disabled. The bad news is that there is a lack of commitment to making those students successful once they are in school. These are the findings of an independent Board of Inquiry[1] commissioned by the National Coalition of Advocates for Students (NCAS) to investigate the status of children of greatest need in public schools. NCAS is a network of child advocacy organizations that address public school issues at the federal, state, and local levels. These groups share a commitment to public education, maximum student access to appropriate educational experiences, and state and local advocacy as a constructive approach to school improvement.

As part of its year-long study, the Board held fifteen days of public hearings in ten cities[2] during late 1983 and throughout 1984. At these hearings, students, dropouts, parents, educators, and other citizens shared their experiences with, and worries about, public schools in their communities. Using information gathered from these hearings and a review of recent research, the Board prepared a report, *Barriers to Excellence: Our Children at Risk.*[3] Here we summarize the Board's findings and present some of their recommendations for change.

RACIAL DISCRIMINATION

In 1985, more than thirty years after the *Brown* decision, 63 percent of America's school children still attend predominantly minority schools. The study found that, compared with white students:

- Black students are three times more likely to be suspended from high school, often for trivial reasons.
- Black students are three times more likely to be placed in classes for the mildly mentally handicapped.

- Black students drop out of school at a rate more than twice that of white students.

CLASS DISCRIMINATION

The income level of a child's family is still the major determinant of the quality and quantity of the education a child receives. The average child from a bottom-quarter-income family receives four fewer years of education than a child from a top-quarter-income family.

Much of the testimony at the public hearings concerned the various forms that class discrimination takes in schools. For example:

- Many districts allocate fewer resources to schools in poor neighborhoods than to schools that serve primarily middle- and upper-income-level students.
- Only half of the almost ten million children eligible to receive Chapter I services actually receive those services.
- Teachers often alter expectations on the basis of students' social class.

CULTURAL DISCRIMINATION

Only half of the 2.7 million students with limited-English proficiency receive the special help they need. That figure falls to 10 percent for Hispanic students. Only 3 percent of teachers are adequately prepared to instruct limited-English-proficient students, although 25 percent of all teachers have such children in their classrooms. Special language-responsive programs are made available to only a small segment of the non-English-proficient population, and existing programs suffer from untrained teachers, inadequate instructional materials, invalid testing, and a lack of administrative support.

SEX DISCRIMINATION

Female students experience lowered expectations in public schools and by high school often function well behind male students in reading, science, social studies, and mathematics. Vocational education programs are often segregated by sex, with females clustered in programs that prepare them for the lowest paying jobs.

Pregnant and parenting teens are the young women most discriminated against in schools. Of the over one million teens who become pregnant each year, 10,000 are under age fifteen. A disproportionate number of these young women are minority students. Teens who are parents are much more likely to drop out of school than are teens who are not, and young, single mothers face almost certain poverty.[4]

SPECIAL EDUCATION

Handicapped students, their parents, and concerned educators described both problems of limited access to special services and problems related to children being inappropriately labeled as handicapped.

When PL 94-142 was passed, Congress assigned high priorities to identifying and serving out-of-school handicapped children and to meeting the needs of the severely handicapped. The Board of Inquiry concluded that schools appear to have met these objectives fairly well with regard to elementary-age children. However, large numbers of three- to five-year-olds, secondary students, eighteen- to twenty-two-year-olds, and emotionally disturbed children of all ages remain underserved, as well as children of migrant families, military dependents, adjudicated and incarcerated youth, and foster children.

On the other side of the coin, many children who are not handicapped end up in the special education system. Sometimes a lack of adequate regular education options designed to meet the needs of children with diverse learning styles results in this misplacement. Biased assessment and evaluation tools may support discriminatory referrals. Poorly defined criteria for entrance into categorical special programs, inferior curricula, and failure to establish exit criteria that clarify what the child must accomplish to qualify for return to the regular classroom also contribute to inappropriate placements.

The children most likely to be mis-classified are minority youngsters who perform adequately in a variety of family and community roles but experience difficulty in school. They are often assigned to special education, having experienced academic failure in the regular classroom, a failure that is routinely ascribed to the child rather than to the classroom setting or the school environment.

The processes by which school districts are usually reimbursed under PL 94-142 require them to declare students handicapped and then determine their needs for special services. Thus, the service delivery system that attaches labels to children in order to ensure that money is spent on students of greatest need also acts as an incentive to school districts to place more children in special classes, often inappropriately.

With its emphasis on higher standards, the current education reform movement may increase the risk of many low-achieving minority and disadvantaged students' being inappropriately labeled as handicapped. Unless higher academic standards in public classrooms are accompanied by additional resources directed toward strengthening mainstream programs, an increasing number of children may be placed in double jeopardy by being assigned handicapped status in addition to their minority status.

MISUSES OF TESTING

Over-reliance on standardized achievement tests as a basis for making educational decisions may have far-reaching effects on students. In districts where testing is in widespread use, the Board urged that the relationship of testing practices to three major, related concerns be carefully examined: (1) the availability of additional resources to assist children who are labeled "failures" as the result of their poor performance on tests; (2) the effects of testing on *what* is being taught and *how* it is being taught; and (3) the effect of tests on school exclusion rates.

The Board of Inquiry found particularly troublesome policies that require school districts to label children as handicapped or academically deficient in order to receive funds needed to provide services to them. The Board considers funding mechanisms of this type to be a contributing factor in the disproportionate placement of minority students in classes for the educable mentally handicapped and the growing number of students being classified as learning disabled. Nationally, the learning disabilities category grew by 125 percent between 1976 and 1982.

Finally, there is a great need for school districts and state departments of education to collect data concerning the effects that intensive testing programs and other school reform strategies have on exclusion rates. Reform legislation does not have monitoring provisions in some states, while other states require the collection of extensive data, but do not require that they be collected by race, sex, or ethnicity.

That school exclusionary practices have always had a disproportionate effect on minority children has been well documented by the Office of Civil Rights' elementary and secondary school surveys carried out during the last decade. Failure at the school, school district, and state level to document that reality is certain to diminish the likelihood of remedy. Because the roots of the problem of disproportionate impact of school suspensions on minority students rest in the ways that teachers make referrals, collection of referral data is an important part of any local self-monitoring effort. Finally, the absence of a uniform system for collecting dropout data is a widely acknowledged problem.

Despite the fact that there is no reliable body of evidence indicating that grade retention is more beneficial than grade promotion for students with serious academic or adjustment difficulties, retention at grade level is a widely employed remedial strategy. Even before the beginning of the national movement to raise academic standards, more than an estimated one million students each year were being retained at grade level.[5]

SCHOOL FINANCE

The quality of education a child receives is profoundly affected by the accident of whether the child lives in a high-tax-wealth or low-tax-wealth school district. Testimony documented vast differences in per-pupil expenditures among states, among school districts inside states, and among school buildings inside school districts. Despite efforts in many states to equalize education expenditures, property taxes are still the primary source of funding for public education. This results in special problems for property-poor districts. Since Robin Hood approaches to equalization are doomed to failure, the most practical solution requires the allocation of massive amounts of state money to districts at lower tax wealth levels. Achieving a satisfactory remedy for the lack of adequate financing for public education is made extraordinarily difficult by the fact that while 90 percent of the nation's children attend public schools, only 27 percent of American adults have children in public schools.

SUMMARY OF RECOMMENDATIONS

Barriers to Excellence: Our Children at Risk identifies 104 strategies for achieving public schools that are both excellent and fair. The following recommendations, excerpted from the report, note appropriate changes in policy and practice that are needed if academic excellence is to be defined in a way that embraces equity issues.

We call for continued, rather than diminished, federal, state, and local attention to the rights of the disadvantaged and those discriminated against because of race, language, sex, or handicapped condition.

We seek:

- To minimize discrimination in the schools by restoring and expanding support for programs serving economically disadvantaged students, recognizing that it is false economy to cut programs which work for poor children.

- To reaffirm commitments to non-discrimination by race by vigorously pursuing efforts to eliminate racially identifiable educational programs and altering school practices that result in minority children dropping out, becoming "push outs," or staying in the educational system but failing to learn.

- To minimize discrimination against students from linguistic minorities by recognizing the importance of bilingual education as a technique that supports their academic development and by moving towards an acceptance of bilingualism as a means of enriching our society.

- To renew commitment to the ideals embodied in Title IX (Education Amendments of 1972) sex discrimination legislation, thereby assuring that female students will have an opportunity to develop their talents and skills fully.

- To promote changes in special education that will improve services for children with moderate and severe handicaps while developing more regular education options for children with milder learning difficulties, so that they can attend school without being labeled handicapped.

We call for greater willingness on the part of those in positions of responsibility to adjust schools to the diverse needs of all students who attend them.

We seek:

- To end tracking and rigid ability grouping, recognizing that such practices work against the best interests of both the most vulnerable and the most able students in the schools.

- To eliminate the use of inappropriate testing practices as a basis for making educational decisions that have far-reaching effects upon the futures of young people.

- To broaden curriculum and teaching practices so that they better meet the needs of diverse student populations, based on the proposition that individual children have differing needs and abilities.

- To move vocational education programs away from the current narrow focus upon job skills and toward the broader goal of preparing young people for a changing world of work.

We call for more democratic governance of schools, which assures parents a significant role in making decisions about the education of their children and teaches children principles of democratic participation and the exercise of constitutional rights.

We seek:

- To reinstate federal mandates for parent involvement in local programs.

- To remove barriers to parental involvement and create opportunities for parents to participate in decisions about school staffing, education programming, school discipline, and resource allocation.

- To assure students of their due process rights in such matters as school suspension and expulsion.

We call for the establishment of comprehensive early childhood education, daycare programs, and in-school support services for children and youth as a means of preventing school failure.

We seek:

- To recognize the usefulness and cost effectiveness of high-quality early childhood education and child care programs as a means of preventing school failure.
- To respond to the needs of an increasing number of young people whose chances of remaining in school would be increased if they had help with serious personal and social problems.

We call for the enactment of more equitable and adequate systems for financing schools, so that the quality of education available does not depend on where a child lives.

We seek:

- To increase tax equity through state systems of raising revenues that are not dependent on regressive taxes and that insulate property poor districts against excessive local taxes.
- To eliminate inequality in educational access, resulting from disparities in funding for schools.
- To raise funding levels for programs serving children at risk, so that every eligible child is assured of adequate services.

We call for more systematic attention to the problems of jobs for youth and dropouts by federal, state, and local education authorities.

We seek:

- To ensure that a comprehensive school-to-work transition program is available for all youth.
- To strengthen counseling services for noncollege-bound youth and develop job-placement services in high schools.
- To encourage broadly based community councils charged with responsibility for examining what could be done locally to revitalize the local economy and create jobs for youth.

Neither the Board of Inquiry nor the advocacy community is naive enough to assume that the changes urged in *Barriers to Excellence* can be accomplished quickly or easily. In all likelihood their achievement may require collaborative energies of more than one generation of educators and concerned citizens. Why is it important for that effort to begin now? Paul Ylvisaker, former dean of the Harvard Graduate School of Education and co-chair of the National Commission on Secondary Schooling for Hispanics, has answered that question simply: "Because we are confronted with a generation of children too precious to waste."

NOTES

1. The Board of Inquiry was co-chaired by Harold Howe, a former U.S. Commissioner of Education, who is now senior lecturer at the Harvard Graduate School of Education, and Marian Wright Edelman, President, The Children's Defense Fund.

2. The ten cities were Boston, Louisville, Chicago, Lansing, New York, Atlanta, Columbus, Cleveland, Seattle, and San Antonio.

3. Unless otherwise noted, documentation for facts and opinions expressed in this article is contained in *Barriers to Excellence: Our Children at Risk.* Copies are available for $5.50 each (prepaid) from: NCAS, 76 Summer St., Suite 350, Boston, MA 02110.

4. The Children's Defense Fund, T*eenage Pregnancy: Some Facts* (Washington, D.C., 1985)

5. Gregg C. Jackson, "The Research Evidence on the Effects of Grade Retention." *Review of Educational Research 45,* 4 (Fall, 1975): 613-635.

VSP: KEY TO MINORITY EDUCATION

1987

PREFACE

On March 19, 1987, I was one of two persons recognized by the League of United Latin American Citizens (LULAC) for our contributions to American education. The text of my acceptance speech was subsequently published in the June, 1987 issue of the IDRA *Newsletter*.

The basic thrust of my speech was the observation that there are enormous differences between successful school programs for atypical students and the dismal failure of these same students in traditional school settings. As a member of, or consultant to, various entities studying these differences, I had ample opportunity to look at many successful school programs throughout the country. I was impressed by the extensive success of some of these innovative programs, and noted the conclusion of Ray Marshalls', former Secretary of Labor in the Carter administration, that the study he co-directed had observed many successful programs, but had not found a single successful educational system in the entire country (*Quality Education for Minorities Project*, 1990).

Up until that time, and even today, it has been noted that students who have been deemed uneducable have enjoyed extensive, and in many cases exemplary success, when participating in some special programs. However, little has been done with this information, other than to conclude that under certain circumstances, students who do not perform well in school can perform in a satisfactory and even exceptional manner. The implication of this conclusion is that there is no inherent impediment to learning in the student. Rather, the impediment arises in relationship to the educational institution.

The various studies consistently stopped short of analyzing the differences between the special programs in which the students excelled and the regular school programs in which the students failed. Looking for these differences, I came to the conclusion that there were always three characteristics of successful programs that were conspicuously absent in the regular school program. These were:

1. In the successful school programs, students were invariably highly valued, and this value was communicated back to the student. Such consistent valuing was *not* found in regular school programs.

2. In the successful programs, students were provided support services not commonly found in regular and traditional schools.

3. In all of the successful programs there were unique interactions among parents, the school, and the community—types of interactions rarely found in the unsuccessful schools.

On the basis of these highly successful school programs for minority, disadvantaged, limited-English-proficient, and other atypical students, I concluded that the key to the education of minorities, and other groups deemed difficult to teach by the school, was "VSP": "V" for valuing, "S" for support services and "P" for unique parent relationships with the school and community.

I regret that administrative matters, litigation, legislation, and other activities precluded my giving more attention to the concept of VSP. Since my retirement as executive director of IDRA, I have given a lot of attention to this topic. So much so, that I feel that the basic concept of valuing and the two additional characteristics of successful programs form the basis for the development of a new educational paradigm for American education, a new paradigm that eliminates past assumptions of minority education and replaces them with new assumptions in keeping with the new paradigm.

The more I look into this, the more convinced I become that there will not be any successful breakthroughs in minority education in the United States until such a new paradigm is developed. The old paradigm is rooted in the assumption that extensive education is a luxury, and that there is a limit on what society perceives as feasible to invest in education. The large portion of the citizenry that found employment in an agricultural and manufacturing economy did not require an extensive education.

The perception of education as the domain of the cultural elite was compatible with dropout rates of 80, 90 and even 100 percent for children outside of the cultural mainstream. With the change of the economic base to information and services, and with the advent of a highly technological society, the country can no longer tolerate a 25 percent dropout rate. Not only must our youth stay in school, but their performance while in school must also strive to meet world competitive standards.

The new educational paradigm must be based on the basic tenet that all children are valuable. It must provide support services never before considered necessary or desirable by the school, and it must incorporate new partnerships among family, school, and community. It eliminates the perception of culturally different children as being culturally and linguistically disadvantaged. It moves away from student and family deficit models and into the basic assumption that all children can learn if the instructional approach is appropriate.

The new paradigm will provide new directions in the training of professional staff, the rationale for innovation, and the framework for the development of new educational programs designed to meet the challenges of the twenty-first century. This paradigm will also contain the basis and sensitivity for the appraisal of the school on its efficiency in educating all children, rather than rationalizing its failure by blaming the victims for the failure of the school.

The development of such a paradigm is a formidable challenge. At most, one can only hope that a framework can be developed in the foreseeable future, and the eventual development will take place over a number of years. But the difficulty of the task should not preclude its undertaking. I am thoroughly convinced that the United States will not see any major breakthroughs in the education of its minority populations in the absence of a new paradigm rooted in the intrinsic value of all children.

It is a moving occasion to be selected for this recognition and honor this evening. I am particularly honored because of the high regard in which I hold the League of United Latin American citizens. It is with LULAC that I had the privilege to plead for the cause of bilingual education in *U.S. v. Texas;* it was with LULAC that I worked with in the case of undocumented alien children (*Doe v. Plylar*), and it was LULAC that provided the necessary backing for many of our efforts for school finance reform in Texas and in other states (*United States v. Texas*, 1971; *Doe v. Plylar*, 1978).

LULAC has always been supportive of IDRA's work in the improvement of educational opportunities for children. I look forward to a long and mutually profitable relationship in activities that continue our work—activities designed to capitalize on the American tradition of upward mobility and the achievement of personal, economic, political, and social success through education.

Just a few months ago, I had the privilege of meeting with the Texas Executive Committee of LULAC in order to provide a personal briefing on our most recent accomplishment—the most extensive and intensive study of school dropouts ever conducted in the state of Texas. The sense of regret I felt then, I feel now, as I communicate to you the deplorable findings of our study.

The dropout rate for the state of Texas was 33 percent, i.e., one out of every three students drops out of school before the completion of the twelfth grade.

This 33 percent figure is an aggregate figure and does not describe sufficiently the inadequacies of education for certain populations. A conservative estimate of the dropout rate for white Anglo students in Texas is 27 percent. Although this figure may be bad enough, the comparable conservative estimated dropout rate for Blacks was 34 percent, and for Hispanics, 45 percent.

Another depressing statistic from our study shows that 30 percent of all students who drop out of school, do so before the ninth grade. For Hispanics, 50 percent of all students who drop out of school, drop out before the ninth grade.

This information leads us to conclude that not only do Hispanics dropout of school in greater numbers, but they also drop out of school at an earlier level and at an earlier age.

This finding of unusually high dropout rates for Hispanics in Texas is not incompatible with dropout information from other states. In New York, the dropout rate for Hispanics was 62 percent as compared to 20 percent for white Anglos.

A study by the Illinois Board of Education put that state's dropout rates at 47 percent for Hispanics and 17 percent for whites.

Hispanic dropout rates in California, 43 percent; Arizona, 35 percent; Colorado, 33 percent; New Jersey, 34 percent,—are all indicative of a massive failure of the schools in responding to the educational needs of Hispanic populations.

The political leadership of our country has stated that dropout rates for Hispanics have increased to about 50 percent throughout the country. I share this concern, although I will be quick to point out that the Hispanic dropout rate has not increased to 50 percent; it has decreased to 50 percent. It is not unreasonable to estimate that the dropout rate for Hispanics in the 1940s, forty years ago, was 80 percent, although accurate data are not available, primarily because nobody really cared.

These indicators of the Hispanic's poor performance in school have led to a renewed interest in the educational performance of Hispanics, with a new cycle of research studies, program development, and pilot test programs throughout the country. Those of us who have been around the educational scene for a number of years are all too familiar with past national awakenings to the educational problems of Hispanics, the national targeting of this group for special study, the development of innovative approaches, and the implementation of new programs all aimed at the improvement of educational opportunities for this segment of the population.

Although the horrible statistics, the innovative approaches, and the new programs are reminiscent of past efforts, the rationale and the roles have changed. Whereas the targeting of Hispanics in the 1960s was related to the civil rights movement of that era, and the targeting of Hispanics in the 1970s was related to the educational equity movement of that era, the targeting of Hispanics in the latter part of the 1980s has changed from a judicial and a political response to an economic response.

The new actor in this traditional play is the private sector—private business and industry concerned with the changing bases for the economy and the impact of educational failure on this private sector. The change in our country from a manufacturing economy to a service and technological economy has created three basic changes that impact on minority education.

1. Business and industry can no longer absorb even a portion of the growing pool of unschooled, untrained, cheap, unskilled labor that formed the backbone of the American labor force in the past.

2. The failure of the schools to educate a large segment of the population has created a financial liability in terms of lost wages, lost taxes, incarceration, rehabilitation, welfare, and delinquency, which will cost many times more than the cost of education. The popular saying, "You pay me now, or you pay me later," is not lost on the private sector. After all, it coined the phrase.

3. The private sector is already experiencing problems in acquiring the skilled labor necessary for the competitiveness, and even the survival, of technology-oriented business and industry. It is anticipated that this shortage of skilled labor will become much more extensive and critical in the years ahead.

Thus we educators find a new ally in the coalition seeking improved educational opportunities for minorities, the disadvantaged and the limited-English-proficient. We welcome this new ally, the private sector, into this coalition, especially since our old ally, the federal government, has very much abandoned us on civil rights as well as equity issues.

Given that the education of Hispanics in this country is characterized by massive numbers of dropouts and underachievement, the most pressing question then is, "What can we do about it?"

There are some who feel no need to do anything about it. The following quotation is from an editorial that appeared in the *Suburban Notebook*, a suburban newspaper in Austin, Texas, immediately following the release of our dropout study:

> Keeping bodies in school is futile and can be damaging to other students. Dropouts often have deep personal problems which they impose on everyone

> around them. . . . According to one recent study, Hispanic students, for instance, are handicapped by church, family, and ethnic peer relationships. Is the [Austin] school district prepared to undertake a massive Americanization of the general attitudes and lifestyles of local Hispanics?. . . .Given the school district's current budget crisis, maybe it would be better to restrict our spending to students who *want* to stay in school.

Thank God that at least the private sector is aware of the social, political, and economic consequences of lack of schooling and is willing to address the problem. But again I ask, "How do we address the problem?"

The answer lies in extensive changes in the school. Extensive changes are needed in the materials and methodologies used in the instruction of Hispanics and other minorities in the schools of this country; changes in the attitudes and relationships between Hispanic students and members of the dominant ethnic group, beginning with the realization and acceptance of the most basic of premises, namely that Hispanics can, want to, and will learn if the school is only willing to accommodate them.

For instance, it is a well-known fact that Hispanics are notoriously poor readers in American schools. Hispanics as a group do poorly in the development and acquisition of reading skills in school, as evidenced by any measure of reading ability in any state in the union. Hispanics as a group have trouble learning to read in Texas. Hispanics have trouble learning to read in California, in New York, in Arizona, in New Mexico, etc. It is axiomatic in American education that Hispanics are poor readers.

Yet Hispanics learn to read with no difficulty in Mexico. Hispanics have no trouble learning to read in Spain. Hispanics easily learn to read in Cuba, in Venezuela, in Argentina and in every other Latin American county. In fact, I am of the opinion that children who go to school in Hispanic countries are better readers than English-speaking children in the United States.

The reality is that only in the United States, of all the countries of the world, only in the United States, does the speaking of Spanish become an impediment to learning to read. Obviously, the problem is not a deficit in the Hispanic population, but a deficit in the American schools.

During the past few years I have had an opportunity to study and visit a large and growing number of programs where an unusual and extensive success has been experienced in the education of Hispanics and other minority populations.

As part of a study conducted by our staff, we looked at successful programs in San Antonio. As part of the *Texas Dropout Study,*we looked at successful programs in all of Texas. As part of the Ford foundation's Dropout Collaboratives, we looked at successful programs in the education of Hispanics and other minorities throughout the country. I have even visited dropout recovery programs such as the Job Corp program in San Marcos and I have made several visits to LULAC's SER model Jobstart Program in Corpus Christi.

Having analyzed the characteristics of successful programs, we were able to identify a common denominator in these programs. This common denominator can become the key to turning around the education of Hispanics and other minorities in this country.

The key to the successful education of atypical populations in American schools is—V S P.

V is for valuing. In all successful programs for the education of at-risk school populations, there is a valuing of the students in ways in which they are not valued in regular and traditional school programs.

In successful school programs, just as in LULAC National Education Service Centers, the student is valued, his language is valued, his heritage is valued, his family is valued, and, most important, the student is valued as a person.

In contrast to successful programs, traditional school programs provide rejection rather than valuing. The Hispanic students speak the wrong language, they belong to the wrong culture. As indicated in the Austin newspaper article I just quoted, it is necessary to Americanize the Hispanic before it is possible to educate him.

S is for support. In all successful programs for the eduction of at-risk youth, there are support mechanisms much more extensive than those that are commonly found in regular and traditional school situations.

These support mechanisms assist the student in coping with problems that would otherwise interfere with schooling. Support mechanisms may be in the form of a program such as bilingual education, which allows the student to continue intellectual development and learning in his native language as he develops proficiency in English as a second language. Or support mechanisms may be in the form of counselling services to overcome personal and social problems, or even in the form of a stipend, a scholarship, or flexible scheduling, which allow the student to cope with financial problems. Regardless of the form of the support mechanisms, they provide assistance not commonly available to at-risk students.

P is for parents. In all successful programs for the education of at-risk youth, parents are involved in meaningful relationships with the school, in types of relationships not commonly found in regular and traditional school situations.

It is ironic that the Austin newspaper editorial reports a study that shows that Hispanic family relationships handicap performance in school.

Of all the characteristics anthropologists and sociologists attribute to Hispanics, in my opinion the most valuable one is the strong family relationships so characteristic in Hispanic families.

All social scientists are in agreement. Sociologists, psychologists, educators, and anthropologists are in agreement, that most of the social problems in this country can be attributed to the dissolution, the breakup, of the family as a social unit. Now, having discovered an ethnic group with a strong family structure, society is determined to destroy it as a prerequisite to Americanization, which has become a prerequisite to schooling.

The school can, and should capitalize on this strong family structure for enhancing the education of Hispanics (Robledo Montecel, 1993).

The key to the successful education of Hispanics and other minorities, the key to the education of disadvantaged children, the key to the education of limited-English-proficient children, is the application of a liberal dose of VSP, valuing of the individual, support mechanisms, and meaningful parental involvement in all aspects of the school program.

It really does not make sense to place a student in a LULAC NESC program or some school remedial program that provides extensive valuing, support, and parental relationships because neither the valuing, nor the support mechanisms, nor the parental relationships were present in the regular program.

It does not make sense to spend 300 to 1,000 dollars per student per year in a supplemental program that provides valuing, support, and parental relationships because the $3,500 spent in the regular program did not provide these characteristics.

A massive effort to restructure the school program by extensive staff training and retraining, revamping of instructional materials, and the use of innovative teaching methodologies would eliminate the majority of the educational problems currently associated with Hispanic and minority education.

I trust that in the near future we will see a drastic change in the education of Hispanics in this country. With the formation of new collaboratives, collaboratives among educators, the private sector and parents, we can reduce the horrendous dropout rates among Hispanics, and we can improve on the low levels of school achievement so characteristic of Hispanics.

I trust that LULAC, and very specifically, the LULAC National Education Service Centers, will continue in your leadership role and serve once again as the catalyst for the improvement of educational opportunities for all of the children of this great country.

I trust that you will take it upon yourselves to see to it that federal, state, and local efforts to improve educational opportunities for our ethic group will include the provision of valuing Hispanic children in all relationships with the school, the provision of necessary support mechanisms, and the involvement of parents in meaningful relationships with the schools.

I thank you again for this recognition and honor that you have bestowed on me tonight. I thank you not only on my behalf and on behalf of my family, but I thank you on behalf of the IDRA staff and the national network of educators and organizations that share our commitment to educational excellence for all children.

STATE EDUCATIONAL LEADERSHIP AND *REYNA v. KIRBY*

1987

PREFACE

In my twenty years with IDRA as an advocate for minority children, there was no incident as distasteful as the court case *Reyna v. Kirby* (*Reyna, et al. v. Kirby, et al.*, 1989). I was involved with the court case when the attorney for the plaintiff—indigent children—requested IDRA assistance in the formulation and negotiation of a consent degree for the settlement of the court case.

It is unbelievable that the need for litigation ever arose. The thought of school children being denied access to books during school hours and forfeiting reading instruction as well as most participation in other school subjects because of their inability to pay for lost books had never entered my mind, even as superintendent of the poorest school district in the state.

At the time of my involvement in the case as a consultant to the plaintiff attorney, progress had been made in settling the court case by agreement to an alternative form of punishment for the children unable to pay for lost books caused by family poverty. I communicated my reservations about the proposed settlement in a memorandum to the attorney on September 10, 1987. In that memorandum I wrote:

> I have severe reservations about the use of discretion in the application of disciplinary action by school personnel. . . . The past insistence on payment in spite of known indigence situations and the severity of past practice to deny [the students] the use of textbooks for extended periods of time and its long range detrimental effects on subsequent learning fails to justify the action as an intent to teach responsibility.
>
> It is probable that the past insistence on payment is a form of non-proportional and unwarranted disciplinary action against the student and his family as a form of penalty for being indigent, for being different, for being an economic or social liability. Removing the payment recourse from the school district may well result in some other form of non-proportional and unwarranted disciplinary action.
>
> *Inappropriate disciplinary action may have more severe and longer lasting psychological implications on the student, than the financial effects of textbook payment.*

Fortunately for all concerned, legislation promoted by Representative Ciro Rodriguez, a former IDRA staff member, made the court case moot.

This article has never been published before. It was a part of a long article entitled "State Educational Leadership in Texas," an article dealing with twenty years of frustration in dealing with a state education agency that opposed all innovation for the improvement of educational opportunities for minorities. Just before publication, the Commissioner of Education resigned and a new commissioner was selected to head the Texas Education Agency. I felt that the timing of the publication would be interpreted as a criticism of staff still with the agency or a belated attack on an official no longer in place, so publication was suspended until a more appropriate time. As is often the case, a more appropriate time never materialized and the remainder of the article remains unpublished.

No analysis of the quality of educational leadership in the State of Texas would be complete without a brief review of the federal court case, *Reyna v. Kirby*.

A long-standing Texas law provides for holding children and their families responsible for state textbooks issued to them and entrusted to their care. Children who lose their books are expected to pay for them before additional books may be issued. It is heartening that school districts take state laws seriously, but occasionally the literal interpretation of the law can create educational problems. In some school districts, the loss of state textbooks resulted in students having no further access to textbooks if the family was unable to pay for the lost books. As testified to in court, children who lost textbooks (some children claimed that the books were taken from their lockers or stolen) spent the entire school year in reading classes with nothing to read, and in arithmetic classes without problems to solve, even when the school was aware that the children were indigent children, participating in the National School Lunch Program, and in both federal and state compensatory education programs for the economically disadvantaged. Over 500 children without access to books in school were identified by plaintiff attorneys.

All attempts to solve the problem of educating children without the financial resources to pay for lost books failed, leading to the case's being filed in federal court. The quality of educational leadership at the Texas Education Agency becomes relevant when the court, reluctant to intervene in a state matter, requested direction from the Texas Education Agency on ways the dilemma could be resolved without the extreme measures of declaring the Texas textbook law invalid or precluding children from poor homes learning to read.

The state education agency responded to the court with a reiteration of the laws of the State of Texas, its support for the district involved, a request that the case be dismissed, and the unbelievable recommendation that the defendant children and their attorneys conduct car washes and bake sales to pay for the missing books.

Reyna v. Kirby became moot through the educational leadership of State Representative Ciro Rodriguez of San Antonio. When informed about the court case he simply submitted an amendment to the Texas textbook law based on what attorneys for the children were seeking:

> Under circumstances determined by the board of trustees, a school district may waive or reduce the payment requirement if the student is from a family of low income. The school district may provide for a method of payment other than lump-sum payment. The school district shall allow the student to use

textbooks at school during each school day" (Sec. 21.031 as amended by Acts 1989, 71st Leg., ch. 357).

Representative Rodriguez' proposed change in the textbook law was adopted with little deliberation and no opposition in the Texas Legislature.

A CULTURALLY DEMOCRATIC LEARNING ENVIRONMENT

1992

PREFACE

In 1992, I was requested by the San Antonio New Schools Foundation to contribute to a proposal to be submitted for the creation of a new pilot school in San Antonio, Texas. The new school was to be a "break the mold" type of school, with innovative features addressing the characteristics of a cross section of the school population in San Antonio (San Antonio New Schools Development Foundation, 1992).

The following article was incorporated into the San Antonio proposal. The basis for the multicultural design of the school is again the 1968 "Theory of Incompatibilities." It is yet another attempt on my part to provide a school environment that responds to the characteristics of atypical children. Unfortunately, the San Antonio proposal was not selected for funding, so the development and implementation of this application for the Theory of Incompatibilities was never realized.

The title of the article comes from a phrase used extensively in the 1960s and early 1970s. It denotes the need for eliminating the elitist characteristic of education by providing improved educational opportunity to all elements in the community.

The developmental matrix I developed for the proposal provided for adapting the ten elements of school activity to the five areas of incompatibilities, but specific examples were only partially addressed in the article. Examples of adapted school responses are provided for only a few of the cells in the matrix. I hope that sometime in the immediate future I will be able to devote the necessary time and effort to conceptualize all of the forms of adaptability found in the developmental matrix and provide specific and simple guidelines for creating a culturally democratic learning environment.

INTRODUCTION

The past performance of San Antonio's schools has not been very impressive. The 230,000 students enrolled in the public schools have performed poorly as a group in terms of commonly accepted indicators of school success. Data on performance on the Texas minimum competency test (TABS, TEAMS, TAAS) indicate that more than 30 percent of the students were unable to meet minimum basic-skill criteria at the various grade levels tested. The weighted mean score for the SAT taken by 40 percent of San Antonio seniors was 850 for the combined verbal and math portions of the test. Various studies of school dropouts using a variety of methodologies consistently show that about one-third of the school population drops out of school before completing the twelfth grade.

There is wide variance in the performance of the students within and among the fifteen school districts in the San Antonio metropolitan area. A considerable number of students perform very well in school, and some of the independent school systems perform much better than others.

The analysis of performance data indicates that in San Antonio, as elsewhere in the country, the performance of the school systems, as well as the performance of the students in all systems, correlates closely with the characteristics of the students. As in all large urban centers in America, aggregate student performance is strongly depressed by the poor performance of certain elements of the school population. Racial and ethnic minorities, the poor, limited-English-proficient immigrants, and migrants are types of school populations that have performed poorly in our schools and are commonly referred to as "at-risk" students, i.e., at risk of dropping out of school.

These characteristics of students play a dominant role in determining school performance. Minority status, socio-economic class, home language, origin, and length of residence completely overshadow mental capability, interest, attitudes, motivation and effort in the determination of school performance.

The poor performance of the aggregate school population in San Antonio reflects the high incidence of at-risk students. Minorities comprise 69 percent of the school population; an estimated 35 percent are limited-English-proficient, and 53 percent meet the poverty criteria of the National School Lunch Program. Although data are not readily available on immigrant and migrant populations, San Antonio is an entry port for immigrants, especially immigrants from Mexico and Central and South America, with limited proficiency in the English language being a common characteristic of both adults and children. A considerable number of families winter in San Antonio and leave the schools in the early spring time as they join the northward migration of migrant agricultural workers.

Although the performance of atypical children in America and in San Antonio schools is characteristically low, it is interesting to note that there is no pedagogical justification for this poor performance. The various social and natural sciences have been unable to identify any reason for a minority student to perform poorly in school because of an inherent physical or mental characteristic of the ethnic group. A similar lack of justification has been found for language characteristics, socio-economic class, or residential status. On the contrary, in controlled learning situations, members of all of the atypical population groups cited above have been able to perform scholastically comparable to white, Anglo, middle-class, geographically stable populations.

This successful school performance of atypical children has been documented in a number of recent studies of "innovative" and "model" school programs throughout the country. Further analysis of successful school programs for atypical students inevitably points out that the "unusual" success is related to the unique characteristics of the successful program. Three such unique characteristics consistently found in successful programs are: the valuing of participating students beyond the valuing provided in traditional and regular school programs; the provision of support services not commonly found in traditional and regular school programs; and unique relationships among the student's family, the school, and the larger community.

DESIGN RATIONALE

The basic characteristic of the Vanguard School for Science and Technology is the creation and implementation of a culturally democratic learning environment. This environment is one in which adaptive responses to the unique characteristics of the students will lead to the elimination of barriers to effective schooling, with the performance of each of the participants being dependent on the interest, motivation, effort, and capability of the individual students rather than on ethnicity, economic class, or residential characteristics.

The Vanguard School for Science and Technology will not be an elitist school comprising superior students "creamed" from different San Antonio school districts. The student enrollment will be reflective of the cultural and socio-economic diversity of the city, and will include all levels of school performance. The Vanguard School for Science and Technology will not be a magnet school with a curricular emphasis on math, science, and technology. The curriculum of the school will be reflective of the diverse curriculum of other schools in the city.

The uniqueness of Vanguard School for Science and Technology will be its recognition of, and response to, the characteristics of its students, creating a culturally democratic learning institution that will develop and keep alive in each student the option of selecting math, science, and technology as a preferred curriculum field. Future careers in math, science and technology will be a feasible alternative for each student, constrained only by self-determined interest and capability, rather than a realistic option for only a predetermined segment of the school population. Similar alternatives for other career choices will be kept open by the development of a sound and strong basic educational experience in all areas of the curriculum.

The key concept of the Vanguard School for Science and Technology is increasing the available pool of students from all segments of the population who can realistically select science and technology as an area of interest and a subsequent career choice.

The Vanguard School for Science and Technology will parallel America's ideal: a free democratic society in which freedom is exercised by freedom of choice, and freedom of choice is made a reality by the existence of feasible alternatives from which to choose.

DESIGN ELEMENTS

The creation of a Culturally Democratic Learning Environment will be based on the school's commitment to the identification, reduction and eventual elimination of the incompatibilities between the characteristics of the San Antonio school population and the characteristics of the proposed school.

For ease of identification, development, and response, the characteristics of the students will be grouped into six distinct areas:

1. Culture;
2. Language;
3. Socio-economics;
4. Mobility;
5. Societal perceptions: How the school perceives the student; and
6. Societal perceptions: How the student perceives him or herself.

In each of the six areas of student characteristics listed above, the proposed school will address the integration of the student characteristics with each of the following ten elements of school life:

1. The school's philosophy of education

   The development of a philosophy of education based on the premise that all students can learn; that current poor performance of students is predicated by inappropriate or inadequate instructional practice; the elimination of student, family, and community deficits as a common rationalization for poor school performance; and making the school accountable for student success.

2. Governance: the rules and regulation of the school

   The development of school policies, rules, and regulations that are equitable for all students, are cognizant of student diversity, and are conducive to successful school performance by students reflecting an extensive community diversity.

3. Scope and sequence of the instructional program

   The development of flexibility in the scope and sequence of the instructional program in order to accommodate students with varying characteristics. The presentation of learning experiences will be compatible with high student readiness for learning, rather than in keeping with an arbitrary, predetermined, chronological sequence.

4. The curriculum: educational methodologies and materials

   The development of an instruction program that is reflective of student characteristics. Instructional activities will be compatible with group and individual student characteristics.

5. The co-curriculum

   Educational experiences in the instructional program will be augmented by supplemental and reinforcing activities. Participation in these activities will reduce the social and academic isolation experienced by students at risk of dropping out of school and will respond to the inherent psychological need for belonging through involvement in socially acceptable group activities rather than seeking to satisfy this need through socially detrimental "gang" behavior.

6. Staffing

   The identification, recruitment, acquisition, and training of educational staff sensitive to the characteristics and needs of students, and capable of identifying, acquiring, modifying, adapting, and creating appropriate instructional activities.

7. Student personnel services

   The provision of the counseling and guidance necessary for the student to be able to cope with individual, family, school, and community problems. These will enhance the student's ability to perform successfully in school and assist the student in exercising new options for further schooling, training, and the selection of career options.

8. The non-instructional needs of students: support services

   Provide necessary assistance or make referrals to other community agencies that can provide the assistance for meeting the student's nutritional, health, social, emotional, and spiritual needs. Meeting these non-instructional needs is essential for the removal of non-school centered barriers to successful school performance.

9. Parent, family, and community involvement

   The mobilization of the family and community in support of the student's educational program. The creation and maintenance of a home environment conducive to learning, and the provision of extensive resources in support of the student and the school.

10. Evaluation

    The acquisition of timely and relevant information for decision-making.

THE DEVELOPMENTAL MATRIX

The intersection of the six areas of student characteristics with the ten elements of a school's life produces sixty cells in a developmental matrix that forms the unique focus of the school. School adaptations in all sixty cells will provide an ideal culturally democratic learning environment that will allow students with non-mainstream characteristics the opportunity for extensive educational success.

The following example is a simple illustration of the content of the school element "Philosophy of Education," with each of the six areas of student characteristics:

CULTURE:

- There is extensive cultural diversity among students attending San Antonio schools. It is not the role of the school to make value judgements about cultural groups, but rather to provide an understanding about culture that will allow students to make intelligent and mature cultural choices.
- There are no group differences in learning capabilities among the various cultural groups in San Antonio.
- It is the responsibility of the school to provide flexibility and to adapt to the characteristics of the various cultural groups.
- Cultural groups have distinct preferred learning styles. An instructional program that is democratic and allows all students the opportunity for successful learning should provide alternative methodologies compatible with different learning styles.

LANGUAGE:

- English being the common and dominant language of the United States, it is an imperative that all students attain complete mastery of the English language and the necessary language skills for its proper and effective use.
- Lack of fluency in the English language need not be an educational barrier. Students throughout the world with no proficiency in the English language have enjoyed successful schooling.
- Proficiency in languages other than English is a desirable educational objective, as evidenced by the emphasis and resources provided foreign language instruction in American schools.
- The use of one language does not preclude the acquisition of a second language. On the contrary, there is extensive research evidence that the use of multiple languages enhances cognitive development and the acquisition of additional languages. Although the United States may be exceptional, there are more people in the world who are multilingual than there are people who are monolingual.
- It is difficult and detrimental to attempt to learn a new language while simultaneously learning basic skills and content material in that same language. Since proficiency in the English language is a prerequisite skill for the learning of basic skills and content material in English, such basic skill and content material instruction must be deferred until such time as the student has mastery of the English language skills necessary for successful participation in the learning activity.
- Language development being crucial to cognitive and educational development, oral and subsequently written language development will be a key component of the curriculum, both in special language developmental classes as well as in all curricular and co-curricular activities.
- Since retardation in the acquisition of basic skills and content material is detrimental to students, as confirmed by the high correlation between overagedness and school dropouts, the development of basic skills and the acquisition of content material may be conducted in a native language other than English while sufficient mastery of the English language is being attained.

SOCIO-ECONOMIC CLASS:

- Students from poor homes frequently have different developmental patterns from students raised in affluent or middle-class homes. These different developmental patterns stem from a lack of academically oriented experiences and adult role models, lack of media, lack of reading materials, and constraints on the amount of adult to child interaction.

- The absence of such middle-class experiences, which are crucial for learning in school, demands a compensating amount of school-enriching experiences.
- It is an educational imperative that the school distinguish between a student's lack of experience and a student's lack of capability. Disadvantaged students are frequently perceived by the school as lacking learning capability rather than experience. Instead of providing a vast quantity of enriching experiences, the school frequently places the student in a low-level, slow-paced, boring, and repetitious program. This misdiagnosis commonly becomes a self-fulfilling prophecy, with school performance consistently and continuously worsening, until the student becomes at risk of dropping out of school.

MOBILITY:

- Many students move from one geographic location to another. Although this phenomenon has long been recognized in immigrant and migrant children, this geographic relocation is now very much a part of central city urban life.
- Educational programs have extensive built-in continuity and sequences that assume that the student in a specific classroom today was here yesterday and will be here tomorrow.
- In order to extend educational opportunity to students who move around, it is necessary that the school provide flexibility in the continuity and sequencing of the instructional program based on characteristics and past school experiences or current needs of geographically mobile students.

SCHOOL PERCEPTIONS OF THE STUDENT:

- It is the belief of the school that all children can learn.
- The school will communicate to the student a valuing of the individual, the student's family, and his or her culture.
- The school will present educational challenges, starting with small, increasing increments of difficulty and with complete assurance that the student has all the necessary prerequisite skills for successful performance.
- All successful student performance will be followed by immediate, strong, and frequent positive feedback to reinforce the successful performance.
- All relationships and communication between the school and the student will be positive and will reflect a belief in the student's dignity and worth.

STUDENT PERCEPTIONS OF SELF:

- The child comes to school with concepts of self and his or her relationship to the world. The school must be sensitive to these self-perceptions, provide positive experiences for the elimination of negative concepts, and provide successful experiences that will develop the student's concept of himself as a successful participant in the learning program.
- The school will prevent experiences conducive to the alienation, isolation, or dysfunctional behavior of the student.

Length constraints preclude a description of the remaining fifty-four cells in the developmental matrix, but the methodology to be followed is similar to the examples presented above. Each of the ten areas of school life will be similarly matched with the six areas of student characteristics.

The contents of the developmental matrix, as implemented in the Vanguard School for Science and Technology, will provide the necessary valuing of the student, support services, and home/school/community interactions found in the most successful innovative schools. The reduction of incompatibilities between the characteristics of the school and the characteristics of the participating students will provide a culturally democratic learning environment conducive to successful performance by students representative of San Antonio's rich cultural diversity.

BIBLIOGRAPHY

American Institutes for Research (AIR), *Evaluation of the Impact of ESEA Title VII Spanish/English Bilingual Education Programs,* Washington, D.C., 1977.

Anderson, Theodore and Mildred Boyer, *Bilingual Schooling in the United States,* Southwest Educational Development Laboratory, Austin, 1970.

Brown v. Board of Education, 347 US 483 (1954).

Cárdenas, Blandina and José A. Cárdenas, "Chicano—Bright-Eyed Bilingual, Brown and Beautiful", *Today's Education,* February, 1973.

Cárdenas, José A., "Education and the Children of Migrant Farmworkers: An Overview," Center for Law and Education, *Inequality in Education,* No. 21, Harvard University, June, 1976.

Cárdenas, José A., "Seven Cities of Gold", Delta Epsilon Sigma, Bulletin, Vol. XV, No. 3, October, 1970.

Cárdenas, José A. and Joan McCarty First, "Children at Risk", Association for Supervision and Curriculum Development, *Educational Leadership,* Vol. 43, No. 1, September, 1985.

Committee for Economic Development, *Children in Need: Investment Strategies for the Educationally Disadvantaged,* New York, 1987.

Doe v. Plylar, 458 F. Supp. 569 (E.D. Tex. 1978).

Edgewood I.S.D., et al. v. Kirby, et al., Case No. 362,516, 250th District Court, Austin, Travis County, Texas, August 27, 1987.

Epstein, Noel, *Language, Ethnicity and the Schools,* Institute for Educational Leadership, George Washington University, 1977.

Fishman, Joshua A., et al., *Language Loyalties in the United States,* Mouton and Co., The Hague, 1966.

Guilford, J. P., *The Analysis of Intellect,* McGraw-Hill, New York, 1971.

Guilford, J. P., *Fundamental Statistics in Psychology and Education,* McGraw-Hill, New York, 1965.

Havighurst, Robert J.,____, 1964.

In Re Alien Children's Education Litigation, 501 F. Supp. 544, 550 (S.D. Tex. 1980).

Intercultural Development Research Association (IDRA), *AMANECER,* San Antonio, 1979.

Intercultural Development Research Association, *Newsletter,* San Antonio, September, 1974, October, 1974, September,1975, October, 1976, November, 1977, January, 1978, September, 1979, August, 1980, March, 1983, and June, 1987.

Intercultural Development Research Association (IDRA), *Nuevo Amanecer,* National Textbook Company, Chicago, 1985.

Intercultural Development Research Association (IDRA), *Successful Schooling for Economically Disadvantaged At-Risk Youth,* Texas Education Agency, Austin, 1989.

Jacobson, Lenore and Robert Rosenthal, *Pygmalion in the Classroom,* Holt, Rinehart and Winston, New York, 1968.

Kagen, Spencer and M. C. Madsen, "Cooperation and Competition of Mexican-Americans and Anglo-American Children of Two Ages Under Four Instructional Sets," *Developmental Psychology,* July, 1971, pp. 32-39.

Kemerer, Frank, *William Wayne Justice: A Judicial Biography,* The University of Texas Press, Austin, 1991.

Keys v. School District No. 1, 576 F. Supp. (D. Colo. 1983).

Lau v. Nichols, 483 F 2d 791 (9th Cir 1973), 412 US 938 (1973).

Lau v. Nichols, 414 U.S. 563 (1974).

Lesser, Gerald S., et al., "Mental Abilities of Children from Different Social-Class and Cultural Groups," *Monograph of the Society for Research in Child Development,* 102, 1965.

Morales v. Shannon, 516 F. 2d. 411 (1975).

National Advisory Commission on Civil Disorders, *Report,* Bantam Books, New York, 1968.

National Education Goals Report, *Building a Nation of Learners,* Washington, D.C., 1991.

Oakes, Jeannie, *Multiplying Inequalities,* The Rand Corporation, Santa Monica, July, 1990.

Overton v. City of Austin, 748 F. 2d, 941 (1984).

Quality Education for Minorities Project, *Education that Works,* Massachusetts Institute of Technology, Cambridge, January, 1990.

Ramirez, Manuel and Alfredo Castaneda, *Systems and Evaluation in Education,* Riverside, California, 1973.

Reissman, Frank, "Overlooked Positives," in Frost, Joe L. and Glen R. Hawkes, *Socially Handicapped Children,* Houghton Mifflin, Boston, 1966.

Reyna, et al. v. Kirby, et al., C.A. No. L-86-44 (S.D. Tex. 1989).

Rios v. Reed, 73 F.R.D. 589 (1977).

Robledo Montecel, Maria, et al., *Hispanic Families as Valued Partners: An Educator's Guide,* Intercultural Development Research Association (IDRA), San Antonio, 1993.

Rodriguez v. San Antonio Independent School District, 337 F Supp 280 (W.D. Tex. 1971).

Ruble, Arthur J., *Across the Tracks: Mexican-Americans in a Texas City,* University of Texas Press, Austin, 1966.

San Antonio Independent School District v. Rodriguez, 411 U.S.1 (1973).

San Antonio New Schools Development Foundation, *Designs for a New Generation of American Schools,* San Antonio, 1992.

Schorr, Lizbeth B., *Within Our Reach,* Doubleday, New York, 1988.

Serna v. Portales Municipal Schools, 499 Federal Reporter, 2d, (10th Cir. 1974).

Texas Advisory Committee to the U.S. Commission on Civil Rights, *Report,* February, 1970.

Texas Department of Community Affairs, *Poverty in Texas—1973,* Austin, Texas, 1974.

Texas Education Agency, *Texas Evaluation Study of PreKindergarten Programs, Preliminary Findings,* Austin, November, 1991.

United States v. Texas, 342 F.Supp. 24 (E.D. Tex. 1971).

DISCUSSION QUESTIONS

1. Define the following terms used in this chapter:

   atypical students
   bilingual education
   dysfunctional responses
   ESL
   immersion
   learning style
   limited-English-proficient
   multicultural education
   scapegoating
   tolerance for turbulence
   VSP

2. What is the difference between a culture of poverty and a poverty of culture? What are the educational implications of this difference?

3. List the cultural assumptions that underlie the structure and curriculum of American public schools. Make a parallel list of the characteristics of minority students in your community. Identify incompatibilities between the two lists. Which of these incompatibilities puts minority students at risk?

4. In 1970, Cárdenas described a deep separation, a chasm, between the needs, values, and aspirations of minority populations and those of the dominant middle class. Review these areas of conflict and assess the participation of the minority groups in your community in community social institutions at the present time.

5. In what ways can the whole language philosophy of instruction, cooperative learning, and portfolio assessment facilitate the school's adaptation to minority students?

6. Develop a plan for including the parents in your school community as resources and as partners in their children's education. How will your plan take into account their cultural, linguistic, and economic realities? What adaptations will the plan necessitate within your school?

7. You are a teacher whose class will be joined by migrant children in the course of the year. Develop a plan for individualized instruction that will enrich both the educational experience of the migrant children and that of the geographically stable population.

8. Identify ways in which Hispanic children and non-Hispanic children are socialized within the family to the values of interdependence and individualism. How can these values be shared in the school? What would such an exchange and adaptation of values contribute to American society?

9. How do your state's current school finance policies serve or not serve minority populations? Why would it be false economy to cut school programs that help poor children?

10. What does "multicultural education" mean for mainstream, middle-class students?

2

Bilingual Education

DEVELOPMENT OF A MODEL FOR BILINGUAL/ MULTICULTURAL EDUCATION

1973

PREFACE

In 1968, bilingual education received its biggest boost by the enactment of Senator Ralph Yarborough's Bilingual Education Act as Title IX of the Elementary Secondary Education Act. By 1973, it was evident that there were varying perceptions of the definition and purposes of bilingual education, as well as the structure of a bilingual program. In order to respond to this lack of consensus, Aspira of America assembled a group of educators and community leaders in Columbia, Maryland, to discuss bilingual and multicultural education in an attempt to provide a Hispanic support model for national implementation. Funds for the meeting, which was attended by members of the Mexican-American, Puerto Rican, and Cuban communities, were provided by the U.S. Department of Health, Education and Welfare (HEW).

I was requested to design and present a model for consideration. The following article is the model which I presented on March 25, 1973 (Aspira, 1973).

A report issued by Aspira included not only the model which I presented, but also a record of the discussion which followed the presentation. This discussion provides an insight into the conflicting perceptions of the nature and purpose of bilingual education—conflicting perceptions that are still with us today. The report also provides insights into Hispanic perceptions of institutional racism, cultural assimilation and the need for political power.

IMPLICATIONS

A model implies a master plan which may be used as a pattern for the subsequent development of programs, as well as facilities for imitation and replication. In addition to this, the model should have the necessary flexibility to be adaptable in a wide variety of situations. The model is a conceptual framework that makes allowances for natural and/or planned variations. Geographical locations, ethnicity of populations, language differences, etc., at the various implementation sites are some of the variables that may be included in a model. Although the foregoing are natural variables which may exist at various implementation sites, the model may and should provide for planned variables. A variety of materials, methodologies, and other factors are examples of the planned variables which may be provided through the model. These planned variables can be utilized to determine the most effective ways of presenting bilingual programs in certain settings to certain types of children.

Political and economic constraints and the availability of personnel resources are examples of other considerations that may affect the development of a model.

MODEL CONTENT

A model for bilingual/bicultural education should contain certain elements imperative for the subsequent development of bilingual programs such as definitions, philosophies, rationale, variables, and evaluation design.

DEFINITION

The first step in the development of a model for bilingual/bicultural education is defining the concept. Although at first glance, definitions of bilingual education are common and the task of defining seems simple or moot, the definition given expands or constrains the model and is therefore extremely important to subsequent model and program development.

For example, a common definition of bilingual education is "education in two languages," or a common definition of bilingualism is "fluency in two languages." For the purposes of bilingual education, both its definition and the definition of bilingualism will be found lacking.

A bilingual education program which responds to the concept of bilingualism in terms of fluency of language deviates considerably from a bilingual program which purports to develop listening, understanding, speaking, reading and writing skills in the language.

A bilingual education program, which under the first definition is transitional in nature; i.e., promotes the use of Spanish as a language of instruction while English is being learned as a second language, makes no effort to further maintain or expand the learner's grasp of the Spanish language, differs considerably from a bilingual education program in which the fluency and communication skills acquired and developed in a native language form a parallel learning system for further skills development and content acquisition. A definition of bilingual education may go further and consider socio-linguistic aspects of language, such as teaching a language and the development of insights into selection of the language to be used in a specific social setting.

A parallel situation exists in the definition of bicultural education; a case in which the sum is greater than the total of the parts. For instance, a bicultural individual is more than the combination of two individuals, each of which functions in a mono-cultural environment. The bicultural individual may develop insights into the relationship of the two cultures and understanding of the similarities and differences in the cultures, and perhaps a facility for movement from one culture to another, depending upon the social situation in which he finds himself, or the cultural options which he may wish to exercise.

Just as too restrictive a definition of bilingualism, bilingual education, and bicultural education forms one end of a continuum, a too elaborate definition may lead the model planner into a philosophical quagmire of issues which have not been resolved by society in general in thousands of years. A definition of bilingual education which attempts to define education, its purposes and goals, may be too exhaustive for a model developed for bilingual education.

It is more practical and definitely safer that social and philosophical issues common to all education be considered at some other time and that the definition of bilingual education be in terms of the unique characteristics of bilinguality and the purposes and goals of education be kept outside of these parameters. Therefore, bilingual education becomes a way of better achieving acceptable goals of education, rather than providing alternatives to these goals. The writer does not exaggerate the issue nor minimize the importance of developing a better set of goals for education. The problem is that the development of a bilingual model may not be the proper kind of setting for resolving larger philosophical issues.

RATIONALE

Avoiding the larger philosophical issues in education, the development of a bilingual model must face some immediate philosophical, pedagogical, social, economic, and political constraints. It is necessary that the development respond to the question, "Why bilingual education?" Unfortunately, too many of the rationales developed for bilingual education are addressed to interested agencies, such as the Office of Economic Opportunity and the Department of Health, Education and Welfare and are not understood nor accepted by the school practitioners. The rationale for bilingual education must address itself to the practical realities and concerns of the local school system administrators, teachers, and community.

The following factors should be included in a rationale for bilingual education:

1. Incompatibilities;
2. Other Language Acquisition;
3. Cultural Pluralism;
4. Development of a Positive Self-Image; and
5. Equality of Educational Opportunity.

Incompatibilities

The dismal failure of American schools in the education of minority groups can be attributed to the incompatibilities which exist between the characteristics of the target minority population and the characteristics of an instructional program developed for a white, Anglo-Saxon, English-speaking, middle-class oriented population. Incompatibilities exist in economic level, mobility, and societal perceptions, but perhaps the most glaring incompatibilities are in the areas of culture, including language. Neither the instructional materials nor the methodologies utilized in the schools reflect or are compatible with the language and the culture of Spanish-speaking Americans.

It seems ridiculously simple to ascertain that a child who speaks Spanish cannot successfully participate in an instructional program conducted in another language. Past efforts of the schools to remedy this incompatibility by placing the child in an English-speaking environment produces a traumatic psychological effect which has been extremely detrimental to the Spanish-speaking children of this country.

The subsequent "English as a Second Language" (ESL) programs have resulted in the delaying of basic skills acquisition or have placed the Spanish-speaking child in the uncomfortable situation of having to master a new language, basic skills in that language, and acquire content in the new language, all at the same time.

It is no wonder that Spanish-speaking children were constantly having to spend several years in school before reaching a level of cognitive development and achievement necessary for placement in the second grade. The resulting retardation and failure connotation did much to establish early in this educational experience a concept of failure with accompanying feelings of inadequacies.

Other Language Acquisition

It can be inferred that our society values and perceives as desirable the acquisition of languages other than English. Seldom can one encounter an institution of higher education or for that matter, a secondary school, in which foreign languages are not only offered, but are required in order to complete the educational program. There is no question but that the school, and indirectly society, perceives the acquisition of a foreign language as desirable. If the foregoing is so, it stands to reason that if a child enrolls in an American school with native-like proficiency in a "foreign" language, it is desirable for the school to nurture, assist in retention, and further develop the Spanish language skills which the child brings to school. It is inconceivable that an educational system should allow the facility in this native language to be lost and at great expense reintroduce it later in the educational sequence as a "foreign" language. That school systems have not only allowed language facility to be lost, but even encouraged the losing of this facility through both administration policies and instructional practices, indicates the eclectic status of the pedagogical mind. Certainly, the right hand cannot possibly condone what the left hand is doing.

Cultural Pluralism

The United States of America is culturally pluralistic. It is made up of many races and ethnic groups. It is desirable that this condition be perpetuated. The role of the school as it relates to culture is two-fold: first, to present alternatives to its clientele, and second, to promote the understanding and appreciation of the variety of lifestyles represented in our society.

Development of a Positive Self-Image

To a large extent, the performance of the child in a school setting is dependent upon the way that the child perceives himself in this setting. The school must accept the child as he is and constantly indicate to him that he is a worthwhile individual. Rejecting a basic characteristic of the child, such as his language or forcing him to reject this aspect of his culture, cannot allow the child to perceive of himself as a worthwhile individual. This traumatic barrier between the home and the school contributes to the development of a negative self-feeling which subsequently manifests itself in self-rejection and poor performance.

Equality of Educational Opportunity

Denial of a bilingual/bicultural education program to a child whose native language is Spanish constitutes a denial of educational opportunity. In the San Felipe/Del Rio intervention suit in the case of *U.S. v. Texas* held in Tyler, Texas, the federal judge for the Western District of Texas ruled that denying access to a bilingual program to the Spanish-speaking children of Del Rio, Texas constituted a violation of the equal protection clause. Judge Justice further ruled that the failure of the school to offer a bilingual program to white, Anglo children constituted an inferior valuing of the Spanish language detrimental to the child and in violation of his civil rights (*United States v. Texas*, 1971).

ELEMENTS OF THE MODEL

The past few years have seen the development of large numbers of bilingual education programs. An analysis of these programs indicates that there are vast differences among the programs. A model for bilingual programs should contain the necessary flexibility for adaptation to a variety of settings. The model should lend itself to both natural and planned variations.

One of the basic assumptions in empirical studies is that cause and effect relationships exist. The effect may be caused by a single stimulus or by a group of stimuli. It is assumed that in a natural setting there are many other stimuli which do not contribute to the effect, therefore, are considered to be independent of the cause and effect relationship. A planned variation model must therefore distinguish between model content or stimuli which will affect the outcome of the bilingual instructional program, and those which will not. Other conditions may have a direct relationship on instructional outcomes, but are so difficult to manipulate that they must be treated as constants within the model. Other factors have such a direct relationship to instructional outcomes or can be easily manipulated and therefore constitute the variables in a bilingual educational model. The following factors should be included as basic variables in the model:

1. ***Language Dominance***: It is dangerous to assume that all of the children from Spanish-surnamed families have dominance in the Spanish language. Assuming that on a continuum from "only Spanish-speaking" at one end to "only English-speaking" at the other end, and with perfect bilinguality in the middle, children will fall at all places along the continuum. A model for bilingual education must allow not only for the qualitative factor of English or Spanish language dominance, but also for the quantitative factor or degree of dominance.

2. ***Staff Utilization***: Many patterns of staff utilization have and may be employed in a bilingual program. Among the alternatives available to a school system are the employment of bilingual personnel exclusively, team arrangements utilizing both bilingual and monolingual staff, the utilization of paraprofessional personnel, and various combinations of these alternatives.

3. ***Staff Training***: Quantitative and qualitative aspects of staff training should be a part of the model. Variables within staff training may include language development of teachers versus methodology; pre-service v. in-service, length of training, and quality of the training program.

4. ***Materials***: The materials utilized in the bilingual education program constitute a fourth variable in the model. Types of materials used in bilingual education programs currently include materials which can be classified in the following categories: (a) materials produced in Spanish-speaking countries, (b) materials produced in this country by publishing companies or rather large institutions, and (c) materials produced by a school system and/or by the individual teacher. For the purpose of the model, the three categories may be labeled as foreign, national (state), and local.

5. ***Methodologies***: The methodologies employed in a bilingual instructional program constitute a fifth variable. Some bilingual programs, particularly those employing materials produced in other countries, tend to follow the prevalent methodology employed in the materials and common to those countries. Frequently, this methodology uses a strong phonetic approach in the development of reading skills. On the other hand, locally produced materials tend to reflect a "basal reader" methodology much better designed for the teaching of reading in a phonetically inconsistent language, such as English. The degree of individualization of instruction is another aspect of methodology.

6. ***Time/Space Factors***: These variables allow variation on the basis of allocation of time and the grouping of children for participation in bilingual instructional activities. Elements in this variable may include the time devoted to instruction in either language, grouping, and organizational patterns for instruction.

   Time/Space factors may also include variations along the integration-segregation of monolingual/bilingual children continuum.

7. ***Community Involvement***: As in staff training, community involvement in the planning, designing, and evaluation of a bilingual program will include quantitative and qualitative factors. The number of parents involved and the length of involvement constitute the quantitative element. The qualitative elements may include the types of involvement which may be informative, advisory, or participatory in decision-making or participatory in involvement.

EVALUATION OF THE MODEL

The last aspect of the model is an evaluation design which provides pertinent and timely information for decision making. Common practices in the implementation of bilingual programs should include both formative and summative evaluation designs. Process and product evaluation should both be included.

As a bilingual program develops instructional materials and methodologies, it is desirable to include a systematic review of such materials. Panels of parents, teachers, and students, may provide valuable input into necessary revisions of instructional materials. Formative evaluation—formative in the sense that it affects the early formation of the program—must include activities for the "debugging" of the program. Classroom teachers utilizing the materials should respond to evaluation criteria including vocabulary level, length, relevancy, appropriateness, pedagogy, feedback, and reward. Information gathered from the formative evaluation must be cycled back to the developers for appropriate revision.

The summative evaluation responds to familiar questions dealing with the success of the program. Comparison of the performance of children participating in the program with the performance of control groups may be analyzed. Similarly, comparisons of pupil performance before and after the intervention will yield summative data. Even as in formative evaluation, the summative evaluation or "field test data" must be cycled back to designers and developers.

Process evaluation gives information to the developer on the success of the new program. Such information must also be cycled back to the decision-makers in order to alter, improve, or re-design programmatic activities.

Product evaluation provides the necessary information for ascertaining the effectiveness of the new program and the alternative provided should extend, supplement, or replace prior efforts.

It is desirable to develop the entire evaluation design prior to the implementation of the developmental program. If possible, the model should contain arrangements for an independent evaluation effort conducted by a responsible organization or institution preferably responsible to the funding agency, in addition to the internal evaluation.

SUMMARY OF THE DISCUSSION ON THE PAPER SUBMITTED BY DR. JOSÉ A. CÁRDENAS ON "DEVELOPMENT OF A MODEL FOR BILINGUAL-BICULTURAL EDUCATION"

Discussion Leader: Hernan La Fontaine

The panel spent a great deal of time discussing racism and its effect on minority groups and on the possibilities of bilingual education. At the end of the session, although they had not discussed it to a great extent, they accepted Dr. Cárdenas' model and appointed a subcommittee to return the next day with an acceptable definition of bilingual education. The discussion was affected by the news that the Rodriguez suit for equal educational opportunity (bilingual) in Texas had been turned down by the Supreme Court on the grounds that education is not a right guaranteed by the Constitution (*San Antonio Independent School District v. Rodriguez*, 1973).

Eduardo Sanchez said that the reason for incompatibility between the WASP culture and culture of minorities who live in this country is racism. American society is pluralistic, but within a narrow racial context that must be broadened, "something we must bring about together" he said.

Miguel Navarrette said that assuming that no culture is superior to any other, the solution lies in mutual adaptability of each culture's members to the other culture when they are exposed to it. "It is the task of educational systems to adapt to the particular characteristics of the typical minority child, not force him to change into something else."

Luis Nieves Falcon questioned Dr. Cárdenas putting aside social and philosophical issues common to education and keeping the definition of bilingual education in terms of the unique characteristics of bilinguality.

Dr. Cárdenas answered that some of the questions are 2,000 years old and the group should avoid getting bogged down in them.

Hernan La Fontaine agreed, but said the Spanish community has been cut out from consideration of the broader goals, therefore, is eager to discuss them in any form.

Marina Mercado pointed out that Dr. Cárdenas included "extraneous" concepts such as culture and academic preparation in this model and these have importance within the sweep of bilingual-bicultural education.

Mario Anglada said, "We are discussing political education because of the political awakening that has taken place among us." But, he added, not enough time is spent analyzing how this political process is transformed into bilingual education.

Dr. Cárdenas said that many minority people seek cultural assimilation and because he wasn't going to make value judgements about such attitudes, models of bilingual education may include alternatives for each group.

Mr. Navarrette objected that the communities may not have the necessary skills to implement the proposed model presently.

Dr. Cárdenas said that he presented four approaches or reasons for bilingual education and there are others, but in the past such rationales seem to have been written in such a complicated way, they have very little relevance for local school staffs.

Henry Casso said that his impression was that no school system has the expertise to implement such a model, but that Latins are now mature enough to realize where this expertise lies, and must strive to develop it.

We are trying to arrive at a different level of analysis, Dr. Seda-Bonilla said, to share experiences and to extend them to our communities. If you take away the political issues of bilingual education, you are taking a self-defeating and even suicidal political stand. Bilingual education is not just an option for us, he said.

Agreeing that the question of racism should be included in an expanded section on cultural pluralism, Dr. Cárdenas said that a fifth rationale should be added to his paper—the equality of educational opportunity.

When we consider bilingual education, Mr. Nieves argued, we have to decide whether we want it as part of a program of assimilation or to preserve our cultural autonomy, requiring value judgments to be made.

But this is nothing but a framework for the development of models for bilingual education, Dr. Cárdenas answered, and therefore, he said, he had refrained from imposing his own value judgments on the definitions, rationale, and philosophical issues. The framework is for anyone to work with and to arrive at their own definitions, rationale, and issues.

Alex Rodriguez called Dr. Cárdenas' job admirable in dealing with the techniques and realities involved. The political needs one sees, he said, will be directly related to the political realities one happens to be closest to. The smaller the bilingual community, the more acceptable bilingual education will be to the dominant group, he said. The huge scale of New York's and California's problems arouses fears.

Those who favor loose definitions may regret them later, he added, because when a case lands in court, a judge will be forced to make a decision.

He may turn to educators for guidelines on bilingual education, so precise definitions are necessary. It is probable, he said, that a judge will rule in the near future on whether it is a violation of the equal protection clause of the 14th Amendment if bilingual education is not provided to a linguistic minority, and that legislation will be written. We want to come up with a precise structural form that may be used in the educational and political systems of various communities.

The discussion leader said it was important to determine at which level pressure must be applied to attain change.

Mr. Rodriguez added that a court ruling that bilingual education in our school systems should measure up to equal protection as defined in the Constitution would be a firm guarantee that bilingual education will exist in this country. Legislation can be repealed and liberal administrations cannot be re-elected forever. We can achieve very good results in one state or another, but such victories can come to an end if the economic and political situation in the state changes. But a court ruling would be effective and lasting, he said.

Severo Gomez asked if the six components of the Texas Statewide Design for Bilingual Education would be acceptable in terms of definitions which include: the child must make the initial adjustment to school in his first language, his language development must take place in his first language; he starts to learn the second language only when he has learned to read and write in the first; and he is taught content in the first language, and the second when he is linguistically ready; and the child's cultural development must transcend all learning experiences. He added that he does not believe in simultaneous development of languages because one language is always relegated to a secondary place and the first language must be the stronger basis for learning.

Mr. Rodriguez said that integration of the two groups, and a way of handling children generationally removed from their own background should be included.

Mr. Gomez said the children are separated under his plan only for their linguistic development. He added that bilingual education ought also to play to the half million Czech-speaking and the equal numbers of German-speaking people in his state.

Ms. Mercado said she did not place as much trust in the courts as Mr. Rodriguez does because there are many ways of interpreting the law. The general attitude among top university officials is that bilingual education is a bastardization of education, she said. Despite New York State's Bilingual Education Act, nothing is done in many branches of City University or in many other universities to implement bilingual education training.

Another speaker said that to achieve something despite racism, the community is going to have to exert the necessary political pressure. "We can ask the school principal to provide the leadership needed to introduce change . . . The only way to get him to act is by exposing him to our views, through his experience in meeting with us."

Since we can't remove him, he added, we will have to change him. "The biggest job in bilingual education is changing the attitudes of people, and mainly of teachers administrators, and deans."

Dr. Cárdenas said the Rodriguez case led him to believe that before going to courts or legislatures, we should seek an amendment to the Constitution, requesting equality of educational opportunity as a right for all minorities in this country. The Supreme Court decision opens the door to so many difficulties. Chicanos, Puerto Ricans, Cubans, Blacks, and others should start trying for amendments to the Constitution.

Another speaker pointed out that some judges have interpreted the question of equal educational opportunity as providing us with the same benefits English-speaking people receive.

César Perales said the Rodriguez decision may not be definitive because a question of wealth was involved, not racial discrimination. This actually gives me some hope if we know how to phrase things when the opportunity arises to go before the courts, he said.

Mr. Nieves added that you have to go to the legislatures and then hope for a court ruling that may extend the state reforms nationally. The state-by-state process will be long and difficult and will succeed in an inverse ratio to the density of the minority population in each state.

The Texas State Legislature may pass legislation to alleviate the funding inequities, another speaker said, because the governor and the school districts are exerting pressure. This is the positive aspect of a negative decision.

Dr. Seda-Bonilla said that underlying the case was a great deal of racism because racism tinges almost all American decisions when dealing with minorities.

Racism is not limited to American society or similar ones, Juana Amelia Hernandez said. It is found in such societies as Mexico and Argentina, she added, and it is not limited to a few groups. "Racism is an important factor in our struggle for recognition, but in my opinion it is not the most important one."

Ms. Delgado said that because racism was overplayed by the Black community throughout the 1960s, coming out strongly with charges of racism will alienate people and do more harm than good.

Agreeing, Adalberto Guerrero said we know there is racism but it is not worth erecting obstacles to bilingual education for the sake of attacking racism. He added that bilingual education will do more against racism in the long run than many of the attacks leveled against it now.

Ms. Inclan said the term racism was abused and applied to everything in which we see discrimination against our side, but not our negative feelings towards any other group.

Ms. Mercado said another aspect to discrimination is the economic attack on minorities. When it comes to reducing funds, minorities really get the ax. Racism is the main factor in our situation. Some of us could "pass" and become Americanized, but what about the others who will never be accepted because of their color? she asked.

Dr. Hernandez said discrimination is suffered by other minorities, particularly Blacks and Indians and the poor white as well. We have to concentrate on politics, she said, and it is important to form solid Latin coalitions that may elect the right political leaders to the posts that matter to bring about the changes we want so badly. Only our Hispanic culture is going to unite Latins, she said. If we base our plan of action on racial considerations, we are going to get entangled in our own racism, and there is plenty of racism among us, with very bad consequences.

Murial Pagan, who sees bilingual education as the only way in which Puerto Rican children can be helped to survive, said, we have to consider the philosophical, political, and educational aspects of bilingual education and to press forward in those areas.

José Luis Hernandez said he was worried about the Bilingual Education Act and that not enough was being done to save it.

Calling for action, Henry Casso suggested planning an approach to H.E.W. Appropriation Subcommittee members and members of the Senate Appropriations Committee in view of the news of the Rodriguez case. He added that he was doubtful that Latins had the necessary political muscle to work for a Constitutional amendment. One thing that was needed, though, was written verification that there is no legislation presently before Congress to continue the existing national appropriations for bilingual education.

Dr. Seda-Bonilla said that there is no question that racism exists among us. He added that the issue should not be skirted because it has been "overplayed" by the Blacks, because "we owe a great deal to the tremendous struggle of Blacks against racism."

It is senseless to pretend we want bilingualism and preservation of our culture for their own sake, as if we were like the Germans or the Dutch who had no trouble at all getting accepted by white America. Not to accept the challenge of American racism is not only immoral, it is detrimental to our efforts, he said.

Mr. Guerrero pointed out, that if we include among the rationales for bilingual education, the racism of those who are discriminating linguistically at the present, we are going to get cooperation only from those who admit that they are racist, which won't be a very big group.

Bilingual education has been more successful in Miami with the Cubans because there the question was never approached as a racial issue, Ms. Cantero said.

Others added that Miami had an advantage because the movement for bilingual education was well organized, there are so many Cubans, and federal money was poured into Miami. As a representative of the Cubans in Miami, Rosa Inclan objected and said that that was an example of prejudice and racism. Luis Alvarez said the statements were not intended to offend or show discrimination, they were objective observations and comments.

Eduardo Sanchez pointed out that Americans themselves are aware of the prejudice in this nation, not only against Hispanic groups but against Jews and even the poor white, and it has been discussed and studied. He suggested burying differences and agreeing on a series of basic questions.

An observer pointed out that there are still $35 million available for bilingual education. People are still working on it.

The discussion leader said the group had to come up with something practical for the use of those who are directly involved in bilingual programs. A statement will give them a little support, he said.

What is taking place is bilingual schooling, not bilingual education, Sylvia Herrera de Fox said, adding that not enough attention has been paid to the educational needs of our children. A careful assessment of their basic educational needs, of what is going to be taught to them and for what purpose, is needed, she said. "Our communities are sadly lacking in individual experiences directly related to the development of our political power as well as our cultural consciousness and the acquisition of economic and social skills needed for survival. I don't think that an education capable of providing these experiences is feasible without more funding at federal, state, and local levels."

She added that "We will have to decide if we need sui generis institutions to provide the kind of education needed in order to survive in a racist society . . . which also manages to neutralize and destroy all cultural values outside its own."

Anthony Santiago said we have to deal with the question of philosophy in order to determine goals and the use of available funds.

Mr. Nieves asked that two categories be incorporated in Dr. Cárdenas' paper—how racial discrimination places the individual in a position of inferiority and the need for minority groups to assume responsibility for their situation and to move into the power structure. He questioned sacrificing basic principles in order to be "practical." In discussing bilingual education's role in cultural preservation, he suggested a type of education that will work with families in order to stimulate the preservation of culture at the family level.

In summing up, Dr. Cárdenas said there has been a conglomeration of bilingual programs under the Bilingual Education Act but that funds were made available very frequently along political, instead of pedagogical lines. He said he had been "burning" because of the absence of models for the development of such programs, but the U.S.O.E. chose not to use bilingual education funds for the development of models, instead funding as many school districts as the money would allow. Much of the money was wasted and hundreds of bilingual education programs have been implemented with teachers who are not bilingual and who do not have the necessary insights to be in bilingual education at all. In higher education, methodologies and materials crucial for bilingual education programs have been by-passed. Consequently, there is a need for a structure for the development of bilingual education programs, which is what he attempted to present, he said.

He agreed with the recommendation that equality of educational opportunity form a part of this rationale and to a certain extent agreed to a further elaboration of the concepts of racism and its detrimental effects upon children and education in general.

He added that political power is a reality to be faced and that unless Puerto Ricans, Chicanos, and Cubans get power, they will continue to be ignored in their efforts.

No objections were voiced to the model, and it was accepted.

At Carmen Delgado's suggestion, Henry Casso for the Chicanos, Luis Nieves Falcón for the Puerto Ricans, and Rosa Inclan for the Cubans were appointed a working committee (open to anyone else to join) to draw up a definition of bilingual education by the next day.

BILINGUAL EDUCATION, SEGREGATION, AND A THIRD ALTERNATIVE

1975

PREFACE

"How can a teacher speak to some in a group of children in English and at the same time speak to others in the group in another language?" This question was asked of me by Judge John Wood following my testimony in the Uvalde, Texas desegregation court case, *Morales v. Shannon (Morales v. Shannon*, 1975). The fallacy in this question is the assumption that teachers need to spend any great amount of time in direct communication with the group as a whole.

At the time this article was written, schools were faced with two distasteful tasks being imposed by the courts: the desegregation of schools, and the implementation of bilingual education programs. The consistent tractiveness of the schools rebelled against the implementation of a response to either dictum. Therefore, in an attempt to do nothing, schools played both ends against the middle by asserting that the two court orders were contradictory. Either they desegregated the language minority children or they responded to the language characteristic with special programs in segregated settings.

To a certain extent, the inability of the schools to reconcile the two orders involved a certain amount of assumed naiveness on the part of the schools. For many years schools had been responding to the varying reading levels of students in a specific class by grouping the students in keeping with reading level. Yet, the apparent paradox was being mentioned so frequently, that I felt the need to respond in the following article.

Although some of the school's failure to respond can be attributed to assumed naiveness, much of the failure can also be attributed to the continued use of outdated instructional practices. Even today, teachers commonly function as a person interacting with a large group of children rather than as directors of a variety of learning activities.

Almost twenty years after the publication of this article, I still observe many classrooms without flexible groupings, without staff differentiation, and without extensive use of the rapidly growing technological assistance available. Where specialized teachers, mentors, aides, tutors, and other differentiated staff, as well as technological aids are available, it is not unusual for this student assistance to be presented independently of the classroom teacher, and in many instances without any extensive attempt at coordination.

The inability of the school to conceptualize a bilingual education program in a desegregated setting is indicative of a lack of imaginative thinking on the part of the school. This lack of imagination will continue to constrain current reform efforts which attempt to increase the educational efficiency of the school.

The Spanish-speaking population in the United States continues to be educationally short-changed as a result of school districts' widespread failures to institute adequate bilingual instruction programs. This failure is most often attributed to organizational obstacles. Educators caught in equality of educational opportunity litigation commonly complain of difficulties in offering bilingual education within heterogeneous groupings of children having varying language dominance characteristics.

Faced with the demand for implementation of bilingual programs, school districts in many areas have tended to project such programs solely for homogeneous groups of monolingual, Spanish-speaking children. Yet they generally have neglected to accept, project or implement bilingual education programs for small numbers of Spanish-speaking children, or for any number when found in heterogeneous settings.

The organizational difficulties that many school districts face are, of course, very real. However, methodologies to resolve them do exist. Unfortunately, it is suspected that some recalcitrant school systems might be using their organizational problems to mask an unwillingness to provide for the educational needs of non-English-speaking children.

Is There a Paradox?

Whatever the underlying reason, one thing is clear: school districts are failing to deliver adequate bilingual instruction for all but a handful of the non-English-speaking school population. Instead, they have proffered two equally dysfunctional alternatives: Spanish-speaking children are either asked to forego the benefits of bilingual instruction, or allow themselves to be segregated in order to participate in a bilingual program.

The school districts' arguments relative to bilingual instruction in a heterogeneous setting are commonly stated as follows: "How can a school system operate a classroom in which a portion of the children speak no English and must be taught in Spanish and a portion of the children speak no Spanish and must be taught in English?" Teaching all children in English denies the non-English-speaker equality of educational opportunity, but reversing the common methodology and teaching all children in Spanish creates a handicap for the non-Spanish-speakers and denies them equality of educational opportunity.

On its face, this paradox seems to present an insuperable problem. It was raised in the Del Rio intervention in *U.S. v. Texas*[1] when the Federal Court for the Eastern District of Texas ordered a bilingual education program implemented in the San Felipe Del Rio School District.

The same argument was made in *Keyes v. School District No.1*, Denver[2] during recent remedy hearings. With the advent of *Lau v. Nichols*[3] and *Serna v. Portales*[4], holding Title VI of the 1964 Civil Rights Act violated by school systems' treatment of non-English-speakers, it can be anticipated that the problem will be a primary consideration in the development of education plans in response to these and related court orders.

Similarly, the new legislative trend making bilingual education mandatory in an increasing number of states will, in all probability, lead to many school districts continuing to cite this paradoxical situation as a rationalization for their failure to implement bilingual programs. Or, districts might apply the equally repugnant alternative, the continued segregation of minority children in the name of bilingual education.

Clearly, many school districts' current practices of offering Spanish-speaking students either segregated bilingual education or integration without bilingual education are counterproductive to a healthy learning climate. Just as clearly, a third option to these practices must be developed as quickly as possible, lest litigation and legislation be unfairly influenced by the paradox we have described.

Before outlining some specific methodologies for teaching Spanish-speaking children in a heterogeneous setting, let us examine the prevailing educational dogma that has led to the often cited bilingual education paradox.

This dogma projects a classroom situation in which thirty children are marched in lockstep through identical instructional activities. Obviously, all children, regardless of ethnicity or language, have different learning abilities ranging perhaps from retarded to genius, varying past achievement rates ranging from retained-in-grade to child prodigy, differing interests, aspirations, motivations, pressures, and learning styles. Yet, in spite of their differences, children are subjected to common instructional activities directed at the mythical average or typical child. It is this methodology, based on an outmoded dogma, that cannot fail to produce the mediocrity for which our schools are becoming famous.

Individualizing Instruction

Coping with varying types and degrees of language dominance is no different than coping with other varying characteristics of children. But in order to do so it is necessary that learning activities be differentiated in keeping with children's varying characteristics. The ultimate goal is an individualized instructional program in which each activity is compatible with each individual child's characteristics, not only as they pertain to economic status, culture, and language, but also to include learning ability, achievement level, motivation, interests, etc.

In order to accomplish this humanizing or individualization of instruction it is necessary to change our perceptions of the classroom teacher. The teacher should no longer be perceived in a "little red schoolhouse" role, interacting with thirty children as they recite their lessons, but rather as a director of learning activities, utilizing diagnostic, prescriptive, and instructional resources in carrying out learning activities for individual, small groups, and large groups of children.

School systems must develop the technical and organizational capability for the implementation of such instructional programs. Clinging to outmoded educational dogma is not only fruitless but dangerous, since it is impossible to adequately train children for living in the twentieth century with eighteenth century methodologies. Neither the Spanish-speaking nor the English-speaking will survive.

Fortunately, the state of the art is such that methodologies are available to deal with the complexities of modern instructional problems. The following methodologies have been successfully applied as responses to the need for providing unique learning situations in keeping with the varying characteristics of children.

Groups: Progressive teachers have learned to utilize the technique of forming flexible and interchangeable groups for implementing some instructional activities. Reading instruction is often presented in small intra-classroom groups. Small groups of children reading at similar levels interact with the teacher while the rest of the class performs other work and play activities. Skilled teachers have no problem in training children to conduct self-directed activities which are neither wasteful nor disruptive as the teacher works with a part of the class. Other areas of the curriculum can be and are being taught in this manner.

There is no reason why similar intra-classroom groups cannot be formed for bilingual instruction on the basis of language dominance.

Exchange: Another response to the varying characteristics of children and teachers is to regroup among different classrooms in the same school for varying periods of time during the day. Thus non-English-speaking children can be regrouped for bilingual instruction during the school day and regrouped heterogeneously for activities in which language dominance is not a critical problem. This practice has been observed in the early elementary grades in certain progressive school districts for many years. In a more sophisticated and institutionalized form it is the basis for most secondary school organizational patterns, although such strict departmentalization is not being recommended here.

Staff differentiation: This favored response to the problem of heterogeneous grouping was found very effective in the Edgewood School District in meeting the unique needs of children. (The Edgewood Independent School District, the poorest of 1149 school districts in Texas and of Rodriguez fame,[5] pioneered in the development of successful instructional programs for economically disadvantaged and minority children in San Antonio, Texas.) The response consisted of providing staff resources for teachers in order to give each child a highly individualized instructional program. Among personnel utilized for individual and small group instruction were assistant teachers, aides, student teachers, interns, practicum college students, volunteer parents, and other school children.

The teacher was given sufficient time to devote to training and planning activities, and most of the actual interaction with children was carried out by trained paraprofessional personnel as described above.

Assistant teachers and teacher aides were paid paraprofessionals employed with funds made available by the state foundation program, Title VII, Title I, Model Cities, Career Opportunities Program (COP), employment and training programs, veterans' programs, Teacher Corps, and a variety of other sources. Since district policy demanded that paraprofessional personnel be recruited from the immediate school community, they invariably reflected the child's economic, cultural, and language characteristics. Although it took several years to recruit an adequate supply of bilingual teachers, each child in the school had immediate and ready access to paraprofessional personnel who could converse in the child's preferred language mode.

Colleges placed a large number of bilingual interns, student teachers, and practicum students. Many of the college students came to San Antonio for this purpose from other cities and from as far away as Michigan and Oregon. This type of staff resource was acquired at no cost to the school district.

High school students in psychology, child care, and homemaking classes participated in Youth-Tutoring-Youth (YTY) programs in the district. Junior high school students were also utilized. The benefits derived by the children being taught were exceeded only by the benefits derived by the secondary school students participating in the program. The Youth Tutors made substantial gains in the subject matter areas in which they taught. Truancy and disciplinary problems among the secondary students before participation disappeared as they found respect and self-fulfillment in helping other children.

The most unexpected payoff in utilizing differentiated staffing was from parents who participated as teaching volunteers. "A parent a day will keep the doctor away" was commonly heard as teachers attempted to meet a goal of at least one parent a day in each classroom. Either the skills needed for conducting simple and routine instructional activities (in English or Spanish) have been grossly overrated, or skills possessed by laymen have been grossly underrated, since the parents experienced success in working with the children. Their success grew as they continued to develop skills under the close supervision of the teachers. Parents who had never had much to do with the school proved that they did care for their children when the relationship with the school became positive, successful, and rewarding.

This elaborate account of successful experiences in implementing staff differentiation patterns is presented in order to demonstrate that such staffing is practical and that the facilitating of a bilingual program need not be constrained by a lack of local wealth or the absence of certified bilingual staff. Many other school systems have experienced similar success in the development and implementation of differentiated staffing.

Resource materials: Individualization of instruction can be achieved by the utilization of a wealth of instructional media which is readily available. Motion pictures, television, slides, and filmstrips can be utilized individually or in small groups. Individual or group language laboratories provide for a variety of instructional activities. Programmed instruction and self-pacing materials can also be utilized, as well as an endless variety of books, games, workbooks and other materials.

SUMMARY

It has been shown that the enrollment of small numbers of non-English-speaking children, time-space constraints, or the lack of a large certified bilingual staff need not be obstacles to providing quality instruction for all children in a bilingual education program.

The self-described helplessness of some school districts in coping with heterogeneous language groupings of children is more of an admission of general educational inadequacies than a problem of bilingual education, although a relationship has been observed between the conservative provincialism of racist school systems and the conservative provincialism of their instructional programs.

With minimal effort and a minimum of cost school districts can offer a third option to the two dysfunctional alternatives, segregation with bilingual education or integration without, which perpetuate the denial of educational opportunities to non-English-speaking children.

NOTES

1. *United States v. Texas*, 342 F. Supp. 24 (E.D.Tex. 1971), affirmed 447 F.2d. 441 (5th Cir. 1971), 466 F.2d. 518 (5th Cir. 1972).
2. *Keyes v. School District No.1*, 380 F. Supp. 673 (D. Colo. 1974).
3. *Lau v. Nichols*, 414 U.S. 563 (1974).
4. *Serna v. Portales Municipal Schools*, 351 F. Supp. 1279 (D.N.M., 1972).
5. In *San Antonio Independent School District v. Rodriguez* the United States Supreme Court rejected a claim that the Texas school financing scheme was inconsistent with federal constitutional provisions. 93 S. Ct. 1278 (1973).

BILINGUAL EDUCATION LITIGATION

PREFACE

You can lead a horse to water, but you cannot make him drink. The truth of this adage was evident in the implementation of bilingual education programs in Texas and in other states.

The court case *Lau v. Nichols* resulted in a unanimous decision by the U.S. Supreme Court that the failure of the schools to respond to the language characteristics of limited English proficient children was a denial of equal educational opportunity (*Lau v. Nichols*, 1973). The court's decision was followed in 1975 by a Department of Health, Education and Welfare memorandum detailing guidelines to be followed for determining the language characteristics of students and prescribing educational responses consistent with these characteristics (Office for Civil Rights, 1970).

Schools in Texas, and generally throughout the country, dragged their feet and did little for language minority children. The initial enthusiasm for bilingual education programs had waned, and schools did not perceive language minority children as valuable enough to warrant the development, implementation and financing of special programs. The common scholastic attitude was the same position rejected by the Supreme Court in Lau, namely, that the schools offer all students the same materials, the same methodologies, the same teachers. If these are not appropriate for some students, it is the responsibility of the students and their parents to adjust to the common educational program, rather than for the schools to adjust to the unique characteristics of children.

This attitude is perceived by minorities as a racist policy, since schools have long adapted to some characteristics of children, such as special education programs for mental and physical handicaps, including mental retardation, orthopedic conditions, blindness, deafness and many others. The racist connotation comes from the willingness of the school to adapt to unique characteristics within mainstream racial and ethnic lines and its unwillingness to adapt to characteristics which are unique to minority cultures.

The lack of interest of the Texas educational and political leadership in providing bilingual and English as a second language programs for language minority children led us to file suit in the federal courts. Professor Mark Yudof from the University of Texas Law School recommended that legal action be taken through the existing *United States v. Texas* court case in which the court still maintained jurisdiction, rather than initiating a new case (*United States v. Texas*, 1971). The Mexican-American Legal Defense and Education Fund (MALDEF) presented the case in the Eastern District of Texas.

In 1981, Judge William Wayne Justice ruled favorably in this case, prescribing guidelines for bilingual education programs for Texas children. That same year, and subsequent to the court order, the Texas Legislature enacted a bilingual education law which paralleled Judge Justice's ruling and prescribed remedy. The ruling was overturned by the Fifth Circuit Court of Appeals and sent back to the district court for additional hearings. No further action was taken by the plaintiffs since most of the original court ordered remedies were included in the Texas legislation.

This litigation is part of a classic example of advocacy through various interrelated efforts. The bilingual education court case led to the convening of an administrative Task Force on Bilingual Education charged with the task of providing recommendations to the Texas Legislature. The Task Force came up with recommendations which paralleled the court findings, and the legislation enacted provided most of the remedies prescribed by the court. The same tractiveness which precludes educational and political bodies from making changes, exerts the same influence once change has been made. In spite of the Fifth Circuit reversal of the lower court's order, no substantial changes have been made in the legislation enacted as a result of the initial court order, in spite of its subsequent reversal.

During the entire period of court, administrative and legislative action, IDRA staff were extensively involved in all three efforts. The similarities among the court order, the task force recommendations and the legislation is not due to coincidence. IDRA staff conceptualized, wrote and recommended major portions of all three.

The decision made by Mark Yudof, MALDEF and me to initiate this court case was partly based on the need for school finance reform. Since the Supreme Court decision in *Rodriguez v. San Antonio ISD* eliminated the possibility of litigation providing relief from the fiscal inequities in the Texas system, we decided to attempt to obtain increased funding through the use of proxies (*San Antonio Independent School District v. Rodriguez*, 1973). In this case funds for bilingual education, not addressed in the state funding system, would provide additional funds for language minority children. We intended for this litigation to be followed by similar cases on behalf of economically disadvantaged students, migrants, immigrants, etc.; so that in time the state system of school finance would provide sufficient funds for the extensive special populations commonly found in low wealth school districts.

Considering that the first of what would have been a long series of federal court suits was undecided and still pending ten years later, the strategy was abandoned in favor of a much more feasible alternative, a direct challenge of the system of school finance in a state court.

STRUGGLE FOR BILINGUAL EDUCATION ENTERS COURTS

1975

The American G.I. Forum and the League of United Latin American Citizens (LULAC) on June 4th filed a motion to enforce decree and for supplemental relief in *U.S. v Texas*. The original suit ordered the Texas Education Agency to take appropriate steps to compel local school districts to desegregate their schools.

U.S. v Texas was brought by the United States Department of Justice against the State of Texas, the Texas Education Agency (TEA), and the Texas Commissioner of Education. As part of the court order by Federal District Court Judge Wayne Justice of Tyler, Texas in 1971, the state was ordered to provide bilingual/ bicultural programs to Mexican-American school children.

Subsequently, the motion of the American G.I. Forum and LULAC to intervene in the suit was granted, and those organizations were certified "for all purposes as representatives of all persons of Mexican-American descent or nationality in the State of Texas." In particular, they represent hundreds of thousands of parents of Chicano youngsters who have been denied an equal educational opportunity in violation of the Constitution and laws of the United States. (*United States v. Texas*, 1971)

According to Professor Mark Yudof and Albert Kauffman, attorneys for LULAC and G.I. Forum, bilingual education in Texas today is a tragic hoax. One of the more than 626,000 Spanish language youngsters in need of bilingual/bicultural education, a mere 26,000, or less than 4 percent, are served by state funded bilingual programs. Of the remaining 600,000, approximately 100,000 are served by federally sponsored bilingual programs. The attorneys added that roughly 500,000 Chicano school children receive no bilingual/bicultural education. Inevitably, this failure poses severe problems in terms of psychological, cultural, linguistic, and social barriers which impede the progress of Spanish language public elementary and secondary school students.

Little legislative aid is anticipated for Spanish language youngsters in Texas since under the new school financing law enacted during the last legislative session, minimal bilingual education is contemplated beyond the third grade in future years. Indeed, it will not be until 1977–78 that third graders will be served.

The motion alleges that only $2.7 million were allocated under the original 1973 Bilingual Act, and by the time administrative and in-service training costs were deducted, only $15 per participating pupil remained for the operating costs of the program. In addition, virtually a third of all so-called bilingual teachers are in fact monolingual, having qualified for the position on the basis of a brief summer institute.

At least twenty-seven districts in Texas which are eligible for assistance under the Texas Bilingual Education Act have failed even to apply for those funds. Fifty-nine districts are under investigation by the Office of Civil Rights for failure to implement legally required bilingual programs.

"The State isn't living up to its obligation. The failure of TEA to take affirmative steps to monitor and implement bilingual/bicultural education programs is apparent," according to Mark Yudof, the University of Texas law professor who served as co-counsel in the *Rodriguez* school finance case. "This stands in sharp contrast to the duties imposed upon it by the Fourteenth Amendment, the Federal Equal Educational Opportunities Act of 1974, Title VI of the Civil Rights Act of 1964, and the recent Supreme Court decision in *Lau v Nichols*," Yudof continued (*Lau v. Nichols*, 1973).

In the *Lau* case, the court unanimously held that the San Francisco school system violated the U.S. Civil Rights Act for failing to insure that all Chinese students with limited English-speaking ability got special attention to overcome the language barrier to effective learning. (Of the 16,000 Chinese youngsters who understood English poorly, less than half were involved in bilingual programs.)

The G.I. Forum and LULAC, through the Motion, have requested that the Court order the Texas Education Agency to:

1. enforce and secure compliance with the Court's Order of July 13, 1971 (Civil Action 5281), which required TEA to ensure an equal educational opportunity for every student in the elementary and secondary public schools of Texas regardless of race, color or national origin;
2. implement, in those districts with 20 or more Spanish language and/or limited English-speaking ability (LESA) students in any one grade, the Court's Order of December 6, 1971, which requires a comprehensive bilingual/bicultural program to include the areas of professional staffing, curriculum, student personnel services, and parent-community involvement;
3. identify all Spanish language and LESA students in Texas by August 1, 1975;
4. assure that all students identified participate in bilingual/bicultural programs in accordance with previous Orders of the Court and the Constitution and laws of the United States; and
5. insure that compensatory services are provided to Spanish language and LESA students to overcome the effects of any denial of bilingual/bicultural education after July 13, 1971.

Plaintiffs in this Motion to reopen *U.S. v Texas* are represented by the Mexican-American Legal Defense and Educational Fund, the Lawyer's Committee for Civil Rights Under Law, the Harvard Center for Law and Education, and Texas Rural Legal Aid. IDRA is serving as educational research consultants for the plaintiffs.

(IDRA, June 1975)

U.S. v. TEXAS IN A HISTORICAL CONTEXT

1981

There are few issues in Texas today which are receiving as much media coverage and administrative, legislative, and judicial attention as the controversy over the federal court decision in *U.S. v. Texas* (*United States v. Texas*, 1971). In the Federal Court for the Eastern District of Texas, Tyler, Texas, Judge William Wayne Justice issued a court order requiring the state of Texas to implement a bilingual education program for all Mexican-American children of limited English-speaking ability. Reactions in the state have varied from applause for the court order to demands for the impeachment of Judge Justice. Reactions have been observed in the Texas Legislature, the Texas Education Agency, the Attorney General's Office and certainly in many of the 100 school districts in the state of Texas. Articles have been written in newspapers and magazines, and news coverage has been provided by radio and television.

It is unfortunate that most of the reaction and almost all of the media coverage has been characterized by limited familiarity with the court case, erroneous assumptions and emotional reactions rather than knowledgeable information on the history and content of the litigation. Almost without exception, media coverage of the opinion of the federal court begins with page 63 of the January 1981 court order and overlooks 62 legal-size pages of legislative history and court findings.

It is difficult to reconcile the court's involvement in the prescription of educational methodology to Texas school districts and the State Education Agency unless one understands the historical context of the Mexican-American educational experience in Texas. During the *U.S. v. Texas* litigation, the Mexican-American Legal Defense and Education Fund (MALDEF), while serving as attorneys for the plaintiffs, presented to the court a series of statements which consist primarily of assertions of: (1) discriminatory treatment of Mexican-American children, (2) problems identified in the education of these children, (3) irregularities in the operation of instructional programs for Mexican-American children, and (4) violations of state laws and regulations related to their education in specified school districts at specified times. Much of the information documenting some 1000 irregularities was obtained by the plaintiffs from the files of the Texas Education Agency. In presenting a defense in this court case, the state of Texas agreed to the veracity of these statements and objected to only twenty-nine of the items. A random analysis of these items to which the state of Texas agreed portrays a dismal picture of educational conditions for Mexican-American children in the Texas educational system. [See a selection of stipulations at the end of the article.]

Despite the concern of education leaders regarding educational opportunities in the state of Texas, and pioneering efforts in the implementation of innovative and responsive programs for Mexican-American children, the state of the art is generally so lacking and the performance of some schools leaves so much to be desired that there is ample justification for an extensive catalytic action to bring about a marked improvement in educational practice. On the basis of the evidence presented in the trial the Court concludes that: *the policy of using English exclusively in the Texas public schools must be seen, not as neutral or benign, but rather as one more vehicle to maintain these children in an inferior position.*

This is an astounding statement, and one may be prompted to voice a strong denial or protest. Before such a denial or protest is issued, however, the person so prompted should read the many stipulations to which the state of Texas agreed.

During the past few months it has been obvious that most of the critics and protesters have read little if any of the various aspects of the trial. Most of their information is based on newspaper, radio, and television coverage of the court case. Unfortunately, the media has been irresponsible in preparing this material which has resulted in extremely shallow reporting, mostly concerned with the contents of the court order but without any effort to relate the court order to findings of fact, evidence and testimony presented in the case, or the stipulations on educational inadequacy.

The Court also states,

> . . . it is a fact that Mexican-Americans in Texas have been subjected to de jure discrimination by the defendants, the state of Texas and the Texas Education Agency, in violation of the Equal Protection Clause of the 14th Amendment.

Again it is recommended that sixty-two pages of court findings be reviewed before an objection is voiced regarding the statement of the Court.

> The state of Texas agreed in the trial that, "The use of an all-English ethnocentric curricula which limited English-speaking ability children have been taught by monolingual English-speaking teachers and English textbooks has resulted in low achievement, frustration and humiliation for Mexican-American children," The state of Texas acknowledges that " . . . negative stereotyping and racial isolation are forms of discrimination which still affect the educational experience of Mexican-American students and contribute to their low achievement."

The Court further states,

> That the defendants' unconstitutional practices have contributed substantially to the special learning problems encountered by Mexican-American children and that vestiges of that past discrimination remain producing deleterious results today, is uncontested. Defendants have conceded the direct, causal relationship between their past actions and current conditions in the Texas public school system. In particular, the defendants' treatment of these children as inferiors, prohibited from using their native language within the schools, was an act of purposeful discrimination with profound consequences. In effect, defendants' past conduct created a learning disability which will continue to impede Mexican-American children until it is completely eradicated."

Criticisms of the court decision and the extensive but inadequate media coverage have focused on three basic issues: bilingual education as an instructional approach, implementation of programs beyond the third grade, and the availability of resources.

BILINGUAL EDUCATION

The first issue concerns the Court's selection of bilingual education as a feasible response to the problems of providing an education to children of limited English proficiency. The Court's position is indicative of its acceptance of the basic thesis of bilingual education, which maintains that it is desirable to provide understandable instruction to children whose English proficiency precludes the acquisition of basic skills and content materials in English. Prior to the selection of bilingual education as an instructional approach, large numbers of children participated in English language instructional activities with deplorable results. The use of the sink-or-swim approach, which constituted total immersion in English language activities with the amount of instructional success dependent upon how quickly a child developed proficiency in English, led to deplorable performance on the part of children and astronomical failure with accompanying underachievement and school dropouts. It has been estimated that as many as 80 percent of all Mexican-American children in Texas failed to swim and drowned in the public schools. The introduction of structured English as a second language (ESL) programs in the late 1950s and throughout the decade of the 1960s was perhaps an improvement for the children. Nonetheless, all cognitive development, acquisition of basic skills such as reading and arithmetic, and development in the content areas was temporarily halted as the child mastered a new language. During these years, virtually all of the Mexican-American population in Texas went through a built-in academic retardation program which assured that they would experience educational frustration and grade retention while the opportunity to master academic subjects was delayed as English language is being learned. The Court notes this in the order when it states,

> The principle criticism of ESL as a substitute for bilingual instruction is its failure to provide students speaking foreign languages with meaningful education in cognitive subject areas until after they have learned sufficient English to participate in their regular classes. While a student enrolled in ESL is likely to benefit substantially during the time special English instruction is being provided, the remainder of the school day, spent without comprehension in English-only classes, may be largely wasted. By the time a student's proficiency in English has improved sufficiently to allow meaningful participation in regular classes, he has fallen far behind his peers" (p. 23).

The advent of bilingual education in the late 1960s and through the 1970s allowed a student continuous development and academic success in his native language until such time as English could be acquired as a second language and a transition could be made into the English language instruction. The rationale of bilingual instruction is educationally sound, although there may be extensive controversy as to its effectiveness. The Court notes, however, that, "Defendants have failed to demonstrate that any alternative medium of instruction would be equally effective."

It is interesting and ironic to note that one of the criticisms being heard about bilingual education is the excessive cost. The $40 per pupil per year currently being expended and the $150 per pupil per year being proposed is considered by critics to be a prohibitive price for the enhanced academic success of children of limited English-speaking abilities. Yet in the absence of bilingual education, the English as a second language approach (with its accompanying built-in retention) costs $1800 per pupil per year the first year and a similar amount for each retention thereafter. It appears that critics of the cost of bilingual education are extremely penny-wise and pound-foolish.

Essentially, the state never argued that bilingual education was educationally unsound or proposed any other methodology as a better alternative.

KINDERGARTEN THROUGH TWELVE COVERAGE REQUIRED

The second issue given extensive coverage is the specification of a bilingual education plan for kindergarten through grade twelve. Critics of the court decision, such as Governor Clements and others throughout Texas, state that because children should be able to master English in a few years, bilingual programs are unnecessary beyond the third grade. The Court notes that the incidence of limited English proficiency is not limited to the early years, but occurs at all grade levels. Testimony presented in the trial indicates that half of the estimated 400,000 limited English proficient children in the state of Texas are in kindergarten through third grades , approximately one quarter or 100,000 are found in grades four through six, and approximately 100,000 are found in grades seven through twelve. Therefore, a program limited to kindergarten through third grade would fail to provide any relief for 200,000 children in the state of Texas. Therefore, until existing conditions are remedied, the Court finds it necessary to address the problem where it exists at all grade levels.
The Court notes:

> But the extensive expert testimony offered at trial demonstrated that bilingual education must be provided for children unable to learn in English, until each child is capable of making the transition to a regular, English language classroom, if learning disabilities borne out of pervasive historical discrimination are ever to be overcome. Dr. Cazden observed: "It is essential that a full plan be available K through twelve for those children who need it." TR 162. Dr. Angel Gonzales, Director of Bilingual Education for the Dallas Independent School District, agreed, TR 275-76, as did Dr. Mary Galvan, Member of a TEA Bilingual Task Force. TR 697. James Lehmann, Superintendent of Schools for the Eagle Pass Independent School District, testified to a tremendous need for bilingual education grades seven through twelve. TR 402. None of this testimony was contradicted or refuted.

AVAILABILITY OF RESOURCES

The third issue is the availability of resources for the implementation of a bilingual education program. Media coverage of the court decision typically presents a school administrator expressing concern over the unavailability of teachers for the provision of services to 400,000 children. The court notes the lack of available teachers to meet such a need. On the basis of testimony presented at the trial, the Court concludes that the state and its school systems have not only failed to meet this need, but are responsible for the limitations on available resources. Certainly the legislative cutbacks in the amount of money available for the development of bilingual education programs have contributed to the unavailability of resources today. The Court notes that evidence presented at the trial indicates that discriminatory employment practices of certain school districts account for the shortage of Spanish language proficiency among instructors.

Yet the Court shows great patience in allowing for a six year phase-in period, as recommended by the plaintiffs, during which time the state may plan, develop and implement programs for the development of resources as bilingual programs are being implemented. The court also provides for some interim measures in order to meet existing needs. The Court's recommendation that the Texas Education Agency provide emergency certification until such time as competent personnel are available is indicative of the sensitivity of the Court to this problem.

Needless to say, there are today and will be in the future many other concerns, issues, and criticisms of the Court's action in *U.S. v. Texas*. It is not expected nor detrimental that such issues, concerns and criticisms be expressed through official channels or through the public media. It is assumed, however, that reaction and criticism will be presented within the historical context of the court case and related to evidence presented in the case, rather than be magnified by irresponsible criticisms made by individuals ignorant of the circumstances leading to the court decision.

SELECTED STIPULATIONS FROM *U.S. v. TEXAS*

The state of Texas and MALDEF agreed to over 1,000 stipulations during the *U.S. v. Texas* litigation, a brief selection of which follows. Stipulations are numbered as they appear in the court pleading.

3. Mexican-American students in Texas are achieving less in the public schools than their Anglo counterparts.

8. Linguistic differences as well as negative stereotypes transmitted by Anglo teachers and students to Mexican- American students contribute to low Mexican-American academic performance.

10. Hispanic students made up approximately 50 percent of the students participating in compensatory education programs during the 1976–77 regular school term.

11. Reading achievement for all students in compensatory education programs indicates that 50 percent of students participating gained less than a month for each month of instruction; and more than 25 percent of the students participating in grades 9–12 gained nothing or lost ground during their participation in said programs.

26. In 1976, the Laredo ISD pointed out that a high percentage of its Spanish dominant students . . . perform at 20–25 percent of their potential.

341. There are fewer total bilingual programs in the state of Texas for school year 1977–78, than there were for the school year 1975–76.

504. In 1974–75, a state survey revealed that 24 percent of the teachers in ESEA Title VII (federal bilingual) programs in Texas were monolingual, English speakers.

505. In 1974–75 a state survey revealed that 32 percent of the teachers teaching in state bilingual programs in Texas were monolingual English speakers.

511. According to the TEA, there are many bilingual teachers in the schools who lack adequate training in the bilingual education concept and, therefore, find it very difficult to implement bilingual programs in their classes.

726. Dropout rates among Mexican-American high school students approached 100 percent until about 1950, and 1/5 of the migrant children never attended school despite compulsory attendance laws.

908. The dropout rate for Mexican-Americans in Texas has decreased where bilingual programs have been properly implemented.

(IDRA, May 1981)

FIFTH CIRCUIT RULES IN *U.S. v. TEXAS*

1982

On the day following the wire service news that the Fifth Circuit Court of Appeals had issued a ruling in *U.S. v. Texas,* a TV reporter came in to tape an interview. The reporter wanted plaintiff reactions to the Fifth Circuit's reversal of Judge William Wayne Justice's ruling on the celebrated bilingual education case *(United States v. Texas, 1971).*

Being hesitant to voice opinions on the Fifth Circuit decision without an opportunity to review it, I was assured by the TV reporter that a copy of the decision was available to them. A few minutes later the reporter came in to my office and started to set up the camera, lights, and sound equipment. When I requested the copy of the decision in order to read it while the equipment was being readied, I was handed a copy of that day's edition of the local paper.

Unfortunately, not one single news article of the dozens in the media that week—on TV, on radio, and in the newspapers—was based on an analysis of the decision. Without exception, coverage was based on a brief synopsis provided by the wire services.

The following analysis is provided to our readers who have been requesting better information than that which is available in the sensationalistic, but limited (and frequently erroneous), coverage in the public media.

SYNOPSIS OF *U.S. v. TEXAS*

On January 9, 1981, Judge William Wayne Justice of the Federal Eastern District of Texas in Tyler issued a ruling on *U.S. v. Texas.* The case, filed by Mexican-American plaintiffs represented by LULAC, the G.I. Forum, and thirty-five individual students, challenged the adequacy of the state of Texas' efforts to respond to the needs of children of limited English proficiency.

After reviewing the evidence and testimony presented in the case by all parties, the judge concluded that Mexican-American children had been subjected to discrimination by the defendants, the state of Texas, and the Texas Education Agency, in violation of the Equal Protection Clause of the Fourteenth Amendment of the federal Constitution. The court also found violations of the Civil Rights Act of 1964 and the Equal Educational Opportunities Act of 1974.

The court in Tyler, Texas then ordered a remedy consisting of an extensive plan for the implementation of bilingual programs. The plan includes availability of program coverage for all grades, a uniform process for the identification of limited English proficient-students, uniform exit criteria, and reform of Texas Education Agency monitoring and enforcement.

THE APPELLATE COURT

Following the court order in January 1981, the Texas Education Agency and the state of Texas appealed the judge's decision to the Fifth Circuit Court of Appeals in New Orleans. In

July 1982, the Fifth Circuit issued an opinion reversing the lower court's findings and remanding (returning to a lower court) the case to Tyler for retrial.

Reviewing the text of the Fifth Circuit's decision, it appears that the reversal was not based on the merits of bilingual education or the findings at trial, but rather on a series of technical issues. The following issues are discussed in the opinion, with the first one receiving the most attention from the appellate court:

1. *Stipulations*—At trial the state of Texas, represented by the Assistant Attorney General, agreed to a large number of stipulations (an agreement that parties will not contest the truth of a factual statement) presented by the plaintiffs. The stipulations consist of more than 400 statements which admit to the statewide historical discrimination of Mexican-American children in Texas schools. Subsequent to the admission of the stipulations at trial, the state requested that they be withdrawn on the basis that the Assistant Attorney General representing the defendants had agreed to them in error and without consultation with the State Attorney General's office or the Texas Education Agency. The motion to withdraw the stipulations was denied by the Tyler court.
2. *Constitutional issues*—Prior to the hearings in *U.S. v. Texas* it had been agreed that the case would be heard on the basis of statutory issues and not constitutional issues. However, at trial, all parties argued constitutional issues, submitted evidence, and filed legal briefs addressing the constitutional violations. On appeal, the state argued that the District Court should not have ruled on the constitutional issues.
3. *District participation*—It was argued by the defendants during the appeal in New Orleans that school districts impacted by the Tyler court orders should have participated in the trial.
4. *Senate Bill 477*—Following Judge Justice's ruling in *U.S. v. Texas,* the state legislature enacted a new law, Senate Bill 477, which revised criteria for the establishment of a bilingual education program for children of limited English proficiency in Texas. Although differing from the court ordered plan, especially at the secondary level, the new law did expand specifications for bilingual education programs in Texas. The new law was much more extensive than the old law, but suffered from two major weaknesses—it placed too much responsibility on the State Board of Education to develop specific regulations and it was grossly underfunded, allowing only $50.00 per child per year for the implementation of the bilingual program.

To summarize, the state of Texas requested that the district court cancel its order on the basis of the new law, making the court order unnecessary. The court's denial of this request was appealed to the higher court.

THE REVERSAL

The Fifth Circuit Court of Appeals found in favor of the defendants, reversed the court order, and sent it back to the district court in Tyler for retrial. As stated previously, the reversal was based on technical questions.

The lower court erred in not withdrawing the stipulations since the Attorney General alleged that: (1) their approval went beyond the authority of the Assistant Attorney General, (2) they were entered into without the consent of the Texas Education Agency, and (3) they were too conclusory to warrant a factual determination of historical discrimination. The Court of Appeals stated that the federal judge should have permitted the state to submit evidence on the above allegations. The case was sent back to Judge Justice for further evidence on the subject matter covered by the stipulations.

The Court erred in its failure to reconsider its court order in light of the 1981 Bilingual Education Act. Therefore, the Court returned the case for further evidence on the adequacy of the 1981 legislation. Additionally, if a remedy in excess of the Bilingual Act is required, local districts must be heard.

These points led to the reversal of the District Court's order and required that the case be retried. One must note that the reversible errors were based on technicalities in the trial and did not really address the substance of the case. Although some of the language used by the Court of Appeals was not too clear, it appears that there was extensive support for the issues decided by the lower court. The following paragraph is a word-by-word transcription of the Fifth Circuit's review of the bilingual case and its findings:

> At trial, plaintiffs' experts presented abundant testimony supportive of the court's finding that the 1973 Texas bilingual program was pedagogically unsound, largely unimplemented, and unproductive in its results. Plaintiffs' experts testified that one hour of intensive English per day for grades four through twelve was not adequate, that the first educational experience of these children had to be bilingual, and that the state's overall proficiency score of 23 percent on a written standardized test did not justify entry into a normal classroom. The evidence was even more overwhelming concerning the TEA's lack of implementation of the existing, under-funded program. Despite evidence that bilingual programs were not actually bilingual in many school districts, sanctions were not being imposed. In fact, the state apparently lacked an adequate monitoring instrument, and limited English-speaking students were not being adequately identified.
>
> To counter these allegations, the state put on only one witness. Undoubtedly there was adequate evidentiary support for a conclusion that in some areas local programs for remedying the educational handicaps of limited English-speaking students were deficient.

AFTERMATH

On the basis of the supportive language quoted above, presentation from the LULAC and G.I. Forum, their attorneys and technical advisers met and decided to retry the case in the Eastern District of Texas. Contrary to media reports, *U.S. v. Texas* is not dead; it is very much alive and undoubtedly will be impacting on bilingual education policy for many more years to come.

(IDRA, August 1982)

LEGAL BASIS OF BILINGUAL EDUCATION

PREFACE

During the 1970s there were many court cases dealing with educational opportunity for language minority children. Prior to education of limited English proficient children becoming a legal issue in *U.S. v. Texas*, a similar court case, *Lau v. Nichols*, had succeeded in California. Both court cases, as well as dozens of others, were based on the indifference of school systems to the language characteristics of minority children (*United States v. Texas*, 1971; *Lau v. Nichols*, 1973).

Edward Steinman, attorney for the plaintiffs in *Lau*, represented some 1,800 Chinese American children in the San Francisco schools who had limited proficiency in English and were receiving no special program in the schools. Although the San Francisco Unified School District did have a number of programs for non-English speaking-students, including a bilingual education program, the implementation of these programs was on a hit-or-miss basis, with some children participating in a program where available, others participating in more than one program, and at least 1,800 Chinese children not participating in any program.

The San Francisco schools argued in court that although they operated several programs responsive to the language characteristics of children, they had no legal obligation to do so. They maintained that the children not participating in any special program were being treated equitably since they were receiving the same instruction by the same teachers as that which was being afforded English speaking children.

For me, *Lau* became a test of The Theory on Incompatibilities which Dr. Blandina "Bambi" Cárdenas and I had conceptualized in 1968. One principle in this theory was that of adaptability. We had argued that when the characteristics of students were incompatible with the characteristics of the instructional program, it was incumbent upon the school to modify materials and methodology to be compatible with student characteristics, rather than to expect students to modify their characteristics in keeping with a standard instructional program. Both Bambi and I served as consultants to the Civil Rights Division of the Department of Justice in preparing a brief which J. Stanley Pottinger presented to the Supreme Court in behalf of the plaintiffs.

The San Francisco schools freely admitted the English language limitation of the Chinese children involved in the lawsuit, but they argued that it was the responsibility of the parents to teach them English. The court noted that most of the parents of the children in question did not speak English and their interest in the children learning the language was one of the prime reasons for sending them to school.

The decision of the lower courts was appealed to the Supreme Court which in 1974, decided unanimously in favor of the Chinese children. Although proponents of bilingual education saw this ruling as a clear cut victory for bilingual education, the Supreme Court did not prescribe a specific methodology, but required that some kind of a special language program be provided limited English-proficient children by the schools. For me, the Supreme Court decision was a victory in upholding the principle of adaptability in our Theory of Incompatibilities.

The *Lau* decision was followed by the establishment of a Lau Task Force by the Office of Civil Rights in the Department of Health, Education and Welfare to develop guidelines for schools to follow in complying with the *Lau* decision. I was appointed a member of this task force as one of the leading advocates of bilingual education in the country. Dr. Edward deAvila, a pioneer in bilingual language testing, was also a member of the group.

The resulting guidelines, the Lau Remedies as outlined in this article, were distributed by the Office of Civil Rights to all state education agencies and were considered national policy. The various regional offices of the federal agencies were assigned responsibility for school compliance with the provisions of the Lau Remedies. Desegregation assistance centers for national origin minority students were given the responsibility for providing technical assistance to school districts in the implementation of the guidelines.

The Lau Remedies immediately became controversial and politicized. School districts opposed the guidelines along some, or all, of three arguments. First, there was an immediate outcry that the federal government was imposing a prescribed curriculum for schools, in spite of education having been consistently upheld by the courts as a function of the individual states. Second, the schools objected to the erosion of local control. School systems have consistently argued that they know best what's good for the child, regardless of the level of performance of the students. Third, the schools argued that the prescribed Lau Remedies required too much effort on the part of the school system. Implied in this argument was the assumption that the target population—language minority children—was not worth the resources required for meeting the Lau guidelines.

Many school systems simply went through the motions and made only token efforts to meet the federal requirements. I was the main witness in an administrative hearing held in Bakersfield, California, where the school system was charged with Lau non-compliance. Officials of the school district testified that the low number of language minority children in bilingual classes was due to most of the students being able to pass an English language proficiency test.

A copy of the test developed by the school system was presented as evidence. If the language minority student could respond to at least three of the items, the student was deemed having sufficient mastery of the English language for placement in an all-English instructional program.

The test included three items which I felt were not indicative of a high level of English language proficiency. One item was telling the student to "sit down." Another item consisted of the command, "Come here." A third item was, "Bring me the pencil." Student compliance with these three requests indicated successful performance on the test and excluded them from participation in a bilingual or any other special language development program.

When asked by the plaintiff attorneys to give my professional opinion on the appropriateness of the test, I testified under oath that I had a dog that could perform all three tasks and therefore in keeping with the Bakersfield language policy required no further language development for placement in the regular instructional program. Under cross examination I was asked in which language could I get the dog to perform the tasks, to which I replied, "In either English or Spanish. My dog is bilingual!"

At the beginning of the Reagan administration the Department of Education rescinded the Lau Remedies, leaving only a brief memorandum previously issued by J. Stanley

Pottinger, a former director of the Office of Civil Rights, on May 25, 1970 as the only federal guidelines for schools to follow in responding to the language characteristics of children.

The absence of the Lau compliance guidelines is very noticeable in the latest, and most nebulous, federal effort in education, the goals developed by the National Education Goals Panel (National Education Goals Report, 1991). The panel established as an educational goal that "By the year 2000, all children in America will start school ready to learn." This goal seems odd considering that every child psychologist in the country is in agreement that all children in America are ready to learn at birth. What is implied in the goal is that by the year 2000 all children in America will start school ready to learn "in the manner in which the school chooses to teach them."

This goal, which places the responsibility for English language mastery by language minority children outside of the school, is most inconsistent with the *Lau* decision which ruled that it is the responsibility of the school to address the language characteristic, as well as all other characteristics of children. Most parents of language minority children do not have any more capability in developing English language skills today, than they had during the *Lau v. Nichols* court case.

The small numbers of language minority children now participating in special language responsive programs indicate extensive lack of compliance with the federal courts' decisions in *Lau*. Schools may know what is best for children, but ignoring the language needs of a large portion of the school population does not indicate that schools do what is best for children.

(IDRA, May 1976)

LAU REMEDIES OUTLINED

1976

In 1975, the Department of Health, Education and Welfare (HEW) issued a memorandum specifying remedies available to school districts for the elimination of past educational practices ruled unlawful under *Lau v Nichols* (*Lau v. Nichols*, 1973).

The effect of this memorandum is that a large number of school districts are in the process of developing plans to submit to HEW on approaches the districts will take in meeting the educational needs of children of limited English-speaking ability (LESA).

Since the *Lau* Remedies were developed for a variety of school situations affecting some 15 million children in most of the fifty states, ethnic groups speaking a variety of languages, and school district enrollments ranging in size from dozens to thousands and constituting from one to ninety-nine percent of the student population, it is understandable that there exists some confusion in the interpretation and implementation of the guidelines.

The understanding of two principles is important if school districts are to develop comprehensive plans responsive to the *Lau* remedies in ways which both adhere to the spirit of the *Lau* decision and allow the school district to develop coherent educational programs for all students.

First, it should be understood that the remedies are minimal and that they have been drawn to adhere to the narrowest legal interpretation of *Lau v. Nichols* on the basis of the most promising current knowledge and thought relating to the education of children of limited English-speaking ability. Thus, while a bilingual multicultural program for all children in a particular area may be best from a pedagogical perspective and most efficient from an administrative perspective, these cannot be required from a legal perspective given the Court's most current ruling on the education of LESA children.

Second, it is important to bear in mind that comprehensive planning to remove past inequities between groups of students is a major effort that requires a realistic assessment of available resources including time, staff, money, space, and curriculum, and the systematic acquisition, redirection, adaptation and utilization of these to meet the new objectives. Thus a comprehensive educational plan may be unacceptable to HEW's Office of Civil Rights (OCR) when it projects unrealistic time-outcome expectations which may in fact be little more than lip service to the requirements of *Lau*. By the same token a school district can establish realistic projects for time-outcome expectations relative to *Lau* giving an indication of an intent to aggressively and systematically pursue the appropriate resources. The *Lau* Remedies require a plan, not a magic trick.

The HEW-OCR has scheduled an extensive number of meetings with school personnel for *Lau* Remedy interpretation, and Office of Education sponsored technical assistance centers (GAC-Type B) have been established to provide assistance to school districts in the implementation of remedies which respond to the *Lau* decision.

In spite of efforts to facilitate the implementation of *Lau* Remedies, some confusion still exists as to the minimum requirements of school districts.

The following processes present the basic requirements of the *Lau* Remedies. Although not an official HEW interpretation, this simplified version based on educational administrative experience is practical, readily understood, and dispels the alarm, confusion and myths surrounding *Lau* Remedies. Furthermore, a plan which provides for meeting the basic requirements outlined should be readily acceptable to HEW as meeting the guidelines stipulated in the *Lau* Remedies.

The development of a compliance plan calls for four phases: student identification; student language assessment; analysis of achievement data; and, program offerings. Additional requirements center on secondary education, staffing, student placement, parent communication, curricular and co-curricular offerings and reporting and evaluation requirements.

Although adherence to a narrow legal interpretation of *Lau v Nichols* has led to the formulation of what appear to be a complex conglomerate of specific requirements, the remedies simply require:

a) that schools systematically and validly ascertain which of their clients are linguistically different;

b) that schools systematically and validly ascertain the language characteristics of their clients;

c) that schools systematically ascertain the achievement characteristics of their clients; and

d) that schools match an instructional program to the characteristics as ascertained.

PHASE I—POTENTIAL STUDENT IDENTIFICATION

The screening process is initiated by the identification of a potential student population. These are students who may be target students as recipients of *Lau* Remedies, although the vast majority may not be affected.

Lau Remedies require three criteria for potential student identification: 1) first language acquired by the student, 2) the language most often spoken in the student's home, and 3) the language most often spoken by the student.

If the answer to all three is "English," the student is not a target student and requires no further *Lau* treatment.

If the answer to any of these three questions is a language other than English, the student is identified as a potential target student, although whether *Lau* treatment is required or the type of treatment to be offered is dependent on further analysis.

School personnel have expressed concern over the method to be used for the identification of potential target students. *Lau* Remedy guidelines are not specific on this question other than insisting on the obviously imperative condition that the assessor have competency in the language or languages to be assessed, and that judgements which are to determine placement be validated through subsequent observation.

In very large school districts with large percentages of minority children this student identification phase may require extensive resources from the district, but a need for such resources may be kept to a minimum by utilizing parental assistance.

IDRA has developed a *Community Language Survey* form intended to be sent home with the children. Parents are asked to indicate the responses to the three questions dealing with first acquired language, language most often spoken in the home, and language most often spoken by the child. Responses given by parents can be expected to be fairly valid, although as stated previously some validation should be conducted since some parents have been known to fear school reprisals for allowing their children to speak a language other than English and project this concern in their responses.

Parental fears may be assuaged through the utilization of professional and/or paraprofessional personnel who, (a) speak the predominant language of the community, (b) reside in the community and/or are known to parents in the community, and (c) can effectively communicate with parents the district's objectives in securing the information.

PHASE II—STUDENT LANGUAGE ASSESSMENT

It follows that regardless of a student's first acquired language, language spoken at home, or in a social setting the type of program best suited for the student is one which is compatible with his language characteristics. Although a student may have spoken Spanish before learning English, if he no longer speaks Spanish placing him in an education program in which basic skills are taught exclusively in Spanish is obviously questionable. Placing him in a linguistically heterogenous bilingual program where the child's dominant language is used for the teaching of basic skills while a second language is developed may have highly positive affective and cognitive outcomes, therefore, it is necessary to assess the language characteristics of potential target students. Such an assessment must be done utilizing a measure of language competence in English and other languages spoken by the student (see "PAL Measures Language Dominance," Sylvia Gil, IDRA *Newsletter*, Nov. 1975). Following such an assessment the student can be classified into one of five categories:

a) Monolingual in a language other than English;

b) Predominant speaker of a language other than English, with some English;

c) Bilingual, i.e., has equal facility in English and another language;

d) Predominant speaker of English, with some other language;

e) Monolingual in English, speaks no other language. Contrary to a concern expressed by some school personnel, *Lau* Remedies require that only elementary school students who are monolingual or are predominant speakers of a language other than English be placed in a bilingual education program.

Students who are bilingual, predominant English-speaking, or monolingual English-speaking need not be placed in a bilingual education program, although other treatment may be required if the student is underachieving.

PHASE III—ACHIEVEMENT DATA

If a potential target student is not required to be placed in a bilingual program because he is in any of the three categories: bilingual, predominant English speaker, or monolingual English speaker, further treatment is dependent on the performance in school. If the student is performing at grade-level expectancy no further *Lau* Remedies treatment is required, and he is dropped from the *Lau* target student population.

If a potential target is underachieving it is required that the school system conduct a diagnosis of the learning problem and develop an individually prescribed educational plan to remedy the existing problem and assure improved performance. Underachievement is defined in the *Lau* Remedies as performing at or below one standard deviation below the mean score for non-minority (Anglo) children. This definition of underachievement implies that school districts must determine achievement norms for non-ethnic/racial minority students. The standard deviation for these scores must be determined and scores of potential target students must be compared with this criterion.

PHASE IV—PROGRAM OFFERING

As discussed previously, the school district must provide two educational services for students under the *Lau* Remedies. Students who are monolingual or predominant speakers of a language other than English must be placed in a bilingual education program, defined by OCR in three ways.

Students who are bilingual, predominantly or monolingual English-speaking must be diagnosed and an individually prescribed compatible program must be afforded.

SECONDARY LEVEL

At the intermediate and high school levels the phases for the identification of the target population are the same as at the elementary level although the fourth phase, Program Offerings, allows for a wider array of options.

Students who are monolingual in a language other than English may be placed in any of four options available to the district:

1. A bilingual education program;
2. A program in which the native language is used exclusively while English is being taught as a second language;
3. A program in which subject matter is taught in the native language and then bridged into English as English is acquired in the subject matter courses;
4. Total immersion in an English as a Second Language (ESL) program or High Intensity Language Training (HILT) program until sufficient mastery of the English language allows the student to be placed in regular subject matter courses.

As in the case of elementary level students, secondary students who are not monolingual in a language other than English and underachieving must be diagnosed and given an individually prescribed program which assures improved performance.

(IDRA, January 1976)

LEGAL STATUS OF BILINGUAL EDUCATION

1976

Recent developments in the area of bilingual education have raised a question concerning the legal status of bilingual education. School administrators, board members, minority populations, state legislators, and federal courts share a concern over the legal issues in bilingual education. Questions concerning the target population or eligibility, types and scope of programs, and minimum legal standards have become an everyday topic for deliberation in many school districts. The answers to these questions have vast implications in terms of programmatic efforts, personnel resources and federal state and local appropriations. The following analysis should prove helpful in determining the current legal status of this educational program.

A legal status can be established on four bases: state legislation, federal legislation, litigation, and administrative regulations.

STATE LEGISLATION

Each of the fifty states has wide discretionary powers in providing an educational system for its population. In exercising its authority for the provision of educational programs, state legislatures may and have prescribed specific programs in bilingual education. At the present time, thirty of the fifty states and three territories have some type of legislative prescription for bilingual education. Eight of the states plus Puerto Rico have mandatory provisions which make it legally binding for the schools of the state to offer a bilingual education program to children of limited English-speaking ability. The remainder of the thirty states allow school districts to offer a bilingual education program. Most of them require local funds for program operation. In most of the states where bilingual education is required, provisions are made for minimum number of students, and a gradual phasing-in of bilingual education programs. Although legislative provisions for bilingual education differ among the various states, most of the programs prescribed by state law are transitional programs which afford native language instruction coupled with English as a second language learning activities until such time as a transition can be made. Maintenance of native language skills is seldom provided for in state legislation.

FEDERAL LEGISLATION

There are two federal laws which have a direct bearing on bilingual education—the Civil Rights Act of 1964 and the Equal Educational Opportunities Act of 1974.

The Civil Rights Act of 1964, recognizes a contractual relationship between the federal government and recipients of federal grants. School districts receiving any form of federal assistance such as funds provided for economically disadvantaged children, vocational education, federally impacted areas, etc., receive such funds under a contract between the school district and the federal government. Under the Civil Rights Act of 1964, these contracts between the federal government and a recipient stipulate that there will be no minority or sex discrimination practiced by the recipient. Evidence of discrimination constitutes a breach of contract with subsequent forfeiture of all federal funds. The Office of Civil Rights in the Department of Health, Education and Welfare is given statutory authority to develop the necessary compliance review procedures to assure the absence of discrimination. The Civil Rights Act of 1964, has been interpreted by the Office of Civil Rights as prohibiting school systems from discriminating against children on the basis of language, therefore, the failure of a school district to make provisions for children of limited English-speaking ability constitutes discrimination which unless rectified by the school district will lead to the loss of all federal funds.

The Equal Educational Opportunities Act of 1974, is much more specific in addressing itself to children of limited English-speaking ability. The Act provides that "No state shall deny equal educational opportunity on account of his/her race, color, sex or national origin by . . . the failure by an education agency to take appropriate action to overcome language barriers that impede equal participation by its students in its instructional program." (20 U.S.C., Section 1703(f)) The Act recognizes the ultimate responsibility of the state for the implementation and monitoring of the bilingual/bicultural programs since, by its own terms, the Act is addressed to the states and the term "education agency" is statutorily defined to include both local and state education agencies (Section 1720 A). Section 1706 of this Act expressly provides that "an individual denied an equal educational opportunity as defined by this subchapter may institute a civil action in an appropriate district court of the United States against such parties, and for such relief, as may be appropriate. . . ."

LITIGATION

Although the making of law is reserved for legislative bodies, the interpretation of statutes as well as state and federal constitutions is performed by the judiciary. Thus the interpretation of a constitution or a statute by the courts provides a legal basis for that interpretation. The following court cases are a few of the many that have provided interpretations of the constitution and federal legislation, and have affected bilingual education.

U.S. v. Texas was originated by the U.S. Department of Justice on March 6, 1970, for the purpose of dismantling the dual system of education in Texas (*United States v. Texas*, 1971). The legal brief for this case was the court's interpretation of the 14th Amendment of the U.S. Constitution and Title VI of the Civil Rights Act of 1964.

In a modified order issued on July 13, 1971, the court in addition to eliminating school segregation in Texas, prescribed equal educational opportunities for every student. The court asked the Texas Education Agency to recommend and implement the curricular offerings and programs to compensate minority children for unequal educational opportunities resulting from past or present racial and ethnic isolation. It specifically ordered the Texas Education Agency to develop and implement programs and curricula developed to meet the special education needs of students whose primary language is other than English. The court prescribed a study of the educational needs of minority children, the development of minimum standards of enforcement procedures, and the submission by the state education agency of annual compliance reports.

In a separate order on December 6, 1971, the court prescribed a much more meticulous program for the San Felipe/Del Rio School District in Texas. In this order the federal court prescribed:

- The vigorous recruitment of Mexican-American administrators and instructional staff;
- Curriculum which recognized the value and cultural environment and language of the Mexican-American students;
- Language programs which develop and reinforced the student's primary and secondary languages from early childhood through the twelfth grade;
- Bilingual counseling;
- Intercultural awareness programs and ethnic studies courses;
- The establishment of multi-ethnic community councils to assist in the formulation and evaluation of the program;
- The development of a plan to insure the hiring and retention of competent bilingual/bicultural staff;
- Recommended provisions for language and cultural awareness training;
- The appointment of bilingual/bicultural teachers for special education classes;
- And, the appointment of an educational consultant team to develop a plan to evaluate the effectiveness of the bilingual/bicultural program, and biannual reports to the Court and the parties on the progress of implementation.

A similar suit in New Mexico produced a strong statement concerning bilingual education. In *Portales v. Serna,* the court rendered a decision based on its interpretation of Title VI of the Civil Rights Act of 1964. The Portales (New Mexico) School District was found to have failed to institute a program which would rectify language deficiencies so that children of limited English-speaking ability would receive a meaningful education. In its review of the case, the federal Tenth Circuit Court of Appeals stated "Under Title VI of the Civil Rights Act of 1964 [children of limited English-speaking ability] have a right to bilingual education" (*Serna v. Portales Municipal Schools,* 1974).

Perhaps the most famous court case dealing with children of limited English-speaking ability was the San Francisco case of *Lau v Nichols* (*Lau v. Nichols,* 1973). The case was filed in behalf of some 1800 Chinese children in the San Francisco Unified School District who were not receiving a special program in spite of being of limited English-speaking ability.

In a decision rendered by Justice Douglas, the U.S. Supreme Court unanimously found the San Francisco Unified School District in violation of Title VI of the Civil Rights Acts of 1964 and in violation of a May 25, 1970 memorandum by the Office of Civil Rights in HEW describing practices ruled illegal in compliance reviews of school districts enrolling children of limited English-speaking ability. This case is of special interest because the San Francisco Unified School District argued the absence of discrimination since the Chinese children were being provided ". . . the same facilities, textbooks, teachers, and curriculum as is provided to other children in the district." The Supreme Court ruled that providing the same program for children who were atypical constituted discriminatory treatment. The court then ruled that San Francisco must provide special treatment for children of limited English-speaking ability or face the loss of all federal funds.

ADMINISTRATIVE REGULATIONS

As mentioned previously, the Civil Rights Act of 1964 authorizes respective agencies to develop the necessary compliance criteria. The Office of Civil Rights in HEW has on two occasions issued memoranda pertaining to the education of children of limited English-speaking ability.

In a memorandum to all school districts on May 25, 1970, the Office of Civil Rights Director J. Stanley Pottinger stated:

> Where inability to speak and understand the English language excludes national origin-minority group children from effective participation in the educational program offered by a school district, the district must take affirmative steps to rectify the language deficiency in order to open its instructional program to these students (Office for Civil Rights, 1970).

The memorandum thus reflects a finding by the federal agency with special competence in the area of education that, where a school system employs English as the basic language of instruction but provides no special assistance to non-English-speaking students who comprise a significant portion of the system's enrollment, those students are impermissibly excluded from participation in, denied the benefits of, and subjected to discrimination under the system's educational program, on account of their national origin.

In the summer of 1975, following the Supreme Court decision in *Lau v Nichols*, the Office of Civil Rights, HEW issued another memorandum concerning educational programs for children of limited English-speaking ability. It is important to note that the Supreme Court in *Lau v. Nichols* upheld this agency's authority to issue such interpretations. This statement by the Office of Civil Rights commonly referred to as the "Lau Remedies" makes special provisions for the identification of children of limited English-speaking ability and prescribes bilingual education programs for elementary school children who are monolingual in a language other than English or who are predominant speakers of a language other than English. The "Lau Remedies" holds school districts accountable for children with English language proficiency, but who may have at one time been of limited English-speaking ability, by requiring diagnostic/prescriptive measures for such children who are currently underachieving. Other provisions of the "Lau Remedies" deal with children of limited English-speaking ability in secondary schools, staffing, student placement, parent communication, curricular and co-curricular offerings, and reporting and evaluation requirements.

SUMMARY

On the basis of federal legislation, court decisions, administrative regulations, and state legislation where appropriate, it appears that school districts must implement bilingual education programs for children of limited English-speaking ability. Methods of identifying the children and the extent of the program is still a matter being reviewed by the courts, but there is no question that children of limited English-speaking ability have a legal right to a bilingual education program. The continued dissipation of school district and state educational agency money, time, energy, and creativity in efforts to circumvent the law should be seriously questioned. Problem solving, planning, resourcefulness, and commitment are needed.

(IDRA, May 1976)

LAU REMEDIES—GREAT WEIGHT

1978

During the past few years, persons concerned with improving educational opportunities for Hispanic and other language minority children have followed the evolution of the legal status of bilingual education.

Legal status is determined by state legislation, federal legislation, Attorney General opinions, administrative regulations, and litigation.[1] The first two, state and federal legislation, have been slow in developing, are frequently permissive rather than mandatory, and have usually followed rather than led in the establishment of policy. With few exceptions, legislators have provided a lackluster performance in bilingual educational reform activities. On the other hand, administrative regulations and litigation have been much more pioneering and dramatic.[2] Judge Wayne Justice's court order of July 13, 1971, in *U.S. v. Texas* was ahead of its time in protecting the educational rights of language minority children and still serves as a model in subsequent litigation.[3] Educators and reformers concerned with the unjust and artificially created paradox between bilingual education and desegregation would do well to go back to the insightful relationship perceived by Judge Justice, namely that bilingual education is a part of the desegregation process. This milestone court order is similarly exemplary in its perception of the role of bilingual education in a much more comprehensive program of multicultural education rather than as a response only to problems of children of limited English speaking ability.

Portales v. Serna,[1] *Keyes v. Denver,*[4] *Aspira v. New York, Overton v. Austin, Morales v. Shannon,* and *Rios v. Read*[5] serve as other landmark cases in the emerging status of bilingual education, each making some contribution toward a global concept of the rights of language minorities.

Perhaps the biggest impact on the legal status of bilingual education was made by the Supreme Court decision in *Lau v. Nichols.* The impact of *Lau* is important for two reasons: first, the courts determined that the provision of equal programs to different children constituted a denial of equality of educational opportunity, (thereby substantiating this author's principle of "adaptability" first promoted in 1969) namely that it is the responsibility of the school to adapt to the varying characteristics of children rather than placing the burden on children to adapt to the characteristics of a single school program. Second, the unanimous decision rendered by the Supreme Court of the United States will hopefully eliminate conflicting opinions of the lower courts forever.

It should be noted that in arriving at its decision, the Supreme Court depended not only on the Civil Rights Act of 1964, but also on the May 25, 1970, memorandum issued by J. Stanley Pottinger, Director of the HEW Office for Civil Rights. In the *Lau* decision, the Supreme Court viewed this administrative regulation as having the status of law.

CINTRON V. BRENTWOOD

On January 10, 1978, a new landmark in bilingual education litigation appeared in the form of a memorandum of decision issued by the United States District Court for the Eastern District of New York. This opinion issued by Chief Judge Jacob Mishler upholds the rights of Hispanic children to a bilingual education program.

In this case the education authorities attempted to reduce bilingual program offerings in the Brentwood Union Free School District following the dismissal of seventeen bilingual teachers as a result of declining enrollment. The court held that the reduced program was not acceptable and that the previous program should be improved.

The legal significance of this case is that in arriving at the decision the court determined the bilingual education program needs of children on the basis of the "Lau Guidelines" issued by the HEW Office for Civil Rights ("Task Force Findings Specifying Remedies Available for Eliminating Past Educational Practices Ruled Unlawful under *Lau v. Nichols*"). The court interpreted the "Lau Guidelines" to require the school district

> . . . to (1) assess the language ability of the student; (2) identify the nature and extent of the students educational needs and utilize the most effective teaching style to meet those needs; (3) implement the type of educational programs dependent upon the degree to linguistic proficiency of the students in question; and (4) train bilingual teachers.

As stated by Herbert Teitelbaum of the New York law firm of Teitelbaum and Hiller, co-counsel with the Puerto Rican Legal Defense and Education Fund in the case, "It is the first opinion that we know of which treats the Lau Remedies in a manner comparable to the way in which the Supreme Court treated the May 25, 1970, Memorandum (of the HEW Office for Civil Rights)."[6] Although the federal court did not give the Lau Remedies the status of law, it did acknowledge that "the guidelines are entitled to great weight. . . ."

Thus, the legal status of bilingual education is further extended, and the legal right of language minority children to a bilingual education program moves one step closer to the closure already prescribed by common sense.

REFERENCES AND RECOMMENDED READINGS

1. Cárdenas, José A., "Legal Status of Bilingual Education," *IDRA Newsletter*, May 1976, pp. 4–6.
2. Teitelbaum, Herbert and Richard J. Hiller, "Bilingual Education: The Legal Mandate," *Harvard Educational Review*, 47:2, May, 1977.
3. *U.S. v. Texas*, Memorandum Opinion, Civil Action No. 5281, U.S. Eastern District of Texas, U.S. District court, Tyler, Texas, July 13, 1971.
4. Cárdenas, José A., "*Keyes v. Denver*," *IDRA Newsletter*, May, 1976, pp. 2–3, 6.
5. Cárdenas, José A., "*Rios v. Read*," *IDRA Newsletter*, March, 1977, pp. 3–5.
6. Teitelbaum, Herbert, Personal correspondence with author.

KEYES V. DENVER

1976

PREFACE

In 1973, I agreed to assist the Mexican-American Legal Defense and Education Fund (MALDEF) to develop an education plan requested by the court in *Keyes v. Denver* (*Keyes v. School District No. 1,* 1983). The education plan was in response to the court's finding that Mexican-American students in the Denver public schools were being denied equal educational opportunities by the failure of the schools to respond to the language characteristics of the children. I testified in court and presented a plan similar to the one adopted by the court in the San Felipe Del Rio intervention suit in *U.S. v. Texas* (*United States v. Texas,* 1971). The plan was again based on the Theory of Incompatibilities, and required a district program responding to all ten of the elements in the developmental matrix.

Judge William Doyle was impressed with the plan and ordered it implemented by the Denver school system. The implementation of the plan raised some interesting questions concerning the relationships between school programs and desegregation. Prior to desegregation there were various schools in the Denver system whose enrollments were predominantly Mexican-American. In most of these schools, the administrators and teachers were mostly Mexican-American. Del Pueblo Elementary School, for instance, had a Mexican-American principal, and the minority student concentration in the school was such that extensive progress had been made in the development of a multicultural environment conducive to bilingual education programs, multicultural education, extensive parental involvement, and many other features supportive of innovative approaches to the education of minority students.

In order to safeguard the innovative programs at these predominantly minority schools, the court excluded them from the district desegregation order. The Tenth Circuit Court of Appeals reversed the desegregation order of the district court on the grounds that bilingual education was not adequate justification for the segregation of students. In the words of the court, " . . . such instruction must be subordinate to a plan of school desegregation."
The entire "Cárdenas Plan" for teaching Mexican-American children in Denver was similarly reversed by the appellate court on the grounds that the findings of the district court did not justify such a massive remedy.

Almost twenty years after the appellate court reversal, the Denver public schools came up with a new plan for addressing the continuous problem of minority student under performance. It is interesting that this new plan has many of the elements which the court prescribed in the original desegregation court order.

The Denver court order brings up an interesting paradox in the history of desegregation. In many school systems segregated schools provided minority populations immediate control of their schools. The dispersal of the minority population into a system-wide desegregation program led to the minority students being a minor part of each school campus. Although district officials were relatively unconcerned with new instructional programs developed in school campuses with predominantly minority enrollments, there was extensive opposition to the implementation of such programs on a district-wide basis to serve students scattered throughout the district in predominantly majority student schools.

School officials, with extensive backing from the courts, presented minority populations with two contradicting alternatives: either attend segregated schools with extensive control of the schools, or attend desegregated schools without this control. Immediately following the *Brown* court order, minority populations eagerly accepted the desegregated option, although in recent years there has been extensive disappointment with the effects of desegregation with a corresponding loss of minority support (*Brown v. Board of Education*, 1954).

There are several fallacies in this no-win set of alternatives. The first is the failure of the courts, minority populations and educators to go beyond the physical movement of students in the desegregation of the schools. As argued by Thomas Pedigrew in the Boston court case, the opposite of segregation should not be "desegregation," the physical blending of different racial and ethnic groups, but rather "integration," the removal of racial and ethnic isolation in all aspects of the school.

Minority students in the desegregation process usually found themselves in culturally isolated situations in the new school environment. The physical desegregation of students placed the displaced students, invariably the minority population which usually carried the brunt of the desegregation process, in alien and hostile educational settings.

I believe that the segregation of minority students is educationally, socially, psychologically, and morally wrong, and I continue to support desegregation. On the other hand, the integration of the minority students into a culturally compatible educational system requires that the school address each of the following elements: philosophy, governance, scope and sequence, staffing, curriculum, co-curriculum, student services, non-instructional needs, community involvement, and evaluation. Without this compatibility there is little chance of improved student performance in a desegregated setting. The cultural isolation is as great as in a segregated school.

Ironically, I cannot help but note that many schools with predominantly minority enrollments have no more cultural compatibility than predominantly white schools. The use of an educational paradigm developed historically for white, middle class, English-speaking students in minority schools makes me classify such schools not as "minority schools," but as "white schools for minority students." As minorities have moved into central city schools vacated by whites moving into suburbia, the educational system has failed to develop and implement new school programs compatible with the characteristics of the new minority population.

The extensive publicity given to the "Cárdenas Plan" in *Keyes v. Denver* led to a large number of requests that I serve as an expert witness in subsequent court cases involving the education of minority children. Usually the courts have been receptive to my suggestions for the creation of a culturally democratic learning environment which allows all students an equal opportunity to succeed. However, school systems have been more than reluctant to accept or implement a drastically new approach to the education of atypical children.

I am thoroughly convinced that until the entire educational community develops, accepts, and implements a new educational paradigm which addresses the needs of all students and leads to the adaptation of schools to the characteristics of the students there will be no significant improvement in the general poor performance of these students in American schools.

In 1973, the U.S. Supreme Court remanded *Keyes v. Denver* to the district court for further proceedings. This case differed from previous desegregation cases in that: (1) it was the first segregation case outside the South, and lacked the clear-cut dual system of education for blacks and whites commonly found in the southern states; (2) made fine distinctions between de facto and de jure segregation; and (3) addressed itself to issues of equality of educational opportunities rather than limiting the integration effort to pupil assignment.

In past hearings in this case, the court had concluded that minority populations in Denver were receiving an inferior instructional program in violation of constitutional and legal rights. After remand from the Supreme Court, the court requested assistance in the development of an instructional program designed to equalize school achievement.

Existing inequalities in the Denver School district were described by the courts as follows:

> The educational opportunity in the minority schools has been proven in our present trial as well as in previous trials to be inferior to that in the majority schools.

The district court's broad interpretation of desegregation was consistent with the Supreme Court's interpretation in this litigation. The Supreme Court had previously noted in this case the close relationship between segregation, curriculum, and other activities.

> The most routine decisions with respect to the operation of schools, made almost daily, can affect in varying degrees the extent to which schools are initially segregated, remain in that condition, are desegregated, or—for the long term future—are likely to be one or the other. These decisions include action or nonaction with respect to . . . the recruitment, promotion and assignment of faculty and supervisory personnel . . . the determination of curriculum including whether there will be "tracks" that lead primarily to college or to vocational training . . . and even decisions as to social, recreational and athletic policies.

THE EDUCATION PLAN

The district court called upon plaintiffs and intervenors to obtain the services of experts in the education of minority personnel in order to formulate a plan to accompany the pupil assignment plan for ". . . a system of compensatory education programs carried out in an integrated environment, designed to equalize achievement." The Mexican-American Legal Defense and Educational Fund obtained the services of Dr. José A. Cárdenas to develop such a plan. After several meetings with Plaintiffs' attorneys, including James Nabrit (NAACP) and Gordon Greiner; attorneys for defendant/intervenors, Sanford Rosen and Paul Baca, the Congress of Hispanic Educators (CHE), and the Denver Black Teachers Organization, an educational plan was developed and presented to the court. The plan drew heavily from a prior education plan developed for the San Felipe/Del Rio District in Texas, and ordered to be implemented by the federal court in the Eastern District of Texas. The Texas plan had been appealed to the Fifth Circuit Court of Appeals where it had been sustained.

The so-called "Cárdenas Plan" was based on the concept of incompatibilities between traditional instructional programs developed for a white, Anglo-Saxon, English-speaking, middle-class population and the characteristics and learning styles of minority children. The scope of the plan was comprehensive, including school district modifications in its philosophy, policy, rules and regulations, scope and sequence, curriculum materials and methodologies, staffing patterns and training, co-curricular activities, student personnel services, pupil non-instructional materials, community involvement, and evaluation activities. The "Cárdenas Plan" as presented to the court was subsequently modified by two addenda. The first addendum was a system for monitoring program implementation and the effectiveness of the program, and a second addendum developed by the Congress of Hispanic Educators in Denver which would provide, on the basis of the framework provided by Dr. Cárdenas, specific and meticulous changes in the Denver public schools.

It is interesting to note that there was virtually no opposition on the part of the defendant school district to the rationale or instructional programs prescribed in the "Cárdenas Plan." Dr. Louis Kishkunas, Denver Superintendent of Schools, testified:

> I found as I read the plan that most of the conclusions that Dr. Cárdenas came to replicated or duplicated the conclusions that I came to a long time ago. . . . I am sure that many of the conclusions he came to, many of the facts that he states are applicable to the Denver situation.

Dr. David Roscoe Davidson, Assistant Superintendent of the Educational Division, also supported the Cárdenas Plan and the addendum in his testimony.

However, school district testimony questioned the implementation of the plan, and the need for extensive resources for implementation. The district court notes, "most of the opposition to the Cárdenas Plan generated during the evidentiary hearings went to the practicality of the plan and to problems of its implementation rather than to the educational principles espoused."

In the final judgement and decree issued by Judge William Doyle, the school district was instructed to:

> . . . further develop a bilingual-bicultural education program in accordance with the model presented by Dr. José Cárdenas or a plan substantially and materially similar thereto and incorporating to the extent feasible the proposals set forth in the Addendum to the Cárdenas Plan. Such program shall consider and treat the matters of educational philosophy, policies, scope and sequence, curriculum, staffing, co-curricular activities, student personnel services, non-instructional needs, community involvement and evaluation.
>
> The defendants shall engage the services of a qualified consultant or consultants to assist in the development and implementation of such program.

> The program shall be implemented at Del Pueblo Elementary School with provisions for voluntary enrollment by Anglo and Black students in September, 1974; the program shall be implemented on a pilot basis at Cheltenham, Garden Place and Swansea Elementary Schools and at Baker Junior High School and West High School. It is anticipated that as these programs are developed and proved, they will be placed in other schools where needed and/or desired

THE TENTH CIRCUIT REVERSAL

Whereas, the Fifth Circuit Court of Appeals had sustained a similar plan for the San Felipe/Del Rio School District, when the education plan ordered implemented by the district court in the Denver Public Schools was appealed to the Tenth Circuit Court of Appeals, the appellate court reversed the lower court's order.

One of the reasons for the reversal was that some of the schools in which the plan was to be piloted were not included in the desegregating pupil assignment plan. The Tenth Circuit stated

> Bilingual education . . . is not a substitute for desegregation. Although bilingual instruction may be required to prevent the isolation of minority students in a predominantly Anglo school system, see *Lau v. Nichols*, 414 U.S. 563; *Serna v. Portales Municipal Schools*, 10 Cir., 499 F2 1147, such instruction must be subordinate to a plan of school desegregation.

The Tenth Circuit further noted: . . .

> The Cárdenas Plan therefore requires an overhaul of the system's entire approach to education of minorities; its proposals extend to matters of educational philosophy, governance, instructional scope and sequence, curriculum, student evaluation, staffing, non-instructional service and community involvement. The plan also proposed a mechanism for comprehensive monitoring of the program's status. Continuing evaluation by ten "Equal Educational Opportunity Committees," each composed in part of persons from outside the school system, is necessary, according to the Plan, because the school system itself "lacks accountability." In the Addendum to the Cárdenas Plan, intervenor CHE details how the Plan would be applied in Denver. These proposals, it must be emphasized, touch virtually every aspect of curriculum planning, methodology, and philosophy presently the responsibility of local school authorities. CHE proposes, for example, the inclusion of specific courses in the curriculum, adoption and publication of specific educational principles, provision of early childhood education (beginning at age three) and adult education for minorities, and provision of adequate clothing for poor minority school children.

> But the court's adoption of the Cárdenas Plan, in our view, goes well beyond helping Hispano school children to reach the proficiency in English necessary to learn other basic subjects. Instead of merely removing obstacles to effective desegregation, the court's order would impose upon school authorities a pervasive and detailed system for the education of minority children. We believe this goes too far.

The Tenth Circuit reversal has been interpreted by many as a reversal of its previous position on the issue of bilingual education. This is not the case. In its Denver reversal, the Tenth Circuit stated:

> Although bilingual instruction may be required to prevent the isolation of minority students in a predominant Anglo school system . . . such instruction must be subordinate to a plan of school desegregation.

The court further states:

> Neither *Lau v. Nichols* . . . nor this court's holding in *Serna v. Portales* . . . is contrary to our position.

The Tenth Circuit Court of Appeals remanded the case to the lower court for a determination of the relief necessary to insure that Mexican-Americans and other minority children will have the opportunity to acquire proficiency in the English language.

THE FUTURE OF BILINGUAL EDUCATION IN DENVER

At present, the lower court is again holding hearings for determination of a court order relating to bilingual/bicultural education. In a February 10, 1976, statement, Judge William Doyle states:

> . . . we are directed on remand to determine the relief, if any, necessary to insure that Hispano and other minority children will have the opportunity to acquire proficiency in the English language. The mandate does not limit this education to children who are unable to speak the English language and thus the school district might consider whether bilingual education is needed to aid children who lack proficiency in the English language. There are undoubtedly other problems and approaches to consider.

SUMMARY

Contrary to arguments being developed in interpretations of the *Keyes v Denver* Final Judgement and Decree by the Tenth Circuit Court of Appeals, the strong legal backup for bilingual education developed in *Lau* and *Portales v Serna* has not been weakened. The Denver reversal merely reinforces (1) the Court's long standing reluctance to administer school districts, particularly to the degree specified in the "Cárdenas Plan" and CHE amendment and (2) its strong support of the concept of integration (through student placement) as essential to eliminating the dual school system.

(IDRA, May 1976)

BILINGUAL EDUCATION: ITS ANALYSIS, NEEDS, AND COST

1977

PREFACE

It was inevitable that IDRA's interest in school finance and its interest in multicultural education would merge into a study on the cost of bilingual education.

Since the enactment of the Bilingual Education Act by the United States Congress in 1968, the federal government has funded a discrete number of pilot bilingual education programs. School systems lucky enough to receive such grants usually have ample funding for the implementation of a bilingual program. If anything, federal grants for bilingual education programs may be excessive in that these funds usually supplant local and state funding, providing for all of the cost of the program, rather than supplementing regular school funding with only the program costs which are over and above the cost of a monolingual program.

In 1975, the U.S. Office of Education provided a grant to IDRA for a study of the cost of bilingual education. The original study in Texas was subsequently replicated in Utah and Colorado with different groups of experts coming up with similar findings. (Cárdenas, et al., 1976)

The studies produced an estimated cost for bilingual education which was subsequently converted into a weighted factor. In Texas, it was determined that the bilingual methodology cost from 25 to 42 percent above a monolingual methodology depending on the grade level and year of implementation. It was immediately obvious that the $45 per pupil per year which the state was allocating for bilingual instruction was most inadequate. As a result of this study the allocation was increased to 10 percent above the cost of regular instruction, a weighted factor of 1.10 which is still in effect. To this day, most bilingual education programs suffer from inadequate funding. The amount commonly allocated in support of these programs is far short of the weighted factor identified in our studies.

As stated in 1977 in the following article, it is understandable that school systems are reluctant to implement a new methodology in the absence of adequate funding. This inadequacy leads to the implementation of an inadequate program or to school system recalcitrance in responding to the needs of language minority children.

(Findings of IDRA's Bilingual Cost Analysis Project were addressed by Dr. José A. Cárdenas at the Texas Association for Bilingual Education (TABE) Conference, December 3, 1976. The research project, funded by the U.S. Office of Education, was conducted during the 1975–76 school year by former State Senator Joe Bernal, with assistance from William Kean. The following is a condensed version of the speech.)

During the last decade federal appropriations for bilingual education have grown from $5 million to almost $100 million, more than thirty state legislatures have made legislative provisions for bilingual education, and at least eleven state legislatures have appropriated funds for the implementation of bilingual education programs. Considering this increased concern for bilingual education, unbelievably no one has addressed this question of: "How much does it cost to provide an adequate program in bilingual education?"

Funding of bilingual education programs has been based on political feasibility, availability of funds, or the cost of alternate programs rather than a direct and realistic analysis of program costs.

LACK OF PRIOR STUDIES

Earlier research in the funding of bilingual education programs failed to turn up a single activity directed toward this purpose. Recommendations made to legislative groups were either based on political considerations or, more commonly, on cost analyses of other programs for atypical children. Both Texas and Florida had performed cost analyses for compensatory education programs, and using the erroneous assumption that bilingual education is a type of compensatory education, made recommendations for similar funding.

BEST PRACTICE METHODOLOGY

Previous studies on educational costs have been based on a "light house" or "best practice methodology" whose rationale is that the cost of an education program can be determined by identifying an exemplary program and its cost. The "best practice" methodology produces two serious problems.

First, the identification of a "best practice" school district is a highly subjective activity and often reflects the strength of public relations departments in competing school districts as well as staff and district popularity. An objective determination of program efficiency and effectiveness is often overlooked.

The second problem which manifests itself in a state like Texas is that expenditures for education are consistently below national averages (usually ranking between 36 and 40th in the nation). Beginning on such a low funding level, the resulting "best program" inevitably will be low also.

IDRA encountered a third problem with its study. Essential elements such as staff preparation, materials development and organizational aspects are in a state of evolution. No program can currently be identified as an exemplary program reflecting the rationale, preparation and practices deemed essential for an adequate bilingual education program.

This does not imply that there are no "good" bilingual programs in Texas. It only reflects that even the best programs have a long way to go in terms of subject matter coverage, curriculum materials and staffing before they can be classified as sound bilingual education programs.

PROJECT METHODOLOGY

To bypass the three problems listed above, the Cost Analysis Project impaneled a group of experts in bilingual education, representing practitioners in the field, institutions of higher education and state and national educational agencies. The experts developed a hypothetical, minimally adequate bilingual education program, identified the personal and material services needed for implementation of the program, and analyzed the cost of providing such support. In every case, the cost of support services was determined on the basis of school district expenditures for monolingual programs, or direct communications with the supplier.

Two concepts complicated matters by distorting and invalidating figures. The first concept was the provision of funds for the education of minority or disadvantaged children on a categorical basis to compensate for inadequacies in the state system of school finance. In such instances, children of limited English-speaking ability may serve as a substitute for distribution of funds in order to reduce disparities in the state system.

The state of New Mexico is a case in point. School districts enrolling children of limited English-speaking ability receive a bilingual education add-on amounting to 50 percent of the district expenditure per pupil. These "bilingual education" funds are made available to each school district regardless of whether or not, and often without consideration to, extent and quality of bilingual education programs to be implemented.

Although Texas does not present such a clear case, it is evident that some compensatory education, special education, and bilingual education funding serves as a substitute for low tax wealth school districts.

Further complicating the analysis of expenditures is the tendency for innovative programs to serve as catalysts for improvements in the general educational program. New programs, particularly federally funded programs, seem to demand a liberal sprinkling of gadgets and gimmicks far above what school districts can afford, or do supply, for the regular programs. It is not uncommon to discover schools in which the "new federal program" provides motion picture and slide projectors, overhead transparencies, tape recorders and duplicating equipment. It is questionable whether the cost of such upgrading should be attributed to the cost of bilingual education. The analysis of bilingual education costs should serve as an estimate of the cost of extending a monolingual program through bilingual offerings, but should not include bilingual education support for the monolingual program itself. Therefore, it was determined early in the study that costs would be analyzed for a minimally adequate bilingual education program, in most cases comparable to the monolingual offerings, and if indirect benefits are accrued to regular instruction programs, it would be a desirable spinoff of the bilingual program, but not at its expense.

FINDINGS

It was assumed at the beginning of the project that the cost of a bilingual education program would be dependent on a variety of characteristics associated with that program. Four variables which influence the cost of a bilingual education program are presented below:

a) **Grade Level**—In general, the cost of a bilingual education program diminishes at each level through the fifth grade.

b) **Year of Implementation**—Start-up costs for a first year bilingual education program at any grade level is significantly higher than in subsequent years.

c) **Prior Staffing Patterns**—Instructional staff played the largest part in determining program cost. School districts which had a plentiful supply of bilingual personnel tended to implement programs at reasonable cost, while districts with few bilingual personnel tended to experience much higher costs.

d) **Size**—The addition of pupils to a bilingual program diminishes the cost of the program on a per pupil basis until the increased size requires hiring more supervisory staff.

After analyzing expenditure areas, project staff and the panel of experts determined that all significant expenditures for bilingual education were concentrated in the five areas listed below. Ranked from highest to lowest, they are:

1) **Staffing**—The cost of staffing a bilingual education program was largely influenced by the availability of bilingual staff in various personnel categories.

   The provision of additional instructional staff for bilingual education programs was deemed imperative for providing one-to-one pupil-to-teacher interactions for modeling in two languages. Although IDRA project staff and the panel exhibited wide disparities on their estimates of the amount of additional instructional staff required for a minimal adequate bilingual program, they recommended that an additional staff of .30 per instructional unit or .30 additional personnel units for each nineteen to twenty-one children (depending on the grade level involved) in average daily attendance. The cost of this additional staff amounted to approximately $160 per pupil per year in kindergarten, first grade, second grade and third grade, and $145 per pupil per year in grades four and five.

   Cost of preservice training was not included as part of the total cost of the bilingual education program, since it is not a recurring cost normally borne by the state or school district.

2) **Materials**—The project identified a need for instructional classroom materials for bilingual education over and beyond materials and supplies generally made available in monolingual programs. The cost for this material was computed at between $11 and $35 per pupil per year depending on the grade level and year of implementation.

3) **Library**—The project identified a need for additional resources. Using current accreditation standards, staff ascertained that a need for seven additional volumes per pupil in bilingual education classes for start-up purposes and an additional $9 per pupil per year in new purchases. The cost for these library resources was constant at $25 per pupil in the first year of implementation and $9 per pupil in each subsequent year.

4) **Equipment**—The wide array of equipment needs of a bilingual education program would be comparable to a monolingual program. The only exception was a need for language masters which record and reproduce models of language for use by students in acquiring a second language. Assuming that such equipment has an average life span of three years, costs were estimated at approximately $20 in grades Kindergarten, first, second and third, $10 in grades fourth and fifth. Replacement cost in

subsequent years were estimated at almost $7 per pupil per year in grades kindergarten through third and $3.50 per pupil per year in grades fourth and fifth.

5) Testing—Additional tests are needed in a bilingual education program. The Cost Analysis Project determined that assessment and testing procedures were necessary for all students regardless of language characteristics and should not be attributed to a bilingual education. The project identified two additional types of tests: a language proficiency test and an achievement test to determine bilingual education outcomes not generally included in regular school testing programs. The cost for testing materials and scoring ranged from $1.32 to almost $3.00 per pupil per year depending on the grade level and year of implementation.

The total cost of a bilingual education program in Texas was estimated as follows:

Bilingual Education Cost

Grade	Year of Implementation			
	1st	2nd	3rd	4th
K	243.77	201.92	199.92	197.91
1	239.96	201.11	199.11	197.10
2	238.07	200.22	197.22	197.21
3	237.08	198.23	197.23	196.22
4	205.69	173.69	172.68	170.68
5	205.77	173.77	172.76	170.76

WEIGHTED PUPIL FACTOR

In order to allow for the utilization of the cost averages presented above for a variety of school districts with high and low expenditure levels, the average costs were converted into a weighted pupil factor which indicates, on an index basis, the relationship between bilingual education costs and the cost of a comparable monolingual education program. The weighted pupil factors were computed on the basis of full-time equivalency. The project staff were in agreement that a bilingual education program is a full-time school activity and not an appendage to an existing program.

Weighted pupil factors for the various grades and years of implementation are presented as follows:

Weighted Pupil Factors for Bilingual Education

Grade	Year of Implementation			
	1st	2nd	3rd	4th
K	1.31	1.25	1.25	1.25
1	1.42	1.35	1.35	1.34
2	1.41	1.35	1.34	1.34
3	1.41	1.35	1.34	1.34
4	1.36	1.30	1.30	1.30
5	1.36	1.30	1.30	1.30

CONCLUSIONS

The tables presented produce two conclusions. The first conclusion is that the $45 per pupil per year being provided in Texas for the implementation of bilingual education programs is most inadequate to meet the needs of even a minimally adequate program. For example, in a kindergarten classroom during the first year of implementation the amount provided by the state of Texas is less than one-fifth the cost of a minimally adequate program. At best, at the intermediate grades (four and five) in the fourth year of implementation the funds being provided comprise about 25 percent of the necessary funds.

The second conclusion is that districts are seeking alternatives for the financing of bilingual programs. It is no wonder that many school districts have been less than eager to comply with state legislation, federal legislation, and court orders demanding a bilingual education program for children of limited English-speaking ability, when such legislation and court orders are accompanied by an appropriation which provides only 20–25 percent of the cost of the mandated programs. The alternatives available to school districts are either to provide a bogus, substandard program which may be misrepresented to meet the letter of the law, or fund the program almost entirely at local expense. Since IDRA has determined in prior studies that the Mexican-American population in Texas and, therefore, children of limited English-speaking ability, tend to reside in the poorest tax wealth districts of Texas, local financing of bilingual education is a dysfunctional alternative to upgrading inadequate programs. It is no wonder that many school district personnel have opted toward a third alternative, namely, opposing bilingual education on a pedagogical, psychological and/or civic grounds, rather than assuming the cost with inadequate resources.

RECOMMENDATIONS

IDRA understands the temporal, personal and fiscal limitations of this study and makes the following recommendations:

1. The replication of this study should be undertaken in other states in order to validate the weighted pupil factors and cost estimates derived by IDRA.

2. Additional studies should be conducted in the area of preservice training for staff of bilingual education programs. Questions pertaining to where, how and how many are in desperate need of answers so that institutions of higher education may address their responsibilities in the training of instructional staff for bilingual education.
3. Further studies should be conducted on the relationship between declining school enrollments in urban school districts and the need for additional bilingual education staff. The declining school enrollments, particularly in school districts with large minority populations, have necessitated reductions in instructional staff at the same time that the school district is needing new staff with the necessary training and competencies for the implementation of a bilingual education program.
4. Further study should be conducted to determine the monitoring of needs of a bilingual education program. Minimum standards must be developed for the identification and enrollment of the target population, the various subject areas to be included in a bilingual program, culturally and linguistically relevant methodologies and the adequacy of curriculum materials and alternative organizational patterns.
5. Plans must be developed for increasing school districts accountability in dealing with children of limited English-speaking ability. It is necessary that the school district determine the extent to which bilingual and other programs are meeting the needs of such children with maximum efficiency and effectiveness.

(IDRA, February 1977)

RIOS V. REED

1977

PREFACE

Rios v. Reed is one of the few court cases in bilingual education in which I was not directly involved, although plaintiffs in this case relied extensively on the findings of previous bilingual education cases (*Rios v. Reed*, 1977).

Rios v. Reed was an important milestone in the development of a legal basis for bilingual education because it affirmed the need for quality in this type of a program. Even in the most successful prior cases, the legal victory seldom resulted in the implementation of an adequate bilingual education program in keeping with the findings of the court and subsequent court-ordered remedies. In *Rios v. Reed*, the legal issue was not so much the right to a bilingual education program, but rather the quality of the bilingual program afforded limited English proficient students.

The decision of the court in this case established bilingual education not as a separate instructional program for language minority children, but as a feasible avenue for equality of educational opportunity.

The *IDRA Newsletter* is currently mailed to some 12,000 persons throughout Texas and the United States, and the organization receives numerous responses from its readers. Although most responses to the *Newsletter* consist of commendations for articles in a variety of topics and an occasional condemnation for the same articles, we do receive additional information which constitutes a national exchange of information concerning various efforts to bring about improved educational opportunities for all children.

A case in point is a communication from Herb Teitelbaum of the Puerto Rican Legal Defense and Education Fund. His letter was accompanied by a copy of a New York court decision in a bilingual education case argued by the Puerto Rican Legal Defense and Education Fund. This recent court decision, rendered on January 14, 1977, should supplement past *Newsletter* articles on the legal status of bilingual education as interpreted by the courts in *Lau v. Nichols, Portales v. Serna, Keyes v. Denver, Otero v. Mesa Valley, Aspira v. New York* and *U.S. v. Texas* (*Lau v. Nichols*, 1973; *Serna v. Portales Municipal Schools*, 1974; *Keyes v. Denver*, 1983; *Otero v. Mesa Valley School District No. 51*, 1975; *Aspira of New York, Inc. v. Board of Education of the City of New York*, 1973; *United States v. Texas*, 1971).

The case of *Rios v. Reed* is being argued in the U.S. District Court for the Eastern District of New York. Plaintiffs in the case are Puerto Ricans and other Hispanic children. Defendants are school officials in the Patchogue-Medford School District in Suffolk County, New

York. The issue addressed by the court is a motion by the plaintiffs to compel the defendant school district to furnish information deemed necessary for presenting the case. The defendant school district argues that the information requested, dealing with the language characteristics of children, their assignment to bilingual and other programs and the subsequent performance of the children, should be made available for three reasons.

First they argue that under the Supreme Court decision in *Lau v. Nichols*, the only issue in *Rios v. Reed* is "whether or not the school district has taken affirmative steps to rectify the language deficiencies of students of Hispanic descent who by reason of such deficiencies are unable to participate in the regular school program." Second, that the Family Educational Rights Act of 1974, (Buckley amendment) prohibits them from disclosing names, or other identifying information of individual students in the Patchogue-Medford schools. And third, that furnishing this information would probably cause great dissension and unrest and create enormous administrative problems for the school district. The court struck down the school district's objections on all three grounds, and in doing so, presented interesting and significant legal precedence for similar arguments as well as for subsequent bilingual and privacy litigation.

The New York Federal District Court found no merit in the commonly heard argument that bilingual education is not a legal *Lau* remedy since the Supreme Court did not specify this type of a program in the *Lau v. Nichols* court case. The court made note that specific remedial programs were not requested by plaintiffs in *Lau v. Nichols*, but rather they requested that the San Francisco Board of Education be directed to apply its expertise to the problem and rectify the situation. The court further notes and reinforces with citations from *Serna v. Portales* (argued by the Mexican-American Legal Defense and Education Fund), *Morales v. Shannon* (*Morales v. Shannon*, 1975) as well as HEW guidelines, that:

> . . . it is not enough simply to provide a program for language disadvantaged children or even to staff the program with bilingual teachers: rather, the critical question is whether the program is designed to assure as much as is reasonably possible the language deficient child's growth in the English language. An inadequate program is as harmful to a child who does not speak English as no program at all.

The court further notes the relationship between the quantity of bilingual programs and the quality of instruction received by the English language deficient child. An ultimate test of a school district's response to *Lau* is the benefits that children of limited English-speaking ability receive from the school's curriculum as compared to the English-speaking students, and not the quantity of the bilingual offering.

It appears that the court is saying that if the Chinese children in *Lau* or other children of limited English-speaking ability are placed in an inadequate bilingual program; or if placed in an English as a second language program without the benefits of bilingual education, which invariably leads to academic retardation; or is placed in some kind of remedial program which accrues less benefits than those gained by the English-speaking student; such placement and instructional offering is unacceptable as a *Lau* response. The court further elaborates on the need to ascertain adequate methodologies for determining language deficiencies and evaluating language progress.

The court ruling responds to various school districts' claims that *Lau v. Nichols*, in failing to prescribe a remedy, places final responsibility on the school district to determine the affirmative steps to be taken. The court not only rejects this concept, but cites the Tenth Circuit Court of Appeals' ruling in *Serna v. Portales* that the Portales School District's remedial action for children of limited English-speaking ability was inadequate in that the proposed plan was only a token program, which would not benefit the children in question.

The second argument presented by the defendants was struck down by a ruling that the plaintiffs had shown a need for the pupil information which the school district did not wish to reveal. The court noted that the federal government has a right to such information in pursuing civil rights litigation. The court then elaborates:

> . . . in view of the significant role of private lawsuits in ending various forms of discrimination in school systems, Section 438 of the 1974 General Education Provisions Act should not serve as a cloak for alleged discriminatory practices simply because litigation to end such practices is initiated by private plaintiffs rather than the government.

The third objection was struck down by suggesting a protective procedure for making information about students available in a court case with reasonable assurances to safeguard public dissemination of the information.

It appears that litigation subsequent to *Lau v. Nichols* is providing additional specificity to the Supreme Court decision. Cases such as *Rios v. Read* provide further clarification of the legal status of bilingual education and appropriate education responses for children of limited English-speaking ability.

(IDRA, March 1977)

AIR EVALUATION OF BILINGUAL EDUCATION

1977

PREFACE

In teaching classes in educational research at the University of Texas, I invariably presented three adages about educational research to my students.

First, research is the scientific determination of that which common sense tells us. Although there are several notorious exceptions to this adage, and I must admit that the sun does not revolve around the earth, nor do I believe that the earth is flat, such exceptions are few and far between. For the most part, research findings are fairly consistent with unbiased and unprejudiced personal observations.

Second, research methodology is easy to manipulate, therefore one can readily prove or disprove any assumption. This is especially true in the social sciences where the absence of laboratory conditions and the moral constraints against many controls and planned variations preclude truly scientific testing.

Third, no research is many times better than poor research. It is much preferable to make educational decisions in the absence of information than to make them on the basis of erroneous information.

There is no better example of the wisdom of these three caveats than the evaluation of bilingual education conducted by the American Institutes of Research (AIR) for the U.S. Office of Education and made public in 1977 (American Institute for Research, 1977). The results indicating mixed findings on the performance of students in federally funded bilingual education programs received extensive media attention at the time of publication and led to the general perception that bilingual education was not a feasible alternative for limited English-proficient children in American schools. Unfortunately, the extensive criticism of the AIR study received little media coverage and did little to offset the damaging effects of the original report.

The AIR study looked at the effects of bilingual education without consideration of problems and inadequacies in the implementation of these programs. To me this has always seemed analogous to a study on the performance of a certain kind of automobile without consideration of any impediments to its successful performance. It is unfair to evaluate the performance of a new Cadillac and conclude that it is inadequate because it does not run, without consideration of the fact that the gasoline tank is empty.

IDRA conducted an analysis of the AIR study and identified major discrepancies in the identification of the target population, the selection of comparable control groups, test instruments used in the study, the amount of treatment between pre- and post-testing, lack of consistency in programs, adequacy of instructional staff, and sources of funding.

In my opinion the most damaging discrepancies were found not in the report made public, but in the technical report which received limited dissemination. The technical report indicated that 50 percent of the bilingual education teachers of the students evaluated indicated that they spoke no language other than English. Since by definition bilingual education is the use of a language other than English for instructional purposes while English is being acquired as a second language, the lack of teacher proficiency in another language precluded the implementation of a bilingual education program. Obviously, the American Institutes of Research evaluated something other than bilingual education.

The technical report indicated that as many as half of the teachers used in the evaluation had received less than three days of training over a five-year span of bilingual program implementation.

By far, the most obvious conclusion of the AIR study should have been that if you take a group of teachers who speak no language other than English and place them in a bilingual program without any additional training, do not expect an exemplary performance from their students.

A second conclusion which could have been reached was the inadequacies of the traditional, non-bilingual program, since students in this category did not do much better than those in the monolingual "bilingual" program. I was dismayed that so many of my colleagues spent so much time debating the interpretations and implications of the AIR findings while giving so little attention to the flawed methodologies which produced these findings. It appears that they swallowed camels and then proceeded to choke on the gnats. The AIR Evaluation of Bilingual Education provides a good example of the danger of disregarding common sense in conducting educational research. The opposition to bilingual education which had surfaced in the U.S. Office of Education and commissioned the AIR study provides a classic example of the ease of manipulating research to sustain a prejudicial assumption. The American Institutes of Research and the U.S. Office of Education proved conclusively in their evaluation of bilingual education that no research is better than bad research.

The U.S. Office of Education recently released interim findings of a study to determine the impact of bilingual education on students. The study, funded through the U.S. Office of Education, was conducted by the American Institutes for Research (AIR) for the Office of Planning, Budgeting, and Evaluation.

A study of this type is rather unique in that it attempts to determine the effects of bilingual education, rather than identifying problems in the implementation of bilingual education programs. It is inconceivable that USOE would conduct a study to determine the effects of reading rather than a study of a specific methodology used in the teaching of reading. It is rather obvious that the difference in treatment is indicative of the USOE commitment to reading as a desirable social value and a lack of similar USOE commitment to bilingual education.

Regardless of implications of this USOE lack of commitment to bilingual education, the report issued by USOE is based on a study which was poorly conceived and even more poorly implemented. However, the study findings were released to the public media, immediately raising questions about the value of bilingual education. Analysis of the study makes it evident that the only issues it can raise are (1) USOE's lack of commitment to bilingual education; (2) USOE's judgment in funding and publishing such a poorly designed and implemented study; and (3) USOE's inadequate supervision of its Title VII bilingual education programs.

An analysis of the AIR study conducted by Intercultural Development Research Association (IDRA) identifies major discrepancies in the identification of the target population, the selection of comparable control groups, test instruments used in the study, the amount of time between pre- and post-testing, lack of consistency in programs being studied, adequacy of instructional staff, and the source of funds being utilized.

Specifically, the following discrepancies were noted:

1. Language classifications were done subjectively by teachers in spite of a body of research which points to the unreliability of teacher judgement as an indicator of the language characteristics of students.
2. One-half of the teachers classifying students in the various language categories did not speak any language other than English.
3. The AIR study did not analyze the performance of children of limited English-speaking ability. The classification, "limited English-speaking ability," included only students who spoke no English whatsoever—monolingual speakers.
4. Comparison groups used as a standard for comparing the performance of Title VII children were "nominated" by Title VII personnel. There is no evidence that the "nominating" process did produce comparable groups.
5. District Title VII personnel were allowed to nominate groups to be used for comparisons from classrooms outside of their own. Differences between school districts, such as organization, teaching methodologies, teacher training, teacher qualifications and competence, and varying financial resources were not controlled.
6. About one-third of the *non* Title VII teachers and aides were involved in a bilingual program. This raises the possibility that the comparison groups had "bilingual treatment," thus invalidating them as a comparison. Instead of concluding that students were not doing well in some aspects of the Title VII bilingual program, an alternative conclusion may have been reached that students do better in state or locally funded bilingual programs.
7. Eighteen out of the thirty-seven projects compared (almost 50 percent) were unable to identify a comparison site. Most of the projects which could not identify a comparison group were in large metropolitan or isolated rural areas. In making comparisons between groups, it is possible that these two significant segments of the sample were excluded.
8. Measures of English reading ability were obtained by the use of English language achievement test given to Spanish monolingual children "just learning to read and write in English."
9. A very large number of children classified as Spanish monolingual did not take the various reading subtests. AIR used total reading scores in

spite of missing subtest scores, thus unfairly lowering reading scores for the entire sample.

10. Although in theory, the interim between pre-testing and post-testing could have been seven months, only six of the thirty-seven projects involved more than six months, and eighteen of the projects (almost 50 percent) were pre-post tested within a span of five months or less.

11. Using a definition based on the placement of students and not on the characteristics of the program itself, the study concluded that most bilingual programs are of the maintenance type. "Maintenance" was not defined.

12. Program characteristics varied considerably as to instructional time, content, and instructional methodologies. Impact findings did not control for such differences.

13. IDRA secondary analysis of the AIR data shows that only 26 percent of the teachers participating in the study reported having a bilingual teaching credential, which is the minimum criteria for adequate training determined by many states.

14. Although the study reports that 93.8 percent of the Title VII teachers had participated in bilingual inservice training, the training could have been taken within a five-year span and could consist of as little as one day or less. IDRA analysis of the individualized project descriptions revealed that 6.6 percent of the teachers involved in the Title VII programs received no training whatsoever, and 7.4 percent received one day or less. It is possible that as many as 46 percent of the teachers received less than three days of inservice training over a five-year span in the implementation of a new and drastically different instructional methodology.

    There is no indication of the extent or quality of such inservice.

15. Analysis of the study indicates that 49.6 percent (almost one-half) of the teachers in the Title VII bilingual programs admit to not being proficient in the other language!

    It is doubtful that USOE would give a second thought, let alone fund, a study of any program presented in the English language if one-half of the teachers did not speak English.

16. An analysis of the study indicates that a cost analysis was not performed, but rather a subjective response was collected from "cognizant local personnel." Conclusions reached did not consider bilingual Title VII funds versus other bilingual funds, developmental costs versus operational, and first year versus continuation program costs.

It is unfortunate and perhaps irresponsible for the U.S. Office of Education to release and give such wide dissemination to findings of such questionable validity just prior to the congressional deliberations on the refunding of the Bilingual Education Act.

The U.S. Office of Education should diligently pursue analysis of the problems identified in the study and channel its available resources into seeking and implementing solutions, rather than undermining bilingual education efforts through the dissemination of invalid findings. A complete copy of the IDRA analysis of the AIR study is available through IDRA.

(IDRA, June 1977)

THE INSTITUTIONALIZING AND FINANCING OF BILINGUAL EDUCATION

1980

PREFACE

"The Institutionalizing and Financing of Bilingual Education" can easily be classified as the best speech I never gave. In 1980, I was requested to present the keynote address for the annual conference of the National Association for Bilingual Education (NABE) held in Anaheim, California. Unlike most keynote addresses that are presented at the beginning of the conference, this one was scheduled for April 22, the last day of the conference. The speech was the last item on the agenda following the banquet and right before the dance.

The last session of the conference included a number of presentations, these were followed by acknowledgements and gifts for the many persons who contributed to the success of the conference. I was seated with Dr. Josue Gonzalez, a colleague of many years, and as speaker after speaker appeared on the program, Josue suggested that I trim down my speech. Reluctantly, I "X"ed out several paragraphs in my presentation. Every time another speaker approached the podium I cut out another paragraph in my speech.

Several hours later as each person who had worked on the conference registration desk was called forward to accept an award and given an opportunity to thank the conference chairperson for this individualized recognition, I was deleting entire pages from my presentation.

By the time the designated person got up to introduce me as the keynote speaker, the dance band in the back of the auditorium was already tuning up. Originally, Freddie Fender was to have played that night, but I believe that there was some kind of a problem, and he did not show up. However, the prospect of dancing to the bilingual singing of Freddie Fender led to every bilingual participant having bought a ticket for the dance. By this time I had boiled down the institutionalizing and financing of bilingual education to no more than two or three double-spaced pages.

When I was finally introduced, many of the participants were already at the back of the auditorium waiting for the band to start playing the first piece. Those still in their seats at the banquet tables were looking over their shoulders, mentally selecting prospective partners for the first dance. I walked up to the microphone, expressed my appreciation for the honor of being selected to give the keynote address, read the last paragraph and thanked the audience for their patience and attentiveness. By the time I got off the stage most of the participants were already dancing most appropriately to Freddie's "Wasted Days and Wasted Nights."

My presentation addressed two very important issues in bilingual education. The first was the institutionalizing of bilingual education, making it a part of the regular school curriculum. In retrospect, most of this part of my presentation was taken from a previous presentation that same year, "The Use of Power: A Double- Edged Sword." For the Anaheim presentation I took the six steps for internalizing shared power and applied them to the internalizing of bilingual education.

The second issue addressed was the financing of bilingual education. This section came from the studies of the cost of bilingual education conducted by IDRA staff in various states and presented elsewhere in this publication.

Although there is extensive redundancy in the inclusion of this article in this anthology, I am adamant in including it in the hope that perhaps some of the Anaheim conference participants will read it and finally bring closure to their 1980 conference experience.

The year 1980 has special significance for me for it is during this year that I conclude thirty years of service as a professional educator. Having started as a teacher at the early age of nineteen, I can now look back and divide my entire life into two segments: my childhood while I was absorbed in the process of growing up and going to school, and adulthood which has been almost totally absorbed in the process of providing educational opportunities for minority populations.

Looking over the thirty years of my professional career, the most demanding activity, the most interesting facet, and the most productive aspect has been my involvement in the development and implementation of bilingual education programs.

Although my involvement in bilingual education may be deemed as accidental, I have no doubt that certain early experiences were extremely conducive for this involvement—my birth to a predominantly Spanish-speaking Mexican-American family; growing up and being educated in a community such as Laredo, Texas, with a higher than 90 percent Spanish-speaking population; growing up with one foot in the United States and the other in northern Mexico; and the early influence of Texas' adopted educator, the late George I. Sanchez of New Mexico, who served as club sponsor, teacher, and dissertation supervisor and who advocated bilingual education in the 1930s.

Perhaps more dramatic an impact was my service as teacher, supervisor and administrator in the educational systems of the 1950s, characterized by overt racism, discriminatory practices, and massive failure in the education of minority children.

All of the experiences which affected me during the growing up period and early adulthood created an environment conducive to involvement in the development of an innovative methodology which could alter the course of educational attainment of language minority children.

The seed was planted in my mind by Dr. Sanchez; the soil on which the seed rested was rich, fertilized by litigation and legislation conducive to the growth of equal educational opportunity; the climate was perfect, with the germinating seed receiving the sun of the civil rights movement and the warmth of the Kennedy-Johnson efforts toward the creation of the Great Society.

The necessary moisture for the growth of the new plant was provided by the federal funds falling upon school districts in the forms of Title I, Migrant, Title VII, ESAP, ESAA and numerous other programs which contrasted dramatically with the drought of state and local funds in the pre-*Rodriguez* era (*San Antonio Independent School District v. Rodriguez*, 1973).

So it is not surprising that in the environment of the 1960s and the 1970s with such propensity for growth, that bilingual education became the single most important development in the education of language minority children in this century.

This is not to say that there were no problems associated with this growth. The reversals of the Cárdenas Plan by the Tenth Circuit Court of Appeals in *Keyes v. Denver* and the loss in a number of prejudicial courts such as in *Otero v. Mesa Valley* acted as hailstones, threatening the loss of the crop, and certainly doing damage to the developing embryo (*Keyes v. School District No. 1*, 1983; *Otero v. Mesa Valley School District No. 51*, 1975).

Needless to say, the young bilingual education plant was almost smothered by weeds, namely those programs hastily implemented in token responses with non-bilingual teachers, with poor training, and void of bilingual instructional materials and with the complete absence of school system support.

Even more damaging was the premature harvesting of the crop by uninformed gardeners such as those from the American Institute of Research, who did not know the difference between the crop and the weeds, and who made hasty, erroneous decisions about their findings.

We also saw the wild birds almost destroy the plants as they satiated their appetites at the expense of the plant. These birds were the non-advocates and sometimes opponents of bilingual education, who, when funding of programs became a reality, became instant experts and fed on the movement, as long as funds continued to be forthcoming.

It is interesting to note that not all programs developed in the favorable environment conducive to bilingualism in education. I remember a summer institute offered by Dr. Theodore Anderson at the University of Texas prior to the enactment of the Bilingual Education Act. Participants in this 1967 institute returned to their school districts in Texas, and without a single penny in bilingual education funds and with little support resources and with special dispensation from the Texas Commissioner of Education since teaching in Spanish was illegal in those days, proceeded to implement bilingual education programs.

I stated that the enactment of Title VII in 1968, provided the first rainfall for the developing program. This was followed in rapid succession by state appropriations which this year total $100 million in support of bilingual education. School districts across the country have appropriated almost $50 million in local funding to supplement the state and federal effort.

Within my professional lifetime I have seen bilingual education develop from an experimental program to a pilot program, to a demonstration program, and even to a full service program in some communities.

Yet bilingual education has not received full acceptance and recognition as an educational methodology for children of limited English proficiency, let alone as a universal methodology for all children, and it will not do so until two additional barriers are overcome—that of institutionalizing and financing bilingual education.

Therefore, I have selected these topics for my presentation here tonight—the financing and institutionalizing of bilingual education. The context of bilingual education in the country today is such that in my opinion it must be institutionalized or it will die. I believe I can substantiate this contention in my presentation today.

I welcome the opportunity to make this presentation, first, because in the dawn of this national age of neo-conservatism, I believe it to be a most timely topic for those of us who care about the fates of language minority children; and secondly, because in order to make this presentation, I am forced to review not the literature, but my own interactions over a thirty year period with the explicit and implicit power centers operating within and upon the institution of education.

I draw upon my experiences as a participant in developing Title VII of the Elementary Secondary Education Act, a participant in *Lau v. Nichols* litigation, a consultant to the Task Force which wrote *Lau Remedies*, and as a witness or resource in over thirty-five court cases dealing with bilingual education (*Lau v. Nichols*, 1973).

From my own experience, I have seen the educational system resisting change through a series of phases. These phases apply, in my estimation, to the mainstream American educational system as a whole, but they also apply specifically to the many individual struggles to bring reform to the educational system and force the doors of opportunity open to a population not previously allowed to enter. These phases apply very specifically to bilingual education which did not develop within the power structure of the educational system, but rather developed outside of the structure and has been forced upon a reluctant and oftentimes recalcitrant system.

I believe the phases operate in almost all cases to a greater or lesser degree, but six phases are usually present in the implementation of this type of innovation. The six phases through which innovation must pass are:

1. the resistance phase;
2. the tolerance phase;
3. the pseudo-acceptance phase;
4. the evaluation phase;
5. the acceptance phase; and
6. the management phase.

1. THE RESISTANCE PHASE

The *resistance* phase is characterized by open hostility on the part of the traditional institutional power centers to the proposed innovation. While this hostility is very likely to be exacerbated when the recipients of the new program are poor and/or minority, the hostility is present in almost all instances, whether the innovation is a spelling program or the teaching of the metric system.

In addition to hostility, the resistance phase is characterized by an extreme preoccupation with the "we/they" complex. Interestingly enough, the atmosphere dominating the resistance phase within the institution often gives license to behaviors previously shunned or barely tolerated. Erroneous information, for example, is almost always rampant in the resistance stage and individuals who would not, under most circumstance give credence or nurturance to error, find themselves doing so in the extreme. Thus, it is possible for the "institution in resistance" to experience some power shifts within itself as the situation calls for or allows changes in behavioral standards among the leadership. Unfortunately this often leads to increased paranoia within the institution and delays the evolution into the next and subsequent phases.

The resistance phase is an important one to the agents of institutional change and can be decisive in terms of final outcomes if it is understood that it is the first of several phases the institutions will pass through in its effort to "shake-off" the invading concept. The strength and discipline and wisdom with which the institution is approached during this period may well set the tone for all future pursuits. Of course the two extreme results of the resistance phase are (1) that the advocates of innovation are successfully put-off, and traditional programs prevail or (2) that the advocates of the innovation are so successful in pressing their case that the institution eliminates all objection. In either of these cases, the subsequent phase is not one of the "institution in tolerance."

2. TOLERANCE PHASE

When the "institution is in tolerance," it is beginning to understand that some yielding will have to occur, although this is almost always accompanied by a collective conviction that the innovation will be neither substantive nor of long duration. One can say that the institution in tolerance is sort of holding its nose—and its breath—firm in the conviction that the turmoil will pass quickly.

The tolerance phase is also characterized by a high degree of solidarity within the institution. Old institutional differences fade away, again perhaps because the innovation is seen as a temporary condition.

The tolerance phase can have important negative consequences for those who are seeking to bring about the institutional change if tolerance is misunderstood for acceptance. Progress and fidelity in the pursuit of the change are both likely to be jeopardized if the advocates of the new program proceed too fast to operationalize the program believing that the institution is keeping pace. When attitudes are revealed with a greater level of honesty, as is inevitable, mistrust can reach irretrievable levels and the struggle for acceptance becomes a winner-take-all struggle which is almost always a lose-lose situation, particularly for poor and minority populations.

3. PSEUDO-ACCEPTANCE PHASE

The resistance and tolerance phases are almost always followed by a significant event or action, either negative or positive in nature, which either terminates or mortally wounds the advocacy for innovation or which moves the institution to a phase of pseudo-acceptance. This action or event may be a legalistic one, i.e., *Lau v. Nichols*, a significant negotiation session, a change in some symbolic condition, a change in significant players through resignation or replacement or the intervention or mediation by some external and usually higher authority, i.e., Office for Civil Rights.

The pseudo-acceptance phase is the beginning of acceptance. The institution begins to behave in ways which begin to get the institution ready for accepting and then managing the innovation. I have called this phase the pseudo-acceptance phase because, in my experience I have found institutional behavior at this point in a change process to be lacking in genuineness while working extremely hard to give the appearance of acceptance. In fact so much energy is spent on giving the appearance of acceptance that significant segments of the institution may begin to believe that the acceptance is genuine. Depending on the level of lingering mistrust generated by the two previous phases, this phase can serve the advocates of innovation well; it provides them the opportunity to first examine the broad repertoire of institutional behaviors which the institution will employ in the inevitable new program as it provides the opportunity to reinforce those behaviors genuinely helpful to the program and begin to extinguish those most abhorrent to the change.

Inevitably the pseudo-acceptance phase is brought to an end when the traditional programs are tested against the innovation and found lacking.

For the advocates of change, it is critical that these transitional phases preceding the evaluation phase be understood. The institution is about to go into the first period of seriously and realistically evaluating its position, its behaviors, its options and the concepts it is being caused to deal with. The messages change advocates give the institution during this period must be clear, complete and strong.

4. THE EVALUATION PHASE

The evaluation phase which follows, then, is one in which the institution assesses, usually with a high degree of clarity, exactly where it stands. In the best of situations it may even genuinely examine the concept of innovation and determine its appropriateness to the institutional mission, but in most cases it does not. It does assess its options in relation to the proposed change, the appropriateness (to its own ends) of its behaviors, the range of strategies appropriate to its goals, and its skills relative to its adopted strategies, including the acquisition of an appropriate language (or the appropriate verbiage) for dealing with the new program.

The products of the evaluation phase may be (1) to go to a new phase of more genuine acceptance, or (2) to return to any one or all three of the earlier stages. If the institution chooses to return to the previous phases, it will likely cycle sequentially through these back to an evaluation phase unless it succeeds in eliminating the advocacy for change altogether. It is important to note however that the return to the previous phases may be very short-lived and may constitute little more than a test of the advocacy position in order to gather more information for making evaluation of the institution's position. Advocates of the change should understand that a return to previous phases is not necessarily bad for their cause, if they understand what is occurring. The "re-learning" of the new realities on the part of the institution may have significant long-term benefits to the innovation. If advocates do not understand the sequential nature of the behavior of institutions when confronting change, they are more likely to be defeated by it.

The inevitable result of the evaluation phase is that the institution becomes a formidable member of a new relationship, a member that behaves in ways that suit its own purposes, does so with great discipline, and utilizes all of the vast institutional resources at its command.

5. THE ACCEPTANCE PHASE

We enter now the period of true acceptance. The institution has determined what it must accept and it proceeds to do so. It may not and probably does not accept the innovation as viewed by its advocates, but it has accepted the concept to the extent that it has assessed it must. At this point the institutional leadership determines that it must now sell the new concept to the many elements of the institution. The institution assumes ownership for the concept as it defines it. Verbiage reflective of the concept becomes a part of the official language of the institution. The concept is discussed in print and thus validated. Personnel skilled in operationalizing the concept are employed. In the best of all institutional worlds, some of the original advocates are employed.

6. THE MANAGEMENT PHASE

As the innovation enters the *management phase*, the institution has determined that it can not only accept this new thing, but that it can manage it. And it does. The first management objective is to contain it, to delimit the parameters of power. The second is to create or reinforce an organism which can cancel any outcome. The third is to manage the information and the organization elements such as time, money and other resources.

At this point, it is interesting to note that the periods of confrontation during early phases commonly makes the original leadership of the advocacy group unacceptable to the institution, and the employment or appointment process always seeks surrogates which are less repugnant to them. When this happens the original leadership finds itself left out, unemployed, and a nonparticipant in further implementation.

The surrogates are more acceptable, less pushy, and in many cases less supportive of the original objectives.

Assuming that the original advocates of shared power are able to withstand this institutional onslaught organizationally, what they will find is that their concept has been taken away from them, it is redefined, reshaped, renamed, and redirected.

It is this management phase which is the toughest of all on the parents of poor and minority children, even when the game is played ethically, and I have seen it played otherwise far too many times. If the previous stages have been more than survived, and if they have been understood as well, the chances of doing constructive work for children are good in the management phase.

The second half of this presentation deals with financing the institutionalized program. Assuming that bilingual education survives the evaluation phase and school systems accept and manage it, where will the money come from to fund a full service program for bilingual education?

The question involves such a great number of children, a minimum of 2.4 to 4.5 million limited English proficiency, plus all others which may eventually desire the program, and such massive resources that one is prone to admit the hopelessness of institutionalization, and I must admit that for some time we have shied away from confronting this task.

Very recently, the reluctance of the Department of HEW to publish the revised *Lau* remedies in the Federal Register without a cost analysis, and the federal prohibitions against an enforcement effort if the new remedies require more than $100 million in new local, state and/or federal funds, have forced us to tackle this problem.

The first question which arises is, "How much does it cost to educate a child in a bilingual education program?"

It is important to distinguish immediately between how much does it cost and how should the funds be distributed. Whether allocation should be made on a formula basis, whether the formula can be based on district expenditures, how to avoid the poorest getting the least and the richest getting the most, how to provide federal assistance in a full-service program without supplanting and with the states withdrawing their support, are all important questions which must be resolved, but they deal with the area of distribution and are not pertinent to determining how much it should cost to implement the program.

On the other hand, there are some basic caveats which one must respect. The two most serious are the proxy and the upgrading concepts.

The proxy concept proposes that oftentimes an institution receives funds for a specific program which acts as a proxy for a more fundamental need. Thus, programs may be funded as a political response, for equalization purposes or for an entirely different purpose.

Thus, we see ESAP funding as a part of President Nixon's southern political strategy to offset the political liability of his limited desegregation efforts. Categorical programs are funded in the various states as a temporary solution for expenditure disparities without having to permanently alter the discrimination system of public school finance during the pseudo-acceptance phase of institutionalizing equity.

Another example of the proxy concept is the state of New Mexico which allocates for bilingual education 50 percent above what it takes to educate a child in a traditional monolingual program, a fine gesture of support on the part of the state, except that although a district need only count and report the number of children of limited English proficiency to acquire the funds, there is no state law or requirement that the district offer a bilingual education program or that the funds be used in its support.

The second caveat deals with innovative programs being used to bring about a general upgrading of the entire educational system. I am quick to admit that Title I programs, migrant programs, bilingual programs and other innovations for minority and disadvantaged children have made a dramatic and worthwhile contribution to the improvement of educational opportunities for all children. The planning, staffing, curricula, training, individualizing, community involvement and evaluation have developed skills, processes, and products.

These skills processes, and products initially associated with minority program planning, staffing, curriculum development, training, individualizing of instruction, community involvement and evaluation have permeated and impacted all educational programs. Their effects have not been contained within the confines of the target population. In some programs the effects on the non-target population have been even stronger. As fifteen disadvantaged students were removed from a classroom of thirty for participation in a Title I funded compensatory education program, the remaining students enjoyed a fifteen to one pupil/teacher ratio which they had never experienced prior to the innovation.

Regardless, the issue is not whether other students benefit from the innovation, but whether the innovation should bear the costs of all the benefits. In analyzing costs of bilingual education programs one cannot fail to note that a particular school spent $800 for the purchase of a motion picture projector. Can one assume then, that a motion picture projector is essential to bilingual instruction but not necessary for a traditional monolingual program? If such an expenditure cannot be justified on these grounds, then one must assume that the cost of the projector represents a general upgrading of the total school program and not an expenditure endemic to bilingual education.

The process which our organization has followed in determining the cost of a bilingual education program is to determine which are the characteristics of a bilingual program and determining the cost of these characteristics.

Using their methodology, IDRA conducted three state studies to determine the cost of bilingual education in Texas, Utah and Colorado. A panel of experts in each of the states with diverse backgrounds including state education agencies, parents, teachers, and administrators, determined the characteristics of a minimally adequate bilingual education program in each of the three states and subsequently determined the add-on or extra cost of these characteristics.

This process identified six elements requiring funding over and above the cost of a monolingual program. Our findings are as follows:

1. Bilingual education programs have staffing needs over and beyond traditional programs.

The development of a second language requires language modeling and child adult interaction which must be reflected in a lower pupil/teacher ratio than in monolingual programs. The bilingual program requires additional administrative/supervisory staff and additional staff development or inservice training activities.

One state (Utah) was convinced that staff resources were not available within the state and required out of state staff recruitment at additional expense.

2. The second element identified in all three states was a need for materials including textbooks, workbooks, consumables and supplies in a second language and comparable to those used in monolingual programs.
3. The third element dealt with educational equipment needed for bilingual instruction. Out of a laundry list of some sixty audiovisual devices, the only one identified as essential by the panelists was a "language master" device which models language and allows the student to record language samples and play back both versions.
4. Pupil testing identified three needs: a) Language proficiency measures; b) Student achievement measures in a language other than English; and c) Program assessment and evaluation measures.
5. A fifth expenditure was for library books and reference materials in languages other than English.
6. The final element identified was support for community involvement activities. This element surfaced very strongly in the Colorado study.

Three variables were identified which may increase or decrease the cost of bilingual education. These were:

1. Start up costs versus continuation costs. The first year of the project required certain expenditures not recurring in subsequent years. Examples of these costs are staff development, some materials, equipment and staff recruitment.
2. A second variable was grade level. In general the cost of bilingual education at specific grade levels paralleled the cost of education at those same levels. Secondary school programs were the most expensive; kindergarten and first grade were less expensive, and third through sixth grades were the least expensive.
3. The third variable was the per pupil expenditure levels for the state and the district. As can be expected, the bilingual program tends to be more expensive in higher level of expenditure districts than in districts with a lower level of expenditure. Teacher salaries, amounts of materials and supplies in the monolingual program tend to affect proportionately the cost of the bilingual program.

The IDRA studies indicate that the cost of educating a pupil in a bilingual program in Texas requires an add-on cost of from $170 to $243 per year depending on grade level and year of implementation, $144 to $298 in Utah, and $209 to $330 in Colorado, although the dollar figures among the three states are not for the same fiscal year.

For the school finance experts, I may add that our studies identified a weighted pupil factor of from 1.17 to 1.42 depending on state, grade level and year of implementation, that is an additional expenditure of from 17 percent to 44 percent of the monolingual program cost for that student.

Having this information, it is now possible to ascertain how much it would cost to implement an institutionalized bilingual education program nationwide.

Using the Texas figures which are based on the largest sampling and conceding a need for more extensive study as well as national validation and update, I am prepared to throw out a ballpark figure for your consideration.

When I was teaching statistics I was frequently asked by my students to define the word "statistics." My favorite definition was, "Statistics is a bunch of numbers looking for an argument." Let me start a national argument by stating that to provide a bilingual education program for each limited English proficiency kid requiring it would cost $500 million a year.

Again such an amount of money may appear prohibitive, and I am frequently bombarded by questions as to where this sum can come from. My response is, "Not to worry, the money is already there."

This year Title VII is expending $135 million in federal bilingual funds. ESAA Bilingual has $8.6 million for a federal total of $143.6 million. State allocations for bilingual education total $93.8 million and local allocations total $46.9 million.

The total amount already appropriated at the federal, state and local levels is $284.3 million. However, I was surprised to find that $229 million is currently being expended for disadvantaged children of limited English proficiency in Title I programs; although only a small portion of this money is in support of bilingual activities. If one were to make the not unreasonable demand that the compensatory education assistance be given in a language which the child understands, over $500 million for the support of bilingual education is currently available. This amount does not represent nor does it include the amount of ESAA, Title IV, and migrant funds being expended on limited English-proficiency children and which should be used in support of bilingual education programs.

If current supplanting or other regulations impede the utilization of the funds for this purpose, the obvious need is to clarify or change the regulations in order to provide bilingual resources and at the same time make the programs responsive to all the characteristics of children.

In conclusion, may I state that after years of struggle in the development of bilingual education programs in this country we are at a point of institutionalizing such programs. We have gone through resistance, tolerance, pseudo-acceptance and are currently at the evaluation phase. Before true acceptance can be reached, the evaluation phase demands evaluative information on the financing of the institutionalized response.

The costing and identification of sources of funding of bilingual education will eliminate one of the few remaining barriers for all children to finally achieving equality of educational opportunity.

I trust that before long and while I am still around, we will see the harvesting of the crop. I trust that the land which has lain fallow will be productive again. And I trust that part of the harvest will be reinvested into future seeding so that the harvest will grow, and bilingual education will not remain a compensatory program for children of limited English proficiency, but an exciting and successful methodology for the expansion of American language facility and the means for perpetuating American leadership worldwide.

THE ROLE OF NATIVE-LANGUAGE INSTRUCTION IN BILINGUAL EDUCATION

1984

PREFACE

Since its inception there has been extensive opposition to bilingual education. The reasons for this opposition vary. To some, the use of a language other than English may seem un-American. To others, language diversity is seen as the basis for social divisiveness and political separatism. And to many, it is seen as an impediment to the learning of English by the language minority populations.

The schools have their own reasons for opposition. As a pedagogical methodology it was developed outside the establishment and is therefore suspect. It is threatening to the majority of teachers and administrators who have no facility in a language other than English. It requires instructional time which is seen as a scarce commodity in an already overcrowded curriculum.

But perhaps the strongest resistance by the school to the use of this new methodology is the fact that it is new, and educational institutions have a long track record of opposing almost every innovation which rocks the boat and changes the order of things.

This normal resistance to change which characterizes the school has been further strengthened by the extensive amount of misinformation about bilingual education. So much so, that bilingual education must be one of the most controversial issues in American education. It is very common for me to mention that I am writing something about bilingual education and immediately hear the statement, "I don't approve of bilingual education." In most cases I ask for the reason for disapproval, and inevitably the reason provided is based on erroneous information about bilingual education.

As the use of bilingual programs in schools is expanded, practitioners have moved further away from its rationale. This neglect of rationale is not unique to bilingual education. If you were to ask a teacher why a specific approach is used for the teaching of reading, spelling, arithmetic or almost any other subject, the teacher would be hard-pressed to provide an adequate answer. In many cases, the school persists in educational methodologies which have little, if any, justification. Why is the spelling bee so popular when there is an abundance of evidence that it provides an extensive allocation of instructional time to the students that need it the least and a minimum of time to the students that need it the most?

The continued use of spelling bees presents no big public relations problem for the school. After all, there is no organized and heavily funded state and national Society for the Elimination of Spelling Bees (SESB). However, this is not true about bilingual education. The methodology is consistently under attack by organized groups of xenophobics whose main purpose in life seems to be to insure and perpetuate foreign language ignorance in America.

As bilingual education is further institutionalized in the presence of continued opposition, it is necessary to reiterate its rationale and relate it to bilingual methodology. In 1984, I responded to this need with this article on the rationale of bilingual education.

This article was originally published in the January 1984, issue of the IDRA *Newsletter*. It was reprinted in the January 1986, issue of Phi Delta Kappa's *Kappan*. More recently, it was included in the 1992 anthology by James Crawford, *Language Loyalties* published by the University of Chicago Press.

The article emphasizes the use of native language for continued cognitive development as the student makes the transition from one language to another. This emphasis is critical since its neglect has been the most detrimental factor to the success of bilingual education programs. Teachers tend to forget that the use of the native language provides the vehicle for cognitive development as a new language is acquired. Due to the influence of academicians, foreign language instruction and the use of foreign textbooks as instructional materials, teachers in bilingual programs have a strong tendency to use the "correct version" of the student's native language. The temptation to teach the student the correct version of his language takes precedence over the use of the vernacular for instructional purposes. When this occurs, and it occurs all too frequently, the native language used by the teacher is just as foreign to the student as the English being acquired. As the use of the vernacular is diminished, so is the ability to communicate, and this lack of communication inhibits further cognitive development.

I see such an extensive failure to use the native language vernacular in bilingual programs, that unless it is consistently addressed in teacher training and inservice programs, the promise of bilingual education as a sound pedagogical methodology for limited English proficient children will not be realized.

Few public issues today produce such a range of diverse reactions as does bilingual education. Proponents of bilingual education programs are vociferous in their demands for it; opponents are equally adamant in their opposition. The reasons for support or opposition are so varied that in the heat of emotional, patriotic, racial, and other arguments, one tends to lose sight of any pedagogical rationale.

Criticisms of bilingual education come from every type of individual and for every conceivable reason. Noel Epstein coined a new phrase, "affirmative ethnicity," to voice his opposition. Others focus on the violation of the official national language (although there is none in the United States), the dangers of language-minority separatism, the unwillingness of newcomers to learn and to speak the English language, and the undesirable need for a crutch in the American and English-language culture. One even hears the perennial resurrection of the totally discredited "Interference Theory" (if individuals are allowed to speak their native language, it will interfere with their learning of English).

An uninformed observer might suggest that part of the problem is the failure of proponents of bilingual education to present an adequate rationale, but such a suggestion would be extremely naive. Actually, the rationale has been presented again and again in journal articles, in the mass media, in court decisions, and in legislation. The fact is that opponents seldom use an accurate definition of bilingual education, a fair description of it, or factual information concerning it. In most cases, the emotional response to the very idea of bilingual education overshadows all rational considerations.

Yet I would be remiss if I allowed those who peruse press releases, news coverage, and letters to the editor to form negative impressions on the basis of information presented solely by opponents of bilingual education. For that reason, I am again presenting some arguments in favor of bilingual education and the pedagogical reasons for the temporary use of native-language instruction in bilingual education programs.

THE EVOLUTION OF BILINGUAL EDUCATION

Bilingual education came into favor as an alternative program in the late 1960s, but my first contact with second-language development occurred much earlier than that. In the mid-1930s, without an adequate knowledge of the English language, I was placed in an all-English first-grade instructional program. I still remember how I felt. The experience was not merely uncomfortable, unpleasant, or challenging, it was traumatic, disconcerting, and terrorizing. This approach to education can best be described as sink-or-swim: either we learned the English language quickly and swam, or we failed to do so and sank. More than 80 percent of us sank. Furthermore, of the few who did not sink, many never really learned to swim well enough to do more than barely survive.

It is interesting to note that, almost without exception, those of us who learned the English language grew up in homes with a strong language capability. Although this capability was usually in a language other than English, the level of language ability within our families was high during our developmental years. This is as true for language-minority persons of my generation who grew up to become legislators, mayors, educators, and successful business people as it is today for the Korean or Vietnamese children who are graduating as valedictorians. The common denominator invariably is extensive competence in the use of some language.

Another significant event in my life occurred in the early 1950s, when I worked as a teacher, supervisor, and principal in the Texas public schools. The performance of children of limited English proficiency in my classes was another traumatic experience. These children, who in any other way would be classified as normal, were unable to perform the most basic classroom activities. I joined the thousands of other teachers frustrated by the fact that despite commitment, caring, and hard work, our teaching of language-minority children did not produce the same type of performance we took for granted with non-minority children.

Still another memory that haunts me concerns the implementation of structured English-language programs in the early 1960s. The main difference between these programs and the earlier sink-or-swim approach was that these programs made a concerted effort to introduce the English language in a structured, non-threatening way. As a result, the trauma of a transition to a new language in the early elementary grades was reduced, but it is difficult to claim that this new methodology was clearly successful.

Although the approach was vastly superior to previous methods, it was evident that children who were exposed to it would suffer cognitive discontinuity, since the learning of skills and content was deferred until they demonstrated a certain level of mastery of the English language. It became common educational practice to postpone cognitive activities until English mastery had been established, but children in such programs were generally a full calendar year behind their English-speaking counterparts—and the cognitive deficit tended to grow in subsequent years, rather than to be reduced or eliminated.

By 1966, the frustrations associated with the instruction of children with limited proficiency in English had become intolerable for many. Language-minority children were dropping out of school at rates of 80 percent and higher, and their achievement levels averaged two grade levels below the norm on standardized tests. Clearly, the English-language programs had not lived up to their promise. In addition, the civil rights movement had awakened the interest of minorities in the education of their children. Students and parents alike were demanding improved educational opportunities, and educators were trying desperately to cope with the growing pressures.

The compensatory education programs of the late sixties and early seventies did little for language-minority children. Such compensatory programs seldom went beyond giving students more of the same inadequate programs that had been in vogue in the fifties. The same methodologies that had served them so poorly during six-hour days for nine months of the year were now extended for a couple of hours each day and for the remaining three months of the year.

Thus it was that a group of concerned educators began to plan alternative teaching strategies. One program that surfaced at the time was a bilingual approach for the teaching of children with limited proficiency in English. It is not sufficient to say that the bilingual approach was merely *accepted* in the late 1960s; it was grasped as the straw that could prevent the continued drowning of children of limited English proficiency in the dark waters of U.S. elementary and secondary schools. The existing situation (the traditional all-English approach), now being widely recommended as a new "alternative" was so bad that anything different was worth trying.

RATIONALE FOR BILINGUAL EDUCATION

The original concept of using a child's native language for instructional purposes while English was being learned as a second language was based primarily on the need for continued learning as the child moved from one language to another. Limited familiarity with the new language made it difficult to attempt to develop reading skills without assurance that a sufficient mastery of the new language enabled the child to understand what was being read. The same was true of the acquisition of mathematical concepts and of learning in the various content fields.

A second consideration was the need to diminish the alienation that children frequently face when they are pushed into an unfamiliar language situation. Not only does the use of the native language lessen the trauma of transition to a second language, but the use of the native language does much to develop and maintain a positive self-concept. The advent of bilingual programs with native-language instruction gave the language-minority child a new sense of acceptance. Suddenly the school appeared to be saying, "We accept your language, your heritage, your culture, your family, your ethnicity." In contrast to previous school experiences, bilingual education gives the language-minority child feelings of worth and self-esteem seldom experienced before.

Recently, I have seen several newspaper articles stating that a positive self-concept should be an outcome of successful learning. In reality, there is a circular relationship between input and outcome. A negative self-concept is detrimental to learning; failure to learn then strengthens the negative self-concept. This cumulative-deficit phenomenon leads children caught in this cycle to do worse and worse in school. On the other hand, a positive self-concept contributes to successful performance, which leads to an improved self-concept and more successful performance.

A third reason for the use of a native language in bilingual programs has received little recognition in the past but now looms as the most important consideration. *The use of language is imperative to the intellectual development of the child.* The extent to which a person develops his or her intellectual capacity depends greatly on the extent of language acquisition and use. By *intellectual capacity* I do not mean the amount an individual learns, but rather the amount of capability for learning that is developed.

Bruce Gaarder, an advocate of bilingual education in the mid-1960s, used an effective analogy to illustrate this point. He compared the used of language to a window through which a person interacts with the environment. The interaction with the environment through this "window" of language provides the experiences that produce learning. The bigger the window, the wider the panorama with which the child is able to interact; the smaller the window, the narrower the view.

Gaarder compared submersion in an all-English curriculum to the closing of the window—eliminating the interaction of the child with the environment and precluding any learning. He compared the minority language to a blue window and the English language to a rose window. The language-minority child who had always used the blue window for communicating with the environment could be placed in a closed room and told, "From now on, you may no longer use this blue window, you will learn to use the rose window in communicating with your environment." Thereupon the blue window would be covered, and the child would stare at a blank wall. Occasionally a child would say, "I don't see any rose window," and the school would respond, "That's because we haven't built it yet, but keep looking at the blank wall, and we will eventually place a rose window there."

Staring at a blank wall does little to produce either learning or the capacity for learning. Bilingual programs allow for continued learning and for a continuing increase in the capacity for learning, even as the transition to a new language is being made.

IMPORTANCE OF THE NATIVE LANGUAGE

Some commentators on the education of language-minority children seem to be obsessed with the concept of an immediate transition to an all-English-language curriculum. Although the school should be concerned with immediate and extensive development of the English language, there are dangers in discontinuing the use of the native language too quickly. Many educators and laypeople recommend that schools discontinue the use of the native language as soon as a child has a basic understanding of English. The danger in this practice is that "a basic understanding of English" is frequently determined by measures of the child's ability to communicate in social situations, which is far from the level of language facility needed for learning activities.

A Hispanic member of the Texas Higher Education Coordinating Board claimed that bilingual education can become a crutch for Hispanic children. Well, crutches are very useful implements when there is a need for them. Crutches provide support until such time as the body recovers from trauma and can function without them. Certainly it is possible to use crutches beyond the time of need, but if one were to err in determining the time of need, most orthopedists would probably prefer that the error be in favor of overuse rather than underuse. The same is true of native-language instruction.

The use of the native language does not preclude the learning of English; on the contrary, research shows that it enhances such learning. Therefore, rather than risk premature restriction of native-language usage and the accompanying loss of language and communication capability, I recommend continuation of the use of the native language until there is complete assurance of sufficient mastery of the English language.

Each person, at any age, has a fund of language that has been acquired over the years. This fund of language has a circular relationship with intellect. People of high intelligence have a large language capacity; people with large language capacity develop high intelligence. A small portion of this language is rather superficial; that is, it is apparent, readily available, and commonly used in everyday social situations, e.g., "I am fine, thank you. How are you?" Each person also has a much larger store of language that is more sophisticated, technical, and not commonly used in social situations. The relationship between the two "types" of language has been described as analogous to an iceberg: only the tip can be seen above the water, leaving the larger bulk hidden beneath the surface.

In learning situations, the learner continuously uses language for discovery. In fact, virtually the entire language capacity of an individual may be used in a learning situation. Determining language development and the capacity for its use in learning on the basis of a working command of the superficial social aspects of language may be detrimental to the learner.

The ability to communicate in a social situation ("I am fine, thank you. How are you?") does not guarantee the existence of the sophisticated, technical language necessary for coping with learning situations.

Some educators believe that at least six years of language development are desirable to allow children to acquire a minimal "reservoir" of language before they begin to learn basic skills in first grade. Research shows that language-minority children may require several years to build the same minimal language reservoir before being able to cope with an all-English language curriculum. Failure to allow sufficient language development before the transition will result in a child's being unable to cope with anything but the most shallow levels of learning and will affect that child's future capability for learning.

Consider the movie portraying the story of Helen Keller's early life, *The Miracle Worker*. Totally deprived of sight and hearing, young Helen lived an animal-like existence—not even aware of the existence of the language that would enable her to communicate with the world. The climax of the movie occurs when she realizes that the hand movements and spellings that her tutor has been trying to teach her constitute language, a method of interpersonal communication. In that scene we see Helen Keller leave her minimally human existence by acquiring the power of language; we see, too, her transformation into an eager and voracious learner.

The placement of a language-minority child into an all-English curriculum before the child has achieved sufficient mastery of the English language is like running *The Miracle Worker* in reverse. We take an eager and voracious learner and remove the power of language, thereby sentencing the child to an animal-like existence until such time as the child acquires sufficient fluency in a different language.

The emerging science of language development substantiates this contention. As educators discover more and more about the role of language in the intellectual development of children, the rationale for bilingual education becomes stronger and stronger. Not only can we prevent academic retardation and negative self-concepts through the use of native-language instruction, but the child's whole future capability for learning can be effectively enhanced.

If the pedagogical evidence is indeed so convincing, why is there so much opposition to bilingual education and the use of children's native languages in the schools? The answer to the question does not rest in pedagogy. Without exception, all experts in language development and second-language acquisition concur regarding the advantages of native-language instruction. The reason must lie elsewhere.

CRITICISMS OF BILINGUAL EDUCATION

After reviewing scores of criticisms of the use of students' native languages in bilingual education programs, I have concluded that these criticisms generally fall into one or more of three categories: emotional, misinformational, or attitudinal.

As I stated above, much of the criticism of programs of bilingual education stems from negative emotional reactions elicited by the idea of using a language other than English for instruction programs in U.S. schools. Reactions range from the affirmative ethnicity of Noel Epstein to the religious objection of Miriam "Ma" Ferguson: "If English was good enough for Jesus Christ, it ought to be good enough for the children of Texas."

Unfortunately, there is little that can be done to ameliorate these strong emotional reactions. Because the source of the irritation is not rational but emotional, rational argument does little good. If a true-blue American patriot feels that it is un-American to speak a language other than English, there is little ground for argument. When I ask, "Which is less patriotic—to allow a child to develop his intellect using a language other than English or to allow a child to grow up deficient in all language and reasoning skills because of an arbitrary English-language limitation?" the common response has been to perpetuate the limitation. It is no wonder, then, that bilingual education programs have come about largely as a result of equal protection litigation and civil rights legislation rather than public support.

It is interesting to note that public school educators have not been exempt from reacting emotionally. The preservation of sacred cows has frequently taken precedence over the need for instructional reform.

Critics of bilingual education also insinuate that advocates of the system have a vested interest in bilingualism and stand to gain financially or professionally through their involvement in bilingual education programs. This is not true. Practitioners of bilingual education have additional training in the area, but they perform in positions that are comparable to those of traditional teachers. The leaders in bilingual education achieved their leadership positions in traditional programs. If the advocacy of bilingual education has had an impact on the financial or professional status of these individuals, that impact has probably been harmful.

If negative emotional responses are the main source of criticisms of bilingual programs, then misinformation must rank a close second. Although it is tempting to conclude that advocates of bilingual education have not done a good job of defining and describing this educational methodology, the fault goes much deeper.

The news media have consistently failed to give extensive coverage to what they perceive as educational (and therefore not newsworthy) material. As a result, articles dealing with bilingual education tend to be short, uninformative, and played down. On the other hand, criticisms of bilingual education—considered controversial and interesting—are given top coverage. A recent article on the shortcoming of bilingual education received wide coverage in the media, including front-page headlines in several prominent newspapers. Subsequent articles on the scandalous methodology used in the study that produced the original article received little or no coverage.

In addition, much of the misinformation about bilingual education is the creation of overly emotional critics. It is not unusual for an article criticizing bilingual education to state or imply that native language is being used in lieu of English-language acquisition. This is simply not so. For example, a writer in the *San Antonio Light* stated, "In many instances, according to reliable published reports, [the teachers of children with limited proficiency in English] are more dedicated to teaching them the correct and literary form of their native language than teaching them English." Again, this is simply not so.

I have observed bilingual classrooms in at least twenty different states, and I have never seen teachers neglect the teaching of the English language in bilingual programs. Furthermore, I have reviewed hundreds of reports on bilingual programs from school districts, state education agencies, federal agencies, and the U.S. Department of Education, and I have never seen a single report (let alone a reliable report) of the practice described in the article. I challenge any reader to show me one report—just one—that documents one case in which a bilingual education teacher was found dedicating more time to the correct and literary form of the native language than to instruction in English as a second language.

The emotional responses to bilingual education sometimes defy all reason. Twice I have seen writers object to the use of the phrase, "English as a second language." Their argument in both cases was that English is the greatest language on earth and therefore second to none. How does one argue with such individuals? How does one make the point that the word *second* refers to a chronological order and that, in the case of a native speaker of a language other than English, English will always follow the native language chronologically?

The third area of criticism of bilingual education is a difficult one to approach. Now that the era of civil rights and equal educational opportunity is past and the word *racist* is no longer considered "in," one is limited in what can be said about certain attitudes toward language-minority children. However, the arguments I mentioned above—on pedagogical rationale, on the need for native-language instruction to prevent educational retardation, on the enhancement of self-concept as a prerequisite to learning, and on the need to use existing language as a means of spurring continued cognitive development—have no effect on some of the opponents of bilingual education. Their opposition has its origin in neither emotion nor pedagogy. It is grounded instead in discriminatory attitudes about the place of racial and ethnic minorities and in the belief, held by some, that equal educational opportunity is not desirable.

Proponents of this point of view seem to be saying that a basic command of the English language is sufficient and should be the desired educational outcome for language-minority children. They agree that it is desirable to afford these children an English as a second language program that allows them to develop sufficient language and intellectual skills to understand and follow basic instructions, to earn a decent living, and to avoid becoming social liabilities. But such programs should not go so far as to develop language and intellectual skills to the point of disrupting the social order. Before you know it (so goes this school of thought), "their" children will be competing with "our" children for admission to medical school, to political office, and to managerial and supervisory positions. This attitude was manifested in the reaction of some community leaders to the introduction of Title I migrant education programs in the 1960s. Their viewpoint was expressed as, "If you give them so much education, they won't want to pick crops for a living."

A recent newspaper item critical of bilingual education exemplifies this attitude. The writer had visited a high school class made up of Asian immigrant children and had observed that, without native-language instruction, the students appeared to be doing fine. The students demonstrated a basic understanding of the English language, she reported, and could communicate with each other in simple English. Here's my point: high school students are not supposed to be communicating with each other in simple English. They are supposed to be communicating about algebra, geometry, physics, and social studies. They are supposed to be reaching near-adult levels of cognition, affective development, and aesthetic appreciation.

Educators frequently express similarly negative attitudes about language-minority children. For the past five years the strongest controversy about bilingual education has been the determination of what level of performance would result in the removal of a child from a native-language support program. Although the 50th percentile on standardized tests is considered average performance for English-speaking children, in this case the state agency was adamant about lowering the acceptable level of performance for language-minority children from the 40th percentile to the 23rd percentile. The 23rd percentile is close to the score a person can make on a standardized test by guessing at the answers, without even looking at the questions. With such abysmally low levels of expectancy, it is amazing that minority children perform as well as they do.

So much of the criticism of bilingual education stems from emotional responses, misinformation, and racist attitudes (I cannot avoid using the word, after all) that one must make a conscious effort to look at this criticism objectively. It is dangerous to formulate an immediate reaction without first asking, "Is the critic emotional, ignorant, or racist?" Yet the vast majority of criticism does indeed fall into one or more of these basic classifications.

Despite all the criticism of bilingual education programs and of the use of native-language instruction for language-minority children, I continue to be a strong advocate to this methodology. I see bilingual education as the best approach for teaching the English language without academic retardation, with a minimum development of negative self-concept, and with a maximum development of the intellectual potential of the individual.

In my thirty-four years as a professional educator working with language-minority children, I have found no better alternative. I will continue to examine alternative approaches, although I see the current push for experimental alternative programs more as an attempt to establish loopholes to avoid complying with current laws and regulations than as a serious attempt at educational experimentation. Certainly current efforts to provide an alternative that echoes the traumatic and disastrous programs of the pre-bilingual era cannot and will not be acceptable to me. Bilingual education with native-language instruction still appears to be the best option for children with limited English proficiency.

(IDRA, January 1984)

OPPOSITION TO BILINGUAL EDUCATION

PREFACE

During the early years in the implementation of present-day bilingual education programs, there was little criticism of this promising methodology. The desire of the Cuban American community to maintain Spanish language skills in their children for an eventual return to the homeland, provided ample political support for education in two languages.

Pedagogical support was found not in the research nor in the track record of the proposed methodology, but rather in the track record of the traditional methodology. Hispanic children in the United States were performing deplorably in the school according to all indicators for school performance. Hence the advent of bilingual education was not so much the adoption of a proven methodology, but the grasping at straws by a minority population seeking upward social and economic mobility for its children.

This last consideration is frequently lost when opponents of bilingual education suggest a change to an all-English methodology. It isn't as if language minority children were performing admirably in the schools prior to bilingual education. Both the sink-or-swim in the new language approach and the English language development with discontinuity of learning and cognitive development had failed to provide any semblance of educational opportunity for language minority children.

Just as bilingual education was beginning to develop into a preferred alternative, the country experienced a strong effort to eradicate bilingual education in this country. In some states the attacks were so strong and so effective that state legislatures and the educational community regressed in support for bilingual education.

One can take the position that opponents of bilingual education are entitled to their opinion, and the issue can be debated in political, educational, or public forums, without strong emotional reactions from supporters, but this is not the case. Although I spent more time than I could afford in defense of bilingual education, I learned over time that debating the issue was a waste of time due to various characteristics of the attacks launched by special interest groups such as U.S. English.

Their attacks on bilingual education were difficult to defend, since such attacks included four characteristics which make debate unfeasible.

The first of these characteristics was the use of false premises in every attack. For instance, members of U.S. English and non-members who have sided with them, invariably begin the attack by defining a bilingual education program as one in which the students are taught their native language and the culture of their native language, but are not taught the English language. Of course if such a situation existed in the public schools of the United States, one could argue that this is not bilingual education, but rather monolingual education in a language other than English. But the discussion of nomenclature, which many supporters of bilingual education are prone to do is counterproductive in that the subsequent discussion proceeds from the assumption that such non-English instruction exists, which it does not.

A second characteristic displayed by opponents of bilingual education is a dogmatic adherence to the false premises. In one public argument a member of U.S. English made the usual comment about English not being taught in bilingual programs. The Texas Commissioner of Education was in attendance, and reassured the participants that there wasn't a single public school bilingual class in which the teaching of English did not constitute the majority of instructional time. The speaker listened politely to the commissioner, and immediately restarted his criticisms with the statement, "Since English is not being taught in bilingual programs . . . ."

Challenging the assumptions presented by U.S. English is difficult since their arguments inevitably are based on erroneous statements such as "Research shows . . . ," when research shows nothing of the kind, or "I have been informed by reliable sources . . . " without ever naming a single "reliable source."

Third, arguments against bilingual education are inevitably irrational, having little to do with reality or the discussion at hand. Arguments based on opposition to government support of affirmative ethnicity or the implementation of a federal prescribed curriculum are difficult to attack in that there is no government support for affirmative ethnicity in bilingual education, nor is there a prescribed federal curriculum in bilingual programs.

The fourth characteristic of attacks upon bilingual education is that any debate on the subject is used as a public forum for the dissemination of erroneous information. When being interviewed on a radio talk show by a host opposed to bilingual education, I was asked, "Is it not true that your success in education is attributed to your support of bilingual education, and have you not made a financial fortune in bilingual education?" The answers to these two questions are fairly evident. I was a successful educator many years before the advent of bilingual education, and bilingual education has never provided me with a significant portion of my income, let alone a financial fortune. I was about to say this when the talk show host cut me off for a commercial. A few minutes later he resumed the interview with the statement, "Since you chose not to respond to my accusations, we can assume that they are true."

Following are four articles that I wrote during the most intensive period of public attacks on bilingual education. The four articles are interrelated in that the latter articles provide a follow-up on the previous ones.

THE ENGLISH ONLY LEGISLATIVE MOVEMENT

1985

An amendment to the federal Constitution has been introduced which would make English the country's official language. Parallel efforts have been initiated in several states, including Texas and Florida.

This dual legislation at the federal and state levels is not a coincidental show of patriotism, or directed at some legal necessity, but rather a coordinated attack upon language minority people and the growing concept of bilingualism.

The initial awareness of the proposed state legislation and the federal constitutional amendment already introduced making English the official language has not produced strong reactions from the various segments of the population. Since English is already the unofficial state and federal language, the enactment of legislation making formal the already obvious appears to be moot. However, the emerging objectives and related provisions of the proposed legislation raises extensive concern. An analysis of the proposed amendments at the federal and state levels indicate a variety of negative effects, which will be prejudicial to the country in general and to language minority people in particular.

LEGISLATION IS DYSFUNCTIONAL

To begin with, the effort is dysfunctional. It does not solve a problem, it aggravates it. Granted, there are hundreds of thousands, very possibly millions, of Americans who are "limited English proficient," and that this lack of English language ability is a national as well as an individual liability. But the solution is to be found in the development of English language skills, not in attacks upon languages other than English. Neither the adult education sector nor the public school sector has developed a sophisticated proficiency or capacity in teaching English as a second language. Adult English language development programs are currently stymied by a demand for English language instruction which far exceeds the capacity of programs to enroll applicants, with their large and growing waiting lists.

The proposed legislation is based on the assumption that there is a vast number of persons who do not want to learn the English language and should be forced to do so; the reality is that there is a vast number of persons who want to learn the English language, but we do not have the capacity to teach them. Denial of the use of their native language while we build the capacity is cruel and counterproductive.

It appears that there is a growing tendency for the country to repeat the mistakes of the public schools. Past efforts to increase English language acquisition through regulations prohibiting the use of languages other than English in the schools did not lead to increased English acquisition but rather to frustration, failure, school dropouts and increased illiteracy.

It is inevitable that the proposed legislation will result in the harassment and punishment of language minority people for something over which they have had little control—the language used in their homes.

CREATES A SECOND-CLASS

Another outcome of the proposals is to give language minority residents an insidious second-class label for their failure to have English language facility. This action not only provides a stigma, it also penalizes them by withdrawing other constitutional guarantees, such as the right to participate in our democracy, the right to vote, the right to equal administration of justice, and even the right to personal well-being and safety. Past efforts to legislate instant English language expertise in Miami, Florida, did not increase the language capability of its Hispanic population, but it did hamper the city's ability to communicate with its people during the crisis of an approaching hurricane.

Proponents of the legislation call for the elimination of the use of languages other than English for instructional purposes in the country's schools. This action guarantees that the use and development of languages other than English will be limited utilization and restrictive vocabularies. In the light of the high penalties which our country has paid because of foreign language limitations, it is incredible that this lobbying group would call for further reductions in the development of foreign language skills. The country has paid a heavy price in terms of social, political, economic and military disadvantages due to a conspicuous lack of foreign language facility. It is inconceivable that this limitation be exacerbated through further scholastic limitations.

It is hoped that the problem of limited English proficiency can be addressed through bilingual, English as a second language and adult education programs, and not by aggravating the problem through dysfunctional legislation.

(IDRA, August 1985)

EDUCATION SECRETARY BENNETT AND THE BIG LIE

1985

If William J. Bennett, Secretary of Education, in his September 26, 1985 address to the Association for a Better New York had stated that the world was flat, if he had stated that the Department's research findings proved that the world was flat, and if he had proposed modifications in American educational programs on the basis that the world was flat, it wouldn't have been as shocking and unbelievable as his statements about the status of bilingual education (Bennett, 1988).

It is impossible to accept that a man with his background and in his position is as ignorant and misinformed as he indicates in his presentation. Although he has already been identified as the James Watt of the Department of Education, his presentation goes beyond the limits of credibility and is an insult to the intelligence and knowledge of his audience.

A few years ago I had the opportunity to participate in an exchange visit to the Soviet Union sponsored by the State Department and the National Institute of Education. During that visit I encountered a slight problem in discussing characteristics of Soviet education with personnel from the Ministry of Education. The problem stems from the facility with which Russian history can and has been changed to accommodate changes in Soviet educational history and practice. Little did I anticipate that the United States Department of Education could and would outdo the Russians in changing history to suit their purposes.

What those purposes are is still to be determined, but at the present there is a gnawing concern that the basis is related to the increases in minority populations and fear of the social, economic, and political potential of these groups.

Regardless of the reason, the Secretary has launched an administrative attack upon one of the few programs that has contributed to the improvement of educational opportunity for children who are limited English proficient. The attack is insidious in that it is based on a distortion of history, based on misinformation, and saturated with half-truths, omissions, and outrageous lies. It is reminiscent of the Nazi propaganda machine of the 1930s and 1940s, which was based on the principle that if you tell a lie, and it is a big one, and you say it over and over again, people will eventually believe it.

There is nothing new in the Bennett attack upon bilingual education either in terms of research findings or program evaluation. The novelty of the attack lies in the extent to which the Secretary has distorted the truth in his arguments for the elimination of the program, the fallacy of his rationale for opposition, and the ease with which he changes history in order to create a basis for concern.

The following are but a few of the points on which I challenge the Secretary's historical perspective:

***Bennett*:** "Teaching non-English speaking children . . . has been performed, with fair success, in communicating across this nation since its beginning."

***Fact*:** The teaching of non-English speaking children has been a dismal failure in this country since its beginning. As great numbers of immigrants arrived in this country they were assimilated into the work force. Schooling was not even a reality for most of the children. Successes in the teaching of English were unheard of, since the schools made little attempt to address these children. The immigrant groups found an abundance of work in the physical labor required for the industrialization and growth of the country. Agriculture absorbed large numbers of these immigrants without an extensive need for schooling. The successes in language acquisition were achieved by second, third, and fourth generations of these immigrants. Among some of the "non-preferred" minorities the reality of success in language acquisition in the schools was even more limited. The federal bilingual education program came as a response to the inability of the schools to develop English language proficiency for vast segments of the population. It is erroneous for the Secretary to imply that language minority populations were doing fairly well in school until the federal government upset their satisfactory performance with the enactment of the Bilingual Education Act.

***Bennett*:** " . . . in the mid-1960s . . . America was . . . engaged . . . in a peaceful revolution—our civil rights revolution. . . . "

***Fact*:** The civil rights movement was neither peaceful nor was it a revolution, and for that matter it was not his. The civil rights movement was wild, bloody, and fiery. Not even the serene Rev. Martin Luther King was able to prevent the hostilities from developing into forceful confrontations between minority and majority interests. To equate the civil rights movement to the evolution of the frog is a disservice to the martyrs who were bloodied and died for the cause of freedom, equality and justice. Mr. Bennett does so in order to create the mistaken notion that the acquisition of civil rights by minority groups was proceeding peacefully and normally without the need for federal intervention.

***Bennett*:** " . . . Americans have always, in their churches and communities, done their part to help give such children (immigrant and refugee) a chance to achieve a brighter future."

***Fact*:** "Always" is inconceivable. "Usually" is too strong. "Seldom" is better. The naiveness of the Secretary displayed in this statement is too much to accept. He is definitely rewriting the history books to suit his, or the administration's purpose.

***Bennett*:** "The Court Found (in *Lau v. Nichols*) that the failure of the San Francisco school system to provide English language instruction to these students denied the students a meaningful opportunity to participate in the public educational program."

***Fact*:** The Court found that the placement of Chinese children in regular English language instruction was a violation of their Constitutional rights. School authorities argued that placement of students in regular classes with regular teachers and regular instructional materials afforded them equal educational opportunities. The Supreme Court, in a unanimous decision, found that the placement of the limited English proficient Chinese children in these regular programs was a denial of equal educational opportunity.

***Bennett*:** "Congress . . . authoriz(ed) . . . funding for programs designed simply to maintain student competence in the native language."

***Fact*:** On five different occasions during his presentation, the Secretary describes bilingual education programs funded by his department as programs using solely the native language. There are no such programs in existence. All bilingual education programs utilize native language for cognitive development and the development of basic skills until the student acquires sufficient mastery of the English language. There is not one program in the entire country funded by the Department of Education in which the bilingual program consists solely of native language instruction. On the contrary, if there is a deficiency which characterizes bilingual education programs, it is the relative or complete absence of native language utilization. This reality is verified by the Department's own findings.

The Secretary certainly demonstrates in this area what I noted previously. If you will repeat a lie often enough, it will eventually be accepted as truth. I believe that Mr. Bennett has accomplished this objective in that the American public is becoming erroneously convinced that bilingual education is a program of native language utilization with the exclusion of English language acquisition. As I have done in the past, I challenge the Secretary to show me one, just one, bilingual program anywhere in the United States, in which the English language is not taught and utilized or where the end objective is not English language acquisition. I have issued this challenge to other critics of bilingual education and they have consistently failed to come up with one such program, but they still maintain that there must be some, because the Department of Education says so.

Bennett: "Indeed the English language skills of students in bilingual education programs seemed to be no better than the skills of those who simply remained in regular classrooms where English was spoken, without *any* special help."

Fact: Consistent with his philosophy of "the big lie," The Secretary repeatedly mentions a research base which indicates that bilingual education has been a failure. This is simply not so. All Department of Education references are based on a research study by the American Institute of Research which has been discredited to the point that it should be discarded as an embarrassment to the Department and a prime example of what Chester Finn, the new research leader in the Department, has described as an incomplete, obsolete, and not very useful research.

Since the Secretary of Education chooses to go back to the 1977 evaluation of bilingual education conducted through the Department, I feel it is only fair to list some of the still unanswered criticisms raised in 1977, when the evaluation report was first released.

- One-half of the teachers classified as bilingual teachers in the Department's study readily admitted that they did not speak any language other than English.
- Forty-six percent of the bilingual teachers in the study indicated that they had received less than three days of bilingual education training over a five-year span in the implementation of this new and drastically different instructional methodology.
- Only twenty-six percent of the teachers studied could meet the local and state requirements for bilingual teacher certification.
- The Department of Education sponsored study did not take into consideration the characteristics of the programs studied in terms of instructional time, content, or methodologies used.
- Half of the projects studied covered a time span of five months or less.
- Students who did not take various parts of the performance tests were assigned a zero for that portion of the test and were included in calculating gains for students in the bilingual program.

- Tests of English reading ability were administered and used in the study for students who had no prior English reading instruction.
- One-third of the students not in a federally-funded bilingual program used as a comparison group were actually in a state or locally funded bilingual program.
- Differences between "bilingual" and "non-bilingual" groups were not controlled as to organization, methodology, teacher training, teacher qualifications, teacher competence, or amount of financial resources.
- Comparison groups were selected by "nomination" by personnel in the group being studied. No validation of the "nominating" process was attempted.
- No limited English-proficient students were included in the study. The study dealt with students who spoke no English whatsoever.

The list of discrepancies continues, but the listing will be limited for the sake of brevity. Yet, the points listed above which have been presented, argued, discussed, published, and documented have absolutely no bearing on the Secretary's continued reference to Department of Education "research" which shows that bilingual education has been a failure.

Bennett: "The recent news of gains by Hispanic students in SAT scores is welcomed indeed, and is a testimony to the impressive efforts of many Hispanic parents and children."

Fact: When SAT scores showed a dismal performance by Hispanic children, it was assumed that bilingual education was to blame, in spite of the fact that at the time none of the students who performed badly in the SAT test had been in a bilingual education program. On the other hand, many of the students now demonstrating gains in SAT scores are the first groups to have gone through bilingual programs.

Bennett: " . . . almost half of all Hispanic high school students in the United States drop out *before* graduation; and of these dropouts, 40 percent never reach the tenth grade. This figure is as tragically high now as it was twenty years ago."

Fact: If only one-half of all Hispanic high school students drop out before graduating it is indeed most welcomed good news. Twenty years ago this figure was as high as 80 percent. Since Secretary Bennett blames the erroneous continued dropout rate on bilingual education, will he be willing to credit bilingual education for the elimination of one-half of the problem?

Bennett: "Two years of data suggest that this method (structured immersion) shows great promise in teaching English."

Fact: There is no data to suggest the success of the structured immersion approach. Although the replacement of bilingual programs by immersion programs has long been an advocacy of the Reagan administration, scholars have never taken this recommendation seriously due to the absence of a single study showing this method as a feasible approach to the education of limited English-proficiency students in the United States.

Bennett: "Our common history is written in English. Our common forefathers speak to us, through the ages, in English."

***Fact*:** This is not so. Mr. Bennett's forefathers may speak to him in English, the forefathers of all the members of the Association for a Better New York may speak to them in English, but all four of my grandparents spoke to me in Spanish. Through the ages, my wife's forefathers, from José S. de la Garza who received the Espiritu Santo land grant in 1735 and contributed to the domination of this hostile territory now known as Texas, to Jose Antonio Navarro who led the effort for the independence of Texas, all speak to us in Spanish. Mr. Bennett is in error in stating that all persons who contributed to the growth and development of this country were English speaking.

It is difficult to argue with an individual whose arguments are based on erroneous assumptions. During the next few months there will be scores of rebuttals to Secretary William Bennett's statements about the status of bilingual education and his attempts to lobby the Congress to abandon initial native language utilization while English is being learned as a second language. I hope that these efforts will not be diluted by arguing recommendations based on the big lie, rather than focusing on the lie itself.

The Governor of the state of Texas, the Commissioner of Education, and countless school district superintendents have responded to Bennett's statements with assurances that bilingual education programs are working, and that perhaps the Secretary and his staff should visit these programs rather than rely on discredited Department of Education studies.

There is no question but that the James Watt of the Department of Education has exceeded the most totalitarian of governments in mastery of the essential elements of promulgating the big lie. The big question is, why does the Secretary of Education deliberately and extensively lie in order to attack one of the few educational programs which has been accepted and successful in the education of language minority children?

(IDRA, October 1985)

AL SHANKER, THE AFT, AND MINORITY ISSUES

1985

The October 1985, issue of the *IDRA Newsletter* carried two articles written by me—one on the Pre-Professional Skills Test (PPST) challenged in a federal court, and the other on Secretary of Education William J. Bennett's remarks on bilingual education.

I am sure that it is a coincidence, but during the same month the President of the American Federation of Teachers published an advertisement, which served as a forum for the union's viewpoints, in which Al Shanker addresses two issues which have recently received extensive coverage in the news media—the PPST litigation and Mr. Bennett's remarks on bilingual education.

Mr. Shanker, who has seldom agreed with the administration on education issues, endorses the administration's position on both issues, agreeing with Mr. Bennett on his attack upon bilingual education, and with the Department of Justice which is challenging the court's position on the PPST and siding with the defendants in the case.

Besides the obvious observation that politics does create strange bedfellows, Shanker's endorsement of Bennett's criticism merits attention.

SECRETARY BENNETT BACKS OFF

The Secretary has backed off from his stated position on seeking a new definition of the role of the federal government in bilingual education programs. News of Bennett's retreat came in a Department of Education briefing in which the Secretary's intentions were described as unnecessary and perhaps illegal.

Although briefings from the Department's legal counsel may have prompted Mr. Bennett to back off, there are probably other reasons for his dropping his bilingual initiative. Certainly the congressional response to his criticisms was much stronger and negative than Bennett had anticipated. His naive attempts to influence the Congress with promises of withdrawing the Administration's opposition to bilingual funding and in turn support increased funding for bilingual education if school districts would not use a bilingual methodology did not prove fruitful. On the contrary, Bennett's unjustifiable attacks on bilingual programs drew a strong negative reaction from Congress.

A similarly strong negative reaction was expressed by the language minorities who have traditionally supported the bilingual education program. Minorities again pointed out to the Secretary that they are very much interested in their children learning English, although the process of learning a new language should not preclude learning basic skills and content material as commonly happens in an all English program. It is doubtful that Secretary Bennett saw the light due to the minorities' criticism of his remarks and his position, but it is possible that the Secretary became aware of the golden rule in dealing with minorities: do anything you want to them, keep them poor, keep them ignorant, mislead them, but never, never get them angry at you.

A fourth element which contributed to the Secretary's decision to drop his bilingual initiative was the extent of the challenge to the accuracy of the Secretary's remarks. His untrue statements on the failure of bilingual education, research findings, the use of native language with the exclusion of English, and the rest of the erroneous data described in my October *Newsletter* article, and reiterated by political figures, school boards, administrators, teachers, and state education agencies, constituted a challenge he did not dare to meet.

SHANKER STEPS IN

It is said that "fools rush in where wise men fear to tread," and as if to prove the truth of this adage, here comes Al Shanker, President of the American Federation of Teachers, in support of a position which the Secretary of Education had just vacated.

Shanker supports the Secretary's prior position on the same erroneous grounds on which the Secretary initially proposed it. With flags waving, balloons floating, and marching to the tune of the *Stars and Stripes Forever*, Al Shanker opposes bilingual education programs taught exclusively in the native language and in the absence of any English language instruction. When the music stops I will ask Al Shanker the same question I posed to Bennett: "Can you show me one bilingual education program in the whole country where English is not being taught?" I suggest that Al Shanker has been spending too much time in his Federation Park Avenue Offices. He should contact Ms. Awilda Orta in the New York City Schools who would be happy to show him American Federation of Teachers members in bilingual programs throughout the city teaching English as a second language.

In his support of Mr. Bennett's criticism of bilingual education, Al Shanker dwells on one topic introduced by Mr. Bennett in his New York City address, but which I did not consider important enough to merit a response in my October article. This topic is that bilingual education programs are unusual and detrimental in that the Congress has mandated a sole methodology to be used in bilingual programs. Both Shanker and Bennett see danger in the United States precedence in prescribing a sole methodology to be used in educational programs. This methodology is the use of two languages in the programs.

Although I, too, do not care to see federal curriculum descriptions, I do not find it so strange that the Congress appropriates funds for bilingual education and expect that programs implemented with such funds be bilingual. The program is not mandatory and neither are the funds. School districts wanting to experiment with bilingual methodologies apply for the funds, implement the programs with federal funds, and terminate the federal programs, since funds are allocated for a specified period and then automatically discontinued. The federal bilingual program was intended, and still remains, a catalyst to assist school districts wanting to implement such a methodology to acquire materials, train teachers, and start programs. It is not compulsory; it is not infinite.

It may surprise both Mr. Bennett and Mr. Shanker that the vast majority of school districts that have initiated and terminated bilingual programs with federal funds, have continued such programs with state and local funds.

Both Mr. Bennett and Mr. Shanker have suggested that the bilingual education regulations be changed so that school districts which apply and receive such funds may use the funds for the continuation of traditional sink-or-swim programs which were disastrous in the past, show no promise for the future, and are detested by the minority populations which responded so strongly to Mr. Bennett's recommendations.

THE SOLE METHODOLOGY ARGUMENT

Although I find this rhetoric boring and frustrating, the number of persons who will oppose federal bilingual programs on the sole methodology argument demands further elaboration. The following analogy may suffice.

The Department of Education provides discretionary funds to stimulate the use of computers in the schools. Being a new methodology, the Department feels that it should play a catalyst role in developing school familiarity with computers, assistance in the acquisition of this relatively expensive technology, help in the identification, acquisition and development of software, and provide support for the training of teachers to use this methodology. School districts wanting to try it out may apply for the funds and implement programs under the regulations established by the Congress and the Department of Education. Mr. Bennett and Mr. Shanker feel that it is wrong for the Department to support this program in that it constitutes support for a sole methodology. They argue that the regulations must be changed in order for a school district to be able to receive the Computer Education funds to implement a computer education program and have the necessary flexibility for the district to utilize the funds to purchase comic books which will be used as the instructional methodology rather than the government-mandated computer methodology. The position of William Bennett and Al Shanker in the bilingual controversy is as ridiculous as in the fictitious example above.

THE PPST LITIGATION

Not being content with making a fool of himself in the bilingual debacle, Al Shanker then proceeds to wave the flag in behalf of teacher standards and the need to protect innocent children from the influence of incompetent teachers, and expresses his support of the defendants in the PPST litigation. I am willing to bet that Shanker has not seen a copy of the plaintiffs' brief or the court opinion in support of the temporary injunction. As a leader of teachers Shanker understands the need for support of teacher standards without realizing, as I pointed out in the October article, that the litigation has little, if anything, to do with teacher standards. It is a discriminatory and unjust attack on minorities wanting to enter the teaching profession in Texas (*United States v. Texas*, 1971).

MINORITY SUPPORT FOR SHANKER

In responding to the Shanker attacks on bilingual education and the PPST litigation, one nagging thought comes to mind which I have dwelt on since I first encountered Shanker's attacks upon minorities many years ago. Why do minority teachers continue to provide the funds for Shanker's forum? His article is an advertisement paid for by the American Federation of Teachers. Why do teachers teaching in bilingual programs or teachers who have been the recipients of inferior educational and teacher preparation programs submit their dues which support the bigotry which Al Shanker has long displayed toward minority populations?

In the past I have had many opportunities to work with John Cole and other fine leaders of the Texas Federation of Teachers. I find them to be reasonable and supportive of programs for the improvement of educational opportunities for minorities, including bilingual education. But I cannot understand their continued affiliation with the bigotry of Shanker.

Perhaps there are sufficient other issues which merit the association, but I would still question minority affiliation with the American Federation of Teachers and the racist policies of their national leader.

(IDRA, November 1985)

U.S. ENGLISH STRIKES AGAIN

1986

During the past year I have written two articles and spoken on various occasions about the concerted efforts of the U.S. English organization to eliminate bilingual education programs from American schools.

In August, 1986, I had my first opportunity to witness the extent to which the U.S. English movement is extending its attacks upon bilingual education programs.

At the meeting of the San Antonio Institute on The Future of a Region, representatives from south and west Texas organized into small discussion groups in order to address the problems of the region. The meeting on primary and secondary education was completely dominated by one participant expressing concern for the large number of language minority children enrolled in bilingual education programs who are being taught in their "ancestral tongues" rather than being taught the English language.

This participant's affiliation did not identify him as representing the U.S. English group; he may or may not be a member of U.S. English, but everything he said and the way he said it was identical to previous positions taken by U.S. English.

The most impressive aspect of this person's participation parallels the most impressive aspect of U.S. English's criticisms of bilingual education, namely that there is no way that they will allow facts to stand between them and their argument.

Never mind that no less an official than the Texas Commissioner of Education gave him reassurances that no children in the public schools of the state of Texas are attending classes in which the native language is used to the exclusion of teaching the English language; never mind that participants expressed concern that students in bilingual programs are being removed from the programs too early rather than too late; invariably, the participant began each of his numerous and superfluous statements with the expression that students in bilingual programs are being taught in their ancestral tongues and being denied the teaching of English.

I am reminded of the U.S. Secretary of Education when he scared the pants off the membership of the Association for a Better New York by stating five times in his presentation that bilingual programs teach the native language and the culture of the native language and do not include English language instruction. Incidentally, when I asked Secretary Bennett at the Cleveland Conference in Chicago to give me one example of a school or a school district where the native language was used to the exclusion of English language acquisition, he responded by saying that I was distorting his perspective and, without responding to my request, continued to criticize bilingual education programs on the same basis.

At the San Antonio Institute the U.S. English espousing participant continued to dominate all discussion. When another participant suggested that students needed higher levels of training in technology, the one-theme participant again intervened with the observation that language minority children are being prevented from mastering useful technology by the teaching of physics and other technological subjects in the ancestral tongue rather than in the English language. A statement by the Commissioner of Education that there is no child in the state of Texas being taught physics in any language other than English had little effect in the ensuing argument.

There is no question in my mind that the distraction and domination of the San Antonio Institute education meetings by the continuous interjection of U.S. English arguments is a preview of things to come.

I can only hope that prior to our next confrontation, U.S. English supporters will be prepared to give me the name of one school or district in which students in bilingual programs are being taught in a native language with the exclusion of English language instruction, but this is too much to expect. By raising the issue with a complete disregard for facts, they have succeeded in getting large numbers of people to question the desirability of bilingual education programs. Why bother with facts? There is sufficient evidence to indicate that if you tell a lie often enough most people will believe it.

(IDRA, September 1986)

BILINGUAL EDUCATION IN HETEROGENEOUS GROUPS

1985

PREFACE

Ten years after the publication of my article, "Bilingual Education, Segregation, and a Third Alternative," language minorities were still being presented with an unnecessary either/or option: desegregation or bilingual education.

In September 1985 I published a second article addressing this issue. The article recapitulates the history of the relationship of desegregation and bilingual education in the federal courts, and the failure of the schools to reconcile the two.

In this article I relied heavily on examples of school districts that had successfully implemented bilingual education programs in heterogeneous settings.

Twenty years after the publication of my first article addressing this issue and almost ten years after the publication of this article, there are still many school systems that have been unable to implement bilingual programs in desegregated settings. As stated in both articles, the failure is more attributable to general inefficiencies of the school system than to the incompatibility of the two responses.

The 1985-86 school year marks the twentieth anniversary of the rebirth of bilingual education programs in this country. Although history shows the existence of bilingual programs through the early part of the twentieth century, following a period of decline and almost total disappearance, the 1966 National Education Association Tucson Conference marks the birth of current bilingual methodology in the United States. It was at this conference that Texas Senator Ralph Yarborough became convinced of the need for federal legislation and appropriations in support of this movement. The resulting Bilingual Education Act of 1968 (Title VII of the Elementary and Secondary Education Act) nurtured the development and growth of bilingual education as a feasible and preferable approach for the education of language minority children.

During the next ten formative years of bilingual education much of the program development was undertaken in schools that enrolled large numbers of language minority children, although by the end of the 1960s Dr. Theodore Anderson, from the University of Texas at Austin, was raising the question about the instruction of limited English proficient children in heterogeneous groupings. His interest focused on the adequacy of the emerging models for use in classroom settings where only a portion of the children were limited English proficient.

This question also surfaced during the formative years of the present legal status of bilingual education. Since the language issue first emerged in desegregation cases, it was inevitable that the courts would address the question of methodologies for the implementation of bilingual programs in desegregated settings. Judge William Wayne Justice found no problem between bilingual education and desegregation in either the San Felipe Del Rio intervention suit in *United States v. Texas* (*United States v. Texas*, 1971), nor in the subsequent bilingual intervention suit in the same case. Judge William Doyle did question the efficacy of bilingual programs in desegregated settings and was so impressed with the bilingual education imperative in *Keyes v. Denver*, that he waived integration requirements at the Denver Del Pueblo school and other schools with very high proportions of Mexican-American children and existing sophisticated bilingual education and multicultural programs. his exemption was overruled by the Tenth Circuit Court of Appeals which issued a strong statement on bilingual education not being a justifiable basis for continued segregation of minority children (*Keyes v. School District No. 1*, 1983).

On the other hand, other federal district judges completely failed to grasp the essence of bilingual education in heterogeneous groupings. Judge John Wood of the Western District of Texas wondered if the teachers in such programs would be expected to speak in both languages at the same time when the subject came up in *Morales v. Shannon* (*Morales v. Shannon*, 1975). Judge Wood's assumed naiveness stemmed from his negative attitudes toward bilingual education. He never understood the need for bilingual education or for the desegregation of minority children for that matter.

The strongest legal base for bilingual education was established in *Lau v. Nichols*, where the Supreme Court ruled that the failure to provide differentiated educational programs to children with different language and cultural characteristics resulted in the denial of equal educational opportunity (*Lau v. Nichols*, 1973). Since the key issue in this court case was not bilingual education per se, it is not surprising that types of student groups were not addressed by the court.

It is interesting to note that groupings of limited English-proficient and English-proficient children for bilingual instruction became more of a legal issue in desegregation cases than a pedagogical issue in the classroom implementation of bilingual programs. By 1973 the legal issue had become so intense that I felt a need to address it in the *IDRA Newsletter*.

The October 1973, issue of the *Newsletter* carried an article by me entitled, "Bilingual Education v. Segregation" which was a condensation of a previous presentation entitled, "Bilingual Education, Desegregation, and a Third Alternative." This presentation was in turn a repetition of testimony in several desegregation court cases. The basic argument in the 1973, article was that bilingual education and desegregation were not paradoxical, and the third alternative was the provision of bilingual programs in heterogeneous groupings of English-speaking and limited English-proficient children. The article argued that "Coping with varying types and degrees of language dominance is no different than coping with other varying characteristics of children."

In the 1973 article I relied on four arguments as justification for instruction and mixed groupings. First, teachers have the skills and experience in forming flexible and interchangeable groups for implementing instructional activities.

Second, teachers must be perceived as directors of learning activities, utilizing diagnostic, prescriptive, and instructional resources in carrying out learning activities for individual, small, and large groups of children. The teacher is not, and has not been for many years, a person interacting simultaneously with all students in one large group.

Third, the teacher can rely on a variety of different staff and material resources in order to group students for specialized instruction. Staff resources may include teacher aides, volunteer parents, interns, team teachers, and cross-age peer tutors. Material resources may include motion pictures, videotapes, slides, filmstrips, programmed instruction, self-pacing materials, books, games, workbooks, and others.

The fourth suggestion is simply to call upon the resourcefulness of the teacher to develop alternative activities for small groups of children. Teachers have an unlimited capacity for resourcefulness which made me very optimistic that they could come up with innovative ideas which I could not begin to conceptualize.

It is interesting to look at educational practice more than fifteen years after this issue surfaced and see how the educational community has responded. During the past few months the National Clearinghouse for Bilingual Education has issued two research memos which address this interest. The first is an article by Annalisa Allegro dated May 31, 1985, entitled, "Approaches for the Mainstream Classroom: LEP and English Proficient Students Learning Together"; the second is an article by Dr. Betsy Hadden dated June 3, 1985, entitled, "Scattered, Diverse, and Fluctuating Minority Language Populations: School District Responses" (Allegro, 1985; Hadden, 1985).

Dr. Hadden uses two school districts to describe efforts which have been made to accommodate various language mixes in classrooms. The first example is the Sacramento City Unified School District in California. This school district has the following characteristics which impact upon the bilingual education program:

- total enrollment of 48,541
- 4,611 language minority children (9.5 percent)
- uneven dispersal of LEPs among 55 school
- as few as two or three LEPs in any one school
- 24 different language groups
- varying dates of immigration
- high incidence of poverty for late arrivals

The Sacramento schools have responded to these characteristics by the establishment of a screening center called the Newcomer Center. The Newcomer Center provides the following special services for minority language students:

- screening—health, academic, English language assessment, native language assessment
- orientation classes
- referrals to schools in students' area with appropriate bilingual and ESL programs
- one year maximum enrollment in the Newcomer School for students from geographic areas not affording appropriate language programs
- instruction in English language skills and content areas
- native language instruction in Cantonese, Hmong, Spanish, and Vietnamese, the most common languages in the district

- individual bilingual or ESL instruction by certified teacher aides for students who speak less common languages
- early exiting from the Newcomer School to available bilingual programs or mainstream classrooms in appropriate attendance areas

In her article Allegro describes various strategies being used for the instruction of students in heterogenous groupings without detriment to students of different language characteristics. Classroom approaches include:

- CI/LEA—the use of student input for the development of instructional materials
- DRTA—a program to enhance reading for meaning in context which utilizes extensive LEP and English proficient student interaction and discussion
- GWP—a special program for use in content areas to teach all four communication processes using special homogeneous and heterogeneous language groupings
- peer teaching
- use of small heterogeneous groups
- general hints and suggestions for classroom procedures which can be used in heterogeneous groupings

Allegro concludes her article with this summary statement: "Special adjustments are often necessary when LEP students share the same class with native English speakers, but through special attention and the application of innovative approaches, classroom activities can be beneficial to all."

These two research reports should defuse past concerns and arguments about the feasibility of teaching children with different language characteristics in heterogeneous groupings. It further emphasizes my observation which concludes the 1973 article and which I used extensively in court cases and administrative hearings: "The self-described helplessness of some school districts in coping with heterogeneous language groupings of children is more of an admission of general educational inadequacies than a problem of bilingual education."

(IDRA, September 1985)

FLEXIBILITY IN BILINGUAL EDUCATION PROGRAMS

1986

PREFACE

Almost since its inception, bilingual education has been attacked within the Department of Education. When William Bennett served as Secretary of the department, his personal opposition to bilingual education led to a massive effort to destroy the program (Bennett, 1988).

One such attack was on the pretext of providing school districts with flexibility. Mr. Bennett attempted to weaken the bilingual program by giving recipients of federal bilingual education funds additional flexibility in the use of the funds.

The following article notes the existing flexibility of bilingual education programs. It is interesting that flexibility is already so extensive that 57 percent of the bilingual programs surveyed did not even meet the common definition of a bilingual program since the native language is not used for instructional purposes.

Secretary Bennett's opposition to bilingual education as a federally prescribed curriculum seems ludicrous if his opposition were applied to any other federally funded program. If the federal government were to provide funds for the promotion of computer utilization in the schools, it is doubtful that he would seek flexibility so that a significant portion of the computer funding could be used for the purchase and instruction in the use of calculators in order to provide school systems flexibility in the use of the funds. Guidelines for the use of funds for expanding library materials should not be so flexible that schools can use these funds for the purchase of band uniforms.

Similarly, funds provided for the development of bilingual education programs should be used for this purpose. Guidelines should not permit schools to use these funds for purposes not consistent with the intent of the appropriation.

The Department of Education's efforts to diminish services to limited English-proficient students in Title VII bilingual education programs is couched in language which purports to provide flexibility to school districts implementing such programs. Education Secretary William J. Bennett has repeatedly stated that the purpose of his recommendations is to allow school districts the flexibility to deviate from the exclusive teaching of native language and culture as well as to teach the English language in bilingual education programs.

What is being taught in bilingual education programs? How much flexibility is being utilized by local school districts in the implementation of programs?

These questions, and others, are answered in the report of a study recently released by the Office of Planning and Evaluation Services in the Department of Education. The study, performed for the Department of Education by Development Associates and the Research Triangle Institute, is part of long-range research into the effectiveness of services for limited English-proficient students in school districts across the nation (Development Associates, et al., 1986).

Contrary to Secretary's Bennett's assertion that bilingual education programs are locked into a rigid, generally prescribed model, the study shows an amazing variety of services being offered to limited English-proficient students. In fact, the study reports difficulties in standardizing types of services being offered, and resorts to forming and identifying clusters in order to group services for their analysis and reporting.

The following information is from the Department of Education report. Copies of the report are available from the department, c/o Dorothy Shuler, Planning and Evaluation Services, Washington, D.C. 20202.

Sections in quotation marks are taken directly from the Development Associates/ Research Triangle report.

- Thirty-nine percent of the school districts in the nation serving limited English proficient students do not have an official definition for a limited English proficient student.

- Twenty-five percent of the school districts did not report having entry criteria for eligibility for special limited English proficient services.

- Of the school districts with official definitions for a limited English-proficient student, forty-three percent had various sub-categories of students.

There was extensive disagreement between district reports and school campus reports on definitions and entry criteria. For example, whereas only 7 percent of the districts reported using only one criterion to define students and program entry, 49 percent of the schools reported using only one criterion. Obviously, schools are not doing what the district offices think that they are doing.

- ". . . both with respect to local definitions of limited English proficiency and to criteria for determining entry and exit from special services, there is considerable variation across schools and school districts. In addition, within these general categories there are important differences in the measurement instruments and procedures used which further add to the variation."

- "Every district offering special services reported that a goal of such services was to bring the English proficiency of LM-LEP (language minority-limited English proficient) students to the level necessary to function effectively in an all-English-medium classroom."

- "More schools had classes in which LM-LEP students were mixed with English-language-background students than had classes for LM-LEP students containing only language-minority students."

- Services for LM-LEP students were clustered to facilitate reporting. The following five clusters, their descriptions, and the percentage of schools offering the type of services were reported:

Type	Characteristics	PCT
A	90 percent or more of the instruction is provided in the native language throughout the entire school year	3%
B	Native language and English are used for instruction throughout the school year	11%
C	Change in language of instruction during the school year	29%
D	All English with Special Instruction in English (to accommodate the limited English Proficient characteristic)	51%
E	All instruction in English with no additional services not provided to other non-LEP students	6%

- The LM-LEP population is being served by 53,299 teachers and 26,474 paraprofessional personnel.
- 50 percent of academic teachers of LM-LEP students reported that they were unable to speak a language other than English.
- 37 percent of the districts had no requirement for English as a second language (ESL) or bilingual certification for teachers teaching LM-LEP students.
- 84 percent of the districts requiring teacher certification in ESL or bilingual allowed waivers for the certification requirement.
- 63 percent of the districts requiring certification had teachers on waivers.
- 14 percent of the districts requiring ESL or bilingual certification for teachers of LM-LEP students had all of their teachers on waivers.
- 40 percent of teachers instructing LM-LEP students had no college or inservice training related to teaching LM-LEP students.
- 44 percent of paraprofessionals instructing LM-LEP students had no college or inservice training related to teaching LM-LEP students.

It appears incredible for Secretary Bennett to seek changes in the federal Title VII regulations in order to afford more flexibility to local school districts in the implementation of bilingual education programs. Department of Education sponsored research clearly shows:

1. There already exists tremendous flexibility in the identification, placement, and services to limited English-proficient children enrolled in bilingual programs.
2. In spite of limited regulations, there are drastic weaknesses in services which more flexible regulations will not correct.

Back in 1967, when Senator Ralph Yarborough introduced the Bilingual Education Act, which subsequently became Title VII of the Elementary and Secondary Education Act, there was a lot of concern that President Lyndon B. Johnson would not support the legislation. An inquiry directed at the White House confirmed the President's opposition to the proposed legislation on the basis that there was nothing in the Bilingual Education Act that could not be provided by Title I programs. President Johnson stated that Title I had sufficient flexibility to provide the type of services which Senator Yarborough wanted for language minority students. Our response was that Title I suffered from too much flexibility, and that language responsive programs would have to compete with dozens of compensatory activities which school districts could opt to implement. The president agreed with us, accepted the bilingual program, and signed the legislation into law.

It would be detrimental now for the Secretary to give the program extensive flexibility which will allow school districts to expend the funds for activities which do not respond to the language needs of the limited English proficient.

(IDRA, January 1986)

CURRENT PROBLEMS IN BILINGUAL EDUCATION

1993

PREFACE

In casual conversations, as well as in formal presentations, persons who are familiar with my twenty-five years of advocacy for bilingual education frequently ask me about the impact of bilingual education programs. "How successful has bilingual education been?" I am always tempted to respond, "I don't know. We have never tried it."

I am reluctant to use this response because in general bilingual programs have been very successful. But success has been severely limited by constraints in the implementation of the programs.

I see nothing wrong with the rationale of bilingual education, nor do I have any reservations about the soundness of the pedagogy. Unfortunately, as a program commonly externally imposed it has not received general acceptance by the education community. Bilingual programs are often reluctantly implemented, inadequately staffed, limited in resources and poorly administered.

The success of bilingual programs in this country would soar if attention were given to problems in implementation. The following article describes ten of the most common problems found in bilingual education programs.

In its simplest form bilingual education is the use of two languages. In a more sophisticated context, such as an educational response to the problems of limited English-proficient students in American schools, bilingual education is the use of the native language for instructional purposes while English is being learned as a second language.

Pedagogues tend to make the rationale of bilingual education unnecessarily complicated. Interrupting and delaying cognitive development and the acquisition of skills and knowledge until a new language is acquired is a waste of time and produces academic retardation and overagedness, which in turn produce underperformance and a propensity for dropping out of school.

At periodic intervals I go out and buy a new suit. Invariably the new purchase has to be fitted and altered before I can use it. It is unnecessary, undesirable and a waste of time for me to sit naked in my house for two or three weeks waiting for the new suit to be delivered. I continue going to work in my old clothes until such time as the new suit arrives. When it does arrive, I simply make the transition from my old suit to the new one, although I sometimes continue to use the old one for certain occasions.

I do not see the period of time in which I am waiting for my new suit to be delivered as the appropriate time to get my old suit dry cleaned, altered or repaired. Doing so would place me back in the house waiting for two suits with nothing to wear.

Using the old suit while waiting for the new one is neither unpatriotic nor divisive; it is simply practical. Contrary to pedagogical myths, wearing the old suit does not delay nor inhibit the delivery of the new one. The continued alternative use of the two suits presents no extensive dilemma, nor am I likely to become schizophrenic. I have developed sufficient judgement to determine which of the two suits to use in a specific social context.

In spite of almost twenty-five years of recent bilingual program implementation in the United States, the status of bilingual education is still unresolved. Although most studies of the impact of bilingual education indicate very positive findings, I am of the opinion that success is still constrained by limitations in program implementation. Having visited bilingual programs in many cities in a large number of states, and having continuous contact with bilingual education personnel throughout the country, I have observed many limitations of bilingual education programs which need to be addressed.

The following ten limitations come immediately to mind:

1. Lack of language development opportunity

There still exists an astounding relationship between language proficiency in general, and English language proficiency specifically, and language development activity in the classroom. As documented by research studies students with the least oral language skills spend the most time in desk-oriented, non-verbal instructional activity. The converse is also true, students with the most oral language skills spend the most time in verbal instructional activities.

Either in bilingual or monolingual programs, the most pressing need of limited English-proficient children is language development. Since oral language development usually precedes written language development, written activity is relatively non-productive without the prerequisite oral language capability. In general, this need is not being met.

It is not unusual to visit a classroom with a large number of limited English-proficient students in which there is a minimum of verbal communication. When asked what is the most pressing need of these students, teachers will invariably respond, "Lack of oral language development."

2. Limited use of the native language

A few years ago, Dr. William Bennett, then Secretary of the Department of Education, criticized bilingual education programs as programs which did not teach the English language, use the native language exclusively for instructional purposes and the instructional content was composed of learning the culture of the native language. In an article I wrote, and in a personal confrontation, I challenged the Secretary to identify one classroom in any public school in any city of the country in which there was native language utilization without English language instruction. The Secretary stated that I had misinterpreted his statement, although I had a copy of it released by his office, but he failed to identify any such program. I knew that he couldn't, because I am certain that such a bilingual program does not exist. On the contrary, I could have similarly challenged the Secretary to identify a bilingual program in which the native language was being used extensively for instructional programs.

In the infamous American Institute for Research study of bilingual education programs, more than half of the teachers with five or more years of experience as bilingual teachers indicated that they knew no language other than English. The shortage of bilingual teachers nationwide indicates that a large number of bilingual programs are staffed by monolingual teachers.

3. Premature transition to English

Where bilingual programs actually use native language instruction, teachers are under tremendous pressures to make a premature transition into English language instruction or to exit the students from the bilingual program into regular English language classrooms.

Premature transitioning is forced by a shortage of bilingual teachers, opposition to bilingual education and early subject matter achievement testing in the English language. Extensive premature exiting from bilingual programs also results from the use of a student's facility with the English language in a social context rather than English language facility in an academic context.

When asked, "How long should a student stay in a bilingual education program?" I invariably respond, "As long as necessary. That is, as long as it takes to be assured that the student has sufficient English language mastery so that it is no longer a variable in the success/failure of basic skill and content material acquisition."

The length of time necessary in a bilingual program will vary from student to student, but I can't help but notice that English-speaking children spend four or five years in English language acquisition in the home before facing academic tasks in school.

4. Inadequacies of instructional materials

In spite of some investments into the development of bilingual instructional materials, there is still a marked shortage in the field. Early native language materials were usually obtained from foreign publishers. Although syntax and morphology were generally acceptable, the lexical characteristics of these materials left a lot to be desired. The context of the materials were also inappropriate, unfamiliar and confusing for the limited English proficient children raised in the United States.

Textbook publishers have been reluctant to invest in the development of materials in any language other than English, with an accompanying limited marketability. The same holds true for supplemental and reference materials. Aside from basic reading materials, children's literature and basic arithmetic, very little is commercially available in support of bilingual education. Above the primary grades, virtually nothing is available.

The lack of appropriate cultural representation in curriculum materials has also been a problem. Early publisher reaction to the need for such materials for use in bilingual and other multicultural programs left a lot to be desired. A common response was to use a little brown or black ink to give color to people in the pictures. This resulted in the typical minority family in the "multicultural" version being made up of Father, Mother, Dick, Baby and their dog, Spot, with all four of the people and the dog having dark complexions.

Bilingual materials were prepared by an all white Anglo staff with a copy made available to a university foreign language professor for translation. I remember getting one such copy of a math workbook which was to be translated into Spanish in which the items for mathematical manipulation were creampuffs. One could conclude that there are dozens of Spanish translations for the word "creampuff," although I am prone to argue that there is no translation for the word "creampuff." Since the English version of the new curriculum was already complete, and the graphics already included the addition, subtraction, multiplication and division of creampuffs, the inappropriateness of this type of pastry for translation resulted in a major disaster.

For the past twenty-five years, a significant part of a bilingual teacher's time has been spent scrounging for appropriate instructional materials in addition to the normal hours teachers spend in instructional and other duties.

5. Lack of bilingual teacher training

In the late 1960s it was common practice to assign teachers to bilingual education programs with little preparation in the use of bilingual materials and methodologies. It was not unusual for the bilingual teachers to be the only staff in the school that could communicate with students and parents in the native language.

The evaluation of bilingual education conducted by the American Institute of Research (AIR), indicated that almost one-half of the teachers studied had received less than three days of bilingual education training over a five-year span in the implementation of this new and dramatically different instructional methodology.

Although I am sure that there has been improvement in the pre-service and in-service training of bilingual education personnel, needs assessment in bilingual education still point to teacher training as a critical need.

6. Lack of administrative support

Back in 1969, as a new superintendent in the Edgewood School District in San Antonio, I implemented one of the earliest bilingual education programs in Texas. I recruited and assigned two teachers to initiate a bilingual program in one of the elementary schools. I always assigned bilingual teachers in pairs, since I found out that it took at least two teachers at any one site to comfort and support each other. After the first day of school, both teachers were back in my office.

"The principal said that if the superintendent wanted to implement a bilingual education program in the district, he would go along with the superintendent and do it. But he also said, `If I catch either of you teachers speaking to the class in a language other than English, I will see to it that both of you will be fired.'"

As is the case in other aspects of bilingual education, perhaps the administration has grown more supportive of this methodology, but the path is still not easy.

Although both the state and the federal departments of education were early supporters of bilingual education, both made abrupt reversals and led a concerted effort to eradicate such programs. It was only through a super-human effort of advocates and advocate organizations in state legislatures and state and federal courts that bilingual education has survived.

Lack of administrative support can also be measured by the resources allocated in support of bilingual programs. For years, the Texas system of school finance provided additional funding in the Foundation School Program in support of bilingual education. School districts received an additional 10 percent of the basic program allotment for each student in a bilingual or English as a second language (ESL) program. However, state law did not require that these funds be expended in support of bilingual or ESL programs. When advocates of bilingual education succeeded in getting the Texas Legislature to amend the law and require that these "bilingual" funds be expended in support of bilingual programs, there was a loud cry from school administrators. Superintendents stood in line to testify in

Austin as to the hardship imposed by the new law requiring that bilingual education funds be spent on educational programs for limited English proficient students.

7. Failure to use the vernacular

The rationale of bilingual education is based on the use of native language for continuous growth while English is being acquired as a second language. Initial efforts were constrained, and are still constrained by the lack of a large pool of trained teachers competent in the student's native language and a complete void of instructional materials in that language. In Texas, instead of addressing the massive pool of native language speakers and facilitating their entry into the teaching profession, the educational leadership opted for two approaches which proved counter-productive. One was to develop other language facility among English-speaking teachers and the other the massive importation of Spanish-speaking teachers from other countries.

The state education agency was assured by a professor of Romance languages, that native-like proficiency could be developed in English-speaking teachers in one hundred hours of Spanish language instruction. Teachers were recruited, enrolled and participated in this one hundred hour program. Unfortunately, supporters of this plan grossly underestimated the amount of time necessary for the acquisition of native-like proficiency, because the teachers, subsequently labeled "One Hundred Hour Wonders" did not develop any extensive proficiency in the Spanish language, certainly not sufficient proficiency to be able to present academic work in Spanish.

It's interesting that teachers who expect students to acquire in a few weeks sufficient proficiency in the English language in order to handle academic work in that language, failed to acquire similar proficiency in one hundred hours of instruction, and even in two hundred hours of instruction when signed up for a second round in the program. It wasn't until some of the participating teachers had acquired three hundred hours of instruction that sufficient proficiency had been developed to permit the teachers to present instruction in the native language.

This approach was eventually dropped, but the state education agency continued to impede the preparation of bilingual teachers by the use of a culturally biased test used as a sole criterion for entry into teacher preparation programs. As a result of poor Hispanic college student performance on the test, large numbers of Hispanics were precluded from enrollment in a teacher training program. A lawsuit seeking to eliminate this barrier to minority entrance into teaching was defended by the state education agency in the courts until the test was replaced by another measure.

It is ironic that following years of excluding minorities from teacher preparation programs, the state education agency subsequently identified the lack of minority teachers as one of the foremost staffing problems in the schools.

The alternative approach, which is still in use, was to import teachers from the various parts of the Spanish-speaking world and place them as teachers in bilingual education programs. This approach presented, and still presents, many problems. To start out with, many of the imported teachers did not have the necessary English language skills to present the English acquisition portion of the bilingual curriculum. Another problem was that pronunciation and vocabulary varied from the children's vernacular, so that the limited proficient students found themselves in trilingual situations, where the English language was being acquired, instruction was conducted in a version of their native language which they didn't understand, and the student's vernacular was still ignored.

This trilingual fiasco still manifests itself, not only with the continued recruitment of teachers from other parts of the world, but with the use of local teachers who insist on purity of language and believe that Castillian Spanish is the only correct language which should be used in the classroom. Since the rationale of bilingual education is continuity of cognitive growth while English is being acquired, the use of a "correct" language unfamiliar to the students defeats the purpose of native language use. The "correct" form of a language is the form used locally and which facilitates communication, with all due respect to the Royal Academy of Spain.

The use of a form of the native language other than the vernacular for instructional purposes while English is being learned as a second language is analogous to my resolving my lack of clothing while waiting for my new suit to be delivered dilemma by wearing my wife's clothes.

The maintenance and improvement of the native language is a desirable, but separate, aspect of bilingual education. Such instruction can be readily justified in that the acquisition of "foreign" languages has been an educational objective in America since colonial days. It seems odd that we would eradicate student native-like proficiency in a language, only to introduce is as a foreign language after the student has lost the proficiency, and at an age when the physiological and psychological propensity for language acquisition has diminished.

8. Xenophobia

As stated earlier, early bilingual efforts received extensive educational, administrative, political and popular support. The key to political support was the large number of Cuban exiles living in the United States while waiting for the overthrow of the Castro regime and their return to their homeland. The acquisition of English was not an imperative at the time for the potential freedom fighters, but there was growing concern that children who came from Cuba at an early age and children born in the United States were attending all English language schools and would therefore be handicapped by a lack of Spanish language skills upon their return to Cuba.

A few Chicano leaders also saw Spanish language competency as a prerequisite for the establishing of Aztlan, a Mexican-American dominated political entity utilizing Spanish as the official language. The number of such leaders promoting a separatist movement was quite small and did not include the language minority educational leadership which saw bilingual education as a pedagogical response to the educational problem created by the lack of English language-proficiency in the children and the lack of Spanish language-proficiency in the school.

This incompatibility of language has not been readily perceived as a problem by the school which tends to present instruction in the English language with little regard for the consequences for non-English speaking children. After all, it did take nine justices of the United States Supreme Court in the unanimous decision in *Lau v. Nichols* to inform the education authorities of the San Francisco Unified School District that if 1,800 children spoke Chinese and no English, and the teachers spoke English and no Chinese, they had an educational problem (*Lau v. Nichols, 1973*). Of course the San Francisco schools readily responded that the problem was not theirs, the problem was with the children who did not speak English. If they wanted to benefit from an all English curriculum, it was their responsibility to learn the English language. Again it was necessary for the Supreme Court to point out that a desire to learn the English language was a basic reason for the children being sent to school.

Progress in the implementation of bilingual programs suffered an abrupt reversal due to the political and public manifestation of the xenophobic characteristic of a large number of Americans. The distrust and fear of foreigners led to a strong, organized counteroffensive against the use of any language but English in American schools. The original attack organized by Senator Hayakawa from California flourished as a new form of McCarthyism with tendrils reaching all the way to Linda Chavez in the U.S. Commission on Civil Rights and Secretary of Education William Bennett.

In spite of the successes of bilingual education and the extensive assimilation of students previously in bilingual programs, the xenophobic attack continues with extensive dissemination of negative propaganda based on misconceptions, distortions and baseless information.

9. Low-levels of expectancy

One of the most serious failures of American schools has been their inability to distinguish between unique characteristics of atypical populations and lack of mental capability. Minority, disadvantaged, migrant and immigrant school populations have over-populated special education classes for the mentally retarded and their close relatives, remedial education classes.

Much of the poor performance of this section of the school population comes about by their placement in remediation programs which are low level, slow paced, repetitious, boring and self-fulfilling.

Limited English-proficient students suffer a similar fate. Lack of English language competency is commonly seen as lack of mental competency, especially so when the determinants of mental capability are developed, normed, administered, scored and interpreted solely in the English language.

Although civil rights legislation requires the determination of lack of English language skills prior to placement in bilingual programs, there is a marked danger that the bilingual program is seen by the school as just another remedial or special education program for low mental capability students. Unfortunately, teachers, parents and the students themselves internalize these low levels of expectancy and convert them into continuous low levels of performance.

10. Rules and regulations

The implementation of bilingual education programs has been accompanied by a host of rules and regulations governing the programs which have served to impede greater success.

Such rules and regulations become a handicap for the successful implementation of the program. Such restrictions include teacher characteristics, language to be used, the relationship between sources of funding and the role of the teacher and paraprofessional staff, time limitations on the use of the native language, and many others.

Addressing these problems in the implementation of bilingual programs would do much for expanding educational opportunities for a large segment of the school population.

(IDRA, September 1993)

BIBLIOGRAPHY

Allegro, Annalisa, *Approaches for the Mainstream Classroom: LEP and English Proficient Students Learning Together*, National Clearinghouse for Bilingual Education, Rosslyn, Virginia, May 31, 1985.

American Institute for Research (AIR), *Evaluation of the Impact of ESEA Title VII Spanish/English Bilingual Education Programs*, Washington, D.C., 1977.

Aspira of New York, *Aspira National Think Tank Report*, Columbia, Maryland, 1973.

Aspira of New York, Inc. v. Board of Education of the City of New York, 72 Civ. 4002, (S.D.N.Y. 1973).

Bennett, William J., "In Defense of Our Common Language," *Our Children and Our Country*, Simon & Schuster, New York, 1988.

Brown v. Board of Education, 347 US 483 (1954).

Cárdenas, Jose A., "An Educator's Rationale for Native-Language Instruction," in Crawford, James, *Language Loyalties*, The University of Chicago Press, Chicago, 1992.

Cárdenas, Jose A., "The Role of Native-Language Instruction in Bilingual Education," Phi Delta Kappa, *Kappan*, Bloomington, 1986.

Cárdenas, Jose A., et al., *Bilingual Education Cost Analysis*, Intercultural Development Research Association (IDRA), San Antonio, 1976.

Cintron v. Brentwood Union Free School District, 455 F. Supp. 57 (E.D.N.Y. 1978).

Development Associates and Research Triangle Institute, *The National Longitudinal Study of the Evaluation of the Effectiveness of Services for Language-Minority Limited English Proficient Students*, Arlington, Virginia, 1986.

Hadden, Betsy, *Scattered, Diverse, and Fluctuating Minority Language Populations: School District Responses*, National Clearinghouse for Bilingual Education, Rosslyn, Virginia, June 3, 1985.

Intercultural Development Research Association (IDRA), *Newsletter*, San Antonio, June 1975, November 1975, January 1976, May 1976, February 1977, March 1977, June 1977, February, 1978, May 1981, August 1982, January 1984, August 1985, September 1985, October 1985, November 1985, January 1986, September 1986, September 1993.

Keys v. School District No. 1, 576 F. Supp. (D. Colo. 1983).

Lau v. Nichols, 483 F2d 791 (9th Cir 1973), 412 US 938 (1973).

Morales v. Shannon, 516 F. 2d. 411 (1975).

National Education Goals Report, *Building a Nation of Learners*, Washington, D.C., 1991.

Office for Civil Rights, *Notice*, U.S.C., 2000d, 35 Fed. Reg. 11595, 1970.

Otero v. Mesa Valley School District No. 51, 408 F. Supp., 162 (1975).

Overton v. City of Austin, 748 F. 2d, 941 (1984).

Rios v. Read, 73 F.R.D. 589 (1977).

San Antonio Independent School District v. Rodriguez, 411 U.S.1 (1973).

Serna v. Portales Municipal Schools, 499 Federal Reporter, 2d, (10th Cir. 1974).

Teitelbaum, Herbert and Richard J. Hillen, "Bilingual Education: The Legal Mandate," *Harvard Educational Review*, 47:2, May 1977.

United States v. Texas, Memorandum Opinion, Civil Action No. 5281, (E.D. Tex. 1971).

United States v. Texas, 342 F. Supp. 24 (E.D. Tex. 1971).

DISCUSSION QUESTIONS

1. Keep a file on multicultural and bilingual education issues as reported in the news media. Note attitudes toward minority education, the role of a child's home language in instruction, English as an official language, policy debates at various levels of government, issues in funding for minority and poor school districts, bilingualism and employment opportunity.
2. Develop your own definition of bilingual education and list what you perceive to be its essential components.
3. List the misconceptions regarding bilingual education that accompany objections raised against public funding for it. Chart these misconceptions beside the rationale presented in the articles of this chapter to challenge the objections. What information about bilingual education should be disseminated in the light of recurring objections?
4. Arrange to visit a school with bilingual programs. Find out the goals and structure of the school's programs and observe at least two classrooms. Is the school providing bilingual education in heterogeneous groups?
5. Work with a group to develop, distribute and analyze an attitude survey on bilingual education. Obtain responses from individuals of varied ethnic background, from parents of different economic levels, from school personnel, from students in teacher education programs, and others. Present and discuss your findings in class.
6. What is the salient point decided by the courts in each of the following cases discussed in this chapter? What effect does each of these cases have on current bilingual education programs?

    a. *Lau v. Nichols*

    b. *U.S. v. Texas*

    c. *Keyes v. Denver*

    d. *Rios v. Reed*

    e. *Cintron v. Brentwood*

3

Undocumented Children

PREFACE

In its advocacy role, Intercultural Development Research Association (IDRA) has been deeply involved in the education of immigrant and alien children. The following article is the fruit of an early attempt to gather research information about the children of undocumented workers. Subsequent to this study, IDRA provided extensive information for the first court case dealing with the education of undocumented children in Texas, *Doe v. Plyler* (*Doe v. Plyler*, 1978). I served as an expert witness for the Mexican-American Legal Defense and Education Fund (MALDEF) during the trial in Tyler.

Since the court decision in *Doe v. Plyler* applied solely to the Tyler School District, the federal decision resulted in similar court cases being filed in a number of other districts. IDRA provided information and testimony in these court cases until it was apparent to both plaintiffs and defendants that it would be advantageous to merge all the court cases into one. IDRA hosted a meeting of the various entities interested in the litigation, and supported the merger of the various court cases. The result was *Multiple District Litigation,* which was heard before Judge Woodrow Seals in Houston (*In Re Multiple District Litigation,* 1980). I provided expert testimony in this case, similar to the testimony I had presented in *Doe v. Plyler.*

The reason for the litigation was due to the exclusion of undocumented children from Texas public schools. During one of the legislative sessions, a representative from the Mexican border area had inserted a sleeper amendment which changed the eligibility for public school attendance by specifying a legal residence requirement. Undocumented children could still attend school, provided the school had the necessary space for them, but they were required to pay tuition upon enrolling. Since few undocumented aliens received even the minimum wage for work performed, the tuition requirement precluded school attendance.

Much of the harsh treatment afforded undocumented aliens and their children was based on myths. In addition, within the individual school districts, children were commonly used as scapegoats for deficiencies in the state educational system. School administrators commonly argued that the poverty status of low wealth school districts was attributed to the extensive number of undocumented children. In contrast, the school finance staff at IDRA found it readily apparent that the districts' poverty status could be attributed to an unfair and inequitable system of school finance, and districts with low local taxable wealth would remain poor with or without undocumented children.

Similar complaints were heard, and are still being heard today. The argument exists that poor school performance of students in low-wealth and minority districts can be attributed to the extensive number of immigrant children, though as in the school finance issue, the performance of native-born children in these districts is far from exemplary. In fact, legal or illegal immigrant children in this country, who have attended school in their country of origin, consistently outperform native-born minority and economically disadvantaged children in our schools.

I consider my participation in the undocumented immigrant children litigation as one of the most satisfying educational experiences of my life. It exemplifies the altruistic nature of IDRA and its staff. I was asked frequently what hidden strategy underlined our participation in the suits, and how such participation related to some master plan. There was no hidden strategy; there was no master plan. The undocumented children were being abused by the educational system of Texas, and as advocates for children we came to their aid.

Although our participation was conducive to the success of the court cases, that undocumented children have a right to equal educational opportunity while in this country, the experience left more than just a bitter taste in my mouth.

The temporary exclusion of the children was contrary to the United Nations' resolution on the rights of children. Although the United States ratified this resolution declaring that all children have a right to be educated, this right was clearly violated in the Texas schools. Legal counsel was aware of this resolution, although the legal implications were not clear enough to pursue this as a legal argument in court. Nevertheless, it is disillusioning to find the United States' commitment to children to be as shallow as was evident during this period of undocumented children exclusion.

To this day, I fail to comprehend the viciousness and tenacity of the educational leadership of this state. The Texas Education Agency and some administrators from affected school districts displayed a callousness to children which defies explanation. The Texas Education Agency fought the case tooth and nail in the courts, pursuing the appellate route through the Fifth Circuit Court of Appeals in New Orleans, and all the way to the Supreme Court of the United States. During the entire litigation, the educational leadership of the state was unique in providing objections, excuses, false estimates, invalid research findings and erroneous testimony in an incomprehensible attempt to exclude these children from the public schools of Texas.

Equally incomprehensible was the short-sightedness of the state's educational leadership. Witnesses from the federal Immigration and Naturalization Service (INS) testified repeatedly that most of the undocumented children would eventually become legal residents under the Fifth Preference section of the immigration code (i.e., most of them had siblings born in this country who would enhance their legal immigration.) Members of the educational leadership continued to oppose the enrollment of the children without regard to the fact that children would subsequently become adult legal residents of this country without any school attendance nor academic skills.

There was extensive irony in the use of a double standard for undocumented aliens. Government agencies were more than aware of the presence of the aliens, although little action was taken for deportation due to their contribution to the workforce; yet, their children were denied school services.

Throughout the litigation the children were treated as scapegoats for school financial and performance problems. This scapegoating of the children paralleled the scapegoating of their parents who were accused of not contributing to the support of government services while helping themselves to generous portions of social programs. In reality, it was the other way around. They made substantial tax payments while making few demands upon government supported social services.

Perhaps the biggest concern is the apparent lack of public understanding and appreciation for the equal-protection clause of the United States Constitution. This protection is extended to all persons in the country, regardless of citizenship, residence or documented status. During the trial, it was mentioned by the state that Mexico and other countries did not extend civil rights nor educational privileges to illegal immigrants. It is demeaning for us to lower our civil rights status in keeping with standards of Third World countries, rather than serve as a model for them to emulate.

The issue of immigrant children and their education comes up again with the imminent ratification of the North American Free Trade Agreement (NAFTA)Although the expected influx of immigrants may not be necessarily undocumented, similar educational problems may be expected to arise. The number of foreign-born children expected to enroll may be as exaggerated as the state estimates of undocumented children during the litigation. Texas educators may have as negative and prejudicial perceptions of the NAFTA immigrant children as was evident during the litigation. And the NAFTA immigrant children may again serve as scapegoats for the inadequacies and inefficiencies of the state system of education.

It would be gratifying to see the educational system projecting and preparing for any new influx of immigrant children. One can only hope that such preparation will prevent the negative stereotyping of the past, and will lead to the development and implementation of sound educational programs responsive to the needs and characteristics of immigrant children.

THE EDUCATION OF ILLEGAL ALIENS

1978

The past few years have seen a growing controversy concerning the education of children of illegal aliens. In recent months, this controversy has been highlighted by extensive media coverage, with television and radio stations transmitting news programs on this topic, and newspapers and magazines publishing extensive information.

Unfortunately, it appears that much of the coverage given to this topic and many of the arguments promulgated, both pro and con, are based on emotional reactions to the problems, conclusions based on erroneous information, and information based on myth rather than the scientific collection of data.

Intercultural Development Research Association (IDRA) was founded in order to provide information necessary for decision-makers to act wisely in affording a better education to all children. In this light, IDRA summarizes the limited information available on illegal aliens, and the impact this information has on the education of children.

LEGALITY OF EDUCATIONAL EXCLUSION

At the present time, limited numbers of illegal children are enrolled in Texas public schools. The exclusion of children illegally located in the state of Texas from free public schooling is based on Section 21.031 of the Texas Education Code, enacted by the State Legislature in 1975. The constitutionality of this law was recently tested in *Hernandez v. Houston Independent School District*, with the State District Court in Travis County supporting the law (*Hernandez v. Houston ISD*, 1977). On the other hand, the Texas Education Agency, on the basis of the federal case of *Silva v. Levi*, precluded the application of this state law to illegal children in the process of legitimizing their residence in this country. The *Silva v. Levi* interpretation applies to children who entered the United States, and whose families have applied for a U.S. visa or residence status between July 1968 and December 1976 and have received a priority date from the U.S. Consulate.

Still pending is the case of *Doe v. Plyler* in the Federal Court for the Eastern District of Texas, in which the 1975 Texas law is attacked as unconstitutional in that it denies equal protection to poor, illegal children, since illegal children with sufficient economic resources to pay tuition continue to be enrolled in the Texas public schools (*Doe v. Plyler*, 1978).

STUDIES OF ILLEGAL ALIENS

Very little reliable information is available on illegal aliens. The nature of this population makes it difficult to study

Attempts to gather data are hampered by the underground characteristic of the illegal population, but also by governmental and economic interests in the population concerned. Therefore, estimates on the number of illegal aliens in this country may range from four to twenty million, depending on who is doing the estimating and the purpose of the estimate. The past practice of collecting estimates from district offices of the Immigration and Naturalization Service, when such estimates also form the basis for budgetary consideration and staff allocations, most probably produced inflated counts of up to five times the number of illegal aliens that could exist. More scientific estimates of the number of illegal aliens in this country indicate that there are some 4 million illegal aliens in the U.S. with approximately 2.7 million of them being of Mexican extraction. Since studies indicate that one-fourth of all illegal Mexicans are located in the state of Texas, it is plausible that there are 675,000 illegal Mexicans residing in that state.

Although few successful studies have been conducted on illegal aliens, the information which has surfaced from these studies is drastically different from popular stereotypes. One example is the Bob Dale cartoon published by the *Express-News* in San Antonio, Texas, showing an illegal alien feasting at a table of welfare benefits and free education, served by a harassed, legal population

One of the most scientific studies of illegal aliens was conducted by David S. North and Marion F. Houston of Linton and Company, Washington, D.C. (North and Houston, 1981). This study is based on the analyses of 793 apprehended illegal aliens, 481 being Mexican. The data from this study indicate that 90 percent came to the U.S. to get a job, 91 percent were male, 17 percent had spouses in the U.S., but only 5 percent had illegal spouses in this country. The Mexican illegal alien averaged a $117 weekly income, even though he worked more (8.6 hours per week more) than legal workers in this country. About 24 percent of the illegals received unlawful wages, less than the minimum wage prescribed by law.

Information on the illegals apprehended indicated that 73 percent paid federal income taxes, 77 percent paid social security, and 44 percent paid some form of hospitalization insurance.

In contrast, one-half of 1 percent received welfare payments, 1 percent obtained food stamps, 1 percent participated in U.S.-funded job training programs, and 4 percent collected unemployment insurance. Although 27.4 percent received medical attention, 83 percent of those who received medical services paid for the medical services with their own funds, their medical insurance, or through their employer. Thus, only 4.7 percent of the illegal aliens received free medical attention.

ILLEGAL CHILDREN

Information concerning the children of illegal aliens obtained in this study also deviates from common stereotypes. Only 3.7 percent of the illegal aliens had children in American schools. Since it has been estimated that there are 675,000 illegal Mexicans in Texas, the number of children one would expect to find is 25,000—substantially lower than the number estimated by the Texas Education Agency. This figure is highly inflated since only 29 percent of the aliens who had spouses in this country had illegal spouses, or of the 25,000 children, 71 percent were from spouses legally residing in the U.S. Therefore, after subtracting probable legal residents, the total number of illegal children in Texas may be no more than 7,243. Still to be subtracted from this number are children not of school age, and since the average age of the illegal adult apprehended was only 28.5, the number of pre-school-age children may be substantial.

EDUCATIONAL CONSIDERATIONS

The information gleaned from the North Houston study and related information indicates that perhaps the state of Texas acted too hastily in attempting to solve the problem through school exclusion.

1. The number of illegal alien children in the state of Texas may not constitute a major problem requiring such drastic measures as absolute deprivation of educational benefits.

2. Total exclusion from school is not a humane manner of dealing with this problem, particularly when the larger society utilizes the work contribution of the illegal adults.

3. Many of the problems in the education of illegal alien children stem from inadequacies in the Texas system of financing schools which are aggravated or compounded by the illegal population. Most school superintendents who have complained about illegal children have done so because of the shortage of school facilities for housing the illegal children . This shortage of school facilities in low property wealth school districts stems from the failure of the state of Texas to provide state funds for school construction, a problem which exists with or without illegal children. A similar situation exists in terms of limited English-speaking ability. There is little hope to meet the language needs of Mexican aliens when very few of the many American citizens having a similar characteristic are being afforded adequate programs.

4. There is evidence to indicate that many of the illegal children in Texas are in the process of legalizing their residence. A study reported by Dr. Gilbert Cárdenas of the University of Texas at Austin indicated that 60 percent of all Mexican immigrants in the U.S., who became legal residents, had been in this country before as illegal aliens (Weintraub and Cárdenas, 1984). The problem of educating illegal children in Texas may be insignificant compared to the problem of educating immigrant children who have been kept out of school for a number of years in previous illegal visits to the state. Other states have better addressed this problem by providing categorical funds for the education of alien children rather than the Texas policy of total exclusion.

5. The illegal alien participates in the support of the school. More than 80 percent of all state taxes which are collected and disbursed for education are consumer taxes which the illegals pay. Local property taxes are paid by the illegals either directly or indirectly

6. Little effort has been exerted in attempting to obtain the resources of the federal government in responding to what is obviously a federal problem. A federal impact program, such as the one directed toward relief of problems caused by concentrations of federal employees, could do much to diminish local problems in the education of alien children.

FEDERAL JUDGE RULES IN FAVOR OF UNDOCUMENTED CHILDREN

SEPTEMBER 1979

Federal Judge D.W. Suttle has issued a temporary injunction ordering the Ector County Independent School District to admit undocumented children into its schools. The hearing was held August 14, 1979, in the United States District Court, Western District of Texas, Midland Odessa Division, for the purposes of determining the judiciability of the case, *Roe v. Holm*, and demonstrating the irreparable harm vested on the excluded class of children.

Section 21.031 of the Texas Education Code, as amended in 1975, provides for the education of children who are citizens or legally admitted aliens and denies undocumented children admission to the state's public schools. Undocumented children are typically excluded from Texas schools unless they can pay a prohibitive tuition. Prior to the injunction, Ector County ISD tuitions were $1,209.39, $1,213.26, and $1,610.42 for admission into elementary, junior high, and high schools, respectively. Tuitions such as these effectively bar the majority of undocumented children from receiving a basic education.

Plaintiffs' attorney in *Roe v. Holm* is Warren Burnett of Odessa, Texas (*Roe v. Holm*, 1979). In his motion for the preliminary injunction, Mr. Burnett stated that the courts have generally looked to four factors in determining the propriety of issuing a preliminary injunction: 1) the plaintiffs' likelihood of prevailing on the merits of the case, 2) the possibility of irreparable harm to the plaintiffs, 3) the counterbalancing risk of harm to the defendants, and 4) the service of the public interest. The first factor does not require absolute certainty before an injunction is issued. *Roe v. Holm* raises serious questions of constitutional and statutory law, and there is sufficient legal support of the plaintiffs' position to suggest that the court *may* rule in their favor. The second factor, the possibility of irreparable harm to the plaintiffs, is of utmost importance in this case. According to Dr. Clarence Kron, chairman of the Education Department at the University of Texas, Permian Basin, who was present to testify at the hearing, children who are deprived of an education during their critical formative years suffer substantial harm in their personal, affective and cognitive development.

With regard to the third factor, Burnett illustrated that any harm to the defendant school district as a result of the injunction would be minimal. According to Burnett, prior to the 1978–79 school year, undocumented children were enrolled in and attended the Ector County schools without apparent harm to the district. Furthermore, after the change in policy and the resulting exclusion of undocumented children, the budget of the Ector County School District did not decrease, school taxes were not lowered, and the district received no perceptible benefits. Therefore, enrollment of the undocumented children would not cause hardships for which the district is unequipped, or which it has not handled adequately and smoothly in the past. The final factor, service of the public interest, clearly lies on the side that believes *extension* of education is to the benefit of society.

As of this writing, there are five other cases of this nature in progress throughout Texas. Affected school districts include Dallas, Houston, Pasadena, Goose Creek, and Tyler (on appeal). Other suits are being contemplated and may have been filed before the publication of this newsletter. With this proliferation of like cases, consolidation is probable for the purposes of statewide application. Perhaps the prohibition on the allocation of state money as enacted by the Sixty-fourth Texas Legislature in 1975 will be removed by the courts, and the human rights of undocumented children will prevail.

THE UNDOCUMENTED CHILDREN CASE AND THE GHOST OF *RODRIGUEZ*

1980

The July 21, 1980, decision by Judge Woodrow Seals in the U.S. District Court of the Southern District of Texas, in the case of undocumented alien children, struck down a state law barring their access to the public schools (*In Re Multiple District Litigation*, 1980). The multidistrict litigation led to a decision, rendering section 21.031 of the Texas Education Code, which permits local school officials to exclude undocumented children from the public schools, as unconstitutional. This finding was not unexpected, particularly since a similar case, *Doe v. Plyler* in the Eastern District of Texas, had resulted in similar findings, although that case affected only one school district (*Doe v. Plyler*, 1978).

The purpose of this article is not to analyze the history, evidence and findings in the case, but to look deeper into social and educational problems related to this matter. Arguments and evidence presented by the Texas Education Agency and the state of Texas raise serious questions as to the structure of public education in Texas, identify problems in the state system of education, and highlight a need for administrative and legislative action.

This analysis of the case of undocumented alien children has been fairly consistent with the purposes and activities of Intercultural Development Research Association (IDRA) these past eight years, and is closely related to most of its project activities. It serves to summarize what IDRA has been saying over the years about problems in the education of atypical populations, the failure of the system to respond to special student characteristics, the absence of equity, and the need for change.

The case of the undocumented alien children is consistent with a past history of dysfunctional responses to educational problems, with the responses frequently aggravating the problems rather than resolving them.

It is surprising and regrettable that the Texas Education Agency (TEA) and defendant school districts would fight so bitterly to exclude undocumented children from the public schools. One would assume that they would have more advocacy for children—any children—but their role in this case belies this assumption. Attorneys, community organizations, the Department of Justice, the Immigration and Naturalization Service, and the public media have shown more humaneness, compassion and understanding than the educators opposed to the education of these children. In opposing the education of undocumented children, defendants consistently displayed amazing naiveness, short-sightedness and misinformation; their tactics relied heavily on playing both ends against the middle.

To start with, defendants have consistently failed to take into account that the population in question is here to stay. Regardless of desirability, arguments on behalf of the education of undocumented children indicate that this is not a transient population, but one that can be expected to remain in the state and the country indefinitely. In both *Doe v. Plyler*, and in the multidistrict case, there was ample evidence that the majority of these children will subsequently become American citizens. The Immigration and Naturalization Service (INS) has given up hope of apprehension and deportation. A former commissioner of INS testified that the inability of INS to deport aliens constitutes a *de facto* amnesty. The administration has recommended legalizing amnesty. As pointed out by Judge Woodrow Seals, the state of Texas has considered and consistently rejected legislation to make the undocumented alien's stay in this country more tenuous.

Considering this reality, one is hard pressed to understand defendants' arguments that the education of these children is a financial imposition. Almost every social scientist involved in the case felt that the non-education of these permanent residents presented more social problems and a higher cost than educating them.

A second characteristic in the defendants' position in this case is the general lack of information concerning the target population. In 1975, the Legislature amended the Texas Education Code, inserting the citizenship requirement. There were no studies conducted on the number of students then enrolled in the public schools, no studies of their impact, special characteristics, or of special programs required. No hearings were held, nor was testimony presented about the cost of their education or the subsequent cost of non-education. The Legislature simply barred them from the schools with a minimum of consideration. During the four years that the undocumented children were barred from the public schools of Texas, no study was conducted on numbers, potential cost, nor location. The one and only study that surfaced was commissioned by TEA for the trial, and the court's analysis of this study would prove embarrassing to TEA and the state of Texas.

This leads one to the arguments presented by the defendants in this case. These arguments center around numbers, quality of education, impact on desegregation, impact on bilingual education, and the cost of education.

NUMBERS

As stated earlier, until immediately before the trial, no studies had been conducted on the number of students involved. The state's study in preparation for this case calculated the number of undocumented children by taking census estimates of Hispanic school-age children in Texas and subtracting from this figure enrollees in public and private schools, and known school dropouts. The resulting figure was the state's estimate of the number of undocumented Hispanic children.

Needless to say, the study's estimate of more than 100,000 undocumented school-age children in Texas did not greatly impress the court.

There are no high quality studies of school dropouts in Texas. School districts' estimates are consistently low. Furthermore, the Court stated that to assume that the children not enrolled in school are undocumented is simply unsound. The Court further criticizes the state's study as using poor methodology, being illogical, unsound and unreliable. At one point Judge Seals notes that using the same TEA methodology on other populations ". . . results in the rather bizarre and untenable conclusion that there are at least 100,000 undocumented black and white children in Texas."

All other studies presented to the Court estimate the number of undocumented school age children at approximately 20,000, or less than one-fifth of the number estimated by the TEA study (This author testified before a U.S. committee on immigration that there were less than 30,000 such children.)

Yet, during the trial, after the trial, and in all state reactions to the court decision, the Texas Education Agency and the state of Texas continued to use the 100,000 figure. Governor Clements, Attorney General Mark White, Commissioner of Education Alton Bowen, and several superintendents argued the need to appeal the case because of the financial impact of having to educate 100,000 additional children. It is this author's opinion that even if there is a concerted statewide effort to enroll undocumented children, less than 10,000 will show up to register in September.

The only area where undocumented children could have an impact would be in the border school districts. The basis for this impact would be that the state has consistently failed to address the long-existing problem of the impact of legally admitted (documented) children. If this issue had been resolved rather than ignored, the impact of undocumented children would be minimal.

QUALITY OF EDUCATION

A second defendant's argument has been that the enrollment of undocumented children would lower the quality of education for all children in Texas. As in the case of numbers of children, no evidence is available to substantiate this claim. Apparently, feeling that turnabout is fair play, Judge Seals notes, "There is no data which show that the academic performance of students has improved since undocumented children were excluded."

In general, the enrollment of undocumented children should have little effect on the quality of education in Texas. As indicated by the early findings of the statewide Texas Assessment of Basic Skills this past year, the quality of education for middle-class white children in Texas has been fairly adequate. The education of Mexican-Americans, Blacks, the disadvantaged, and language minority children leaves a lot to be desired. The inclusion of undocumented children could not make matters much worse, no more than their exclusion will make it any better. Instruction, resources and teacher training for these groups will have to be improved with or without undocumented children. In fact, the experience of Texas educators dealing with immigrant children shows that if these immigrant children have attended school in Mexico prior to coming to Texas, they will consistently outperform native-born Mexican-American, Black and disadvantaged children. This phenomenon should be intensively studied by Texas educators.

BILINGUAL EDUCATION AND DESEGREGATION

A third argument used by defendants concerns the impact of the admission of undocumented children on bilingual education and desegregation. The Court was not impressed by the arguments presented in these areas. There is nothing in the desegregation process that could suffer from an influx of minority undocumented children. The majority of these children will probably enroll in impacted districts, that is, districts in which the percentage of Mexican-American children is so high that there aren't enough non-minority children for any practical desegregation.

Similarly, the impact on bilingual education should be minimal. The border districts have no shortage of bilingual teachers, whereas districts where shortages exist have never had any great pressure from the state to comply with federal and state bilingual education legislation.

The motion to enforce in *U.S. v. Texas* recently heard in Tyler should soon reveal the extent of state concern in providing understandable instruction to children of limited English proficiency (*United States v. Texas,* 1971).

It is interesting to note that in a recent session of the Texas Legislature, the TEA recommendation for the funding of bilingual education was little more than one-half of the amount appropriated in the preceding session.

Of much more consequence than the defendants' arguments regarding desegregation and bilingual education needs is the growing tendency of defendants to play both ends against the middle. Desegregation, bilingual education, and undocumented alien children are three problems to which the state and school districts must respond. Instead, there is a growing tendency to play one against the other. For some time now, one has heard the argument that desegregation and bilingual education are contradictory. One school district in Texas presented testimony in its desegregation court case that Mexican-American children of limited English proficiency could not be desegregated because bilingual education legislation at the state and federal levels prohibits the desegregation of children in bilingual education classes. This testimony was presented to the Court in spite of the fact that both federal and state regulations explicitly prohibit the segregation of children in bilingual programs.

It now appears that the undocumented children will be played against both of the other programs. One can even visualize the state of Texas testifying in future desegregation and bilingual education cases that their inability to meet the requirements of the law is due to the presence of undocumented children, in spite of the fact that these past four years without undocumented children have not been exceptional as far as the state's response to desegregation or bilingual education.

FINANCING

The fourth argument presented by the defendants in the multidistrict litigation on undocumented children is the argument most closely related with the past goals and activities of IDRA.

The state of Texas and the defendant school districts argued that the cost of educating these children is prohibitive. Reading defendants' press releases and media announcements, one would conclude that the state was at the point of bankruptcy and that the inclusion of undocumented children would push it over the brink.

This assumption is just not true. In the first place, the fiscal situation is not even bad. As noted by the Court, the Texas General Revenue Fund has had a surplus for the last twelve years—over $600 million a year for at least the last three years. The cost to the state of educating 20,000 undocumented children would be as little as $16 million a year.

Much of the public controversy over this case centers on the concept of educating, at the public's expense, kids whose parents do not pay taxes. Nothing could be further from the truth. Evidence in this case and in *Doe v. Plyler* shows conclusively that parents of undocumented children pay as much in taxes as any other group of their own economic level. In addition, the clandestine nature of the population leads to their making less demands on state services

Undocumented children counts contribute to the allocation of federal funds, such as Title I, although in the past four years undocumented children have not been included in these benefits.

The most frustrating aspect of the fiscal impact arguments, in that what the state of Texas claims as the inability of the state to finance the education of undocumented children, is really a criticism of the inadequacy, the unfairness, and the lack of equity in the Texas system of school finance.

Judge Woodrow Seals in this case joins Judge William Wayne Justice in *Doe v. Plyler* in noting that "any spectator watching the state's presentation might easily have mistaken it for a retrial of the *Rodriguez* case, with the state of Texas acting as *amicus curiae* for the plaintiffs, emphasizing the plight of property-poor border school districts under the state's educational financing scheme" (*San Antonio ISD v. Rodriguez*, 1973).

In the *Rodriguez* case, the state defended the existing system of school finance in Texas. According to the state of Texas, all school districts had sufficient resources for an adequate education. In the multidistrict litigation, the state paraded a host of witnesses from property-poor and inner-city schools showing the drastic unavailability of resources in these districts.

I repeat what I think could be the most important outcome of this case, namely that the financial problems in the education of undocumented children should be attributed to the inadequacies in the present finance system and to a lack of interest in its reform, rather than to the inability of the state to afford.

For the past three sessions of the Texas Legislature, bills have been introduced to provide state aid for school construction desperately needed in the border districts, with or without undocumented students. In the last legislative session, not one single state official, not one single TEA official, not one single school district official testified on behalf of the bill. The bill again died in committee, with the author bitterly noting that there was not enough interest on the part of school officials to bring it up for consideration. To exclude the education of undocumented children in Texas (which is one of the few states without any form of state aid for school construction) on the grounds that the school districts cannot afford the facilities for them, reminds one of the story of the young man who murdered his parents and requested leniency from the courts on the grounds that he was an orphan. It appears that educators in Texas have their share of *chutzpah*.

The children of the state of Texas deserve better. The entire state needs better. In the light of the increasing need for education in this technological society, a failure of the state to educate any segment of the population has severe implications for all.

Arguments concerning the quality of education in Texas are moot. The education of atypical populations, specifically the minorities and the disadvantaged, needs vast improvement. The state of Texas needs educational leadership. It is high time that this leadership be acquired or developed. Foot-dragging, scare tactics based on exaggerations, red herrings and rationalizing will not bring about this improvement. Only through the efforts of concerned educators, laypersons and decisionmakers at the local and federal levels, in finding functional solutions to the problems of educating children, will Texas see the arrival of equal educational opportunities for all children.

THE IMPACT OF *DOE v. PLYLER* UPON TEXAS PUBLIC SCHOOLS

José A. Cárdenas and Albert Cortez

INTRODUCTION

Up until 1973, undocumented alien children had been enrolled in Texas schools without a special classification. It is doubtful that many teachers or other school authorities were aware of the immigration status of most of the Hispanic children in public schools. The only awareness of a problem existed in border cities where large numbers of Mexican children routinely crossed the state line for the sole purpose of attending public schools in Texas.

The controversy surrounding the exclusion of undocumented children from Texas public schools was created by a 1975 revision in the state's public school admission and funding statute which limited eligibility for some state funds to students who are legally admitted aliens or citizens of the United States. Before 1975, all children between the ages of six and twenty-one years of age were required to be enrolled; in fact, in 1975 (before the revision in state law) the attorney general ruled that alien children were entitled to attend public schools whether they were legal or illegal residents. However, with the 1975 revision, undocumented children were subsequently excluded from tuition-free admission to Texas public schools.

As currently written, the statute reads:

> All children who are citizens of the United States or legally admitted and who are over five years and under the age of 21 years shall be entitled to the benefits of the available school fund [and]. . .shall be permitted to attend the public free schools of the district in which he resides or in which his parents, guardian, or the person having lawful control over him resides at the time he applies for admission.[1]

By nature of the wording, the state determined that children not meeting the criteria were not entitled to tuition-free admission; they may not be counted by the district in reports used to calculate their state aid entitlement. Decisions concerning the admission or exclusion of these students, given the absence of state aid for them, were left to the individual school district's discretion. In response to these developments, many school districts initiated policies which called for the total exclusion of undocumented children, usually basing their rates on the average amount spent for each student enrolled in the school system.

Within two years, growing parental and interest-group concern with the impact which the state's exclusionary policy was having on undocumented children led to legal challenges of the provisions.

The Legal Challenges

In February 1977 the parents of children who were denied admission to the Houston Independent School District filed suit in state district court, arguing that the exclusionary provisions in the state's admission law was unconstitutional. In *Hernandez v. Houston Independent School District*,[2] the state court ruled in favor of Houston and the Texas Education Agency, which were co-defendants in the action.

Although *Hernandez* was recognized as a serious setback in the challenge of state and local policies concerning undocumented children, advocates recognized that federal courts were available as alternative courses of action. In September 1977 a new wave of litigation was triggered with the filing of *Doe v. Plyler* in the United States District Court for the Eastern District of Texas. In his final ruling, delivered in September 1978, Judge William Wayne Justice struck down the state and local district's exclusionary policy as it applied to the Tyler Independent School District, and issued a permanent injunction forbidding Tyler's continued enforcement of the policy.[3] The case was appealed to the United States Fifth Circuit Court of Appeals, where it awaited consideration. Although significant as a precedent-setter, Judge Justice's ruling was restricted solely to the Tyler school district; by implication, the issue remained open to individual challenges in school districts throughout Texas.

The second wave of litigation was initiated by the filing in Houston of *Garza v. Reagan*,[4] which challenged the exclusionary provisions enforced by the Houston school district. Following closely on its heels were *Roe v. Holm*[5] which challenged the exclusion of undocumented children by the Ector County school system; *Boe v. Wright*[6] which dealt with the exclusionary policy of the Dallas Independent School District; and *Doe v. Lodestro*[7] which challenged similar policies of the Port Arthur school system.

In the cases involving the Ector County and Port Arthur school districts, the federal judges for the respective cases granted a preliminary injunction and mandated that the plaintiffs and the class of undocumented children residing in the district be allowed to enroll in the school systems in question.

In each case, the court also mandated that the state agency provide the corresponding state aid which the added enrollment would qualify the school systems to receive. In Houston, the federal judge involved allowed the named plaintiffs to enroll; however, action on the class of undocumented children residing in the Houston Independent School District was postponed for a future hearing on the matter.[8]

In Dallas, Federal Judge Robert Hill broke the pattern established by his predecessors and denied the plaintiff class a preliminary injunction which would have allowed them to enroll in the Dallas Independent School District.[9] The cases against the state were eventually consolidated, and the trial was conducted in the Federal District Court for the Southern District of Texas in Houston before Judge Woodrow Seals. The case is hereafter referred to as *In Re Alien Children's Education Litigation*.[10]

The trial required twenty-four days of testimony and arguments, with the court requiring an additional three months to consider the record of proceedings and render its conclusions. On July 21, 1980, the court ruled in favor of the plaintiff children. The order permanently enjoined the state and selected school systems from denying admission and from charging tuition to the class of children involved.[11] The state requested a postponement which was denied by Judge Seals. The state then proceeded to appeal the decision.

To fully understand the rationale for the judge's decision requires a review of the court's opinion. What follows are selected excerpts from the court's eighty-seven page opinion.

> Maintaining the fiscal integrity of the public schools is an important and legitimate state interest. States have the responsibility of safeguarding all monies entrusted to them by the taxpayers and these demands are increased when a fundamental state function such as education is involved. That does not mean that any measure which saves money is constitutional. The court has concluded that the absolute deprivation of education should trigger strict judicial scrutiny, particularly when the absolute deprivation is the result of complete inability to pay for the desired benefit. When strict judicial scrutiny is appropriate, important or legitimate governmental interests are not sufficient to justify legislative classifications. The classifications, if they are to be upheld, must be shown to be necessary to promote a compelling governmental interest.
>
> Additionally, the factor which is the basis for differentiating between persons otherwise equal may not be capricious or irrelevant; it must be germane to the effectuation of the State's interest. . . .Finally, the State is required to show that there are no less restrictive alternatives available. . . .The State has not carried this heavy burden of justification. (Citations omitted.)[12]

With regard to the state's asserted rationale for section 21.031, Judge Seals indicated that:

> In defense of its decision to exclude undocumented children from the public schools, the State presented evidence concerning (1) the number of undocumented children in Texas; (2) the financial impact of educating undocumented children on the quality of education and on compliance with desegregation orders. The State contends that the equal protection clause does not apply to undocumented aliens and thus that the discrimination against members of that class is permissible no matter how invidious. Nonetheless, the State offered evidence which it believes demonstrates that section 21.031 is supported by a rational basis.
>
> At the outset, the evidence demonstrated that prior to the passage of the amendment to section 21.031 in 1975, the State never had attempted to determine the number of undocumented children attending Texas public schools, nor the impact of educating these children upon the school districts. The current commissioner of the Texas Education Agency was the Deputy Commissioner at the time section 21.031 was enacted and he was then primarily responsible for its implementation. He testified that no one from the Texas Legislature contacted anyone at the Texas Education Agency prior to the amendment. No studies were conducted to determine the number of undocumented children throughout the state, or the fiscal impact of educating them. No one attempted to compare the amount of taxes paid by undocumented aliens with the cost of educating undocumented children.

> Since the law was amended, the State has done very little to monitor the implementation of the statute by the local school districts. There is no evidence that the State has ever determined the number of local school districts which are excluding undocumented children, the number of school districts that charge tuition, or the number of school districts that provide tuition-free education to all children within their jurisdiction.
>
> Because this basic information has not been gathered, no effort has been made to determine the number of children actually affected by section 21.031. There are no data which show that the academic performance of students has improved since undocumented children were excluded.
>
> Indeed, the evidence in this case indicates that the State has been concerned primarily with the impact and number of documented Mexican children. With the exception of a study commissioned in connection with this case, the State sponsored studies have concentrated on the characteristics and number of documented immigrant children. . . .[13]

Commenting on the state-financed study conducted by Criterion Analysis, Inc., of Dallas in estimating the potential number of undocumented children residing in the state, the court observed:

> The State's assumption concerning the potential impact of undocumented children on the public schools is based on an estimate of the number of undocumented children presently residing in Texas. It must be emphasized that only the current figure is of concern; no evidence was offered which implied that the number of undocumented children living in Texas and attending the schools in 1975, had an impact on public education. Thus the State does not argue that the number was so great in 1975 that it was necessary to exclude undocumented children, but that once they had been excluded there are too many to incorporate them once again.[14]

On the adequacy of the study itself, the opinion stated that "[t]he court finds that the Criterion study does not represent an accurate estimate of the number of undocumented children in Texas."[15]

Responding to the state's contention that free public education will be a magnet which will attract increasing numbers of undocumented persons, the court noted that Texas was the only state with exclusionary legislation, yet "[t]here is no evidence that other states have a disproportionate number of undocumented persons who have been drawn to those states because of the availability of free public education."[16] Thus, "the court [found] that free education would not serve as a significant attraction for undocumented persons."[17]

Turning to the question of fiscal impacts which will result from the enrollment of these children, the court commented:

> Permitting undocumented children to attend the public schools clearly would affect state and local resources. The evidence does not indicate, however, that the State or the school districts lack the necessary funds. Indeed, as counsel for the State noted in closing arguments:
>
> There is no place in this pre-trial order that the State has said the State of Texas doesn't have enough money. Not one place. Texas can come up with the money. If we want to get the legislature to fund certain projects, we will go down and get them to fund it. The State never said it didn't have money in its budget.
>
> Without a reliable estimate of the number of undocumented children in the State, it is difficult to gauge the precise financial savings that can be expected to accrue as a result of excluding children from school pursuant to section 21.031. Nonetheless, the evidence indicates that both the State and the local school districts together have sufficient funds to educate the undocumented children.[18]
>
> The current estimate by the Comptroller is that the General Revenue Fund will have a cash balance of $324.4 million at the end of the current biennium. This projected surplus is sufficient to finance completely the education of all undocumented children in Texas even if the State correctly estimated the number of undocumented school age children.[19]

Recognizing that the impact will be more significant in border areas and major urban centers, the Court observed:

> The impact of admitting undocumented children on the local independent school district would not be uniform. It appears that the wealthy metropolitan school districts in which local funds support a larger percentage of the total educational cost and the poor school districts in which local dollars are stretched to the limit would be the most affected. These problems are very real. The conditions in Brownsville require the use of temporary buildings having no air conditioning. In districts like Dallas the high cost of living requires the school districts to adopt a salary structure which exceeds that contemplated by the Foundation School Program. These difficulties are addressed by current school finance laws in only one respect. The school finance laws do not attempt to aid a district like Brownsville with its construction problems . . . and they do not attempt to compensate for the higher cost of living and of municipal government in the large cities. Instead, the Legislature has attempted to ameliorate these conditions by reducing the number of students.

> The State often stated during the hearing that Texas has the duty to protect the fiscal integrity of the local independent school districtsAs Judge Justice noted in *Doe v. Plyler*, 458 F. Supp. [at] 589, "[a]ny spectator watching the state's presentation might easily have mistaken it for a retrial of the Rodriguez[20] case, with the State of Texas acting as amicus curiae for the plaintiffs, emphasizing the plight of property poor border school districts under the State's educational financing scheme."

> The Legislature's approach to alleviating overcrowding in the border school districts and to assist the metropolitan school districts with teacher salaries is a drastic one. It is to exclude children from the schools.[21]

The Court concluded with the observation that:

> [W]hether it be [at present] in the form of modest increases in tuition, in public school operating cost, or . . .in terms of social cost. . .fifteen years from now, we will pay this bill. It is, of course, the prerogative of the State Legislature to saddle the public with such a future public burden, provided that they do so in conformance with the Constitution. That they have not done.[22]

The final result of Judge Seal's ruling was that undocumented children were to be admitted, and the corresponding state aid was to be provided to school districts throughout the state.

Dissatisfied with the district court's interpretations of the law, the state of Texas decided to appeal the decision to the Fifth Circuit Court of Appeals. At the circuit level, a three-judge panel reviewed the findings in *Doe v. Plyler* and summarily upheld Judge Justice's ruling;[23] a short time thereafter it also upheld Judge Seal's decision in *In Re Alien Children's Education Litigation*.[24] Determined to exhaust all levels of appeal, the state decided to appeal to the United States Supreme Court, where the cases were consolidated and arguments were heard from all parties to the suit.[25] In a five to four decision, the Court upheld the lower court rulings and permanently enjoined the state from excluding these children from tuition-free enrollment in Texas Public schools.[26]

1981 LEGISLATIVE ACTION

Prior to the Supreme Court ruling, State Representative Albert Luna introduced legislation which would allow undocumented children to enroll in Texas schools. During the 1981 Texas legislative session, not one single state official, not one single Texas Education Agency Official, not one single district official testified on behalf of the bill. The bill again died in committee, with the author bitterly noting that there was not enough interest on the part of the school officials to bring it up for consideration. To exclude the education of undocumented children in Texas (which is one of the few states without any form of state aid for school construction) on the grounds that the school districts cannot afford the programs or facilities for them, should remind one of the story of the young man who murdered his parents and requested leniency from the courts on the ground that he was an orphan. It appears that educators in Texas have a similar nerve.

UNDOCUMENTED STUDENT COUNTS

Of critical interest to both proponents and opponents of the enrollment of undocumented children in Texas schools is the number of such children attending public schools within individual districts. Prior to their enrollment and throughout the legal battles, speculation abounded on this issue. Due to the clandestine existence of undocumented families, however, little hard data had been available.

Estimates regarding the actual number of such students varied tremendouslyIn a state-commissioned study by Criterion Analysis, Inc., a Dallas-based firm using census data, it was found that as many as 110,000 such students were present in Texas.[27] Fear exhibited by the state and some school officials of an influx of such magnitude served to fuel the debate concerning their enrollment. Contrary to such inflated projections, Intercultural Development Research Association (IDRA) and other researchers proposed that the estimated counts, based on data regarding the numbers of undocumented persons who migrated with their families, would total no more than 25,000 students statewide.

Moreover, IDRA and others proposed that the students would be concentrated in those areas with large numbers of Hispanics, a pattern already observed by previous studies on immigration into the United States. Debate regarding the accuracy of all estimates continued throughout the litigation.[28] Following the mandated enrollment of these students, a result of Judge Seal's decision, actual data regarding the number and distributional characteristics became available.

THE TEA STUDY

Following the district court order in the Houston case, the Texas Education Agency (TEA) conducted a survey in which school districts were asked to indicate the number of undocumented children enrolled in their public schools. IDRA subsequently acquired the data which had been compiled by TEA. These data were merged with official TEA figures on districts' refined average daily attendances (ADA) for the 1979-80 school year, in order to assess the proportion of a district's ADA which was composed of undocumented students. The resulting data base was subsequently analyzed. The following are excerpts from the results of IDRA's analysis of the data pertaining to the registration of undocumented students in Texas school districts.

Most noteworthy among these early statistics is that only 332 of the 1,080 Texas school systems reported the presence of any undocumented students. The majority of Texas school systems (or 748) reported no impact from the court ruling (see Table 1). Of the 332 districts reporting undocumented student enrollment, 204 (61 percent) reported having ten or fewer undocumented children enrolled (see Table 1). In contrast, only thirteen school districts reported counts in excess of 100 pupils. Not surprising to anyone, the major urban/suburban school districts, which have the greatest pupil enrollment in the state, also had the greatest undocumented student enrollment.

Table 1

Distribution of Undocumented Students by Concentrations Within School Districts

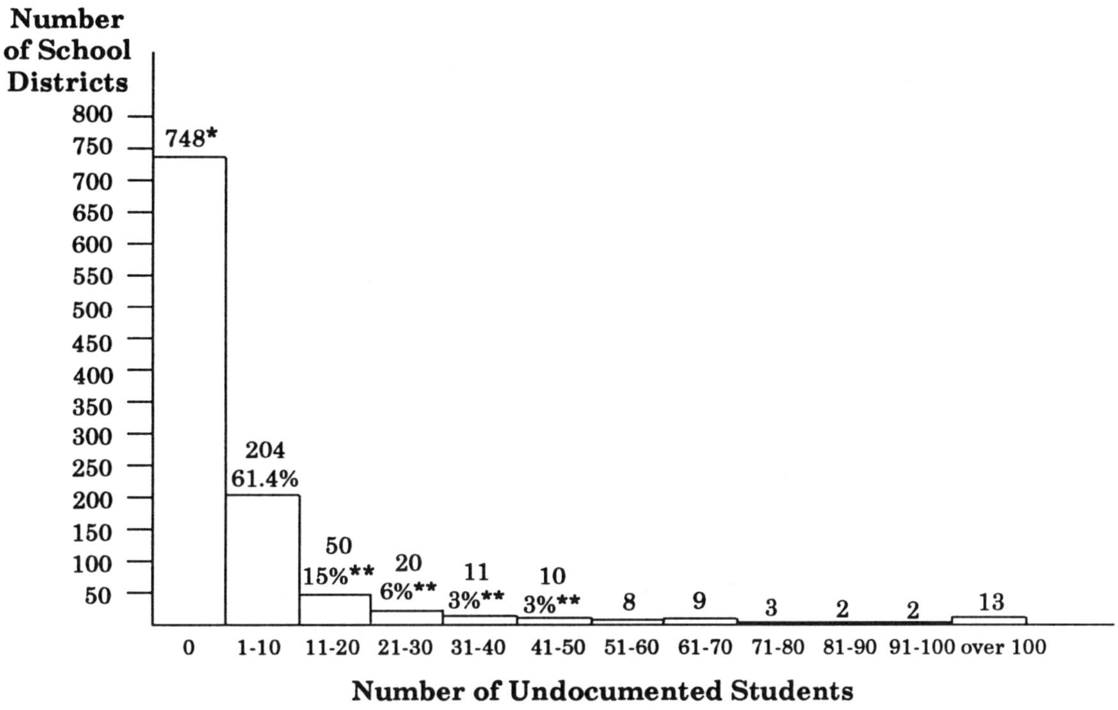

* Not reporting any undocumented students to TEA.

** Computed as a percentage of the 332 school districts reporting undocumented counts to TEA.

Source: Reports submitted by school districts to Texas Education Agency, Oct. 1980.

CONCENTRATION CHARACTERISTICS

The IDRA analysis also examined what proportion the undocumented pupils constituted in a district's existing enrollment and, more specifically, the percentage that such pupils represent in a district's ADA. To arrive at these figures, IDRA staff acquired district-refined ADA data for the preceding (the latest available) school year and calculated the percentages. The resulting variables revealed distribution patterns of concentration levels of undocumented pupils within Texas schools. The most striking of these statistics indicates that undocumented students represented less than one percent of the district's ADA in 239 (or 72 percent) of the 331 districts reporting (see Table 2). In forty-one of the remaining ninety-two districts, undocumented students constituted between 1 percent and 2 percent of a district's

ADA. At the opposite end of the scale, undocumented students represented more than 5 percent of a district's ADA in only eleven (or 3.3 percent) of the 331 districts reporting undocumented enrollment.

Table 2

Statewide Distribution of Undocumented Pupils by Percentage of Undocumented Pupils to District's ADA

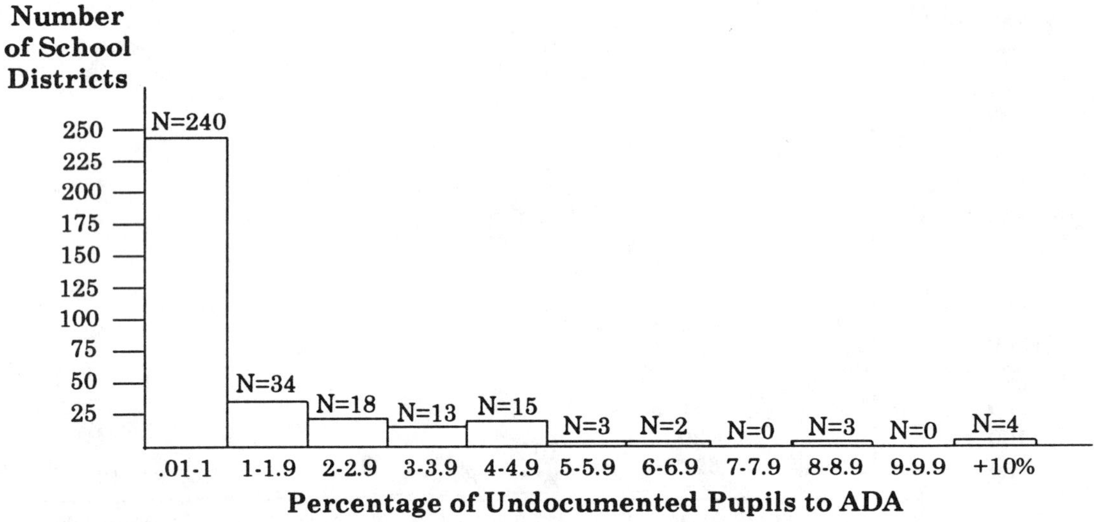

Statewide Ave. 1.2%
Total N = 332

* Computed as a percentage of the 332 school districts reporting undocumented student counts.

Source: Reports submitted by school districts to Texas Education Agency, Oct. 1980.

The relatively low proportions of a district's total attendance, which these students represent, are perhaps most apparent in the accompanying summary listing which ranks districts according to the percentage of undocumented pupils within the school systems. Inspection of the figures reveals that relatively high counts of undocumented students are generally found in relatively high-enrollment districts, with the proportional relationships reflected in the school district's low percentage. Close inspection of districts with unusually high percentages of undocumented pupils reveals that, for the most part, they tend to be low-enrollment districts in which small numerical increases in enrollment constitute substantial proportional changes.

Summary Listing
Selected School Districts
Reporting High Counts/Percentages of Undocumented Students

SCHOOL DISTRICT	1979-80 ADA	UNDOCUMENTED STUDENTS REPORTED	PERCENT UNDOCUMENTED
Houston	173,861	2,506	1.4
Dallas	114,877	810	7
Ector County	20,996	684	3.3
El Paso	53,697	486	9
Mission	6,390	207	3.2
Pasadena	32,244	186	.6
Brownsville	23,314	182	.6
Goose Creek	13,887	158	1.1
Aldine	29,489	123	.4
Spring Branch	31,081	122	.4
Edgewood	16,239	92	.6
Grandfalls-Royalty	219	11	5.0
Sivells Bend	37	2	5.4
Lockney	848	47	5.5
Talpa Centennial	969	6	6.1
Doughtery	24	2	8.3
Booker	289	24	8.3
Dell City	298	25	8.4
Sharyland	1,511	170	11.3
Valley View	294	401	3.6
McFaddin	15	3	20.0
Carta Valley	4	1	25.0

GENERAL OBSERVATIONS

The preceding analysis leads the authors to the following conclusions:

- The actual counts of undocumented students who enrolled in Texas public schools fell far short of many original projections with 1980 enrollments totalling an estimated 13,000 students.
- With the exception of major urban and a few high-enrollment large-city school systems, undocumented students represented insignificant numerical increases in most districts' ADAs
- For the most part, the percentage of undocumented pupils in proportion to a district's ADA was insignificant, falling below 5 percent in 97 percent of all districts reporting undocumentedstudent counts.

Following the mandated enrollment of undocumented children, some school districts modified their position and withdrew their opposition to such enrollment. A few, however, maintained that the enrollment of these undocumented children detracted from the quality of educational programs available to citizen children residing in their districtsAlthough this may be the case in some very limited instances, these positions were not supported by the data for the great majority of school systems in the state.

PERCEPTIONS OF THE IMPACT OF UNDOCUMENTED ENROLLMENTS

Dating back to Justice Powell's 1980 denial of a stay[29] of the injunction in the *In Re Alien Children's Education Litigation,*[30] Texas policymakers, educators, and special interest groups have debated the fiscal and programmatic implications which the mandated enrollment of undocumented alien students would have on Texas public schools. In an effort to shed light on the issue, Dr. Leonard Valverde, Director of the Office for Advanced Research in Hispanic Education, and Albert Cortez, Director of IDRA's Division of Research, Development and Evaluation, conducted research designed to acquire school district personnel's perspectives on these issues. Districts canvassed in the survey included those which had reported fifty or more undocumented students, and those in which undocumented enrollments accounted for 3 percent or more of a district's average daily attendance (ADA). The survey form collected information relating to the districts' undocumented student enrollments; perceptions about the effect of undocumented students on school operations such as personnel needs, school budgets, and local facilities; and school administrators' preferences regarding impact aid associated with undocumented student enrollment.

The major findings of the study follow:

1. Enrollment counts had decreased in nineteen school systems, while nineteen others reported increased enrollmentsIt was not possible to establish the net increase or decrease in the remaining districts due to a lack of updated estimates. Districts with decreasing counts were primarily rural districts, while major urban and south Texas systems reported relatively small tomoderate increases in undocumented enrollment.
2. Forty-nine percent of respondents felt that these children had unique needs, with the majority noting these children's limited English proficiency as a need area.

3. Nine school systems observed that undocumented children had unique positive characteristics, with most perceiving those students as being more motivated than some native-born children.
4. When asked to indicate the areas most affected by undocumented student enrollments, districts cited (in order of frequency): (a) need for bilingual personnel, (b) facilities, (c) other personnel, and (d) support services.
5. The data reflect that in the majority of districts responding, undocumented student populations were relatively stable, with the great majority remaining enrolled in the same schools. When transferring, most transferred to other schools in the district.
6. When asked if undocumented students helped offset declining enrollments, thirty-two of forty-nine districts indicated that they did not, while seven districts perceived that they did.
7. When queried as to what they considered an adequate level of impact aid to offset the effects of undocumented enrollments, the majority proposed funding levels equal to or over $400 per pupil. The majority of respondentsfavored use of a formula which considered the percentages that undocumented students comprise of a district's ADA, with respondents divided between the percentage (i.e., ten, five, or one percent) which should constitute the eligibility cutoff.
8. When asked to indicate how such impact aid funds would be used, the majority of districts cited personnel, materials, and facilities; eight districts cited a preference for unrestricted funding.
9. The majority of school personnel responding (69 percent) felt that such aid should be incorporated into existing foundation school program funding.[31]

THE CLUSTER HYPOTHESIS

In studies of the characteristics of undocumented aliens, a specific characteristic surfaced so frequently that social scientists labeled it as a hypothesis and targeted it for further study. This characteristic is the tendency of undocumented aliens entering the United States to cluster among members of their own ethnic and language group. Thus, undocumented aliens coming from Mexico and Central America tend to locate among the Spanish-speaking Mexican-American population, whether the host population is similarly undocumented or enjoys legal status.

The testing of this hypothesis was included in a research study conducted by the Washington D.C.-based firm of Reyes and Associates for the Immigration and Naturalization Service.[32] Although this study was beset by many problems and never achieved the scope originally envisioned, assumptions made about the cluster hypothesis held true during the implementation of the study.

The tendency of newly arrived immigrant groups to locate among their cultural peers has positive impact upon the ability of the educational systems to respond to the characteristics of the new population. Seldom, if ever, do newly arrived undocumented aliens settle in communities where their characteristics appear conspicuous and introduce new problems in school participation. The vast majority of undocumented aliens are impoverished and looking for employment. They do not settle in the affluent sections of town where the recipient schools are strangers to compensatory education. Schools which they attend are very familiar with the problems of poverty, minority education, and limited English-proficiency. Schools which have attempted to address these problems in the past are able to cope with the characteristics of the new arrivals. Schools which have failed to address these problems with their legal minority populations fail to cope with the undocumented children. In either case, the impact of the new students is minimal. They fit in with the children of the previous residents to such an extent that in many cases the school is completely unaware of the legal status of the children.

In spite of the similarity of characteristics between the native-born Mexican-American and the immigrant child—regardless of documentation status—there is a difference in their performance in school. On the whole, immigrant children who attended school in their native country tend to out-perform native-born Mexican-American children. It is easy to speculate on the reason for this phenomenon. The alien children have attended school in their native country without the negative expectations associated with Spanish-speaking populations in this country. Their extensive use of native language in school and out of school situations allows for an extensive cognitive development not commonly found in Texas schools with native language restrictions. In general, alien children enrolled in Texas schools, regardless of difficulties encountered in the changeover of language, will out-perform native born children in proportion to the amount of schooling which they received in their native country.

FINANCIAL IMPACT

The financial impact of undocumented alien children on Texas schools in the post-*Doe v. Plyler* era has been minimal. One quick and relatively easy way to measure the impact is to take the average per pupil expenditure in the state and multiply it by the number of undocumented children. Since estimates of per pupil expenditures indicate some $2,000 per pupil is being expended for elementary and secondary education in the state of Texas, this amount can be multiplied by the 13,000 such children estimated to be enrolled in Texas schools. This calculation produces a maximum of twenty-six million dollars a year as the total cost for education services. Comparing this figure to an annual state expenditure for education of three billion dollars, the cost of education for undocumented alien children is relatively small.

Since approximately 50 percent of school expenditures in Texas comes from state sources and 50 percent from local sources, the twenty-six million figure is probably equally divided between state and local expenditures. The state of Texas expends some thirteen million dollars annually, and the other thirteen million is expended from local funds by the estimated school districts enrolling alien populations.

Unfortunately, enrollments are not evenly divided throughout the school districts enrolling undocumented alien children; therefore, the cost is not evenly divided among these districts. For the most part, both school districts in geographic proximity to the border and school districts with the largest Mexican-American populations, tend to attract the highest numbers of undocumented aliens. This is also true for large urban centers, although the undocumented aliens may be a blessing in disguise for urban centers whose predominant problem has been declining enrollments.

Border cities and urban centers bear the brunt of the numbers of undocumented alien children. Certainly many of the criticisms of the pre-1975 legislation and the support for the exclusion of undocumented children has come from these districts. However, it is dysfunctional to place the blame for financial hardships on the undocumented children. Texas' system of school finance, denounced as "chaotic and unjust,"[33] places a financial burden on low-tax wealth school districts. Districts like Brownsville, McAllen, Laredo, and El Paso would have financial hardships if no undocumented students were to be enrolled in any of these districts. The presence of undocumented alien children aggravates an already bad situation. The undocumented children may aggravate the problem, but they are not the cause of the larger disparities in local money existing under the state system of school finance.

In considering the cost of educating undocumented alien children, it is well to keep in mind certain realities not commonly considered by the state of Texas during the exclusionary years.

The immigration and naturalization service has consistently maintained that most undocumented children old enough to attend public schools in Texas have younger siblings born in this country. By virtue of the American birth, these siblings are United States citizens. Members of the family then qualify for preferential citizenship status under the immigration and naturalization laws.

For this reason it has been substantiated that most of the undocumented school-age children will remain in the United States for the rest of their lives and will eventually attain citizenship. Assuming that this testimony presented by the Immigration and Naturalization Service is accurate, one must wonder about the cost of educating undocumented alien children as compared to the subsequent cost of non-education. Problems of welfare, health, unemployment, underemployment, incarceration, and rehabilitation, would cost the state of Texas many times more than the cost of education. It is generally agreed that including undocumented alien children in educational systems is much more cost-efficient than exclusion, if they remain in this country.[34]

SUMMARY OF FINDINGS

In general, the impact of *Doe v. Plyler* and subsequent court decisions facilitating a free public education for undocumented alien children has been minimal. t is apparent that throughout the litigation, the Texas Education Agency consistently over-estimated the number of such children enrolled in Texas schools and the extent to which findings in behalf of the children would attract others. Rather than the 110,000 increase in enrollment predicted by the Texas Education Agency during litigation, the actual count was closer to 13,000, and even this number is questionable since school figures did not allow for single student enrollments in multiple districts. The actual enrollment of undocumented alien children was dispersed over a large number of districts, so that no single school district absorbed a large percentage of the population.

The impact upon curriculum and instructional programs was similarly minimal. The bulk of the undocumented children enrolled were in school districts with large numbers of Mexican-American children displaying similar cultural, economic, and language characteristics. The extent to which school districts were able to meet the special needs of the immigrant group was largely dependent on the extent to which they have been able to meet the unique needs of the already existing minority populations

The enrollment of undocumented alien children did not create a problem in school finance. The only exception to this was in low tax wealth school districts near the border. But, it is generally conceded that a financial problem exists because of the inadequacies of the Texas system of school finance, rather than because of the presence of undocumented alien children.

The children of Texas deserve better. The entire state needs better. In the light of the increasing need for education in this technological society, a failure of the state to educate any segment of the population has severe implications for all.

Arguments concerning diluting the quality of education in Texas are moot. The education of atypical populations, specifically the minorities and the disadvantaged, needs vast improvement. The state of Texas needs educational leadership. It is high time that this leadership be acquired or developed. Foot-dragging, scare tactics based on exaggerations, red herrings and rationalizing will not bring about this improvement. Only through the efforts of concerned educators, laypersons and decision makers at the local and federal levels, in finding functional solutions to the problems of educating children, will we see the arrival of equal educational opportunities for all children.

NOTES

1. Tex. Educ. Code Ann.. s. 21.031 (Vernon 1985 Supp.). The restrictive language was added by 1975 TEX. GEN. LAWS, ch.334, s. 4.
2. 558 S.W. 2d 121 (Tex. Civ. App. 1977), *application for writ or error refused, id.*
3. 458 F. Supp. 569 (E.D. Tex. 1978).
4. C.A. No. H-78-2132 (S.D. Tex. 1978).
5. C.A. No. MO-79-CA-49 (W.D. Tex. 1979).
6. C.A. No. 3-79-0440-D (N.D. Tex. 1979).
7. C.A. No. B-79618-CA (E.D. Tex. 1979).
8. See *In Re Alien Children's Education Litigation*, 501 F. Supp. 544, 550 (S.D. Tex. 1980).
9. See *Boe v. Wright*, 648 F.2s 432, 433 (5th Cir. 1981). The district court reversed itself on this point after Justice William F. Powell's decision sitting as Circuit Justice in *Texas v. Certain Named and Unnamed Non-Citizen Children*, 448 U.S. 1327 (1980) (vacating the Fifth Circuit's stay of Judge Seal's injunction in *In Re Alien Children's Educ. Litigation*, 501 F. Supp. 544 (S.D. Tex. 1980). 648 F.2d. at 433, 433 n.4.
10. 501 F. Supp. 544 (S.D. Tex. 1980).
11. *Id.*
12. *Id.* at 582.
13. *Id.* at 574.
14. *Id.* at 575.
15. *Id.* at 577.

16. *Id.* at 578.
17. *Id.* at 579.
18. *Id.*
19. *Id.* at 582.
20. *San Antonio Indep. School Dist. v. Rodriguez,* 411 U.S.1 (1973) (upholding the Texas school finance system).
21. 501 F. Supp. at 580-81.
22. *Id.* at 597.
23. 628 F.2d 448 (5th Cir. 1980).
24. See *Plyler v. Doe,* 457 U.S. 202, 210 (1982).
25. *Texas v. Certain Named an Unnamed Undocumented Alien Children,* 452 U.S. 937 (1981).
26. *Plyler v. Doe,* 457 U.S. 202 (1982).
27. Criterion Study, *Estimates of the Undocumented Hispanic School Age Population* (1980), Defendant's Exhibit No.2-1, *In Re Alien Children's Educ. Litigation,* 501 F. Supp. 544 (S.D. Tex. 1980).
28. See, e.g., 501 F. Supp. at 575. For a critique of the statistical evidence in *In Re Alien Children's Educ. Litigation,* supra note 25, see generally, Flores, *The Impact of Undocumented Migration on the United States Labor Market,* 5 Hous. J. Int'l L. 287 (1983).
29. *Texas v. Certain Named and Unnamed Undocumented Alien Children,* 448 U.S. 1327 (1980).
30. 501 F. Supp. 544 (S.D. Tex. 1980).
31. Valverde and Cortez, *Children of Undocumented Residents in Texas Public Schools: A Follow-Up Survey,* 3 Memo. Hisp. 15 (1982).
32. See generally Flores, *supra* note 27.
33. *San Antonio Indep. School Dist. v. Rodriguez,* 411 U.S. 1, 59 (1973) (Stewart, J., concurring.) The majority in Rodriguez did not seriously contend that the Texas financing system was "fair" or that there were not inequities. Id. at 54. The state conceded that the system could withstand careful scrutiny. Id. at 16–17. The majority only held that the system did not discriminate against an identifiable suspect or semi-suspect class, id. at 40, or that it burdened a fundamental right, id. at 37, and that the system was in pursuit of legitimate state goals of providing some educational resources for all children and encouraging local control and encouraging local control and participation in the educational system. Id. at 49. The dissenters concurred with Justice Stewart's assessment of the system. Id.at 70. (White, J., dissenting) Id. at 71 (Marshall, Jr., dissenting).
34. See generally *Plyler v. Doe,* 457 U.S. 202 (1982).

BIBLIOGRAPHY

Boe v. Wright, C.A. No. 3-79-0440-D (N.D. Tex. 1979).

Criterion Analysis, Inc., *Estimates of the Undocumented Hispanic School Age Population*, Dallas, 1980.

Doe v. Lodestro, C.A. No. B-79618-CA (E.D. Tex. 1979).

Doe v. Plyler, 458 F. Supp. 569 (E.D. Tex. 1978).

Flores, Esteban, *The Impact of Undocumented Migration on the United States Labor Market*, 5 Hous. J. Int'l L. 287 (1983).

Garza v. Reagan, C.A. No. H-78-2132 (S.D. Tex. 1978).

Henandez v. Houston Independent School District, 558 S.W. 2d 121 (Tex. Civ. App. 1977).

In Re Multiple District Litigation, 501 F. Supp. 544, 550 (S.D. Tex. 1980).

North, David S. and Marion F. Houston, *The Characteristics and Role of Illegal Aliens in the United States Labor Market: An Exploratory Study*, Unpublished monograph, Washington, D.C., 1981.

Plyler v. Doe, 457 U.S. 202, 210 (1982).

Roe v. Holm, C.A. No. MO-79-CA-49 (W.D. Tex. 1979).

San Antonio Independent School District v. Rodriguez, 411 U.S.1 (1973).

Silva v. Levi, 76 C 4268, (N.D. Ill., 1978).

Texas v. Certain Named and Unnamed Undocumented Alien Children, 448 U.S. 1327 (1980).

United States v. Texas, 342 F. Supp. 24 (E.D. Tex. 1971).

Valverde, Leonard and Albert Cortez, *Children of Undocumented Residents in Texas Public Schools*, 3 MEMO. HISP. 15 (1982)

Weintraub, S. and G. Cardenas, *The Use of Public Services by Undocumented Aliens in Texas*, Lyndon B. Johnson School of Public Affairs, The University of Texas, Austin, 1984.

DISCUSSION QUESTIONS

1. Identify three frequently held stereotypes regarding illegal aliens. What data does the author present to unmask these generalizations?
2. Explain and substantiate the claim that undocumented immigrant children have been used as scapegoats for inadequacies in the state system of education. In what ways does the author characterize past educational policy for undocumented children as "dysfunctional?"
3. On what grounds did the Texas Legislature exclude undocumented children from public schools?
4. How did Mr. Burnett's arguments in the 1979 hearing of *Roe v. Holm* address the Texas population?
5. List the arguments for exclusion of undocumented children as presented by the state in Judge Seals' court and specify the court's position on each argument.
6. Explain the "cluster hypothesis." How does this affect school program and finance planning?
7. What explanations can you give for the observed superior school performance of immigrant children over native Mexican-American children?
8. References to immigrants often use water metaphors, e.g., . . . stem the *tide* of the new *wave* of immigrants *flooding* our schools. . . . What does the data presented on undocumented students in Texas schools tell us about the "inundation?"
9. Suppose children from outside the U.S. enroll in your local school. You, with interested parents, are looking into how best to draw on their language, culture, and life experience as a resource to enrich your school's learning environment. Brainstorm with a group about how to tap this resource.

4

School Dropouts

PREFACE

One of the common indicators of the performance of the school is the number of school dropouts, the number of students that quit school prior to graduation. Nationwide, about one out of every four students that enroll in school does not stay around long enough to complete high school.

I first became aware of the problem as the first vice-principal of Edgewood High School in San Antonio, Texas in 1955. Although I had a general feeling since my own student days that many students weren't around as we moved from one grade to the next, the magnitude of the problem was unsuspected until I looked at the number of students in each of the high school grades. Although the district at that time was a growing school district, the discrepancies between the class sizes could not be attributed simply to a tremendous growth in the number of students entering the ninth grade each year. Having enrollment data readily available, and to satisfy my own curiosity, I initiated an informal study of student attrition over a three-year period. As suspected, even with an adjustment to compensate for district growth, the data indicated that three-fourths of the students in any given cohort disappeared between the ninth grade and graduation almost four years later.

My interest in the number of students dropping out of school remained dormant for many years, until I had the opportunity to address the problem at IDRA in a series of state and national studies on this problem. In 1985, IDRA contracted with the Texas Department of Community Affairs to conduct a study of school dropouts in Texas (Cárdenas, et al., 1986). The Texas Education Agency (TEA) joined in the study subsequent to its beginning. Participation by TEA not only provided additional funds for expanding the scope of the study, it proved instrumental in providing necessary data and opening doors for the acquisition of information.

After the completion of the Texas study, Ed Meade of the Ford Foundation provided the necessary funds for conducting a national study on the characteristics of school dropouts (Cárdenas, et al., 1988).

IDRA was also awarded a contract to conduct an intensive study of school dropouts in the Dallas School District. This study allowed us to contact students in and out of school, as well as their parents and school personnel, in order to compare characteristics and attitudes concerning the two groups (Robledo, 1989).

The Texas study was the first attempt in the state to measure the extent, characteristics, and economic impact of school dropouts. Initially, three methodologies were selected to determine the extent of student dropouts. The first was an analysis of dropouts on a performance report required from all of the school districts in the state. The second was the analysis of census data, and the third was a longitudinal study on the basis of school enrollments over a long period of time.

The analysis of school district self-reports on the number of students dropping out turned out to be a dismal failure. There was no standard definition of a school dropout, nor was there a standard methodology for computing the number. Although Texas and other states have since adopted better definitions and reporting methodologies, the problem has not been completely eliminated since individual districts still make different interpretations of both. At the national level, differences in state definitions and reporting methodologies still impact the validity of institutional information.

The analysis of census data proved more fruitful, although school systems and the general public immediately attributed the high number of students of school age not enrolled in school on immigration and migration patterns, rather than to students dropping out of school in the state and individual communities.

The longitudinal studies which produced what we called "school attrition rates" rather than "school dropouts" provided the best information in the absence of standard definitions and reporting methodology. This methodology consisted of taking the difference between enrollments at the ninth grade level and enrollments three years later at the twelfth grade level, determining the percentage of students missing and adjusting this percentage by the change in total high school enrollments during this same period.

Educational research literature on school dropouts downplays the validity of longitudinal attrition studies, although we believe that the methodology is much better than one would infer by the treatment given in the literature, at least for large entities such as the state and counties. We concede that the validity of longitudinal studies may drop somewhat, such as in very small communities, larger communities with a multiplicity of small local districts and at the school campus level.

The report on the state dropout study was released on October 31, 1986, and a summary was published in the following article, "The Texas School Dropout Survey Project: A Summary of Findings," written by José A. Cárdenas, Dr. María R. Robledo, Project Director, Ms. Josie Supik, Project Research Coordinator, and other project staff, which appeared in the November 1986 issue of the IDRA *Newsletter*.

As indicated in the following article, the attrition rate was estimated at 33 percent for all Texas students, 27 percent for white, non-Hispanic students, 33 percent for Asian Americans and Pacific Islanders, 34 percent for African Americans, and 45 percent for both Native American Indians and Hispanics.

The completion and report on the Texas study was preceded by a preliminary report for Bexar County, Texas, as described in the following article, "School Attrition Rates in Bexar County."

Although we anticipated that the education community would not be pleased with the findings on the magnitude of the problem, we did not anticipate the magnitude of the school district response. Researchers should anticipate challenges to their findings, but we did not anticipate challenges to our veracity, our motives and our professional integrity.

A school board member informed the media that the attrition rates for her district had been manipulated by the researchers and then suggested that the study should have been altered in order to avoid embarrassing the district. Many administrators and board members charged that IDRA had inflated attrition rates in order to obtain foundation funds to address the non-existing problem.

Perhaps the weirdest response was a call from a school district superintendent asking how we had calculated the dropout figure for his district. I informed him that his district had 100 students in the cohort at the ninth grade level. Three years later there were only fifty students in the class. Since the number of students in the high school had not increased or decreased, no adjustment had been made for enrollment changes. We simply calculated an attrition rate of 50 percent.

"Yes, but how do you calculate it?" he asked.

"Do you mean how is a percentage calculated?"

"That's right."

"You take the fifty and divide it by the 100 and then multiply it by 100."

"Just a minute. Let me try it." After a pause, "It does come out at fifty percent, but it seems very high to me."

"That's because it is high. You did lose half of the students in the three-year period."

With a sigh, he concluded, "I guess you are right, but it still seems high to me."

After the original explosion from our attrition study tapered off, criticisms of the study focused on the methodology. The education community insisted that the attrition rates were invalid because they did not account for the number of students in the cohort who transferred out of the district. We maintained that they did. The adjustment for changes in high school enrollment did provide a gross estimate of the number of students that transferred out of the district. If enrollment remained constant during the three-year period, we assumed that the number that transferred out of the district was offset by the number that transferred into the district. School districts then maintained that the adjustment was invalid in that students transferred out from the cohort being tracked for the three-year period, but students transferred into the high school grades were not included in the cohort. We found this argument hard to swallow, especially since no school district could provide us with any extenuating circumstances in support of such a unique transfer pattern. Any support for this argument disappeared as we replicated the study for six consecutive years with very similar findings. A unique transfer pattern would show up in subsequent years. It did not.

A second criticism of the study focused on our failure to take into account student retentions in grade. School personnel still maintain that the diminishing of the cohort is not due to students dropping out of school, but rather to students dropping out of the cohort when retained in a grade. This could happen even though we originally assumed that the reduction in the cohort due to students being retained in any specific year was compensated for by an increase from students retained in previous years. For example, if there were 100 students in the ninth grade and ten of them were retained at the end of the year, the 10 percent loss can be attributed to this retention. But if the cohort is similarly increased by the addition of ten students retained the previous year, the size of the cohort would remain the same.

Just to be sure, we tested this assumption in a sampling of school districts. We found that although the number of students retained varies greatly from one grade level to another (many students are retained at the end of the ninth grade; few are retained at the end of the eleventh grade), the number of students retained at any grade level is surprisingly constant over a large number of years.

We concluded, and still maintain, that neither the transfer nor the retention of students accounted for the high attrition rates indicated by the study. Over the years the validity of our original study, and six subsequent annual studies, has stood up. When TEA implemented a more standard definition and reporting methodology, school district self-reports on dropouts show a *higher* rate than our attrition studies. This higher rate is also reflected in the performance indicators released by the Department of Education for the National Education Goals Report (National Education Goals Panel, 1992). This supports our original and continuous contention that the attrition methodology used by IDRA is a *conservative* estimate of the number of school dropouts.

The bad feelings resulting from the dissemination of our Texas School Dropout Survey can be attributed to a difference in orientation between IDRA and many members of the education community. IDRA believes that the first step to the elimination of a problem is a context evaluation which identifies the existence of a problem and addresses the nature of that problem. Many educators prefer to act like ostriches, burying their heads in the sand, and denying the existence of a problem. Although the manner in which the dropout problem has been addressed in Texas leaves a lot to be desired, it is preferable to continue seeking feasible solutions, than to pretend that the problem does not exist.

Inadequacies in addressing the school dropout problem in Texas and nationwide can be attributed to inadequacies in the identification of the causes of the problem. Just as it is reassuring to the schools to maintain that there is no dropout problem, when research evidence leaves no doubt about the existence of the problem, it is equally reassuring to the schools to maintain that it is a problem not of their own making.

I have maintained for many years that the basic reason for the continued poor school performance of minorities, the economically disadvantaged, the limited English proficient, and the immigrant and migrant students is the use of a deficit model by the schools. Such students are seen as being deficit in traits essential for school success. This school perception becomes a self-fulfilling prophesy in the poor performance of the students, and evades accountability since the poor performance is attributed to student factors over which the school has little control. A corollary of the student deficit model is the parent (family, home, ethnic group) deficit model in which the deficit in essential traits is not directly attributed to the student, but rather to the parents or the home.

This deficit model is passed on from one generation of educators to the next. Robert J. Havighurst, one of the United States' foremost social scientists stated in 1964, "There is substantial doubt that the socially disadvantaged children in our big cities have any positive qualities of potential value in urban society...."

In 1993, a college textbook for the preparation of teachers stated, "The relationship of education to economics and social mobility is not perceived by black youth." It also stated, "Children from [Spanish-speaking] families frequently do poorly in school because of language difficulties, impoverished cultural backgrounds, and a highly transient lifestyle....Their cultural background makes it hard for them to succeed economically in a highly technical society."

Deficit models permeate all aspects of American education. The problem of school dropouts is no exception. The National Center for Educational Statistics (NCES) of the U.S. Department of Education recently conducted a research study on school dropouts for the National Educations Goals Panel, a group which has developed educational goals and is providing direction for the improvement of education in the country today. As a consultant to Panel II dealing with school dropouts, I was given a copy of a survey form used by NCES to determine the causes of school dropouts. The survey, to be completed by former students who had dropped out of school, provided twenty-six reasons for dropping out. Out of these twenty-six reasons, all but one was based on a deficit model. Twenty-five of the reasons which the students could select provided a negative trait which accounted for dropping out of school, such as "I didn't like school," "I didn't like my teachers," or "I could not perform the work." There were no parallel causes which focused the reason for dropping out on the school, such as "My teachers did not like me" or "The instruction was inadequate." In spite of my objections, the survey was conducted, data were analyzed, and findings were reported. It is not surprising that the NCES findings indicate that student deficits account for the large number of students dropping out of school.

Since the reasons for dropping out of school are commonly attributed to deficits in the segments of the population with high dropout rates, it is not strange or unexpected that subsequent efforts to reduce the number of school dropouts have been unsuccessful. The term, "unsuccessful," needs to be further qualified. In the intervening years since IDRA conducted the first study on school dropouts in Texas, the magnitude has been slightly reduced. Attrition rates have declined for white Anglo students, but the rates have increased for minority populations.

A common assumption in deficit models is that students who dropout of school do so because of lack of motivation to stay in school or because the students, as stated in the college textbook for teachers, do not understand the importance of an education. Therefore, dropout prevention programs commonly aim at addressing such deficits by subjecting the students to motivational sessions. One school district contracted with some well-meaning retired professional athletes who conducted pep-rally type sessions in which the students repeatedly yelled, "Stay in school! Stay in school!"

Although motivation certainly has its place in making scholastic decisions, such programs frequently fail to address much more basic causes for school dropouts, namely, poor school performance and factors which impede improvement in student performance. One school district in cooperation with a community organization made a massive effort to contact students no longer in school to encourage them to return to school. Since several thousand dropouts returned to school, the program was deemed a big success. However, since nothing was done to address the basic problems which led to the original dropping out of school, in a few weeks not a single one of the students who re-enrolled was still in school.

Minority student dropouts have increased in Texas since the advent of dropout prevention and school reform efforts. The increase in dropouts is not *in spite of* state efforts, the increase is *because of* the school efforts. The simplistic rationale of the 1986 Texas school reform legislation that an increase in standards would bring about an increase in performance did not hold true. Increasing the standards without providing special assistance to students who are having trouble meeting the previous lower standards has not led to improved school performance for the Texas school population. Last year, 8,138 seniors were unable to graduate because they could not meet the new minimum performance standards. This year, the number increased to 13,337.

Educators appear to have few insights as to why students drop out of school. Legislatively mandated annual performance reports require school systems to list the reasons for students who dropped out of school. In a recent analysis of school district reports on 82,325 students that dropped out of Texas schools in one year, the reasons for dropping out provided by the schools included "Reason not known" for 54,080 students, 66 percent of the students who were reported as having dropped out of school. An additional 11,059 students (13.43 percent) were reported as having dropped out of school due to poor attendance. Poor attendance is not a reason for dropping out of school; it is the beginning of the process for dropping out of school.

This information indirectly provides the basic reason for students dropping out of school. When the school system has such a tenuous relationship and such limited communication with students who are prone to drop out, it is not surprising that the system has no knowledge of the reason why two out of every three students leave.

I believe that the basic reason for students dropping out of school is their poor performance in school. Schools are prone to magnify family economic problems and the need for students to join the work force. Seldom does a student who is performing well in school drop out in order to go to work. Extensive interviews with students who are prone to drop out, or who have already dropped out of school, consistently uphold our contention that the basic problem is poor school performance.

Other reasons commonly cited for dropping out of school include drugs, pregnancy, gang involvement and crime. However, I believe that all of these anti-social behaviors, along with dropping out of school, are the effects of poor school performance, rather than the causes for dropping out of school.

THE IDRA VALUED YOUTH PROGRAM

IDRA's research into school dropouts inevitably resulted in the development of a program for dropout prevention. As superintendent of the Edgewood School District in 1969, I implemented a cross-age tutoring program to address high school dropouts. The program was initiated through the efforts of Mary Conway Koehler, a retired juvenile court judge from New York City. Judge Koehler provided the district with encouragement, technical assistance and some funding for the implementation of the program in 1970. Ms. Marlene Simon, a former student of mine at St. Mary's University and Rebecca "Becky" Barrera, who subsequently worked many years at IDRA, were selected to manage the various aspects of the program. The rationale of the program was based on research information gathered by Frank Reissman on the use of student tutors to help other students in school. The program evaluations concluded that the students being tutored made small but significant gains as a result of peer and cross-age tutoring, but the student tutors made substantial increases in school performance as a result of their tutoring experience (Reissman, 1966).

Implementation of the Youth Tutoring Youth program at Edgewood High School provided amazing results. During one school year none of the students involved in the program dropped out of school, in spite of having been recruited for the program because of a certainty that they were going to dropout by the end of the year.

In spite of the success of the program, I had to discontinue it. Student stipends were being paid from federal funds, and the Texas Education Agency (TEA) ruled that such payments to students and other program expenditures were not authorized under federal and state guidelines. Since the district was the poorest one in Texas, funding of the program from local and state funds was out of the question.

The Edgewood Youth Tutoring Youth program did not die from a lack of interest or available funds. It was killed by a bureaucratic educational system which has frequently opposed innovation in the schools, in spite of the dismal track record of regular and traditional programs.

In November 1983, I was asked by Mayor Henry Cisneros to represent him at a meeting in San Antonio where Coca-Cola USA was to announce grants to several cities important to their Hispanic marketing. I attended the meeting where I was informed by Ms. Marife Hernandez, from a public relations firm in New York City that was doing Hispanic marketing work for Coca-Cola USA, that Coca-Cola was donating $500,000 for the improvement of education for Hispanic children in five of their major marketing sites: Los Angeles, New York City, Miami, Chicago and San Antonio. $100,000 was earmarked for San Antonio, but there was some confusion on who to give the money to since there are fifteen independent school districts in the San Antonio area. I was asked if our non-profit organization could receive the money and dispense it to local school districts with large Hispanic enrollments.

IDRA staff immediately drew up a plan for the development and implementation of a dropout prevention program similar to the successful Youth Tutoring Youth program which I had initiated in Edgewood. Marife Hernandez and the Coca-Cola USA representatives were impressed with our plans, and $100,000 was allocated for each of four years beginning in the 1984–85 school year. Over 90 percent of these funds were passed through to the participating school districts in support of the program. Although IDRA budgeted 10 percent of the $100,000 each year for IDRA organization, coordination, training and evaluation services, much of this amount was also passed through to the school districts for unanticipated expenses.

The program was so successful that, at the end of the third year, the U.S. Department of Education provided IDRA with a three-year grant to continue the program and determine the reasons for its success.

In 1990, the Coca-Cola Foundation contacted IDRA with an offer to fund the program for an additional five-year period in five sites: San Antonio, McAllen, Los Angeles, New York City and Miami. Other sources of funding have led to its implementation in six school districts in San Antonio and additional districts in New York, California, Florida, Montana, Oregon, and Idaho.

Throughout its history, the Coca-Cola Valued Youth Program has enjoyed the same success which the Youth Tutoring Youth program experienced in Edgewood. Thanks to its generous funding, the program has developed extensive training materials for all elements of the program, including an extensive parental involvement component.

The implications of this success are awesome. In each and every community in which IDRA has implemented the program, we have taken the worst performing students on the verge of dropping out of school. No more than 2 percent of the students involved have dropped out of school, and in most cases, the few that did drop out of school did so for family rather than school reasons. Many of the students graduated as honor students, a striking comparison with their performance prior to participation in the Valued Youth Program.

After twenty years as advocates of children, IDRA has completely demolished the erroneous child and parent deficit myths which have been used for years as a rationalization for the failure of the school in the education of minority and disadvantaged students.

In school after school, in nineteen communities throughout the country, we have taken the worst performing students and turned them into successful and responsible youth. It is no wonder that the program has been extensively recognized in the media, including all three major national TV networks and was selected by *Ladies Home Journal* as one of the ten best school programs in America (Lewis, 1988).

We believe that the success of the program lies in our faith in and our value of youth. Youth's success in school is dependent on three basic characteristics commonly found in successful school programs. The students are valued in ways not commonly found in regular school programs, students are provided support mechanisms not otherwise available, and the program provides unique interactions among the home, the school and the community.

Program mechanisms provide for the assignment of middle and high school students at risk of dropping out of school as tutors of elementary school children at nearby schools. After receiving extensive training, the secondary school students are given released time and a stipend for tutoring the small children under the direction of cooperating teachers. Tutoring activities are complemented by extensive rewards and supplemented by field trips and interactions with successful community adult role models.

Program success did not come about without problems and frustrations. Although participating schools have been more than cooperative in the implementation of the program, there are three constraints commonly encountered.

First, the school has to value these poor performers sufficiently in order to want to exert a special effort in their behalf. After all, it is easier to argue that the students are deficient and uneducable, than to go to the trouble of organizing and implementing a special program for them.

Second, since the participating students receive financial stipends for the time spent tutoring younger children and extensive, positive reinforcing feedback has to be provided, there is a tendency for the school to select better students for participation in the program, rather than providing rewards for the poorer performing students. This tendency, which we call "creaming," can lead to the inclusion of students who need this type of program the least and the exclusion of students who need it the most. It is regrettable that many so-called dropout prevention programs address the students who are in no danger of dropping out of school.

Third, although the school is usually willing to supplement regular school activities with special programs, it is very difficult to get the school, along with regulating agencies, to supplant regular school activities with special programs. Educational programs which do not work are so institutionalized that it is extremely difficult to re-allocate time, money and personnel resources to alternative programs that will work.

The eight articles in this section provide a time-lapse picture of IDRA's ten-year involvement in addressing the large and growing problem of minority and disadvantaged student dropouts.

SCHOOL ATTRITION RATES IN BEXAR COUNTY, TEXAS

José A. Cárdenas, María del Refugio Robledo, and Albert Cortez

1986

Editor's note: *Through various funding sources, Intercultural Development Research Association (IDRA) is conducting dropout-related research and development activities involving the State of Texas and specific school systems within the State. Administratively, activities are housed within IDRA's Center for the Prevention and Recovery of Dropouts (CPRD). Current activities focus on the magnitude of the problem, the causes for which students drop out of school, the characteristics of dropouts, the cost and impact of the problem, and the identification, development, and evaluation of school and community programs addressing high-risk student populations. This article is the first in a series of articles concerning IDRA CPRD research.*

A study on the magnitude of the dropout problem was conducted for the Education Policies Committee of the Greater San Antonio Chamber of Commerce. The study looked at attrition rates for twelve school districts in Bexar County, Texas, and related these attrition rates to various other demographic characteristics of the districts. Attrition numbers and attrition rates were computed on the basis of an adjustment formula developed by Intercultural Development Research Association (IDRA) and used in various research studies.

Due to changes in population among the various school districts in Bexar County, an adjustment in the number of students expected at the twelfth-grade level must be made in order to eliminate increases or decreases due to growing or declining district enrollments. The formula used to make adjustments for population changes in this study is to multiply the ninth grade enrollment by the total high school enrollment ratio, the enrollment of the high school when the group of students being studied was in the twelfth grade in 1984–85 divided by the enrollment of the high school when the group of students being studied was in the ninth grade in 1981–82. An assumption is made that the number of high school students transferring in and out of the district are fairly evenly distributed among the high school grades. No adjustment was made for racial or ethnic enrollment changes in the districts. Three special districts in the area were not included in the study because they enroll children of military personnel, have an unstable enrollment, and do not have a tax base in support of the school program.

The study looked at a cohort of high school students enrolled in Bexar County high schools at the ninth grade level in the 1981–82 school year through the twelfth grade level in 1984-85. The enrollment figures in Table 1 indicate that total enrollments in the high schools of the twelve Bexar County districts increased by one percent over the three-year period, from 60,019 students to 60,597. During this same three-year period, the size of the 1981-82 freshman class diminished from 16,754 to 11,490. Assuming that the enrollment growth is fairly evenly distributed over the four high school grade levels, one would expect that the 1981-82 freshman class would have increased by one percent to 16,829. Therefore, the number of students lost from the ninth to the twelfth grade levels is the difference between the expected number (16,829) and the number enrolled at the twelfth grade level (11,490), or a loss of 5,339 students.

Although the adjustment made by multiplying the original size of the class by the ratio of the total high school enrollment in the last year over the total high school enrollment in the original year is small and has little effect on total county school population fluctuations, the adjustment must be made in analyzing individual school district attrition. In general, school districts in the central city areas show decreasing enrollments, and school districts in the suburban areas indicate increasing enrollments. A failure to make an adjustment for changing school district sizes would make it impossible to estimate the number of students lost to attrition, and probably closely related to dropouts, and the number of students lost through transfers to other districts. The opposite is also true. In growing school districts, the estimate of students lost could be diminished by students transferring into the district.

The attrition for each of the twelve school districts can be determined using a similar adjustment formula, i.e., by subtracting the number of students in the twelfth grade from the expected number of students (the number of ninth graders three years before) and multiplying by the district's total high school population change ratio.

Table 2 presents the attrition percentage rates for each of the twelve school districts and the county as a whole. The attrition rate for Bexar County high schools for the group of freshmen students in 1981-82 was 32 percent. Rates varied for the individual districts from a low of 7 percent for Alamo Heights to a high of 49 percent for the Southside School District. In general the twelve school districts could be grouped into three categories, those with below county average attrition rates (Alamo Heights, East Central, Judson, and North East), those with average attrition rates (Edgewood, Harlandale, Northside, and Somerset), and those with above average rates (San Antonio, South San Antonio, Southside, and Southwest).

Table 2 also presents the dropout rates for the individual school districts as reported in December 1985 to the Texas Education Agency in the Annual Performance Report prescribed by House Bill 72. The differences between attrition rates calculated in this study and the district self-reported dropout rates is very marked, with the percentage of students missing in the 1985 senior class being three times larger than the number of dropouts reported by all of the districts. The self-reported figure represents the number of students that the school district knows dropped out of school. The attrition data indicates, however, that for every such student, there are two others that disappeared and cannot be accounted for. It is unlikely that the students enrolled in other area districts, considering the stability of total county high school enrollments. In the absence of a local, state, or national student tracking system, one can only assume that many of the missing students dropped out of school without any notification to the high school. The large number of such students may demand some form of an interdistrict tracking system or perhaps the development of a better communication system between the schools and the potential dropout population, their families, and the larger community.

Attrition rates were also calculated for the three major ethnic groups enrolled in the high schools of Bexar County. White non-Hispanics had an attrition rate of 15 percent. The attrition rate for Blacks, 34 percent, is more than double the attrition rate for the white non-Hispanic populations. The attrition rate for the Hispanic population for high schools in

Bexar County, 43 percent, is almost three times the attrition rate for the white non-Hispanics (see Table 2).

In order to assess the relationship between selected school system characteristics and attrition rates, IDRA compiled and tabulated the latest data available on:

1. a school district's taxable property wealth per ADA;
2. percentages which economically disadvantaged students comprised of district enrollments;
3. percentage minority as well as percentages of Black and Hispanic pupils;
4. expenditures per pupil; and
5. percentages of eleventh grade pupils achieving mastery on the 1985-86 state-mandated TEAMS examination.

Analyses included tabulation of descriptive statistics on all major variables, correlations, and multiple and step-wise regression analyses.

Table 3 presents a summary of the descriptive statistics. The data indicate that the overall percentage of pupils passing the TEAMS language and math exams was comparable to the state average, with county means of 89 percent and 84 percent on each respective measure. Within school systems, the range of students mastering the language section ranged from a high of 97 percent to a low of 79 percent. In mathematics the mastery levels ranged from 97 percent to 74 percent. Review of the county's minority percentages reveals that the overall minority mean is approximately 64 percent, with individual district totals ranging from 98 percent to 28 percent minority. The mean per pupil expenditure in 1984-85 was $2,241. District expenditures ranged from a low of $1,751 in Somerset, to a high of $3,650 in Alamo Heights. The mean percentage of free lunch eligible pupils for Bexar County was 48.6 percent with individual school system concentrations ranging from 14 percent to 84 percent.

In order to assess the inter-relationships between selected variables, Pearson product moment correlations were calculated for the entire set of variables included in this study. The correlation matrix is presented as Table 4. Review of these data indicates that attrition is highly, positively correlated to the percent of free lunch eligible students ($r = .89$), percent minority ($r = .86$). Conversely, the statistics indicate that a district's student attrition is negatively correlated to its property wealth per ADA ($r = -.75$). Other variables which reflect significant relationships include: percentage of students mastering mathematics where the r value was .92; percentage of free lunch eligible pupils and percent minority ($r = .95$); percent of free lunch eligible pupils and percentage Hispanic enrollment ($r = .96$); and percent minority enrollment and Hispanic enrollment ($r = .97$).

Further review of the correlations reveals some important negative relationships between selected district characteristics. Among the major variables which were significantly negatively correlated were:

1. district attrition rates and percent mastering language ($r = -.80$);
2. district attrition rates and percentage of eleventh grade students mastering TEAMS math ($r = -.84$);
3. percentage free lunch eligible students and percentage of pupils mastering TEAMS language section ($r = -.87$);

4. percentage of free lunch eligible pupils and percentage mastering TEAMS math (r = -.88); and
5. percentage Hispanic enrollment and percentage of students in a district mastering either TEAMS language (r = -.86) or TEAMS math (r = -.89).

In order to examine the extent to which particular district characteristics contributed to or account for variations in attrition levels, regression analyses were conducted. According to the data, the combination of TEAMS language, TEAMS mathematics, percent minority, per pupil expenditure, property wealth and percent free lunch students account for 94 percent of the variance in attrition levels in Bexar County school systems.

In a step-wise regression, the relative effects of percent free lunch eligible pupils, property wealth, and percent Black and Hispanic on attrition were analyzed. Results of these analyses indicated that percent free lunch eligible accounts for the majority (R^2 = .80) of the variance noted among Bexar County school districts.

The data in this study supports other research findings which indicate that minorities and the disadvantaged are at high risk of dropping out of schools and that poor school performance is associated with dropping out of school. Since the percentage of disadvantaged and minority students shows a very high correlation with TEAMS performance, it is evident that dropout prevention strategies must target disadvantaged and minority populations, and that strategies must place the highest priority on academic school performance.

Table 1

Enrollment Declines[1]
Bexar County School Districts: 1981–82 to 1984–85
Adjusted for Changing District Enrollments

District	H.S. Enroll. 1981–82	H.S. Enroll. 1984–85	9th Grd. Enroll. 1981–82	12th Grd.[2] Expected 1984–85	12th Grd. Enroll. 1984–85	Attrition[3]
Alamo Hts.	1203	1136	288	272	253	19
East Cent.	1429	1503	346	364	288	76
Edgewood	4520	3660	1395	1130	707	423
Harlandale	4539	4116	1373	1245	845	399
Judson	2892	3317	708	812	696	116
North East	11772	12226	2832	2941	2604	337
Northside	10931	12642	3003	3473	2495	978
San Antonio	17521	16588	5200	4923	2654	2269

Somerset	439	452	124	128	83	45
South San	2926	3033	930	964	544	420
Southside	596	561	185	174	88	86
Southwest	1251	1363	370	403	232	171
Total Bexar	60019	60597	16754	16829	11490	5339

1. Based on data furnished by the Texas Education Agency
2. Estimates based on IDRA adjustment formula
3. Number of students no longer with class

Table 2

Attrition Percentage Rates[1]
Bexar County School Districts: 1981–82 to 1984–85
Adjusted for Changing District Enrollments

District	Black	Hispanic	White Non-Hispanic	Total District	Reported[2] Dropout Rate
Alamo Hts.	N/A[3]	12%	6%	7%	4.0%
East Central	18	42	14	21	3.7
Edgewood	38	37	N/A	37	8.1
Harlandale	N/A	36	0[4]	32	7.7
Judson	11	14	16	14	8.5
North East	14	14	11	11	1.4
Northside	21	38	23	28	3.1
San Antonio	42	49	39	46	20.7
Somerset	N/A	32	39	35	16.4
South San	36	42	54	44	16.2
Southside	N/A	50	46	49	25.2

Southwest	25	49	35	42	—
Total Bexar	34	43	15	32	10.5

1. Expected size of class minus actual size, divided by expected size
2. High School Dropout Rate reported to TEA on Annual Performance Report for 1984 85
3. Enrollment too small to estimate
4. Number enrolled exceeds estimate

Table 3

Descriptive Statistics
Bexar County School Districts

Variable	Mean	Minimum	Maximum
Percent Mastering Language	89.0	79	97
Percent Mastering Math	84.5	74	97
Attrition Rate	30.5	7	49
Percent Minority	64.2	28	98
Percent Hispanic	57.4	21	94
Percent Black	5.1	.1	13.4
Percent Free Lunch Eligible	48.6	14.2	84.8
Per Pupil Expenditure	$ 2,341	$ 1,751	$ 3,650
Property Wealth Per ADA	$ 143,655	$ 38,889	$ 501,502

Table 4

Correlations Between
Attrition Indices And Related Variables

	Attrition	TEAMS/L	TEAMS/M	PW/ADA	PPE	% Disadvantage	% Minority
Attrition	—	–.80	–.87	–.75	–.58	.90	.87
Teams/L	—	—	.93	.72	.60	–.88	–.86

Teams/M	—	—	—	.75	.60	–.88	–.84
PW/ADA	—	—	—	—	.88	–.66	–.71
PPE	—	—	—	—	—	–.38	–.49
% Disadvantaged	—	—	—	—	—	—	.95
% Minority	—	—	—	—	—	—	—

THE TEXAS SCHOOL DROPOUT SURVEY PROJECT: A SUMMARY OF FINDINGS

1986

The following is an excerpt from the Texas School Dropout Survey Project: A Summary of Findings Report. The research was conducted by Intercultural Development Research Association (IDRA) through a contract with the Texas Department of Community Affairs (Cárdenas, et al., 1986).

The problem of school dropouts has achieved unprecedented urgency at national, state, and local levels. The importance given to the issue may reflect not a dramatic increase in the number or rate of students dropping out of school before completing the twelfth grade, but the increasing educational needs of our society. Whereas only a few years ago a low-skilled labor pool formed the basis of the economy, recent years have seen a trend toward technology and services as the most important labor need for business and industry. Today, the typical blue-collar job requires skills for reading and interpreting instructions, tables, graphs, and manuals.

Texas has experienced a similar change in the composition of its labor force. The oil, minerals, and agriculture sectors of the economy have relinquished their demand on labor in favor of technology and a service economy. A recent analysis of the Texas labor market projects that, while the state economy will grow by 21.8 percent between 1982 and 1990, technology intensive occupations will grow by 32.0 percent over the same time frame (Texas Department of Community Affairs, 1986). The ability of the state to absorb an illiterate and unschooled labor force has become so limited, that there is a state imperative to keep students in school long enough for them to acquire the extensive basic skills, knowledge and competencies necessary to function in our new society.

To address this imperative, the Texas School Dropout Survey Project was initiated in order to establish an information base for analyzing the dropout problem in Texas and to formulate recommendations to the 69th Legislature based upon research findings. The Project was mandated by House Bill 72 and was funded in the Spring of 1986 by the Texas Department of Community Affairs (TDCA) in collaboration with the Texas Education Agency (TEA). Intercultural Development Research Association (IDRA) was contracted to conduct three of the project's four research tasks:

Task 1 Measure the extent of school dropouts in Texas through valid and reliable dropout indices (Research Task 1).

Task 2 Collect and analyze benefit-cost data on the impact of dropouts on the criminal justice and human service systems in Texas (Research Task 3).

Task 3 Identify and evaluate in-school and alternative training programs for dropouts in Texas (Research Task 4).

In addition to these three major research areas, the measurement of the extent of school dropouts was supplemented by three tasks in response to requests made by the TDCA and the TEA. These additional research tasks included the following:

1. Conduct a meta-analysis of existing school district dropout documentation.
2. Design and implement procedures for tracking of student withdrawals in a sample of districts.
3. Generate estimates of macrocommunity dropout rates in the state.

The research which examined the principal causes for school dropouts (Research Task 2) was conducted by Texas A&M—Prairie View University, under a separate contract with that institution. No causal data were included in this IDRA report.

This report summarizes only the studies conducted by IDRA as part of the Texas School Dropout Survey Project. Comprehensive reports for each area of study are available in seven volumes.

Volume 1: Magnitude of the Problem—Census Analysis
Volume 2: Magnitude of the Problem—Attrition Analysis
Volume 3: Magnitude of the Problem—Tracking Study
Volume 4: Magnitude of the Problem—School District Research and Procedures
Volume 5: Benefit-Cost Impact of the Dropout Problem
Volume 6: Program Responses—Their Nature and Effectiveness
Volume 7: Study Methods and Procedures

In conducting the research, several methodological concerns were addressed. The variability and general unavailability of dropout data required multiple methods of analysis in order to generate valid and reliable dropout estimates. Both micro- techniques and macrotechniques were used to examine the magnitude of the problem. Microtechniques included, (a) collecting data on district dropout identification procedures, (b) examining available district research on dropouts, and (c) conducting a student tracking survey. Through these techniques, intradistrict and interdistrict issues of measurement and definition were identified. Macrotechniques were used to estimate dropout rates. Estimates were generated by developing attrition indices using 1982-1983 and 1985-1986 Fall Survey data provided by the Texas Education Agency. Estimates were also generated by analyzing the 1980 Census 5 percent Public Use Microdata Sample.

The assessment of the economic impact of the dropout problem to the state was derived from data from state agencies, including the Texas Department of Human Resources (TDHR), the Texas Department of Corrections (TDC), the Texas Department of Community Affairs (TDCA), and the Texas Education Agency (TEA).

In-school and out-of-school alternative training programs for dropout prevention and recovery were identified through surveys sent to school districts, community colleges, service delivery areas, colleges and universities, and private industry councils. Information on the types of programs and services provided was collected and organized into a state-wide directory. A meta-analysis of evaluative programs data was deemed inappropriate due to the small number of programs with evaluation data.

EXECUTIVE SUMMARY

This report presents the results of the dropout studies conducted by Intercultural Development Research Association (IDRA). The major research tasks were designed to examine three primary questions:

1. What is the magnitude of the dropout problem in the state of Texas?
2. What is the economic impact of the dropout problem for the state?
3. What is the nature and effectiveness of in-school and alternative out-of-school programs for dropouts in the state?

The research was conducted during the period of May through October, 1986. Given the paucity of reliable data on dropouts, research methods included primary analyses of data collected by IDRA and secondary analyses of available databases including Fall Survey and Annual Performance Report information collected by TEA and census data collected by the U.S. Bureau of the Census. Major findings are listed below.

MAJOR FINDINGS

Magnitude of the Problem

1. The 1985-1986 attrition rate for Texas high schools was 33 percent.
2. One in five Texas youth (nearly half a million), ages sixteen to twenty-four, were not enrolled in school and had not completed the twelfth grade in 1980.
3. Three out of ten Texas dropouts—152,000 young people—had completed fewer than nine years of schooling when they left school.
4. Approximately 85 percent of Texas dropouts were born in the United States; less than 15 percent were born in a foreign country.
5. Of the nearly half a million Texas dropouts ages sixteen to twenty-four, more than half (52 percent) were male.
6. Among females, attrition rates ranged from a low of 26 percent for white females to 43 percent for Hispanic females.
7. Attrition rates differed markedly for three racial/ethnic groups in the state: 27 percent for white, 34 percent for Blacks and 45 percent for Hispanics.
8. Hispanic youth, ages sixteen to nineteen, were twice as likely, and youth ages twenty to twenty-four, were nearly three times as likely to have left school prior to the completion of the twelfth grade as their white counterparts.
9. Nearly half of Hispanic dropouts had completed less than the ninth grade when they discontinued schooling, compared to 18 percent of white and Black drop-outs who discontinued schooling before the ninth grade.
10. Black male dropouts were less likely to be employed than either Hispanic or white male dropouts; two in five Black male dropouts, ages sixteen to nineteen, in contrast to one in five of white and 26 percent of Hispanics in that age group, were not in the labor force.

DROPOUT ACCOUNTING PROCEDURES

11. Thirty-nine percent of Texas school districts have a system for identifying dropouts.

12. The majority of districts follow similar, but not identical, forms of the TEA dropout definition.
13. Sixty-two percent of districts do not use a dropout formula for calculating their dropout rate; among districts who have a formula, 9 percent use Average Daily Attendance, while 24 percent use Average Daily Membership as the base figure.
14. Only 3.5 percent of districts have conducted some form of dropout research with only nine districts conducting formal research studies on dropouts.
15. Sixteen percent of the students tracked who were presumed dropouts had not dropped out of school.
16. Twenty-eight percent of the students tracked were employed; of these, most worked at labor-intensive, minimum wage jobs.
17. The majority of the students tracked left school because of poor grades, marriage/pregnancy, or financial problems.

AVAILABLE DROPOUT PROGRAMS

18. Approximately 12 percent of Texas school districts reported having a dropout program; the number of programs reported by colleges, service delivery areas and other agencies was not commensurate with the magnitude of the problem.
19. Approximately 89 percent of dropout programs in Texas reported having no evaluation data.
20. The dropout problem is costing the state $17.12 billion in (a) foregone income and lost tax revenues, and (b) increased costs in welfare, crime and incarceration, unemployment insurance and placement, and adult training and education (for each cohort of dropouts). Every dollar invested in educating potential dropouts is estimated to result in a return of nine dollars.

IMPLICATIONS OF THE RESEARCH

1. There is a need to develop and use a standardized dropout definition with explicit identification procedures.

Findings from the district dropout identification and procedures surveys, the dropout research reviews, and the student tracking surveys point to a need for a standardized, uniformly applied dropout definition with necessary identification procedures. Only 61 percent of districts reported having a system for identifying dropouts. Among these districts, definitions were similar but not uniform. The lack of standard definitions effectively precludes aggregating individual district data campuses within a particular school system.

Any definition and identification procedure at the state level must accommodate contextual variables at the district level and also be rigorous enough to result in reliable aggregation across districts. In addition, the definition must be sensitive to such issues as summer versus school-term withdrawals, non-attenders, often carried on membership rolls, verifiable transfer procedures and completion of graduation requirements.

State efforts at standardizing dropout identification procedures were initiated in the TEA 1985 Annual Performance Report requirements. Dropout reporting requirements for 1986 focus on a district-wide base figure for grades seven through twelve. Student identification and tracking procedures are also being put in place with the Public Education Information Management System (PEIMS) being developed by TEA. Both of these efforts can serve as a springboard for further standardization.

2. There is a need to develop standard procedures for calculating the dropout rate.

As a corollary to the development of a standard dropout definition, calculation procedures must be standardized and clearly specified. IDRA research findings indicate that 62 percent of districts do not use a formula for calculating the dropout rate, despite current reporting requirements developed for local use.

Critical manipulable factors involved in the calculation of dropout rates include: (a) the time frame during which the number of students is counted, e.g., annual versus longitudinal, (b) the range of grade levels included in the dropout rate calculation, i.e., the greater the grade span, the lower the dropout rate, and (c) the student accounting procedures used by the district, e.g., average daily attendance versus average daily membership.

While calculations of district dropout rates must remain useful at local levels, state level rates must be used to guide policy deliberations and monitor the effects of state and local intervention strategies.

3. There is a need to develop a centralized and standardized system for collection of dropout data.

The extensive variability in district dropout definitions and calculations noted above makes comparability across districts difficult at best. Even with standardization, however, it will become important to develop and maintain a centralized means of aggregating and analyzing dropout data across districts. With a centralized data base, the overall effect of intervention strategies as well as the effect of these efforts on particular populations can be monitored.

4. There is a need to develop tracking mechanisms which will increase the reliability of dropout counts and will result in more appropriate program interventions.

Research findings clearly indicate that current communication between and within districts does not facilitate tracking of students who withdraw from a particular school. Approximately 16 percent of the presumed dropouts tracked across the state by telephone or mail reported having never dropped out of school but either transferred or were still enrolled. Within districts, procedures for tracking of students are varied and depend, in part, on district size and resources. Across districts, standard record-keeping and transfer documentation and follow-up procedures for student withdrawals would greatly facilitate tracking of students as they move from one district to another.

The Migrant Student Record and Transfer System (MSRTS) is the only national longstanding system for tracking students. The centralization of achievement and other data at a single location currently required by the MSRTS might be circumvented through the use of a computer bulletin board concept with subsequent transfers of records remaining at the district-to-district level. Whatever the configuration of a feasible tracking system, it is imperative that tracking mechanisms be identified which will enhance monitoring the progress in addressing the dropout problem.

5. There is a need for early dropout intervention efforts given the large numbers of students who leave before the ninth grade.

IDRA research evidence reveals that three out of ten Texas dropouts had completed fewer than nine years of schooling. Among Hispanic dropouts, almost half had discontinued schooling before completing the ninth grade. Reviews of existing dropout prevention programs in Texas revealed that few focused on pre-high school students. If dropout prevention efforts are to impact effectively at-risk populations, prevention efforts must begin at earlier levels. In doing so, strategies must be program focused and avoid merely labeling and stigmatizing students at earlier grades.

6. There is a need for developing and replicating model dropout prevention and recovery programs for particular types of high-risk groups.

Reviews of available literature and IDRA findings related to existing state programs indicated that information on "what works" is generally fragmented. While some exemplary or model programs are in operation across the country and in the state, there is little systematic and generalizable information which would permit program replication. It is, therefore, important to develop and replicate prototypic programs which have the components which are known to be successful: teaching of basic skills, survival skills training, work/study programs, individualized instruction, strengthened guidance and counseling, highly committed and caring teachers with high expectations for their students, and community/parent/business liaisons.

7. There is a need to expand the pool of available dropout prevention and recovery programs in order to service the large and diverse dropout population in the state.

Research on existing dropout programs in Texas revealed that the number currently in operation is inadequate when contrasted with the magnitude of the dropout problem in the state. There is a dearth of formal, structured programs specifically targeted at dropout or dropout-prone youth both within and outside the state's public school systems. In addition to developing and replicating model programs, successful models and strategies must be incorporated into a substantially larger number of diverse programs which will service diverse needs within the dropout population.

In order to serve the diverse migrant population, for example, a Graduation Enhancement Model is being developed by TEA and the Texas Migrant Interstate Program. According to data compiled by the coordinator of the program, migrant dropout rates are estimated to be in the 60 to 90 percent range. It is obvious, then, that more and varied programs are needed.

8. There is a need to develop systematic approaches to the evaluation of dropout prevention and recovery efforts.

The survey of dropout prevention and recovery programs indicated that 89 percent had no evaluation data. In the absence of such data, conclusions about program effectiveness are not possible. In developing guidelines and standards for evaluation, it is important to ensure that evaluation designs serve to identify programs that work for particular types of participants in particular types of situations. Strategies and results in a prevention program may differ from strategies and results in a recovery effort. Success in a prevention program for non-migrant students may differ from that for migrant students. The enormity of the dropout problem leads to the inevitable conclusion that all students do not leave school for the same or similar reasons or under the same or similar conditions. Neither the reasons nor the solutions can be the same. Evaluation designs must be able to generate information about what works, for what target group, and under what conditions.

9. There is a need to develop and link public and private sector initiatives which are proportionate to the massive number of dropouts in the state.

There are on-going substantive efforts directed at the dropout issue in the state of Texas. State agencies, including TEA and TDCA, have already begun initiatives designed to address the problem from both a prevention and recovery perspective. Private corporations, including Coca-Cola USA and Southwestern Bell, are sponsoring efforts designed to raise awareness of the issues and to develop program alternatives. Foundation support is also being directed at the dropout problem. The Ford Foundation, for example, has established a national dropout initiative which involves public and private sector collaboratives. Further development of communications networks and other linkages between private and public sector initiatives is central to effective dropout interventions. Coordination is also crucial to maximizing the return on the investment which must be made.

The linkages and networking which are necessary to producing results in the area of school dropouts will be facilitated by working within the concept of the educational pipeline. A focus on students, as they progress through the pipeline, i.e., kindergarten through public schooling and on to a college education, provides context and continuity. The Dallas County Community College District, for example, has established Adopt-A-School partnerships with area middle schools. College faculty are given release time in order to provide staff development and technical assistance to schools.

10. There is a need to make an investment in dropout prevention and recovery efforts which is commensurate with the magnitude of the problem and its economic impact in the state of Texas.

The number of dropouts for the graduating class of 1985-1986 was estimated to be 86,000. This represents a 33 percent attrition rate for a single group of high school students over a three year period. Over the course of their lifetime, projected losses in tax revenue averaged $58,930 per dropout. The estimated cost of keeping each of these students in school was $3,859 per averted dropout. In addition, the state would have realized a savings of $652 million in social expenditures related to crime, welfare, incarceration and unemployment costs. Every dollar invested in educating potential dropouts will result in a return of nine dollars. An investment in human capital yields substantial short and long-term results.

ATTRITION RATES AS INDICATORS OF SCHOOL DROPOUTS

José A. Cárdenas, Ed.D. and
María del Refugio Robledo, Ph.D.

1987

THE TEXAS DROPOUT SURVEY

Under a contractual relationship with the Texas Department of Community Affairs and the Texas Education Agency (TEA), Intercultural Development Research Association (IDRA) has recently conducted an extensive state-wide study of school dropouts. The study included estimates of the magnitude of the problem, the long range cost of school dropouts to the state of Texas, and an analysis of school programs related to dropout prevention and rehabilitation (Cárdenas, et al., 1986).

The study of the magnitude of the problem included several approaches—reviews of prior studies, an analysis of dropout information submitted by Texas school districts to TEA in the Annual Performance Report, analysis of Bureau of the Census data, and student surveys in a sampling of Texas school districts.

PURPOSES OF THE MAGNITUDE STUDY

The study of the number of dropouts in the state of Texas served three purposes:

1. To determine the magnitude of the problem, and to indirectly weigh the extent of dropout prevention efforts against the magnitude;
2. To develop baseline data and a methodology for evaluating the success of subsequent dropout prevention efforts; and
3. To provide base information for further inquiry.

PRACTICE CONSIDERATIONS

In the selection of a methodology for estimating the magnitude of the dropout problem in Texas, it was necessary to take into account several factors which presented severe limitations for this study.

The selection of methodology was in part based on the general unavailability of reliable and valid data at the local level. Only 39 percent of Texas districts reported having a system for identifying dropouts. Among these districts, definitions of school dropouts were similar but not uniform. 62 percent of the districts reported having no formula for calculating the dropout rate. The lack of uniformity in definition and procedures precluded aggregating data from individual school systems.

It was necessary to generate an estimate in a very short period of time. Although the Texas Dropout Survey was originally conceived as a one-year study, various constraints resulted in less than half of the original time line being available for the study. Funding limitations further constrained the amount of effort which could be expended on the study, and there was throughout the project a serious attempt to make a minimum of data demands to the school districts and other agencies participating in the study.

ATTRITION RATES

The Texas Dropout Study analyzed enrollment figures made available by the Texas Education Agency for a cohort of students who were in the ninth grade in 1982-83 and followed them for three years up to the twelfth grade in 1985-86. The attrition rate was calculated by dividing the number of missing students by the size of the group in the ninth grade to produce an attrition percentage rate.

Changes in high school enrollments during the three-year period of the longitudinal study were taken into consideration by adjusting the attrition rate. The number of ninth graders in 1982–83 was multiplied by the high school enrollment in 1985–86 and divided by the high school enrollment in 1982-83. This adjustment produced an "expected" twelfth-grade enrollment which was subsequently used to produce the attrition rate adjusted for the change in the number of high school students caused by increasing or declining enrollments.

The methodology described above produced estimates of school dropouts at the state, regional, county, and district levels. Various assumptions were made in determining the attrition rates for the various entities, but a subsequent testing of the assumptions substantiated their validity.

An assumption was made that the data available for the Texas Dropout Study were valid and correct. Several discrepancies in the data were found and corrected by contact with the respective school districts. Enrollment data, as well as attrition rates produced, were mailed to each of the one thousand school districts in Texas with an attached card requesting that discrepancies be reported. Although some fourteen school districts responded with requests for additional information on the methodology used, no cases of erroneous data were identified.

An adjustment for retentions did not have to be made. Even though retention rates at some grade levels (end of ninth grade) were higher than at any other grade levels, this lack of uniformity was found consistent from one year to the next for the three years studied. If a high percentage of the students were retained at the end of a grade level, the loss was compensated for by an equally high percentage of students retained the previous year. In a test sample of school districts, not one single district showed a significant change in the rate of retentions from year to year at any of the grade levels studied.

The entire methodology was tested against actual student data in a small sampling of school districts, including the second largest school district in Texas. As in the test for the impact of retentions and changes in enrollment, no discrepancies were identified.

A separate study of the magnitude of school dropouts was conducted using data furnished by the Bureau of the Census. The incidence of youth aged sixteen to twenty-four years not enrolled in school districts with less than high school completion validated IDRA attrition data at the state, regional, and metropolitan levels. No comparable data were available for analysis in metropolitan areas served by several school districts.

The state attrition rate (33 percent) was comparable to the dropout estimate produced by the analysis of the National Center for Educational Statistics of the *High School and Beyond* data set (34 percent).

EXAMPLES

The following sample cases from school districts in Texas demonstrate the methodology used in the study:

A. In one school district there were 1,157 students in the ninth grade in 1982-83. Three years later there were 546 students in the twelfth grade (1985-86). During these three years the high school enrollment held constant, with 2,894 in 1982-83 and 2,892 in 1985-86. Since there is virtually no fluctuation in the high school population, the number of students no longer in the cohort (1,157 minus 546 = 611) was divided by the number of students in the original group (1,157) to produce an attrition rate of 53 percent.

B. In another school district, there were 3,168 students in the ninth grade class in 1982-83. During the next three years the high school enrollment for the district increased from 10,736 to 13,370, a 22.67 percent increase in enrollments. In order to determine how many students should be in the ninth grade group by the time they would be seniors in 1985-86, it is necessary to adjust the ninth grade number by the 22.67 percent increase in enrollment. Making this adjustment produces an expected enrollment of 3,886 in the twelfth grade in 1985-86, assuming that the increase in high school enrollment was evenly distributed throughout the four grade levels.

Since only 2,594 students were enrolled in the twelfth grade in 1985-86, there are 1,292 students missing from the expected enrollment of 3,886. This produces an attrition rate of 33 percent.

If the increase in high school enrollments were not distributed evenly throughout the four grade levels, and none of the 2,434 additional students were enrolled in the class which was followed from 1982-83 to 1985-86, the number of students missing from the original group is 18 percent, although it is ludicrous to assume that none of the additional students were enrolled in the group being studied.

Given two assumptions: 1) that the additional students were evenly distributed among the four grade levels, and 2) that the additional students were enrolled in all grade levels except the one under study, it is the latter assumption that appears much more improbable, statistically invalid, and pragmatically unreasonable. On this basis it stands to reason that the 33 percent attrition rate figure is a much more valid estimate than the 18 percent.

C. In a third school district the enrollment at the ninth grade level in 1982-83 was 1,226. At the twelfth grade level three years later the enrollment was 629. The number of missing students (597) divided by the number in the original group indicates that 49 percent of the original group was missing. But during the same three-year period the high school enrollment declined from 3,928 to 3,442. Assuming that a proportionate number of students were lost in each of the four grade levels, the original number is adjusted to 1,074. Subtracting 629 from the adjusted estimate of unaccounted students and dividing the result by the adjusted estimate produces an attrition rate of 41 percent.

CAVEATS

As is the case with any type of statistical analysis, the reader is warned of factors which may not have been taken into consideration in the analysis. The reported attrition rates constitute a good estimate, but should be further interpreted in the light of district information not available to the researchers. The following factors should be considered in estimating the number and rates of students dropping out of school.

A. The attrition rates produced by this study are extremely conservative estimates. Actual dropout rates may be expected to be much higher. The study followed a group of students for a three-year period in grades nine to twelve.

Yet, another portion of the study which analyzed census data indicated that 30 percent of all students who dropout of school do so before the ninth grade, i.e., before the beginning grade of the longitudinal study. For some ethnic groups, such as Hispanics, the percentage dropping out of school prior to the ninth grade was 50 percent.

The longitudinal study was terminated at the twelfth grade level with no attempt to determine how many additional students may have left the school at this level or subsequent years without graduating.

A third factor producing conservative estimates is the use of net growth/decline figures in adjusting for changes in the high school population. The amount of change in total enrollment due to dropouts was not factored out prior to making the adjustments.

B. School districts in Texas reported differences in the definition of a school dropout and used a variety of methodologies in computing self-reported dropout rates. Rates reported to the Texas Education Agency in the Annual Performance Report and following the methodology recommended by the agency constitute one-year dropout rates rather than cumulative longitudinal rates as estimated and reported in the Texas Dropout Study.

A dropout rate reported by a school district using the entire enrollment of the district (K-12) represents the average number of dropouts at each grade level. Therefore, a reported figure of 5 percent, for example, would indicate that 5 percent of ninth graders, 5 percent of twelfth graders, 5 percent of kindergarten and second grade students, etc. dropped out of school during that year. Since there are reasons to believe that few dropouts occur at the early elementary grades, rates computed by such a formula may not reflect the holding power of the school.

Instructions from the Texas Education Agency for the calculation of dropout rates have been modified, with the recommendation that districts use the secondary school enrollment figure rather than the entire district enrollment in computing the dropout rate. Districts following this recommendation will see their dropout rates doubling and even tripling this year.

G. Alfred Hess, Jr., in reporting variations in dropout reporting methodologies, uses the rule of thumb that annual reports of school dropouts should be multiplied by the number of grade levels in the study in order to convert annual reports to longitudinal figures (Hess, 1986). Therefore, districts reporting dropout figures compiled on the number of students enrolled in grades K through twelve should multiply the dropout rate by thirteen in order to make the rate comparable to a longitudinal rate. Districts using the new TEA recommended procedure of dividing the number of dropouts by the number of students enrolled in grades seven through twelve should multiply the annual dropout rate by six to produce a comparable longitudinal figure.

C. Districts using the attrition rates submitted to them as a follow up of the study should use caution in interpreting the data, particularly when the number of students is exceedingly small. Although the original intent of the study was not to compute attrition rates for individual school districts, the availability of the data in calculating a state rate facilitated the calculation of attrition rates at regional, county and local levels.

It can be assumed that attrition figures reported in the Texas Dropout Study are valid, although conservative, at the state and regional levels, for heavily populated counties, and for large school districts. The data may become questionable in sparsely populated counties and in very small school districts. The abundance of school districts in Texas with high school enrollments of less than 200 students demands caution in local interpretation of the findings.

Similarly, ethnic breakdowns which result in very small numbers of students in some ethnic groups may affect the validity of attrition estimates for those groups. In a large school district with a small number of Black, Hispanic, Asian or white Anglo students, rates for the total district population may be highly valid, but the rates for a very small number of students of an ethnic subgroup may be questionable.

D. Extenuating circumstances may exist in some school districts which should be taken into consideration in the interpretation of local attrition rates. For example, discussions with school superintendents in districts along the Mexican border indicate that there may be large numbers of students from Mexico that enroll in Texas school districts for the sole purpose of learning English. Having accomplished this objective in a year or two, the students return to Mexico, and any further school attendance is now beyond the control of the Texas school districts.

Another unique circumstance identified during the study was the effect of court-ordered school desegregation on enrollment patterns. If the reaching of an age or grade level influenced by desegregation results in large, uneven distributions of students leaving or returning to a school district, the validity of attrition rates is questionable.

CONCLUSION

The calculation of attrition rates for the state, regions, counties and school districts proved to be a simple, fast, economical and valid method of determining the magnitude of school dropouts, providing baseline data for the subsequent evaluation of prevention efforts, and providing school districts with basic information for subsequent analysis and validation.

The availability of these data should provide a sound framework for the development of educational policies at the federal, state and local levels aimed at eliminating, or at least greatly reducing, the existing school dropout problem.

FORMULATING A PLAN FOR DROPOUT PREVENTION

1988

It has become a national and state concern over the number of students that are not completing a high school education as a result of dropping out. This increased concern has led to legal intervention that makes this a priority issue in education.

In Texas, House Bill 1010, enacted in 1987, provides the educational system with a clear mandate for the implementation of a program for the identification of at-risk children and the development of school responses for diminishing the likelihood of these children becoming school dropouts.

Most school districts have responded to the state mandate for the appointment of an "at-risk" coordinator, established a more uniform system for determining the extent of the problem, and are in the process of developing a plan of action which will guide the district in addressing the problem.

The development of a district's plan of action can be a difficult undertaking. The reasons for students dropping out of school are pervasive. The reasons are multiple, and they are interrelated.

A simplistic plan cannot address adequately a large and complex problem. The plan of action must be comprehensive, coordinated, and involve the commitment and the efforts of all segments of the school district.

A commitment by the school board or the top level administrative officers has little chance of success unless it is accompanied by an equal commitment and effort by the practitioners in contact with the target populations. A strong effort by teachers and support personnel can be dissipated in the absence of district policy in order to prevent a failure in the allocation of the necessary resources in support of the effort.

A plan of action for the high school may prove unsuccessful, because in many school districts the highest incidence of students leaving school takes place at the middle school level. On the other hand, a plan for the middle school may be unsuccessful if academic underperformance, which is so characteristic of school dropouts, is allowed to develop during the early elementary school years.

In order to facilitate the difficult task of developing a comprehensive campus or school district plan for addressing the dropout problem, it is desirable to organize responses into discrete areas. The use of these subdivisions will allow school personnel to assess existing conditions in the school system, determine the extent to which that portion of the school plan has been addressed, identify areas in which further action is required, and proceed with the development of additional school responses addressing the dropout problem.

The following categories are broken down into five organizational school levels form a matrix with fifty cells (see Figure One) which can be used as a framework in the development of the action plan for the school district. Key phrases have been provided in each of the ten categories to assist in the initiation of the planning process.

AREAS OF DROPOUT PREVENTION ACTIVITY

1. *Philosophy of Education*

The district, its staff and programs display a philosophy which is conducive to all students succeeding and staying in school.

The district is *committed* to the prevention of school dropouts and will provide the necessary support and resources for addressing this problem.

The district is aware that the solution to the dropout problem requires new and different behaviors on the part of the at-risk student, as well as on the part of the school system.

The district is willing to change traditional concepts and practices in order to facilitate student success, continuation in school and eventual graduation.

2. *Governance*

The district reviews policies for ways to ensure a student continues in school.

The district identifies any existing barriers which may impede student success and continuation in school.

The district considers alternative and new policies, procedures, rules, regulations, programs and organizational patterns conducive to dropout prevention.

3. *Scope and Sequence*

The district analyzes existing programs to determine the extent to which they are responsive to the needs of at-risk students.

The district expands its services to facilitate school attendance and success for students in unique circumstances.

The district seeks new partnerships with business and community agencies for providing resources and support mechanisms conducive to school success and completion for at-risk students.

The district implements new services in support of at-risk students. These new services may include pre-natal instruction and care, extension of pre-school programs, alternative programs for problem students, alternative schools, special programs for pregnant teenagers, and child-care services.

4. *Staffing*

School personnel identify the staff competencies and skills needed in programs addressing the needs of at-risk students.

The administration identifies, recruits and assigns adequately prepared staff to regular programs and special programs for at-risk students.

The district utilizes flexible and differentiated staffing patterns in order to address the problem of educating at-risk students.

The district implements a program for the in-service training of new staff and for staff assigned to new, innovative and model programs to be used as dropout prevention strategies.

5. Curriculum

The system conducts an analysis of the existing curriculum and determines ways in which it may be deficient for at-risk students.

The district identifies, acquires, adapts and modifies curriculum in order to make it appropriate for at-risk students.

The district develops and implements new programs and school offerings which respond to the characteristics and needs of at-risk students.

6. Co-curriculum

The district uses co-curricular activities to attract and retain at-risk students, particularly those students who appear to be isolated from their peers and have few personally rewarding experiences in school.

The district de-emphasizes demonstrated talent and emphasizes student need as a criterion for student participation in co-curricular activities.

7. Student Personnel Services

School personnel provide guidance, counseling, mentoring and other services as support mechanisms to assist at-risk students in coping with personal, family and academic problems.

8. Non-instructional needs

All school personnel assist the student in meeting basic physiological and psychological needs not directly dealt with in instructional programs.

The school system networks with other community institutions for the provision of services which can diminish the impact of personal, family and social problems on school performance.

9. Parental Involvement

School personnel develop and increase opportunities for positive communication with parents.

The district develops and implements special programs to assist parents in providing the home support necessary for school success. These special programs can include parenting training, adult basic education, adult English development, family literacy programs and others.

10. Evaluation

The school system provides for the acquisition of timely and pertinent information on at-risk student needs and performance for diagnostic and prescriptive purposes.

The school system provides sufficient feedback mechanisms to provide immediate and strong positive reinforcement to students immediately following satisfactory performance.

The district implements a systematic process of continuous self-evaluation in order to provide for the successful education of at-risk students.

The district implements an accounting system which monitors the success of its efforts in dropout prevention.

AREAS OF DROPOUT PREVENTION ACTIVITY

Figure One

	Pre-school	Elementary School	Middle School	High School	Adult
1. Philosophy					
2. Governance					
3. Scope and Sequence					
4. Staffing					
5. Curriculum					
6. Co-curriculum					
7. Student Personnel Services					
8. Non-instructional Needs					
9. Parent Involvement					
10. Evaluation					

ATTRITION RATES FOR STATE SCHOOLS SHOW INCREASE

1988

In October 1986, the Texas Department of Community Affairs and the Texas Education Agency released a study conducted by the Intercultural Development Research Association of student dropouts in the state of Texas (Cárdenas, et al., 1986).

One aspect of the study was an estimate of school dropouts at the state, county and district levels based on high school student attrition over a three-year period, from the ninth-grade class in 1982-83 to the twelfth-grade class in 1985-1986. The study indicated that an estimated 33 percent of the students in the group dropped out from all Texas high schools during that period.

The longitudinal attrition rate derived in this study is the cumulative amount of student decline during the three-year period, and it is not comparable to the annual rates calculated and reported by school districts.

A subsequent study for the next group moving through Texas high schools has just been completed. The study compares the ninth-grade class in 1983-84 with the twelfth-grade class in 1986-87.

Using an identical methodology, the new study indicates a longitudinal attrition increase in Texas of one percentage point, from 33 percent to 34 percent, a three percent state-wide increase.

Texas Education Agency enrollment figures from district enrollment reports indicate that 826,176 students were enrolled in Texas high school grades nine through twelve in 1983-84. Three years later, in the 1986-87 school year, there were 871,725 students in Texas high schools, an increase of 45,549. During this same period, the class of 1987 decreased from 252,964 to 177,037, a loss of 75,927 students, or 34 percent of the ninth graders, as adjusted for the increase in the high school population.

Further analyses on the basis of ethnicity, race and sex indicate a 3.7 percent decrease in the attrition of white, non-Hispanic students, from 27 percent to 26 percent. On the other hand, Hispanic attrition increased by 2.7 percent, from 45 percent to 46 percent, and the attrition of Black students increased 11.8 percent, from 34 percent to 38 percent.

The attrition rate for total males, 35 percent, and the attrition rate for total females, 32 percent, did not change from 1985-86 to 1986-87.

Increases in attrition rates in the state's large urban counties parallel the 3 percent state increase and may account for much of it. The following changes were noted in the six largest urban areas:

Texas Counties' Attrition Rate Changes By Percent

County	1985-86	1986-87	Change
Nueces	26	30	+ 15.4
Bexar	37	39	+ 5.4
El Paso	38	40	+ 5.3
Tarrant	29	30	+ 3.4
Dallas	36	37	+ 2.8
Harris	38	39	+ 2.6
Travis	41	40	– 2.4

ADDRESSING SCHOOL DROPOUTS

1989

"School Dropouts" has become the dominant theme of American education in the second half of the 1980s. Efforts at the local, state, and national levels are focusing on the reduction of the number of students leaving the schools prior to graduation.

Although the high incidence of students dropping out of school justifies the attention this aspect of education has been receiving, it is neither a new nor a separate phenomenon of this era. Dropout rates have been higher in the past without demanding a fraction of the national attention now being given to the problem.

"School Dropouts" is a new label and a new emphasis brought about by the appearance of a new interest in the schools, the interest of the economic sector and its need for a better educated work force. The disappearance of the need for unskilled labor and the emerging need for skilled labor in a more technical and service-oriented society has led to an extensive concern for a better educated work force, which in turn is dependent upon a significant improvement in the quantity and quality of elementary and secondary education.

Basic to the prevention of a massive exodus of students from the schools prior to graduation is the need for drastic improvements in the performance of students in school. Although teenage pregnancy, substance abuse, gang activity, and other social ills may be identified as reasons for high dropout rates, these problems are usually secondary, and in many cases, a result of the much more basic problem of poor performance, frustration, and hopelessness in school work.

For the past three years, IDRA has conducted an intensive study of Hispanic dropouts in a Texas urban school district. Hispanic students were targeted for the study because local, state, and national studies indicated that Hispanics have the highest dropout rate of any ethnic group in the country. During this study, information was gathered through 746 individual interviews and 337 telephone interviews of students who had left school, students who remained in school, and parents of these two groups. Information was also collected through surveys of and meetings with principals, teachers, and counselors in twenty-seven middle and high school campuses in the district. Additional data were obtained through district archival records, reviews of documents related to dropout prevention and recovery, and sessions with district personnel and advisory committees.

As a result of this research effort, substantial information surfaced which is useful in addressing the dropout problem. Past efforts to remedy this problem have often been dysfunctional and counterproductive in that school and community responses were not compatible with research findings on the characteristics of school dropouts.

A sensible way of addressing the dropout problem is to start with research data on the fundamental causes and contributing factors to dropping out of school. The next logical step is to develop responses which address these causes and contributing factors.

The following information gathered in our three-year study provides a sound beginning for the formulation of appropriate responses.

RESEARCH QUESTION 1:

What student and parent characteristics affect a student's propensity to stay in or dropout of school?

Age (at time of interview)

- Overagedness at grade level increases the propensity for dropping out of school. Students who had been retained in grade had almost double the dropout rate than students not retained.

Birthplace and Length of U.S. Residence

- The majority of school leavers and school attenders are U.S. born and not immigrant children.
- Students whose mothers were not born in the U.S. had a lower dropout rate than students whose mothers were U.S. born.
- Dropout rates for students whose mothers were not born in the U.S. diminished after the mother had been in the U.S. for at least ten years.

Parent's Education

- A parent's level of education affects the chances of dropping out of school. In general, the lower the parent's educational level, the greater the chances the student will dropout.

Employment

- Most parents of Hispanic students, whether school attenders or school leavers, work. Most mothers work in service maintenance jobs, such as house cleaning. Most fathers work in skilled labor jobs, which include mechanics and carpentry.
- A students' chances of staying in school are also affected by whether or not the father works. If the father is not working, the odds of a student dropping out are increased.

Household Characteristics

- Students who live in households with both parents have better chances of staying enrolled in school.
- Students who have children of their own at home run a greater risk of leaving school.

Youth's Current Status

- Over half of all students who have left school are not working. One in five is married and has children.
- Most students who have left school are not re-enrolled in school, are not pursuing a GED, and have not entered job-training programs.

RESEARCH QUESTION 2:

Does language determine whether or not a student stays enrolled in school?

- Most students, both school leavers and school attenders, speak English and Spanish at home.
- If students believe that they do not read or write English very well, they are more likely to dropout of school.
- Hispanic students whose first language is Spanish have a better chance of remaining in school.
- Hispanic students whose parents encouraged bilingualism are also more likely to remain in school.

RESEARCH QUESTION 3:

Do a student's attitudes and perceptions determine whether or not he/she stays in or drops out of school?

Youth's Likes and Dislikes

- Students tend to remain in school if they like school personnel, feel positively about teachers and administrators, and perceive both school personnel and other students as liking youth with positive attributes (e.g., "good," "polite").
- Students who have left school perceive teachers as disliking Hispanics.
- Students who have left school perceive teachers and other students as linking negative characteristics in students (e.g., gang members, drop-outs).

Helps and Hindrances

- Most students believe study skills are most helpful for staying in school while peer pressure and harassment are the greatest hindrances.

Importance of Finishing High School

- Although the majority of students recognize the importance of finishing high school, those who leave attach less importance to it and feel that their parents think likewise.

Leaving School: First Thoughts and Reasons

- Students have a greater chance of leaving school if they first considered leaving during the transition school years (grades seven and nine).
- Students who had left school indicated they left because school work was too difficult, and they had to work.
- Among students who left school, problems with school personnel and pregnancy were the principal reasons for leaving.
- Students still enrolled in school cited pregnancy and the need to work as reasons for leaving school if they were to decide to leave.

Ethnic Composition

- Most school leavers and school attenders would change their school's ethnic composition: Hispanic students enrolled in school feel there are not enough white students; Hispanic students who leave school feel there are too many white and Black students.
- Both school attenders and school leavers feel there are not enough Hispanic teachers.

Parents' Perceptions

- Parents' belief that both they and the school can do something to help students stay in school is conducive to students remaining in school.
- Parents perceive that they and the school can make the greatest contribution to students staying in school by providing support in classroom and instructional organization.

RESEARCH QUESTION 4:

What is the relationship between participation in school and out-of-school activities, and staying in or dropping out of school?

Youth

- Most students, both school attenders and school leavers, participated in middle and high school activities (mainly sports).

- Involvement in school and out-of-school activities increases a student's chances of remaining in school.
- Encouragement from parents for students to participate in school activities is conducive to staying in school.

Parents

- Most parents visit the school for meetings with teachers and would visit more often if parents had more time, were more interested, or if meetings were held at more convenient times.
- Students have a greater chance of staying enrolled in school if their parents visit the school for positive reasons (such as awards ceremonies).
- Students have a greater chance of staying in school if their parents show an interest in school programs.
- Students whose parents visit school mainly for discipline problems and teacher/parent meetings have a greater chance of leaving school.
- Parents of school dropouts feel they visit the school too often for disciplinary purposes.
- Most parents of both school leavers and school attenders feel there should be more visits for parent meetings and school programs.

RESEARCH QUESTION 5:

What is the relationship between school history and dropping out of school?

Mobility

- The more times a student changes schools, the greater are the chances of leaving school.

Work

- Working more than fifteen hours per week while in school increases the chances of a student leaving school.
- Most students who work while in school do so in service maintenance jobs in order to have spending money or to help with home expenses.
- Most students who work while in school earn slightly above the minimum wage.
- All students who worked more than forty hours per week while in school ultimately left school.

Grades and Retention

- Receiving failing grades at the elementary, middle or high school level increases the chances of dropping out of school.
- Being retained at grade level increases the chances of dropping out of school during the middle and high school years.

Absenteeism

- A high absentee rate (i.e., more than eleven days per school year) increases the chances of a student leaving school.
- Students who leave school frequently cite "feeling out of place" and boring classes as reasons for absenteeism.

Early Schooling

- Children who attend nursery school tend to remain in school through graduation.

RESEARCH QUESTION 6:

What is the relationship between a supportive environment and dropping out of school?

Relationship with Others

- Most students, both school leavers and school attenders, get along with parents and friends, but students who remain enrolled in school feel more comfortable discussing school or personal problems with school personnel, parents, and friends.

Encouragement

- Most school attenders and school leavers are encouraged to remain in school, but those who remain enrolled receive multiple encouragement from their family and school and church personnel.
- Most students know good friends or family members who have dropped out of school.
- A student's peers are the most likely persons to encourage a student to leave school.
- Students who leave school are encouraged by school personnel to do so.

Classroom Participation

- Students who do not ask questions when they do not understand a lesson tend to leave school.

Study Aids

- Odds of staying in school are increased if study aids, such as a quiet place to study, encyclopedias, a typewriter, and books, are available in the home.

Family

- Family problems, including conflicts with parents and relatives, household responsibilities, or financial concerns, increase the odds of leaving school.
- Most parents of students who left school report no notification by the school regarding problems with their children and maintain there were, in fact, no problems to report.

RESEARCH QUESTION 7:

What is the relationship between involvement with gang activity, substance abuse, or criminal behavior and staying in or dropping out of school?

- Students who participate in gang activity, use alcohol or drugs, and are involved in criminal activity are more likely to leave school.

RESEARCH QUESTION 8:

What effects do student and parent aspirations and expectations have on students' propensity to dropout or stay enrolled in school until graduation?

Future Employment

- Students who believe they will reach their career goals stand a greater chance of remaining in school.
- Most student leavers and attenders expect to be working in five years and want to work as professionals, technicians, or office and clerical staff.
- Students enrolled in school expect to work as professionals; students who leave school have lower expectations and believe they will be employed as skilled craft workers rather than as professionals.
- Students who believe their parents expect them to work in order to support the family run a greater risk of dropping out.

Future Education

- Most students who leave school expect to earn a GED, while most students who remain in school expect a college degree.
- Most students who have left school are planning to return to school the next fall but need support (e.g., child care, financial, counseling) in order to be able to return.

Parents' Aspirations and Expectations

- Most parents of students in school have high expectations for their children and believe their children will attain their goals.
- Most parents of school dropouts have similarly high expectations for their children and believe their children will attain their goals.
- The odds of leaving school are increased if parents expect their children to join the military or marry before high school graduation.

RESEARCH QUESTION 9:

What student, school or family/community characteristics have been found to predict dropping out?

Dropout Profile

The typical Hispanic dropout:

- Was seventeen years old when he/she left school; however, almost 40 percent of school leavers were under age sixteen.
- Was single; however, 11 percent of school leavers were married.
- Had parents who were married when he/she left school; however, 19 percent were in homes with one parent.
- Had a father working full-time as a skilled worker; however, 16 percent were either working part-time, not working, or retired; 14 percent had no father or male guardian in the home.
- Had a mother working full- or part-time in the field of service maintenance; however, 44 percent were not working; 3 percent had no mother or female guardian in the home.
- Is unemployed.
- If working, was doing skilled labor or service maintenance work to help out at home financially.
- Would require school-related assistance in order to return to school, i.e., different school, nice teachers, GED assistance, flexible hours, and school safety.

Parent Notification

- Over one-third of the parents were not notified by the school that their children had dropped out of school.
- Most parents report their children left school in the ninth grade and want them to return to school.
- Most parents believe their children want to return but need support in order to do so.

Predictive Variables

Multiple regression analyses were conducted on parent and student survey data and student archival records for the purpose of identifying variables which would predict which students were most likely to dropout of school.

Results showed that the chances of a student leaving school before graduation were increased if the student:

- Was overage for the grade level.
- Did not discuss problems with counselors.
- Had fathers who were born outside the U.S.
- Changed middle schools.
- Used drugs.

RECOMMENDATIONS

Recommendations for the prevention and recovery of dropouts were formed on the basis of current research literature, this study's findings, and the result of focus-group interviews conducted with a group of administrators, counselors, and teachers selected from each of the twelve campuses participating in this study. The focus-group interview used a force-field structure for a guided discussion about needs and solutions to the Hispanic dropout problem.

All this information points to the fact that comprehensive measures are needed to keep Hispanic students in school and succeeding with their studies. To frame our recommendations and give them a comprehensive context, IDRA has diagrammed the basic relationships in the education of children with a triangle: the student, the school, and the family/community. These recommendations call for changes in all three points and are couched in a set of guiding principles. Each principle is positive and visionary, interrelated, and interdependent. These principles are:

1. Strategies must be family-centered;
2. Strategies must be student-centered;
3. Strategies must be campus-focused; and
4. Strategies must accelerate learning.

Family-centered strategies consider parental involvement crucial, recognizing the value and strength of the Hispanic family. Student-centered strategies focus on the student rather than on the program or curriculum; student motivation, engagement, and achievement become the measures of success. Campus-focused strategies involve the entire campus in responding to the needs of students, rather than to a set of programs for students labeled "at-risk" of dropping out. Accelerated learning strategies ensure that at-risk students are taught at a faster pace and are targeted for success.

Our recommendations address each major audience in the outline and the three points of our triangle. They also give each group validity, support, and responsibility.

Specific recommendations are made to each audience. The first audience addressed is the community. External organizations, the private sector, public/private social services, and other groups outside the educational system constitute the community. For this specific audience, a coordination of services, activities, schedules and information must be provided to each campus with at-risk students. This involves utilizing existing resources and finding additional ones to provide support.

The next audience is the school board. This body must expand policy that promotes the utilization and coordination of all outside resources, encourages access to schools, and allocates the necessary resources needed for training and support. Another recommendation is that continuous reporting be done in order to assess progress.

The third audience is the superintendent and central office staff. Overall recommendations to this group include directing a coordinated effort of all services, implementing and monitoring plans district-wide, and providing the resources necessary for full implementation of plans addressing at-risk students.

At the campus level, the major actors (principal, support staff, teachers, parents, and students) are given very specific recommendations. In general, however, the campus should have a team approach which provides support, interventions, outreach, training, and resources to all of the parties in order that viable solutions are found and implemented. The campus principal is charged with implementing them. There must be a partnership which helps all students.

The plan incorporates such important variables as new instructional options, cross-departmental coordination, a recovery initiative, and the identification of new funding sources or better use of existing resources.

TEXAS SCHOOL DROPOUTS: 1986 TO 1989

1990

In 1986, under a contract with the Texas Department of Community Services (now the Department of Commerce) and the Texas Education Agency, the Intercultural Development Research Association (IDRA) conducted a study of school dropouts in Texas. This study was the first comprehensive analysis of school dropouts ever conducted in Texas, and included studies on the magnitude, economic impact and dropout prevention programs in the state (Cárdenas, et al., 1986).

The study on the magnitude of school dropouts utilized three methodologies: district self-reports to the Texas Education Agency, an analysis of census data and estimates of dropouts based on school enrollments and longitudinal attrition.

The dropout study based on districts' self-reports was abandoned in its early stages. At the time, districts were using a variety of definitions of school dropouts and an even wider variety of methodologies for counting and reporting data to the state education agency. The census data and attrition studies were continued and resulted in similar, mutually validating findings.

Subsequent to the 1986 report, the Texas Education Agency implemented standard methodologies for defining and reporting school dropouts. The latest reports based on the new definition and methodology have validated school dropout data produced by IDRA using the attrition methodology.

Since 1986, IDRA has conducted the annual longitudinal attrition study for each district and county in the state. Information derived from these annual studies becomes more important since it is the only data available which have been derived using a constant methodology. Thus, we are now able to see trends not discernible in any other recent dropout data.

The attrition methodology looks at school district enrollments in the ninth grade for a specific year, and compares this enrollment with twelfth grade enrollments three years later. Differences in enrollment are adjusted by the growth rate of total enrollment in the high schools.

Figure 1 below presents four years of state total attrition rates from 1982-83 to 1985-86, 1983-84 to 1986-87, 1984-85 to 1987-88, and 1985-86 to 1988-89. The annual rate is identified by the ending year.

These data in Figure 1 indicate that attrition rates have diminished in Texas during the past four years, from a 33 percent loss of students from 1982-83 to 1985-86 to a 31 percent loss in students from 1985-86 to 1988-89. This is a 6 percent improvement over the last four years.

On the other hand, the analysis of the data on an ethnic basis indicates that all of the improvement has been concentrated in the white, non-Hispanic population, with a 26 percent improvement in the holding power of the school, while the Black and Hispanic populations have experienced a 9 percent and 7 percent *increase* in attrition rates, respectively.

It is my belief that the initial increase in attrition for twelfth graders in 1986-87 can be attributed to the implementation of House Bill 72, the Texas school reform legislation, in 1984-85 and 1985-86. Subsequent to the initial increase for all ethnic groups, the reform legislation which was very much white, non-Hispanic oriented has led to a very significant improvement in the school performance of white, non-Hispanic students.

On the other hand, minority students not adequately addressed in the reform legislation of 1984 have not only continued to perform poorly in school, but the provisions of the legislation have exacerbated school problems for minorities, leading to a continuous increase in attrition rates. This unfortunate finding was predicted at the time of its enactment, since many of the provisions of the reform legislation were dysfunctional and counter-productive for minority students.

State concern over school dropouts will require a further examination of past legislation and school efforts in order to develop alternative responses to the dropout problem which will produce improved school performance and diminished dropouts for all students in the state.

Four-Year State Longitudinal Attrition Trends

Year	Black	White	Hispanic	Total
1985-86	34	27	45	33
1986-87	38	26	46	34
1987-88	39	24	49	33
1988-89	37	20	48	31
% Change (1985 to 1989)	+9	-26	+7	-6

(Similar data for each of the 254 counties are available upon request)

VYP CELEBRATES FIFTH SUCCESSFUL YEAR

José A. Cárdenas, Ed.D. and Merci G. Ramos, M.A.

1989

An awards luncheon marked the ending of the fifth year of the Valued Youth Program, a year as successful as the previous four. The Valued Youth Program, initiated in San Antonio through a grant from Coca-Cola, USA, continues to provide an innovative and sound approach to the school dropout problem.

The Valued Youth Program received special recognition last year when *The Ladies Home Journal* selected it as one of the ten best school programs in America (Lewis, 1988).

The program was implemented this year in middle and high schools in the South San Antonio and Harlandale school districts. Students deemed at risk of dropping out of school were recruited into the program where they received special training and were assigned as tutors for younger at-risk kids in nearby elementary schools. The tutors were paid minimum wage for the hours spent in tutoring activities.

At the middle school level, the U.S. Department of Education's Office of Bilingual Education and Minority Languages Affairs (OBEMLA) funded the Innovative Approaches Research Project (IARP) and selected Development Associates, Inc., a governmental management and consulting firm, to administer the project. Development Associates IARP Project Staff includes: Dr. Charlene Rivera, Project Director; Dr. Paul J. Hopstock, Acting Associate Director; and Richard Ottman, Contracts Administrator.

Although the original Coca-Cola funding of the program has terminated, IDRA and the participating school districts have been able to continue the program through the generous donations and support by personal and corporate friends of IDRA, as well as the extensive cooperation and support of the participating school districts.

Support services for students in the program included extensive involvement by parents, special training in the basic skills which were necessary for providing the tutoring services, designing and making tutoring materials, field trips, role modeling guest speakers, and extensive student recognition through special ID tags, feedback sessions, photo albums, films of field trips, media publicity at the local and national level, certificates of participation, awards, and, of course, the weekly paychecks.

Evaluative information indicates that the program was very successful. Out of the 117 students participating in the program, only two dropped out of school. (We may add that both students were lost due to home problems not related to school performance.) One student was promoted to a higher grade during the school year. Two students made the honor roll in April. Nine students came within one grade of making the honor roll. One student was awarded a $600 scholarship for being the most improved student in the school.

Tutoring groups in each school developed an identity and a "family" network that provided extensive mutual support. Members of the groups became protective of each group member.

Additional data indicates that grades improved, absences were reduced, test performance went up, and discipline problems declined. The school performance of the elementary school kids being tutored also improved.

The success of the program can be attributed to the inclusion of the three basic elements common to all successful programs for at-risk students: the valuing of the student in ways not found in the regular school program, the provision of support services not commonly available to these students, and the interaction among the school, the family and the larger community to provide a strong base for student success.

Participation in the program in itself communicates to the student that he/she is valued. Teachers, counselors, and administrators have singled out the student for a positive special purpose. The assignment to tutoring duties may often be the first and only responsibility given to that student. Tutors take this role very seriously. In evaluation interviews, one of the most commonly expressed statements is that the tutor feels that his/her behavior has to improve in order to live up to the image of a teacher of elementary school children. Student tutors not only perform better, they dress better; they speak better; they look better.

Opportunities for improving self-concept are continuously capitalized on by frequent and strong positive feedback. The appreciation of the elementary school kids, the teachers they assist, membership in a select group, guest speakers, certificates of accomplishment, achievement awards, all convey a strong message of appreciation, of recognition, of acceptance—a startling recognition that school can be a rewarding place, in spite of past limitations and a history of failure and frustration which are frequently brought into the program.

This year's award luncheon was purposely held at Palo Alto Community College, a member institution of the Alamo Community College District. It was a memorable occasion for most of the students. For many of them, it was their first contact with an institution of higher education, a type of institution not only foreign to them, but not a part of the family experience. Being greeted by the president of the college, touring the campus, hearing presentations by the admissions office on what will be required for college attendance to become a reality, and hearing from the Student Financial Aid officer what financial assistance can be expected were part of the morning's activities. Our hope was that as early as the seventh, eighth, and ninth grades, graduation from high school and subsequent college enrollment would become feasible alternatives and goals for these kids at risk of dropping out. It was very rewarding to hear several students make a commitment to Palo Alto Community College President Dr. Terry Dicianna that they would be back as students in a few years.

In addition to valuing the student, the program provides extensive support services. The money earned compensates for financial limitations of the family. Post-program interviews indicate that the money earned has been used by the students mainly for the purchase of school clothes and school materials.

Teachers and other school personnel working with the program provide extensive support services including individual and small group instruction and academic and personal counseling.

IDRA research on school dropouts indicates that students who dropout of school tend to be both academic and social isolates in school. Their school history indicates a lack of identification with and participation in school activities other than class attendance, and even this participation was fairly inconsistent. Participation in the tutoring program developed peer relationships in the school which did not previously exist. In each campus, the group of tutors became an extended family for each member. They developed peer group norms which were academically oriented, positive, and unlike many out-of-school gangs, demanded socially acceptable behavior.

For the fifth consecutive year, the evaluation shows that the valuing of students and the provision of support services in the context of extensive and meaningful school/parent/community relationships can alter student behavior and reduce, if not eliminate, school underachievement and the subsequent dropping out of school.

BIBLIOGRAPHY

Cárdenas, José A., María del Refugio Robledo and Josie D. Supik, *Texas School Dropout Survey Project*, IDRA, San Antonio, 1986.

Cárdenas, José A., María del Refugio Robledo and Dorothy Waggoner, *The Undereducation of American Youth*, IDRA, San Antonio, 1988.

Hess, G. Alfred, Jr., *Metropolitan Education*, Fall, 1986.

Lewis, Anne C., "America's Ten Best School Programs," *Ladies' Home Journal*, Vol. CV No. 9, September 1988.

National Education Goals Panel, *The National Education Goals Report*, Washington, D.C., 1992.

Reissman, Frank, "Overlooked Positives," in Frost, Joe L. and Glen R. Hawkes, *Socially Handicapped Children*, Houghton-Mifflin, Boston, 1966.

Robledo, María del Refugio, *The Answer: Valuing Youth in Schools and Families: A Report on Hispanic Dropouts in the Dallas ISD*, IDRA, San Antonio, 1989.

DISCUSSION QUESTIONS

1. Among the research methodologies explored to study the school dropout problem, IDRA found that longitudinal studies which identify school attrition rates were the most effective. Describe this approach and its application.
2. What is meant by a "deficit model" for explaining poor school performance among certain populations? How does such a model impact on efforts to remedy the school dropout problem?
3. Identify specific features of the IDRA Valued Youth Program that underlie its success. What does participant performance in the VYP tell you about the deficits assumed by some educators to explain school failure and dropouts?
4. Why are co-curricular activities and parental involvement considered to be necessary components of successful dropout prevention programs?
5. Suppose you are an executive of a major national corporation. Prepare a brief for your Board of Directors outlining a rationale for the investment of corporate funds in school dropout prevention.
6. Consider a student who is a potential school dropout. Sketch a financial profile showing the cost to the state of keeping him in school and the cost of letting the student leave school. Compare the cost with respect to this individual at age 12 and at age 30.

5

Retentions in Grade

PREFACE

The retention of students at specific grade levels is one of the most perplexing problems in the schools. It is perplexing for a variety of reasons.

First, it is a very pervasive practice. Though there are no accurate reporting procedures, therefore no accurate records of the number of students who are not promoted to the next higher grade level at the end of each year, it has been estimated conservatively that at least 10 percent of the school population is retained each year in the Texas public schools.

Second, it is a very expensive practice. If 10 percent of the school population is retained, the cost of this practice is one-tenth of the approximately $16 billion a year currently being expended for education. One-tenth of this annual expenditure amounts to $1.6 billion—a substantial sum.

Third, current research conducted on the results of school retentions concludes that the practice does not work; that is, there is no general improvement as a result of this $1.6 billion annual expenditure.

The belief that students who repeat a grade do better the second time around is a myth. For years, research studies have concluded that 50 percent of the students who repeat a grade do no better the second time, and 25 percent of the students actually do worse the second time. Since only one-fourth of the students retained show any improvement, three-fourths of the money expended in this practice, $1.2 billion annually, is a waste of money.

The retention practice is not supported by modern pedagogy. Retention in grade is a negative psychological experience which tends to develop or substantiate negative feelings of self. Students retained tend to see themselves as failures and develop negative self-concepts which tend to depreciate subsequent school efforts and levels of expectancy.

The psychological impact of this failure may be even stronger for Spanish speaking populations for whom the Spanish word for retention, *reprobar,* has stronger negative connotations than the corresponding English word. "Reprobar" also means "to condemn strongly as unworthy, unacceptable, or evil," "to reject," "to exclude" and "to damn."

The rationale of the retention practice is based on the assumption that the repetition of a grade leads to improved performance. There is no pedagogical basis for such an assumption, other than a corollary assumption that learning is acquired through osmosis, and if a student is repeatedly exposed to instruction, enough learning will be absorbed so that the cumulative effect becomes sufficient for the mastery of the content of a specific grade level.

Unfortunately, little is done by the school to identify or remove impediments to learning, so that the same impediments encountered during the initial exposure are usually present during all subsequent exposures. For example, if a student does poorly in the first grade because the student does not have sufficient English language skills to cope with the English language curriculum, it is extremely inefficient to have the student repeat the grade until such time as the student has acquired sufficient English language mastery. It is much more efficient, programmatically and financially, to provide extensive English language development in order to eliminate this as an impediment, or teach the content in the student's language until such time that English language competence is sufficient for a transition to English language instruction, as is common in a bilingual program.

The common myth that the repetition of a grade will lead to improved performance for most students is founded in obsolete school concepts that no longer hold true, if they ever did. The following are some of these concepts:

1. The threat of retention may have been much more effective as a motivational device when the public schools enrolled a more elitist and homogenous school population.

2. Holding just the students accountable for school performance may be a carryover from the old principle of state infallibility. Since the state could do no wrong, and the school is an extension of the state, the school could do no wrong. Therefore, any failure of students must rest solely in the students.

3. The retention of students is consistent with a student deficit model. It is assumed that the student has total control over the learning situation, and the failure to learn is attributed to student negligence or unwillingness to do so.

4. Retention is perceived as a punitive device. For minority, disadvantaged and other atypical students, retention can be perceived as punishment for being atypical rather than punishment for lack of effort.

Research efforts by IDRA indicate that the number of students retained in a specific grade is consistent from year to year. Assuming that ten percent of all students are retained each year, it is interesting that little effort is expended by the school in analyzing and addressing this failure. It is possible that the retention rate is so institutionalized that the school may perceive itself as being inefficient if the rate is diminished. If this is the case, school personnel, who are notorious in their use of subjective criteria for student performance evaluation, may be manipulating grading criteria in order to keep constant the number of students retained each year.

The educational problem of retention in grade has been compounded by recent findings of a strong relationship between student overagedness and dropping out of school. Though this relationship may not be causal, the relationship is so strong that it is worth seeking alternatives to retention in grade in order to address the dropout problem.

The following six articles published over a twelve-year period are indicative of IDRA attempts to address this issue. Although the Texas Legislature and the Texas Education Agency have attempted to address this issue, no significant change in the number of students retained has taken place. Politically, alternatives to retention are consistently viewed as attempts to institute a social promotion policy, the mass movement of students from one grade to another, regardless of student performance.

Neither retention in grade nor social promotions constitute an adequate response. The ideal response lies in determining and addressing reasons for the poor school performance of such a large segment of the student population.

RETENTION IN GRADE —A DYSFUNCTIONAL PANACEA

1981

At the time that the Texas Legislature was considering mandating a statewide criterion-referenced competency testing program, the proposed legislation was accompanied by a provision allowing the results of the standardized testing to be used for determining promotion or retention of students at grade levels dependent upon their performance on the test. On the basis of hearings and testimony before the Education Committees, the legislature dropped the provision for a mandatory promotion/retention policy on the basis of this testing program. Many school districts, however, established district guidelines which incorporated the results of this testing as criteria for pupil promotion.

It is anticipated that in the near future Texas will be inclined to use the results of the Texas Assessment of Basic Skills (TABS) as a criterion for retention in grade. It is difficult, however, to estimate what levels will be used to determine failure, because 28 percent of all white students in the ninth grade level failed at least one of the three portions of the test, as did 61 percent of all Hispanic students and 70 percent of all Black students in Texas. Certainly retaining 28 percent of white students, 61 percent of Hispanic students and 70 percent of Black students appears inappropriate. A decision by the Texas Legislature to use the results of TABS for retention purposes should prove interesting because New York, Florida, and other states have been experiencing long court battles over the legality of using standardized testing to determine student retention.

In expressing concern over the use of standardized testing for determining retention in grade, or for that matter in expressing concern over the use of retention as an education response, one is immediately perceived as favoring the elimination of all standards for education and as advocating a social promotion policy. Though it is desirable to establish and maintain high standards for the education of children, the attainment of these levels rests upon the improvement of instructional programs, teaching practices and educational resources and not on the utilization of a dysfunctional response such as an extensive dependence upon retention policies.

The stark reality is that the use of retention or repeating a grade in order to improve educational performance simply does not work. Educational research has been consistent in its findings which indicate that about one-half of the children retained do not improve in performance and do no better at that grade level than they did the first time. Only about one-quarter of the children who repeat a grade show some amount of improvement. Because the odds are three to one against a child receiving educational benefits from repeating a grade, retention should be used sparingly and only where there is overwhelming evidence and justification for it as a method of improving educational performance.

Probably the reason for the lack of success of retention as an educational response is that it is negative in nature. The child and the school develop a perception of failure, and the repetition of a grade reinforces this negative perception. Though it may tend to teach a child what not to do to succeed, it definitely does not teach the child what needs to be done. At its worst, retention may lead to the punishment of a victim of the educational institution rather than of the perpetuators of the crime. Extensive poor test results are an indictment of the educational system, not an indictment of the individual students.

Perhaps the most convincing argument against retention as an educational response is its cost ineffectiveness. The repetition of a grade by a retained child costs approximately $1800 per year. Considering that the allocation for special programs is $50 per child per year (for programs such as bilingual education and compensatory education), it would appear to be much more cost-effective to drastically increase educational resources to improve student performance and eliminate the need for retention, rather than to expend many times as much in an ineffective remediation approach.

It is hoped that Texas will react to the eye-opening results of the Texas Assessment of Basic Skills with a strong strategy for improving educational programs for that segment of the population which performed poorly on the test. It is further hoped that the basic strategy will be an improvement of educational programs and not the dysfunctional panacea of retaining children in grade for their failure to perform.

EDUCATIONAL EXCELLENCE AND SCHOOL RETENTIONS

1985

During the entire history of our country we have seen a cyclic phenomenon of national interest and concern for education. Periods of disinterest and neglect are followed by periods of intense interest and activity. At present the cycle is at the intense interest and concern level, as the country moves in its search for excellence in education necessary to support technological development.

This movement differs from past eras of national concern in that the response has been much more decentralized. We have witnessed massive legislative activity at the state, rather than the federal, level. An "Educational Reform Act" is a familiar piece of legislation in more than three-fourths of the state capitols. In the last two years, forty-three states have raised graduation requirements in their search for excellence.

The quest for educational excellence in its initial efforts has produced state legislation which can be described as overdue, necessary, and in good faith, but not necessarily predicated on sound educational research or the most modern pedagogy. In striving for educational reform, there is a danger that the reformers (educators and non-educators alike) will lose sight of the essence of quality education in the formulation of reform responses, and address many of the institutional mechanisms rather than the essence of education.

It is important to remember that the quality of education is based chiefly on the quality of the interaction between the teacher and student. Educational improvement comes about primarily through the improvement of this interaction and only secondarily through improvements in the quality of support mechanisms. Seldom, if ever, does the quality of the teacher/student interaction improve as a result of changes in administrative policies, particularly when the changes are not directly related to instruction. In fact, many such administrative policies are dysfunctional, not only not producing the desired improvement, but in many cases aggravating the learning situation and creating additional problems.

RETENTIONS INCREASING

One such dysfunctional response is the attempt to improve the quality of education by simply increasing performance standards. One result of this action is the increasing number of retentions in grade at the end of the school year. There has been a significant increase in the number of retentions as a result of state and national quests for excellence. Yet retaining students is a poor response to existing educational problems and will not lead to the excellence being sought.

To begin with, retention is a negative educational act. No matter how it is explained to children and parents, the word "retention" is perceived as synonymous with "failure." "The child was retained in the second grade" means "The child failed the second grade."

The act is punitive. At best, retention is the punishment given when the child's school efforts have been insufficient. At worst, it is the punishment given to a child for not having received the normal allocation of mental capabilities at birth. Though it is not being suggested that inadequate performance, insufficient effort, or lack of capabilities be rewarded; by far the most important objective of any school is to teach children, not punish them.

Retention and the accompanying feelings of failure may instill or aggravate feelings of inadequacy, contributing to a negative concept of self. One of the most important causes of poor school performance is a negative self-concept. The inability of the child to perceive himself or herself as a successful learner in a learning situation leads to low levels of expectancy that tend to become self-fulfilling prophesies. Not only does the failing child tend to develop a negative image of himself, his immediate family and peers quickly adopt his attitude, creating an environment of failure.

RETENTION FAILS TO MOTIVATE

One argument for retention is that the threat of it motivates students to improve their school performances. This simply is not so. The threat of retention proves to be a weak psychological impetus for improved performance. Psychologists are quick to point out that there is an important time relationship between performance and reward in order for the reward to impact upon the performance. In laboratory settings a delay of minutes, and often seconds, in the reinforcement seriously diminishes its impact upon performance. The threat of retention at the end of May has little or no impact on the performance of children in September. Parents do not expect improved behavior in children during the month of March by the threat of Santa Claus' absence in December. Children simply do not have sufficient temporal maturity for such motivational gimmicks to work.

There is a possibility that the increased retention of students will lead to a diminishing number that stay and finish school. Though this may be attractive to some people, it cannot be accepted in the new technological age, with our country becoming much more dependent on human resources than on natural resources. The last thing we need is more uneducated, unskilled, and unemployable persons for society to support.

It is a mystery why retention is still pursued as an educational response to poor performance. Research has consistently shown that at least half of all children retained do no better the following year in school, and about one-fourth actually do worse. The negative psychological impact of retention, as described previously, is so strong that research shows that less than one-fourth of all children retained make subsequent educational gains the following year.

THE COST OF RETENTION

The last, but an important, factor in considering retention as a means of attaining educational excellence is its cost effectiveness. The cost of retaining a student is equal to the annual per pupil expenditure for the school system. In a school year in which the average per pupil expenditure is $3,000, the cost of retaining a child will be $3,000. This is ten times the amount spent on the most liberal preventive programs. Three thousand dollars per child per year could be spent in much better ways; attracting and retaining better teachers, smaller class sizes, more and better instructional materials, extensive teacher training, and hiring resource teachers are a few of the much more cost-effective approaches than the placement of the child in the same learning situation which has already proved inadequate. If a state such as Texas would increase the retention rate by 10 percent in its quest for excellence (the Houston School District recently reported an increase in the elementary school retention rate to 12 percent for 1984-85) the total cost of elementary and secondary education would go up by another 10 percent. In Texas this would be an additional one billion dollar increase in annual expenditures without any hopes of bringing about a proportionate improvement in the quality of education.

These arguments should not be misconstrued as support for the social promotion of all students. The lockstep promotion of students regardless of how little they have learned in order for them to continue in the company of their peers is not a feasible alternative. Neither social promotion nor retention will do much to improve the relationship between teacher and student which is the key for improved performance. There may be some instances in which immature and slow developing children may benefit from retention, but the application of such a measure should be carefully and judiciously applied and not as a massive response to inadequacies in the system. Retention is not the panacea it is being perceived to be in the quest for educational excellence.

NEW STATE REGULATIONS ON SOCIAL PROMOTION

1985

New regulations enacted by the Texas Education Agency (TEA) circumvent the state law prohibiting social promotions, segregate classes of children and institutionalize poor performance in Texas public schools.

Prior to the appointment of a new State Board of Education as called for by the Education Reform law (House Bill 72), enacted by the Texas Legislature in special session during the summer of 1984; the old State Board of Education established a tracking system for secondary school students in the state of Texas.

Provisions of the new regulations allow for students with high performance records to go into an academic track and students with poor performance records to go into a vocational track with limited opportunities to overcome academic subject deficits. Perhaps the worst aspect of the Texas tracking system is that career options are being forced upon students at too early an age, years before they have had sufficient opportunity to overcome barriers presented by slow development or the effects of disadvantaged homes, minority status, or home language characteristics.

The hope that the newly appointed State Board of Education would eliminate the tracking system created by its predecessor proved fruitless. Not only has the new board not acted to rescind tracking in the secondary schools, they have now extended it downward to the second grade.

At the July 1985 meeting of the State Board of Education, regulations were enacted for the implementation of the House Bill 72 section dealing with social promotions. Students may be promoted only on the basis of academic achievement. "A student who has not maintained a grade average for a school year equivalent to at least 70 on a scale of 100 may not be advanced from one grade level to the next."

Texas Education Agency provisions for the implementation of the law and presented to the State Board at the first and second readings called for two categories of students in Texas schools—those who are normal and are expected to adhere to the letter of the law, and those who are in special education and are exempt from the letter of the law.

At the third reading of the regulations in July, a new section was added which creates a new category of students for promotion purposes. This new category contains students of normal capabilities who are performing poorly in school, the "remedials." Students in the new category can now be placed in "special remedial or compensatory classes or programs where deemed appropriate."

The grade level placement of these students under the new regulations will be nebulous, since the new regulations use voodoo language. They provide that "the district shall fully inform the parent or guardian that the student was not promoted but placed at the next grade level." Perhaps the Texas Education agency will issue a memorandum which will assist school districts in explaining to parents the difference between "promotion" and "placement at the next grade level."

Assignment into this limbo, called "The Special Remedial Category," is determined by a committee consisting of, at a minimum, the student's teacher, the principal, and one other professional staff member deemed appropriate by the district." The basis for the assignment will be the meeting of at least three of the four following criteria:

1. "Specific factors exist over which the student has no control which limit the student's achievement." I presume that race, ethnicity, socio-economic status, divorced parents, parental indifference and home language will easily meet the requirements for this criterion.
2. "The student's performance on standardized achievement tests falls in a range that the district recognizes as below acceptable standards." This means that the student did poorly on the test developed in New Jersey.
3. "The student has a history of non-performance and the majority of grades are failing." This can be interpreted as "We've never been able to teach him/her, why try now?"
4. "The student has a history of non-mastery on the Texas Assessment of Basic Skills or on the Texas Educational Assessment of Minimum Skills test" (Similar to number 2 above.)

The worst feature of the new regulations is that they make no attempt to distinguish between poor student performance and poor school performance. A student encountering poor instruction by a single teacher in an elementary school can become labeled "Special Remedial Category" and spend the rest of his or her life in the quagmire of educational inadequacy.

The results of the new regulations enacted by the State Board of Education will lead to the following:

1. The virtual elimination of the social promotion prohibition established by the Texas Legislature in House Bill 72. The new law states that a student may not be promoted to the next grade if the student is performing poorly. The new regulations keep this standard, but it is not applicable to students who are normal but performing poorly.
2. The creation and institutionalization of a new class of students, "the remedials," earmarked for failure by lower levels of expectancy. It is possible that as many as 49 percent of the students in Texas could go into this new category, all students performing below average.
3. The elimination of any accountability for the poor performance of students. If the students do not learn or the school does not teach them, the simple placement in the special remedial category absolves everybody.
4. The allowance for the increased segregation of students. Although the new regulations allow for the placement of students in regular classes, this provision applies only if the student is "achieving at a level that is not significantly lower than other students at the grade level so that placement in a class will not disrupt or overly complicate instruction for other students of the teacher." This provision guarantees the segregation of the low-performing students.

5. A false perception of student performance. They call for a "special report card or attachment to the report card that clearly explains that the grade reflects that the student is below expectations for the age and grade and the level at which the instruction is being provided." The student may have lots of "A"s on the report card, but they really mean "D"s and "F"s.
6. It can be expected that once assigned to the Special Remedial Category, these students will continue to underachieve for the remainder of their lives. Such placement in the new category can begin at the second grade.

Even though these new regulations appear to provide for lower standards of performance expected from mentally handicapped children, in reality they are lower standards of performance for perfectly normal children who can be expected to have high levels of performance, but are not reading at those levels.

The recent enactment of these regulations by the State Board of Education makes reform efforts and reform legislation in Texas a travesty undeserved by the reformers and certainly not deserved by the children of Texas. While other states continue to reform, to improve, to set new standards, the state of Texas institutionalizes poor performance on the part of children and schools.

MORE ON SCHOOL RETENTIONS

1985

The August issue of the Intercultural Development Research Association (IDRA) *Newsletter* carried an article on the negative effects of school retentions and the danger that this response would be a favored option in addressing educational reform in Texas. Since the publication of that article, our office has obtained an extensive amount of material which substantiates the claim that retention in grade may be doing more harm than good.

One such item is the June 1985 report of the Illinois Fair Schools Coalition on their research on retentions as a reform response (Smith and Shepard, 1985).

The report, which gives forty citations as sources for their study, comes to a startling conclusion: ". . . a substantial body of research about the effects of retention programs indicates clearly that **RETENTION IS AN ENORMOUSLY COSTLY PRACTICE THAT DOESN'T WORK**" (Emphasis theirs).

The following is their summary of findings:

- Research studies indicate that low-achieving students who are held back in school do worse than students with similar records who are promoted.
- Research studies indicate that retention increases the dropout rate and would undermine current efforts to keep students in school.
- Retention coupled with special remedial help is a false solution. Often, promised special help isn't provided, but even when it is, retained students do not do significantly better than promoted students with similar profiles. The ineffectiveness of retention, when it involves massive expensive doses of remedial education, was most recently demonstrated by the failure of the Promotional Gates Program in New York City.
- The students most likely to be retained are poor, minority and handicapped students. Since they are hurt rather than helped by retention, retention constitutes a massive assault on equal educational opportunity.
- A single test score is a particularly inappropriate means for deciding who will be held back. Often two or three wrong answers spell the difference between being promoted and staying in the same grade for another year.
- Retention programs cost enormous amounts of money. One detailed cost analysis of the program being proposed for Illinois estimates annual costs as being between $392 million and $436 million per year. This is

> more than the state's political leaders indicate will be available for all aspects of the proposed educational reform package.

The Illinois Fair School Coalition proposes that extensive retentions be abandoned as an educational response and replaced with another alternative, *prevention*.

In lieu of massive retentions, they propose two short-term responses and four reform strategies. The two short-term responses are:

- Summer school
- Promotion with remediation

The four reform strategies are:

- Early childhood education
- Effective school and classroom practices
- Early remediation
- Multi-grade groupings

It is certain that a similar research effort in Texas would result in similar findings on the extent, effects, cost, and effectiveness of retention as a reform measure.

MASSACHUSETTS FOCUSES ON GRADE RETENTION

1990

Concerned with the growing problems of overage children in the schools of Massachusetts, the Commonwealth initiated a study on retention in grade. Under the direction of the Massachusetts Board of Education, an extensive and exhaustive study was conducted by a team from the department of education, school personnel and other experts in the field (Massachusetts Board of Education, 1990).

Interest in this topic has increased in Massachusetts, Texas and virtually every state in the country as a result of mounting evidence on the relationship between grade retention and school dropouts. Intercultural Development Research Association (IDRA)'s research on school dropouts indicates that one retention in grade, resulting in a student being one year overage for grade, doubles the propensity for the student dropping out of school; more than one retention in the school life of a student just about guarantees that the student will drop out of school prior to completion of the twelfth grade.

The Massachusetts study notes that the high retention rate in the United States is two to eight times higher than that of other industrialized nations. The study also notes increases in retention rates in urban districts and in the early grades. The study states:

> In some districts up to 15–20 percent of kindergarten and first graders were recommended for retention, and up to 25-35 percent of ninth graders.

By far the most interesting aspect of the report is the contrasting of research findings with assumptions about retention made by the public and school personnel. The chapter contrasting assumptions with reality concludes with the following summary:

> In reviewing the research, overwhelming evidence is presented that widespread use of grade retention is not an effective practice in raising student achievement. On the contrary, grade retention may retard academic progress, undermine student self-esteem, and ultimately contribute to a student's decision to drop out of school. Those who continue to retain pupils at grade level do so despite cumulative research evidence showing that the potential for negative effects consistently outweighs positive outcomes. As with many other school practices which sort students, grade retention impacts disproportionately upon low-income and minority students, and, in most cases, reduces their future opportunities to lead productive lives. Consequently, schools should consider the weight of the evidence against grade retention prior to retaining any child.

The following are five assumptions about retentions commonly made, summaries of research findings and excerpts from the Massachusetts research study:

ASSUMPTION ONE:

> *Grade retention improves academic achievement by focusing upon the mastery of sequential basic skills and by giving students an extra year to master academic course work.*

What the Research Shows:

A. No evidence suggests that grade retention for low-achieving students promotes academic achievement more than promotion.

> Over one-hundred studies and six major literature reviews have been conducted on the effects of grade retention, and not one has found that grade retention is more beneficial than promotion for low-achieving students.

B. Schools are not able to accurately predict which students will benefit most from grade retention.

> . . . educators have not been able to predict with any degree of accuracy or consistency which students actually will benefit from this (retention) practice. Thus, schools are retaining students without any sound or reliable evidence that the retention will benefit the student.

C. In most cases, the type of instruction delivered to retained students may hinder, rather than enhance, their achievement rate.

> Rarely do retained students receive a new program of instruction and curriculum tailored to the student's learning style and strengths and geared to accelerating achievement. This lack of instructional response often leads to student boredom and ultimately retards academic progress for many retained students.

D. Grade retention represents a grouping arrangement that is not helpful to many students.

> Essentially, grade retention is a form of ability grouping, in that low-achieving students are held back a grade and placed with younger students who are thought to be closer to their achievement levels. The research concludes, however, that ability grouping retards the academic progress and negatively influences the affective development of low-ability grouped students, and can result in these students receiving an inferior education.

E. Retention coupled with remediation generally is not successful in bringing students back up to grade-appropriate academic achievement.

> Too often, promises of remediation go unfulfilled. Rarely do retained students receive consistent and substantial instructional support during their retained year. . . .
>
> Despite these [New York City Public Schools] impressive resources, retained students achieved no better than their promoted peers. On the other hand, the largest academic gains by low-achieving students have occurred when students have been promoted and provided with instructional support.

F. The harmful effects of grade retention upon achievement levels increase over time. This results in a knowledge gap, which widens with each successive year, between students who have been retained in grade and their promoted peers.

> Rarely are retained students promoted back to their age-appropriate grade level. Thus, a cycle of failure is created, and most retained students spend the rest of their academic careers unsuccessfully trying to catch up to their grade-appropriate peers.

ASSUMPTION TWO:

> *The self-esteem personal adjustment, academic confidence, and motivation of retained students increases as they are placed in academic settings in which they become one of the high-performing students.*

What the Research Shows:

No evidence exists that the social and psychological adjustment of retained students is better than that of promoted students, while substantial evidence exists that the self-esteem of retained students suffers.

> The retention is viewed by most students as punishment, regardless of how it is presented. In fact, students have ranked grade retention as the third most feared life experience, behind blindness and the death of a parent.

ASSUMPTION THREE:

> *Enrolling children in kindergarten or first grade a year later than the eligible age enhances a child's academic achievement and ability to succeed, and gives children a competitive advantage over other classmates.*

What the Research Shows:

There are no long-term academic benefits to enrolling children in kindergarten a year later than their eligible age.

> Any differences in achievement scores based upon age differences [for children placed in kindergarten or first grade a year late] disappear by the end of the third grade.
>
> . . . educators charge that this practice creates inequities for low-income families. Most poor families cannot afford to enroll their children a year later than their age eligibility due to day care and other costs. Consequently . . . the younger students tend to be low-income and the older students tend to be more affluent. Such a trend creates classroom dynamics where low-income children are the ones most likely to be retained.

ASSUMPTION FOUR:

Transition classes provide low-achieving students with a more appropriate learning environment in which to succeed and catch up academically with their grade-appropriate peers while avoiding the stigma of being retained in class.

What the Research Shows:

In reality, most transition classes are no different than grade retention.

Transition classes are classes for low-achieving students that are viewed as a step between two grades—usually between kindergarten and first grade, and more recently, between eighth and ninth grade. Transition classes are usually characterized by a smaller class size and a basic skill focus.

In most cases, transition room students achieve no better than their retained counterparts and rarely rejoin their grade-appropriate peers. While short-term gains may be greater in some cases, the achievement advantage disappears over time. . . . Interestingly, promoted students who received more individualized reading instruction have achieved at higher rates than comparable students who were placed in transition rooms.

While most transition room students do not benefit academically, they do suffer psychologically. Transition room students have been found to have lower self-esteem and lower self-confidence than comparable low-achieving students who were promoted.

ASSUMPTION FIVE:

Schools that retain high numbers of students are effective schools because they have high standards for academic achievement, thus ensuring the value of the district's high school diploma.

What the Research Shows:

A. No evidence suggests that students in high-retaining schools fare better academically than students in lower-retaining schools.

The average standardized achievement test scores in schools with little or no retention are equal to those in high-retaining schools.

B. Students who are retained in grade have an increased chance of dropping out of school; thus, high-retaining schools probably have higher dropout rates than low-retaining schools.

C. Promotional "gate" tests (or basing promotion on passing a standardized test) may merely result in the inappropriate retention of students, rather than raising overall academic achievement.

D. Grade retention may in fact be a practice that discriminates according to socio-economic background, race, and language.

> In Massachusetts, Black and Hispanic students are three and one-half times more likely to be recommended for retention than white students. Such trends question whether appropriate educational experiences are being offered to these groups of students.

E. Grade retention is a costly and ineffective practice of addressing the problem of low-achieving students.

RECOMMENDATIONS:

Unlike many other studies, the Massachusetts report follows up its conclusions on the negative aspects of grade retentions with an abundant list of recommendations for alternative strategies. The recommendations are preceded by a warning against simplistic approaches based on limited alternatives:

> Rather than adopting merely one of these recommendations, districts are encouraged to adopt a comprehensive approach that combines a variety of strategies that best address student needs.

The following are the general headings in the section on recommendations in the report:

- *Reaffirming the School and District Mission*
- *Recommendations For Assessment and Planning*
- *Recommendations For Curriculum and Instruction*
- *Recommendations For Grouping of Students*
- *Recommendations For Promotion Policies*
- *Recommendations For Staff Development*
- *Recommendations For Student and Family Support*

Other chapters in the Massachusetts study provide examples of nationally-recognized exemplary school programs which have been successful in reducing grade retentions, statewide data on students recommended for grade retention in Massachusetts, an annotated bibliography, and footnotes citing specific research studies used in the compilation of this report.

> (The report provides a telephone number, 617-770-7589, which can be called for additional information.)

IMPLICATIONS

The conclusions drawn by the Massachusetts study are not new nor unusual. Similar findings have been obtained in research studies on grade retention for the past thirty years. The Massachusetts study is much more comprehensive and thorough than previous efforts.

What is very unusual is that the practice of extensive retention in grade has continued and even has been exacerbated in recent years, in spite of an overwhelming body of knowledge showing it to be expensive, dysfunctional and even counterproductive.

It is ironic that in Texas, the number of retentions has been deliberately increased by reform efforts of the Texas Legislature. House Bill 72, enacted in 1984, mandated increased retention rates in Texas schools, making this piece of legislation one of the most counterproductive efforts in the history of education in Texas.

It is even more ironic that the Texas Legislature has spent so much time and effort addressing the two biggest educational problems in Texas, school dropouts and inadequate financing, when the school dropout problem was exacerbated by state-mandated retentions, and the state is expending over $1 billion in support of grade retentions.

Without exception, every study on grade retentions has concluded that it is a very expensive response that does not work. The Massachusetts report provides ample evidence about the inadequacy of grade retentions as a response to the poor performance of children. It also provides some interesting guidelines for the cost of this ineffective response.

Research studies indicate that the average cost of grade retentions in the United States is 8 percent of the cost of education. In Texas no data on the number or percentages of retentions has been found, but since retentions have been encouraged and legislatively mandated it can be safely assumed that the retention rate is much higher than for the country as a whole. Since most of the students being retained are in "at risk" categories, the cost of repeating a grade is higher than the average cost of education in the state.

Using the very conservative estimate of the retention rate being 8 percent in Texas, this means that some 264,000 of the state's 3.3 million students are being retained each year. The repetition of the year, which has been estimated to cost $4,000 per pupil in 1990-91, will cost the state of Texas an estimated $1.056 billion. Over one billion dollars in state resources needed for the improvement of educational opportunity, as well as for providing for the cost of school finance adequacy and equity, is being expended in an educational response which nationwide research shows does not work.

EARLY-GRADE RETENTION IN TEXAS

In July 1990, the State Board of Education took a positive first step in addressing the question of retention in Texas. It adopted a rule prohibiting the retention of children in pre-school or kindergarten classes. The newly enacted rule has been placed on the October agenda of the State Board of Education for reconsideration because State Board members and the Texas Education staff were flooded with contacts from teachers and administrators upset about the new rule.

In view of the obvious undesirable effects of grade retention cited in all educational research, why are Texas teachers and administrators so supportive of this practice? This is a difficult question to answer. The Massachusetts Board of Education concludes that "While the vast majority of school practitioners believe that grade retention is an effective practice, rarely do they examine whether this practice does, in fact, promote accelerated academic achievement for low-achieving students."

Rigidity of curriculum content at grade levels may account for some of the support for early-grade retentions. Instead of adapting school curriculum to the developmental characteristics of the child, the schools find it easier to adapt the children (through retentions as well as other means) to a uniform program offering.

Another reason for the popularity of grade retentions is continued dependence on student deficit models to account for the massive failure of the schools. The Massachusetts report states, "Implicit in the practice of grade retention is the notion that the student is to blame for failing to achieve." Grade retention reinforces the erroneous concept that curriculum and methodology are adequate for all students, the failure to perform is placed on the victim.

And finally, facetious as it may sound, educators favor grade retentions, and especially early-grade retentions, because it allows the school to red-shirt kids out of the alternate year state-mandated testing program. Educators erroneously conclude that if the student is kept out of the testing program until he/she is one year older, student performance will appear better on this measure of accountability.

TRANSITIONAL PROGRAMS

In recent years a new strategy has been implemented to deal with students considered by the school to be too immature for first grade. This strategy consists of placing the student in a "transition" class for one year prior to enrollment in the first grade.

Actually the strategy is not new, but merely resurrected. Some years ago, prior to the advent of bilingual and English as a Second Language programs, it was common practice to place limited English-proficient children in "Pre-primer" programs for one year to prepare them for entrance into the first grade. The practice was mostly abandoned when bilingual education programs demonstrated that automatic retention and overage could be circumvented.

My first awareness of the new transition programs was when a parent requested my opinion on whether his child should be placed in such a program. My inquiry into the transition programs led me to the conclusion that the practice is worse than grade retentions in that the decision to retain the student in the first grade (I find it hard to accept the euphemism "transitioned to the first grade") was made *before* the student was allowed an opportunity to perform in class. In the case in question, a recommendation had been made to place the student in a transition class on the basis of the student "appearing immature" and the suspicion being validated by a counselor's evaluation of the picture of a man drawn by the child in a Florence Goodenough type of test.

An inquiry on the number of children from the previous year's transition class indicated that not one of the students had been placed in the second grade at the end of the first year.

The growth of transition classes is difficult to understand in the light of the Massachusetts report that most transition classes are no different than grade retentions.

CONCLUSION

The most interesting aspect of the Massachusetts study on retentions is not the findings, recommendations and conclusions, but rather the process of taking educational assumptions and matching them to educational research *before* making policy decisions.

How nice it would be if the Texas Legislature had looked into the vast amount of research on school dropouts before following Ross Perot's simplistic recommendation that the performance of students in Texas schools could be drastically improved by massive retentions.

If grade retentions are at least partially accountable for subsequent school dropouts, and the cost of grade retentions is financially prohibitive, it would behoove other states to address this problem. The following recommendations should be considered:

1. Include the number of students retained at the end of each year in the annual school district performance reports in order to assess the extent of the problem and provide baseline data for the evaluation of subsequent efforts to address the problem.

Data gathered should be broken down by gender, race/ethnicity, home language and economic class to insure that aggregate data does not overlook certain types of at-risk students. A 1983 retention study conducted by the Austin school district found varying percentages of retention among the various campuses, with some having less than 1 percent and other campuses with rates as high as 15 percent (Austin Independent School District, 1983).

2. Establish a goal for reducing the number of retentions in grade in Texas schools. If the retention rate is indeed as high as 8 percent, and research consistently shows that more than three-quarters of students retained do no better or even worse when repeating a grade, future retention rates should not exceed 2 percent of the student population. This should produce a savings of about $750 million dollars a year in the cost of grade repetition.

3. Establish a mechanism for determining whether a student should be retained or promoted to the next grade. Such mechanisms are now in place for determining admission and dismissal from special education programs (Admission, Review and Dismissal [ARD] Committee), and for placement and existing bilingual education programs (Language Proficiency Assessment Committee [LPAC]). As in ARD and LPAC committees, the group should represent teachers, parents, administrators, counselors and other specialized staff.

4. Establish criteria for determining whether a student should be retained or promoted to the next grade. Decisions should be made on multiple criteria rather than solely on teacher recommendations.

5. Establish a retention policy for school districts to follow. Some innovative districts in Texas have already developed model policies on retention.

6. Develop and implement an accelerated learning plan for students who are retained lest the retention lead to further underperformance as is now the case with more than three-fourths of the students being retained.

7. Develop strategies for addressing the learning needs of underperforming children in keeping with the recommendations presented in the Massachusetts study and summarized above. Strategies should address both underperforming students who are retained and those promoted to a higher grade.

The successful implementation of a state program can impact on the cost of education, improve educational opportunities for children, diminish academic and behavioral problems, and ameliorate the number of students dropping out of the schools prior to graduation.

TEXAS LEGISLATURE REVISES RETENTION POLICY

1991

The November 1990 issue of the Intercultural Development Research Association (IDRA) *Newsletter* featured an article on grade retention. This article included the findings of a Massachusetts' nation-wide study of retentions in grade and presented the following summary:

> In reviewing the research, overwhelming evidence that widespread use of grade retention is not an effective practice in raising student achievement. On the contrary, grade retention may retard academic progress, undermine student self-esteem, and ultimately contribute to a student's decision to drop out of school.

House Bill 1314 introduced by Representative Ciro Rodriquez and carried in the Senate by Senator Gonzalo Barrientos replaces a simplistic retention policy established under House Bill 72 in 1984, which stated, "A student who has not maintained a grade average for a school year equivalent to at least 70 on a scale of 100 may not be advanced from one grade level to the next." Solely using a grade of 70 on teacher-made tests as the determinant of success or failure is the epitome of irresponsibility. As any student of measurement and evaluation can attest, teacher-made tests are notorious in their lack of reliability and validity. Test difficulty varies from school to school, teacher to teacher, and for each teacher from one day to the next. A grade of 70 is as meaningless as a distance measured with a rubber band.

The new legislative policy on retentions should not be viewed as a return to the old policy of social promotions. The alternative to retention is the improvement of instructional practice and increased student learning. As long as inadequacies and inefficiencies in instructional practice can be perpetuated by blaming and punishing the victim, there is little hope for reform and improvement of our educational institutions.

Opposition to past retention policy stemmed from three problems: (1) retention does not produce improved student performance, (2) a strong correlation has been established between retention in grade and school dropouts, and (3) it is a prohibitively expensive approach to poor student performance. All studies of students retained in a grade, including students retained through placement in euphemistic "transitional classes," indicate that one-half of the students retained do no better the second time around, and one-fourth of all students retained actually do worse the second year.

Studies of school dropouts conclude that students retained once have double the propensity for dropping out than students never retained. Students who have been retained two or more times are almost certain to drop out of school. A Texas Education Agency (TEA) study on school dropouts found that 70 percent of all students who dropped out of school last year had been retained at least once prior to dropping out. Ninety percent of the students who had been retained twice dropped out of school. It is difficult to determine the cost of school retentions since no data exists on the number of students retained in the state. A conservative estimate is that the cost of school retentions in Texas is over $1 billion a year.

The Rodriquez/Barrientos law contains four provisions which may not only reduce the number of students retained and provide a massive financial savings to the state, but should lead to a drastic improvement in educational practice.

1. House Bill 1314 requires school systems to maintain records on the number and reasons for retention and submit them to the state education agency every two years.
2. School districts may now use multiple criteria when making a decision to retain or promote a student. The new criteria may include:
   - A student's overall grade average;
   - Grade averages in individual subjects;
   - Extenuating circumstances which may account for inconsistent, poor student performance; and
   - Any other factors the district considers important.
3. Before deciding to retain a student from one grade to the next, a district may consider one or more alternatives for providing the student remedial assistance, including:
   - An extended school day;
   - An extended school year;
   - Specialized tutorial support, including peer and cross-age tutoring, student mentoring; and
   - Summer programs.
4. The new law makes special provisions for dyslexic students under rules to be adopted by the Texas State Board of Education.

In conclusion, the enactment of House Bill 1314 is a giant step toward providing a professional basis for educational decisions of severe importance to the students involved.

BIBLIOGRAPHY

Austin Independent School District, *A Matter of Time: Retention and Promotion*, Austin, 1983.

Massachusetts Board of Education, *Structuring Schools for Student Success: A Focus on Grade Retention*, Boston, April 1990.

Smith, Mary and Lorrie Shepard, *Illinois Fair Schools Coalition Report*, Chicago, June 1985.

Intercultural Development Research Association (IDRA), *Newsletter*, San Antonio, November 1981, August 1985, September 1985, November 1985, November 1990, August 1991.

DISCUSSION QUESTIONS

1. Develop an inventory of the data presented to support arguments *against* retention in grade. What data can you present to argue *for* retention in grade.
2. The author comments that "it is a mystery why retention is still pursued as an educational response to poor performance." What attitudes held by educators and the general public in general are brought to the support of retention policies? Which of these attitudes do you share?
3. Develop strategies that you as a professional educator can employ to challenge attitudes in support of present retention policies.
4. The author charges that some educators fail to distinguish between poor student performance and poor school performance. Outline program and instructional strategies designed to remedy poor school performance in multicultural settings. Include a rationale for each strategy presented.

6

Early Childhood Education

PREFACE

I became a believer in childhood education during the early stages of my professional career with minority and disadvantaged children. My first experience in early childhood education was fifty-eight years ago. My mother enrolled me in a kindergarten program at St. Peter Parochial School in Laredo, Texas, hoping that I would learn some English before starting the first grade.

Before the development of bilingual programs in schools, Spanish-speaking people who could afford pre-school tried to provide this experience for their children. The League of Latin American Citizens (LULAC) established and provided financial support for English development experiences in an educational movement for disadvantaged children called "The School of 400." The purpose of these programs was to develop a basic English language vocabulary of 400 words, prior to enrollment in the first grade.

The advent of President Lyndon B. Johnson's War on Poverty provided a government subsidized pre-school program, Headstart. This program was much more sophisticated than prior privately funded efforts. Headstart provided programs for the physical, intellectual, emotional and social development of disadvantaged children giving them a "headstart" for enrollment in the first grade.

The startling results of the Ypsilanti Program and the writings of Jerome S. Bruner and other psychologists made me an early believer and supporter of early childhood education (Bruner, 1961; Weikart, 1971). In recent years, I have concluded that too much emphasis is placed in preparing the child for a standard instructional program in the first grade. Not enough emphasis is placed on making the first grade program more flexible to accommodate children with differing individual and group characteristics. However, I still support the concept of early intervention and stimulation for maximum growth and development.

My interest in early childhood education was heightened in 1967 when I went to work for the Southwest Educational Development Laboratory (SEDL) in Austin. SEDL pioneered the development of bilingual and early childhood education materials and methodologies for minority children. One of my first tasks at SEDL was the development of a handbook for use as a guide in providing pre-school programs for Mexican-American children.

One aspect of my responsibilities at SEDL during the 1968-69 school year included assisting the San Antonio and Edgewood School Districts in the conceptualization of an early childhood center. This concept would be used as the key element in a Model Cities educational program. Both districts decided against the implementation of the program. But in the summer of 1969 I was selected as superintendent of the Edgewood School District in San Antonio. The early childhood education center became the key element of the Edgewood Model Cities program.

This program was one of the most successful activities during my very successful tenure in the Edgewood School District. It became a national showcase. In 1972 when I obtained Model Cities funding for a physical plant, community, teachers, administrators and Richard Moore, the architect, collaborated on the building of one of the most unique educational structures in the country. The entire building was dedicated to early childhood programs, with facilities for research, training and materials development. When the facilities opened in 1992, at the request of the community, the Edgewood board named it the José A. Cárdenas Early Childhood Center.

Not surprisingly, the educational leadership of the state of Texas took issue with the nomenclature and ruled that the school was ineligible for state or state-allocated federal funds because the name of the school did not carry the designation "school." It was necessary to change the name to "José A. Cárdenas School" in keeping with the State Department of Education's interpretation of State Board of Education regulations. Ironically, this intervention in the renaming of the school was the only help I received from the state in the operation of this unique program.

After leaving the Edgewood School District my interest and support for early childhood education carried over to my new position at Intercultural Development Research Association (IDRA). One of the first three programs at IDRA was the development of a bilingual early childhood education program. The organization has had an early childhood education component ever since, with and without external sources of funds. IDRA produced *Amanecer*, one of the first bilingual early childhood programs in the country. (IDRA, 1979) This instructional program was subsequently revised and is currently distributed as *Nuevo Amanecer* by the National Textbook Company (IDRA, 1985).

In 1978 I was appointed by President Jimmy Carter to the United States Commission on the International Year of the Child. The Commission produced a comprehensive national agenda for children emphasizing the need for pre-school programs for all children.

IDRA was also involved in the development of Texas legislation for the establishment of public school pre-school programs. Unfortunately, upon implementation, the schools have stressed academic content rather than the child development emphasis of Headstart programs. The article, "Early Childhood Education in the Public Schools," which I wrote and was published in the January 1992 issue of the IDRA *Newsletter*, describes the effect of this academic emphasis.

HAPPY NEW INTERNATIONAL YEAR OF THE CHILD

1979

In 1976, the United Nations General Assembly proclaimed 1979 as the International Year of the Child, encouraging countries around the world to set aside this one-year period to focus attention on the needs of all children.

The United States responded to this program by the appointment of a U.S. National Commission to evaluate the status of American children and give attention to programs and policies which will enhance the well-being of children.

One of the first tasks of the U.S. Commission was to collect information about American children. Although many children in this country enjoy the fruits of our bountiful land, it was immediately evident that many American children are the victims of indifference, poverty, and neglect. Frequently, the problems that beset children cut across social, cultural and economic lines, touching all classes of children; problems are not limited to the poor or minority child.

Initial findings of the U.S. Commission reveal startling statistics concerning the status of children in this country. There are approximately 66 million citizens of the United States under the age of eighteen, comprising almost one-third of the population. Of that total number, many are experiencing problems with health, nutrition, pregnancy, abuse and other forms of neglect.

Analyses of similar information for Texas indicate similar problems exist in this state. A recent publication by Jeannette Watson, Director of the Early Childhood Development Division of the Texas Department of Community Affairs, provides sufficient food for thought concerning the status of children in Texas. It is immediately evident that there are neglected needs and plenty of room for state and local improvement.

In light of startling evidence of children's needs, and in keeping with the international, national, state and local dedication to the International Year of the Child, Intercultural Development Research Association (IDRA) renews its commitment to the improvement of educational opportunities for all children. During the International Year of the Child, 1979, we will rededicate our resources, our energies and our attention to the neglected needs of all children until the most pressing problems are resolved.

IDRA asks all concerned citizens to join together in 1979 in support of programs, policies, and efforts which will enhance the well-being of all children.

AN OPEN LETTER TO OUR READERS

1979

During the last decade we have seen tremendous strides in early childhood education programs, particularly in those directed at low-income children. We have seen, and have been involved in, a continuous quest for curricular materials designed for Spanish-speaking children. As educators, we have sought materials which honor and respect these children, their language and their culture, while meticulously attending to the developmental needs that Spanish-speakers share with all children.

Building on the work of many people over the last decade, Intercultural Development Research Association (IDRA) has developed a bilingual/multicultural curriculum model for use in early childhood education programs. We believe that the IDRA AMANECER model, *A Multicultural Action Network for Early Childhood Education Resources*, represents an important refinement of curriculum development efforts for Spanish-speaking children (IDRA, 1976).

The *AMANECER* curriculum has been developed with the practitioner point of view. It represents an operationalization of sound early childhood theory. Throughout the *AMANECER* development and pilot-test phases, we sought to develop a product which works, not only with the highly skilled, but with the teacher who wishes to become highly skilled. We sought to develop a product that does not grow old and cold on a shelf, but that is fully utilized and is revitalized by people's creativity and the dynamic growth of culture. *AMANECER*, therefore, is a process-oriented, personalized model designed to develop teachers of children and not teachers of curriculum.

As you analyze the specific needs of your program, your teachers and your children, I encourage you to analyze early childhood education policy in this country. I encourage you to examine all of the existing curricular and training responses to young children's needs. I encourage you also to examine *AMANECER*. After a three-year developmental effort, the *AMANECER* Bilingual/Multicultural Pre-school Curriculum Model is available for dissemination.

AMANECER is a Spanish word which means the beginning of a new day—a new day of learning, a new day of respect for children's culture and language, a new day of hope, and a head start for their future. If you believe we can work together to fulfill the promise of *AMANECER*, we would be pleased to hear from you.

José A. Cárdenas
IDRA Executive Director

THE INTERNATIONAL YEAR OF THE CHILD: A BEGINNING

1980

On April 21, President Carter received the report of the United States National Commission on the International Year of the Child (IYC). In the letter of transmittal which accompanied the report, Commission Chairperson Jean C. Young stated:

> We are not calling our report a final report. There was nothing final about the Year of the Child; it was only a beginning. In these pages we share with you some of the many marvelous efforts of individuals and groups to observe the Year of the Child. The challenge is to continue what they have begun (U.S. National Commission on the International Year of the Child, 1980).

The report is a compilation of the IYC Commission's year-long study, during which the commission worked to define and stimulate discussion about children's needs, increase public awareness of these needs, and organize action for them. Through White House briefings, workshops, public forums, and reports from state/local governments and national organizations, the commission sought to become the eyes and ears of the American people on issues affecting children.

The following discussion of the commission's findings on the status of minority children in the United States is excerpted from *Agenda for Change*, part two of the report.

Although our major concern this year has been the fundamental qualities that unite all children and families in the United States, we have also reflected on the racial and cultural diversity of this society and on the special contributions and special problems of minority group families and children.

The minority population is, of course, many populations. These populations consist of 24.8 million Blacks; 12 million Hispanics, not counting the residents of the territory of Puerto Rico, 3 million Asian-Americans and Pacific Islanders, 827,000 American Indians and Alaskan Natives; and numerous other, smaller minority populations. Even within each group, there is striking diversity. For example, of the 12 million Hispanics (who are also called Latinos), 7 million are of Mexican origin, 1.7 million are Puerto Ricans living in the continental United States, 774,000 are Cubans, and the remaining 2.5 million come from a variety of other Spanish origins. The Asian-Americans and Pacific Islanders include Chinese, Japanese, Koreans, Filipinos, Vietnamese, Hawaiians, Guamanians, Samoans, Laotians, Thais, Cambodians and others who differ in religion and language as well as in place of origin. The American Indians and Alaskan Natives represent well over 150 separate tribes, organizations, and communities.

Although we have cited figures, the numbers in the country's minority populations are difficult to estimate because, for various reasons, the census undercounts these groups. For instance, the United States Census Bureau acknowledges that as much as 7.7 percent of the

Black population went uncounted in 1970. Beyond baseline population counts, data on the facts of life of minority children and families are, to a great extent, either uncollected, unanalyzed, or unpublished. Currently, data on the populations and conditions of Hispanics, American Indians and Alaskan Natives, Asian-Americans, and Pacific Islanders are poor to nonexistent.

Over the course of this year, we heard a great deal about what it means to be a minority child in the United States. Again and again, we saw how minority children and families have benefited from the unique strength and human resources of their cultural and ethnic communities and traditions. But we also saw evidence of the discrimination that has set the context in which minority children grow up.

... *Perhaps the greatest obstacle that many minority children in the U.S. face is the poverty of their families*. The proportion of Black families with incomes less than $5,000 is almost three times the proportion of white families; for Hispanics, the proportion is almost twice that for the rest of the white population. Minority adults suffer a higher unemployment rate than do whites, earn less than non-minority workers, and are more likely than whites to be employed in hazardous or unsafe occupations. A young Black college graduate has the same chance of being unemployed as does a white high school dropout; a Black high school graduate has the same chance of being unemployed as a white grade school dropout. All of this, translated into family income, means that minorities are less able than others to purchase health care or medicine, adequate food, decent housing, and services such as counseling or baby-sitting for their families and children. These aspects of living in a family with low income have a cumulative effect on most minority children's present lives and future hopes.

The historical denial of equal opportunity to minority children persists in the present. A few facts highlight this reality:

- Among children aged one to four, minority children die at a rate 70 percent higher than white children; minority children aged five to nine die at a rate 40 percent higher than white children.
- American Indian children are twice as likely to die from heart disease, influenza, and pneumonia than other children.
- For every two Black high school graduates, one Black child drops out of school. The same rate holds for Hispanic children. For every ten American Indian children who graduate, eight drop out. Black children are more than twice as likely to be suspended from school and to receive corporal punishment in school as are white children.
- Black and Hispanic children are more likely than white children to grow up in a female-headed family.

The personal experiences of individuals often tell an even more powerful story. Last year, we heard about a Sioux Indian teenager who was pregnant. When she went into labor her friends took her to a city hospital's delivery room. Upon arrival, she was told that her Indian health card was not acceptable at the hospital and that she should find an Indian Health Care Hospital or go back to the hospital on the reservation. Enroute back to the reservation hospital, she started to hemorrhage. By the time she arrived, she was critically ill and the baby was dead.

A pervasive lack of recognition and respect for cultural and language diversity destroys children's sense of identity and acceptance. Nowhere around them in the mainstream culture are minority children, no matter from what background, likely to find material from which to build a positive self-image. The printed and electronic media do little to depict people from their backgrounds as they really are. Television may be the most obvious offender, but printed materials, books, and textbooks are no better.

Minority children often encounter attitudes and practices hostile to retaining their own culture and language. Few services, for example, are offered in a language other than English. An illustration of the challenge to a child who does not speak English comfortably was related to us by a young Chinese immigrant:

> Imagine for a moment that you have lost your power of speech and that it will take a great deal of effort on your part to regain it. At that same time, in order to survive and carry on your daily activities you have to communicate. Sign language, body language and pantomime will work to a degree, but how can you tell someone in sign language that George Washington was the first President of the United States? If you can imagine this perhaps you can feel for the immigrant child who has to deal with the total adjustment of being uprooted and transplanted in a new country, but also with the sudden loss of almost all of his ability to communicate.

Government policies do not respond to the diversity of minority populations nor to their individual characteristics. Although it is undeniable that minority populations differ greatly, government programs do not sufficiently reflect or respond to their differences. The strengths of each community are neither recognized, nor utilized. Health care services for American Indians do not draw on traditional healing methods. In immigrant populations, programs for translating and interpreting differences between native cultures and practices and the American approach in a variety of areas are needed but rarely exist. For example, the situation of the 250,000 refugees from Southeast Asia with an estimated 40 percent children, is unique; apart from leaving their home countries far behind, these refugees have undergone traumatic experiences of war, of risking their lives in the process of escape, and of losing family members. Services designed for this population must be responsive to these experiences.

Present assistance programs tend to undermine populations for which they were originally intended. For example, policies that deny services to undocumented children force families to choose between getting the help they need and risking involvement with immigration officials. American Indian families often must send their children away from home for schooling because no school has been provided nearby. Some foster care regulations deny reimbursement costs to agencies that place children with relatives or extended family members, so children are often sent to live with strangers when the extended family wanted to keep them.

In December 1979, we convened a special conference on minority children and families to learn more about the situation of minority children. This was an exciting undertaking in which representatives of different minority groups met with a common focus on children. One hundred and twenty participants attended. Representatives met in general sessions, as well as separating into various caucuses. Workshops were offered featuring topics such as intergroup cooperation, strategies for making public agencies responsive to minority children's concerns, and current legislation.

What emerged from these intensive two days of deliberation and debate was a fresh picture of the special and diverse needs of minority children and a recognition that by working together minority groups can address those needs for all minority children more effectively. Those who attended insisted that the continuing racial and cultural discrimination that victimize minority children and families within our education, health care, juvenile justice, child welfare, social services, welfare, and employment systems must be eliminated. Toward that goal, participants put forward several specific principles for action:

- Accurate up-to-date and reliable data on minority groups must be collected while protecting the privacy rights of individuals.

Good data is essential for obtaining appropriate services. Poor data can underplay the need altogether. Therefore, federal agencies must gather, analyze, and publish information on the needs of diverse minority group children and on how well those needs are being met. In particular, increased data on conditions of Hispanics, American Indian and Asian American children are required. Moreover, major reporting systems should break down each group into its component populations. Unless differences between and within minority groups are known and documented, tailoring services to specific needs will be impossible. For example, the Census Bureau recently reported the percentage of children who were under eighteen and living with a single parent; the report was broken down by Hispanic sub-population groups. There were significant differences among these groups, with 15 percent of Mexican-American children living in single-parent families, as contrasted with over 45 percent of Puerto Rican children. Clearly, the needs of these groups differ.

- The design and implementation of programs must recognize, respect, and build upon the contributions and strengths of minority families and communities. Programs to help minority children and families must have strong minority participation and direction and be sensitive to the varying needs, languages, cultures, traditions, values, and informal support systems of the minority populations being served.

- Greater minority-group unity in advocating for improved policies for minority children is needed, focusing in particular on the budgetary and resource allocation processes and calling for increased funding for programs that will meet the needs of minority children.

- Internal and cross-cutting communications coordination, and action networks must be established within and among diverse minority groups in order to use the political process effectively to achieve specific goals for minority children. Minority communities must rely on themselves, their votes, their strengths in ensuring that their children's needs are visible and responded to by policymakers and political leaders.

NOTES

1. "Population Characteristics," U.S. Department of Commerce, U.S. Census Bureau, Washington, D.C. April 1979.
2. Public Information Office, Bureau of Indian Affairs, Telephone Interview, Thomas Oxendine, Jr. December 19, 1979.

3. *Health United States, 1979*, U.S. Department of Health, Education and Welfare, Public Health Service, Office of Health Research, Statistics and Technology, Washington, D.C., 1979.

4. Ibid.

5. *The Social and Economic Status of the Black Population in the United States: An Historical View, 1790-1978*, U.S. Department of Commerce, U.S. Census Bureau, Current Population Reports/Special Studies Series, P-23, No. 80, Washington, D.C.

6. Children's Defense Fund,"Doctors and dollars are Not Enough," Children's Defense Fund, 1520 New Hampshire Ave., N.W. Washington, D.C. 20036, 1978.

7. "Towards Policies for Children and on Agenda for the Media," Forum, National Council on Children's Television, Winter 1979, vol. 2, No. 1.

8. Edelman, Marina Wright, "The status of Black children in the United States." *Children: Mankind's Greatest Resource*, Congressional Black Caucus, Ninth Annual Legislative Weekend, September 21-22, 1979.

9. Ibid.

10. "National Indian Child Care Conference," Public Forum for National commission on the International Year of the child, 1979 in cooperation with save the Children's Federation, Phoenix, Arizona, November 27-28, 1978. (Information in the commission's unpublished conference file, National Archives.)

11. Sung, Betty Lee. *Transplanted Chinese Children*. Department of HEW, Administration for Children, Youth and Families, under Grant Number 90-C-920, 1979.

TEA PRE-SCHOOL TEXTBOOK ADOPTION: THE LAST STRAW

1986

There has never been any love lost between the Texas Education Agency (TEA) and minority populations in Texas. But, TEA's action on the adoption of textbooks for the State Pre-School Program triggered an unprecedented strong, loud, and negative response from minorities across the State.

In a letter addressed to the chairman of the State Board of Education (SBOE), Jose Rodriguez, President of the Rio Grande Valley School Board Association representing thirty-one school districts, charged the Texas State Board with blatant disregard of the educational needs of Hispanic pre-kindergarten students. "Once again, we realize that we cannot always rely on state officials to be sensitive to the needs of our growing Hispanic student population," stated Rodriguez.

A separate resolution was drafted admonishing the state education agency about testing practices which may be unfair to language minority children and undermine the state's bilingual education program.

The action of the Rio Grande Valley group closely followed the enactment of a similar resolution protesting the SBOE's pre-school textbook adoption by the Texas Association for Bilingual Education (TABE).

Both education groups expressed strong support for the sentiments of minority SBOE member, Ms. Mary Helen Berlanga, as expressed in a letter to Jon Brumley, Chairman of the State Board of Education. "The commitment of this Board to the resolvement of problems inherent in the education of these (Hispanic) children is once again questionable."

In a speech to Rio Grande Valley board members and administrators, Ms. Berlanga identified issues having a negative impact on the education of Hispanic children and the failure of TEA to provide support for these children. In addition to the textbook adoption, Ms. Berlanga addressed TEA staffing, the state's dual tracking system, discriminatory testing, and lack of support for minority programs.

Berlanga's presentation, which was interrupted at regular intervals as she tried to hold back tears of frustration, resulted in a standing ovation from the predominantly Hispanic audience.

THE PRE-SCHOOL TEXTBOOK ADOPTION

The Texas Education Agency put out a call for textbooks for the pre-school program for four-year-olds created by House Bill 72. This program is already operational, but no textbooks have been furnished by the state, although most school districts enrolling disadvantaged and limited English-proficient children in the program have purchased instructional materials at local expense.

TEA then appointed a Textbook Committee to review materials and make recommendations to the State Board. The Textbook Committee did not include anyone knowledgeable in early childhood education, nor any Hispanics involved in pre-school programs.

The Textbook Committee's recommendations created a furor among minority educators and teachers of pre-school programs. Though the state program is solely for disadvantaged and limited English-proficient children, none of the choices selected by the committee were developed, nor had any special strengths, for the type of students enrolled in the program. Though the committee could have recommended five sets of materials for adoption, they chose to recommend only three sets of materials. The fourth set of materials in the priority listing compiled by the committee was the *Nuevo Amanecer* program published by the National Textbook Company and developed by Intercultural Development Research Association (IDRA) specifically for minority, disadvantaged, and limited English-proficient populations (IDRA, 1985). The National Textbook Company materials received only one vote less in the committee than the third set recommended for adoption.

Educators from throughout the state took issue with the failure of the Textbook Committee to select any materials which could be used in bilingual and compensatory education programs. Their feeling was that over the years bilingual and compensatory education programs have been hindered by the lack of appropriate materials for the children. The action of the Textbook Committee in not selecting appropriate materials was seen by minority populations as an attempt to undermine these categorical programs.

When the adoption of the pre-school materials came up for a vote in the SBOE meeting, minorities called upon the Board members to reject the recommendations of the Textbook Committee and re-start the textbook selection process. TEA staff defended the recommendations of the Textbook Committee, showing an unbelievable ignorance and lack of sensitivity to the need for materials for the education of minority populations.

The vote of the State Board proceeded along ethnic lines, with minorities (comprising a minority on the Board) voting against the recommendations of the Textbook Committee and all-Anglo Board members voting for the adoption of the three sets recommended by the committee.

TEA STAFFING

Berlanga's criticism of TEA was not limited to the SBOE's textbook adoption. Berlanga identified TEA staffing as a basic problem in the agency's insensitivity to the educational problems of Hispanics. In her address to the Rio Grande school people, as well as in her letter to Brumley, she singled out four persons detrimental to TEA policymaking concerning minority populations. These four TEA staff members were Vickie Bergin (Deputy Commissioner), Tom Anderson (Deputy Commissioner), Henry Perry (Textbook Director) and Grace Grimes (Assistant Commissioner). Berlanga particularly singled out Vickie Bergin because of Bergin's prior testimony in the PPST court case in which she identified the poor performance of minority populations on the Pre-Professional Skills Test as attributed to a low level of intellectual ability. Ms. Bergin then testified before the SBOE on the adequacy of the instructional materials recommended by the Textbook Committee.

CURRICULUM TRACKING

The failure of the new SBOE to address the dual tracking system implemented by the old Board was similarly criticized by Berlanga. This policy allows students to pursue an academic track in Texas high schools which prepares the student for further training in higher education, or an alternative track which becomes an educational dead end. "You are sorting people into these tracks at age 13 . . . the students who are going to hurt the most are the Hispanics," said Berlanga.

TEAMS TESTING

Berlanga also took issue with TEA policy which requires that limited English-proficient children enrolled in bilingual education programs are required to take the TEAMS standardized achievement test prior to their transition to an English curriculum. Teachers, knowing that they will be evaluated on the basis of their students' performances on an all-English test are forced to introduce English language instruction before the students are ready for it. This TEA policy serves to undermine bilingual education programs, in that student achievement, even exceptionally good student achievement, in a bilingual program is deemed unacceptable if it is evaluated only in English-only achievement tests.

The Rio Grande Valley educators expressed concern that the administration of invalid English language tests to non-English dominant students will result in psychical violence to the self-esteem and self-worth of very capable and intelligent students.

OTHER CONCERNS

The action of both the Rio Grande Valley Association and the Texas Association for Bilingual Education was predicated on a continued lack of TEA sensitivity to the educational needs of minority children.

The following have created an ethnic gap between the Agency and minority educators in the state: (1) the continued opposition of TEA to bilingual education programs as expressed in their pursuit of the bilingual suit in *U.S. v. Texas*; (2) the elimination of 66 percent of Hispanic college students and 73 percent of Black students wanting to go into teacher education programs by the use of the questionable PPST examination; and (3) the TEA opposition to school finance reform in the Legislature and subsequently in the court case *Edgewood v. Kirby* (*United States v. Texas*, 1971; *Edgewood ISD, et al. v. Kirby, et al.*, 1987).

Although the question of adoption of inappropriate instructional materials may have set off an unprecedented outcry from the state's minorities, this action may be but the tip of the iceberg if minority political and educational entities perceive the SBOE's action as the straw that broke the camel's back.

EARLY CHILDHOOD EDUCATION IN THE PUBLIC SCHOOLS: THE TEXAS EDUCATION AGENCY EVALUATION

1992

During the last three decades there has been a dramatic increase in the number of pre-school age children enrolled in the public schools. Prior to the 1960s the public schools had virtually no contact with pre-school age children. Following the enactment of the Elementary and Secondary School Act of 1965, a limited number of pre-school age children were served under the various federal programs. Since then, a number of states have made heavy investments in the education of young children.

The overriding rationale for early childhood education has been that much of a person's development takes place prior to enrollment in school at age six. Unfortunately, many children spend their early years in home environments which provide limited stimuli for maximum development. The purpose of the early childhood education program is to provide enriching experiences to compensate for prior deprivation, and lead to maximum physical, intellectual, social and emotional development before encountering the curriculum of the first grade.

Extensive evaluations of children in Headstart, and other types of early childhood programs substantiate the value of this early intervention. The investment in the early development of children prior to regular school enrollment produced sufficient dividends to justify the investment. The payoff in improved subsequent student performance was big enough to lead a number of states to provide early schooling for five-, four-, and even three-year-olds in the public schools. In Texas, half of the school districts are providing pre-kindergarten education to low-income and limited English-proficient four-year-olds.

The Texas Education Agency (TEA) has just completed an evaluation study of pre-school programs in Texas. A preliminary report has been issued which includes a statewide survey and a case study of ten pre-school programs (TEA, 1991). Initial findings of longitudinal studies of 2,000 students will be available in 1993.

The results of the preliminary report are not encouraging. Although student performance data are not yet available, it was generally recognized that the Texas pre-school programs differed considerably from traditional early childhood programs. The difference is explained in the TEA evaluation report as an implementation of a "pushdown" model. Instead of the pre-school program focusing on the development of the child's physical, intellectual, social and emotional development in order to prepare the child for the academic curriculum of the first grade, Texas programs have pushed down the academic curriculum of the first grade to the kindergarten and the pre-school level. As a result of this early focus on academic skills, the failure previously experienced in the first grade is being encountered by children at the ages of four or five.

The TEA study compared early childhood programs to standards established by the National Association for the Education of Young Children (NAEYC). The following is the "Comments and Conclusions" section of the TEA report:

> The call for developmentally appropriate programs stems from the growing recognition that schools must become more responsive to the unique needs of young children, rather than forcing young children to conform to traditional and often inappropriate expectations and practices. Knowledge of how young children develop is essential in designing pre-kindergarten programs.
>
> The NAEYC has identified three conditions that must be met in educational programs for young children. First, teachers of early childhood programs must receive specialized preparation in early childhood development/education. Second, teachers must have practical experience teaching this age group. Third, the adult/student ratio should not exceed 2:16.
>
> Although administrators and teachers in pre-kindergarten programs in Texas are receptive to the concept of developmentally appropriate practices, little evidence of their implementation was apparent. Several barriers currently impede the implementation of these practices. First, pre-kindergarten programs did not appear to be grounded upon sound beliefs/theories about how young children learn, nor did a framework exist at the state level to identify program quality standards. Second, staff typically did not receive the training in early childhood development/education that is necessary to implement developmentally appropriate programs. In programs with teacher assistants, training for them in early childhood was minimal or nonexistent. Third, in many classrooms the adult-child ratio of 1:22 which exceeded the NAEYC recommended 1:8 adult-child ratio, did not support individualized instruction and adequate supervision of children. Fourth, the programs for limited-English-proficient students appeared to focus on moving children into English, rather than ensuring that children first had a strong foundation in their native language. Finally, parents, although strongly supportive of pre-kindergarten, did not appear to have a partnership relationship with the districts.
>
> To address the barriers impeding implementation of developmentally appropriate practices, preliminary recommendations in the following broad areas were made: 1) staff development at both the preservice and inservice level; 2) lowering the mandated class size; and 3) the development of an early childhood education framework, including identification of program quality standards, by the Agency.

The implications of the TEA evaluation findings and the summary presented above allow few options for Texas school districts. Lowering the mandated class size will be difficult, since funding levels are not based on a 8:1 pupil-teacher ratio. Furthermore, pre-school programs have not been fully funded under the state Foundation School Program. This places a heavy burden for support on the school districts, with the heaviest burden on low wealth school districts which have the most children in need of pre-school assistance and the least resources for meeting this need. The continued failure of the state to provide resources for school buildings compounds the problem of providing small enrollments in each class. Though existing funds can be reallocated to meet the desirable pupil-teacher ratio, it is doubtful that educational systems in Texas can continue to meet some needs by taking funds away from others. The only feasible solution is the legislation of new and adequate funding by the state, a long—standing recommendation in Texas, but one which continues to fall on deaf ears.

The development of an early childhood education framework should not be a formidable problem, either at the local or state level. Excellent models for early childhood education are readily available, including the NAEYC standards which are universally accepted and utilized.

The challenge to the school districts in responding to this unfavorable evaluation of pre-school programs is in the training and retraining of school administrative and teaching staff.

IDRA SERVICES

Intercultural Development Research Association (IDRA) has provided technical assistance, materials, development, training and evaluation services in early childhood education since 1975. Assistance can currently be provided in a variety of areas. School districts eligible for participation in currently funded programs can receive assistance at no cost to the district. Non-eligible school districts can receive assistance at a nominal cost.

The following are examples of training and technical assistance topics in early childhood education most frequently provided by IDRA Staff:

- The determination of student goals and the identification of developmentally appropriate activities for meeting these goals.
- The use of teacher observation and parent interviews for the identification of multiple approaches for language proficiency assessment.
- The use of developmental screening instruments and informal assessment measures for the determination of individual growth and development.
- The identification and utilization of age-appropriate curriculum materials.
- Organization of teacher and child-initiated thematic instructional activities.
- The development and implementation of a culturally relevant developmental program.
- Guidelines for the use of native and English language in the instructional program.
- The use of appropriate learning centers and manipulatives in the pre-school environment.
- Parent involvement in early childhood education activity.
- An evaluation model for pre-school programs.

BIBLIOGRAPHY

Bruner, Jerome, *The Process of Education*, Harvard University Press, Cambridge, 1961.

Edgewood ISD, et al., v. Kirby, et al., Cause No. 362,516, 250th District Court, Austin, Travis County, Texas, 1987.

Intercultural Development Research Association (IDRA), *AMANECER*, San Antonio, 1979.

Intercultural Development Research Association (IDRA), *Newsletter*, San Antonio, November 1981, August 1985, September 1985, November 1985, November 1990, August 1991, January 1992).

Intercultural Development Research Association (IDRA). *Nuevo Amanecer*, National Textbook Company, Chicago, 1985.

Texas Education Agency, *Texas Evaluation Study of PreKindergarten Programs, Preliminary Findings*, Austin, November 1991.

United States v. Texas, 342 F. Supp. 24 (E.D. Tex. 1971).

U.S. National Commission on the International Year of the Child, *Report to the President*, Washington, D.C., March 1980.

Weikart, David P., *Early Childhood Special Education for Intellectually Subnormal and/or Culturally Different Children*, National Leadership Institute in Early Childhood Education, Washington, D.C., 1971.

DISCUSSION QUESTIONS

1. List reasons why an early childhood education program is especially valuable for atypical children. In what ways can the cost of an early childhood education program be offset in subsequent schooling?
2. Describe a "pushdown" model of early childhood education. What would motivate a school to employ such a model?
3. Why is a "pushdown" model especially counter-productive among children from poverty and minority homes?
4. Make a study of early childhood programs in your area. Rate the programs in terms of "developmentally appropriate" practices. Keep in mind the needs of economically disadvantaged and minority children when rating the programs.
5. Review the early childhood teacher training programs in your area to identify strengths and weaknesses in the light of the issues raised in this chapter.

7

Science, Math and Technology

PREFACE

I started my teaching career as a science teacher. My first teaching assignment was teaching science at a junior high school in a low wealth school district with a large percentage of minority and disadvantaged students. The experience was rather disappointing. Although interactions with students were, and continue to be, very rewarding, the performance of the students left a lot to be desired.

The classroom where I taught science was indistinguishable from any other classroom in the school. There wasn't a single piece of equipment or any instructional materials for the teaching of science, except for a science textbook which most of the students found difficult to read.

Subsequent employment at Edgewood High School in San Antonio, Texas, was equally frustrating. General science and biology were taught in a crowded government surplus barracks with nothing in it remotely resembling a science laboratory. When a new building was built in 1954, I had the opportunity to teach in a science lab, although the low wealth school district did not have a budget for the purchase of any scientific equipment, materials or supplies. In the new building it was at least possible to put together some semblance of science equipment made up of discarded bottles, cans and any other recyclable junk that I could get my hands on. Still, it is difficult to teach a biology class and tell students about protozoa without access to a microscope where they can actually see an amoeba or a paramecium grown in a jar of stagnant water.

Having been personally involved in the teaching of science and mathematics in low wealth minority school districts, it was no surprise to review the Rand Corporation publication, *Multiplying Inequities,* in which Jeannie Oakes reports on the Rand research on minority student performance in math and science. As indicated in a following article, the Rand Corporation study concluded that the three principal factors for poor minority and disadvantaged student performance in math and science could be attributed to three factors: lack of access to quality programs, lack of access to quality teachers and lack of access to adequate resources (Oakes, 1990).

Intercultural Development Research Association (IDRA) has been involved in a number of projects for the improvement of science and math instruction in minority and low wealth schools. In cooperation with the Control Data Corporation, we conducted an evaluation of the use of the Plato computer programs for teaching math in a large minority urban school district. The district was grasping at straws in the use of the computer-based math program. At the time of its implementation, the district did not have a single certified math teacher in any of its three high schools and five middle schools. The superintendent felt that at least the computer program had the familiarity with mathematics which most of his teachers lacked.

In this early assessment of computer assisted instruction, it was learned that better performing teachers improved their performance through the use of the computer program. Poorly performing teachers did no better with the use of this instructional aid.

IDRA also conducted a study of computer use by minority students funded by the Carnegie Foundation. As in the Plato experience, we learned that those students who could profit most from the use of computers had the least access to computers. Analysis of computer instructional software indicated that its usefulness was diminished for atypical students. Limited proficiency in English and lack of reading skills precluded the effective use of the computer materials. The content of the programs reviewed was compatible with social and cultural characteristics of white, Anglo, middle-class, male students. Few adaptations were available for use by minority, disadvantaged and female students.

In our desegregation technical assistance center, we noted that the popularity of magnet schools designed to provide minority students access to better math and science programs tended to be counterproductive. Although a small number of students gained access to these superior programs, the removal of the students with the highest interest, background and performance in math and science from the regular schools seriously diminished the quality of math and science instruction for the students not transferring to the magnet schools.

In recent years IDRA has pilot-tested a program for the improvement of math instruction for Hispanic girls. This program has demonstrated that facilitating access to quality programs, qualified teachers and adequate resources produces a proportionate increase in the interest and performance of Hispanic girls in the male-dominated world of math.

As indicated in the following articles, the fields of science, math and technology are widening the gap between the performance of mainstream and atypical students. It will be difficult for these students to enjoy any upward mobility without science, math and technological skills in an increasingly technological society.

HIGH TECHNOLOGY AND EQUAL EDUCATIONAL OPPORTUNITY

1983

The review of the literature in education today leaves no doubt that the decade of the 1980s will be known as the decade of high technology. The literature is replete with articles, books, and materials dealing with the impact of the new technology on education. Recent advances in electronics, in computers, in automation, and even the more recent robots preclude any other topic surfacing to match technology as the predominant educational concern.

The impact of technology has been felt in industry with hundreds of communities attempting to attract the silicon chip, in business with electronic inventions becoming more commonplace, and in education with its recent infatuation with the computer.

As in the other two fields, industry and business, the impact of the computer is reciprocal. The computer plays a part in the outcomes of education and is also a growing part of the process of education. Computer skills will continue to become an important aspect of educational activity, with no student being considered as educated without being well-versed in computer language and having a sufficient amount of "hands-on" time at the computer terminal. It is conceivable that in a few years simple languages such as BASIC and its many derivatives will be as common in the school as foreign languages, even at the elementary school level. FORTRAN, COBOL, RPG, and other computer languages will be taught at appropriate levels. This knowledge will then be combined with careers subjects for student entrance into the work force, or be utilized for subsequent learning.

The process of education is similarly being impacted by the computer; that is, the computer is being utilized as a technical tool for instructional purposes. Computer assisted instruction (CAI) is being used for the teaching of reading, language, mathematics, sciences, social studies, and almost every other area of the curriculum.

It is inconceivable that such a drastic change in educational process and product will come about without an accompanying change in federal intervention in education. Although education has been perceived as a state function and a local responsibility, it historically has been a federal interest. The implications of high technology in industry, business, politics, and the military are such that we can soon expect a new federal policy in education which will make computers in education a national priority. This prioritizing will be accompanied by the necessary legislation providing massive funds for the acquisition of hardware, the development of software, the training and retraining of teachers, and any and all resources needed for the schools to respond to the new priority.

These predictions do not require a unique psychic or a polished crystal ball. History repeats itself, and the history of the relationship between the federal government and education is full of similar examples of federal intervention to accompany an intense federal interest.

The Northwest Ordinance of the eighteenth century, the Morrill Act of the Civil War, the Smith-Hughes Act of World War I, the National Defense Education Act of the 1950s, and the Elementary and Secondary Education Act of the 1960s teach us that the federal government engages strongly in education in a time of national crisis. History also teaches us that when the crisis subsides, education again becomes a state right and the federal government disengages. Perhaps there is one other lesson to be learned, and an important one at that; namely, that national crises previously occurred at intervals of several decades, the interval between such occurrences is diminishing and one crisis is hardly ended before the next one takes place. Thus the civil rights crises of the last three decades, even though ameliorated, have not ended before the country has had to face the challenge of the technological revolution. While the federal government has started to implement the disengagement from education as part of the ideology of the new federalism, powerful new forces are pushing it into the new engagement of high technology.

It appears that the federal government will have come full cycle with one generation if the demands of the new technology are met by the government. It seems like only yesterday that the national priority was technological. The schools appeared wholly absorbed with the development of science, mathematics and the technology necessary for building atomic submarines and getting an American to the moon first. We built the submarines, missiles, atomic bombs, and laser beams, and we walked on the moon. In the process, we also changed to the new math and the new approaches to science, although it was inevitable that someone would question whether the mathematics most appropriate for submarine building and moon walking was also not appropriate for the millions of children who would not participate in either.

So the new math died on the vine although few people noticed because the country was involved in a new national priority—the issue of educational equity. This issue continued as a national priority for two decades and is about to be plucked from the vine just before it ripens as the country moves into a new national educational priority.

As one reads over the profusion of literature on the high technology, some of it appears vaguely familiar and some of it appears very familiar. The professional demands of the new technology for engineers, electronic experts, and computer experts is similar to the earlier needs for submarine builders. The need for fluency in computer languages is similar to the foreign language fluency needs addressed by the National Defense Education Act of the 1950s. The retraining of teachers to teach or to simply use computer science is reminiscent of the massive retraining in the new mathematics. What initially appears to be a flashback is in truth a cycling of national priorities in education, with the sole exception that the silicon chip rather than the atom is the basic unit of instruction.

The cyclic re-emergence of technology as a national priority is not undesirable nor is it detrimental if, and this a very big if, education proceeds from its place in time and does not regress thirty years. There is no reason to believe that the emergence of equity as a national priority in the '60s and '70s was undesirable, nor was it detrimental. It provided improved educational opportunities for millions of children and, in my opinion, was on the verge of a dramatic breakthrough in the realization of educational equity as past investments were starting to produce returns when the federal government initiated ill-timed disengagement from their equity endeavors.

The key to the federal engagement in the new technology is that it be coordinated with past and present efforts in the equity issue rather than being implemented as a replacement for the equity issue.

Differences in educational opportunity are going to be exacerbated by the new technology. Disparities in educational funds between affluent and low-wealth school districts and differences in personal resources between rich and poor kids will widen the achievement levels between the two. Studies of the dispersion of computer equipment in the nation's schools today show that the distribution is already extremely lopsided. Computer equipment is concentrated in the wealthiest schools and few students from low-income homes have seen one, let alone accumulated hands-on time.

If we look at the three roles of the computer in education, we can predict a continuous worsening of the existing situation over the next few years.

1. The role of the computer in the management of instruction will increase the advantage of pupils in high-wealth school districts. Teachers and support personnel are receiving powerful instructional tools which will expand their ability to teach, while the lack of computer availability in low-wealth schools will perpetuate their inability to cope with the existing problems of teaching the disadvantaged, the minorities, and the limited English proficient.

2. The role of the computer as a product of education will similarly hamper the employability and further training of the disadvantaged. Funding limitations in low-wealth schools are so severe that it is conceivable that years from now, in the midst of the age of high technology and computers, these schools will be graduating pupils who have never seen nor had access to a computer. It is not exaggeration to make this analogous to a school graduating a secretary today who has never seen or had access to a typewriter.

3. The role of the computer in the process of education will again penalize students in low-wealth school districts. There is every indication that computer assisted instruction will revolutionize the quality and the quantity of educational programs. This impact will not be felt in schools without the resources for the implementation of the new technology for instructional purposes. A brief review of the emerging software indicates that, similar to the curriculum of the pre-equity ear, it is a curriculum developed for white, Anglo-Saxon, English-speaking, middle-class children. The computer assisted instructional programs make no attempt to bring about any compatibility between them and the characteristics of atypical student populations.

One concern regarding the impact of the new technology on equality of educational opportunity rests on the assumption that the new technology will preempt educational equity as the dominant and almost exclusive national priorities. Needless to say, this does not necessarily have to be so. A preferred alternative is the integration effort involving the two concerns without a detrimental exclusivity.

During the next few years educators, social scientists, politicians, and technicians will be gathering at various conferences to map out a plan for the fulfillment of the next decade or two as a new era in education. It can only be hoped that in these sessions there will be concern for the continued expansion and development of all of the resources of this country, and that the new educational strategies developed and implemented will be conducive for giving expanded opportunities to all children.

HIGH TECHNOLOGY AND EQUAL EDUCATIONAL OPPORTUNITY—PART II

1983

In February 1983, the IDRA *Newsletter* carried an article by Dr. José Cárdenas entitled "High Technology and Equal Educational Opportunity." Since the printing of the article several things have happened. First, IDRA has received an unusually large amount of correspondence in response to the article. Most of the feedback supports the theme of the article and requests further inquiry into the potential problems. Second, Intercultural Development Research Association (IDRA) has been involved in extensive activities related to computer assisted instruction (CAI) and special populations. Third, additional information has surfaced regarding the impact of technology on education equity. In the light of these subsequent developments, this article is intended as an expansion of the issues presented in the previous article.

Synopsis of the original article: The author traces the history of federal government involvement in education and identifies three dangers which tend to increase the opportunity gap between the haves and have-nots in our society. The three dangers are: 1) the replacement of educational equity by technology education as a national priority, 2) existing difference, in educational opportunity being exacerbated by disparities between affluent and low-wealth school districts and the impact of these disparities on the ability to acquire technology, and 3) the differences in personal resources between students from affluent and poor homes and their personal ability to acquire technology in the home.

NARROWING THE TECHNOLOGY GAP

The widening of the opportunity gap as a result of the new technology continues. Unfortunately, the growth in disparities will not diminish until several steps are taken to remedy the existing situation. The first necessary step is the development of a policy concerning educational technology utilization in the schools. The acquisition of technical equipment by the schools has occurred for the most part in the absence of any national or state leadership. In fact, recent studies indicate that the bulk of microcomputers currently found in the nation's schools was acquired with local funds, most often purchased by PTA's and other local support groups. Yet, if the microcomputer will impact education to the extent being claimed in all the media, PTA purchases (which are based upon a wide range of PTA purchasing power) are too haphazard a resource for the introduction of educational innovation. As is the case for almost any type of educational expenditure, if it is important enough to justify the expenditure of funds, it is important enough to include in the school finance structure. It is regrettable that what is considered the most important innovation in education in the last few decades should come in through the back door in the absence of state and national policy and support.

The second step needed to forestall a widening of the technological opportunity gap is the equalization of resources between high- and low-wealth schools. This problem has been with us for half a century and, after much litigation and legislation, remains a problem in all but a few of the fifty states with favorable post-Rodriguez court cases. Suffice it to say that the opportunity gaps existing prior to high technology utilization in the schools will grow exponentially in future years.

The third step in reducing the impact on educational opportunity is enhancing the appropriateness of technological developments for utilization by atypical populations. The three most significant special populations requiring appropriate technological tools are minorities, the economically disadvantaged, and the limited English proficient (LEP). The remainder of this article will deal with computer assisted instruction (CAI) for non-English speaking populations who are commonly minority and disadvantaged.

CAI RESPONSIVENESS TO LEP NEEDS

Demographically, the growing limited English-proficient population is significant enough to warrant special consideration in the field of computer assisted instruction. The 1980 U.S. Census identified 30 million non-English speaking persons in the country. There is every reason to believe that undocumented aliens and missed counts would result in an even larger figure. This population is expected to increase to 40 million in the next sixteen years under normal conditions, and even more so if proposed immigration policy changes are implemented in the future. In 1976 school-age children ages five to fourteen who did not speak English constituted 2.5 million. By the year 2000 this number is expected to increase to 3.4 million, with over 95 percent of the increase occurring in the Spanish-speaking population. In contrast, there are only some 32,000 certified bilingual teachers nationwide, and a current need for 72,500 additional bilingual teachers to meet the educational needs of LEP children.

The potential for CAI as an educational response for the limited English proficient is large, not only because of the size of the population and the lack of teacher resources, but because the characteristics of CAI make this educational tool appropriate for special populations. The varying characteristics of the limited English proficient from absolutely no English proficiency to slightly below grade-level proficiency is multiplied by a similar range in fluency in the native language. CAI can easily identify these characteristics and present an individualized program compatible with the existing needs. Differences in individual ability to acquire a new language can best be accommodated in self-paced computer programs.

It is important to note that the author is most conscious of the limitations of CAI in the acquisition of new languages. The most effective technique for language acquisition is extensive, meaningful and profitable interaction between the learner and a trained speaker of the new language. It is doubtful that any but the most sophisticated multimedia approaches even approximates the ideal. However, CAI is an important response for two reasons. First, it can provide an extensive amount of reinforcement and practice as a supplement to the teacher's efforts, and second, it provides extensive relief and release time for the teacher to devote to intensive interaction with very small numbers of students. It is a constant frustration to see teachers who are working with small numbers of children in language development activities assign unimportant and often trivial busy work to the rest of the students. CAI is far superior as a reinforcing activity for children in English as a second language programs than the prevalent coloring assignments that appear to dominate the time LEP children spend not interacting with the teacher.

CRITERIA FOR CAI SUITABILITY

In reviewing the available information concerning the use of computers by special populations, IDRA staff identified a number of studies and publications which have addressed this topic. In addition to the available literature, several surveys of in-school computer utilization have been conducted which shed some light on the status of computer utilization by special populations, although most such surveys were not intended to focus on special populations.

Lindsey reports severe limitations on the availability of software for handicapped populations in spite of extensive attention given in other publications to the potential special benefits of CAI for this target population. Another thought-provoking work on the use of microcomputers by the disadvantaged was performed by John P. Lipkin of Litigation Support Services under a National Institute of Education contract. His analysis for various studies led him to conclude that, "... micro-computer purchases are closely tied to the ability of the school districts to afford them" (Lipkin, 1983).

In determining equity in the use of microcomputers in schools, much of the available literature uses a model provided by Brookover and Lezotte (Brookover & Lezotte, 1981). They provide three criteria for determining the equity in computer utilization: (1) the access criterion, which is the equality of accessibility by all students, (2) the participation criterion, which is the extent to which practices and programs guarantee equal participation, and (3) the benefits criterion, which is the extent to which all users benefit in a nondiscriminatory manner. To these three criteria, IDRA staff would add a fourth criterion—the appropriateness criterion, which is the extent to which the materials are appropriate for use by special populations.

In spite of the limitations of information available, the application of the access criterion indicates that children in higher wealth school systems have at least twice as much accessibility to computers as do children in low-wealth school systems. In addition to the findings stated previously, Lipkin concludes that funds used for the purchase of microcomputers by the schools appear to break down as follows: 10 percent from federal funds, 20 percent from state funds, and 70 percent from local funds.

Local funds are fairly evenly divided into voluntary contributions (30 percent of total) and local school funds (40 percent of total). Local school funds come primarily from materials and supplies budgets with an additional source being contingency funds. It should be noted that low-wealth school districts have very limited materials and supplies budgets and contingency funds are non-existent.

Further observations should be made of federal funds as a future source of funding for microcomputer acquisition. First, federal funds provide only about 8 percent of total school budgets, an amount too small to be consequential in the future distribution of computer equipment. Furthermore, the percentage of federal funds in education is at the lowest level in ten years and there is a good possibility that it may go lower. In addition to these concerns, it should also be noted that other studies indicate that the allocation of federal funds in block grants has resulted in an increase in the use of the money for the purchase of microcomputers by the schools. This implies that the use of federal funds for computer acquisition has been at the expense of funding for special populations. Because most computer programs fail in the appropriateness criterion, it appears that the use of federal funds for purchasing computers has resulted in a diminished supply of resources for special populations without providing benefits in use to these populations.

The application of the participation criterion indicates limited and inequitable participation by special populations. In the case of the LEP population, there is almost a complete absence of programs available for non-English and limited English speakers. A review of various source books and catalogs failed to identify all but one or two software programs which may be used by LEP children. Several of the limited listings for English language development were studied with disappointing results. For the most part, the programs were intended for use by adults having a high level of literacy (usually a post-secondary educational background) in some other language. Even though some of these programs may have value for newly arrived immigrants with professional status, they are worthless for LEP children in elementary and secondary schools. Several school district responded to my previous article with information about local efforts at computer curriculum development focusing on English as a second language, but most of the programs are in the formative stages and are not nearly extensive enough to impact on the problem.

It is already apparent that the application of benefits criterion will indicate so few current benefits for special populations that the promise of a technological revolution in educational programs for them not only did not materialize, but is not prone to occur in the foreseeable future.

Nonetheless, a model program for limited English-proficient children can be easily conceptualized. The acquisition of financial and personnel resources for its development is a much more formidable problem. The model should contain four elements commonly found in bilingual education programs. An English as a second language (ESL) program presented in a systematic structured process and compatible with recent findings in the field of language development and linguistics should be included, as should a program of native language instruction to continued cognitive and basic skill development while English is being acquired. A transition program for the transfer of skills and learning to the newly acquired English language is also essential. The fourth element is an ESL program for young adults and adult populations, who differ from children in language acquisition characteristics. The ESL program can be developed by a team of experts in the areas of ESL, linguistics, curriculum development, and computer applications. The biggest problems in development will probably be the aggregation of experts in the identified areas and the possibility that only simplistic materials will emanate due to the constraints of available resources. The old adage, "Don't plan vast projects with half-vast resources," certainly appears to hold true in the development of ESL software programs.

Another potential pitfall is the possibility that an extensive amount of material development will occur at the lowest levels of learning. Contrary to popular opinion, CAI is not limited to drill and practice. The computer lends itself to far more intricate forms of learning. Learning forms ranking above drill and practice that are suitable for computer applications are tutorial, simulations, problem solving, and educational games. To a certain extent, the application of Brookover and Lezotte's participation and benefit criteria already identifies an overabundance of drill and practice (the lowest from of computer learning) in programs utilized with the less affluent, the rural, and the inner-city populations. D. Watt observed this phenomenon along with significant variations in the utilization of the computer in the context of programming and computer awareness (Watt, 1982). The following observation by Watt surfaces frequently in the literature on equity and computer utilization: "Affluent students are thus learning to tell the computer what to do, while less affluent students are learning to do what the computer tells them." In other words, the rich are manipulating computers, while the poor are being manipulated by computers. Program development for the limited English proficient must make a strong conscious effort to resist the temptation of producing simplistic drill and practice and tutorial programs and aspire to the production of the more sophisticated computer applications, such as simulations, problem solving exercises, and educational games.

Above all, the computer materials development team must exercise extreme caution in differentiating between material which can best be presented through teacher/student interaction. Student/computer material must be supportive of teacher/student interaction; therefore, there is a great need for the effective coordination of the two. The CAI program must be able to support and supplement the teaching program. Independent and non-classroom related ESL materials may only be appropriate for a very small portion of the LEP population.

There has been some speculation about the possible use of audio in English development computer programs. The use of multimedia controlled by the computer is appropriate and feasible for use by LEP populations. These programs are more difficult to develop, however, and can be utilized effectively only with the more sophisticated computer systems, such as the Control Data Plato software. Unfortunately, at the present time, few school districts are opting for the acquisition of sophisticated mainframe computers for instructional purposes and most of the CAI is through the use of microcomputer equipment which offers limited flexibility for multimedia utilization. Needless to say, the microcomputer voice synthesizers are far from adequate for language development purposes.

The development of native language instruction materials for computer utilization presents some unique situations which should be addressed in the materials development process. Some of the LEP children may have a low level of native language development in their native language. If this is the case, it is necessary to make an allowance for this characteristic in the instructional materials. Previous educational errors of assuming language facility that did not exist in the English language should not be repeated in native language instruction. In some cases it may be preferable to include native language development prior to basic skill and content acquisition in that language. In other cases, it may be preferable to go directly into English language development as the shortest distance between two developmental points. At any rate, the final determination would have to be made by a trained instructor on the basis of information available at the time of placement.

Similarly, following transition to English language instruction, the school must make a choice between continued native language maintenance and development or allowing the loss of the native language followed by the less cost-effective and unproficient reintroduction of the native language as a foreign language. Unfortunately, in the past, this decision has been heavily influenced by myth and misinformation. For years school systems opted to reduce or eliminate the use of the native language in the belief that its use detracted from the ability to acquire a second language. Recent evidence indicates that not only is this not so, but fluency in a language enhances the learning of subsequent languages. Therefore, maintenance and development of the native language will enhance English language acquisition.

The period of transition from native language to English presents unique problems of its own. My biggest concern is that the materials must effectively establish that English language acquisition precedes the transfer. The last thing desired is a repetition of yesteryears' attempts to teach a child a new language, basic skills in that new language, and content material—all at the same time. Lack of coordination of English language acquisition with skill transfer can result in the deplorable educational situations of the pre-bilingual education era.

APPROPRIATENESS OF CURRICULUM

Throughout this article it has been stressed that curriculum materials should be appropriate for the target population. The points made about special curriculum materials for computer utilization with LEP children must also take into account the other characteristics of these children.

Children whose native language is not English tend to have strong cultural orientations which differ markedly from those of mainstream Americans. Instructional materials especially designed for their use must ensure that there is compatibility between the cultural characteristics of the students and the instructional materials. The fact that the materials are designed for CAI does not diminish the need for cultural propriety. This propriety must be reflected in both the content of the materials as well as the methodology utilized.

A similar propriety criterion must be utilized in matching the content and methodology of the materials to the socio-economic background of the learner. Differing developmental patterns exhibited by economically disadvantaged children must be reflected in the content and methodology employed.

PSYCHOSOCIAL ADJUSTMENT

Minority, disadvantaged, and LEP children frequently develop negative concepts of self in school situations. This condition accompanies the frustration and failure encountered by the slew of inappropriate instructional programs. Regardless of whether this negativism toward self is developed during the transition from home to school, or developed and reinforced as the child falls further behind in age/grade achievement levels, the fact that it exists has a strong impact on future learning situations. A child's self-perception as an unsuccessful learner influences the outcome of new learning situations, thereby creating the cumulative deficit phenomenon so characteristic of special populations.

It is interesting to note that this author and Dr. Blandina Cárdenas Ramírez described this problem in 1969. It was suggested that instructional activities for minority and disadvantaged children must not only address the skill or content material being taught, but that they must also respond to the negative perceptions of self which may form formidable barriers for future learning. Fourteen years ago we recommended that instructional materials for minority children be designed with a built-in mechanism which could modify these negative perceptions of self. These mechanisms included several suggestions to be incorporated in order to reduce the chances of failure and enhance opportunities for success, such as:

1. Complete assurance that all necessary prerequisite skills necessary for success in the new learning activity be mastered.
2. Small increments of increasing difficulty in order to minimize chances of failure due to too big a jump in difficulty.
3. Necessary reinforcement or other assistance to prevent further failure and the strengthening of the negative self-concept.
4. Continuous and frequent feedback on performance as the child proceeds through a learning task.
5. Strong, positive reinforcement of correct performance.

It is amazing how CAI can address these needs in the instructional programs for minority children. It appears that technology has finally given the teacher the right tool to develop the positive concept of a successful learner, which in my opinion is the largest stumbling block in minority education.

IMPLICATIONS AND RECOMMENDATIONS

The analysis of microcomputer utilization in the public schools reveals the CAI educational programs will definitely have some implications on the opportunity gap existing between the haves and the have-nots in our country's schools. If the movement toward the increased use of high technology in education is not to exacerbate differences already existing, it is necessary that preventive steps be taken. These steps should address the following points:

1. The development of national and state policies on the use of technology in the schools. Policy must be accompanied by the necessary funds and resources for adequate implementation.
2. There is a serious disparity in the accessibility of computers among schools attended by students from varying socio-economic levels.
3. The amount and the type of participation in the utilization of educational computer programs differs among the various segments of the population.
4. Not all children stand to acquire benefits from the haphazard introduction of computer technology into the schools.
5. Available computer software is not appropriate for special populations such as minorities, the disadvantaged, and the limited English proficient.
6. There is a need to develop new software and to modify or adapt existing software for use by special populations.
7. Computer assisted instruction can make a contribution to the improvement of educational opportunities if existing problems are addressed.

TEXAS, TAXES, AND HIGH-TECH

1984

Recently I received a copy of an article which appeared in the Houston *Chronicle* on February 14, 1984, written by Bernard L. Weinstein, Assistant Director of the John Gray Institute in Beaumont. In this article Weinstein notes the aspirations and efforts of the state of Texas in the development of a high-tech economy. The theme of the article is that there is little chance of this occurring unless there is a drastic change in the elementary and secondary schools of the state. The key to past economic development in Texas has been the plentiful production of oil, gas, food, and fiber. However, the key to the development of a high-tech economy is not natural resources, but rather human resources. In the development of these resources the state of Texas has not excelled.

Weinstein notes the following seven points to illustrate the inadequacy of Texas' human resources.

1. Only 16 percent of the adults in Texas are college graduates. This figure is slightly below the national average, and substantially below high-tech economy states, such as California and Massachusetts.
2. Only 61.4 percent of the adult population of Texas are high school graduates. This figure is about five percentage points below the national average and more than ten percentage points below California and Massachusetts.
3. Graduates of Texas high schools rank fifth from the bottom in combined SAT scores.
4. Only 68 percent of ninth graders in Texas finish high school. This percentage is twelfth from the bottom in rankings among the fifty states.
5. Per-pupil expenditures in Texas schools average 15 percent below the national average.
6. Teacher salaries in Texas are still 5 percent below the national average.
7. The state of Texas ranks last in the country in the percentage of personal income spent on public education.

Weinstein concludes that the low educational performance of the state of Texas is incompatible with the human resource demands of a high-tech economy. The obvious solution is a strong concerted effort in the improvement of education in the state before it can aspire to develop a high-tech economy.

Opposition to higher taxes for public education, which can be expected from many politicians, business leaders, and citizens must be countered with the argument that educational outlays should be viewed not as a tax, but rather as an investment in the future productivity of Texas and its work force.

SCIENCE AND MATH EQUITY IN THE SCHOOLS

1991

As local communities, states and the entire nation grapple with issues relating to the quality of our educational systems, there are few areas of education which contrast the performance of the *haves* and *have-nots* as severely as science and mathematics.

The most dramatic point in the original court trial of *Edgewood v. Kirby*, the Texas school finance equity case, was testimony presented by Superintendent Allen Boyd of the San Elizario Independent School District in the El Paso area (*Edgewood I.S.D. v. Kirby*, 1987).

Mr. Boyd testified about the absence of high school subjects due to the financial limitations of the school district. Activities such as football, music and choir, taken for granted in most schools, were not available to students in the low-wealth school district. But there was an audible gasp from participants and audience alike when Mr. Boyd testified to a limited science and mathematics offering due to the lack of resources and the inability of the school district to afford or attract qualified teachers of geometry, calculus, chemistry, physics and other subjects commonly deemed essential in American schools.

Studies of school dropouts in Texas and in other states consistently identify poor school performance as the leading cause of school dropouts. Of all subject matter characterized by poor performance of students at risk of dropping out of school, science and math are at the forefront. Performance in science and math is not only less than satisfactory, a large percentage of the at-risk population does not even enroll in most of these courses, certainly not master them. School dropouts seldom abandon the school while enrolled in advanced algebra, calculus, trigonometry, biology, chemistry or physics. For the most part they drop out of school while still enrolled in remedial arithmetic or at best some watered down course in business math.

Reasons for minority, disadvantaged and other at-risk students doing so poorly in science and math can be found in a recent publication by the Rand Corporation, *Multiplying Inequities: The Effects of Race, Social Class and Tracking on Opportunities to Learn Mathematics and Science*, by Jeannie Oakes (Oakes, 1990).

Jeannie Oakes is a familiar name to educators interested in the education of the disadvantaged, having published a number of articles and books on the subject. In *Multiplying Inequities* Oakes reports on a Rand study sponsored by the National Science Foundation on educational opportunities in mathematics and science among various groups of students. Oakes' study should be required reading for every educator interested in causes of and solutions to contemporary problems in the education of at-risk students. Her insights into the issues are backed by the study's research findings.

MULTIPLIER EFFECT

The Rand study looks at minority and disadvantaged performance in science and mathematics in a continuum from pre-school to college. Poor performance is a cumulative phenomenon beginning in the home and compounded as the student moves up the educational ladder, with each subsequent year producing an increased deficit in the student's performance.

When perceived in a cumulative deficit continuum, it is obvious that addressing the poor performance of minority and disadvantaged students calls for the development of a comprehensive approach addressing the entire continuum, rather than a strategy aimed at a specific age or grade level.

HOME DIFFERENCES

Each individual is a member of a group or class from the moment of birth. The individual at birth becomes a member of a racial and ethnic group, a social and economic class and a type of community.

Different groups have different achievement and participation levels which impact upon the child in its early stages of development. With limited exceptions, children born into minority and disadvantaged homes have limited or different experiences in the fields of science and math. As a result, by the time the child is ready to enroll in school for the first time, the achievement and participation levels in science and math, as well as virtually all other areas of the school curriculum, differ significantly from the achievement and participation levels of children from non-minority middle-class homes.

At this point it is necessary to note that atypical children have no shortage of experiences, even in science and math. It is probable that non-middle-class homes provide extensive experiences applicable to all areas of the curriculum. But the middle-class school has difficulty in perceiving, recognizing and accepting these experiences in the context, format or language in which they are found.

It is not unusual for limited English-proficient children to be treated by the school as if their total experiential base is zero on the basis of the child's performance on an English language experiential base. Inability to communicate in English becomes equivalent to inability to communicate. Unfortunately, little research has been conducted as to how much learning takes place in atypical homes since the school is totally ignorant of the context and format of such learning.

Regardless of the quality and quantity of learning in atypical homes, it is obvious that children in such situations have developmental patterns which are different from those that the school has learned to expect from children from middle-class homes.

This difference in developmental patterns calls for an appropriate response by the school. It is relatively easy for the perceived or real limitations of achievement and participation to be overcome by a simple and short period of enrichment experiences which can develop the science and math experiences and understandings which appear to be absent in the home.

Unfortunately, the school has been notoriously ineffective in distinguishing between achievement and capability. The lack of science and math achievement brought to the school by the child with limited exposure in the home is consistently interpreted by the school, and larger society, as a lack of capability on the part of minority and disadvantaged children.

Instead of enrichment experiences to offset the curricular differences and/or limitations of the home, the school provides slow paced, watered down, intellectually unchallenging, limited and boring experiences compatible with the erroneously perceived low capability of the child. Thus the temporary deficit attributed to an initial limitation in the home becomes an increased, prolonged and oftentimes permanent deficit due to an extended limitation in the school.

Differing developmental patterns of low-status children are immediately converted into low-level expectations for these students in the school.

The low level of expectancy for atypical children turns into a self-fulfilling prophecy. This happens when the school experiences are based on the erroneous assumption that these children have limited capability and are therefore exposed to limited and limiting instructional experiences.

Oakes identified in her study three types of schools, with the type closely correlated to the geographic location of the schools in metropolitan areas. The three types are inner-city schools with enrollments made up primarily of minorities and disadvantaged, suburban schools in which minorities and disadvantaged students are underrepresented, and mixed schools with mixed enrollments.

ACCESS TO PROGRAMS

Quality science and math instruction is not accessible to minority and disadvantaged school populations due to three exclusionary mechanisms: lack of enrollment in quality classes, the low quality of science and math instruction in classes in which they are enrolled, and the subsequent effect of non-enrollment in "gatekeeping" classes.

The high socio-economic status schools with few minority and disadvantaged students were found to have the best science and math programs. The reason for the quality programs found in high socio-economic status schools is the quality and extent of science and math program offerings, the quality of the instructional staff, and the availability of resources in support of high quality programs. Although little research exists on the performance of the few minorities and disadvantaged enrolled in high status schools, Oakes found that even low-capability minority and disadvantaged student enrolled in high-status schools performed better in science and math than high-capability minority and disadvantaged students in lower status schools.

Although the quality of science and math programs in mixed schools was superior to that of low socio-economic status central city schools, minority and disadvantaged students seldom benefited from such programs. For the most part these students are excluded from participation in higher quality classes by two exclusionary practices at the mixed schools: ability grouping and "gatekeeping" courses.

The inability of the school to distinguish between past science and math experiences and student capability for learning results in students lacking in science and math achievement, participation *being perceived* as students with low capability, and placement in classes commensurate with this misperceived lack of ability. Ability grouping eventually leads to tracking, with the latter defined as "placement in a differentiated program without the option of changing to another program, thereby being locked into the differentiated program." This locking out of mainstream programs frequently happens in science and math because of the prerequisite learning required for advanced courses.

The Rand study identifies prerequisite courses as "gatekeepers" which lock out students from further science and math participation. Students who did not take algebra in the freshman and sophomore years are precluded from enrollment in trigonometry and calculus in subsequent years. Even though schools maintain that the option to enroll in an academic track still exists, the option may be in theory only, since it is not practical for a senior desiring to change from a non-academic to an academic track to enroll sequentially in ninth grade algebra, tenth grade geometry and eleventh grade trigonometry, prior to taking calculus. Exclusion at an early level guarantees continued exclusion throughout school and possibly throughout a lifetime. Subsequent and long-range exclusion becomes more tragic when one considers that early exclusion was based on erroneous perceptions.

Gatekeeping courses are commonly found at the senior high school level, although the Rand study identified similar exclusionary courses at the early middle school level. Exclusion from quality experiences in science and math often originated at the early elementary school level; the exclusion was then compounded throughout subsequent schooling.

ACCESS TO QUALIFIED TEACHERS

The Rand study found significant differences between the quality of science and math teachers available to high and low socio-economic status students.

Schools with large proportions of minority and disadvantaged students have fewer high-quality science and math teachers than schools enrolling mixed or large proportions of minority and disadvantaged students. The schools with lower socio-economic status students had less financial resources for attracting and hiring highly qualified teachers, and, in cases where financial resources were adequate, highly qualified teachers did not opt to teach in such schools.

Science and math teachers with large enrollments of minority and disadvantaged students indicated a lack of teacher interest in the student population, inadequate preparation for the teaching of science and math, and less confidence in their ability to teach science and math.

Comparisons of science and math teachers in the various types of schools and in varying tracks in mixed schools indicated that the minority and disadvantaged students consistently had the teachers with the least advanced degrees, lowest certification status, the least academic background in science and math, and the least teaching experience.

ACCESS TO RESOURCES

The Rand study compared resources other than teachers available to students in schools of different socio-economic status. In general, the study found large discrepancies in facilities and equipment in the elementary schools and even larger discrepancies in the secondary schools. Schools enrolling high socio-economic status students invariably had the better access to resources deemed necessary for the teaching of science and mathematics.

Significant differences were found in availability of computers to students, availability of specialized computer utilization staff, laboratories, special equipment, and even in the quality of science and math textbooks available to the students.

Instructional staff in schools enrolling low socio-economic level students frequently identified the lack of instructional resources as a critical problem in the teaching of science and math.

CLASSROOM OPPORTUNITY

The study analyzed curricular goals emphasized by teachers and the use of instructional strategies in high and low student status schools.

Curricular goals deemed essential for adequate performance in science and mathematics, such as the development of inquiry and problem-solving skills, were conspicuously absent in classes made up of minority, disadvantaged and inner-city students.

Findings did not identify differentiated curricular goals and instructional strategies in keeping with different student ability levels. As stated in the study, "On the contrary, students in low-track classes simply have less exposure to the teaching goals and strategies that are most likely to generate interest and promote learning among students at all achievement levels." The over inclusion of low-income and minority students in low-track classes decreases educational opportunity and performance in science and math.

IMPLICATIONS

The Rand study concludes that differences in performance of high and low socio-economic status students in science and math are attributed to significantly different educational opportunities available to the two groups.

Inferior opportunities are afforded to low socio-economic status students from minority groups, the economically disadvantaged and the inner cities. The inequality is initiated by common and extensive misclassification of low socio-economic status students as being limited in capability. The inequality is continued by inferior and inadequate instruction in elementary school and by limited access to quality science and math programs, teachers and instructional resources in the remaining school years.

The poor performance of minority and disadvantaged students in science and math occurs in a context of diminished resources and low expectations.

RECOMMENDATIONS

The recommendations for remediation of an unjust and unsound discriminatory treatment of a portion of the school population is pertinent to all state and local school systems. It is particularly pertinent to states like Texas in which the allocation of resources through the state system of school finance has been determined unconstitutional, and the state is seeking methods of correcting the existing inequities.

In addressing the inequities in resources for science and math programs in schools of varying wealth, the Rand study identifies three possible solutions which coincidentally parallel three attitudes toward school finance inequities which have characterized Texas finance reform efforts in the past twenty years.

Oakes presents three alternatives for eliminating the resource inequities: First, ". . . through legislative action and local district decisions, policy-makers and educators could redistribute the available resources to schools by shifting equipment, materials, and staff away from schools that now have more to schools that have less."

This is reminiscent of the "Robin Hood" approach to the school finance dilemma, and is rejected as a feasible alternative by the Rand publication as politically disastrous, in that "powerful constituencies would undoubtedly work to prevent a withdrawal of resources from currently advantaged schools."

The second alternative considered by the Rand study is the increase of the overall levels of educational resources so that all schools could command sufficient facilities, equipment, materials, and qualified staff to develop and sustain high-quality programs.

This alternative also parallels a common viewpoint on school finance reform efforts. Aside from the few plaintiff school districts in *Edgewood v. Kirby*, most school administrators and the majority of the Texas Legislature have favored increased resources for all school districts rather than equitable funding.

It is interesting that the Rand study also dismisses this alternative as a feasible solution for providing equitable science and math resources. This alternative "... holds little promise, since even as resources increased, the communities and parents who are now more advantaged would undoubtedly use their political clout to garner the lion's share of those resources for their schools and children."

The Rand study adds to the response to the second alternative that "... the notion of 'advantage' is a relative, rather than an absolute designation. Schools with better science and mathematics programs may still have legitimate needs for additional resources." This prediction in the study has become a reality in states that have attempted to equalize financial resources available to the various school systems. In Texas, this approach has led to billions of dollars in new funding since 1973, with the disparities between high- and low-wealth districts still as large or larger than before. Five billion dollars in 1984 did not reduce funding disparities.

The third alternative considered in the Rand study is an increase in educational resources with the new resources allocated on a priority need basis. It is this alternative which is considered both politically acceptable and potentially effective, although there is still some doubt about policymakers and educators supporting this preferential distribution to schools with large enrollments of low-status students.

Support for this preferential distribution in school finance litigation has come from the courts in the absence of political and educational leadership.

The prospect for school finance reform in Texas leading to an equitable distribution of resources for the improvement of science and math instruction for low-status students in low-wealth school districts is far from becoming a reality. Not a single legislative action to reform the system has included funding for facilities and equipment.

Multiplying Inequalities makes some additional recommendations for the improvement of science and math opportunities for children. Recommendations are grouped within the following topic headings:

- *Focusing on the Importance of Students' Opportunities*
- *Generating Resources and Devising Improvement Strategies*
- *Changing Priorities for Resource Allocation*
- *Improving the Use of Resources Within Schools*
- *Monitoring the Distribution of Opportunities and Accountability for Equal Opportunity*

PERSONAL RECOMMENDATIONS

In addition to the recommendations made by Ms. Oakes in the Rand study, there are additional recommendations which can be made which were not included in the study. These recommendations which should be considered in any attempt to improve opportunities in science and mathematics for at-risk school populations include:

The Elimination of Ability Grouping

Low levels of expectancy arise from the erroneous notion that school personnel have the capacity to distinguish between low achievement due to constrained or different experiences and low achievement attributed to lack of capability. Since there is an abundance of evidence that most children are misclassified and are therefore denied challenging and enriching school experiences, it is desirable to eliminate such groupings in the schools.

Ability grouping continues to be popular in the schools because it is conducive to lockstep methodologies, where students are expected to adapt to a predetermined curriculum, rather than undergo the inconvenience of the school having to adapt the curriculum to the varying capabilities, experiences and characteristics of children.

The whole concept of grouping children is pedagogically wrong and unsubstantiated by research. Studies indicate that regardless of the criteria used for grouping, the resulting subgroups rarely attain less than 75 percent of the original range, and in many cases the resulting range in the subgroups is almost identical to the range in the original group.

Ability grouping is commonly based on one curricular area, with reading being the most commonly used criteria. The subgroups formed frequently become constant for all other areas of the curriculum. Since there is a lack of evidence that students doing poorly in reading do so because of a lack of capability, let alone that the poor performance in reading is indicative of lack of capability in math, science, social studies, art, music and physical education, groups formed for one area of the curriculum are not valid for other areas. Even when subgroups may be reorganized for other curriculum areas, the stigma of low-ability grouping carries over and affects levels of expectancy in all areas of school activity.

Addressing School Tracking

Since so much of the determination of which science and math courses a student is able to access is dependent on past achievement in these areas and the successful completion of gatekeeping courses, it is desirable that students be subjected to minimum tracking. Options should be kept open until the last possible moment in students' school programs and even into post-secondary opportunities.

Since most students placed in non-academic tracks find themselves in such programs due to past academic experiences, rather than because of a lack of capability, one can only hope that sometime during the academic sequence or even after the termination of secondary schooling, the individual will be able to escape from the cumulative deficit situation and reverse the pattern of depreciating performance. Tracking assures that the unjustified effects of inadequate early schooling will be non-reversible regardless of changes in student perspectives brought about by maturity or experience.

QUALITY OF PROGRAMS

As indicated throughout the Rand study, the quality of student performance is drastically influenced by the level of expectations held for the student. Desires on the part of the school to present a higher quality of science and math program are mitigated by constraints and pressures applied to the school. State educational monitoring and accountability is frequently counterproductive in that public information concerning the performance of the school is frequently expressed in terms of student performance. This includes basic skills and minimum competencies, rather than in science and math or the higher-level cognitive skills, including the inquiry and problem-solving skills found missing in classes for low-status students in the Rand study.

QUALITY OF STAFF

The quality of instructional staff is an amorphous and pervasive variable. Although training, experience and attitudes among science and math teachers may be immensely important in determining the quality of science and math programs. It is apparent from the Rand study that teachers' attitudes toward minority and disadvantaged students has a strong effect on the levels of expectancy for such students and subsequently on their performance.

The inability of teachers to distinguish between achievement backgrounds and student capability usually initiates the long-lasting continuum of poor student performance. Much of the inability of teachers to distinguish between lack of achievement and capability is determined by teacher perceptions of the target population. It is therefore disheartening to note in a recent study published by the Metropolitan Life Insurance Company which indicates that new teachers have low expectations for a large portion of their students. The study, *New Teachers Speak Out*, consists of a poll by Louis Harris and Associates of new teachers in the 1990-91 school year (Metropolitan Life Insurance Company, 1991).

When asked to respond to the statement, "Many children come to school with so many problems that it's very difficult for them to be good students," 75 percent of the new teachers agreed with the statement. In response to the statement, "Even the best teachers find it difficult to really teach more than two-thirds of their students," 45 percent of the respondents expressed agreement with the statement.

It is evident that these new teachers polled as participants in teacher education programs are entering the teaching profession with low levels of expectancy for a portion of their students. Although the study does not delve into student characteristics, it is not difficult to guess which students the teachers will identify as having difficulty being good students or which students comprise the two-thirds who will be difficult to teach.

An aspect of staff quality not addressed by the Rand study is the impact of poor student performance on teacher attitudes, performance and subsequent decisions on career choice. It is my opinion that desertions from the teaching profession are frequently and erroneously attributed to the lack of tangible rewards in teaching, such as teacher salaries and fringe benefits, even though a much more viable reason for teachers leaving the profession is lack of job satisfaction, specifically the lack of success in teaching.

The elimination of teaching failure by the elimination of predestined student failure in groups erroneously grouped by ability could go far in retaining qualified teachers in the profession, particularly in the critical fields of science and math.

CONCLUSION

As is the case in so many new studies concerning the education of students at risk of dropping out of school and performing poorly while in school, the Rand study cites cases of success for students in programs which address the problems identified in the study. Although such successes are usually limited to small programs in specific systems, the exceptions serve to challenge the rule that poor performance in science and math is attributed to inherent characteristics of student populations; therefore such underperformance should neither be expected nor acceptable.

BIBLIOGRAPHY

Brookover, W. and L. Lezotte, "Educational Equity: A Democratic Principle at a Crossroads", *The Urban Review,* Vol. 13, No. 2, 1981.

Edgewood I.S.D., et al. v. Kirby, et al., Cause No. 362,516, 250th District Court, Austin, Travis County, Texas, 1987.

Lindsey, M., *State of the Art Report: Computers and the Handicapped,* Medford, OR: Northwest Regional Educational Laboratory, 1981, pp. 143–144.

Lipkin, J.P., *Equity and Microcomputer Use in the Public Education,* Litigation Support Services, Washington, D.C., 1983.

Metropolitan Life Insurance Company, *New Teachers Speak Out,* 1991.

Oakes, Jeannie, *Multiplying Inequalities: The Effects of Race, Social Class and Tracking on Opportunities to Learn Mathematics and Science,* The Rand Corporation, Santa Monica, July 1990.

Watt, D., "Education for Citizenship in a Computer-Based Society," in *Computer Literacy,* Seidel, R., R. Anderson and B. Hunter, eds., Academic Press, New York, 1982, p. 59.

Weinstein, Bernard L., in *Chronicle,* Houston, February 14, 1984.

DISCUSSION QUESTIONS

1. In 1983, the author made three predictions regarding the future role of the computer in education. Survey a local school district to assess the extent to which this forecast as been realized with respect to:

   (a) the presence of the computer for the management of instruction;

   (b) the job preparedness of the students for today's workplace;

   (c) the availability of computer software programs to serve atypical student populations.

2. How is Computer Assisted Instruction (CAI) uniquely suited to the needs of minority students?

3. If you were about to graduate and were prepared to teach science or math, what considerations would affect your choice of a school or a school district for employment?

4. Work with a group to prepare and carry out a survey of area teachers regarding the policy of ability grouping in schools and their expectations for student achievement. Compare your findings with those of the Louis Harris poll reported in this chapter.

8

Standardized Testing

PREFACE

During the six years that I was employed in the teacher education program at St. Mary's University, I was responsible for teaching the required course in standardized testing. Teaching this course and others, such as Individual Intelligence Tests, I came to appreciate the value of standardized tests for student diagnosis, program evaluation, research and other common uses.

In the intervening years I have developed extensive concern over the increased use of standardized tests in the schools and the defaulting of educational decision making to the results of these tests. Specifically, I have six major reservations about the role of standardized tests in the schools.

1. OVER-UTILIZATION

Although I personally went through the entire elementary and secondary grades without once taking a single standardized test, it appears that such testing has become an extensive part of the educational process. The types and numbers of tests now being used in the schools make extensive demands upon time and resources available for instruction. At periodic intervals new tests are required for different purposes and at different grade levels. The preparation for, administration, scoring and reporting of test data make a demanding effort on the part of school staff.

When I was serving on the National Commission on Testing and Public Policy two years ago, George Madaus of the Boston College based Center for the Study of Testing, Evaluation, and Educational Policy presented us with an estimate of 120 to 327 million tests being administered annually in education. In their 1993 book, Th*e Fractured Marketplace for Standardized Testing*, Haney, Madaus and Lyons have revised this estimate to between 400 and 500 million tests administered in 1981 (Haney, et al., 1993). Since their source estimates 5 million educational tests administered in 1930 and 100 million in 1960, the rate of growth in test administration is as astounding as the number of tests being administered.

Second only to the students who take all of these tests, teachers rank the highest in the amount of inconvenience associated with testing. Students spend a considerable amount of time preparing and taking these tests, time which would otherwise be spent on instructional activities. Teachers are commonly responsible for preparing the students for the tests, organizing and administering the tests, and in some cases scoring the tests and reporting test results.

This year I was asked to deliver a speech to a group of teachers in a large urban school district. I was preceded on the podium by the District Director of Evaluation who presented a list of tests to be administered that spring, and instructions on how and to whom the various tests were to be administered. The presentation was not lost on me. When introduced by a friend who informed the audience that I had finished high school and enrolled at the University of Texas when I was only fifteen years old, I started my presentation by confirming the introduction and then stated, "The reason I was able to finish high school at such an early age was that they didn't have standardized tests at that time, and my teachers spent all of their time teaching me." Needless to say, the standing ovation I received was very helpful in establishing good rapport with my audience for my subsequent presentation.

2. INFLUENCE ON EDUCATIONAL POLICY

This extensive amount of testing and the public dissemination of test results have had a strong impact on educational policy. Schools now have a "test driven curriculum." What is taught and how it is taught is heavily influenced by what will be tested. The importance given to the results of standardized testing and limits on the amount of instructional time leads to the conclusion, "If its not on the test, it's not worth teaching."

Since most of the standardized tests are based on multiple choice items, there is a strong tendency to teach only subjects, content and levels of learning which can be easily tested in a multiple choice test.

The extended period of time in which school testing emphasized the basic skills led to a deplorable emphasis on basic skills to the exclusion of the more important higher forms of learning.

The use of tests which determine student mastery of minimum levels of competency has led to minimum competency becoming an educational objective, rather than the maximum realization of all of a student's potential.

Standardized testing drives the curriculum in other ways. Past state policy which required English language testing for students using native language instruction in bilingual programs all but eliminated the use of the native language and promoted early exiting from the program in a futile attempt to produce immediate improved test performance in the English language.

Standardized tests have made innovation a high risk in the schools. The potential of any new approach must be weighed carefully on the effect that new content, methodologies or materials may have on that year's test results.

Not only the curriculum is test driven. More and more the making of educational decisions is heavily influenced by the impact on test results. Decisions on the placement in or the removal from a special education program, promotion and retention policies, graduation and other educational decisions have to take into consideration their impact on aggregate test scores.

Just like "the computer says" has become a rationalization for defaulting on making decisions, "the test says" is now commonly used for the justification of unpopular educational policy.

3. RELIABILITY

Reliability is the consistency with which an instrument measures. A clock which performs erratically, getting ahead and behind the actual time, is deemed as having low reliability, being invalid and therefore worthless. Tests as measuring instruments must have high reliability, making this concept of importance to test publishers.

Unfortunately, standardized tests do not have the reliability commonly assumed. I believe that many of the fluctuations in test results from year to year and which form the basis for elation when scores increase and frustration when they decrease, may be simple indications of lack of test reliability rather than changes in the performance of the schools.

Test item changes, cultural and societal changes, types of students tested, and other elements can account for a significant portion of longitudinal variations in test scores.

4. VALIDITY

Validity is the extent to which the test measures that which it is supposed to measure. Lack of test reliability is a cause of lack of validity. Time reported by an inaccurate clock is invalid since the time reported by such a clock is more an indication of the inadequacy of the clock than an indication of the correct time.

Standardized tests measure many things not intended by the test maker. Tests commonly measure the extent to which the student being tested is consistent with the type of student for whom the test was originally intended. Cultural traditions and orientations, socio-economic background, language idioms and geographic locations have a severe impact on test performance by a variety of students.

Although test salespersons make incredulous claims on the cultural fairness of their products, there is no such thing as a culturally fair test, since standardized tests are dependent on language, and language is inseparable from culture.

The biggest problem in the use of standardized testing is the failure of test users to understand that there is no such thing as inherent test validity. The best test in the world is only as valid as the circumstances under which it is administered. The best test in the world will not measure accurately what a student knows about a subject if the student has a massive bellyache while taking the test. Room temperature, lighting, noise levels, seating comfort, and neighboring students are but a few of the limitless test situations which can impact upon a student's performance on a test. Some students just cannot perform well on standardized tests, due to apprehensiveness or some other factor. It is therefore dangerous to make educational decisions which can alter a student's entire life on the basis of test performance.

Test publishers are aware of this and constantly caution the schools about the use of the test as a sole criterion for making educational decisions. Political, and oftentimes the educational leadership, commonly forget this warning and make bad decisions on the basis of bad test data. This error was dramatically demonstrated during the PPST litigation in which evidence was presented where students with the highest grade point averages, honor student designations, and highly recommended by their teachers were precluded from entering the teaching profession solely on the basis of poor test performance on this one standardized test.

5. STIGMATIZING OF STUDENTS

One of the worst aspects of standardized testing is the effect which test results have on students. Not only do they go through school in dread of failing the test, poor performance is often the realization of their worst fears. Negative concepts of self are commonly developed or reinforced on the basis of invalid test results. Thousands of students in Texas schools are being denied graduation on the basis of poor performance on test content based on subject matter not even encountered in their educational experiences. The political and educational leadership defends such action on the grounds of educational accountability, even though it is readily evident that it is the student who pays the penalty in this system of accountability rather than the school.

If the purpose of administering 400 million standardized tests is school accountability, this is the biggest waste of time and money in the history of education in this country. No other segment of the community does universal testing in order to determine adequacy of product. Accurate estimates of the adequacy of school performance can easily be obtained by a small sampling of the school population. It is inconceivable that the television industry would call every home in America in order to determine the success of a television program.

6. GATEKEEPING

Underlying the popularity of standardized tests is the concept of gatekeeping. More and more standardized tests are being used to deny access to opportunity to a large segment of the school's population. Civil rights legislation has made overt discrimination in providing equal opportunity more difficult. Covert discrimination is facilitated through the use of discriminating standardized tests.

During the more than thirty years since I was teaching college courses in the use of standardized tests my viewpoint has not changed. I still feel that such tests can be useful for diagnosing student needs, assessing student and school performance, evaluating school programs and for other purposes. I am very concerned over the extensive misuse of standardized tests and their negative effects on students.

BILINGUAL INTELLIGENCE TESTING

1972

The past few years have seen increased concern over the testing of intelligence of minority children, and particularly the assessment of mental abilities of non-English speaking or bilingual children.

Various national, regional, and local studies have ascertained that bilingual children are over-represented in classes for the mentally retarded. In some cases, the traditional underachievement characterizing minority children in the public schools has been rationalized on the basis of below normal mental abilities.

The unfair practice of administration of invalid intelligence tests to bilingual/bicultural populations has been noted and addressed by the courts and various civil rights agencies. In general, both the courts and regulatory agencies have understood at least some of the reasons for the lack of test validity and have consistently ruled against the use of language incompatible testing.

However, the remedy formulated by the courts, often at the insistence of plaintiffs, has resulted in equally discriminatory or, in some cases, even more discriminatory testing practices.

Courts have consistently ruled the use of English intelligence tests to be unfair to children of limited English speaking ability, but have then ruled that intelligence testing must be conducted in the language spoken in the child's home.

Such a response has not proved to be an ideal solution to the problem, and in most cases, has resulted in worse testing practices than those being replaced.

In order to understand why such responses are dysfunctional, it is necessary to review the rationale and methodology utilized in intelligence testing.

In general, intelligence testing is based on the following four assumptions:

1. Intelligence being an intangible cannot be measured directly, therefore, it must be measured indirectly and on the way intelligence influences certain behaviors. An intelligence test item is a situation in which the behavior of the testee is dependent on his mental abilities.

2. The test itself is a series of situations which represent ways in which intelligence is utilized. The test items are samples of activities influenced by intelligence.

For example, it is assumed that a person's vocabulary is influenced by his intelligence. An individual's mental abilities determine how many and which (quantity and quality) words he understands.

Since it is difficult and time consuming to determine all the words an individual knows, a sampling of words is used, and the ability of an individual to understand words on this list is then generalized to estimate his entire vocabulary.

3. It is assumed that the individual has been exposed to certain common experiences and that his knowledge is not dependent on his exposure to experiences, but rather to the amount that he gained or retained from these experiences.

In the vocabulary example used above, it is assumed that each of the words presented in the sample are words commonly perceived by the testee. If the testee failed to master the word, it is because in spite of having encountered the word, the testee was intellectually unable to conceptionalize it, or his ability to retain the concept is lacking.

4. It is assumed that the testee has all the necessary skills and competencies necessary for responding to the test situation: the only variable is the level of mental functioning. If in a test situation, a testee is required to write an answer, it is assumed that the testee knows how to write and that his ability to manipulate a pencil does not influence his behavior.

The four assumptions listed above immediately ascertain the invalidity of intelligence tests for persons who have atypical language, cultural, and socio-economic characteristics. In fact, the invalidity is so obvious that one wonders about school personnel who persist in the utilization of these tests when it is obvious even to lay judges, administrators, and community groups that the tests are biased, unfair, and invalid.

Testing the intelligence of a Spanish-speaking youngster through a sampling of English words penalizes the testee. He may not have had the opportunity to have heard the word in English, and the test does not measure any vocabulary that he has acquired in Spanish.

The assumption that the testee has been exposed to experiences basic to test activities similarly leads to invalidity. For the most part, experiences utilized in intelligence test items are taken from typical white, Anglo-Saxon, English-speaking, middle-class situations. Test critics go further and claim that the test items are biased in favor of northeast, urban populations. For example, one test item requires that a child associate a hill of snow with the type of vehicle used for transportation on this snow. A child from Key West, Florida; Brownsville, Texas; or San Diego, California may not have the experience of sliding down a snowy hill which the test assumes everybody has. His failure in the item may be attributed to this lack of experience rather than the low level of intelligence implied by the test.

Culturally different children experience the same failure due to not having the experiences assumed by the test items rather than lack of intelligence.

When an intelligence tester asks a Mexican American or Puerto Rican child, "What would you do if your mother sends you to the store to buy a loaf of bread and the grocer does not have any?" it is assumed that the child is acquainted with the concept of bread among other things. If the child is better acquainted with home-produced flour tortillas or tostones and does not know how to react to the problem situation, it is dangerous to assume a low intellect.

Intelligence tests often require special skills and abilities commonly acquired at the age or grade level at which the test is administered. A fifth grade intelligence test may require third grade reading skills. The tester assumes that a fifth grader can read at least at the third grade level. However, if the fifth grade student were academically retarded because he did not learn to read in the first grade due to his having to develop fluency in the English language, and subsequently did not possess third grade reading skills at the fifth grade level, the assumption that he possesses the necessary skills is false and the test item, and subsequently the test, and the score(s) produced are invalid.

As stated previously, courts, unlike educators, have not experienced difficulty in understanding the reasons for the lack of validity tests developed for white, Anglo-Saxon, English-speaking, middle-class populations when applied to non-white, non-Anglo-Saxon, non-English-speaking, or non-middle-class populations.

However, the remedy implemented by the courts has frequently been equally dysfunctional and invalid.

In one case involving Mexican American children, the court addressed the administration of English language intelligence tests to be replaced by the administration of Spanish language intelligence tests. It is assumed that the results were disastrous.

In the first place, there are no Spanish language intelligence tests developed for or standardized for Mexican American children. In the second place, language is not the only invalid characteristic of intelligence tests used for minority populations.

In order to illustrate the ramification and complexity of the problem, the writer will draw from his experience in the measurement of mental abilities of Mexican American children. Using a very simple test of mental abilities in order to avoid the complexities of analyzing a test such as the Wechsler or Binet which require and assume much more sophisticated testee skills and experiences, the writer did extensive testing of Mexican American elementary school children using the Peabody Picture Vocabulary Inventory.

The Peabody utilizes a simple rationale and methodology. The testee is presented a test kit which has been divided into four compartments, with each of the four compartments containing a picture: at the lower levels of the test it depicts a simple object and at higher levels an activity or some complex concept.

The tester gives an oral stimulus word and the testee is to indicate which of the four pictures on the plate depicts the stimulus word. For example, a plate may depict a butterfly, a bird, a baseball bat, and an elephant. When the testor says, "Show me "butterfly," the child is expected to point to the picture of the butterfly. Assuming that he has experienced the objects depicted, it is assumed that his response to the stimulus word is dependent on, and solely on, his mental abilities. It is assumed that he has seen a butterfly, and that he has previously heard and perhaps used the word "butterfly."

The fallacy of these assumptions mentioned previously holds true in this test situation. It is not only possible, but extremely common that a child from a Spanish-speaking home has never heard this insect being referred to as a butterfly. Although he may have heard it referred to by a Spanish word, which incidentally in no way resembles the phonetic elements of butterfly (*mariposa*) and may be able to identify the word if the stimulus word were to be presented in Spanish, his failure to respond correctly assumes a low level of mental ability. Incidentally, many children from Spanish-speaking environments who are highly fluent in English have never heard the test words in the English language.

The opposite of this situation is also true. Mexican American children who are fluent in Spanish frequently have never heard the Spanish equivalent of some English words, either because there is no commonly utilized Spanish language equivalent or the concept is extraneous to the race, ethnic or socio-economic culture of the child. For instance, the writer has never heard a commonly used Spanish language equivalent for the English language words "marshmallow," "cream puff," "hot dog," or "bush."

For bilingual children, the validity of Spanish language testing depreciates tremendously. The bilingual child by definition is one who has fluency in two languages. Testing in English does not reach the vocabulary content the child may possess in Spanish; testing in

Spanish does not sample the child's English vocabulary. Similarly, English sampling does not identify words associated with a child's Mexican (Spanish, Indian, Hispanic, Latin) culturally related concepts; Spanish sampling does not identify words associated with a child's English (American) culturally related concepts.

Many attempts have been made to validate intelligence tests through translations. For the most part, such attempts have proved fruitless. The writer has seen, at some time or another, at least a dozen attempts to translate the Peabody test. The following example illustrates the reason for the failure of translations to validate intelligence measures:

1. The Spanish language competency of some translators have left a lot to be desired. In one do-it-yourself translation of the Peabody test called to the attention of the writer, the stimulus word "hot dog" has been translated "un perro caliente" which at best means "a dog which is warm" and at worst means "a dog in heat."

2. Translators have a difficult time identifying dialectic characteristics of the second language, often peculiar to an area or region in which the translated test is utilized. In the administration of the Peabody, the writer had translated the stimulus word "tree" into the Spanish "arbol." In one school, almost every Spanish-speaking student had failed the test item. After a test administration, I asked a child, "What is that?" while pointing to the tree. The child replied, "Es un palo." I subsequently found that in that area the word "arbol" was never used; "palo" was the accepted terminology.

As we have seen previously, the assumption that the testee is acquainted with the word and the concept did not hold true, therefore, the item was invalid.

3. A third problem encountered in the translation of tests is retaining the level of difficulty of a test item. In the development of a test, the items must possess a certain level of difficulty to distinguish between age or grade levels. A test item using a stimulus word must ascertain the word is commonly known by the members of an age group (such as eight-year-olds, but not commonly known by seven-year-olds). If an eight-year-old does not know the word, it is assumed that he has inferior intelligence. If an eight-year-old knows the word he is assumed to be of average intelligence. If a seven-year-old knows the word, he is assumed to be of superior intelligence.

In general, words are ranked by difficulty. The level reached by a child in relation to his age constitutes his intelligence.

The translation of a word frequently changes the level of difficulty for that word. For example, the Peabody uses the stimulus word "tumble" which must be associated with the picture of a child "tumbling" down a hill. As stated previously, there is no commonly used Spanish language equivalent for this word.

Translators have used the words "tropezar" and "caer" as stimulus words in Spanish. Yet, "tropezar" means "trip" which may or may not be at the same level of difficulty as tumble. It may be easier (at a lower level) or it may be harder (at a higher level). The alternative "caer" means "fall" and is generally at a much lower level of difficulty than "tumble."

Levels of difficulty for vocabulary words change from language to language and when one word has several translations the level of difficulty changes from one translation to the other. Such a situation most definitely invalidates each such test item.

4. A similar situation exists in the index of discrimination for test items. The value of a stimulus word in a test item is dependent on its ability to discriminate, that is, high-intelligence testees will consistently get it right, low-intelligence testees will consistently get it wrong.

In the development of a test, huge quantities of test items are discarded due to their inability to produce this discrimination. The ones that are retained have been found to make the discrimination consistently. The translation of a test item changes the index of discrimination. The translated word may favor the low-intelligence child and penalize the high-intelligence individual. Therefore, translated test items must be re-analyzed for their ability to discriminate.

The four problems listed above make it virtually impossible to utilize a translation of an intelligence test with any degree of validity. In order to utilize such a test, it is necessary to conduct the necessary item analysis, and re-norm the test for the intended population. The amount of work involved would be almost identical to the effort made in the original development of the test.

It should be noted that the lack of validity holds true regardless of language characteristics or ethnicity of the administrator. There is no basis for assuming that an invalid instrument becomes valid when used by experts, sensitive or skilled individuals, or by sympathetic or empathetic administrators. The claim by school personnel that translated tests are valid because the administrator has a "high degree of knowledge of Mexican American children" is asinine, and is not substantiated by reason or research.

Assuming that a test publishing company came up with a high-quality translation of an intelligence test for bilingual children, the administration of such a test would still present some formidable problems.

In attempting to obtain more valid administrations of the Peabody, the writer tried administering two tests to the testee. The first administration was in English, the second in Spanish.

It was found that when the English version was given, several items were missed by the testee due to the language described previously. Surprisingly, when the test was administered in Spanish, the testees tended to make the same mistakes in the Spanish language, even when subsequent investigation indicated that the testees knew the right answers. They consistently made the same wrong choice when retested in a more familiar language.

It appears that the behavior of selecting a choice from the four pictures presented turned out to be self-reinforcing. Having made that choice there was a strong tendency to stick to that choice even when he subsequently discovered it to be a wrong one.

In order to prevent wrong choice reinforcement, the two tests were administered simultaneously, that is, the stimulus word was given in English and in Spanish in order to prevent the first response from becoming self-reinforcing. The testee was not allowed to respond until the stimulus was presented in both languages.

Performance on such administrations improved dramatically, even though some new problems were discovered.

Administrations were made where the English stimulus word was presented before the Spanish word, and in some administrations the sequence was reversed, with the Spanish being used before the English word. The results showed significant differences in the measurement of intelligence depending upon which language cue was used first. In general, through the first three grades, Spanish followed by English produced higher results; in grades four to six, English followed by Spanish produced significantly higher results.

Perhaps this finding can be attributed to language dominance, although no attempt was made at the time to explain the phenomenon.

The foregoing evidently supports the contention that it is difficult, if not impossible, to measure with a high degree of validity the intelligence or mental abilities of children who speak two languages or by the use of a test in a second language. Past efforts to do so proved to be detrimental and led to the over-inclusion of minority children in classes for the mentally retarded. It can be assumed that low levels of expectancy for a child assumed to be mentally retarded led to a self-fulfilling prophecy much to the life-long detriment of minority children.

Recent attempts to remedy the situation by the administration of "translations" are equally dysfunctional and will perpetuate an unfortunate situation.

If school personnel persist in their efforts to evaluate the mental abilities of minority children, or, for that matter, the economically or educationally handicapped, it is necessary that an extensive research and development effort be undertaken.

Alternative ways of assessing mental abilities must be identified which will probably have to differ considerably from past practices. Psychometrists have gone so far up the wrong creek in the assessing of minority mental abilities that it is wise to heed the National Education Association's recommendation that all intelligence testing of minority children be suspended until alternative ways may be explored.

USE OF TESTS: EDUCATIONAL ADMINISTRATION

1972

(Originally published in the Report of *the Tenth National Conference of Civil and Human Rights in Education*, National Education Association, 1972.)

The most serious problem in the assessment of intelligence and the use of intelligence tests is the assumptions that are made. One assumption is that intelligence is intangible and not directly measureable. Secondly, intelligence can be indirectly measured by assessing some form of behavior related to other variables such as related understanding, prior learning, and motivation. Thirdly, evaluation of behavior and performance requires written, oral, or nonverbal interaction between tester and testee. Fourthly, test results give little information unless a comparison is made between the performance of the tester and the norm group.

Research indicates more is unknown than is known about intelligence and that the assumptions and methods of testing are not always valid. Performance can be based on more than the one variable of intelligence. Our assumption that all other factors are equal or that nondependent variables have nothing to do with intelligence is false. Language facility, reading ability, and cultural compatibility all influence test scores.

Too many intelligence tests assume that all children have had common experience, for example, a question on the Wechsler Intelligence Scales for Children (WISC) asks, "If your mother sends you to the store for a loaf of bread and there is none, what do you do?" The child who answers "I go back home," is considered to be intellectually inferior to the child who says, "I go to another store." However, in rural areas, there is no place else to go. In some families, the parent and not the child is supposed to make such a decision. A second major problem in testing is the dysfunctional responses we sometimes use to try to remedy our invalid assumptions. It is simplistic to give a Puerto Rican child a Spanish translation of the WISC. Some English stimulus words become Spanish paragraphs when translated properly. I have never heard a one-word translation of "cream puff" yet this word is on the Spanish version. Also, the Spanish equivalent of an English word may be an entirely different level of difficulty. No matter how good the Spanish translation of a test, it must take into account the regional variation of the language.

In conclusion, we must protect all students against invalid testing. We must reeducate educational personnel and perhaps discontinue intelligence testing. We must develop new and functional techniques for measuring intelligence and establish different criteria for making decisions.

TABS AND THE EMPEROR'S NEW CLOTHES

1981

Once upon a time an emperor was hustled by a phony tailor who sold him a set of clothes which were supposed to be magnificent, except that they were invisible to fools. The emperor walked around naked, "showing off" his new clothes and receiving the compliments of all his subjects. Neither the emperor nor anybody else would admit that they could not see the new clothes for fear of being considered fools. The farce was concluded when an innocent little boy remarked that he could not see any clothes on the emperor. Soon everyone, including the emperor, realized that they had been had.

I was reminded of this amusing story some years back when Governor Dolph Briscoe was addressing a joint conference of the Texas Association of School Administrators and the Texas Association of School Boards. In his speech, Governor Briscoe complimented participants by stating that Texas has the finest system of schools in the country.

Much to my surprise, the audience reacted by giving Mr. Briscoe a long and loud standing ovation. I say "surprised" because although I am as patriotic and proud as any other Texan, there is no way that I can perceive the Texas educational system as the finest or the best one in the country. In essence, the standing ovation given by board members and administrators constituted a compliment of the emperor's magnificent new clothes, although I for one could not see them.

If one looks through the invisible garments, one can't help but note that Texas expends an unusually low amount of state funds for the support of the public schools. Texas is one of the few states which provides absolutely no funds for school construction. The distribution of state and local funds creates greater disparities between "wealthy" and "poor" school districts. Texas is a national leader in the percentage of students who drop out of school prior to completion of the twelfth grade. Programs in vocational education, compensatory education, and for the gifted and talented are few in number and commonly suffer from inadequate resources. Teachers' salaries are low as compared to other states and even lower as compared to other professions and businesses in Texas. Teacher availability, turnover and inadequate preparation constitute problems which resurface periodically. Schools have not learned how to cope with the special characteristics of atypical populations such as Blacks, the limited English proficient and the disadvantaged.

The list of unsolved problems goes on and on, but it is certain that our state does not have a fine educational system, much less the best in the country.

The subjects of this state have two options: one, to make believe we have the best in the country and "ooh" and "aah" over the invisible and nonexistent; or two, to identify the weaknesses in the Texas educational system and correct them. Although many educators and school personnel have traditionally, and perhaps subconsciously, elected the first option, it is becoming increasingly difficult to do so. One reason for this is the surfacing of information showing us the shortcomings of the Texas system.

In this case, the analogy of the little boy in the story who ended the pretention about the emperor's new clothes may well be the Texas Assessment of Basic Skills (TABS). TABS is an assessment program enacted by the Texas legislature in 1979. It requires a standard criterion-referenced test to be administered to all students in grades three, five, and nine. It is a criterion-referenced test of basic skill mastery in mathematics, reading, and writing. During the first administration of TABS, which occurred in the 1979–80 school year, several problems surfaced in the content, administration, and scoring of the test. An improved revised form was utilized during the 1980–81 school year.

Improvements in the instrument, however, did not yield significant improvements in the relative performance of the students. The results of the testing program were exemplified by math and reading scores for ninth graders. The percentages of White children mastering the basic skills at this grade level were 84 percent for math and 84 percent reading. The percentages of Hispanic children mastering the basic skills were only 60 percent for math and 52 percent for reading. Black children mastering the skills totaled only 45 percent in math and 45 percent in reading.

Economically disadvantaged children throughout the state fared poorly with only 54 percent mastering math and 47 percent mastering the reading skills. The percentages of students demonstrating mastery of all three portions of the test (math, reading, and writing) were 72 percent for whites, 39 percent for Hispanics, and 30 percent for Blacks.

On the basis of ethnic/racial breakouts by regions and specific school districts, one must conclude that the minority and economically disadvantaged populations fared poorly in the statewide testing program. A correlation analysis of school districts in the San Antonio area comparing the mastery of the skills tested and the percentage of student ethnicity resulted in a coefficient of .86. This indicates that the performance of a school district was largely influenced by the percentage of minority children in that school district. This relationship has to be viewed cautiously lest one conclude that a school district did poorly because there were many minority children in it and fail to follow through with the added observation that a school district did poorly because there were many minority children *and* minority children are not being taught adequately.

A cursory glance at district and regional scores indicates that a relationship also exists between the low property wealth of certain school districts and their low level of performance on the Texas Assessment of Basic Skills.

Although the performance of white middle-class children in Texas schools may be judged borderline, with 28 percent of them failing at least one area of the test, there is no question as to the inadequacy of performance for the minority and disadvantaged children. It is impossible for Texas to shrug off this unsatisfactory performance in the light of the political, social and economic consequences of this underperformance. Although few studies have been conducted on the cost of non-education, one can assume that Texas will be burdened by the results of unemployment, underemployment, rehabilitation, incarceration and welfare for many years to come. The quality of life and standard of living will continue to be substandard in proportion to the failures of the educational system.

The results of the Texas Assessment of Basic Skills indicate an urgent need for a statewide strategy to address the educational needs of minority and disadvantaged children. A statewide plan must be developed to address inadequacies in instructional programs which make them dysfunctional for the culturally different, limited English proficient, and economically disadvantaged children. There is a desperate need for the reallocation of state resources in support of this strategy.

As further analysis of the Texas Assessment of Basic Skills is developed, more information should be obtained which will provide additional insights into the inadequacies of our state system of public education. By the time the Texas Legislature reconvenes in 1983, the groundwork should be prepared for a retesting of the state's commitment to equality of educational opportunity.

THE STATE BOARD OF EDUCATION AND THE PPST LITIGATION

1985

On August 27, 1985, the Federal District Court for the Eastern District of Texas issued a temporary injunction prohibiting the use of student performance on the Pre-Professional Skills Test (PPST) as a barrier to enrollment in teacher education courses in Texas colleges and universities (*U.S. v. Texas*, 1985).

The PPST requirement originated in a 1981 Texas law which specified that the State Board of Education issue rules for a competency exam of basic skills as a condition for a student's admission into an approved teacher education program. In February 1984 the State Board of Education (SBOE) adopted test regulations, set cut-off scores, and informed colleges of the new requirement. Actual testing in colleges and universities began in March 1984.

By July 1985 more than 18,000 students had taken the test, with failure rates of 27 percent for whites, 66 percent for Hispanics, and 77 percent for Blacks.

Plaintiffs argued in court that the cut-off scores on the PPST were adopted arbitrarily, and that the exclusion of massive numbers of minority students from teacher education programs without regard to other factors, such as grades or bilingual language fluency, diminished the number of new minority teachers at a time when Texas faces severe shortages of teachers in general and bilingual teachers in particular.

The issuance of the preliminary injunction was determined by four factors: irreparable harm to minority students from failure to issue the injunction; the relative lack of harm to the state of Texas from issuance of the injunction; the public interest; and the probability that plaintiffs will ultimately succeed on the merits in the subsequent trial of the case.

The effect of the injunction is that students performing below the Texas Education Agency (TEA) cut-off scores cannot be precluded from enrollment in teacher education courses until a decision is rendered by the courts.

TEA REACTION

The reaction of the Texas Education Agency was predictably swift. Within ten days after the preliminary injunction had been issued by the court, TEA and the Attorney General had filed a request for a stay, had presented arguments in its behalf, and had been turned down by the appellate court.

This action by TEA was predictable because it is in keeping with a long tradition at the agency to make an all-out effort to oppose any litigation, as well as legislation and regulations, which pose a threat to the status quo.

The Texas Education Agency fought the *Rodriguez* case, which found the Texas system of school finance unconstitutional, all the way to the Supreme Court where they finally prevailed with a five to four questionable victory, only to conclude a few years later that the biggest single problem in attempting to offer a minimally adequate education to all children in Texas was the unfair and inequitable system of school finance (*Rodriguez*, 1971). This problem, institutionalized by the TEA victory in *Rodriguez* is still with us, since the recently enacted HB 72 only diminished interdistrict disparities by 10 percent and teacher salary disparities by 12 percent. Much of the credit for the persistence of this problem must be given to the Texas Education Agency which fought so hard in its defense.

The Bilingual Motion in *U.S. v. Texas* is still dragging out in the courts more than twelve years after it was filed, and at a horrendous cost to the taxpayers of the state of Texas (*United States v. Texas*, 1971). Efforts to negotiate a settlement have been unsuccessful, and we can anticipate another round of hearings, appeals, and court orders.

Doe v. Plyler, and the accompanying Multiple District Litigation is unusual for the viciousness with which the Texas Education Agency fought it all the way to the Supreme Court where the Plaintiffs finally prevailed (*Doe v. Plyler*, 1978; *In Re Multiple District Litigation*, 1980). Civil rights attorneys are still shocked at the opposition given to the education of undocumented alien children in spite of the fact that virtually every expert who testified in the case was of the opinion that the children in question would eventually become legal citizens whose educational deprivation would have disastrous implications for the state of Texas. Even the calloused Immigration and Naturalization Service took drastic measures to prevent the schools from becoming the focal point for the identification of undocumented aliens, lest the parents become reluctant to send their children to school. The vicious defense of the TEA was based primarily on a paranoid concept that allowing children to attend school would lead to an influx of hordes of undocumented children. After the courts forced the state of Texas to educate these children, fewer than 10 percent of TEA's estimate of 112,000 appeared in the schools.

THE COST OF LITIGATION

There are many reasons why a decision to pursue litigation should be given serious and extensive consideration. Not the least of these reasons is the cost involved. Attorneys for plaintiffs in *Doe v. Plyler* state that the state of Texas paid almost $500,000 in costs allocated by the court. Assuming Texas expended an equal amount in the defense, the bill totaled approximately one million dollars.

U.S. v. Texas presents a worse scenario. Almost $500,000 has been paid in court costs to the plaintiffs. It can be assumed that an equal amount has been expended in legal costs for the defense. At one point TEA stated that the response to interrogatories, questions to be answered prior to the trial, entailed staff time equivalent to some $450,000. Using a conservative estimate that an additional $550,000 has been expended by plaintiffs and defense since costs were last paid, it is estimated that Texas has expended $2 million in the defense of a case in which many of the differences between plaintiffs and defendants were resolved by the subsequent enactment of Senate Bill 477, the bilingual education law, and the remaining differences could have been negotiated.

Lawyers for plaintiffs in the PPST case asserted that the ten day period of the TEA request for a stay of the temporary injunction cost them $20,000. Adding an equal amount for state expenses would indicate that $40,000 of public money was expended in the ten day period if plaintiffs are awarded costs. Having lost the request for a stay, TEA is currently working on an appeal of the injunction. It can be estimated that the entire bill for this court case will be in the millions of dollars.

Although financial considerations should not be the sole determiner for decisions on litigating actions, the cost of requests for stays, appeals for temporary injunctions, and hearings at the various levels would demand a careful consideration of the merits and implications of each case, before initiating a quixotic defense of the status quo.

STATE BOARD OF EDUCATION INVOLVEMENT

The swift action of TEA and the Attorney General's Office in the PPST case does not reflect a careful consideration of the merits and the implications of the case. I had the opportunity to speak to several members of the State Board of Education after the TEA request for a stay on the temporary injunction had been denied. Much to my surprise their familiarity with the case was limited. Three board members had not seen the opinion rendered by the Federal District Court. This raises two interesting questions:

- Does the Commissioner of Education have the legal prerogative to initiate legal action in behalf of the Texas Education Agency without prior consultation and approval of the State Board of Education?
- Should the State Board review the merits of the case before the initiation of an almost automatic response involving further litigation?

RELATED ISSUES

In deciding the appropriateness of expending several million dollars in the defense of the PPST case, there are several important issues that should have been considered. The following are but a few of the prime concerns which should be addressed:

- The plaintiffs are not seeking to overturn the law which establishes the PPST. It does not challenge the right of the state nor the Texas Education Agency to impose minimum standards to guarantee the quality of teachers in the classroom. They do take issue with the speed of implementation and the effect that it had on minority populations. Is it possible that the former State Board of Education acted unwisely in finalizing test regulations in February 1984, and beginning testing in March 1984, with little warning or time for preparation? The judge states in his court order, "It is clear from the correspondence emanating from the Texas Education Agency (Plaintiff-intervenors' Exhibits 4, 5, and 6) that the requirement was adopted in a rather disorganized fashion, with insufficient publicity or clarity." Should not the Texas Education Agency and the Attorney General's Office review exhibits 4, 5 and 6 for the possibility that the implementation procedure was flawed?
- It is reported that TEA paid Dr. James Popham and IOX Associates $250,000 for the validation of the PPST. Regardless of the amount, the court heard testimony which cast doubts on the appropriateness of the validation. Since two-thirds of the minority students who took the test (2,299 out of 3,031) were kicked out of teacher education programs and the state of Texas has a drastic need for minority and bilingual teachers, should not the Texas Education Agency review the test validation

procedures which the court found so inadequate before spending several million dollars in their defense? Should the state of Texas be exploring the possibility of recovering the funds paid Dr. Popham?

- In discussing some aspect of the case with an attorney representing the state of Texas, an attorney for the plaintiffs was informed that he should communicate with the attorneys for the Educational Testing Service (ETS), authors of the PPST, since ETS was in charged of the case. If this is true, is the state of Texas and the Texas Education Agency only providing funds and a forum for the Educational Testing Service to protect its financial investment in the development of the test?

- The plaintiffs maintain that the cut-off scores that determine eligibility for entrance into teacher education programs were arbitrarily set. Although nobody is in favor of placing incompetent teachers in the classroom, what guarantees are available that the cut-off scores adequately distinguish between competency and incompetency? The minority students who flunked the test were not a random sampling of the population. Various studies indicate that 60 percent of the minority population in Texas drop out of school prior to completion of the twelfth grade; half of those that graduate go to college; half of those that go to college attend only community colleges and do not enroll in junior or senior courses. The conclusion is that the 3,031 who took the test, with 76 percent of them failing, is a sampling from the best performing 10 percent of the minority population in Texas. Either the test is extremely invalid, the educational system of the state leaves much to be desired, or probably "all of the above."

- The Texas Education Agency has a long history of mistrust of the use of a single criterion in formulating educational decisions. The IQ score which was used for the placement of mentally retarded students in Special Education classes was replaced with Admission, Review and Dismissal (ARD) committees to prevent misclassifications. In a similar action TEA promoted and required LPAC committees for placement and removal from a bilingual program in lieu of the use of a language proficiency score. Is the Texas Education Agency contradicting itself in defending the use of a single test score to determine who will make a good teacher and who should be kept out of the profession? Some of the students who testified in the court hearings were A and *B* students in their colleges. Either the test score is an invalid measure, or the problem of teacher preparation is much deeper than what the PPST can resolve.

- The defense of the Texas Education Agency in accounting for the poor performance of 67 percent of Hispanics and 73 percent of the Blacks taking the test is unbelievable. The judge notes TEA officials reflect an attitude ". . . that minority students were themselves to blame for their poor performance." Reasons given for the poor performance included lack of intellectual ability on the part of the students, failure to listen in class and do homework, teacher lack of basic skills, and the income levels of the students. If no further action on the PPST is taken by the State Board of Education, it would behoove it to pursue these simplistic and prejudiced deficit models presented to the court by the Commissioner and the Deputy Commissioner of Education.

- One topic not covered in the hearings is the role of the Texas education Agency in the monitoring and regulating of teacher education programs in the state. The Commissioner of Education made a statement to the media that the injunction would be appealed in order to guarantee the quality of teachers available to our children. However, this has been the responsibility of the Texas Education Agency since its inception. The Agency monitors, visits, accredits and supervises teacher education programs throughout the state. If indeed the teaching ranks are full of illiterates and incompetents, is it not an indictment of the responsible state agency? If teacher quality can be controlled by the PPST, it would make the Deputy Commissioner for Education Quality, the Assistant Commissioner for Professional Development and the Divisions of Teacher Education and Accreditation superfluous.

The following statement is expressed in the court opinion by the judge who will hear the case: ". . . it is concluded that they (plaintiffs) have a substantial likelihood of success on the merits of this claim."

It appears that the Texas Education Agency is retracing its steps in *Doe v. Plyler*. It is blindly defending an issue which may be indefensible. It would be much preferable in deference to both parties' interest in the education of children to proceed cautiously, study the issues, and take the necessary steps to guarantee the improvement of educational opportunities than to expend time, effort, and resources in defense of an unjust action.

If nothing else, the Texas Education Agency's decision to appeal the PPST case further polarizes the mainstream and minority communities in the state. It lends support to the widely-held belief that TEA plays an adversative role to the minority quest for improved educational opportunities. It provides substance to the minorities' beliefs that they must resort to the courts in order to be protected from the agency which could do the most to improve the quality of their life.

BIBLIOGRAPHY

Doe v. Plyler, 458 F. Supp. 569 (E.D. Tex. 1978).

Haney, Walter M., George F. Madaus and Robert Lyons, *The Fractured Marketplace for Standardized Testing*, Kluwer Academic Publishers, Norwell, 1993.

National Education Association (NEA), *Report of the Tenth National Conference of Civil Rights and Human Rights in Education*, Washington, D.C., 1972.

In Re Alien Children's Education Litigation, 501 F. Supp. 544, 550 (S.D. Tex. 1980).

Rodriguez v. San Antonio Independent School District, 337 F. Supp. 280 (W.D. Tex. 1971).

United States v. Texas, 342 F. Supp. 24 (E.D. Tex. 1971).

DISCUSSION QUESTIONS

1. Develop a list of pitfalls to avoid in the development and the use of intelligence tests and basic skills tests for students from atypical populations.
2. Outline a proposal for your state education agency for the fair and responsible assessment of students who are:
   (a) culturally different;
   (b) limited English proficient;
   (c) economically disadvantaged.
3. Review the various obstacles to educational success among minorities as presented in this and previous chapters.
4. How do state policies and attitudes regarding teacher education and certification reflect chronic official resistance to providing equal educational opportunity to all students?

9

School Reform

PREFACE

The massive underperformance of large segments of the school population cries out for drastic changes in the schools. Minorities, disadvantaged, limited English proficient, migrant, immigrant children are leaving the schools in large numbers without the necessary skills for earning a decent living. The number of such children is further augmented by a sizable percentage of mainstream students experiencing little success in school and the inability of the schools to provide gender equity in male-dominated fields.

The outlook for race, national origin and gender equity is not bright, since the lack of value placed on such populations by the larger society and reflected in the performance of the school, places a low priority on addressing the problem. School reform efforts at the national, state and local levels adhere to a "trickle down" philosophy which demands that these efforts be focused on reforming the basic structure of the school, with a built-in assumption that when the efficiency of the school is improved, educational benefits with trickle down to all elements in the population. This "trickle down" approach in education reform is not too different from the trickle down economic policy of the past decade which exacerbated rather than diminished the economic plight of the disadvantaged in the United States.

The school reform leadership of the country shares the same position as the educational leadership. As I testified in *Keys v. Denver* more than twenty years ago, educators generally have little insight into the cultural characteristics of minority students and their impact upon school performance (*Keyes* , 1983). Those few that develop such an understanding do nothing about it in terms of educational practice. The insignificant number who attempt to address the problem, invariably do the wrong thing.

Problems in the education of atypical students are so pervasive and the effect is so massive that there exists an urgent need to develop a new educational paradigm based on the old and the new needs of American education. The Jeffersonian imperative of an educated citizenry for the effective performance of a participatory democracy is still with us, although the dissolution of the family and the growth of social problems gives education a more important role.

Equal educational opportunity remains an unfulfilled promise in a land based on the concept that all men are created equal. Two other forces require drastic reform in the schools: the changes in the economic bases at the national, state and local levels, and an equally drastic change in industrial efficiency.

The change of the economy from agricultural, mineral and industrial production to information and services, while the need for unskilled labor has diminished to the point of disappearing, demands an efficient educational system to provide the work force needed in support of the new economy.

In their book, *Thinking for a Living*, Ray Marshall and Marc Tucker make a strong argument for a movement away from assembly line labor to a more sophisticated development-oriented work force if the United States is to meet world competition in industrial production (Marshall and Tucker, 1992). The present educational goals of producing a worker with proficiency in the basics of reading, writing and arithmetic, who can follow simple directions and knows how to behave is an anachronism in our new technological world.

I can predict without any reservations that a drastic breakthrough in the education of atypical populations cannot and will not come about under the existing paradigm for American education. Education is caught in a vicious cycle of deficit perceptions of atypical students, leading to a deficit performance, rationalized by the deficit perceptions. Present reform efforts are cosmetic, changing the appearance of education but doing little for the basic inadequacies.

During its twenty-year history, Intercultural Development Research Association (IDRA) has been extensively involved in addressing the educational problems of atypical students. For the most part, this involvement has been too small a tail for wagging a very big dog. Success in a massive reform of education lies in advocacy organizations like the IDRA who are meeting two goals. The first is to demolish the current educational philosophy that deficits in atypical populations account for their poor performance in schools. This requires the development and establishment of pilot programs which demonstrate that under appropriate conditions the performance of atypical students can parallel the performance of mainstream students. The second is the development of a framework for a massive restructuring of education, that is, the development of a new educational paradigm which will provide the conditions necessary for equal educational opportunity and comparable educational success in the schools.

THE USE OF POWER: A DOUBLE-EDGED SWORD

1980

(This article is a presentation made to the Second Statewide Migrant Education Management Training Workshop in San Diego, California, on February 6-7, 1980. The "Six Phases of Institutional Change" may be original with the author, or the concept may have been borrowed from some contemporary publication. Unfortunately, citations are seldom given in oral presentations, so if the information was taken from some outside source, I can only tender my apologies for my failure to give credit where credit is due.)

One of the most intellectually challenging and rewarding aspects of my involvement in the last two decades of educational reform has been in responding to the way in which that movement demands the timely and honest examination of the concepts it pursues. Today, I have been asked to examine the use of power, which has been characterized as a double-edged sword.

I welcome this opportunity, first, because in the dawn of this national era of neo-conservatism, I believe it to be a most timely topic for those of us who care about the fate of the children of the most powerless; and secondly, because in order to present an honest view of my understanding of the workings of power within education, I am forced to review not the literature, but my own interaction over almost one-third of a century with the explicit and implicit power centers operating within and upon the institution of education.

Anyone involved in migrant education ought to know about those arid lands in south Texas which are home to many migrant families. They are also home to me as a jet-set migrant who has spent much of his energy and creativity trying to bring about change in the power relationship that exists between the migrant child of south Texas and the social, political, and economic ecology which has heretofore dominated, and far too often defeated, the migrant child and his family.

Those lands also represent a microcosm of the several extremes in the use of power that can affect the lives of migrant and the poor in general. One can see the ravages of feudalism in south Texas counties where the power of all institutions is vested in a very few. One can see the effects of a situation in which power is so transitory that no one perceives of themselves as sufficiently powerful to do anything other than try to hold on to power. In short, one can see counties which seem to have slept for the last two decades, remaining as unchanged in terms of power relationships as if they were a small South Pacific island. One can see the noblest concepts of the Great Society of the Sixties run amuck, and one can see experimentation abandoned.

In spite of evidence on a national level of far too many examples of lack of change, I need only look at the reality of migrant life in south Texas to conclude that the sharing of power between institutions and the people they serve is imperative, particularly among people as grossly lacking in power as migrant families in the United States. As an educator,

I am convinced that schools cannot empower children to control their own destinies if the families of those children are not vested with some individual or collective power to interact with the institutions which are impacting their children.

As we face the 1980s grasping for solutions to problems that loom overly large because we cannot yet describe them, it is all too easy to long to return to the days when life and institutional functioning were simpler. But it would be as wrong to do so in education as it is to do so in the areas of personal freedom and international relations—and particularly if you are Black or Brown—it would be disastrous to return to the old power relationships that dominated all of our social institutions in my youth. To return to the past because power is a double-edged sword, which many of the "newly" empowered have misused, would make sense only if the evidence of the past reveals that an equal or greater number of the "traditionally" empowered had been any more skilled at using that same sword.

Yet, for those of us who do care about the fate of the children of the powerless, the present resurgence of conservatism should call us to question the appropriateness of our change strategies within the context of current social and political forces, and to strengthen those strategies where appropriate, rather than abandoning them in the first face of criticism.

I believe strongly that the concept of shared and balanced power is good for our schools and good for our children; that the concept has hardly begun to live; and that it should be pursued with vigor and dedication to the super ordinate goals the concept pursues. Thus, as I proceed with my examination of the "Use of Power," I do so explicitly stating my bias and therefore with the following alteration in the title, "The Use of Power: A double-edged sword—and a sword well worth having."

My examination of these concepts will focus on the following: the examination of power and power relationships in the educational system; a review of power and power relationships as experienced by the poor; and finally with some thoughts on optimizing the use of power for the benefit of children within the educational system.

POWER AND THE EDUCATIONAL SYSTEM

This nation's educational system together with the many Community Action Programs (CAPS) of the War on Poverty provided the laboratory for experimentation in consumerism, one-issue activism, and neighborhood control which have always worked so very well for the middle class of this country. The legitimization of power-sharing among the schools and the communities they serve is still slow in coming. At the time that the concept was introduced in the early 1960s, it was as alien to the way in which schools had operated as the financial bounty which accompanied it. Looking back, it is a wonder that any vestige of community participation survived. Not only were teachers, administrators and school board members required to talk with and accept the views of non-teachers, non-administrators and non-school board members, but these newer players in the school scene were often non-white, non-English-speaking, and non-middle-class people. No, they were Black and Brown and Native American and they were poor. Many of them didn't even speak English.

The maintenance of power has historically been an imperative for educational professionals. In spite of lip service to the principle of "local control," institutional power in education has traditionally rested with the professionals. The advent of the War on Poverty introducing the concept of shared and balanced power only began to open up the system. In fact, it is likely that an examination of the specific power sharing activities with federal incentives would reveal that, in those activities, very little power-sharing occurred. Equally likely is that an analysis of the last 10-15 years would reveal that because of those federal activities in which incentives were provided (through grants, court orders, regulations and experiments), power-sharing achieved a legitimization in the schools which worked very well for teachers' unions, middle-class parents' organizations, and single-issue groups such as those concerned with textbook content. The truth of the matter is, these groups had power all along. What the activities of the 1960s did was teach them how to operationalize their power and to tell them it was all right to do so.

For the most part, however, the basic power centers in the educational system have relinquished little of the absolute power they have held throughout the history of universal education in the United States. As in most areas of our society, that history is characterized by early periods of many years with little change, followed by a Toffler-like ever-accelerating rate of change through the present (Toffler, 1970). It is that period following the introduction of the concept of shared power which is most relevant to us now.

SIX PHASES OF INSTITUTIONAL CHANGE

From my own experience, I have seen the educational system struggling to maintain power with even more sophistication, through at least six phases. These phases apply, in my estimation, to the mainstream American educational system as a whole, but they also apply very specifically to the many individual struggles now unfolding in education related settings where the institution is being enticed or forced to relinquish some of its power. I believe the phases operate, in almost all cases, to a greater or lesser degree. The six phases of institutional change to shared and/or balanced power are:

1. the resistance phase,
2. the tolerance phase,
3. the pseudo-acceptance phase,
4. the evaluation phase,
5. the acceptance phase, and
6. the management phase.

1. THE RESISTANCE PHASE

The *resistance* phase is characterized by open hostility on the part of the traditional institutional power centers to the concept of shared power. While this hostility is very likely to be exacerbated when the agents of shared power are poor and/or minority persons, the hostility is present in almost all instances, whether the agent of shared power is a teacher's union or an anti-metric system organization.

In addition to hostility, the resistance phase is characterized by an extreme preoccupation with the "we/they" complex. Interestingly enough, the atmosphere dominating the resistance phase within the institution often gives license to behaviors previously shunned or barely tolerated. Rumor, for example, is almost always rampant in the resistance stage and individuals who would not, under most circumstance give credence or nurturance to rumor, find themselves doing so in the extreme. Thus, it is possible for the "institution in resistance" to experience some power shifts within itself as the situation calls for or allows changes in behavioral standards among the leadership. Unfortunately, this often leads to increased paranoia within the institution and delays the evolution into the next and subsequent phases.

The resistance phase is an important one to the agents of institutional change and can be decisive in terms of final outcomes if it is understood that it is the first of several phases the institution will pass through in its effort to "shake-off" the invading concept. The strength and discipline and wisdom with which the institution is approached during this period may well set the tone for all future pursuits. Of course the two extreme results of the resistance phase are: (1) that the advocates of shared power are successfully put-off, and power remains absolute within the institution or, (2) that the advocates of shared power are so successful in pressing their case that the institution relinquishes substantial power. In either of these cases, the subsequent phase is not one of the "institutions in tolerance."

2. TOLERANCE PHASE

When the "institution is in tolerance," it is beginning to understand that some power sharing will have to occur, although this is almost always accompanied by a collective conviction that the sharing will be neither substantive nor of long duration. Neither the concept of shared power nor the exercise in tolerance are viewed as worthwhile. One can say that the institution in tolerance is sort of holding its nose—and its breath—firm in the conviction that the turmoil will pass quickly. The tolerance phase is also characterized by a high degree of solidarity within the institution. Old institutional differences fade away, again, perhaps because this is seen as a temporary condition.

The tolerance phase can have important consequences for those who are seeking to bring about the institutional change if tolerance is misunderstood for acceptance. Progress and fidelity in the pursuit of a shared power relationship are both likely to be jeopardized if the advocates of the new relationship proceed too fast to operationalize the relationship—believing that the institution is keeping pace. When attitudes are revealed with a greater level of honesty, as is inevitable, mistrust can reach irretrievable levels and a struggle for shared power can become a struggle for absolute power which is almost always a lose-lose situation, particularly for poor and minority populations.

3. PSEUDO-ACCEPTANCE PHASE

The resistance and tolerance phases are almost always followed by a significant event or action, either negative or positive in nature, which either terminates or mortally wounds the advocacy for shared power or moves the institution to a phase of pseudo-acceptance. This action or event may be a legalistic one; a significant negotiation session; a change in some symbolic condition; a change in significant players through resignation or replacement; or the intervention or mediation by some external and usually higher authority.

The pseudo-acceptance phase is the beginning of acceptance. The institution begins to behave in ways which begin to get the institution ready for accepting and then managing shared power. I have called this phase the pseudo-acceptance phase, because in my experience, I have found institutional behavior at this point in a change process to be lacking in genuineness while working extremely hard to give the appearance of acceptance. In fact, so much energy is spent on giving the appearance of acceptance that significant segments of the institution may begin to believe that the acceptance is genuine. Depending on the level of lingering mistrust generated by the two previous phases, this phase can serve the advocates of shared power well; it provides them the opportunity to first examine the broad repertoire of institutional behaviors which the institution will employ in the inevitable new relationship as it provides the opportunity to reinforce those behaviors genuinely helpful to the relationship, and to begin to extinguish those most abhorrent to the relationship.

Inevitably the pseudo-acceptance phase is brought to an end when the institutional behaviors are tested against the criteria of shared power as perceived by its advocates and found lacking. At this point, you can count on someone in the institution leadership impatiently asking, "Well, just what do you people want?"

You can also count on little understanding of what has happened to and within the institution in the previous three phases. There is generally genuine bewilderment as to what has occurred. The institution is functioning much as a person does in an interpersonal power struggle. Levels of anger and frustration are genuinely high, although it is unlikely that one would see demonstrations of open hostility as are usually seen in the resistance phase.

For the advocates of change, it is critical that these transitional behaviors preceding the evaluation phase be understood. The institution is about to go into the first period of seriously and realistically evaluating its position, its behaviors, its options and the concepts it is being caused to deal with. The messages of change advocates give the institution during this period must be clear, complete and strong. The parameters for negotiating the shared power relationship are set at this time.

4. THE EVALUATION PHASE

The evaluation phase which then follows is one in which the institution assesses, usually with a high degree of clarity, exactly where it stands. In the best of situations it may even genuinely examine the concept of shared power and determine its appropriateness to the institutional mission. But in most cases it does not. It does assess its options in relation to the proposed change, the appropriateness (to its own ends) of its behaviors, the range of strategies appropriate to its goals, and its skills relative to its adopted strategies—including the acquisition of an appropriate language (or the appropriate verbiage) for dealing with its new situation.

The products of the evaluation phase may be: (1) to go to a new phase of more genuine acceptance, or (2) to return to any one or all three of the earlier stages. If the institution chooses to return to the previous phases, it will likely cycle sequentially through these back to an evaluation phase unless it succeeds in eliminating the advocacy for change altogether. It is important to note, however, that the return to the previous phases may be very short-lived and may constitute little more than a test of the advocacy position in order to gather more information for making an evaluation of the institution's position. Advocates of the change should understand that a return to previous phases is not necessarily bad for their cause, if they understand what is occurring. The "re-learning" of the new realities on the part of the institution may have significant long-term benefits to the inevitable shared power relationship. If advocates do not understand the sequential nature of the behavior of institutions when confronting change, they are most likely to be defeated by it.

The inevitable result of the evaluation phase is that the institution becomes a formidable member of a new relationship, a member that behaves in ways that suit its own purposes, does so with great discipline, and utilizes all of the vast institutional resources at its command.

5. THE ACCEPTANCE PHASE

We enter now the period of true acceptance. The institution has determined what it must accept and it proceeds to do so. It may not and probably does not accept the concept of shared power as viewed by its advocates, but it has accepted the concept to the extent that it has assessed it must. At this point, the institutional leadership determines that it must now sell the new concept to the many elements of the institution. The institution assumes ownership for the concept as it defines it. Verbiage, reflective of the concept, becomes a part of the official language of the institution. The concept is discussed in print and thus, validated. Personnel skilled in operationalizing the concept are employed. In the best of all institutional worlds, some of the original advocates are employed.

At this point, it is interesting to note that the periods of confrontation during early phases commonly make the original leadership of the advocacy group unacceptable to the institution, and the employment or appointment process always seeks surrogates which are less repugnant to them. When this happens the original leadership finds itself left out, unemployed, and a non-participant in further implementation. The surrogates are more acceptable, less pushy, and in many cases less supportive of the original objectives.

I was told by a Mexican American hired by an oil company foundation that as a result of militant Mexican Americans burning their oil company credit cards in a public forum, if there was one thing he couldn't stand, it was militant Mexican Americans.

Assuming that the original advocates of shared power are able to withstand this instructional onslaught organizationally, what they will find is that their concept has been taken away from them; it is redefined, reshaped, renamed, and redirected.

6. THE MANAGEMENT PHASE

The institution has determined that it can not only accept this new thing, but that it can manage it. And it does. The first management objective is to contain it, to delimit the parameters of power. The second is to create or reinforce an organism which can cancel any outcome—in the state of Texas, a school board *cannot* delegate certain explicit powers. The third is to manage the information, the organization elements such as time, money and other resources.

It is this management phase which is the toughest of all on the parents of poor and minority children, even when the game is played ethically, and I have seen it played otherwise far too many times. If the previous stages have been more than survived, and if they have been understood as well, the chances of doing constructive work for children are good in the management phase.

PRINCIPLES OF INSTITUTIONAL RESISTANCE

In my own experience interacting with the education system around power relationships, I have found the following five principles operating:

First is the principle that power is never freely relinquished. Power never relinquishes power. It is an axiom of democratic theory that people need to pull and push, by any variety of ways, in order to get into the process of exercising some modicum of influence over the institutions which affect their lives.

The second principle is that when there is no other recourse, only the smallest possible amount of power is given up. The institution invariably delimits the power sharing to a specific program or activity with the smallest possible effect on the total structure.

The third is that in any struggle for power, time is an important tool. It is those individuals or groups who make time and timing their ally, that will prevail.

The classic example of the concept of using time is the course of desegregation efforts in the country's schools. Litigation, appeals, dysfunctional plans, rejection and replanning, have delayed any substantial desegregation in hundreds of cities for a quarter of a century. In most school districts, the original plaintiffs grew up and a new generation has similarly gone through the system with little change.

The classic example of timing is the *Rodriguez v. San Antonio ISD* which was heard by the Supreme Court at the worst possible time (*San Antonio ISD*, 1973). Two years sooner or two years later, the school finance reform case would have succeeded at the federal level.

Fourth, institutions employ a myriad of institutional defense mechanisms in order to maintain power. The defense mechanisms closely parallel personally utilized psychological defense mechanisms, including the various forms of withdrawal, aggression, and compromise.

And fifth, when institutions do share power, there is almost always an accompanying increase in the organizational complexity of the institution.

This institutional reorganization usually tends to neutralize the power it has yielded. For example, for years minority groups have been clamoring for minority employment at decision-making levels. At the acceptance phase, educational institutions compromise and appoint a minority person in an assistant superintendent position, but this concession is usually accompanied or immediately followed by the creation of a new and higher level in the hierarchy, with the decision-making powers being moved up to the newly created level.

Thus, when the Hispanic or Black is appointed assistant superintendent, a white Anglo fills the new and higher position of associate superintendent. The process is repeated with the subsequent creation of the Office of Deputy Superintendent. Each of the new levels in the hierarchy requires an increased organizational complexity.

POWER AND THE POOR

When President Carter first sent his bill for a Department of Education to Congress, he included in the new department a number of programs whose inclusion threatened to kill the department altogether. Among them was the Head Start Program, now fifteen years old and perhaps the most politically effective human service constituency in the country. It was not the first time a President was to have tampered with Head Start and lost. Mr. Nixon had attacked the program on several legislative, budgetary and administrative forays and was rebuffed every time by politicized, organized and effective parents lobbying their Congress. It is a remarkable and moving story: these are the poorest and most powerless parents in the country, yet they've effectively thwarted the wishes of two presidents when they have felt those presidents to be wrong.

There is no reason why the Head Start story cannot or should not be replicated in terms of a vast number of educational issues such as school finance reform, bilingual education, and vocational education. No reason, except that three-fourth of Head Start's 1500 programs operate not in schools but out of community agencies.

There are many good reasons why parents should be encouraged through the schools to learn to exercise power as advocates for the well-being of their children. The exercise of such advocacy would reduce the feelings of powerlessness parents feel daily which K. Keniston described in *All Our Children* (Keniston, 1977). It would reduce the chasms which exist between family and institution and between community and institution. For poor parents, the effect would be to increase the feelings of control over their environment—so essential to healthy child development. In my experience as a school superintendent, I suffered all of the headaches of sharing power with community persons and few of the joys. Yet in retrospect, I have to say that the personal growth experienced by many individuals involved in those activities and their impact on their families and community will live way beyond the effect of the specific activity, and the empowerment of those individuals makes the headaches worthwhile.

Perhaps the most compelling reason for advocating expanded power roles for the parents of poor children, however, is a simple one: they represent an efficient and effective use of the human resources available to do a job well. In my estimation, their capacity to use power well is as great or greater than that of persons now exercising absolute power over the lives of children. Take the average state superintendent of schools and rank in order, the issues that concern him, according to the amount of advocacy (in terms of time) he dedicates to that issue daily. Where do you think "advocacy for children" would rank against advocacy for "other bureaucrats," finances, management systems, evaluation issues, personnel matters, legislative matters, etc.? Who best to advocate for children than their own parents? In short, parents have the capacity to exercise power on behalf of their kids. They have the stake and they have the skills. What they need is an institutional setting which is accessible in terms of resources and genuinely supportive.

In the absence of institutional support, the double-edged sword indeed becomes bloody and the following problems arise.

- Obfuscation purpose—Why the power struggle in the first place?
- Delimited leadership—There are fewer leaders and fewer participants, with both leaders and participants playing the same non-productive role.
- Unguided missile phenomenon. The movement losses direction and frequently undertakes purposes and activities completely unrelated to its original goals.
- Lack of perspective over time as to the relationship of the original institution to problems.
- No understanding of power on the part of the community and the inability to utilize it once it has been acquired.
- Loss of touch with broader community—the participants spend all their time talking with school personnel and are frequently institutionalized themselves.

MAKING POWER WORK FOR CHILDREN

Obviously the question for all of us is, "how do we make power work well for children?" How do we create, through shared power, better schools and visibly better schools that the public in general can support and that can serve our children?

From my own perspective, I have found that the most effective parents and professionals, for that matter, are effective not because of what they do but because of the philosophical understandings which they bring to the task. It is not so much a matter of strategy as it is a matter of approach. It is the depth and clarity of motivation rather than the daring of the tactic. The philosophy and the motivation can emanate from one or two individuals and envelop a whole group. I have seen in such individuals, regardless of their economic or educational achievement, an intelligence and a dignity that pervades all that they do in the name of children, and it is neither transitory nor occasional. These individuals have demonstrated to me that the philosophical base must be put into operation by at least the following elements if it is to work well enough and long enough for children.

The first element is that of a significant amount of *purposefulness*. The individuals making up a group must share a commonality and a clarity of purpose. That purpose, advocacy for children, must be clearly identifiable as the primary objective over any significant period of time.

The purposefulness must be compatible with an accurate *perspective* on the part of the group as to the parameters for policy or programmatic improvement that can be achieved by interacting with a particular institution over a designated time period.

The *leadership* of the group must be dedicated to the development, nurturance and maintenance of the group's strength; sharing information, visibility and rewards generously and diligently. A significant number of individuals in the group must operate from a secure level of *self*-knowledge and knowledge of each other that will enable them to deal with unfamiliar, ambiguous and rapidly changing situations with success. The group must institute its own checks on itself, particularly in terms of purpose and product.

Finally and perhaps most difficult, both individuals and the group as a whole must have the capacity to relinquish power when their retention of the instruments of power is no longer in the best interest of their purpose, and thereby improve the lives of children and the institutions which serve them.

EDUCATIONAL REFORM AND DYSFUNCTIONAL RESPONSES

1984

There are few national and state news topics which receive the media coverage given recently to the revamping of our educational systems. At the national level we have seen a proliferation of commissions, committees, and study groups directing their attention to the assessment of our educational institutions and offering a host of recommendations for improvement.

The phenomenon is neither unprecedented nor undesirable. Many positive characteristics of our educational system were developed by intense efforts during periods of national stress in which the outcomes of education impacted directly on specific emergencies. The Civil War, the two World Wars, the launching of the Russian Sputnik, and the civil rights movement all launched periods of frenetic educational activity in order to respond to social, political, or military crises. However, it must be noted that almost without exception, the period of frenzied activity was preceded by a period of educational neglect.

The current period of frantic educational activity has included a host of commissions which have come up with an abundance of recommendations. Many of the recommendations appear desirable and feasible, but far too many lack sufficient specificity and detail to be practical guidelines for reforming our educational systems.

The state of Texas is no exception in the quest for educational excellence, and it is a shining example of educational neglect. The state of Texas has been blessed by its supply of natural resources. Oil, gas, other minerals, and productive land have provided a solid base for its past economy. However, the Texas economy is following the national trend in moving away from a product economy to a new service and information economy.

For a state like Texas, which is aspiring to make a niche for itself in the "high tech" economy (as well as for any other state which may have similar aspirations), it is well to note that the early and rapid transition of California and Massachusetts into the high tech strongholds was not based solely, nor primarily, on the existence of technological research centers in their institutions of higher education. There is overwhelming research evidence and professional opinion that the transition of California and Massachusetts into magical "silicon valleys" was based primarily on the excellent quality of their elementary and secondary schools.

In contrast, Texas is not blessed by an abundance of a highly trained and skilled population. Not only does the state not have the human resource pool, it doesn't even have a system for developing it. The previous neglect of its educational system now finds the state in competition with other states in the race for high tech industries, handicapped by unbelievably high levels of adult illiteracy, large numbers of school dropouts, and an underachieving school population. It is no wonder, then, that the state of Texas is following the national movements toward educational reform.

There is a great danger, though, that precipitous action on the part of the reformers may result in the implementation of irrelevant and dysfunctional responses which do not necessarily address the source of educational problems and may not offer solutions for them. The dangers of this happening are augmented by the non-rational mood in which solutions appealing to the public are being offered without the benefit of a rationale or relating the solutions to the source of the problem. Many of the recent commissions and study groups have yielded to this tendency, offering general solutions with a high level of public appeal but with no empirical evidence to support the recommendation and little specificity as to how the solution is to be implemented.

Abolishing the federal Department of Education, reducing federal involvement in education, prayers in the classroom, and tuition tax credits may all be very appealing—but they are a far cry from a blueprint for improving educational outcomes. The reduction of disciplinary problems may be a desirable goal, but it may do little for the increased mastery of basic skills.

The quality of education is largely dependent on the quality of the interaction between the teacher and the learner. In general, the more a reform effort impacts on this relationship, the greater the chances of bringing about improvements in educational outcomes. Improvements in the skills and knowledge teachers bring to the learning interaction can be expected to have a strong impact on student learning. Thus, reform efforts aimed at identifying, recruiting, training, and rewarding good teaching are conducive to improvement. The same is true for improvements in the curriculum, parent participation, pupil-teacher ratios, the elimination of distractions, and enhancing the learning environment.

On the other hand, if a student cannot add and subtract at the sixth grade level, the adding of an additional year of mathematics at the junior high or senior high school level will have a minimal impact on remediation. If a student cannot read or write upon entering high school, a fourth year of English does not comprise adequate remediation. The implementation of such responses may look good and make for good copy in the media, but they do not respond to the state's educational problems.

In addition to irrelevant and dysfunctional responses to the real problems of education, there is currently a great danger of enacting responses which aggravate and compound problems. A good example of this is the recent action of the State Board of Education in creating a multiple track system of education in the state's secondary schools. Objections to the proposed new system appeared in the *IDRA Newsletter* article, "Curriculum Tracking: An Ill-Conceived Panacea," which appeared in the September, 1983 issue (IDRA, 1983). It is noteworthy that this article received the second highest number of reader responses in the ten years of *IDRA Newsletter* publication and that all responses expressed opposition to the concept of a tracking system for Texas schools.

In spite of the opposition, the Texas State Board of Education has seen fit to implement such a system. Instead of vocational, general, and academic, the new system uses the euphemisms general, academic, and honors to identify the three tracks, but the concept is still the same. A label is being placed on a child which will stick for the rest of his or her life.

The main objection to this labeling is that it is virtually impossible to predict the learning capabilities of future adults during their secondary school years. As noted by Pat Longoria of the Mexican American Legal Defense and Educational Fund (MALDEF), both Albert Einstein and Thomas Edison would have been severely handicapped in their adult lives by such a system because neither did particularly well in school. This problem will manifest itself with children from all socio-economic classes who mature at a later date. It will be especially bad for minority, disadvantaged, and limited English-proficient children who take longer than average to reach their full potential. In fact, if the state of Texas were to design a school program to push out and eliminate minority, disadvantaged, and limited English-proficient children from its schools, it couldn't do much better than to design a multiple track system of education much like that recently enacted by the Texas State Board of Education.

The student population is a mass of undetermined and unrecognized potential. It is made up of individuals who are brilliant, gifted, average, and below average. Unfortunately, schools do not have the skills and insights needed to determine validly which is which. It is wrong to prejudge students and lock them into a corresponding track for the rest of their lives. A simple test of the fallacy of curriculum tracking is to pick up an old high school yearbook and match the career aspirations commonly expressed by students with reality many years later. It is not unusual for the student who said he was going to be a doctor to be playing a saxophone in Las Vegas, and the one who was going to be a fireman to be an astrophysicist in Houston.

The guidance and counseling programs in our schools are not equal to the task of assisting students in career choices. Until maturity, many students tend to take the path of least resistance, looking at high school as a place to have fun and enjoy life until the demands of adulthood, employment, marriage, or military service awaken them to the realities of career choices.

Females will probably suffer from curriculum tracking more than males—both from the sexist culture which steers them away from certain subjects, as well as from the common illusion that it is a woman's goal to coast through life until a knight in shining armor sweeps her off her feet and provides for her. CETA, the new Job Training Partnership Act, commercial colleges, and community colleges are full of such sleeping beauties awakening to the realities of earning a living, the need for second incomes, single parent families, and making a career away from the drudgery of home and kitchen.

For years I have maintained that the biggest problem in the education of special populations has been the low level of expectancy which schools have for such populations. The low level of expectancy is subsequently internalized by these students and becomes a self-fulfilling prophecy. The guidance and counseling system cannot compensate for this syndrome; rather, it is a part of the syndrome. Expecting the guidance programs to steer female, minority, disadvantaged, limited English proficient, and handicapped students, away from the lowest career tracks is too much to expect.

Years ago, IDRA advocated for the inclusion of undocumented alien children in the Texas educational system on the grounds that abundant evidence indicated that the bulk of such children would eventually attain U.S. citizenship and constitute a heavy liability on the state's social services. Church groups, civic organizations, educators, the general public, and even the federal Immigration and Naturalization Service agreed to the need for educating this group at the state's expense. The only entity which consistently and persistently opposed the concept was the Texas Education Agency, who fought it until the Supreme Court of the United States finally crammed it down their throats. Similarly, we can expect the state education agency to support the new concept of curriculum tracking until the legislature or the courts abolish it in Texas.

Since the State Board of Education has established a tracking system, it is hoped that the legislature will abolish it before it is even implemented. Should the legislature fail to act in remedying this evil, the concept of curriculum tracking should be attacked in the courts as a violation of the equal protection clause of the U.S. Constitution.

ALTERNATIVES TO DIPLOMAS

1986

At the July 1986 meeting of the Texas State Board of Education (SBOE), members of the Board discussed the issuance of a certificate of completion and a certificate of attendance in lieu of a high school diploma for students unable to meet requirements for graduation, including successful performance on the state-prescribed TEAMS test.

The issue arose as a possible response to the problem of slow learning children who may not be able to meet the state requirements for graduation.

Although IDRA is very sympathetic to the problems of slow learning children, we see grave dangers in the provision of an alternative diploma. Basic to our opposition to the proposals provided for SBOE consideration is the difficulty, if not impossibility, of distinguishing between slow learning children who have a permanent disability and children who are learning slowly because of a temporary disability. Neither intelligence tests, nor psychologists, nor professional education personnel have been able to make reliable discriminations between students in these two categories. For years, students with limited English proficiency, students from economically disadvantaged homes, minority students, and countless students from the cultural and economic mainstream have been erroneously identified as slow learners, with the erroneous classification subsequently becoming a self-fulfilling prophecy through low levels of expectancy erroneously imposed by the school. This inability to distinguish between innate permanent disability and temporary environmentally imposed limitations has been thoroughly documented and is cautioned against by the most prestigious psychology and education professional associations. Given that the school does not have the capability of distinguishing between these temporary and permanent conditions, it goes against reason for the state of Texas to stamp a permanent and life-long label on a person on the basis of a temporary disability.

If there is any question about limitations on the ability of school systems to distinguish between permanent and temporary disabilities, note the following from testimony presented to the Committee for Students of the State Board of Education immediately before the July meeting of the Board:

> While the district would like the SBOE (State Board of Education) to consider a differentiated diploma for Special Education students and maybe certain students who are identified as English as a Second Language (ESL) students, . . .

IDRA is adamantly opposed to the issuing of a certificate of attendance or a certificate of completion for students who are unable to meet graduation requirements. Although we recognize that a high school diploma should signify some level of achievement and many students are currently unable to meet this level, a "certificate of incompetence" for students unable to meet graduation requirements constitutes a simplistic and superficial quick-fix for a difficult and complicated educational problem.

Even though the state of Texas has been unable to address the achievement problems of many of its students, the issuing of a certificate of incompetence will not remedy the existing situation. It merely relieves the pressure created by the inability of the schools to educate a large segment of the population. The alternative diploma will surely lead to a diminishing effort to develop and implement appropriate educational programs for a large number of students. The proposed certificates severely penalize the students who failed to meet the requirements for graduation in that, regardless of the reason for failure, the students will be labeled as incompetent for the rest of their lives.

The issuing of an alternative diploma will tend to increase the number of students who drop out of school, and rightly so, since it is deemed preferable for the student to drop out and leave the status of his/her competency in question, than to receive a certificate which attests to the incompetence. Although some students may not have the necessary competencies for graduation *at this time*, it is unfair, unnecessary and undesirable to place a label or a brand which will follow them for a lifetime. There are many persons who did not complete a high school education and subsequently have been able to succeed in further schooling, in work, and in life. The certificate of incompetence will be a formidable barrier to such subsequent rehabilitation.

At the present time minority, disadvantaged, and limited English-proficient students will be the main target group for receiving this type of certificate. These are the students who are performing most poorly in the state's public schools, who require additional resources, and whose educational needs have barely been addressed. However, these types of students will not be the only ones damaged. Many students from all cultural and economic groups who may be temporarily disabled by slow development, lack of motivation, family problems, work, and even by temporary distractions caused by an awareness of the existence of members of the opposite sex or a car, can be permanently damaged.

It is hoped that Texas will continue it efforts to improve educational opportunities for all students rather than choosing one of two alternative evils: allowing them to drop out of school or pushing them out with a label of incompetence.

RESTRUCTURING OF EDUCATION: THE CHICAGO EXPERIENCE

1988

On January 1987, the Intercultural Development Research Association (IDRA) *Newsletter* featured an article on a position paper issued by a broad coalition of Chicagoans concerning education problems in the city's schools and drastic efforts to restructure the school system (IDRA, 1987). Eighteen months after publication, it is interesting to note that the Illinois General Assembly enacted legislation for Chicago which implements most of the recommendations made by the reform coalition.

Unlike most state legislation which calls for the reform of education within the context of the existing system of education, the Chicago legislation incorporates dozens of changes which drastically affect the governance of schools, with a greatly increased power base for parents, community, teachers and school principals.

Two major problems were identified by the coalition of parents, community groups and businesses which were expressed in the previous IDRA article:

- Almost half the students who enter the Chicago Public schools drop out. Of those who still remain as high school seniors, only one-third are reading at or above the national average. In our segregated high schools, the situation is even worse. Only 8 percent of the students who enter these high schools as ninth graders graduate and read at or above the national average.

- Despite its failure to educate our children, the school system bureaucracy concentrates primarily on its own care and feeding. The present superintendent of schools has created more than 240 new job positions for bureaucrats in various administrative offices who provide no direct services to children.

DRASTIC CHANGES MADE EXPLICIT

The following changes are spelled out in the 114 page legislative package:

- The Central School Board is stripped of most direct authority over local schools, while a Local School Council at each of the 590 Chicago schools is given authority that approaches that of a separate school board.

- The powers of these Local School Councils which are composed of six elected parents, two elected community residents, two elected teachers, and the school's principal include: appointing and removing the school principal; controlling the school's budget; and fashioning a plan that must be carried out that spells out priority steps for improving student performance.

- Principals no longer have life time tenure, but are selected for a three-year performance contract. If a principal fails to improve student performance another principal can be hired.
- Principals have authority to supervise all school staff; to hire teachers, teacher aides, and other educational staff for vacant positions without regard to seniority; and to define the school's curriculum and teaching methods.
- Unsatisfactory teachers can be removed by the principal after a forty-five day remediation period.
- The current Central Board of Education will be disbanded, and a new one, selected by the mayor from nominees screened by a citizen nominating committee, will be put in place.
- The budget of the central administration will be cut by $46 million and permanently capped.
- Through plugging loopholes in an existing state funding program, approximately $100 million will be shifted to low- income schools over four years.
- A School Reform Oversight Authority will be established to oversee the transition. This Authority has the right to approve and monitor a school board plan for carrying out the reform, to void proposed collective bargaining agreements and other contracts that conflict with the reform plan, and to suspend or remove administrators who resist reform.

The final reform bill submitted to the governor follows the plan recommended by the Alliance for Better Chicago Schools, a coalition of forty business, community, and parent organizations, who drafted the legislation and lobbied for its passage. Out of twenty-nine specific requirements spelled out by the coalition, two are partially and twenty-seven are fully incorporated into the legislation.

In keeping with constitutional provisions of the state of Illinois, the governor may sign the bill, veto the bill, or make line item changes before approval. Should most present provisions of the legislation be retained, it would most certainly be one of the most radical changes in the governance of big city school districts in recent years.

POLITICAL LIMITS TO AN EDUCATION OF VALUE: THE ROLE OF THE STATE

(This article is included in *Access to Knowledge: An Agenda For Our Nation's Schools*, by John I. Goodlad and Pamela Keating, College Entrance Examination Board, New York, 1990.)

PRÉCIS

The needs of students whose cultural and ethnic backgrounds tend to be outside the traditional mainstream are typically not met by what might be characterized as one-size-fits-all education. Although extension of services to special groups of middle class, English-speaking students—the gifted and the physically handicapped, for example—has proceeded now to the point of general acceptance, much less has been done in response to special conditions related to variables of race, culture, national origin, and gender. To the extent that equity concerns in these terms are going to be advanced in the next decade, state government will play a pivotal role, maintains José Cárdenas. The states are the emergent power in education today, particularly state education agencies, public officials who shape state policies in education, and quasi-public groups that influence these policies. Only a few pioneering states have pushed for a shift from a traditional regulatory role (the length of the school year, required units of American and state history, for example) to a role of real leadership. Furthermore, an inverse relationship seems to exist between state attention to compliance with regulations and political and professional commitment to devise innovations that enhance all students' learning experiences.

It is obvious that a new pattern of state leadership must be developed and designed to enhance the educational opportunities of students who currently are not well served. State officials need to devote their energies to equitable tax policies and fair resource allocation, to the enlightened exercise of their regulatory functions, and, perhaps most important, to policy leadership.

Political and economic forces in each state should be brought to bear on concerns for children in such a way that positive opportunities will result. Only when all students can equitably access state resources, Cárdenas claims, can there be a reversal of the current situation, in which (as the population deviates from the white Anglo-Saxon mainstream) the chances for appropriate educational program responses to special needs diminishes.

José Cárdenas, former School Superintendent, is currently executive director of the Intercultural Development Research Association in San Antonio, Texas.

—The College Board

The absence of the topic of education from the U.S. Constitution and from the Reserve Clause of the Tenth Amendment has formed a strong legal basis for treating education as a function of the state. Although the federal government has had a historical concern with the responsibilities incurred by provisions for the general welfare as well as First Amendment guarantees,[1] the Equal Protection Clause of the Fourteenth Amendment, early local and state ordinances, educational practice, and an unbroken sequence of court findings have consistently confirmed the sovereignty of the state in the provision of educational programs to its citizenry.

Education is a function of the state. This unique feature of American education marks it apart from almost every other system of education throughout the world. Although the state may assign wide prerogatives to local school districts and accept information and resources that reflect the national interest and concern, it is the individual state that is responsible for the quantity and quality of education in that particular state.

This concept of state sovereignty in education was created during the historical development of education in this country. Education was a concern in each of the thirteen original colonies prior to the formation of the country, and this concern led to early legislation in each of the colonies that subsequently became states.

In the formative years of the country, the educational effort was as loose a confederation as was the first political attempt at unifying the newly independent country. Subsequent attempts to create a stronger union did not include education as one of the responsibilities granted to the central government under the new Constitution, thereby preserving the decentralized character of American education.

LEGAL BASIS FOR THE STATE ROLE IN EDUCATION AND LOCAL RESPONSIBILITY

Although legally education is a state function, the operation of educational programs traditionally has been a local responsibility. State constitutional provisions to establish an efficient system of education seldom led to more than cursory legislation for the establishment of schools at the local level, with little direction or resources for the townships to do so. And even though romantic notions prevail about the high quality of schools in the absence of state regulation, the reality is that the local districts provided poor schools and managed them badly.[2] It was not until the beginning of the twentieth century that school districts in most states started to receive extensive state assistance for the operation of the public schools.

The extensive early delegation of responsibility to the local schools created two characteristics that have greatly diminished in recent times, extensive parental and community involvement and almost unlimited local control.

As late as 1930, the local school districts in the United States bore the brunt of the cost for the support of the schools, with 83 percent of the funds being generated at the local level. State interests in education, which led to the establishment of comprehensive state systems of school finance, also led to extensive legislation concerning the operation of the schools in order to protect the state investments. State participation in the making of educational decisions, in turn, preempted parental and community involvement in the affairs of the school. Trends for the construction of large urban schools resulted in bureaucratic structures much more concerned with responding to mandates from the state capital than to the wishes of the school constituency.

Judging by the reams of new legislation being enacted by the state legislatures, erosion of local control and initiative will not only continue but will accelerate in future years.

Although the continued existence of the local school district does not appear to be in jeopardy, it seems that direction for the operation of the schools will continue to shift from the local community to the state level.

THE FEDERAL CONCERN

Although the absence of a provision for education in the federal Constitution and in the Reserve Powers Clause of the Tenth Amendment makes education a function of the state, there is sufficient legal basis for the involvement of the federal government in education. Providing for the general welfare and defense, securing the freedoms of the First Amendment and ensuring the equal protection provided for in the Fourteenth Amendment serve as firm bases for federal concern and involvement.

Historically, federal involvement in education has been cyclic, with federal engagement intensifying during periods of national stress or crisis and diminishing after the crisis has subsided. In recent years federal crises leading to increased involvement in education have come about with more frequency and have lasted for a longer time. It appears that the last cycle of intervention has not subsided before a new crisis initiates a new cycle.

Economic recessions, the rise of technology, marketing competition, military and political commitments, and deficits in the balance of payments have combined to maintain a strong federal contribution to education. Although the style of federal involvement in educational activity has changed in the last decades, the federal commitment of financial resources has not. Federal funds for education have increased from $834 million in 1964 to $19.5 billion in 1986. This tremendous increase in absolute dollars may be attributed both to a federal commitment to education and to the growing realization that the federal government has the best financial structure with a broad tax base to support the rising costs of education.

Federal involvement in education has changed in the amount of aid provided, in the scope of intervention, and in the style of intervention. Percy Burrup and Vern Brimley cite five general categories of federal aid to schools: aid to promote the cause of education, aid to broaden the scope of education, aid to educate individuals for whom the federal government accepts responsibility, aid to improve the quality of education, and aid to compensate for deficiencies in the school tax base.[3] Michael Kirst adds four additional categories of federal action in education: regulation, discovering knowledge and making it available, providing technical assistance, and exerting moral persuasion through use of the bully pulpit.[4] Table 1 summarizes Kirst's description, and adds the characteristics of pre-1964 federal advocacy for education.

Limitations on the growing national interest and intervention in education were clearly established in *San Antonio Independent School District v. Rodriguez,* where the federal Supreme Court yielded jurisdiction to the state political process.[5] Legal constraint on federal intervention in education has been supplemented by the changing characteristics of federal intervention as depicted above, giving the individual states in recent years more responsibility in their control of educational activity.

THE STATE ROLE IN EDUCATION

The absence of education in the federal constitution is more than made up for by its extensive coverage in state constitutions. Invariably the state government is charged with establishing a system of free public schools. Originally conceptualized as essential for

Table 1

Characteristics of the Federal Administration's Advocacy for Education Since 1964

Pre–1964	1964 to 1980	Post–1980
Small Role	Large and influential role	Mitigated role
Little regulation	Detailed and prescriptive regulation	Deregulation
Faith in local and state systems	Mistrust	Renewed faith
State and local options	Equity concern	Efficiency with state and local options
Small, unrestricted grants	Large categorical grants	Large and unrestricted grants
Minimum support to private education	Minimum and indirect support	Significant support to private education

participation in a democratic society, education has now become an economic imperative in each of the fifty states.

With education being a function of the state, it is expected that the role of the state in education would be very large. As stated previously, this was not true until the beginning of the twentieth century. Whereas the state contribution for the support of education in 1930 was only 16.9 percent of total costs, by the 1986-1987 school year the state share grew to an even 50 percent at a cost of $80.4 billion.

Much of the responsibility for the implementation of the educational program has been delegated to local school districts, quasi-corporations especially created by the state for this function.

In spite of the delegation of responsibility for implementation of school programs, the state continues to increase its participation in education. State participation in education can be subdivided into three roles: the provision of fiscal and material resources, regulation, and leadership. The extent to which the emphasis is placed on any one or more of these roles is very much a matter of style in each of the individual fifty states, but the state plays a part in each.

RESOURCES

Because the state is the entity charged with responsibility for the implementation of a public educational system, each state faces the responsibility for providing the necessary funds for implementation and operation. Although the relationship between the two appears to be obvious, the history of education in the various states indicates that the responsibility for creating a system of education was not always accompanied by the resources for doing so. Although the responsibility for funding education has been dealt with much more seriously by the states in the second half of the twentieth century, existing systems of school finance in many of the states are less than ideal.

The responsibility for the operation of schools at the local level has frequently been granted to school districts with the accompanying responsibility for acquiring the necessary funds in support of the educational program. Since local school districts have no inherent taxing authority, it must be given by the state to the individual school districts.

The granting of taxing powers to school districts, usually as a tax levied on real and personal property within the boundaries of the district, may have seemed sufficient during periods of predominantly agricultural and industrial economies, but by the middle of the twentieth century it was apparent that local property taxes were insufficient to support a state system of education, requiring the commitment of large amounts of state funds in support of the schools. The large taxing base of the state and the various options for taxation at the state level made it feasible for states to increase their share of the cost of education to the present 50 percent level. Aside from the 6.2 percent contributed by the federal government, approximately half of the cost of education today is paid for by taxes collected at the state level and half by taxes the state authorizes the local districts to collect.

Extensive variations on the location of taxable property have led to wide variation in the amount of wealth available for local taxation. Simplistic systems of funding education have led to wide disparities in the amount of wealth accessible to local school districts, wide variations in the extent to which local districts can fund education, wide variations in the amount expended for education, and wide variations in the amount of tax effort necessary for the support of at least a minimum-quality educational program.

In 1971 a federal district court ruling in *Rodriguez v. San Antonio Independent School District* declared the Texas system of school finance unconstitutional, and by implication most of the systems of school finance in the other states.[6] Although this decision was subsequently reversed by the Supreme Court in 1973, individual state systems of school finance were found wanting by a succession of state courts.

The legal basis of school finance suits stems from a determination that the state constitutional provision for the establishment of a state system of education gives the state the role of distributing resources on an equitable basis. State funding of education, and by implication, the quality of education afforded by the state, must give each school system access to the wealth of the state as a whole rather than being highly dependent on the wealth of the individual local school system.

The provision of other resources by the state in an equitable manner is even more complicated than the distribution of funds. Whereas equity in the distribution of money involves only the concept of quantity, the distribution of other resources may involve the additional concept of quality. Such a dilemma is immediately obvious in states that have established and maintained a system for the distribution of textbooks and other instructional materials.

This argument surfaced at the local level in *Lau v. Nichols* in which the San Francisco Unified School District was found to be denying equal educational opportunities to Chinese children who had limited proficiency in English by affording them the same teachers, materials, and instruction given to English-proficient children.[7] In keeping with this unanimous decision by the United States Supreme Court, it can be inferred that the state distribution of educational resources would also have to be compatible with known characteristics of minority and other classes of children.

REGULATION

The second role played by the state in the educational enterprise is the regulatory role. Much of this responsibility is vested in the central education agency which acts as an agency of the state in regulating education. In this role, the state education agency is responsible for the distribution of financial and material resources, the pre-science and in-service development of personnel resources, the monitoring of educational services, holding school systems accountable for the proper and efficient use of resources, and applying punitive measures through the processes of resource allocation and accreditation.

The capability to regulate education varies from state to state, but in general most states have extensive capability in monitoring input measures although they tend to be much less efficient in the regulation of teacher-learner interactions.

The historical concept of local control tends to become a buck-passing mechanism when it comes to the regulation of instructional activity. Although state departments of education can be bureaucratically meticulous in the enforcement of school laws, rules, and regulations dealing with teacher-certification requirements, subjects taught, days and hours of school operation, and even the number of minutes spent on each curricular area, this meticulousness seldom extends to the outcomes of education.

Recent national attempts at determining the number of school dropouts and research studies on the causes of such dropouts have been stymied to the point that the efforts were dropped in favor of determining the definition of school dropouts and methodologies for counting them.

Perhaps the biggest failure of the states in the regulation of education has been in meeting its responsibility for the implementation of equitable school programs. Just as financial equity provides for equal access to wealth, the concept of equity in educational programs provides for equal access to learning opportunities. School districts failing to provide an appropriate educational program should be held accountable by the state.

The concept of appropriateness of educational program has been readily understood, if not adequately implemented, by local school districts and by the state during the latter part of this century. Concepts of special education for students with mental and physical handicaps have been generally accepted by educational systems.

The extent of a handicapping condition which must be responded to may still be in discussion and litigation, as is the case in determining the school's responsibility to multiple-handicapped children, children needing controlled environments such as air conditioning or a plastic bubble, or in recent cases, children who have been exposed to the dreaded AIDS disease.

When culture, race, national origin, or sex is the variable under consideration, the educational systems have been much more lax in accepting and implementing the concept of equity in educational programs. As a population deviates from majoritarian, white, Anglo-Saxon, Protestant culture characteristics, the chances for fair and appropriate programs are diminished considerably.

The growth of the American public school has paralleled the growth of the American middle class. Prior to the existence of an extensive middle class, there was no extensive American system of education. As in the European system which served as a model for early American education, private schools educated the children of the upper class, philanthropic institutions looked after the needs of the disadvantaged, and the church schools taught the basic skills as a prerequisite for religious instruction.

Although initially extremely limited in the ability to offer services to atypical children, as the need for education and for the development of salable skills has increased in the American economy, the ability of the American school to expand its offerings to atypical populations has increased similarly.

Still grounded in the fundamental concept of serving the middle class, schools started developing special programs to serve a wider range of people within the middle class. States developed and implemented special services for atypical middle-class populations not previously served. Classes for the mentally retarded, originally the educable mentally retarded, and subsequently, the trainable mentally retarded, were developed and implemented. Soon "special education" programs began to differentiate between mentally retarded, emotionally disturbed, learning disabled, dyslexic, slow learners, and a variety of other impediments for effective middle-class participation in the public schools. The growth of specialized educational services for the mentally atypical was paralleled by a similar growth in services for the physically handicapped. Original state-operated schools for the blind and the deaf led not only to mainstream services for this group, but also to a bountiful number of special programs addressing other handicaps.

The amount and types of services offered to middle-class populations have been constrained only in the extremes, where the cost of the service or the amount of service has been deemed to exceed a reasonable cost-benefit ratio or has created a physical or moral risk to the rest of the middle-class school population. The education of children requiring elaborate environmental controls such as air conditioning or a plastic bubble are examples of handicapping conditions deemed too expensive or troublesome by the school. The education of children exposed to the AIDS virus is an example of concern for physical risk; the education of pregnant teenagers is an example of moral risk.

The extension of educational services to special cases of middle-class children has sometimes required legal intervention by the state or federal government or both, yet the implementation of such services has proceeded with general support, acceptance, and success. Unfortunately, this has not been the situation in the development and implementation of educational responses for children not associated with the white, Anglo-Saxon, English-speaking middle class.

Almost 100 years after the termination of slavery and the granting of full rights to Blacks, most of the Black children in the United States were attending segregated schools offering vastly inferior educational programs. Ten years after the U.S. Supreme Court order in *Brown v. Board of Education*, more than 90 percent of Black children in the South were still attending segregated school facilities.[8] The Civil Rights Act of 1964 and the Elementary and Secondary Education Act of 1965 were a carrot-and-stick combination by the Congress of the United States to bring states into compliance with the *Brown* decision.[9]

Although there has been a certain amount of reluctance and even recalcitrance in accepting the concept of extending educational services to mentally and physically handicapped children, the negative response has been nothing compared to the reluctance, recalcitrance, and even defiance of the concept of extending educational opportunity to minorities, those with limited English proficiency, and the disadvantaged.

It took nine justices of the United States Supreme court in *Lau v. Nichols* to inform the school authorities of the San Francisco Unified School District that having 1,800 Chinese children who spoke no English being taught by a proportionate number of teachers who spoke no Chinese constituted a serious educational problem. It was also necessary for the Supreme Court to determine that it was much more reasonable for the school to adapt its educational program to accommodate the Chinese language than for the Chinese children to adapt their language to accommodate the San Francisco schools.

In one state, the state education agency issued a report some years ago on dropout rates for selected school districts. One district was reported as having a dropout rate of 90 percent with a 10 percent margin of error, making the true dropout rate somewhere between 80 and 100 percent. It was not surprising that the specific school district had a 90 percent dropout rate. The quality of its educational programs for Hispanic students, who formed the vast majority of the student population, had been the subject of extensive litigation in federal courts and in Office of Civil Rights administrative hearings. What was amazing was that the school district had been monitored, visited, reviewed, and accredited by the state education agency. Minority educators in the state at the time were heard to murmur that the accredited status of the school district was related to the fact that most of the students who dropped out were minority students. It is doubtful that a school district with a predominantly white, Anglo student population would stay accredited for long with a 90 percent dropout rate.

Neither the state, which has the responsibility for education, nor the local school districts, which are delegated the responsibility for the operation of school programs, have been subjected to any rigorous demands for accountability in educational outcomes as a result of state regulation. Although school districts have experienced extensive failure in the education of large segments of the population, there have been few penalties associated with this failure. If anything, school systems have been rather successful in having the victim of the educational inadequacy held accountable for the crime, and in many cases they have even been extremely successful in having the victim agree to the culpability.

LEADERSHIP

Aside from the regulatory role, the state serves as the focal point for school leadership, which should lead to the improvement of educational opportunity. Ways in which this leadership is exercised include the provision of technical assistance for local school systems leading to an improvement in educational programs, the conducting of research and development activities, and the identification, acquisition, modification, and dissemination of innovative instructional practices.

There is an inverse relationship between state leadership and the state regulatory roles. In states where state leaders have clearly defined goal-oriented roles, the need for regulation diminishes. State default in its leadership role increases the pressure for responsiveness and leads to extensive and intensive regulation.

Unfortunately, central education agencies sometimes lack a sufficiently dynamic orientation to fulfill the leadership role. Central education agencies can be tractive institutions, much more aware and concerned with legislative and practical constraints to change than with innovative practice. Rather than visualizing ideal educational environments, the state education agencies can be the strongest defenders of the status quo, expending much of their energy in the defense of that which is, rather than in the conceptualizing of that which should be.

As with the state capacity for meeting its regulatory role, states vary in their capacity to meet their leadership role. The fifty states could be sorted into three groups that describe the quantity and quality of educational leadership provided by state education agencies, with a plentiful supply of cases for each of the three groups.

The first group would include states that provide extensive direction and leadership for education. These states function in the historical tradition of Horace Mann (Massachusetts), Henry Barnard (Connecticut and Rhode Island), Caleb Mills (Indiana), and Calvin Wiley (North Carolina), organizing, developing, and improving educational programs within the state.

The second group would consist of those states that seldom pioneer in educational innovation or reform, but eventually accept and internalize the no-longer-new innovation and reform.

The third group would be made up of those states whose central education agencies fight any attempts to alter the existing system of education. These education agencies resist all innovation and reform until forced to accept it, usually by legal enactment, at which time the state education agency immediately institutionalizes the new program and diligently protects it from removal or from any further modification.

NEW PRESSURES FOR EDUCATIONAL ACCOUNTABILITY

In recent years two new pressures have manifested themselves, demanding extensive changes and increased accountability in the educational system, thereby creating new demands on the states' educational leadership. The first is the equity movement as described in the states' regulatory role; the second is the loud voice of the business and industrial community demanding nationally, as well as in each of the states, a better product from the educational system.

The change our country is undergoing as it moves from a manufacturing, mineral, and industrial economy to a service and technological economy has resulted in three altered characteristics of American labor that are extremely significant for education. First, business and industry can no longer absorb even a portion of the growing pool of unschooled, untrained, cheap, unskilled labor that formed the backbone of the American labor force in the past. Second, the failure of the schools to educate a large segment of the population has created a financial liability in terms of lost wages, lost taxes, incarceration, rehabilitation, welfare, and delinquency which costs many times more than the cost of education, and the private sector has become very aware of the burden of its share of the cost. The slogan "you pay me now, or you pay me later" is not lost on the private sector, after all, it was the private sector that coined the phrase. Third, the private sector is already experiencing problems in acquiring the skilled labor necessary for the competitiveness, and even the survival, of American technology-oriented business and industry. It is anticipated that this shortage of skilled labor will become much more extensive and critical in the years ahead.

It is surprising that this crisis in American labor needs has been relatively lost on the schools. Many educators are unable to interpret and understand the new demands that the private sector is making on them. In the past, the schools have enjoyed a nice relationship with the private sector, easily meeting the demand for cheap, unskilled labor. If the schools have not succeeded in anything else in the past, they have certainly been extremely successful in providing business and industry with an extensive supply of unskilled labor. The new demand for skilled labor has been much more difficult for the schools to meet.

The problem of meeting the demand for skilled labor is further compounded by the shrinking of the white middle class and the rapid growth of minority populations, providing the schools with a higher number and a higher proportion of the type of student with which the schools have consistently experienced the most failure.

In states in which educational leaders have communicated with the private sector and joined hands in the struggle for educational reform, the results have been encouraging. Where state educational leadership has been lacking, the results have been disastrous.

State attempts to bring about educational reform in the absence of equitable allocations of resources and instructional fairness have proved counterproductive. A focus on outcome measures, particularly achievement-test requirements for promotion and graduation, rather than on input equity, has exacerbated rates of failure and school dropouts among minority and disadvantaged students.

CONCLUSION

As our country has grown, we have seen a change in the responsibility and support of education. Originally provided at local initiative, education has become a central responsibility of the states and a major federal interest. Although the interest and support of education at the federal level increased and decreased periodically, the interest and support of education at the state level has consistently increased over the years.

The extent to which the various states will flourish politically and economically is very much dependent on the extent to which the individual state meets its educational responsibilities. Vigorous commitment is required in discharging the three major educational responsibilities of the state: the furnishing of adequate and equitable resources for the support of education, the enlightened exercise of its regulatory role, and the provision of educational leadership resulting in further state growth and improvement.

NOTES

1. The Constitution of the United States. Preamble: "We the people of the United States, in Order to form a more perfect Union, establish domestic Tranquility, provide for the common Defense, promote the general Welfare, and secure the Blessings of Liberty to ourselves and Our Posterity, do ordain and establish this Constitution for the United States of America."

   The Constitution of the United States. Amendment 1. December 15, 1791: "Congress shall make no law respecting an establishment of religion, or prohibiting the free exercise thereof; or abridging the freedom of speech, or of the press, or the right of the people peaceably to assemble, and to petition the Government for a redress of grievances."

2. Newton Edwards and Herman G. Richey. *The School in the American Social Order* (Boston: Houghton Mifflin, 1947). 248.

3. Percy E. Burrup and Vern Brimley. Jr., *Financing Education in a Climate of Change* (Boston: Allyn and Bacon. 1982). 160.

4. Michael W. Kirst. Jr., *The Federal Role and Chapter 1: Rethinking Some Basic Assumptions* (Washington, D.C.: Research and Evaluation Associates, 1986), 4.
5. *San Antonio Independent School District v. Rodriguez*, 411 US 1 (1973).
6. *Rodriguez v. San Antonio Independent School District*, 337 F Supp 280 (WD Tex 1971).
7. *Lau v. Nichols*. 483 F2d 791 (9th Cir 1973), cert. granted. 412 US 938 (1973).
8. *Brown v. Board of Education*, 347 US 483 (1954) David L. Kirp and Mark G. Yudof, *Educational Policy and the Law* (Berkeley Calif.: McCutchan, 1974), 307.
9. The Civil Rights Act of 1964, 42 USC, Sec. 2000c-2000d; The Elementary and Secondary Education Act of 1965, Title I, 20 USC, Sec. 241.

SELECTED REFERENCES

Brown v. Board of Education. 347 US 483 (1954).

Burrup, Percy E., and Vern Brimley, Jr. *Financing Education in a Climate of Change*. Boston: Houghton Mifflin, 1947.

The Civil Rights Act of 1964. 42 USC. Sec. 2000c-2000d.

Edwards, Newton, and Herman G. Richey. *The School in the American Social Order*. Boston: Houghton Mifflin 1947.

The Elementary and Secondary Education Act of 1960. Title I, 20 USC. Sec. 241.

Kirp. David L., and Mark G. Yudof. *Educational Policy and the Law*. Berkeley, Calif.: McCutchan, 1974.

Kirst, Michael W., Jr. *The Federal Role and Chapter 1: Rethinking Some Basic Assumptions*. Washington, D.C.: Research and Evaluation Associates, 1986.

Lau v. Nichols. 412 US 938 (1973).

San Antonio Independent School District v. Rodriguez. 411 US 1 (1973).

NO PASS, NO NOTHING

1990

(This article was originally published in the May 1990, issue of the Intercultural Development Research Association (IDRA) *Newsletter*. It was subsequently published in *Texas Coach*, a publication of the Texas High School Coaches Association [Texas High School Coaches Association, 1991.] It was selected for a recognition award as the best article written by a non-member in 1991.)

In 1984, the Texas Legislature, under heavy pressure from the business community to improve the education system of the state of Texas, enacted its infamous "No pass, no play" legislation. The goal of this law was to motivate students participating in athletic activities, particularly the major competitive sports, to do better in their school work or lose the opportunity to play. Unfortunately, the poor conceptualization of the law and its wording has resulted in many students not participating in any extra-curricular activities including many activities which are closely related to and enrich the academic program, activities not meant to be targeted under the law.

Five years later the "No pass, no play" legislation was expanded to include "No pass, no drive" which denies a driver's license to a student of school age not enrolled in school. In other states the "no drive" provision has been modified to include students not doing well in school in addition to those who have dropped out. "No pass" legislation and regulations have become a fad, with states and school districts enacting similar legislation as fast as other states and school districts are abandoning them.

The main criticism of "No pass" regulations is that it is an extremely simplistic approach to improving school performance. The rationale of this approach is that the student has the power to do better, and the threat of not being able to participate in extra-curricular activities or not being allowed to drive a car can lead to substantially improved performance on the part of the student. Although there are undoubtedly some students who may profit from such drastic negative motivation, it does little to improve school performance for the bulk of the student population that is currently under-performing and dropping out of school.

The rationale of "No pass, no play" is based on a deficit model which attributes to the target population deficit or negative characteristics which account for their poor performance in school. It assumes that everything the school is doing is adequate; if the student does not benefit, then the student is solely to blame.

A deficit rationale is inconsistent with every basic principle of education and most of contemporary research findings. Atypical students for the most part do poorly in school because of the failure of the school to address the characteristics and developmental patterns of atypical populations, and in most cases underperforming students are unable to control their performance or cope with problems associated with school activity.

The "no play" and "no drive" provisions is society's way of punishing the victim for the crime and leads to further alienation of the at-risk school population.

IDRA studies of school dropouts in Texas identified the potential dropout as an academic and social isolate, a student who is alienated from the school and seldom a participant in the academic activities of the classroom or the more socially oriented activities in extra-curricular programs.

Rather than attempting to integrate the isolated at-risk student into school activities as an attempt to diminish the risk of dropping out, "no pass" prohibitions push the potential school dropout further away from school activities and exacerbate the isolation so typical of school dropouts.

Although many school systems and entire states have enacted "no pass" regulations, it is difficult, if not impossible to assess the impact of such regulations. Much of the assessment of these programs is entirely subjective, with advocates of the "no pass" regulations perceiving success and opponents perceiving failure.

Not only is there an absence of empirical data, the amount of subjectivity in determining the adequacy of student performance makes a scientific determination of the impact of "no play" or "no drive" policies very difficult. The following circumstances impair valid assessments of "no pass" regulations:

1. Most grades are given on subjective criteria with little control for level of difficulty which can provide assurance of cross section or longitudinal equivalency in measurement. A teacher may grade "hard" one year and "easy" the next. Variations in teacher grading have been found to exist between classes and between students. In fact, grades given to the same test paper on different occasions by the same teacher have been found to be notoriously inconsistent. Such a lack of reliability and subsequent lack of validity makes it difficult to determine if students are really doing better or worse on the basis of teacher based subjective evaluations.

2. At the time of the enactment of "no pass" regulations, teachers tended to be extremely harsh in their evaluation of school athletes. After all, there had been no love lost between school coaches and school teachers who perceive the coaches as privileged employees with much higher salaries, an abundance of fringe benefits not found in the classroom, and commonly exempted from the non-instructional chores of education (hall duty, cafeteria supervision, etc.). The enactment of "no pass" regulations was seen by classroom teachers as the chickens finally coming home to roost with the teacher finally being given a form of power over the rival athletic program personnel.

   Now it is difficult to determine to what extent student improvement in grades can be attributed to better performance on the part of the student, rather than to the coaches learning to eat crow and make their peace with classroom personnel.

3. There is abundant evidence that students have learned to distinguish between advanced, difficult, honors type courses and the easier courses and non-academic tracks in school. Improvement in student grades and a diminishing of "no play" conditions may be indicative of a student shift away from the more difficult, and therefore more dangerous, curriculum.

Ways have been devised to handle the difficult courses which every student is required to take. One way is to sign up baseball players during the fall semester when poor performance does not impact on the baseball season, and sign up football players for difficult courses during the spring semester after the football season has ended. If wouldn't be surprising if basketball players are encouraged to take the hard courses during the summer months.

4. In required courses, students and their athletic mentors have learned to identify teachers who tend to give higher grades to students. One teacher in an orientation function informed a group of parents that she was not very demanding, gave little or no homework, did not require the students to read the book, and nobody ever failed her classes. She also assumed that the kids of the parents present were in competitive interscholastic activities. "I don't know why," but all the ball players, band members, pep squad girls and cheerleaders always wind up in my classes."

   It would be naive to assume that "no pass, no play" is successful in that school on the basis of the diminished number of participants found ineligible.

5. There are reports that the number of students trying out for school teams has diminished since the enactment of the exclusive legislation. A diminished number of students ruled ineligible to participate may be indicative of students eliminating themselves from participation, rather than letting the school do it for them.

   Coaches are loath to sign up players who are at risk of becoming ineligible. As a coach said to a student who had been dropped from the football team due to low grades and after improving his grades was trying out for the baseball team, "No way, I don't want losers on my team." The student committed suicide a few days later.

IDRA monitoring of student attrition rates in Texas schools during the past five years following full implementation of the Texas reform legislation, including the "no pass, no play" provision, presents a much more scientific assessment of the impact of the legislation. White, non-Hispanic student attrition rates have diminished by 23 percent. On the other hand, the attrition rates of Blacks has increased by 9 percent; the attrition rate for Hispanics has increased by 7 percent. There is no evidence to indicate that the performance level of at-risk students who stay in school has made any significant improvement since the enactment of the legislation.

A second phenomenon which has manifested itself since the enactment of the "No pass, no play" legislation in Texas has been the number of school districts asking IDRA for assistance in dealing with undesirable gang activity. Such a topic had never been requested until the last few years and has led IDRA staff to develop training modules addressing this problem.

Since belonging is an inherent psychological need which becomes very dominant during the adolescent years, it stands to reason that much of a student's drive will be directed toward the satisfaction of this need—if not in school sponsored socially acceptable activity, then in unacceptable and often destructive gang activity.

Although no empirical evidence has surfaced, it may well be that the reported increase of problem gang activity is the result of "No pass, no play" legislation.

On the basis of school experiences one can only conclude that "No pass, no play" policies are definitely not a panacea for improving student performance in school and may very well be counter productive—creating more problems than those which it purports to solve.

SCHOOL-BASED MANAGEMENT: ARE WE READY?

Gladys J. Gibbs

(The following is a summary of a study conducted by the author as part of the requirements of a practicum in applied research at the University of Texas in San Antonio. Dr. José A. Cárdenas, Visiting Professor in Educational Leadership, supervised the study conducted during the Fall 1990, semester. It was published in the April 1991 issue of the IDRA *Newsletter*.)

INTRODUCTION

Educators are continually faced with contradictory messages from the public. The public usually views the schools as inferior institutions and holds them responsible for a variety of social, economic and political problems. On the other hand, the public sees schools as the major institution for the dispersal of information in order to solve national problems—AIDS, drug abuse, teenage pregnancy, highway deaths—and much more.

Citizens have high expectations for their schools and feel that schools should be places where *all* children can learn. Many innovative techniques are constantly being tested. One innovation that has had impressive results, including improved teacher and student attitudes, improved test scores, a restored sense of professionalism among teachers and decreased vandalism, is school-based management (SBM).

State legislators pass laws and school officials administer them in all the school districts in the state. District school boards set goals and policies for the schools. But the actual teaching and learning takes place in the classrooms of each local school. The rationale of school-based management is to place more responsibility for making decisions at the campus level—close to where the teaching-learning interaction is located.

This research study will focus on the various aspects of school-based management and test a school district's readiness for its implementation.

WHAT MAKES A SCHOOL EFFECTIVE?

The correlates of effective schools are closely related to the rationale of school-based management. "In their now classic review of the effective schools literature, Purkey and Smith (1983) drew attention to school-site management as one of the most important organizational-structural variables' connected with effective schools" (Radius, 1988). As the research on SBM unfolds, it will become evident that this management system complements the effective schools correlates.

Effectiveness among schools, defined in terms of student performance on tests of basic skills, can be accounted for by the following five factors identified by Cohen (Cohen, 1982):

- Strong administrative leadership by the school principal, especially in regard to instructional matters;

- Clear instructional focus with school-wide emphasis on basic skills instruction, in which there is agreement among the professional staff that instruction in the basic skills is the primary goal of the school;
- High expectations of student performance; principal and teachers believe that students can reach high levels of achievement regardless of pupil background;
- A school climate conducive to learning: i.e.,a safe and orderly school free from discipline and vandalism problems;
- A system of monitoring and assessing pupil performance which is tied to instructional objectives.

SCHOOL-BASED MANAGEMENT

Goldstein states:

> In its purest form, school-based management is a remarkable, simple idea. It calls for each school to create its own council consisting of the principal, teachers, parents, and students, if appropriate. Other members of the community, such as neighboring business persons or local clergy, are sometimes included. The idea is to put more decision-making authority at the local school level, where the kids are, so that those who must implement decisions have a hand in making them (Goldstein, 1989).

David, Purkey and White add:

> "SBM is different from past decentralization efforts because it changes the entire system of district and school organization and restructures most roles in the district" (David, Purkey and White, 1988).White states, "The purpose is not to just reorganize administrative responsibilities, but to make changes in the traditional structure of authority, developing new relationships among teachers, administrators, parents and students" (White, 1989).

The ultimate goal of SBM is to improve the learning and teaching environments for the students.

ELEMENT OF SCHOOL-BASED MANAGEMENT

School-based management requires a reorientation in the way one thinks and operates in local schools and at the district level. The superintendent is the key to initiating and continuing SBM in a school or district. Without superintendent and school board support, and some budgetary flexibility, a context conducive to SBM does not exist. They must support the concept and be willing to share some of the decisions they would normally make. Their continued support is vital to the success of a SBM program in the district. Muthler reports:

> A district seeking full implementation of school-based management will decentralize authority to the greatest possible extent and provide broad

> discretion at the campus level. The state and district set broad goals and standards and provide resources, but the employment of resources and the path toward achievement are determined by school-site participants (Muthler, 1989).

The principal must be willing to share decisions with faculty and parents. Failure in this willingness to share would block any SBM program initiated by the central office. Effective school research attributes success to strong instructional leadership by the principal. Successful schools need to create a collegial or shared work attitude, combined with a norm of continuous improvement.

Lortie states, "Studies of classroom management and decision making suggest overwhelmingly that teaching is fundamentally a process of making decisions in situations that are highly unpredictable and interactive" (Lortie, 1975). Teachers are decision makers. It is a natural step to involve the people that are affected by decisions into the decision making process. Research of both effective schools and SBM shows an increase in professionalism among teachers when they are allowed ownership in the process. Increased authority at the school site can improve morale, self-esteem and efficiency of school personnel.

According to Caldwell and Wood:

> Several factors that show promise for success in implementing school-based improvement are: first, each superintendent must be deeply committed to improving instruction in the schools. Second, each district needs to have already been shifting some control to individual schools. In addition, funds for staff development in some districts need to be decentralized to support school-based improvement and inservice education. Finally, teachers and administrators need to recognize that (1) professional growth and in-service education are important components of any plan to increase effectiveness, and (2) school-based improvements require changes in roles, with accompanying professional development for all district personnel (Caldwell and Wood, 1988).

The move to school-based management and school improvement requires changes in the roles of board members, the superintendent, central office administrators, principals, teachers and staff development personnel. The new roles are described subsequently in this article.

Strategic planning is the vehicle that will help administrators journey into the future. According to Herman, the keys to successful strategic planning include:

- Involving stakeholders;
- Scanning for relevant data;
- Identifying critical success factors;
- Developing vision and mission statements;
- Doing an analysis of site manager's supports and constraints;
- Arriving at strategic goals and objectives;
- Developing action plans and allocating resources;
- Arriving at monitoring structures (Herman, 1989).

Training and staff development are crucial to the success of school-based management. Principals, teachers, parents and community members that are involved in the decision-making process must participate in a staff development program. The training is an ongoing process that should continue throughout the program.

White found:

> Budget, curriculum, and staffing decisions are three areas of decision making most commonly decentralized under SBM. School-based budgeting allows the principal, teachers, and community representatives to allocate funds across a variety of categories according to the priorities of the campus (White, 1989).

School personnel are better able to meet the needs of students by purchasing supplies and equipment necessary for students' specific needs.

White added:

> School-based curriculum development enables school staff to develop the instructional program, to select instructional materials and textbooks, and to design in-service training programs. Granting greater discretion over curriculum development and methods allows school staff to develop curricula most appropriate to the needs of their students.

> Participation in staffing decisions allows principals, teachers, and other school staff to determine the distribution of full-time and part-time positions, and the number of regular teacher, lead teacher, and teacher aide positions. Advocates of SBM argue that if school personnel are involved in making hiring decisions, they will select like-minded staff that reflect their own values, goals, and objectives (White, 1989).

According to Goldstein:

> Successful SBM takes parental encouragement a step further and involves the parents and community business leaders in the school decision making process. Outreach is important. While the initial SBM council may consist of the principal, teachers and staff, this group then must design an effective plan for attracting parent participation (Goldstein, 1989).

The 22nd Annual Gallup Poll addressed parental control of public schools. As reported by Elam, "The 1989 poll showed that more than 40 percent of the public believed that parents should have a greater say regarding the allocation of school funds, the content of the curriculum, the hiring of teachers and administrators, and the choice of textbooks and instructional materials" (Elam, 1990). These findings indicate the public is ready for SBM and willing to take part in its implementation.

SBM cannot be initiated overnight. White suggests, "Districts with successful SBM programs refer to the gradual transition process" (White, 1989). Research states that it would take a year of planning, and then from three to five years to completely implement a school-based management program.

PROBLEMS IMPLEMENTING SBM

Although efforts to improve schooling through councils and empowerment at the building level are theoretically attractive and may help bring about positive reform, they are also inherently problematic. Some of the problems and obstacles that researchers have identified are listed below by Levine and Eubanks:

1. Inadequate time, training, and technical assistance.
2. Difficulties in stimulating consideration and adaptation of inconvenient changes.
3. Unresolved issues involving administrative leadership on the one hand and enhanced power among other participants on the other.
4. Constraints on teacher participation in decision making.
5. Reluctance of administrators at all levels to give up traditional prerogatives.
6. Restrictions imposed by school board, state and federal regulations and by contracts and agreements with teacher organizations.

IS TEXAS READY?

Since 1984, Texas public schools have been subjected to an onslaught of educational reform from the Texas Legislature and the State Board of Education. This attack began with an educational reform committee headed by H. Ross Perot and led to the 1984 enactment of House Bill 72.

A district or campus that is considering the possibilities of developing a SBM program might be concerned that state control might be too great to allow such a system to exist effectively. A close look at the newest Texas reform laws, Senate Bill 1 (SB 1) enacted in 1990, might help alleviate these concerns.

In Texas, some aspects of curriculum are mandated in the form of essential elements which must be addressed. However, proponents of SBM are quick to point out that school-based management does not mean that federal and state guidelines on curriculum could be eliminated. SBM does not offer carte blanche to schools to teach whatever they want, however they want. It instead offers an opportunity to teach the mandated curriculum in a more original and locally-specified fashion.

SBM research also indicated that it is an advantage for individual campuses to choose textbooks and instructional materials appropriate to their needs. SB 1 provisions allow for a district or campus to be exempted from the state textbook selection requirements. Although not automatically exempted from state textbook regulations, the waiver procedure can allow the purchase with state money textbooks not on the state-adopted multiple list (SB 1, Art. IV, Sec.401, 11.272[f]).

SB 1 also created a Public Education Development Fund in order to support the implementation of innovative programs. Seventy percent of the money disbursed from this fund can be used for projects designed to achieve academic excellence for low-performing students. This provision in SB 1 is indicative of Legislative confidence in local campus innovations (SB 1, Art. III, Sec. 3.03).

SBM research states the need for the school council team to have authority in staffing decisions. SB 1 also addresses this. It states, "Each principal shall approve all teacher and staff appointments for that principal's campus from a pool of applicants selected by the district . . . based on criteria developed by the principal after informal consultation with faculty. . . ." (SB 1, Art III, Sec. 3.05, 13.352 [d]).

Another provision in SB 1 that supports SBM states that ". . . the principal of each school campus . . . with the assistance of parents, community residents, and the professional staff of the school . . . shall establish academic and other performance objectives. . . ." SB 1, Art II, Sec. 2.16, 21.7532). A district or campus interested in the development of a school-based management program could work within the guidelines set down by the Texas Legislature and would find extensive support from the Texas State Board of Education.

SUMMARY

School-based management is not a fixed set of rules. It is the opposite. By definition it may operate differently from one district to the next and from one school to the next, and from one year to the next. Due to its autonomy, school-based management is not for everyone. Even within a district it is not necessary, and it may be undesirable, for every school campus to participate.

There are three key terms elements that must be present for the successful implementation of site-based management: motivation, professionalism and leadership. It is the administrators, teachers and parents with these three traits that drive SBM. Since it places severe demands on the precious resource of time, restructuring needs to include sufficient planning time in the regular work week for site-based management to be implemented properly.

THE RESEARCH PROJECT

The research that follows will attempt to determine the knowledge, experience, and attitudes of principals and vice-principals in a large suburban school district in south Texas. It is appropriate for a district this large to have its administrators participating as the research population group. There is a wide variety of socio-economic groups among the student population. Districts that are large in size, with extensive student diversity, can benefit the most from SBM.

By the development and use of a survey instrument the investigator will determine the district administrators' levels of knowledge and attitudes about school-based management. Responses from elementary and secondary principals will be compared for group differences. Comparisons will also be made on the basis of length of administrative experience. The analyses of the survey findings should determine if the administrators in the district perceive the presence of central office support for the district, as well as possess the basic knowledge and positive attitudes to move towards the implementation of a school-based management system.

DATA COLLECTION

The survey instrument was distributed through the office of the district's deputy superintendent to approximately 100 campus administrators in the district. The deputy superintendent wrote a cover letter indicating the district's interest in the results. The respondents were given one week to return the survey form to the district office. Survey forms were received at the deputy superintendent's office in a sealed envelope and turned over to the investigator. A total of eighty-eight completed surveys were collected at the end of the one-week period.

DATA ORGANIZATION

Survey information was transferred to electronic scored answer sheets which were subsequently scored and analyzed by Charles Cavazos of the Research and Evaluation Department of the Intercultural Development Research Association (IDRA). The survey section measuring knowledge of site-based management (items 1-11) was analyzed for mean score, range in scores and individual item analysis.

In the section determining the attitudes of the survey population (items 12-28), the data were analyzed for mean score and standard deviation.

Data were then analyzed by level (elementary, middle or high school), position (principal or vice-principal), and experience (0-5, 6-10, 11-15, or 16+ years) of the respondents.

DATA FINDINGS

Results of Section 1

The analysis of section 1 of the survey provided the following demographic information:

FIGURE 1

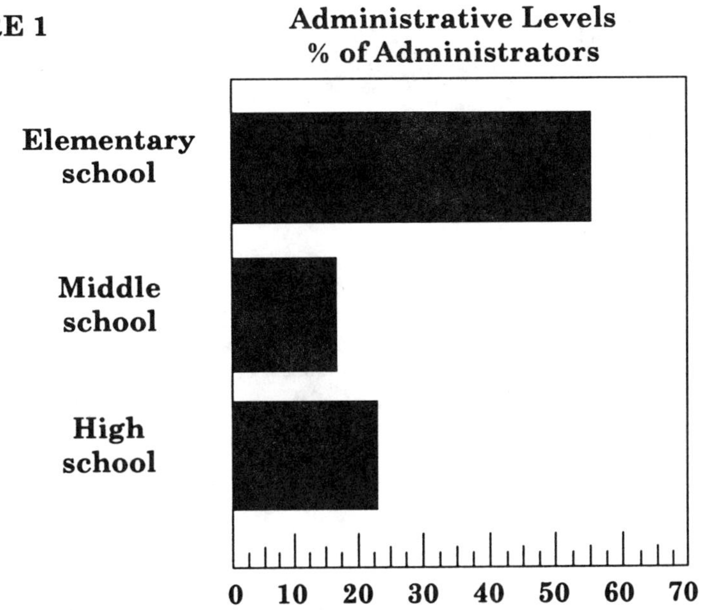

FIGURE 2

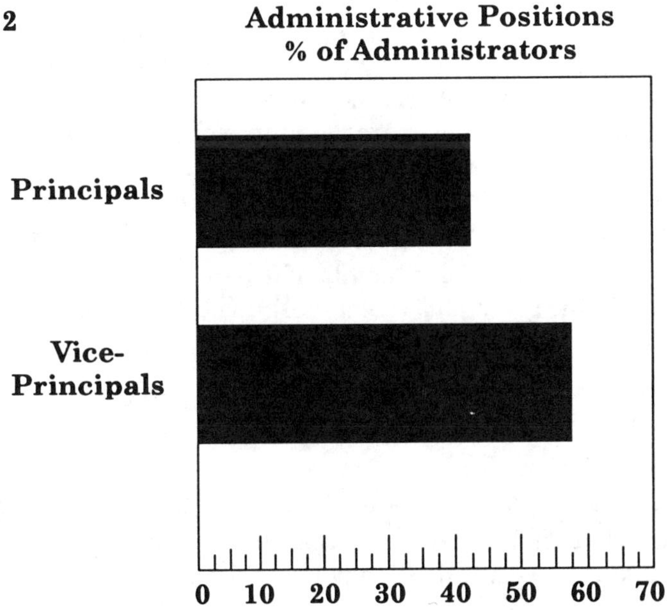

FIGURE 3

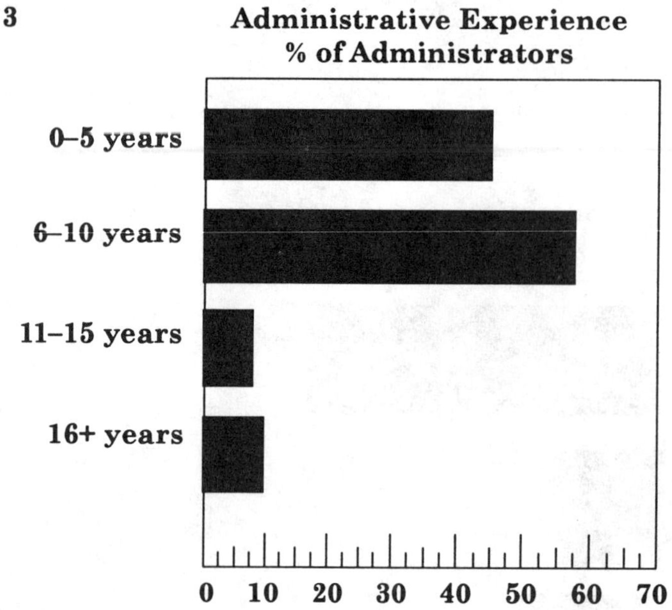

Results of Section 2

Analysis of the survey section on knowledge about the subject provided the following information: The eleven items produced a mean test score of 8.65 correct with a standard deviation of 1.29. Individual administrators scored on a range of 7, with a minimum of 5 and a maximum of eleven correct. Results indicate a mean of 78 percent mastery of the knowledge tested. On the basis of this finding it can be concluded that the majority of the administrators have a working knowledge of school-based management.

There were no significant differences in scores among elementary, middle and high school administrators. Nor were there significant differences between principals and vice-principals or among the levels of experience. An analysis of the eleven items on knowledge about site-based management included in the survey indicates three major areas of concern:

- Responsibility for instructional leadership (90 percent of the respondents felt that in SBM the principal is solely responsible for instructional leadership).
- The ultimate goal of school-based management (85 percent of the respondents felt that the goal was to improve relations between central office and campus personnel).
- The role changes necessary for the implementation of SBM (47 percent of the respondents felt that the primary role changes are required of members of the board and central office personnel).

Results of Section 3

Analysis of data from the third section of the survey, attitudes of administration toward SBM, produced the following findings concerning the implementation of school-based management:

- 70 percent of campus administrators in this district felt that increased autonomy at the campus level would be welcomed.
- 80 percent of the respondents felt that increased authority at the campus level would improve morale, self-esteem and efficiency of school personnel.
- Only about half (50 percent) felt that teachers would be willing to invest the time and energy necessary for the development of a SBM program.
- The administrators surveyed seemed to have faith in their teachers' abilities to make decisions and solve problems.
- Campus administrators do not feel that at this time they have sufficient control over budgeting to implement SBM.
- A higher percentage felt that they had more control over curriculum development (52 percent) and staffing decisions (78 percent).

RESTRUCTURING WITH SBM REQUIRES A REDISTRIBUTION OF POWER

- 39 percent of the campus administrators felt that central office personnel would be reluctant to reduce their own power.
- 45 percent felt that campus administrators would be reluctant to empower other participants in SBM.
- 59 percent of the respondents felt that they would be more than willing then most to empower others.

All of the campus administrators surveyed (100 percent) realized the importance of commitment of the school board and superintendent toward school-based management.

- Only 25 percent of the respondents agreed or strongly agreed that the school board would be willing to back SBM in the district.
- Only 31 percent agreed or strongly agreed that the superintendent would back the implementation of SBM.
- Over 50 percent of the respondents indicated a neutral position on the two preceding statements.

In comparing scores of items 12 to 28 that deal with administrator attitudes, no significant differences were found among elementary, middle and high school administrators. All three levels felt that increased autonomy would be welcomed at the campus level.

Middle school administrators perceived more backing from the superintendent and school board than the elementary and high school administrators.

Elementary school administrators appeared more receptive than other administrators to shift more control to teachers, parents and community members. All three levels agreed that increasing authority at the campus level would improve morale, self-esteem and efficiency.

In comparing scores on items 12 to 28 dealing with attitude, no significant differences were identified among administrators with varying years of experience.

- Administrators with the longest levels of experience (11 to 15 years and 16+ years) felt that they had more control over the hiring of staff.
- Administrators with sixteen or more years of experience had lower expectations for shifting control from the central office to the campus level, or at the campus level from the principal to the teachers, parents and community members.

The survey indicated the following perceptions of the district's current involvement in school-based management.

- One-third of the respondents felt that the district office was already shifting control to the schools.
- 57 percent felt that there was shifting of control at the campus level.
- 51 percent of the respondents felt that campuses already have committees for curriculum development.
- Only 10 percent indicated the existence of campus committees for staffing decisions.
- Only 26 percent indicated the existence of campus committees for budgeting decisions.
- 48 percent of the administrators surveyed indicated that they were definitely interested in receiving training in SBM.

CONCLUSIONS AND RECOMMENDATIONS

The majority of the administrators in the research district have a working knowledge of school-based management. These campus administrators have a positive attitude about the benefits of SBM. The majority feels that they have a staff that would benefit and be willing to invest the time and energy in SBM. There is a need for a visible show of commitment to SBM on the part of the school board and superintendent. Central office administrators have to be willing to delegate power to the campus level. Campus administrators have to be willing to delegate power to teachers, parents and community members. Not all administrators indicate a willingness to empower others.

Those campuses that have innovative administrators, staffs that are willing to delegate powers and go through SBM training, would probably benefit from the immediate implementation of SBM. Since SBM can be implemented one school at a time, it is possible to begin the implementation on those campuses that already have innovative and willing administrators, as well as school staffs that are willing to delegate powers and participate in SBM training.

Research studies indicate that those attempts to implement SBM that have failed, have done so due to the tremendous demands on the time of the teacher and administrator, and lack of staff training. It would be advantageous for the district to address the need for sufficient time during the work week for those involved in the implementation of SBM. It is an energy and time-consuming management method, and it will require many hours of staff training and other meetings for proper implementation.

It is recommended that a staff development program in the fundamentals of school-based management be made available to the school board, central office administrators and campus administrators. If there is sufficient support among these groups, then campus administrators interested in implementation of SBM need to provide fundamental training to school staff, parents and community participants. Following campus training, it is desirable to survey campus personnel to determine interest in participation.

Campus and central office administrators, teachers, parents and all others that will be involved in the transitional process should receive intensive training in the various aspects of school based management implementation.

ROLES FOR SCHOOL BOARD MEMBERS

Members of the board of education:

- establish and revise current policies to promote and support effective decision making and improvement of programs and practices in district schools;
- identify improvement goals to address major educational problems affecting the district;
- identify any improvement goals that all schools must address;
- establish a climate supportive of school-based improvement;
- establish performance expectations for central administration that support school-based improvement;
- monitor progress toward achieving the district's goals;
- allocate funds to support the achievement of the district's improvement goals;
- serve as public advocates for both the school improvement process and the effort to achieve the district's improvement goals.

ROLES FOR CENTRAL OFFICE PERSONNEL

Central office administrators (the district management team):

- translate board policy and priority goals for improvement into short- and long-range district plans for implementation;
- provide data related to the district's major problems and goal areas identified by the board;
- provide and manage district resources to support school instructional improvement plans;

- approve and monitor school instructional improvement plans;
- evaluate all aspects of the district improvement operation;
- provide staff development to accomplish desired goals and objectives of approved school improvement plan;
- model, in all aspects of their operations, the behaviors expected of principals and their school-based improvement teams.

ROLES FOR PRINCIPALS

Principals:

- ensure the positive climate necessary for gaining commitment to school improvement decisions;
- involve their staff and those clientele served by the school in developing goals and program plans for improvement;
- ensure that staff development programs designed for their staffs are related to their school improvement goals;
- participate in staff development with their faculties; ensure that the design of the school improvement plan addresses the major educational problems in their schools;
- implement and reevaluate school instructional improvement with their planning teams.

ROLES FOR TEACHERS

Teachers:

- work collaboratively with the principal, central office staff, and representative parents (as well as students themselves), to consider district and school priorities and to select goals to achieve over the next four or five years;
- help identify the programs and practices necessary to achieve school goals;
- assist in the implementation of these programs and practices by participating in staff development designed to help them achieve goals;
- conduct inservice for peers;
- help collect and interpret evaluation data related to improvement goals;
- assist the principal in managing the resources to assure improvement plans are successful.

ROLES FOR STAFF DEVELOPMENT PERSONNEL

Staff development personnel:

- assist principals and school faculties in developing improvement plans;
- collect and coordinate inservice needs from teachers, school planning teams, principals, and district-level administrators to support each school's improvement plan;
- work with principals to plan and manage inservice training for their school staffs related to assessed needs;
- work with central office administrators to plan and manage training for principals, district-level personnel, and the board;
- train district trainers and coaches to support staff development plans;
- assist in the evaluation of school-based inservice training;
- design and deliver new teacher and principal staff development programs;
- identify and keep school faculties aware of trends, programs, and research related to student achievement (Wood, et al., 1984).

REFERENCES

AFT Center for Restructuring, "School-Based Management," *Radius*, Vol. 1, No. 1, May 1988. Caldwell, S.D. and F.H. Wood, "School-Based Improvement—Are We Ready?" *Educational Leadership*, Vol. 46, pp. 50-53, October 1988.

Clune, W. H. and P.A. White, *School-Based Management*, Center for Policy Research in Education, Rutgers University, New Brunswick, 1988.

Cohen, M., "Effective Schools: Accumulating Research Findings." *American Education*, pp. 13-15, 1982.

David J., S. Purkey and P. White, "Restructuring in Progress: Lessons from Pioneering Districts," Paper prepared for the National Governors' Association, Washington, D.C., 1988.

Duttweiler, P.C. and S.M. Hord, *Dimensions of Effective Leadership*, Southwest Educational Development Laboratory, Austin, Texas, 1987.

Elam, S.M., "The 22nd Annual Gallup Poll of the Public's Attitudes Toward the Public Schools," *Phi Delta Kappan*, p.45, September 1990.

Goldstein, Robert, *Improving Schools One by One Through School Based Management*, Citizens Education Center, Northwest, pp. 1-39, 1986.

Herman, J.J., "A Vision for the Future: Site-Based Strategic Planning," *NASSP Bulletin*, pp. 24-27, September 1989.

Levine, D.U. and E.E. Eubanks, "Site-Based Management: Engine for Reform or Pipedream?" *Problems, Pitfalls, and Prerequisites for Success in Site-Based Management*, pp. 1-25, July 1989.

Lortie, D.C., *School Teacher: A Sociological Study*, University of Chicago Press, Chicago, 1975.

Mutchler, S.E., "Shared Decision Making: Harnessing the Energy of People," *Insight*, pp. 1-3, December 1989.

Texas Education News, "Major Provisions: SB 1," Austin, Texas, June 1990.

Wells, A.S., "Teacher, Principal, and Parent Involvement in the Effective School", *ERIC Clearinghouse on Urban Education*, Vol. 38, pp. 3-4, December 1987.

White, P.A., "An Overview of School-Based Management: What Does the Research Say?" *NASSP Bulletin*, pp. 1-7, 1989.

Wood, C.J., "Participatory Decision Making: Why Doesn't It Seem to Work?" *The Education Forum*, 49 (1), p. 61, 1984.

AMERICA 2000: WIDENING, NOT NARROWING, THE GAP

1991

(This article was printed in June 1991 in the IDRA *Newsletter*. It was subsequently published in *Voices from the Field* by the William T. Grant Foundation Commission on Work, Family and Citizenship and the Institute for Educational Leadership. *Voices from the Field*, is a 1991 collection of thirty expert opinions on America 2000, the Bush administration strategy for reinventing America's schools [National Education Goals Report, 1991]).

"The America 2000 initiatives fall far short of a comprehensive plan to address current educational problems. They fail to address the most severe problems of the educational system: the perception of atypical students as being deficient, the inability to distinguish between lack of experiences and lack of capability, low levels of expectancy and incompatible materials and methodology."

It is satisfying to see the President of the United States finally establish an agenda which addresses education—one of the most pressing problems on the domestic scene. It is high time. But it is doubtful that the nine features of *America 2000*—even with their seeds of promise—will alleviate, let alone resolve, the multitude of problems facing educational institutions.

As has been characteristic of prior educational reform efforts, some of these features may make a small impact on the problem. Many will be dysfunctional, and some may be counterproductive, creating more problems than solutions.

EDUCATION SEQUENCE

Education can be organized into three sequenced phases: inputs, processes and outcomes. *America 2000* emphasizes outcomes, with little attention given to inputs and a complete neglect of processes. In doing so, it mirrors the attitude of the National Education Goals Panel, which targets outcomes based on the erroneous assumptions that education needs to establish new goals and that once established, education is capable of achieving them.

Three major initiatives focus on educational outcomes: the establishment of new standards, nationwide tests, and the use of report cards to compare schools, districts and states.

The creation of new standards has been a common element in state school reform efforts. In general, the new standards provide a desirable goal for the schools to pursue. Past experience, however, has shown that setting higher standards without assisting the students who could not meet the old standards to achieve at higher levels tends to be counterproductive.

The commonly used example may seem trite, but it still serves to illustrate the problem: If a runner cannot jump a hurdle three feet high, raising the bar to four feet without providing any additional training or instruction can only lead to increased frustration and failure. New standards must be accompanied by new strategies so that the extensive number of students who have failed under the old standards can succeed.

Developing new indicators of the massive failure of large segments of the school population is unnecessary. It is doubtful that minority, disadvantaged, limited English proficient, immigrant and migrant students will do any better or any worse on a new national exam than they are doing on the standardized national and state examinations currently in use.

Comparisons of schools, districts and states will demonstrate what is already known: that some segments of the population perform deplorably in the education process. School, district and state characteristics will be reflected in these comparisons.

Schools with large numbers and concentrations of minority, disadvantaged, and other atypical populations will do worse than schools enrolling white, middle class, English-language background students. Central city and rural districts will perform more poorly than suburban districts. States with homogeneous white populations will out-perform states with heterogeneous populations. The challenge is to provide assistance to students not performing well, not to further stigmatize them.

CHOICE

Without a doubt, the weakest part of *America 2000* is its expectation that choice will solve our most pressing educational problems. Choice is based on the assumption that a free marketplace will lead to the selection and utilization of those schools which are successful and the atrophy of those which are not. While this notion may be attractive, its lack of adequate conceptualization and refinement forebodes catastrophe.

The knee-jerk support which this methodology has received in the absence of performance information is amazing. The models which are widely utilized in support of choice are mostly untested. What little evaluation has been done relies on deplorable research methods.

The most compelling argument against "choice" as the panacea for educational improvement is the *lack* of choice available to those segments of the school population most in need of an alternative. Existing models assume that all students have the wherewithal to make their choice a reality. Many poor families may have difficulty in allocating funds to make up the difference between government subsidies and the cost of private education. Not every student has access to the necessary transportation, or a parent with the time to help them make an informed "choice." This absence of choice for the school segment most in need of educational opportunity will lead to the mass exodus of only the white middle class from the central city schools, resulting in the dual system so common in other countries: The upper and middle classes attend private schools, and the public schools resemble charity institutions for those who have nowhere else to go.

In order for a choice program to be effective, *all* families must have equal opportunity to choose. This demands a guarantee of adequate transportation to the school of choice—with support transportation to ensure student participation in extracurricular activities—transportation for parents to be meaningfully involved with the school.

The mind-boggling logistics of desegregation seem insignificant compared to the logistics of implementing a democratic choice program. At the present time, successful schools are not so plentiful that all students could be guaranteed placement. Balanced distributions of minority, disadvantaged, limited English proficient children and other atypical populations will require advanced planning and careful implementation.

Advocates of choice shrug off these caveats with the simplistic assurance that all of these concerns will be addressed eventually. None of the existing models have addressed them as yet, however. Nor is there any readily available model to respond to these concerns in future programs.

INNOVATIVE SCHOOLS

Perhaps the strongest element of *America 2000* is the provision for 535+ new, experimental schools. The concept of creating innovative new schools, with creative teachers and administrators unfiltered by the traditions and tractiveness of existing institutions, is indeed challenging.

Reviews of educational literature show an extensive array of successful school programs in every sector of the country and for every segment of the population. During the past decade we have been thrilled by reports of school success among students deemed uneducable in the traditional school. The Committee for Economic Development's *Strategies for the Education of the Disadvantaged*, Lizbeth Schorr's *Within Our Reach*, and very recently the Quality Education for Minorities Project's report, *Education That Works*, are three recent efforts documenting the success of pilot, model and innovative programs (Committee for Economic Development, 1987; Schorr, 1988; Quality Education for Minorities Project, 1990). The innovative schools project proposed by the federal administration should be at least as successful.

We should note, however, the observation of former Secretary of Labor Ray Marshall, who chaired the Quality Education for Minorities effort: even though QEM found an abundance of successful *projects* in its nationwide survey, it did not identify one single successful educational *system*.

The three elements found in all of these successful projects provide important clues in addressing educational reform. In all of the successful projects, (1) children were valued in ways not commonly found in regular and traditional schools; (2) students were provided support services not commonly provided in regular and traditional schools; and (3) there were unique relationships among the school, the community and the family not commonly found in regular and traditional schools.

The proposed innovative schools will probably be extremely successful with the students they serve. The problem will lie in transferring the success of the innovative school to the traditional school campus. As noted by Marshall, no school system operating a successful project was successful in transferring this success to the regular school program. Neither the valuing of students, nor the supportive structures, nor the unique school/community/home relationships characteristic of successful programs will automatically transfer to non-participating schools. A federally-sponsored innovative school with the most dedicated, innovative, creative, sympathetic and best-trained teaching and administrative staff may have little impact on the thousands of schools in each of the 535 congressional districts not participating in the project.

America 2000 fails to address the common barriers to schooling. It inadequately values students and does not reflect the priority, attention and resources allocated to other national issues. The initiatives fail to address the need for sufficient investment in the education of children, let alone the innovative and equitable distribution of limited existing resources. Providing incentives for better performance by rewarding exemplary schools violates a basic principle of school finance. Performance is a poor basis for the distribution of resources. Rewarding high performing schools may deny resources to the entities which most need them. Providing funds for under-achieving schools may reward inefficiency and incompetence.

The *America 2000* initiatives fall far short of a comprehensive plan to address current educational problems. They fail to address the most severe problems of the educational system: the perception of atypical students as being deficient, the inability to distinguish between lack of experience and lack of capability, low levels of expectancy, and incompatible materials and methodology. Direction, support and resources are needed to address these inadequacies in existing schools.

HOMEWORK AND THE EDUCATION OF THE DISADVANTAGED

1992

Among the most important problems in the education of economically disadvantaged children are recognizing the ways that these children differ from middle-class children and adapting instructional practices to respond to these differences. The failure to recognize these differences inevitably leads to the erroneous assumption that the unique characteristics impair learning; therefore, the child is incapable of learning. There is an important difference between concluding that some children cannot be educated and concluding that they cannot be educated through conventional methods. An educational example of the failure of conventional methods is homework.

Homework is a middle-class institution which has been very successful in providing reinforcement for school learning, and in expanding the temporal and geographic horizons of the school. In keeping with the proven impact of homework, early school reform efforts focused on increasing the amount of homework assigned in order to improve student performance in school.

Unfortunately, homework is not often a very successful methodology in poverty homes. Such environments seldom can provide students with space, time, privacy, isolation or proper assistance in doing the homework. There is no specified children's room where homework is to be done; space constraints place both the homework and the educational materials in physical jeopardy; and parents who may not even speak the language used in the school, nor have an extensive academic background, may not have the skills to provide any amount of assistance to the student.

Instead of homework providing reinforcement for school work or expanding temporal and geographic impacts of the school, homework can be difficult, frustrating and dysfunctional. Homework can even be counterproductive as in the case of a student repeating an incorrect way of doing long division fifty times. Such a situation provides extensive reinforcement of an incorrect and undesirable response.

This does not mean that school instruction cannot be reinforced or expanded; it means that the school should opt for alternative ways in which to do it. Tutors, individualized assistance and adequately staffed study periods may be much more effective than the assignment of massive amounts of homework for students facing constraints in doing it adequately.

The most important implication of this example is the continued and extensive need for adapting educational materials and methodologies to the characteristic of atypical populations, and ultimately to the unique characteristics of each individual child.

DENIAL OF DIPLOMAS LEGALIZED IN FLORIDA

1983

On May 4, 1983, Judge George C. Carr issued a decision in *Debra P. v. Turlington* which is bound to impact on educational issues in a majority of the states (*Debra P.*, 1981). Judge Carr decided that scores on the state of Florida's minimum competency test could be used legally to deny graduation to high school seniors and to award them a "certificate of completion" instead of a regular diploma.

The Florida standardized achievement test, which measures proficiency in communication and math skills, is first administered at the tenth grade level. The results of the test administration last October may preclude regular graduation for approximately 3,800 students, almost two-thirds of whom are Black.

Minimum competency testing is gaining in popularity in some 38 states which are administering this type of proficiency test in the schools. To a great extent it is difficult to take exception to the use of these tests, although like almost every other type of test, problems abound in the utilization of the results.

As long as the tests are used for determining problem areas in the school's curriculum and instruction, as well as for the identification of areas of possible student weaknesses, one cannot argue against their use. But when used for judging student success and for determining student promotion and graduation, they leave much to be desired.

Before any number of states respond to the Turlington decision by jumping on the standardized proficiency test bandwagon and by starting a massive substitution of certificates of completion in lieu of diplomas, it is well to consider the following points:

1. Excellence in education—a much sought after goal these days— is not brought about by testing or the application of sanction on the basis of test performance. Excellence is brought about by the appropriateness and quality of the interaction between teachers and learners. Failing one-half of a class does not bring a measure of excellence to the educational process.

2. In Florida, the courts spent considerable time determining that the specific proficiency measure covered material which was taught in the schools. Throughout the case, the question of instruction/test relations was established prior to proceeding with the other legal issues involved. Proficiency tests used in the other thirty-seven states may not be as closely related to actual instruction, leaving a wide gap for possible litigation.

3. The wide use of proficiency standardized tests has inevitably led to an overemphasis in teaching the test. This is most unfortunate because such tests tend to measure the lower forms of learning. Although assessing

the extent to which basic skills are acquired is desirable, an extreme preoccupation with the basic skills can easily lead to an under emphasis on far more important cognitive and affective areas of learning.

4. The disparity of test results and teacher grading leaves a serious question about the ability of school personnel to evaluate student performance objectively, to identify failure, and to communicate the information to the student and his parents. The 3,800 Florida students in question should not have to discover at the tenth grade that their performance in school is substandard. If the results of the minimum competency tests indicate that the student is a functional illiterate, how did they manage to amass the necessary credits and units in English, math, science, social studies and other requirements to reach senior status in high school? Perhaps the school is letting the "test" communicate to the student and the family what school staffs do not have the nerve and/or the skills to communicate.

5. The issuing of certificates of completion in lieu of a diploma is a dysfunctional response. Already identified as "Jim Crow diplomas" because of the high incidence of Blacks scheduled to receive them, these certificates of completion are bound to become "certificates of incompetence" which will haunt the recipients for the rest of their lives. Critics of the Florida policy point out that such graduates will be denied jobs and access to further education. The recipient will have been tracked forever by this dubious award. I would not hesitate to advise a potential candidate for a certificate of completion to drop out of school, leaving the door open for future remediation, rather than be branded and tracked for life as an incompetent.

6. Court cases on educational malpractice where a student sues the school for its failure to teach him have not been very successful, because courts have been very reluctant to place the entire blame on the school. The courts have noticed a sensitive balance between the school's willingness and capability to teach and a student's willingness and capability to learn. By the same token, I would be very reluctant to go to the other extreme and punish the student for his failure to learn and completely absolve the school in this failure. Yet the Florida educational system is doing exactly this. By using the minimum competency test for the denial of high school diplomas in an accountability movement, the Florida educational system penalizes the student and completely absolves the teacher. In keeping with the court-identified balance between student and school, perhaps the denial of a student's diploma should be accompanied by a 10 percent forfeiture of pay for all school personnel involved. I can imagine the teacher unions and associations screaming that the fault may not lie with the teacher, yet the system is quick to assume that the fault lies with the student. Unilateral blame is equally unfair to the teacher and to the student.

7. Retention and denial of graduation are the least cost effective means of coping with under achievement. The repetition of a grade costs the average school system approximately $2,000 per student. A much lesser investment in smaller pupil/teacher ratios, higher quality of teachers, compensatory and remedial programs, and more adequate instructional materials would produce much better results without the negativism associated with the Florida response.

It is hoped that these seven points will be kept in mind by decisionmakers during the next few months as the impact of the Florida decision is felt throughout the country. Some educators in each of the states will view denial of diplomas as a panacea for the inadequate educational performance being criticized so commonly and so frequently in educational reports. Yet that is a fallacy that should not be perpetuated.

Florida has chosen and legally succeeded in lowering the quality of its educational process through this "quick fix" approach. I trust it will not be a model for the rest of the country.

8,138 WAYS TO MESS UP SCHOOL REFORM IN TEXAS

1992

At a time when the entire country has become keenly aware of the inability of the schools to respond to the educational demands of an information, service and technological economy, and hordes of educators, politicians and community leaders strive to bring about a much-needed reform in our schools, the state of Texas proceeds with its own brand of school reform.

Instead of addressing inadequacies in the level and distribution of school funds, inadequacies in the preparation of teachers, inadequacies of curriculum and methodology, the state of Texas takes a direct and simplistic approach to school reform.

The Texas Legislature directs that standards be raised by the implementation of a new test, the Texas Assessment of Academic Skills (TAAS). This new test legislated in 1989, and implemented in the 1990-91 school year differs from the two previous tests in that it measures a wider range of curriculum areas, and it measures more sophisticated learning than the minimum competency tests of yesteryear.

The TAAS was administered twice to high school juniors in the 90-91 school year, and twice again in 91-92 to seniors who did not pass the test in the junior year.

In its rush to meet the educational demands of the twenty-first century, the state of Texas overlooked one very important detail. Raising the standards without improving the quality of the instructional program does little for the performance of students, other than increase difficulty, frustration and failure.

As a result of the TAAS requirement there are now 8,138 seniors who cannot receive their diplomas because their performance on the test is below the high standard determined by the State Board of Education. Incidentally, more than 85,000 students did not stay in Texas high schools long enough to take the final test.

The political and educational leadership of the state is now at a standstill, not knowing how to proceed. The commissioner suggests that the students keep taking the test until they pass it, but it is doubtful that simply retaking a test will result in any improvement in these students' performances. He further calls for remedial instruction in preparation for subsequent administrations of the test, but again, it is doubtful that twelve or more years of educational neglect and a progressive decline in the performance of the students will be reversed by a test coaching program. Nor are the young adults who have completed their high school program prone to linger for several additional years in hopes of remediating their educational shortcomings, passing the test and receiving their high school diplomas.

The Texas approach to school reform demands high performance on the part of the students—subsequent to the students' completion of most of the course work on which the new examination is based. Concepts tested by the TAAS were not often part of the instructional program available at the time of student attendance. Some of the concepts should have been taught in courses not required and/or not available at the time the students were enrolled in school.

Many of the students unable to pass the TAAS in order to graduate were enrolled in "below level courses," i.e., the course offering's content was below the level now being measured by the new test. The Texas commissioner of education is certainly aware of the inadequacies in course offerings since he is currently advocating the elimination, or severe restriction, of these watered-down offerings in Texas schools.

The improvement of instruction which will lead to improvement in student performance is being phased-in over a period of years. Legislated improvements, such as restrictions in class size and special assistance programs, have been waived continuously since their enactment in 1986 due to the inability of many schools to acquire the financial, personnel, physical and other resources to implement a better instructional offering. Yet, the expected outcomes of this not yet realized improvement have not been waived.

The Texas Education Agency (TEA) is in the process of developing new accreditation standards which include the higher performance on the TAAS, but the TEA monitoring part of the plan will not be ready until the 1993-94 school year. Even then, it is too much to hope that the schools will be able to meet the new accreditation standards for several additional years.

It is unreasonable to hold the students accountable for their failure to perform at a level which the state's schools hope to reach around the year 2000.

The improvement of instructional practice must proceed step-by-step with an improvement in the resources available to the school. Increases in financial support for Texas schools have been limited. What little overdue catch-up increases the state has provided in recent years have been more than eroded. This is indicated by the state's ranking in expenditures per pupil slipping back to number forty among the fifty states.

New appropriations for education have not only been meager and far between, but a portion of the appropriations have never materialized. Texas schools are operating in this biennium under a shortfall of an estimated $574 million dollars; $231 million dollars short in 1991-92 and $343 million dollars in 1992-93. This means that the state is $574 million dollars short in meeting its share of the state/local formula for funding the basic school program tested by the TAAS.

The ability of low wealth school districts to have access to an equal portion of public funds is still a dream. An attempt to address reform of the still inadequate and unconstitutional system was dropped earlier this month in the absence of legislative support for any reform plan. Many of the students who cannot perform adequately in the TAAS are students in school districts whose administrators testified in the school finance case. They testified that inadequacies of funding precluded consistent offerings of courses and course work now being measured in the TAAS.

Data available from the Texas Education Agency indicate a positive correlation of .63 between low district wealth and the number of students still unable to pass the TAAS. This correlation increases to .71 when controlled for district size. A correlation of this magnitude indicates that continued poor student performance on the TAAS is simply a fairly good representation of the wealth of the school district the students attend.

Some school districts have already requested assistance in resolving the problem created by graduating seniors who cannot graduate, even though some of their requests are based on the worst of reasons: the enrollment of large numbers of minority and disadvantaged students—the type of student that the Texas system has consistently deemed uneducable.

Perhaps the worst aspect of the TAAS mess is the mistaken notion by the political and educational leadership of the state that waiving TAAS requirements for students who went through most of the system before the implementation of the test constitutes a decrease in accountability. There is no relationship between denial of a diploma to the student and school accountability.

The denial of the diploma is a misdirected punitive measure. Students who have already been victimized by poor educational opportunity in a poorly funded, poorly operated educational system are now being further victimized by being punished for their poor performance on the test.

Punishment for victimized children is particularly grating when there is no parallel punishment for those teachers who can't teach, administrators who can't administer, school boards that consistently expect and accept poor performance and inefficiency; short-sighted taxpayers reluctant to invest in education, a state education agency that provides no leadership save what is ordered by the courts, legislators unable to distinguish between investment in human resources and government waste; and a political leadership incapable of leading. The deplorable condition of education in Texas is the fault of years of neglect on the part of the entire state. Now we hold the students accountable and punish them accordingly.

One can only hope that one day Texas will conceptualize and bring about a superior educational program which addresses the current and future social and economic needs of the state. When this comes, and it surely will not be in the immediate future, it will come as the result of a better conceptualized, better operated and better funded educational system. It will come by rewarding educators for being successful and persevering. Educational standards cannot and will not be raised by simply punishing students.

THE VOICE OF THE ELECTORATE: WHAT DID IT SAY?

1993

The voters have spoken. Saturday, May 1, 1993 marked the end of the statewide elections which included a vote on three constitutional amendments dealing with school finance: legalizing wealth neutral county education districts, a prohibition against requiring state education mandates without adequate funding, and the sale of $750 million in revenue bonds.

The result of the vote is now history. The Texas voters clearly rejected all three of the proposed constitutional amendments, the first one by a very decisive margin. More than two million voters turned out to defeat the three propositions by 63 percent, 51 percent, and 56 percent, respectively.

What caused Texas voters to reject the three propositions? And what are the short-term and long-term effects of this rejection?

Opponents of the proposed amendments will be quick to assert that the vote was indicative of public sentiment against taxes. Proponents will be equally quick to assert that the vote is indicative of a lack of concern over the education of the state's 3.5 million public school children. Perhaps both sides will be right, but I believe the issue is much more complex than this. Simplistic conclusions give few insights into the nature of the problem and none into future action or direction.

It would be nice to have the time and resources to conduct a massive survey of voter attitudes and subject them to multiple regression analysis in order to identify and weigh the various factors which influenced the election. It is doubtful that anyone will attempt this, so in the absence of empirical data, I will conduct my own analysis of the reasons for the defeat.

There may be hundreds of reasons for people voting as they did, but I believe that there are five major influences that led to the rejection of the three propositions.

1. Opposition to the elimination of the elitist system of schooling which has always characterized the state educational system

Texans have always liked to glory in the past with their erroneous myths and obsolete traditions. Educational opportunity in Texas has been a scarce commodity since colonial days, and the majority of the state still feels that universal education is a waste of time and money. Although the entire world is cognizant of the shift in economic base from agriculture, minerals and manufacturing to services, information and technology, many Texans would like to continue living in the past with an educational system ranking fortieth among the fifty states and precluding quality education for all but a few.

The *Rodriguez* court case in 1971, signaled the beginning of a movement for an efficient system of schooling based on an equitable system of school finance (*Rodriguez*, 1971). The *Edgewood* court case today demands equity or it will close the schools (*Edgewood I.S.D.*, 1987).

During the entire election period, opponents of the amendments called for "less drastic measures" for compliance with the court order. This call comes in spite of the courts having already rejected three less drastic measures and obviously losing its patience with the failure of the legislature to reform the system.

Opponents of reform called for the defeat of the amendments and proposing that inequities in the system be eliminated by giving low-wealth districts' revenue from the Texas lottery to bring them up to the level of their richer neighbors. As the Texas Legislature discovered, it would take some $45 billion to bring all Texas schools to the level of their richest neighbors, an amount which cannot be feasibly raised by an extensive income tax, let alone with the limited revenues of a state lottery.

The failure of the legislature to reform the system can be attributed not to the lack of available reform measures, but to its desire to change the system of school finance just enough to meet the equity standards imposed by the court while still maintaining a privileged position for privileged students and privileged taxpayers. However, the number of privileged under the existing system of school finance cannot account for the overwhelming defeat of the amendments, so there must be other reasons for the decisive vote.

2. Opposition to taxation

There can be no question that some of the negative vote resulted from the universal state opposition to taxation. Ever since Proposition 13 in California reversed the trend toward higher and higher taxation, vested-interest groups in Texas banded to oppose all forms of taxation. There is some irony in this since Texas, unlike California, ranks forty-ninth among the fifty states in per capita taxation.

Although it is easy to conclude that the wealthy are most prone to oppose the taxation of wealth, I do not believe that this group was a key element in the school finance amendments' defeat. With notable exceptions, the business leadership of the state is convinced that future economic growth is now dependent on a skilled work force. The business community is aware that there can be no economic survival for Texas by attempting to compete with Third World countries as a provider of cheap labor. Cheap, unskilled labor is an obsolete commodity in this country. The Texas business community is now shopping for skilled labor, and either importing the supply which Texas schools cannot produce or doing without and defaulting in national and world economic competition.

As evidence of business community support for an improved educational system, we can note that the main support for the proposed constitutional amendments in Bexar County came from Save Our Schools and the Greater San Antonio Chamber of Commerce, both organizations substantially subsidized by the business community.

The opposition to taxation now comes from the older, retired community, and from a rapidly aging population. I cannot help but be sympathetic to their plight. They have worked in an era in which there was little investment in retirement, and find themselves in a situation where the family structure has changed so that taking care of grandpa and grandma has little priority in their children's budgeting. Furthermore, the inability of the elderly to earn a living has become a nightmare with increased and regressive taxation. Persons over sixty-five years of age living on Social Security checks look with horror at consistent increases in sales taxes, annual increases in county, city and school taxes, and the unconstrained growth of taxing entities. To them, the last straw probably was the construction of a domed stadium with a transit company sponsored sales tax. Fear of additional taxation is no longer tempered by the civic purpose of the tax; for many, it is a question of survival.

This need not be an indictment of taxation; it is an indictment of regressive taxation which has replaced the progressive taxation of the past. The current trend is to levy taxes on those segments of the population which can afford them the least.

3. Misinformation

Unfortunately, the voters of Texas were subjected to more misinformation about the proposed constitutional amendments in this last election than in any other election I can remember.

Proposition 1 was a simple amendment which would have allowed the state to use high, relatively untaxed wealth in the richest of school districts to partially finance the cost of education in the other 90 percent of the state districts. Opponents of taxation would probably be surprised to learn that the continued exemption of property in very high wealth districts will result in $440 million in additional state and local taxation to compensate for this loss, or it will further reduce the quality of education in the state by $440 million which legislators are now not prone to produce.

The current system of school finance places a legislative limit of $1.50 on local school tax rates per $100 valuation (with some exceptions for past bonded indebtedness). Included in this $1.50 cap is the amount being raised by the tax-sharing County Education Districts. In Proposition 1, County Education Districts were limited to a $1 rate within the legislated maximum.

Opponents of this proposition quickly informed the public that the $1 limit was in addition to the $1.50 maximum already imposed by the state. Homeowners were warned that passage of the proposition would lead to an immediate school property tax rate of $2.50 per $100 valuation, a 67 percent increase.

A newsletter distributed by Texans Against Robin Hood asserted that the proposition was part of a carefully crafted plan by the governor to implement a state income tax when the public reacted negatively to the $2.50 property tax.

A similar newsletter by the same group falsely identifies Texas as the only state in which there is a court mandate for school equity. It falsely describes Proposition 1 as an attempt to make equitable funding a part of the Texas Constitution. It questions the constitutionality of the judge's decision in the *Edgewood* court case, in spite of the decision being upheld by the Texas Supreme Court. It asserts that passage of Proposition 1 will free billions of dollars which would go into the pork barrel. It also predicts the creation of a whole new state-appointed bureaucracy to administer funds created within the county districts.

The fearmongers did an excellent job in private communications as well as in the public media to lead 62 percent of the voters to reject equitable taxation in a small number of districts with distribution of the revenues in lieu of state funds.

4. The conspicuous absence of educational leadership

Almost every day the media carried stories which conveyed the erroneous and irresponsible assertions made by the opponents of Proposition 1. Conspicuous by its absence was a strong denial or rebuttal by the education community.

As a group, educational administrators stayed out of the discussion. The main concern of the educational leadership in Texas has always been a plentiful supply of money—with little regard for its equitable distribution or the educational needs of students in low-wealth districts.

While Proposition 1 addressed the equitable distribution of funds, school boards focused on the inadequacy of funding. They dream of an ideal system in which the state will provide 80 percent of the operational costs—making it relatively easy for them to raise only 20 percent at the local level. The leadership's lukewarm support of Proposition 1 was due to the failure of the state to provide sufficient funds to ease the local effort. Since the percentage of the cost of education in Texas provided by the state has already peaked at 50 percent and has been declining during the past ten years, the expectancy that the state provide the majority of educational costs is very unrealistic.

At a meeting of community business people and school district leaders concerning the upcoming election, not a single one of the lowest wealth districts was in attendance. At a better represented meeting a week later, the representative from one of the poorest school districts in the state was asked by the business community where the district stood on Proposition 1. He shocked the participants with the qualified statement, "I think our district will support the amendment, but it will not come up for board consideration until the end of April."

Although other low-wealth school districts did support the amendment, this support can be tritely described as "too little, too late."

School officials will be quick to point out that state law prohibits the expenditure of school money in support of any election. This may be so, but I will be equally quick to point out that this has never been an impediment when the schools have had a sufficient interest in the outcome of an election. There are many things that could have been done without the need to expend school money.

In the months preceding the election and during the election itself, critics of the amendments repeatedly raised the charge that most educational funds are being wasted in that teachers comprise less than 50 percent of school staffs, with most of the money going to the bureaucratic administrators. It is surprising that no denial surfaced from the educational leadership.

By simply looking at Texas Education Agency's report, *Snapshot '92*, it can be immediately ascertained that of the 72 percent of Texas school employees which are professional staff, (i.e. eliminating the 29 percent comprised of janitors, cafeteria workers, bus drivers, etc.), 74 percent are teachers and 11 percent are teacher aides, making the total instructional staff 85 percent of the educational task force (Texas Education Agency, 1993).

During the entire election I did not hear a single person from the education community, or outside the education community for that matter, provide this rebuttal to a very commonly heard criticism.

The administrative leadership could not even carry Proposition 2 which provided no new state educational mandates without additional new funding, a compromise amendment proposed by the legislature at the districts' requests.

Proposition 3 would have provided state money for school construction in below-state-average-wealth districts. The representative of a large school district eligible for funding under this proposition, desperate for new schools in keeping with his district's rapid growth for which a bond issue election was only recently soundly defeated, could not bring himself to state that the district supported Proposition 3.

Although teacher groups took positions either for or against the various proposed amendments, neither the educational leadership nor the 1,000 plus school boards provided a voice of strong positive leadership in the election.

5. School accountability

Although perhaps lost in the tumult, it appears that there is a strong voice in the state calling for no additional funds for education until such time as educators become accountable for funds already supplied.

There is no question that education is sadly in need of an accountability system. Unlike other professions, educators do not attempt even a semblance of regulating its own members. The best teachers I have observed seldom raise a voice against their numerous colleagues that accomplish nothing. It is not uncommon for a nominee for the national Superintendent of the Year award to come from a school district with a student dropout rate of over 50 percent. Just a few years ago the Texas Superintendent of the Year award was given by the profession to the superintendent of the school district with the highest dropout rate in the state!

The public, particularly the taxpaying public, is sick and tired of seeing media releases by the public relations departments of districts describing the success of its schools in order to cover up the ineffectiveness of its programs. The public is sick and tired of reading about this year's "innovative" programs created to move the public focus away from last year's innovative programs that did not work. An Intercultural Development Research Association (IDRA) analysis of the state's seventy-five most promising innovative programs revealed that seventy-three of these programs did not even include an evaluation component to determine program success.

The Texas voter is sick and tired of listening to school officials attribute minuscule improvements in student performance to the leadership of the administrators and the board (never to the teachers), while unable to account for massive deterioration in student performance. Each account of progressively poorer student performance in state and national indicators is invariably followed by the appointment of a task force to determine the reason for the poor performance. I have never seen in the media the findings of such task forces. I doubt that such reports are ever issued.

The same Texas Education Agency report on professional positions also informs us that 60,000 students dropped out of Texas schools during 1991-92, a number which I can prove is actually much higher than reported. Of these students reported by Texas schools as dropping out during the 1991-92 school year, 27.3 percent came from economically disadvantaged homes. This means that 72.7 percent of the dropouts, 39,210 students, came from middle- and upper-class homes.

Performance in the state mandated Texas Assessment of Academic Skills (TAAS) leaves much to be desired. In 1991-92 only 44.6 percent of the 1,133,871 Texas students who took the test passed all three sections in reading, writing, and arithmetic. Only 58.5 percent of white, non-Hispanic students passed the tests, while only 21.2 percent of Hispanics and only 17.5 percent of African Americans passed.

At the seventh grade level, only 36.3 percent of all students passed all three tests: 49.4 percent of white, non-Hispanic; 21.2 percent of Hispanics; and 17.5 percent of African Americans.

Performance on the SAT college entrance examination is sadly summarized in the report as "lower than the national average" which is already disgustingly low.

In spite of these statistics, the Texas educational establishment calls for increases in salaries, increases in state funds for education and increases in property taxes, without any accountability for their failure to produce. When the political leadership does call for increased accountability, it is usually demanded from the "schools," a conglomeration of bricks and mortar that has little sensitivity to the needs of children or influence on their performance. Recent suggestions for accountability focus on penalizing low performing "schools" by giving them less money and reward high performing "schools" by giving them more money. This only results in withholding funds from the children that need them the most and giving additional funds to the children that need them the least.

School administrative personnel play musical chairs, constantly moving from one school district to another before accountability can catch up with them. My visits to school districts are usually prefaced by a superintendent saying, "I am new to this school district, don't blame me for anything you find wrong." I can't help but believe that in whatever district the new superintendent came from, there is another superintendent making an identical statement.

Successful school practitioners simply move up the built-in career ladder, moving away from the low paying jobs in the poorest school districts and into the higher paying jobs in the wealthier districts.

Although I believe that the relationship between money and performance is cyclic, and that Texans are reaping the harvest of years of financial neglect of their schools, I also believe it is incumbent upon school personnel to take some initiative in addressing their deplorable performance.

Additional resources made available through a more adequate and equitable system of school finance must be targeted for the development of better programs for poor performing children. This will attract more qualified and better trained personnel into the profession and the massive retraining of existing staff. There is a critical need to raise expectations for pupil performance and replace current programs with excessive emphasis on basic skills with challenging curricula which focus on the development of thinking skills.

The first step for the reform of Texas schools is the recognition and acceptance that there is a problem. Massive changes in the economy and the threat of world competition demands a move away from the development of a cheap labor work force to the development of a skilled labor force capable of a creative contribution to product development, production and marketing. Texas not only lacks a work force in support of a global competitive technology, Texas does not even possess the schools capable of developing it.

Texas educators must understand and accept the need for a massive reform of our schools, rather than resisting all forms of change while waiting for the return of oil and cotton to make Texas schools adequate for meeting the labor needs of the prevailing economy.

Texas educators must abandon the past practice of finding deficits in the students to account for poor performance. All other social sciences, and the general public as well, reject the school's argument that the failure of 80 percent of the minority population can be attributed to the genetic or cultural characteristics of that population. Schools must address the inherent potential of all students, instead of letting socio-economic class be the prevailing determiner of school success.

The most tragic scenario which can be created for Texas schools is to allocate more money and have this money used for the expansion of "remedial" programs which are low level, slow paced, repetitious, dull, boring, and self-fulfilling. It is ridiculous for the school to presuppose that all children from minority, poverty and language minority homes that differ from white, middle class, English-speaking children are mentally deficient and should be taught like the mentally retarded. These children need enriching experiences to expand their mental horizons, not the further confinement in dull, mentality constraining drills.

Educators, as well as the rest of the state population, must quit looking for simplistic "quick fixes," which cost nothing, achieve nothing and even tend to be counterproductive. Assuming that teachers who are unsuccessful all year will encounter extensive success by doing the same things for an additional few weeks is most unrealistic and not the solution to the problem. A drastic improvement in the state's student performance in the TAAS test or the SAT will surely not come about through the use of a cute new hand puppet which the teacher and students spent all of their instructional time in making.

THE IMMEDIATE FUTURE

The opponents of the constitutional amendments have not killed school finance reform in Texas. All they have succeeded in doing is giving taxpayers in a few rich school districts a continued $440 million tax break.

The legislature has one month in which to enact an equitable system of school finance. About the only feasible option still available is to increase equitable funding by reforming the system within the existing constraints of the constitution. It is a simple matter to reduce inequities by doing away with tax haven school districts and at the same time recovering the $440 million in revenues lost in the election. There are already several school consolidation bills available for accomplishing this, the only difference among them being which districts are to be consolidated with which.

I do not believe that the legislature will seriously consider placing unrealistic caps on school district expenditures as a way of achieving the court-ordered equity. Although this would make the opponents of taxation very happy, it would be a tragedy for the future of the state.

An impasse in the legislature may lead to the closing of the schools, but even if this should come to pass, the closing will be extremely temporary. If the legislators allow the courts to close the schools, 3.5 million kids will be sent home. It would be only a matter of days before the Texas electorate would realize that there are worse things in life than taxation.

THE LONG-RANGE FUTURE

Having tasted victory in this constitutional amendment election as well as in a number of recent school bond elections, there is no question that education is going to have a harder time reaching into the public's pocket for additional funding.

Support for a larger investment in education will have to be coupled with an identifiably larger return on the investment. It is unreasonable to assume that the public will continue to pick up the tab for an educational system that cannot turn out half of the student population with sufficient skills to pass a minimum competency test in reading, writing and arithmetic. There not only must be a measurable improvement in the basic skills, there must also be comparable success in computer literacy, science and technology. The future success in meeting the work place needs of the economic sector will be the key to an adequate level of public school finance.

School personnel must develop the capability of responding quickly and accurately to the massive amount of misinformation about the schools and related issues. School public relations specialists, which every medium and large school system seems to have, must spend their time promoting education rather than promoting administrative officers and the school board. There is no reason for the massive amount of misinformation which surfaced during the last election to go unchallenged.

Educators, in cooperation with the economic sector and the family, must develop a new educational paradigm which rejects the erroneous and false assumptions of the past and is compatible with the educational needs of the remainder of this century and of the new one to come. This paradigm must create an educational system responsive to a diverse clientele, rather than perpetuating the elitist system utilized in the past.

Although we have no guarantee that additional funding will bring about a dramatic improvement in school performance, it is a certainty that such an improvement will never come about in the absence of adequate resources.

BIBLIOGRAPHY

AFT Center for Restructuring, "School-Based Management," *Radius*, Vol. 1, No. 1, May 1988.

Brown v. Board of Education, 347 US. 483 (1954).

Burp, Perky E. and Van Jr., *Financing Education in a Climate of Change*, Allyn and Bacon, Boston, 1982.

Caldwell, S.D. and F.H. Wood, "School-Based Improvement—Are We Ready?" *Educational Leadership*, Vol. 46, October 1988.

Clune, W.H. and P.A. White, *School-Based Management*, Center for Policy Research in Education, Rutgers University, New Brunswick, 1988.

Cohen, M., "Effective Schools: Accumulating Research Findings," *American Education*, 1982.

Commission on Work, Family and Citizenship, *Voices from the Field*, The William T. Grant Foundation, Washington, D.C., 1991.

Committee for Economic Development, *Children in Need: Investment Strategies for the Educationally Disadvantaged*, New York, 1987.

David J., S. Purkey and P. White, "Restructuring in Progress: Lessons for Pioneering Districts," National Governors' Association, Washington, D.C., 1988.

Debra P. v. Turlington, 644 F. 2nd 397, 1981.

Duttweiler, P.C. and S.M. Hord, *Dimensions of Effective Leadership*, Southwest Educational Development Laboratory, Austin, Texas, 1987.

Edgewood I.S.D., et al. v. Kirby, et al., Cause No. 362,516, 250th District Court, Austin, Travis County, Texas, August 27, 1987.

Edwards, Newton and Herman G. Richey, *The School in the American Social Order*, Houghton Mifflin, Boston, 1947.

Elam, S.M., "The 22nd Annual Gallop Poll of the Public's Attitudes Toward the Public Schools," *Phi Delta Kappan*, September 1990.

Goldstein, Robert, *Improving Schools One by One Through School Based Management*, Citizens Education Center, Northwest, 1986.

Goodlad, John I. and Pamela Keating, *Access to Knowledge: An Agenda for Our Nation's Schools*, The College Board, New York, 1990.

Herman, J.J., "A Vision for the Future: Site-Based Strategic Planning," *NASSP Bulletin*, September 1989.

Intercultural Development Research Association (IDRA), *Newsletter*, San Antonio, June 1983, September 1983, April 1984, August 1986, January 1987, September 1988, May 1990, April 1991, June 1991, February 1992, June 1992.

Keniston, Kenneth and The Carnegie Council on Children, *All Our Children*, Harcourt Brace Jovanovich, New York, 1977.

Keyes v. School District No. 1, 576 F. Supp. (D. Colo. 1983).

Kirp, David L. and Mark G. Yudof, *Education Policy and the Law*, McCutchan, Berkeley, 1974.

Kirst, Michael W. Jr., "The Federal Role and Chapter 1", *Rethinking Some Basic Assumptions*, Research and Evaluation Associates, Washington, D.C., 1986.

Lau v. Nichols, 414 U.S. 563 (1974).

Levine, D.U. and E.E. Eubanks, "Site-Based Management: Engine for Reform or Pipedream?" *Problems, Pitfalls, and Prerequisites for Success in Site-Based Management*, July 1989.

Lortie, D.C., *School Teacher: A Sociological Study*, University of Chicago Press, Chicago, 1975.

Marshall, Ray and Marc Tucker, *Thinking for a Living*, BasicBooks, New York, 1992.

Mutchler, S.E., "Shared Decision Making: Harnessing the Energy of People," *Insight*, December 1989.

National Education Goals Report, *Building a Nation of Learners*, Washington, D.C., 1991.

Quality Education for Minorities Project, *Education that Works*, Massachusetts Institute of Technology, Cambridge, 1990.

Rodriguez v. San Antonio Independent School District, 337 F. Supp. 280 (W.D. 1971).

San Antonio Independent School District v. Rodriguez, 411 U.S. 1 (1973).

Schorr, Lizbeth B., *Within Our Reach*, Doubleday, New York, 1988.

Texas Education Agency, *Snapshot '92*, Austin, 1993.

Texas Education News, "Major Provisions: SB 1," Austin, Texas, June 1990.

Texas High School Coaches Association, *Texas Coach*, Austin, 1991.

Toffler, Alvin, *Future Shock*, Random House, New York, 1970.

Wells, A.S., "Teacher, Principal and Parent Involvement in the Effective School," *ERIC Clearinghouse on Urban Education*, Vol. 38, December 1987.

White, P.A., 'An Overview of School-Based Management: What Does the Research Say?" *NASSP Bulletin*, 1989.

Wood, C.J., "Participatory Decision Making: Why Doesn't It Seem to Work?" *The Education Forum*, 49 (1), 1984.

DISCUSSION QUESTIONS

1. What would you include on a list of symptoms of dysfunctional educational institutions?
2. What do you believe to be the essential components of a new educational paradigm for American schools?
3. Devise an accountability report card for your state education agency.
4. Devise an accountability report card of local school districts based on a list of symptoms of dysfunctional educational institutions.

10

A New Educational Paradigm

A NEW EDUCATIONAL PARADIGM

INTRODUCTION

To say that there is extensive dissatisfaction with current school performance would easily be the understatement of the year. There is an extensive amount of dissatisfaction with the performance of the school at the local, state and national levels. This dissatisfaction is evident even in the traditional clientele of the school, the mainstream middle class, whose performance may not be optimal, but at least much of the group is still between tolerable limits.

Much less recognized, and even less seldom addressed, is the performance of students from non-mainstream school populations. The school performance of atypical students such as ethnic and racial minorities, the economically disadvantaged, immigrants, limited English-proficient and migrant students goes substantially below the tolerance limits—not only of the atypical populations themselves—but within the tolerance limits of a nation striving to maintain and capitalize on its traditional world leadership role.

The education of female students is another area of unacceptable performance in today's schools. Girls as members of the dominant cultural group tend to do well in areas of education compatible with the historic role of women in our society. However, there are areas of education traditionally perceived as masculine in which the performance of girls leaves much to be desired. These areas include math, science, technology and the specific curriculum and career areas associated with these.

The performance of female students from atypical populations exemplifies the worst failure of the school. Minority and disadvantaged girls are commonly the recipients of the worst forms of discrimination in the schools. They are discriminated against by predominantly male-policy formulation. They are discriminated against because of their minority or disadvantaged status. They are also discriminated against within their own racial, ethnic and socio-economic group.

Since female students commonly receive minority status within their own cultural group—regardless of ethnicity or class—these students will be included in references to atypical school populations and in the development and implementation of new strategies for achieving equal educational opportunity.

The school performance of most atypical populations is characterized by low grades, deplorable performance on any type of achievement measure, extensive retention in grade and overagedness and an appalling school dropout rate.

This poor performance by a large and growing segment of the school population takes on a new importance in the light of the recent economic transformation in our country. The minorities and disadvantaged who were not served adequately by the schools forms the nucleus of a cheap, unskilled labor pool necessary in an agricultural, mineral and industrial economy. Urban centers, where 80 and 90 percent of the non-mainstream students dropped out of school without acquiring even a minimal literacy capability, even capitalized on the inefficiency of the school by advertising cheap, unskilled labor in attempts to bring business and industry into the community.

The change in the economy to information, services and technology creates two new problems in dealing with the failures of the schools. First, the cheap, unskilled labor is no longer marketable. Industries requiring cheap labor can acquire it in third world countries at a fraction of what it costs in the United States. The implementation of new international free trade agreements will institutionalize the acquisition of cheap labor elsewhere and accentuate the obsolescence of a cheap labor force in the United States.

Second, the cost of non-education continues to rise, creating a budget crisis at each level of government. The cost of unemployment, underemployment, welfare, police and security forces, crime, the administration of justice, prison systems and rehabilitation is already prohibitive. Not only are the school failures increasingly non-productive, they have also become a serious drain upon the productive segment of our communities.

The social and economic implications of school failure have led to a call for an extensive reform of the school. Unfortunately, school reform measures have not led to a reversal in the performance of the school. On the contrary, it is not unusual for reform measures to exacerbate school problems—with the lowest performing segment of the population doing even worse after the implementation of the reform effort than they were doing before.

School reform efforts are usually accompanied by massive infusions of additional funds with so little improvement, that increased funding in itself has become suspect as a reform measure. In an article by David Osborne, co-author of *Reinventing Government*, Osborne identifies the greatest obstacle to innovation in government: the power of outdated ideas (Osborne, 1993; Osborne, 1992).

"It's easy to dream up new approaches to problems." states Osborne. "People do it all the time. The hard part is selling them to those who still see the world through old lenses."

If the greatest obstacle to innovation in government is the power of outdated ideas, the greatest hope for innovation in government, and in schools, is the power of new ideas.

The performance of the schools will not improve until such time as a new paradigm is developed, accepted and implemented. This new paradigm must be realistic in prescribing educational practice through new lenses which see the school in a new and different context, the social and economic realities of our country today, rather than the realities and the myths of yesteryear.

The new paradigm must be comprehensive in that it is not based on a segment of population which traditionally formed the core of the school. This new paradigm must address the educational needs and characteristics of a cross section of the school population, both male and female, and especially the characteristics of the minorities, the disadvantaged, the limited English proficient, the immigrants, the migrants and the homeless.

The old paradigm assumes that most children are valuable; the new paradigm assumes that all children are valuable.

The new paradigm must be in keeping with the current and future role of the school in a new social and economic order, rather than continue to be based on outdated social and economic ideas.

PARADIGMS

As described by Osborne, the word "paradigm" was popularized by Thomas Kuhn in his 1962 book, *"The Structure of Scientific Revolutions."* A paradigm is an accepted model or pattern with a set of assumptions about reality (Kuhn, 1970).

Kuhn describes human behavior as consistent with a paradigm, seeing and conceptualizing not what is seen, but what is expected to be seen in keeping with previous experience. Kuhn's description is most adequate for education in that the behavior of the school is consistent with past paradigms, and what educators see and conceptualize is inconsistent with reality, but based on expectations from previous experience.

Osborne's application of Kuhn's paradigm to government needs little transformation for application to the American school. Like government, there is little hope for improvement in the schools unless we restructure our thinking about the schools—particularly our thinking about the schools in the reality of a new American social order.

So much of school activity functions under an obsolete paradigm that it is relatively easy to list examples of this obsolescence. Schools still operate in keeping with a school calendar based on the need for summer child labor in an agricultural society decades after this labor need quit being a reality. Schools still participate in spelling bees designed to produce and identify a spelling champion long after pedagogy pointed out that an extensive amount of time is being expended on the development of unusual spelling skills among the students who need them the least and an early and total exclusion of students who need spelling lessons the most. School finance systems in a majority of the states are based on elitist principles which concentrate resources on a privileged class which needs the resources the least—with less resources committed to those students who need them the most.

School extracurricular activities are better suited for providing inexpensive entertainment in local areas not able to sustain a professional team than in supplementing the educational needs of students. The typical large high school has a larger budget for the 5 percent of the students who participate in team sports than for intramural and co-curricular activities for the 95 percent of the students not in the interscholastic athletic program.

As indicated by Kuhn and Osborne, not only do schools operate on old ideas, but educators tend to perceive realities in the schools in terms of obsolete paradigms, with an absolute failure to see a need for conceptualizing new paradigms based on a new and accurate set of realities.

EDUCATIONAL PARADIGMS FOR ATYPICAL STUDENTS

To the school clientele not coming from the cultural mainstream the American school is seen as an elitist, middle class institution. Early in the history of American education, the schools reflected educational models of mother countries in Europe. Colonists and early immigrant groups introduced the European system of education which placed the school in one or more of three historical roles: private institutions supported by the parents of the children who could afford them, religious institutions which provided basic skills deemed necessary for Bible reading as an avenue to spiritual salvation, and philanthropic institutions which provided limited educational experiences as charitable undertakings.

The advent of the industrial revolution and the rise of the American middle class required a new paradigm for education. The inability of educational institutions to function under the old paradigms led to the development of the American public school which was able to deal with such concepts as universal education, compulsory school attendance, expensive financing, public policy inputs, monitoring and regulation, standardization and transferability.

In the absence of this new paradigm conducive to the development of a system of public education, neither the private schools, nor the religious schools, nor the charity schools could have addressed the educational needs accompanying the industrial revolution. The American concept of public school education was based on new realities incompatible with the paradigms of early educational systems.

Unfortunately, the new paradigm in support of the new system of public education was not as universal as it has been believed. Universal education was restricted to the upper classes. Although the industrial revolution led to the development of a new and large middle class, the schools made no attempt to accommodate minority, poverty and disenfranchised populations.

African Americans, Hispanics, other minorities and disadvantaged children were not perceived as equal participants in the public school. Children from these groups often did not attend school, attended school for a limited number of years, or attended inferior segregated schools in keeping with the social standards of the era. Educational opportunity for minority and disadvantaged students continued in conformity with the pre-industrial revolution concepts of public education.

There is an existing myth in the United States that the public schools of the industrial revolution era provided for the cultural assimilation and upward mobility of large immigrant groups. This is simply not so. Opportunity existed mainly in the private church supported schools. Integration into the larger society and upward mobility were provided in the work force. Public educational opportunity and cultural assimilation did not occur until the second or third generation.

Inadequacies in the education of atypical populations continued until the period following World War II. The impact of a massive fight against tyranny in other parts of the world, and the participation of minorities in this fight led to a determination to acquire first class citizenship in this country. *Brown v. Board of Education* led the beginning of the end for second-class education for second-class citizens (*Brown*, 1954). The new era of social justice and civil rights led to extensive social litigation and legislation which weakened the fabric of the public school paradigm.

The movement away from separate and unequal led to an unprecedented awareness of the inadequacies of the schools. Although there was some amount of movement of students in order to bring about racial and ethnic mixes, particularly after the one-two punch of the stick and the carrot, the Civil Rights Act of 1964 and the Elementary and Secondary Education Act of 1965, respectively, the desegregation of public schools did not usher in a new era of improved performance for minority populations (Civil Rights Act of 1964, 1964; Elementary and Secondary Education Act, 1965). The movement of students was not accompanied by any systematic attempt to bring the minority students into an integrated learning environment. The schools continued to operate under a paradigm established for a white, Anglo, English-speaking, middle-class school population.

If anything, educational performance declined for everybody. The inability and unwillingness of the school to make any adaptations for the characteristics of atypical students led to extensive underperformance and failure. The problem was further compounded by large increases in both numbers and percentages of atypical students. This resulted in the abandonment of the public schools in central cities to the atypical populations as the middle class moved to the suburbs and established new institutions compatible with the traditional paradigm.

Unfortunately, as the middle-class moved out of the central cities they left behind a middle-class paradigm which was not substantially altered for the influx of minority and disadvantaged students, especially since there was little empowerment of minority and disadvantaged parents for control of the schools. Past educational practices were continued with little effort at adapting them to an entirely different, non-middle-class populations.

Following the abandonment of the dream of a Great Society, new attempts to bring about educational equity proved harder to implement. The quest for social justice was impeded in 1973 when the judiciary reversed its prior support for atypical populations with a reluctance to interfere in the affairs of the school, and it was abandoned by 1980 along with the administrative effort for civil rights compliance.

All hope for a major breakthrough in the education of atypical populations would have ended a dozen years ago if it were not for the changes in the economic base of the country, the necessity for increasing the productivity of the labor force and reducing the cost of the effects of a lack of education.

The current educational paradigm provides such a thorough exclusion of atypical students that they make little impact on the evaluation of the school and the subsequent accountability measures. It is inconceivable that a school would be tolerated fifty years ago where less than 20 percent of the students could meet the minimum competency requirements for the basic skills. It is also equally inconceivable that a middle-class school would be tolerated today with a similar level of student underperformance. However, such a situation is common and accepted in schools for minority and disadvantaged children. It is not unusual for a school administrator with a minority and disadvantaged school population to have 80 percent of the students unable to meet minimum performance standards and a dropout rate of over 66 percent and still be considered successful. In fact, such administrators are commonly honored by the community and their colleagues for their outstanding performance.

A NEW PARADIGM FOR MINORITY EDUCATION

During the past decade, Intercultural Development Research Association (IDRA) participated in a number of local, state and national studies on the vast number of successful programs for minority and disadvantaged students which have been implemented in very recent years (Zamora, 1986; Committee for Economic Development, 1987; Quality Education for Minorities Project, 1990). It was surprising that a large number of successful programs were identified. The number of such programs conclusively proves that atypical students can perform successfully in school and that common school perceptions of negative characteristics of minority and disadvantaged students are quite erroneous and do not hold true under certain conditions.

Although the studies identified many successful school programs, it is important to note that the studies did not find a single successful educational system. Without exception, successful performance of atypical children was limited to students participating in a special program or a special school. The remainder of the students in that school or system, however, exhibited the same underperformance characteristic of atypical students elsewhere.

It is regrettable that the studies did not delve into the environment in which the successful programs were operating, nor did they attempt to identify variables which were responsible for bringing about successful performance, or how students participating in a successful program in an educational system differed from students not participating in the innovative program.

If such a study had been conducted it would show three consistent characteristics of successful programs for atypical children. First, in each of the successful programs, and without exception, students participating in the program were valued by program staff in ways not found in traditional school programs. Second, students participating in the successful program commonly received support services which were not provided in the traditional school program. Third, successful innovative programs provided unique home-school-community relationships not found in traditional school programs.

These three characteristics and their impact upon student performance can be explained in terms of educational paradigms. It appears that in innovative, model, pilot or experimental programs, program staff have the freedom to establish and operate under a different, and often times temporary, educational paradigm. Staff is not bound by the negative perceptions of the students held by the regular school staff. They are allowed to value the students, if for no other reason because they are "special" students in a "special" program. School activities are conducted under different game rules which are relatively uninfluenced by the current educational paradigm and its accompanying set of erroneous perceptions. Students can be expected to perform satisfactorily, they may be praised and given other forms of positive reinforcement. They are important enough to merit individual attention and individual assistance in keeping with educational need. Ethnic, racial and socio-economic characteristics of students may be addressed. Instructional materials and methodologies may differ from traditional textbooks and practices and may even be individualized.

In these innovative programs support services may be provided both in support of the instructional program as well as meeting the non-academic needs of the child. Innovative programs may include school materials, health and nutritional services, special guidance and counseling and even financial assistance in the form of special stipends.

Innovative programs inevitably provide exemplary relationships among the home, the school and the community. Parents are given an opportunity to participate with the school as equals in the formulation and implementation of the program. Mentors, role models, field trips are commonly provided as various segments of the community are not only allowed to participate in the program but are actually encouraged to participate.

Although the innovative program operates under a new and different educational paradigm leading to extensive success in the performance of the student, the remainder of the school system continues to operate under the old educational paradigm in which the schools serves a middle-class population and will not accommodate students with other than middle-class characteristics.

In the development of a new educational paradigm it is not only possible but almost certain that each person involved in school reform efforts will perceive the program being advocated as a new paradigm conducive to the success of minority and disadvantaged students. New programs or ideas are not necessarily indicative of a new paradigm.

Much of the failure to bring about a major breakthrough in the education of minority and disadvantaged students can be attributed to new approaches under the same old paradigm. Much of the school reform effort in existence today displays this limitation. School reformers are attempting to bring about better practices for middle-class school populations in the erroneous belief that as educational practice improves the benefits will trickle down to other school populations. This trickle down approach to educational reform has not been, nor will it be, any more successful than the recent trickle down approach to economic reform.

Reform efforts are being conducted in what may be a new paradigm for middle-class students, but it is the same old dysfunctional, discriminatory and ineffectual paradigm for minority, disadvantaged, limited English proficient, immigrant and migrant students.

One such reform movement exemplifies the perpetuation and exacerbation of an outdated paradigm. Advocates of choice in the selection of schools are either purposely misleading public opinion or have absolutely no idea of the lifestyles and constraints of disadvantaged families. Advocates of choice state that the purpose of school choice is to give the minorities and the disadvantaged the same opportunity to choose, as is now enjoyed by the middle-class. These advocates are constrained by middle class perceptions that each family has two cars in the garage and a nonworking parent to facilitate transportation to the school of their choice. They assume that the prestigious schools will give the same opportunity for participation to all student that apply. They assume that the partial stipend provided by government will be accompanied with the balance of the tuition payment which in some cases may be more than the annual family income.

Educational choice is far from being a new paradigm for the education of American children. It is a conservative paradigm designed to perpetuate the differences in educational opportunity made available to children from different segments of the population. It is an elitist attempt to preserve a privileged education for privileged children. It insures the middle class of the traditional choice they have always enjoyed, while giving the lower classes through the payment of taxes, the opportunity to help finance this choice.

Site-based management is another example of an educational innovation stifled by having to operate under an obsolete educational paradigm. I applaud the attempt to decentralize educational decisionmaking. It is inconceivable, however, that such decisionmaking can be meaningful under legal constraints which give centralized school boards the responsibility, the authority, accountability and the legal liability for decisions which have been made.

A third example of innovation constrained by the old educational paradigm is the unfulfilled promise of pre-school programs. The value of early childhood education was proved conclusively many years ago in the Headstart program. The successes of Headstart made it inevitable that the public schools extend educational opportunity to students from atypical homes at the early ages addressed in Headstart. The educational program offered in Headstart and other successful community programs, however, operated under a much different paradigm than programs in the public school.

Whereas the typical Headstart program is developmental, concentrating on the physical, emotional, social and intellectual development of the child, the typical pre-school program was academic. It consisted of a "push down" curriculum where the educational activities which disadvantaged and limited English-proficient children would not master at the age of six were presented at the age of three and four. The operation of the pre-school program in the public schools in the absence of the Headstart developmental activities provided poor performance, frustration, failure, and negative concepts of self at an earlier age.

ADAPTABILITY IN THE NEW PARADIGM

As stated previously, schools tend to operate under an old paradigm built for the white, Anglo, English-speaking middle class. A new paradigm requires the school to adapt to the racial and ethnic cultural characteristics of minority students. Similar cultural adaptations should be made for female and immigrant students. The school should also adapt to the language characteristics of limited English-proficient students and to the socio-economic characteristics of economically disadvantaged students. A similar adaptation should be made for the geographic instability of migrant and other mobile students.

To illustrate the effects of a failure to adapt to student characteristics, we can analyze the common status of language minority students in our school. Personal observations as well as student performance records from throughout the country indicate that students who speak a native language other than English have extreme difficulty in acquiring English language reading skills. Spanish-speaking children in San Antonio, Texas are notorious for their difficulty in learning to read. The same is true of Spanish-speaking children in Los Angeles, Seattle, Chicago, Washington and Miami. One can conclude, as have the schools, that the speaking of Spanish is a linguistic deficit which precludes learning to read. Thus, the solution to this educational dilemma is the eradication of the Spanish language, preferably before the student begins schooling.

On the other hand, Spanish-speaking students in Mexico City have no such difficulty in acquiring reading skills. On the contrary, personal observation indicates that Spanish-speaking children in Mexico City read better, per unit of instruction, than English-speaking students in the United States. The same phenomenon has been observed in Spain, Guatemala, Ecuador, Peru and all other Spanish-speaking countries.

Only in the United States is the speaking of Spanish an impediment to the learning of reading. Obviously the reading problem is not a deficit on the part of language minority children, but a deficit on the part of American schools.

It is quite an indictment of American schools when the Supreme Court of the United States issued a finding in *Lau v. Nichols* that an educational program for 1,800 Chinese children who spoke no English presented by teachers who spoke no Chinese constituted a problem; and that school rationalizations that the parents should have taught the children to speak English prior to sending them to school were dysfunctional, in that most of the parents did not speak English, did not have the resources for teaching the children the English language, and the primary purpose of sending the children to school was for the children to learn the English language (*Lau*, 1974).

Lau v. Nichols not only substantiated the need for adapting educational practice to the characteristics of students, it made the schools legally responsible for doing so.

The adaptation of educational practices in the new paradigm should also be extended to societal perceptions: the way the school perceives the student and the way the student perceives himself/herself.

CHARACTERISTICS OF THE NEW PARADIGM

For a new paradigm to be successful, it is necessary that it incorporate the three characteristics which have been so successful in innovative programs: the valuing of students, the provision of support services and the inter-relationships among home, school and family.

The first characteristic, the valuing of students, is key to the attainment of the two subsequent characteristics. It is similarly key to any school reform efforts as well as to any other attempt to provide adequate educational opportunities for any and all children.

The past callousness and unresponsiveness of the school to the educational needs of atypical children accounts for the underperformance of the children and their eventual exclusion from the schools. Future success in the education of such children will be determined by the extent to which the school will value them.

It is hoped that the school values all children because of their intrinsic worth. This has not been the case in the past, and there is little reason to hope that it will be the case in the future. If anything, exposure of the school to a wider variety of children has resulted in increased resentment of these elements of the population which has challenged the performance of the school.

There is, and it can be expected to continue and increase, a wish by the school to return to the days of yesteryear when its clientele was more homogenous. This yearning has resulted in a narrowing of the parameters of student variation which the school feels a need to respond to—with increased segments of the population being perceived as deficits which dilute and misdirect the resources and efforts of the school.

Yet, it is impossible for the school to return to a mythical era that never existed; therefore, the necessity is for the school to wake up to the reality of the democratization of education and of the need for change in order to accommodate segments of the population never before perceived as an important target of schooling.

The problem of valuing children in the schools is further compounded by a lack of value, or even negative valuing, given children in the larger society. Regardless of the shortcomings of the school, it must be admitted that the attitudes and prejudices of the school simply reflect the attitudes and the prejudices of the larger society.

If children cannot be perceived as valuable by the larger society, and subsequently by the school, for their intrinsic worth, then it is necessary and desirable that they be valued for their extrinsic worth. To a certain extent this has happened already, as evidenced by the growing awareness of the economic sector of the need for a much better prepared and competent work force. In many communities across the country there is a growing alienation between the schools and the economic sector. The schools have failed to understand the reason for this growing alienation and wonder why businesses and industries which provided strong support for education have suddenly become uncooperative and hostile. It appears that the school is saying, "Why is the economic sector so down on us? We are still providing them with a huge supply of cheap, unskilled labor," while the economic sector seems to shout, "We don't need, we don't want a supply of cheap, unskilled labor. We can get cheap, unskilled labor in Third World countries for thirty-five cents an hour. We need skilled labor in our work force, and you are not supplying it."

In recent years I have gotten into philosophical arguments over the concept of valuing children for economic reasons. I sympathize with these arguments, but there is no question that I would rather have children valued for economic reasons, than not valued at all.

One can only hope that all schools and school personnel would value all children for their intrinsic worth. If this does not come about, then it is necessary that schools and school personnel be made to value children for their extrinsic worth. This can be brought about, and is being brought about, by increased accountability for the performance of the school.

Exorbitant dropout rates of 80 and 90 percent, and even 100 percent for certain segments of the population, is no longer acceptable by the larger society. Many states are enacting accountability measures which are being externally imposed on the schools. Performance indicators in the form of standardized tests, dropout rates and other measures are becoming popular. This is evident in the products of the National Education Goal Panel, its new and ambitious goals for education, and its use and development of performance indicators for determining the performance of the school.

Unfortunately, the entire concept for the implementation of the national goals, Goals 2000, has two major flaws which will preclude extensive success. It assumes that education has the competency for meeting the higher goals which have been established, and it assumes that education has the necessary resources for getting there.

The extrinsic valuing of children may be viewed as the only feasible vehicle for bringing about a drastic change in the performance of the school. It does not, however, preclude a long-range strategy for the intrinsic valuing of children.

If the people of this country can get so involved in the preservation of our resources in terms of mineral deposits, timber lands, and the lowly spotted owl, it is more than possible that they can get involved in the preservation of our most valuable resource—our children.

In 1979, advocacy for children reached a high level through the efforts of the U.S. Commission on the International Year of the Child. It is possible that in this country each year can become "A Year of the Child," an annual celebration of children as our most precious commodity (U.S. National Commission on the International Year of the Child, 1980). An extensive effort by children's advocacy organization can produce a focus on children in our mass media. A focus on children in the mass media can easily result in sensitivity and response to children's issues in our entire political system, the administration, the legislative bodies and the courts. A re-commitment to children and youth in the larger society will inevitably lead to a re-commitment to children in the schools and the valuing of children which is the single most essential need for an improvement in the performance of all children, mainstream and atypical alike.

The valuing of children will lead to the development and implementation of adequate support structures inside and outside of the school. The rationale for the development of support services in the school should be the realization that there are many conditions which impede the performance of students in school, and that satisfactory performance can only come about with the removal of these impediments.

It is not necessarily the responsibility of the school to provide for all the non-instructional needs of children and their families, but it is the responsibility of the school to communicate with the larger community and its service agencies to insure that any obstacles affecting school performance are adequately addressed. Although they may not be direct responsibilities of schools, problems in nutrition, physical health, mental health, housing, employment, transportation, family financial and social conditions are of utmost concern to the school because of their impact on school performance.

The third characteristic of a new educational paradigm is the creation of a partnership relationship among the school, the home and the larger community. Such a partnership does not currently exist in spite of the need.

An IDRA research effort in mental health research sponsored by the National Institute of Mental Health, aimed at increasing the interface between school and community mental health services, revealed a complete absence of any interface (IDRA, 1980). Our research showed conclusively that community mental health agencies provided services to students and families without the schools even suspecting that such services were being provided. On the other hand, school student personnel services were commonly provided to students without the community coordinating agencies being aware of it. In my early role (1967) as director of the Texas Migrant Educational Development Center of the Southwest Educational Development Laboratory (SEDL) I learned that there were thousands of agricultural migrant children enrolled in schools without the school being aware of the migrant status of the children. A 1993 IDRA study of immigrant children indicated the presence of thousands of immigrant children in the schools without the schools' knowledge of the children's recent immigration (IDRA, 1993).

IDRA has found that students commonly drop out of school without the school being notified by the parents, nor the parents being notified by the school. Students are incarcerated without notification given to the school. Students are expelled from school without notification given to relevant community agencies.

The ideal partnership relationship among school, home and community cannot exist with the closed door isolation of any of the partnership participants. No kind of partnership relationship can exist as long as the participants take unilateral action which usually transfers the problem from one entity to another without anybody addressing the problem. In an ideal partnership not only is unilateral action without notification undesirable, unilateral action itself is undesirable.

The formation of the unique partnerships which characterized successful school programs requires at least the following to reduce the polarization and alienation which currently exists:

- A mutual respect among the school, the home and the community based on the assumption that each of the three entities has a vested interest in the successful schooling of the child.
- The clarification of the overlapping roles of the school, the home and the community in the education of the child.
- An opening and widening of doors to facilitate extensive interaction and the planning of cooperative activities.
- Extensive communications among the three entities.
- Participation by the three entities is making decisions impacting upon the child.

ELEMENTS OF THE NEW PARADIGM

A comprehensive educational paradigm must address all aspects of the student's interaction with the school. The following ten elements used by José A. Cárdenas and Blandina Cárdenas since 1968 in their "Theory of Incompatibilities" can serve as a guideline for the basic attitudes and assumptions which the school should make about all children, but specifically about atypical children in the development of the new paradigm (Cárdenas and Cárdenas, 1973).

These ten elements interact with areas of incompatibilities, producing a matrix with seventy cells. The area of societal perceptions in the original "Theory of Incompatibilities" has been subdivided into the school's perception of the student and the student's perception of self. Another area of incompatibility, gender, has been added.

The table, DEVELOPMENTAL MATRIX, illustrates the organization of the seventy cells in the matrix, and it is followed by a description of the contents of each of the seventy cells. The content of each cell is illustrative of the responsibilities of the school and is not intended to be exhaustive. On the contrary, educators are urged to continue seeking ways in which the adaptability of the school can be extended for each of the seventy cells in the matrix.

THE DEVELOPMENTAL MATRIX

AREAS OF INCOMPATIBILITY

ELEMENTS	CULT	LANG	SES	MOB	GEND	SCH PERC	STU PERC
PHILOSOPHY							
GOVERNANCE							
SCOPE & SEQ							
CURRICULUM							
CO-CURR							
STAFFING							
STU PERS SVC							
NON-INSTR							
PARENTAL							
EVALUATION							

CULTURE

A1: CULTURE/PHILOSOPHY

- There is extensive cultural diversity among students.
- Cultural diversity is an asset to society. It provides an extensive array of options in values, traditions and orientations for dealing with societal problems.
- It is not the role of the school to make value judgments about cultural characteristics, but to provide a culturally democratic learning environment in which there is respect for different cultural characteristics and to insure that these characteristics do not become an impediment to learning.

- It is the responsibility of the school to provide an understanding about all cultures and to safeguard the freedom of the student to make intelligent and mature cultural choices.
- It is the responsibility of the school to be flexible in educational practice and to adapt materials and instruction to the characteristics of the various cultural groups.
- Cultural groups often have distinctive learning styles. An instructional program which allows all students equal opportunity for successful learning will provide alternative methodologies compatible with different and preferred learning styles.
- Students from all cultural groups have the potential for learning.
- Much of the past poor performance of minority students can be attributed to inappropriate instructional practice rather than to the characteristics of the minority students, families and communities.

A2: CULTURE/GOVERNANCE

- Successful performance in school requires that the school establish school policies, rules and regulations which are equitable for all students, are cognizant of student diversity, and are conducive for success by students reflecting an extensive cultural diversity.
- The school can minimize student alienation through student and parent participation in school governance.

A3: CULTURE/ SCOPE & SEQUENCE

- Multiculturalism requires an extensive and sequential treatment in the curriculum of the school.
- Instruction is based on the students' socio-cultural backgrounds and begins with the experiences they bring with them to school.
- Random treatment of culture in association with national and state designated periods is insufficient.

A4: CULTURE/ CURRICULUM

- There is no such thing as a culturally neutral curriculum. The various materials and methodologies utilize content, language and concepts that have strong cultural connotations.
- The instructional program is reflective of the cultural characteristics of all students.
- Materials and methodologies are identified, acquired, modified or adapted in order for the student to be able to identify with them.

A5: CULTURE/CO-CURRICULUM

- Educational experience in the instructional program is augmented by supplemental and reinforcing co-curricular activities.
- Co-curricular activities are compatible with and have respect for the cultural characteristics of students.
- Student participation in co-curricular activities will reduce the social and academic isolation experienced by minority students.
- Rather than have the student seek to satisfy this need through socially detrimental "gang" behavior, participation in co-curricular activities satisfies the inherent psychological need for belonging through involvement in socially acceptable group activities.

A6: CULTURE/ STAFFING

- The educational system identifies, recruits, acquires and trains an educational staff with positive perceptions sensitive to the characteristics and needs of minority students.
- The system provides training to staff in the identifying, creating and adapting of culturally appropriate instructional activities.
- The school provides adult role models from the racial and ethnic groups represented in the student population.

A7: CULTURE/STUDENT PERSONNEL SERVICES

- The school provides personnel resources capable of enhancing the student's ability to perform in school.
- The school provides the counseling and guidance necessary for the student to be able to cope with individual, family, school and community problems.
- School staff assist the student in exercising new options for further schooling and training and the selection of feasible career options.

A8: CULTURE/NON-INSTRUCTURAL NEEDS

- The educational system recognizes that students have non-instructional needs which should be addressed in order to remove barriers to successful schooling.
- The provision of this type of support is compatible with the values, traditions and orientations of the family.

A9: CULTURE/PARENT INVOLVEMENT

- The educational system is supportive of the home and family structures and values.
- The school mobilizes the community in support of the student's educational program.
- The school works with parents for the creation and maintenance of a home environment conducive to learning.

A10: CULTURE/EVALUATION

- Evaluation of the school's programs is made in light of the cultural characteristics of students.
- Evaluation instruments which purport to measure student learning are culturally fair and do not penalize the student for unique cultural characteristics.

LANGUAGE

B1: LANGUAGE/PHILOSOPHY

- With English being the common and dominant language of the United States, it is imperative that all students attain extensive mastery of the English language and the necessary skills for its proper and effective utilization.
- Lack of fluency in the English language need not be an educational barrier. Students throughout the world with no proficiency in the English language have enjoyed successful schooling.
- Proficiency in languages other than English is a desirable educational objective as evidenced by the emphasis and resources provided for foreign language acquisition in American schools.
- The use of one language does not preclude the acquisition of a second language. On the contrary, there is extensive research evidence that the use of multiple languages enhances cognitive development and facilitates the acquisition of additional languages. Although the United States may be an exception, there are more people in the world who are multilingual than there are people who are monolingual.
- Language is not just a cognitive skill. It reflects social identity and ethnicity.
- Superior or inferior attitudes or animosities associated with language can create severe psychological barriers to learning.

B2: LANGUAGE/GOVERNANCE

- The school recognizes and is sensitive to the reality that the English language may not be understood or spoken in language minority homes.
- Rules and regulations respect the use of a language other than English in the home.
- Communications with the home are commonly provided in the language spoken in the home.
- The school recognizes the value of communication for cognitive development and encourages students to communicate regardless of the language used.

B3: LANGUAGE/SCOPE AND SEQUENCE

- Language development, like all other forms of learning proceeds from the known to the unknown. Beginning instruction, therefore, commences with the language background of the student.
- It is virtually impossible to master a new language, by learning basic skills in that language and acquiring content material at the same time. All skill and content instruction is presented after determining that the student has the necessary language skills necessary for successful performance.

B4: LANGUAGE/CURRICULUM

- It is difficult and detrimental to attempt to learn a new language while simultaneously learning basic skills and content material in that same language.
- Since proficiency in the English language is a prerequisite skill for the learning of basic skills and content material in English, such basic skills and content material instruction in English is deferred until such time as the student has mastery of the English language for successful participation in a learning activity.
- Retardation in the acquisition of basic skills and content material is detrimental to students; therefore, the development of basic skills and the acquisition of content material is conducted in a native language other than English while sufficient mastery of the English language is being attained.

B5: LANGUAGE/CO-CURRICULUM

- The co-curriculum presents unique opportunities for the natural development of language skills.

- Students with limited language proficiency are encouraged to participate in co-curriculum activities which present opportunities for language development.
- Students frequently acquire more language competence through interactions with other students than through the best planned instructional program of the school.

B6: LANGUAGE/STAFFING

- The student is provided with school staff that can communicate with the student in his native language.
- Limited English-proficient students have access to staff trained and experienced in bilingual education.
- Although not all instructional staff may be bilingual, it is necessary that all instructional personnel dealing with limited English-proficient students be knowledgeable about linguistics and the language needs of such students.
- The school provides adequate training to all staff in the instruction of limited English-proficient and bilingual students.

B7: LANGUAGE/STUDENT PERSONNEL SERVICES

- School support personnel are able to communicate with limited English-proficient students and their families in their native language.
- Support personnel and programs are sensitive to unique language characteristics of students.

B8: LANGUAGE/NON-INSTRUCTIONAL NEEDS

- Language is not a barrier in assisting the family in meeting the non-instructional needs of children.
- The school is able to identify and make referral to community agencies with the necessary language competency to facilitate the provision of services.

B9: LANGUAGE/PARENT INVOLVEMENT

- Language characteristics of parents are not ignored in school/parent relationships.
- The school has the necessary language resources to facilitate communications with parents and other members of the family.
- Participation in parent involvement activities provides for participation in languages commonly utilized in the community.

B10: LANGUAGE/EVALUATION

- Evaluation of students in all areas of the curriculum, except English language instruction, is language neutral.
- Neither native language nor English language measurement is valid for bilingual students. Evaluation should sample the entire language capability of the student.

SOCIO-ECONOMIC

C1: SOCIO-ECONOMIC/PHILOSOPHY

- Students from economically disadvantaged homes frequently have different developmental patterns from students raised in affluent or middle-class homes. These different patterns may stem from a lack of academically oriented experiences, a lack of academic-oriented role models, constraints on available media and reading materials, constraints on adult/child interaction and other factors.
- The absence of middle-class developmental experiences in the home requires that such experiences be provided in school.
- It is an imperative that the school distinguish between a student's lack of experience and a student's lack of capability.
- The placement of students with normal capability and lack of experience in low-level, slow-paced, boring and repetitious programs commonly becomes a self-fulfilling prophesy leading to poor and worsening school performance.

C2: SOCIO-ECONOMIC/GOVERNANCE

- The school recognizes the impact of poverty on school participation, attempts to lighten this burden, and avoids making poverty a larger impediment to schooling.
- The school does everything possible to minimize the impact of poverty on effective school participation.
- The school is sensitive to the impact of the cost of fees, fines, materials, supplies, dress, fund-raising activities and extracurricular activities on students and their families.

C3: SOCIO-ECONOMIC/ SCOPE & SEQUENCE

- Economic deprivation frequently fails to provide middle-class experiences which are prerequisites to successful performance in school.

- It is the responsibility of the school to determine the developmental levels of the student and to provide the necessary enrichment experiences which will be subsequently required in the instructional program.

C4: SOCIO-ECONOMIC/CURRICULUM

- There is a vast difference between lack of developmental experiences and lack of learning capability.
- All learning is dependent on certain prerequisite skills. In all learning situations, the school determines the extent to which these prerequisite skills exist or are lacking and insures that they are developed sequentially throughout the curriculum.
- All learning activities are interesting, exciting and challenging to the student.
- Levels of expectancy are high, but the student is given the proper assistance in reaching these high levels of expected performance.

C5: SOCIO-ECONOMIC/CO-CURRICULUM

- The co-curriculum provides unique opportunities for students from economically disadvantaged homes to acquire extensive experiences otherwise not available.
- The social isolation of students from poverty homes can be addressed through participation in co-curricular activities as a prelude for participation in the instructional program.
- Participation in co-curricular activities does not create a financial burden for students from economically disadvantaged homes.

C6: SOCIO-ECONOMIC/STAFFING

- School staff is sensitive to the limitations of poverty and is trained to eliminate these limitations as barriers to successful school performance.
- School staff is provided extensive training on the characteristics and needs of children from poverty homes.
- School staff is provided extensive training in distinguishing between the deprivations of poverty and the lack of learning capability.

C7: SOCIO-ECONOMIC/STUDENT PERSONNEL SERVICES

- The deprivations of poverty which often include broken homes, single parents and atypical role models, require that economically disadvantaged students be given extensive individual and personal assistance.

C8: SOCIO-ECONOMIC/NON-INSTRUCTIONAL NEEDS

- Student nutritional, health, physical, social and emotional needs are important to academic success.
- The system provides necessary support services or makes referrals to other community agencies which can assist students and their families in meeting their needs.

C9: SOCIO-ECONOMIC/PARENT INVOLVEMENT

- The involvement of parents in meaningful relationships with the school is crucial for successful student performance.
- Low socio-economic-class parents are no less interested in successful schooling for their children, although financial limitations and the effort of surviving sometimes impede the amount of time and effort which they can dedicate to school support.
- Negative relationships between the parents and the school and the subsequent alienation form formidable barriers for the school and family to form effective partnerships in the education of the children.
- Schools provide ample opportunities for parents to participate as equals in the development and implementation of school programs.
- Establishing positive relationships with parents requires personal and extensive outreach in a location, such as the home, which is perceived as non-threatening.

C10: SOCIO-ECONOMIC/EVALUATION

- The school determines the developmental levels of the child and compares them to the developmental levels assumed in the instructional program.
- The school evaluates the appropriateness of instructional materials and methodologies used with economically disadvantaged children.
- Lack of successful performance is analyzed in terms of instructional program inadequacies, rather than as deficits in the child.
- The school maintains the same levels of expectancy for the performance of economically disadvantaged children as for other children.

MOBILITY

D1: MOBILITY/PHILOSOPHY

- Many students move from one geographic location to another, producing a parallel movement from school to school. Although this movement has long been recognized in immigrant and agricultural migrant students, this continuous geographic relocation is now very much a part of central urban city life.
- Educational programs have extensive built-in continuity and sequence which provide sequential learning experiences for students. Moving from one school to another disrupts the normal sequencing of educational experiences.
- In order to extend educational opportunity to students experiencing geographic mobility, it is necessary that the school provide flexibility in instructional programs, so that the scope and sequence is maintained for individual students.

D2: MOBILITY/GOVERNANCE

- School rules and regulations are flexible in order to accommodate students with high geographic mobility.
- The school facilitates the transfer of records and information between schools and school districts.

D3: MOBILITY/SCOPE AND SEQUENCE

- The school program is flexible in order to accommodate students with varying experiences.
- The presentation of learning experiences is compatible with high student readiness for learning, rather than in keeping with an arbitrary chronological sequence.
- A system of partial credits culminating in full credits is made available to students who complete only portions of academic periods.

D4: MOBILITY/CURRICULUM

- Irregular enrollment patterns demand flexibility in the organization and presentation of the curriculum.
- The instructional program is highly diagnostic and prescriptive. Instructional activities are based on personal and individualized assessment and programming.

- Students withdrawing from school early are given self-paced materials that they can utilize while away from the school.
- Supplemental help and enriching activities are a part of the curriculum.
- The curriculum is accelerated at the home base school, not necessarily by extending the school day, but by providing the resources for enriching the student's school activities.

D5: MOBILITY/CO-CURRICULUM

- Irregular enrollment patterns do not preclude student participation in all co-curricular activities.
- New students can be sponsored by their classmates in order to facilitate participation in co-curricular activities.

D6: MOBILITY/STAFFING

- The irregular enrollment demands flexibility in staffing patterns.
- Pupil/teacher ratios are as low as possible.
- All school staff are sensitive to the characteristics and needs of mobile students.
- The unique enrollment patterns require extensive training of school personnel to meet unique needs of students.

D7: MOBILITY/STUDENT PERSONNEL SERVICES

- The movement of a student from one school to another requires the immediate and effective transfer of information about the student.
- Problems associated with mobility and economic deprivation require extensive personal assistance for mobile students and their families.

D8: MOBILITY/NON-INSTRUCTIONAL NEEDS

- School staff assist the family in obtaining necessary social services available in the community.
- Continuity in social services is provided for mobile populations.

D9: MOBILITY/PARENT INVOLVEMENT

- The school provides an effective program for contacting new families moving into the community.
- Parent involvement activities are flexible in order to facilitate effective participation for mobile parents.

D10: MOBILITY/EVALUATION

- The organization and implementation of the evaluation program are synchronized with the enrollment patterns of mobile students.
- Evaluative information is transferred to the various schools enrolling the mobile student.

GENDER

E1: GENDER/PHILOSOPHY

- The role of females in our society has undergone extensive changes in recent years.
- It is the responsibility of the school to provide equitable learning opportunities for both male and female students.
- It is not the responsibility of the school to make decisions about curricular or career options for female students. It is the responsibility of the school to extend career options and allow female students to make feasible personal choices from a wide variety of options.
- Pregnancy or parenthood are not barriers to schooling.

E2: GENDER/GOVERNANCE

- Rules and regulations are equitable and equally fair for male and female students.
- Students from both sexes have equal opportunity for participation in all curricular and co-curricular activities of the school.
- The school creates policies and procedures to prevent the sexual harassment of students.

E3: GENDER/SCOPE AND SEQUENCE

- Gender equity is developmentally integrated and age appropriate in all areas of the curriculum and across all age levels.

E4: GENDER/CURRICULUM

- All curriculum materials reflect equitable treatment of males and females.
- Instructional materials avoid the use of sexual stereotypes and discriminatory language.

- Instructional programs enhance self-esteem through visible inclusion and an equitable balance of male and female source materials.
- Instructional methodologies provide equitable attention, treatment and support for male and female students.

E5: GENDER/ CO-CURRICULUM

- The school takes the responsibility for providing and encouraging student participation in a wide range of choices for physical education, sports, organizations, clubs and other co-curricular activities.
- The school encourages female participation in co-curricular activity historically precluding such participation.

E6: GENDER/STAFFING

- The school provides student accessibility to female role models.
- School systems review hiring and promotion practices to insure that employment opportunity is not denied due to gender, marital status, or parenthood.
- The school is especially sensitive to the need for female personnel in non-traditional staff positions.

E7: GENDER/STUDENT PERSONNEL SERVICES

- Guidance and discipline are equitable for both sexes.
- Career guidance for students include non-traditional options.
- Schools prevent the tracking of students on the basis of gender.

E8: GENDER/NON-INSTRUCTIONAL NEEDS

- The school assists students in meeting needs which may be unique for each gender.
- Schools provide support services for victims of sexual harassment, acts of violence and rape.
- Schools provide information and support services for dealing with the prevention of unwanted pregnancy and sexually transmitted diseases.

E9: GENDER/PARENT INVOLVEMENT

- The school provides for the extensive involvement of parents of students of both sexes.

- The school makes an extra effort to involve parents from non-traditional families such as teen parents, single parents and extended family members.
- Parents are encouraged to perceive their children's pursuit of non-traditional educational and career choices.

E10: GENDER/EVALUATION

- The school disaggregates performance data to compare the performance of students from both sexes.
- Evaluation techniques are varied to prevent sex biases.
- Test items are analyzed for inherent sex bias.

SCHOOL PERCEPTIONS OF THE STUDENT

F1: SCHOOL PERCEPTIONS/PHILOSOPHY

- It is the belief of the school that all children can learn.
- The school will communicate to the student a valuing of the individual, the student's family, ethnic and racial group.
- The school will present educational challenges only with the complete assurance that the student has all the necessary prerequisite skills for successful performance.
- All successful student performances are immediately reinforced with strong and frequent positive feedback.
- Relationships and communications between the school and the student are positive. It demonstrates the school's belief in the dignity and worth of the student.

F2: SCHOOL PERCEPTIONS/GOVERNANCE

- All school personnel are flexible in their perceptions of students and avoid the existence or use of negative stereotypes.
- The school recognizes and respects the rights of individual students.

F3: SCHOOL PERCEPTIONS/SCOPE AND SEQUENCE

- It is the responsibility of the school to integrate the personal characteristics of students with the organization of school activities.

F4: SCHOOL PERCEPTIONS/CURRICULUM

- Atypical children are often exposed to hard work early in their lives. The school is challenged to channel such experiences into meaningful educational activities.
- There is a meaningful relationship between the curriculum of the school and the characteristics of its students.
- The instructional program is based on connecting new knowledge to knowledge which the student already possesses.
- The instructional program provides a positive reflection of the student's cultural characteristics.
- Instructional personnel hold high expectations for the capabilities of students.

F5: SCHOOL PERCEPTIONS/CO-CURRICULUM

- All students have access to school activities which are compatible with their life styles.
- The school holds high expectations for the performance of all students in co-curricular activities.

F6: SCHOOL PERCEPTIONS/STAFFING

- The school is staffed by personnel who are cognizant, sensitive and responsive to the characteristics of the student.
- School personnel receive extensive training in distinguishing between educational impediments attributed to atypical student development patterns and a student's lack of capacity for learning.
- Training is provided in adapting instructional materials and methodologies in order to make them compatible with the characteristics of students.

F7: SCHOOL PERCEPTIONS/STUDENT PERSONNEL SERVICES

- Atypical students may have personal, family and social problems which need to be addressed by the school.
- It is the responsibility of the school to assist the students in overcoming the many barriers to successful schooling.

F8: SCHOOL PERCEPTIONS/NON-INSTRUCTIONAL NEEDS

- The school is cognizant and sensitive to the non-instructional needs of students.

- The school assumes the responsibility for providing referrals to community agencies which can assist the student and his family in coping with problems which can become barriers to successful participation in school.

F9: SCHOOL PERCEPTIONS/PARENT INVOLVEMENT

- The school views and treats parents as equals in the joint endeavor of educating children.
- The school assumes that parents of atypical children have the same care and concern about their children as other parents.

F10: SCHOOL PERCEPTIONS/EVALUATION

- The school has the same high levels of expectancy for the performance of atypical children as it has for the performance of all children.
- Instrumentation used for diagnosis and performance is carefully analyzed for cultural bias.

STUDENT PERCEPTION OF SELF

G1: STUDENT SELF-PERCEPTION/PHILOSOPHY

- The child comes to school with preconceived concepts of self and his/her relationship to the world.
- The school is sensitive to these student self-perceptions. Positive perceptions are reinforced; negative perceptions are altered.
- The school provides the student with positive and successful experiences which will enhance the student's concept of self as a successful participant in the learning program.
- The school prevents negative experiences conducive to the alienation, isolation or dysfunctional behavior of the student.

G2: STUDENT SELF-PERCEPTION/GOVERNANCE

- All interactions between the school and the student in the instructional program, co-curricular activities, and administrative relationships reflect a high value given to each student.
- Parents, teachers and students participate in school decisionmaking in order to feel in control and be a part of the school community.
- Penalizing students without intervention to help them resolve their problems is psychologically detrimental to the students.

- Students are encouraged to be proud of themselves, their families and their community groups.

G3: STUDENT SELF-PERCEPTION/SCOPE AND SEQUENCE

- A narrow instructional scope or strict adherence to a particular sequence which alienates the student imposes constraints which, in turn, develop negative concepts of self.

G4: STUDENT SELF-PERCEPTION/CURRICULUM

- Student participation in the school instructional program has a strong impact on the way in which the student perceives his/her self.
- In order to develop a positive concept of self, or to change a negative concept of self, it is necessary that the student have success in learning situations.
- Success in learning situations is usually determined by reasonable increments of difficulty in sequential learning tasks and the possession of the necessary prerequisite skills.
- Teachers use extensive cuing and other forms of assistance to prevent unsuccessful student performance.
- Successful performance in school activities is followed by positive, immediate, strong and frequent feedback to the student.
- A curriculum which conveys a negative message about the student's cultural heritage, economic circumstances, language, community or family is conducive for the development of negative concepts of self.
- Instructional materials do not present models (such as the two-parent family) which serve as standards and which the student has no control over and cannot meet.
- Participation in additional programs and services is perceived by the student as a necessary resource and not as punishment for being different.

G5: STUDENT SELF-PERCEPTION/CO-CURRICULUM

- Every student is provided the opportunity to be a successful participant in some co-curricular activity.
- The co-curriculum appeals to a wide variety of interests and experiences.
- Student talent, academic achievement or economic class are not justifications for excluding students from effective participation in co-curricular activities.
- Cooperation in co-curricular activities is as important as competition.

G6: STUDENT SELF-PERCEPTION/STAFFING

- The focus of staffing is on meeting the individual needs of students rather than that of organizational needs.
- School communications in the form of grades, attention and praise and other rewards send the student powerful messages about self.
- The schools implement affirmative action and aggressive recruitment of school staff which are sensitive and empathetic to student characteristics and needs.
- School staff receive the proper training in building self-esteem in students. Training programs address the need for the training of new teachers and the periodic retraining of experienced staff.

G7: STUDENT SELF-PERCEPTION/STUDENT PERSONNEL SERVICES

- The school provides the necessary counseling and guidance for each student to develop capacity for meeting the basic physiological and psychological needs.
- Successful student personnel services result in student awareness of the school's interest and concern over their well-being.

G8: STUDENT SELF PERCEPTION/NON-INSTRUCTIONAL NEEDS

- The provision of assistance to students and their families in meeting their non-instructional needs is rewarding to the participants without their being stigmatized for receiving such assistance.
- The receiving of assistance is of concern only to the agency providing the assistance and to the student and family receiving such assistance. All information concerning participation in school or community assistance programs should be held in strictest confidence.

G9: STUDENT SELF PERCEPTION/PARENT INVOLVEMENT

- The acceptance of a student's ethnicity, cultural heritage, language, community and family is basic to the acceptance of the student.
- The school provides the medium for parent participation as valued partners in the education of their children.
- Participation in school activities is a satisfying and rewarding experience for students and parents.

G10: STUDENT SELF-PERCEPTION/EVALUATION

- The focus of student assessment is on identifying weaknesses in the school program, rather than weaknesses in the student.
- Evaluation focuses on the identification of adequate instructional strategies compatible with the characteristics of the student.
- School personnel are trained to see various qualities of student work as indications of different needs rather than an indictment of either the teacher or the student.

CONCLUSION

As stated previously, a paradigm is an accepted model or pattern with a set of assumptions about reality. What new assumptions about reality in the education of minority and disadvantaged children should be included in the new paradigm? The new paradigm should begin with a complete rejection of Robert J. Havighurst's assertion that "There is substantial doubt that the socially disadvantaged children in our big cities have any positive qualities of potential value in urban society..." and it should begin with the basic premise that there is absolutely no doubt that minority and disadvantaged children in our big cities have many positive qualities of extreme value in urban society.

Not only do these atypical populations have qualities of extreme value, it is incumbent upon the school to identify and capitalize on these qualities in developing a mature individual with knowledge and skills necessary for a productive life and contributing to the social, political and economic needs of our country.

BIBLIOGRAPHY

Brown v. Board of Education, 347 US 483 (1954).

Cárdenas, Blandina and José A. Cárdenas, "Chicano—Bright-Eyed Bilingual, Brown and Beautiful," *Today's Education*, February, 1973.

Civil Rights Act of 1964, 42 USC, 1964.

Committee for Economic Development, *Children in Need: Investment Strategies for the Educationally Disadvantaged*, New York, 1987.

Elementary and Secondary Education Act, 20 USC, 1965.

Intercultural Development Research Association (IDRA), *A Research Study on the Projected Impact of the North American Free Trade Agreement (NAFTA) on Texas Public Schools*, Prepared for Texas Education Agency, Austin, 1993.

Intercultural Development Research Association (IDRA), *A Review of the Literature on the Underutilization of Mental Health Services by Mexican Americans: Implications for Future Research and Service Delivery*, San Antonio, 1980.

Kuhn, Thomas S., *The Structure of Scientific Revolutions*, 2nd Edition, The University of Chicago Press, Chicago, 1970.

Lau v. Nichols, 414 U.S. 563 (1974).

Osborne, David, "Comment," *San Antonio Express-News*, San Antonio, Texas, January 9, 1993.

Osborne, David and Ted Gaebler, *Reinventing Government*, Addison-Wesley, Reading, 1992.

Quality Education for Minorities Project, *Education that Works*, Massachusetts Institute of Technology, Cambridge, 1990.

U.S. National Commission on the International Year of the Child, *Report to the President*, Washington, D.C., March 1980.

Zamora, Gloria, et al., *Dropout Prevention: A Resource Booklet of Student Incentive Programs*, Intercultural Development Research Association (IDRA) in Cooperation with the Institute for Educational Leadership, Inc., San Antonio, 1986.

DISCUSSION QUESTIONS

1. Review and summarize the data and rationale presented to support the following elements of the proposed new educational paradigm:

   a. It is the responsibility of the school to be flexible in educational practice and to adapt materials and instruction to the characteristics of the various cultural groups.

   b. Since language development, like all other forms of learning, proceeds from the known to the unknown, beginning instruction in the school must commence with the language background of the student.

   c. The social isolation in school of students from poverty homes can be addressed through participation in co-curricular activities as a prelude for participation in the instructional program.

   d. Pupil/teacher ratios should be as low as possible.

   e. The school should make an extra effort to involve parents from non-traditional families such as teen parents, single-parents and extended family members.

   f. There should be a meaningful relationship between the curriculum of the school and the characteristics of the students.

   g. The focus on staffing is on meeting the individual needs of students rather than meeting organizational needs.

2. How would you as a professional educator demonstrate the advisability and the feasibility of the author's educational paradigm to decisionmakers for American education?

3. Develop a statement based on the changing nature of the American workplace and demographic projections for minorities to make the case for the urgency of school reform that includes adapting to the realities of atypical student populations.

APPENDIX I

INTERCULTURAL DEVELOPMENT RESEARCH ASSOCIATION

Intercultural Development Research Association (IDRA) is an independent non-profit organization dedicated to equity and excellence in education for all children. Founded in 1973, IDRA has worked since its inception for the rights of minority and other special populations. IDRA fulfills its mission through the provision of training and technical assistance, targeted research and evaluation projects, the development of appropriate instructional materials, and the aggressive dissemination of information.

IDRA targets specific pressing concerns through its Center for the Prevention and Recovery of Dropouts, which seeks to turn the dropout tide through in-school programs such as the national Coca-Cola Valued Youth Program. The IDRA Institute for Policy and Leadership informs decision-makers on school finance and other policy issues.

As IDRA enters a new century, it maintains its commitment to educational equity, the potential within each student and the right of every child to the brightest possible future as only such equity can provide.

INDICES

AUTHORS

COURT CASES

LEGISLATION

ORGANIZATIONS, AGENCIES AND INSTITUTIONS

TOPICS

About the Author

It was inevitable that José Angel Cárdenas spend most of his professional life working in the development of multicultural and bilingual education programs.

PHOTO CREDIT: CHRISTINE CÁRDENAS BOEHME

He was born in Laredo, Texas in 1930, with an extensive number of relatives residing on both sides of the United States/Mexico border. A large variance in the economic circumstances of members of his extended family provided an early source of familiarity with a diversity of socio-economic levels. Family interactions led to an early immersion in a variety of cultural contexts. The extensive use of Spanish and English in the community led to a high level of proficiency in both languages.

Cárdenas graduated from the University of Texas at Austin in 1950. He obtained a Master of Education degree from Our Lady of the Lake University in San Antonio, Texas in 1955 and a doctorate from the University of Texas at Austin in 1966. His teaching experience includes elementary school, junior and senior high schools, and higher education. He has been a high school vice-principal, elementary school principal, district math and science supervisor, and superintendent of schools.

In 1973, Cárdenas established Texans for Educational Excellence (TEE), which later became the Intercultural Development Research Association (IDRA), where he dedicated twenty years as an advocate for the improvement of educational opportunities for children. In 1992, he retired as Executive Director of IDRA and was named Director Emeritus for life. José A. Cárdenas now spends most of his time writing about educational issues at IDRA, raising cattle in South Texas, and studying America's pre-Columbian civilizations.

Dr. Cárdenas is married to Laura Tobin Canales, a descendant of early 18th century immigrants to Texas, and has five children.